Hugh Johnson's
Pocket Wine Book

2003

MITCHELL BEAZLEY

Acknowledgments

This store of detailed recommendations comes partly from my own notes and mainly from those of a great number of kind friends. Without the generous help and cooperation of innumerable winemakers, merchants, and critics, I could not attempt it. I particularly want to thank the following for help with research or in the areas of their special knowledge.

Gerard Basset MW
Dr Ernö Péter Botos
Gregory Bowden
Bruce Cass
Michael Cooper
Rupert Dean
Michael Edwards
Jacqueline Friedrich
Denis Gastin
Rosemary George MW
James Halliday
Shirley Jones
Annie Kay

Chandra Kurt
Gabriel Lachmann
Gareth Lawrence
James Lawther MW
John Livingstone-
    Learmonth
Nico Manessis
Richard Mayson
Kathryn McWhirter
Charles Metcalfe
Adam Montefiore
Jasper Morris MW
Vladimir Moskvan

Stuart Pigott
John and Erica Platter
Carlos Read
Jan and Maite Read
Emma Rice
Daniel Rogov
Lisa Shara Hall
Stephen Skelton
Paul Strang
Marguerite Thomas
Daniel Thomases
Simon Woods

Hugh Johnson's Pocket Wine Book 2003

Edited and designed by Mitchell Beazley, an imprint of Octopus Publishing Group Limited, 2-4 Heron Quays, London E14 4JP.

© Octopus Publishing Group Limited, 1977–2002.

First edition published 1977
Revised editions published 1978, 1979, 1980, 1981, 1982, 1983, 1984, 1985, 1986, 1987, 1988, 1989, 1990, 1991, 1992, 1993, 1994, 1995, 1996, 1997, 1998, 1999, 2000, 2001, 2002.

A CIP record for this book is available from the British Library.

ISBN 1 84000 611 0

The author and publishers will be grateful for any information which will assist them in keeping future editions up to date. Although all reasonable care has been taken in the preparation of this book, neither the publishers nor the author can accept any liability for any consequences arising from the use thereof, or from the information contained herein.

Editor: Emma Rice
Executive Art Editor: Yasia Williams
Design: Fiona Knowles, Nicky Collings
Production: Julie Young

Printed and bound by Toppan Printing Company, China

Contents

Agenda 2003	4
How to use this book	6
Vintage report 2001	7
A closer look at 2000...	8
Grape varieties	10
Wine & food	17
Food & finest wine	30
France	32
Châteaux of Bordeaux	80
Italy	106
Germany	134
Spain & Portugal	156
Sherry, Port, & Madeira	176
Switzerland	184
Austria	188
Central & Southeast Europe	194–209
Hungary	196
Bulgaria	199
Former Yugosalvia/Czechoslovakia	201
Romania	205
Greece	206
Cyprus	209
Asia, North Africa, & The Levant	210
England & Wales	213
North America	216–243
California	217
The Pacific Northwest	235
East of the Rockies & Ontario	239
The Southwest & Rockies, Texas, etc	242
South America	244
Australia	251
New Zealand	265
South Africa	272
A little learning...	282–288
A few technical words	282
Wines for drinking in an ideal world	283
And the score is...	285
Quick reference vintage charts	286-7
The right temperature	288

Agenda 2003

Revising this book (and this is my 26th shot at it) is like plotting the swirling Sahara sand. There are, thank goodness, oases here and there which re-emerge each time the sand settles (or we pretend it has settled; the new edition is going to press). But the dunes around them have shifted; the landscape is different, however familiar. There are new high points, new depressions – and new routes to where you want to go.

For ten years now it has been the New World that has set the agenda. Uninhibited experiments by countries without the baggage of regulation and tradition are more exciting to watch. They make the contortions of appellations and the laws to enforce them look painful. To many the effort seems pointless. "If you grow Chardonnay, why not say so?" is a question that still shocks growers in Chablis or Meursault. It has only one possible answer: the consistent uniqueness of what the growers bottle.

Two arguments today seem to point in opposite directions. One says that wine is too complicated; that big, well-advertised, often-discounted brands are the only things the public can be bothered with. The other says that a bit of a puzzle is the very essence of wine. Strip it of its mystery, its complexity, even the racy hint of risk, and it's just a drink. Certainly restaurants with wide-ranging wine-lists that dip into more obscure regions, suggesting inside knowledge, do well out of it. And producers with successful simple brand ideas are rarely content to leave them alone. They soon complicate them with premium notions.

Inherent in the idea of an Australian Riesling or a California Cabernet is the possibility of a Clare Riesling or a Napa Cab; a closer focus giving a better wine... until you name the vineyard, regulate the labelling – and presto, you have an appellation.

Are all old appellations good appellations? The challenge is thrown down by the organic movement. If what is unique about Meursault (or Margaux, or Montalcino) is its soil, you had better not mess with it. All the fertilizer you chuck on, the effects and residues of anti-fungal treatments over the years, the stuff you use to kill red spiders – they all alter the subtle biochemistry of the place. The very thing you call terroir. It is a serious case that farmers have to answer. Many are taking self-denying steps, if not to fully organic or "bio-dynamic" farming, at least to what the French call "*lutte raisonée*", a controlled campaign using minimum artificial treatments consistent with reasonable returns.

What else is on the agenda? On mine there is the rising alcoholic strength of many wines. Why is stronger seen as better? There is a simple answer – from the taster's, and certainly the professional critic's, point of view. More alcohol can make wine taste sweeter, more important, more prestigious. The French wines that have always been the benchmarks can achieve a magic balance of total flavour ripeness with moderate alcohol. But in hot climates the sugar comes easily; ripe tannins less so. Wait until the grape is fully ripe and the sugar content inevitably spells high alcohol. More so with new breeds of yeast that are unfazed by it.

The result, especially in parts of the New world where high sugar levels are all too easy to achieve – California above all – is headachy wines of thuggish strength as the new norm. They stand out in tastings. Their muscle, and their glycerol content, make them "big", smooth, rich and important. But who wants instant oblivion? Or is that a silly question?

Comparative tastings have certainly become silly. The prime example is the race to be first with judgements on each new vintage in Bordeaux. Scores of experts rush to Bordeaux in spring, taste hopefully representative samples of wines that won't be finished for another twelve months, and publish their findings. The success of a whole vintage, and the profitability of many wineries, can ride on the opinions of one man. It was Robert Parker's idea. He and his 100-point system have provided America with the authority it craves; an easy solution to the unsettling subtleties of wine. Give it college marks. (For more on this see page 285.)

The rest of the world is less susceptible. But it cannot ignore a force that drives a market as big as the USA. The sad result is a trend among winemakers deliberately to make wines that appeal to US journalists: dense, oak-flavoured and, yes, strong. The very antithesis of wines Bordeaux was built on: classic claret.

The other agenda item that is getting bigger every year is cork. The traditional way of plugging a wine-bottle is a survivor of seventeenth century technology. If our ancestors had had screwcaps for their bottles they would have used them – and so should we. Corks, unfortunately, can taint wine with a specific mould at an alarming rate. Some estimate between five and ten per cent of all bottles are more or less "corked". If the public recognized even half of the affected bottles wine-producers would go bust. Nor is there any argument for a permeable stopper for the ninety per cent of wines that will be opened within months or so. Except nostalgia. Is the romance of wine worth a one in ten chance of a bad bottle? You decide. And when you do, buy your daily wines from suppliers with the courage to use modern stoppers.

Laying aside the broader issues, though, this micro-encyclopedia looks closely at the present position in this fast-changing world. Even readers who bought the last edition (others, I'm afraid, only come back to the well at intervals of two or three) will find thousands of changes of detail, emphasis, and evaluation.

This is intended to be a practical guide; theory has no place here. In essence, it compresses all the useful information you can't possibly carry in your head – and neither can I. My information is gleaned, as ever, from many sources, from tastings, visits, and never-ending correspondence. Revision is continuous. As you read this I will have a scribbled-on proof for next year's edition. The book is designed to take the panic out of buying. You are faced with a daunting restaurant wine list, or mind-numbing shelves of bottles in a store. Your mind goes blank; out comes your little book. You can start with what you propose to eat, see pages 17–31, or where you are by turning up a national section, or a grape variety you like. Just establish which country a wine comes from, then look up the principal words on the label in that country's section. You should find enough information to guide your choice – and often a great deal more. Even after twenty-six editions I can browse for hours...

A declaration of interest

Readers should be told that I have an interest in the Royal Tokáji Wine Company in Hungary. (It's hard not to be interested in many friends' vineyards, too.)

How to use this book

The top line of most entries consists of the following information:

Aglianico del Vulture Bas | r dr (s/sw sp) | ★★★ | 88 90' **91 92** 93' 94' 95 96 (98)

① Wine name and the region the wine comes from.

② Whether it is red, rosé or white (or brown/amber), dry, sweet or sparkling, or several of these (and which is most important):

r	red
p	rosé
w	white
br	brown
dr	dry*
sw	sweet
s/sw	semi-sweet
sp	sparkling

( ) brackets here denote a less important wine
*assume wine is dry when **dr** or **sw** are not indicated

③ Its general standing as to quality: a necessarily rough-and-ready guide based on its current reputation as reflected in its prices:

★	plain, everyday quality
★★	above average
★★★	well known, highly reputed
★★★★	grand, prestigious, expensive

So much is more or less objective. Additionally there is a subjective rating:

★ etc   Stars are coloured red for any wine which in my experience is usually especially good within its price range. There are good everyday wines as well as good luxury wines. This system helps you find them.

④ Vintage information: which of the recent vintages can be recommended; of these, which are ready to drink this year, and which will probably improve with keeping. Your choice for current drinking should be one of the vintage years printed in **bold** type. Buy light-type years for further maturing.

95 etc   recommended years which may be currently available

90'etc   vintage regarded as particularly successful for the property in question

87 etc   years in **bold** should be ready for drinking (the others should be kept)

89 etc   vintages in colour are the ones to choose first for drinking in 2001 – they should be à point. (See also Bordeaux introduction, page 78.)

(98) etc   provisional rating

The German vintages work on a different principle again: see page 137.

Other abbreviations

DYA   drink the youngest available

NV   vintage not normally shown on label; in Champagne, means a blend of several vintages for continuity

CHABLIS   properties, areas or terms cross-referred within the section

A quick-reference vintage chart appears on pages 286-7

Vintage report 2001

The 2001 vintage started the new century on a quiet note. It was always going to be in the shadow of the much-hyped millennium vintage. Producers who hoped to make another killing were forced to be more realistic. Happily 2001 produced many useful unspectacular wines that we will drink with pleasure relatively soon. A few, especially on the Right Bank, will be much better than that.

In Bordeaux the running battle between the Bordelais and trade buyers became acute. Buyers of the 1998 and 1999 vintages are disillusioned. There is no reason to buy 2001 en primeur – except to keep the producer's goodwill – and in a buyer's market there should be enough of even this to go round. Sauternes was the glorious exception and many wines are outstanding, tasting wonderful even at this early stage. The dry whites of Bordeaux are also very promising.

Elsewhere in France the vintage was reasonable but unspectacular. Burgundy, from Chablis through the Côte d'Or to Beaujolais, was too cool in August for intense ripening, but fine in September until the harvest Whites, including Chablis, are generally better than all but the best reds (just as they were in 2000). In the Loire, Muscadets were virtually perfect and there are some good wines from those in other areas who took the risk and picked late. Champagne suffered from severe harvest rains and, although Chardonnay generally did well, there will be no 2001 vintage declared. The Northern Rhône did well for both reds and whites. The Southern Rhône was less consistent. In Italy, a cool September in both Tuscany and Piedmont means irregular quality in both, though Nebbiolo and Barbera may be exceptional. Spain had an excellent vintage from north to south and, while yields in Portugal were high, the standard is generally good. Though it may not be a vintage year for port.

Germany had a good year throughout with the Mosel producing superb wines, including ausleses.Central Europe and eastwards had poor ripening weather.Tokaji, after two excellent vintages in 1999 and 2000, failed to produce good aszu, though Austria, like Germany, did well; the September rains caused a moment of panic but an Indian Summer more than compensated – there should be some excellent wines.

Northern California and the Central Coast suffered very erratic weather from spring heatwaves to April frost to extreme summer heat. Not the most consistent vintage but overall very high quality. Lower acidity and concentration in thePacific Northwest means the wines are approachable earlier than previous vintages. Chile had a smaller harvest this year with a perhaps consequent rise in quality. Argentina saw rain at harvest time for the second year in a row and although the results were varied some excellent reds were produced.

The extreme temperatures of the Australian summer were most in evidence in the Southeastern regions. The "cooler" areas of Western Australia fared better with the best conditions in Great Southern. The North Island of New Zealand suffered from heavy rains and the reds of Hawkes Bay and Gisborne saw tiny crops. The South Island had better results with Sauvignon Blanc but they are still variable; Pinot Noir should be excellent. South Africa again had a great year for big reds that should age well.

A closer look at 2000...

The millennium vintage carried all sorts of hopes, expectations, and symbolic meanings for wine producers around the world. Looking back, a year after our initial summary, a few were disappointed but many wines have proved outstanding.

In Bordeaux these hopes were realized with a vintage to rival 1990. On the Left Bank very few properties failed to maximize the potential of the vintage. A few exceptions in Graves do not mar the overall result, but the best wines come from the classic communes of St-Julien, Margaux, and Pauillac. For the Right Bank conditions were slightly trickier and required more intervention in the vineyard. A damp, steamy spring and early summer threatened mildew but hot dry weather later in the season saved the day. The harvest was straightforward and the resulting wines, in St-Emilion, are exceptional. The wines of Pomerol are not far behind but lack the distinction of their neighbours. Sauternes was sadly left out of the party; severe rainstorms in October dampened any chances of 2000being a great year. It suffers further by comparison with the good 1999 and potentially brilliant 2001.

Burgundy was not as fortunate as Bordeaux but the vintage is by no means a write off. The Côte de Nuits was the more fortunate half of the Côte d'Or and some reds will rival the excellent 1999s. The Côte de Beaune was hit by storms during the harvest (which also affected the more southerly Côte Chalonnaise) and, coupled with bad weather earlier in the summer, meant rot in the Pinot Noir was a problem. Careful selection allowed growers to salvage the crop but the wines generally do not have the potential to age – enjoy them in their youth. The Chardonnay harvest was similarly affected by the weather but rot was not such a problem as the vines were picked earlier than the Pinot Noir. Again, not destined for an very long life, but a pleasant one nonetheless. Chablis has produced some good wines.

After the disappointing weather of 1999 Champagne will no doubt be declaring 2000 as a vintage. The weather came good at harvest and produced some well-balanced wines. The sweet wines of the Loire had a tough time with too much rain and not enough sunshine; the results are variable but rarely more than good. Cabernet Franc produced some very decent reds but appearances can be deceptive –ß the deeply coloured wines promise a richness that simply isn't there. Drink them young, they won't age.

The Rhône had a mixed bag with the southern areas coming out particularly well. Not to say the northern Rhône didn't have some good results; many reds are clean and well-made, they just lack the luxuriance normally associated with the wines of that region. But the southern Rhône reds are rich and ripe and well-structured. The whites of Châteauneuf are beautifully elegant. Continuing south, Provence, Languedoc, and Roussillon all enjoyed a warm summer that resulted in ripe fruity wines throughout. The Southwest suffered from heavy rain late in the season so only those producers who got their harvest in early will have made good wines. The rains effectively washed out the sweet wines.

Germany is not shouting about the 2000 vintage either. Rain fell on the harvest in most areas. Late-ripening Riesling had a late weather break and made some fine wines in the Mosel. In Italy the overall production was down because of the sporadic weather. Piedmont and northern Italy in general suffered periods of heavy rain followed by a drought. But a warm and dry late summer and autumn rescued the harvest. The whites are weak but there are some splendid reds to be found. In Tuscany and further south total production was reduced by mildew, but on balance producers were more than satisfied.

In Portugal most of the major port houses have declared 2000 as a vintage year – the concentration and structure of the wines has already caused quite a stir. The lack of rain during the summer and autumn was also good news for other red wines but the whites suffered from the heat and stress and are generally not up to scratch. The drought also affected Southern Spain, bringing down the quantity of the crop but also meaning that quality was high – the vines escaped the ravages of disease and healthy grapes mean good wine. Northern Spain saw more rain. The results in Rioja are hit and miss. 2001 is the Rioja vintage to wait for.

Further analysis of the vintage in Central and Eastern Europe has not dampened the enthusiasm which greeted it this time last year. Bulgaria, Austria, Hungary, and Romania are all still celebrating. But even with better raw materials it was still down to the winemaker to follow through.

California led the way in North America and, with less than ideal weather conditions, managed to produce an enormous crop of excellent quality grapes – the reds do not have the ageing potential of previous vintages but will provide much pleasure. Cool weather in the Pacific Northwest produced powerful tannic reds with huge structure; patience is required. In South America, Argentina had to contend with three times the normal rainfall and coped remarkably well – some of the wines are superb. Chile also suffered unusual weather patterns but still produced some excellent wines.

Australia's harvest was considerably smaller than predicted, thanks to the unusually difficult conditions, but we are not going to notice a drought of Australian wine. New vineyards are still being planted at a phenomenal rate and total production continues to grow. By the time harvest came along in New Zealand the grapes were at optimum ripeness and balance. But problems in the spring had reduced the crop in the South Island. By contrast, on the North Island, Hawke's Bay had a record vintage. In South Africa drought reduced the crop quite considerably from last year. The quality is much better, particularly the well-structured reds.

Grape varieties

In the past two decades a radical change has come about in all except the most long-established wine countries: the names of a handful of grape varieties have become the ready reference to wine. In senior wine countries, above all France and Italy (between them producing nearly half the world's wine), more complex traditions prevail. All wine of old prestige is known by its origin, more or less narrowly defined, not just the particular fruit-juice that fermented.

For the present the two notions are in rivalry. Eventually the primacy of place over fruit will become obvious, at least for wines of quality. But for now, for most people, grape tastes are the easy reference-point – despite the fact that they are often confused by the added taste of oak. If grape flavours were really all that mattered this would be a very short book.

But of course they do matter, and a knowledge of them both guides you to flavours you enjoy and helps comparisons between regions. Hence the originally Californian term "varietal wine" – meaning, in principle, from one grape variety.

At least seven varieties – Cabernet Sauvignon, Pinot Noir, Riesling, Sauvignon Blanc, Chardonnay, Gewürztraminer, and Muscat – have tastes and smells distinct and memorable enough to form international categories of wine. To these you can add Merlot, Malbec, Syrah, Sémillon, Chenin Blanc, Pinots Blanc and Gris, Sylvaner, Viognier, Nebbiolo, Sangiovese, Tempranillo... The following are the best and/or most popular wine grapes.

Grapes for red wine

Agiorgitiko (St George) Versatile Greek (Nemea) variety with juicy damson fruit, velvety tannins. Sufficient structure for serious ageing.

Baga Bairrada (Portugal) grape. Dark, tannic; great potential; hard to grow.

Barbera Most popular of many productive grapes of N Italy, esp Piedmont, giving dark, fruity, sharp wine. Gaining prestige in California and Italy.

Blaufränkisch Austrian reputed GAMAY but at best (in Burgenland) a considerable red. LEMBERGER in Germany, KEKFRANKOS in Hungary.

Bourboulenc This and the rare Rolle make some of the Midi's best wines.

Brunello South Tuscan form of SANGIOVESE, splendid at Montalcino.

Cabernet Franc, alias Bouchet (Cab F) The lesser of two sorts of Cab grown in Bordeaux but dominant (as "Bouchet") in St-Emilion. The Cab of the Loire, making Chinon, Saumur, etc, and rosé. Used for blending with CAB S, etc, or increasingly, alone, in California, Australia.

Cabernet Sauvignon (Cab S) Grape of great character: spicy, herby, tannic, with characteristic "blackcurrant" aroma. The first grape of the Médoc; also makes most of the best California, S American, E European reds. Vies with Shiraz in Australia. Its wine almost always needs ageing; usually benefits from blending with eg MERLOT, CAB F, or SYRAH. Makes aromatic rosé.

Cannonau GRENACHE in its Sardinian manifestation: can be v fine, potent.

Carignan By far the most common grape of France, covering hundreds of thousands of acres. Prolific with dull but harmless wine. Best from old vines in Corbières. Also common in N Africa, Spain, California.

Carmènere An old Bordeaux variety now virtually extinct in Europe. Widely used in Argentina where until recently it was often mistaken for MERLOT.

Cinsault / Cinsaut Common bulk-producing grape of S France; in S Africa crossed with PINOT N to make PINOTAGE. Pale wine, but quality potential.

Dolcetto Source of soft seductive dry red in Piedmont. Now high fashion.

Gamay The Beaujolais grape: light, very fragrant wines, at their best young. Makes even lighter wine in the Loire Valley, in central France, and in Switzerland and Savoie. Known as "Napa Gamay" in California.

Grenache, alias Garnacha, Alicante, Cannonau Useful grape for strong fruity but pale wine: good rosé and vin doux naturel, esp in S France, Spain, California. Old-vine versions are currently prized in S Australia. Usually blended (eg in Châteauneuf-du-Pape).

Grignolino Makes one of the good everyday table wines of Piedmont.

Kadarka, alias Gamza Makes healthy, sound, agreeable reds in Hungary, Bulgaria, etc.

Kékfrankos Hungarian BLAUFRANKISCH, said to be related to GAMAY; similar lightish reds.

Lambrusco Productive grape of the lower Po Valley, giving quintessentially Italian, cheerful sweet and fizzy red.

Lemberger See Blaufränkisch. Württemberg's red.

Malbec, alias Cot Minor in Bordeaux, major in Cahors (alias Auxerrois) and esp Argentina. Dark, dense, tannic wine capable of real quality.

Merlot Adaptable grape making the great fragrant and plummy wines of Pomerol and (with CAB F) St-Emilion, an important element in Médoc reds, soft and strong (and à la mode) in California, Washington. A useful adjunct in Australia, lighter but often good in N Italy, Italian Switzerland, Slovenia, Argentina etc. Grassy when not fully ripe.

Montepulciano Confusingly, a major central-eastern Italian grape of high quality, as well as a town in Tuscany.

Mourvèdre, alias Mataro Excellent dark aromatic tannic grape used mainly for blending in Provence (but solo in Bandol) and the Midi. Enjoying new interest in eg S Australia, California.

Nebbiolo, alias Spanna and Chiavennasca One of Italy's best red grapes; makes Barolo, Barbaresco, Gattinara, Valtellina. Intense, nobly fruity, perfumed wine but v tannic: improves for years.

Periquita Ubiquitous in Portugal for firm-flavoured reds. Often blended with CABERNET S and also known as Castelão Francês.

Petit (and Gros) Manseng The secret weapon of the French Basque country: vital for Jurançon; increasingly blended elsewhere in the SW.

Petit Verdot Excellent but awkward Médoc grape now found lgely elsewhere.

Pinot Noir (Pinot N) The glory of Burgundy's Côte d'Or, with scent, flavour, and texture unmatched anywhere. Less happy elsewhere; makes light wines rarely of much distinction in Germany, Switzerland, Austria, Hungary. But now splendid results in California's Sonoma, Carneros and Central Coast, Oregon, Ontario, Yarra Valley, Adelaide Hills, Tasmania, and NZ.

Pinotage Singular S African grape (PINOT N x CINSAUT). Can be very fruity and can age interestingly, but often jammy.

Refosco Possibly a synomym for Mondeuse of Savoie. Produces deep, flavoursome age-worthy wines, esp in warmer climates.

St-Laurent Dark, smooth and full-flavoured Austrian speciality. Also in the Pfalz.

Sangiovese (or Sangioveto) Main red grape of Chianti and much of central Italy. BRUNELLO is the Sangiovese Grosso. Top quality potential now in California.

Saperavi Makes good sharp very long-lived wine in Georgia, Ukraine etc. Blends very well with CABERNET S (eg in Moldova).

Spätburgunder German for PINOT N – a very pale shadow of burgundy.

Syrah, alias Shiraz The great Rhône red grape, giving tannic purple peppery wine which matures superbly. V important as Shiraz in Australia, increasingly successful in Midi, S Africa, and California. Has a growing fan club.

Tannat Raspberry-perfumed, highly tannic force behind Madiran, Tursan, and other firm-structured reds from SW France. Also for rosé. Now star of Uruguay.

Tempranillo The pale aromatic fine Rioja grape, called Ull de Llebre in Catalonia, Cencibel in La Mancha. Early ripening.

Touriga Nacional Top port and Douro grape, travelling further afield in Portugal for full-bodied reds.

Zinfandel (Zin) Fruity adaptable grape peculiar to California with blackberry-like, and sometimes metallic, flavour. Can be gloriously lush, but also makes "blush" white wine.

Grapes for white wine

Albariño The Spanish name for N Portugal's Alvarinho, emerging as excellently fresh and fragrant wine in Galicia. One of Spain's new delights.

Aligoté Burgundy's second-rank white grape. Crisp (often sharp) wine, needs drinking in 1–3 yrs. Perfect for mixing with cassis (blackcurrant liqueur) to make a "Kir". Widely planted in E Europe, esp Russia.

Arinto White central Portuguese grape for crisp, fragrant dry whites.

Blanc Fumé Alias of SAUV BL, referring to its "smoky" smell, particularly from the Loire (Sancerre and Pouilly). In California used for oak-aged Sauv and reversed to "Fumé Blanc". (The smoke is oak.)

Bourboulenc (now in red)

Bual Makes top-quality sw Madeira wines, not quite so rich as Malmsey.

Chardonnay (Chard) The white burgundy grape, the white Champagne grape, and the white grape of the New World, partly because it is one of the easiest to grow and vinify. All regions are trying it, mostly aged (or, better, fermented) in oak to reproduce the flavours of burgundy. Australia and California make classics (but also much dross). Those of Italy, Spain, New Zealand, South Africa, New York State, Chile, Argentina, Hungary and the Midi are all coming on strong. Called Morillon in Austria.

Chasselas Prolific early-ripening grape with little aroma, mainly grown for eating. AKA Fendant in Switzerland (where it is supreme), Gutedel in Germany.

Chenin Blanc (Chenin Bl) Great white grape of the middle Loire (Vouvray, Layon, etc). Wine can be dry or sweet (or very sweet), but with plenty of acidity – hence its long life and use in warmer climates (eg South Africa and California). See also Steen.

Clairette A low-acid grape formerly widely used in the S of France as a vermouth base. Being revived.

Colombard Slightly fruity, nicely sharp grape, hugely popular in California, now gaining ground in SW France, South Africa, etc.

Fendant See Chasselas.

Folle Blanche High acid/little flavour make this ideal for brandy. Called Gros Plant in Brittany, Picpoul in Armagnac. Respectable in California.

Fumé Blanc (Fumé Bl) See Blanc Fumé.

Furmint A grape of great character: the trademark of Hungary both as the principal grape in Tokay and as vivid, vigorous table wine with an appley flavour. Called Sipon in Slovenia. Some grown in Austria.

Gewürztraminer, alias Traminer (Gewürz) One of the most pungent grapes, distinctively spicy with aromas like rose petals and grapefruit. Wines are often rich and soft, even when fully dry. Best in Alsace; also good in Germany, E Europe, Australia, California, Pacific NW, NZ.

Grauburgunder See Pinot Gris.

Grechetto or Greco Ancient grape of central and S Italy: vitality and style.

Grüner Veltliner Austria's favourite (planted in almost half her vineyards). Around Vienna and in the Wachau and Weinviertel (also in Moravia) it can be delicious: light but dry, peppery and lively. Excellent young, but the best age 5 years or so.

Hárslevelü Other main grape of Tokay (with FURMINT). Adds softness and body.

Italian Riesling Grown in Northern Italy and Eastern Europe. Much inferior to Rhine RIES, with lower acidity, best in sweet wines. Alias Welschriesling, Olaszrizling (no longer legally labelled simply "Riesling").

Kéknyelü Low-yielding, flavourful grape giving one of Hungary's best whites. Has the potential for fieriness and spice. To be watched.

Kerner The most successful of recent German varieties, mostly made by crossing RIESLING and SILVANER, but in this case Riesling x (red) Trollinger. Early-ripening flowery (but often too blatant) wine with good acidity. Popular in Pfalz, Rheinhessen, etc.

Loureiro The best and most fragrant Vinho Verde variety in Portugal.

Macabeo The workhorse white grape of N Spain, widespread in Rioja (alias Viura) and in Catalan cava country. Good quality potential.

Malvasia Known as Malmsey in Madeira, Malvasia in Italy, Malvoisie in France. Alias Vermentino (esp in Corsica). Also grown in Greece, Spain, W Australia, E Europe. Makes rich brown wines or soft whites, ageing magnificently with superb potential not often realized.

Marsanne Principal white grape (with Roussanne) of the N Rhône (eg in Hermitage, St-Joseph, St-Péray). Also good in Australia, California and (as Ermitage Blanc) the Valais. Soft full wines that age v well.

Müller-Thurgau (Müller-T) Dominant in Germany's Rheinhessen and Pfalz and too common on the Mosel; a cross between RIESLING and SILVANER. Ripens early to make soft aromatic wines for drinking young. Makes good sweet wines but usually dull, often coarse, dry ones. Should have no place in top vineyards.

Muscadelle Adds aroma to many white Bordeaux, esp Sauternes. Also the base for Australian Liqueur Tokay. Apparently not a true MUSCAT.

Muscadet, alias Melon de Bourgogne Makes light, refreshing, v dry wines with a seaside tang round Nantes in Brittany. (California "Pinot Bl" is this grape.)

Muscat (Many varieties; the best is Muscat Blanc à Petits Grains.) It is universally grown, easily recognized, pungent grapes, mostly made into perfumed sweet wines, often fortified (as in France's vins doux naturels). Superb in Australia. The third element in Tokay Aszú. Rarely (eg Alsace) made dry.

Palomino, alias Listán Makes all the best sherry but poor table wine.

Pedro Ximénez, alias PX Makes very strong wine in Montilla and Málaga. Used in blending sweet sherries. Also grown in Argentina, the Canaries, Australia, California, South Africa.

Pinot Blanc (Pinot Bl) A cousin of PINOT NOIR; not related to CHARDONNAY, but with a similar, milder character: light, fresh, fruity, not aromatic, to drink young; eg good for Italian spumante. Grown in Alsace, Northern Italy, Southern Germany, and Eastern Europe. Weissburgunder in Germany. See also Muscadet.

Pinot Gris (Pinot Gr) At best makes rather heavy, even "thick", full-bodied whites with a certain spicy style. Known (formerly) as Tokay in Alsace; Ruländer (sweet) or Grauburgunder (dry) in Germany; Tocai or Pinot Grigio in Italy and Slovenia (but much thinner wine).

Pinot Noir (Pinot N) Superlative black grape (See "Grapes for red wine") used in Champagne and occasionally elsewhere (eg California, Australia) for making white, sparkling, or very pale pink "vin gris"

> ### Riesling
>
> It is a strange irony that Riesling is making its re-entrance on the world-stage through, as it were, the back door. No serious commentator disagrees that Riesling stands level with Chardonnay. They are the world's best white wine grapes, in diametrically opposite styles. While Chardonnay gives full-bodied but aromatically discreet wines, Riesling offers a range from steely to voluptuous, always positively perfumed, and with ageing potential far beyond any Chardonnay. Germany is the great Riesling protagonist and makes the greatest Riesling in all styles. Yet its popularity is being revived, of all places, South Australia, where this cool-climate grape does its best, in body at least, to ape Chardonnay. Holding the middle ground, with forceful but still steely wines, is Austria. Meanwhile lovers of light and fragrant, often piercingly refreshing Rieslings have the Mosel as their exclusive playground. Also grown in Alsace (but absurdly grown nowhere else in France), Pacific NW, Ontario, California, and South Africa.

Ruländer Obsolescent German name for PINOT G used for sweeter wines.

Sauvignon Blanc (Sauv Bl) Makes very distinctive aromatic grassy – or gooseberry – sometimes rank-smelling wines; at its best in Sancerre. Blended with SEMILLON in Bordeaux. Can be austere or buxom. Pungent triumph in New Zealand, now planted everywhere. Also called FUME BLANC or vice versa.

Savagnin The grape of Vin Jaune of Savoie: related to TRAMINER?

Scheurebe Spicy-flavoured German RIES x SYLVANER, very successful in Pfalz, esp for Auslesen. Can be weedy in dry wines.

Semillon (Sem) Contributes the lusciousness to Sauternes; subject to "noble rot" in the right conditions but increasingly important for Graves and other dry white Bordeaux. Grassy if not fully ripe, but can make soft dry wine of great ageing potential. Formerly called "Riesling" in parts of Australia, where it is also often blended with CHARDONNAY. Old Hunter Valley Semillon can be great wine.

Sercial Makes the driest Madeira (where myth says it is really RIESLING).

Seyval Blanc (Seyval Bl) French-made hybrid of French and American vines. V hardy and attractively fruity. Popular and reasonably successful in eastern States and England but dogmatically banned by EU from "quality" wines.

Steen South Africa's most popular white grape: good lively fruity wine. Said to be the CHENIN BL of the Loire and now often so labelled.

Silvaner, alias Sylvaner Germany's former workhorse grape: wine rarely fine except in Franken where it is savoury and ages admirably, and in Rheinhessen and the Pfalz, where it is enjoying a renaissance. Gd in the Italian Tyrol; now declining in popularity in Alsace. Vg (and powerful) as "Johannisberg" in the Valais, Switzerland.

Tokay See Pinot Gris. Also a table grape in California and a supposedly Hungarian grape in Australia. The wine Tokay (Tokáji) is made of FURMINT, HARSLEVELU and MUSCAT.

Torrontes Strongly aromatic, MUSCAT-like Argentine grape, usually dry.

Traminer See Gewürztraminer.

Trebbiano Important but mediocre grape of central Italy (Orvieto, Chianti, Soave etc). Also grown in S France as Ugni Blanc, and Cognac as St-Emilion. Mostly thin, bland wine; needs blending (and more careful growing).

Ugni Blanc (Ugni Bl) See Trebbiano.

Verdejo The grape of Rueda in Castile, potentially fine and long-lived.

Verdelho Madeira grape making excellent medium-sweet wine; in Australia, fresh soft dry wine of great character.

Verdicchio This grape gives its name to potentially good dry wine in central-eastern Italy.

Vermentino Close to Malvasia, but makes a sprightlier wine in Liguria, Tuscany, etc – still with satisfying texture and ageing capacity.

Vernaccia Grape grown in central and S Italy and Sardinia for strong smooth lively wine, sometimes inclining towards sherry.

Viognier Rare Rhône grape, grown at Condrieu for v fine fragrant wine. Drink ASAP. Much in vogue in the Midi, California, etc, but still only a trickle.

Viura See Macabeo.

Weissburgunder See Pinot Blanc.

Welschriesling See Italian Riesling.

Wine & food

The dilemma is most acute in restaurants. Four people have chosen different dishes. The host calculates. A bottle of white and then one of red is conventional, regardless of the food. The formula works up to a point. But it can be refined – or replaced with something more original, something to really bring out the flavours of both food and wine.

Remarkably little ink has been spilt on this byway of knowledge, but 25 years of experimentation and the ideas of many friends have gone into making this list. It is perhaps most useful for menu-planning at home. But used with the rest of the book, it may ease menu-stress in restaurants, too. At the very least, it will broaden your mind.

Before the meal – aperitifs

The conventional aperitif wines are either sparkling (epitomized by Champagne) or fortified (epitomized by sherry in Britain, port in France, vermouth in Italy, etc). A glass of white or rosé (or in France red) table wine before eating is presently in vogue. It calls for something light and stimulating, fairly dry but not acidic, with a degree of character; rather Riesling or Chenin Blanc than Chardonnay.

Warning: Avoid peanuts; they destroy wine flavours.

Olives are also too piquant for many wines; they need sherry or a Martini. Eat almonds, pistachios or walnuts, plain crisps or cheese straws instead.

First courses

Aïoli A thirst-quencher is needed for its garlic heat. Rhône, sparkling dry white; Blanquette de Limoux, Provence rosé, Verdicchio. And marc, too, for courage.

Antipasti Dry or med white: Italian (Arneis, Soave, Pinot Grigio, Prosecco, Vermentino); light red (Dolcetto, Franciacorta, young Chianti).

Artichoke vinaigrette An incisive dry white, eg NZ Sauv Bl; Côtes de Gascogne or a modern Greek; young red: Bordeaux, Côtes du Rhône. With hollandaise Full-bodied slightly crisp dry white: Pouilly- Fuissé, Pfalz Spätlese, or a Carneros or Yarra Valley Chardonnay.

Asparagus A difficult flavour for wine, being slightly bitter, so the wine needs plenty of its own. Sauv echoes the flavour. Sem beats Chard, esp Australian, but Chard works well with melted butter. Alsace Pinot G, even dry Muscat is gd, or Jurançon Sec.

Aubergine purée (Melitzanosalata) Crisp New World Sauv Bl eg from Chile or NZ, or modern Greek or Sicilian dry white. Or Bardolino red or Chiaretto.

Avocado with seafood Dry to medium or slightly sharp white: Rheingau or Pfalz Kabinett, Sancerre, Pinot Grigio; Sonoma or Australian Chard or Sauvignon, Cape Steen, or dry rosé. Or Chablis Premier Cru. With vinaigrette Manzanilla sherry.

Bisques Dry white with plenty of body: Pinot Gris, Chard. Fino or dry amontillado sherry, or Montilla. West Australian Sem.

Boudin Noir (blood sausage) Local Sauv Bl or Chenin – esp in the Loire. Or Beaujolais Cru, esp Morgon.

Bouillabaisse Savoury dry white, Marsanne from the Midi or Rhône, Corsican or Spanish rosé, or Cassis, Verdicchio, California unoaked Sauv Blanc.

Caesar Salad California (Central Coast) Chardonnay. Top California Chenin Blanc.

Carpaccio, beef Seems to work well with the flavour of most wines, incl reds. Top Tuscan vino da tavola is appropriate, but fine Chards are good. So are vintage and pink Champagnes. (See also Carpaccio under fish.) **Salmon** Chardonnay, or Champagne.

Caviar Iced vodka. Champagne, if you must, full-bodied (eg Bollinger, Krug).

Ceviche Australian Riesling or Verdelho, Chile or NZ Sauvignon Bl.

Charcuterie Young Beaujolais-Villages or Bordeaux Blanc, Loire reds such as Saumur, Swiss or Oregon Pinot N. Young Argentine or Italian reds.

Cheese fondue Dry white: Valais Fendant or any other Swiss Chasselas, Roussette de Savoie, Grüner Veltliner, Alsace Ries or Pinot Gris. Or a Beaujolais Cru.

chowders Big-scale white, not necessarily bone dry: Pinot Gris, Rhine Spätlese, Albariño, Australian Sem, buttery Chard. Or fino sherry.

Consommé Medium-dry amontillado sherry, Sercial Madeira.

Crostini Morellino di Scansano, Montepulciano d'Abruzzo, Valpolicella, or a dry Italian white eg. Verdicchio, Orvieto.

Crudités Light red or rosé: Côtes du Rhône, Minervois, Chianti,-Pinot Noir; or fino sherry. Or Alsace Sylvaner or Pinot Blanc.

Dim-Sum Classically, China tea. For fun: Pinot Grigio or Riesling; light red (Bardolino or Beaujolais-Villages). Or NV Champagne or good New World fizz.

Eggs See also Soufflés. These present difficulties: they clash with most wines and spoil good ones. But local wine with local egg dishes is a safe bet. So *→** of whatever is going. Try Pinot Bl or straightforward not too oaky Chardonnay. As a last resort I can bring myself to drink Champagne with scrambled eggs.
Quail's eggs Blanc de Blancs Champagne.
Seagull's (or gull's) eggs Mature white burgundy or vintage Champagne.

Escargots Rhône reds (Gigondas, Vacqueyras), or St-Véran or Aligoté. In the Midi, vg Petits-Gris go with local white, rosé or red. In Alsace, Pinot Bl or Muscat.

Fish terrine Pfalz Riesling Spätlese Trocken, Chablis Premier Cru, Clare Valley Ries, Sonoma Chard; or manzanilla.

Foie gras White. In Bordeaux they drink Sauternes. Others prefer a late-harvest Pinot Gris, Riesling (incl New World), Vouvray, Montlouis, Jurançon Moelleux or Gewürz. Tokay Aszú 5 puttonyos is the new Lucullan choice. Old dry amontillado can be sublime. But not on any account Chard or Sauv Bl.

Gazpacho A glass of fino before and after. Or Sauvignon Bl.

Goat's cheese, grilled or fried (warm salad) Sancerre, Pouilly-Fumé or New World Sauv Bl. Chilled Chinon or Saumur-Champigny or Provence rosé. Or strong red: Ch Musar, Greek, Turkish, Australian sparkling Shiraz.

Gravadlax Akvavit or iced sake. Or Grand Cru Chablis, orCalifornia, Washington, or Margaret River Chard, or Mosel Spätlese (not Trocken).

Guacamole California Chardonnay, Sauvignon Blanc, dry Muscat or NV Champagne. Or Mexican beer.

Haddock, smoked, mousse or brandade A wonderful dish for showing off any stylish full-bodied white, incl Grand Cru Chablis or Sonoma or NZ Chardonnay.

Ham, raw or cured See also Prosciutto. Alsace Grand Cru Pinot Gris or good, crisp Italian Collio white with Spanish Pata Negra or Jamon, fino sherry or tawny port.

Herrings, raw or pickled Dutch gin (young, not aged) or Scandinavian akvavit, and cold beer. If wine essential, try Muscadet.

Hors d'oeuvres See also Antipasti. Clean, fruity, sharp white: Sancerre or any Sauvignon Bl, Grüner Veltliner, Hungarian Leanyka, Cape Chenin Blanc, English white wine; or young light red Bordeaux, Rhône or Corbières. Or fino sherry.

Houmous Pungent, spicy dry white, eg Hungarian or modern Greek white.

Mackerel, smoked An oily wine-destroyer. Manzanilla sherry, proper dry Vinho Verde or Schnapps, peppered or bison-grass vodka. Or good lager.

Mayonnaise Adds richness that calls for a contrasting bite in the wine. Côte Chalonnaise whites (eg Rully) are good. Try NZ Sauvignon Bl, Verdicchio or a Spätlese Trocken from the Pfalz.

Melon Strong sweet wine (if any): port, Bual Madeira, Muscat de Frontignan or vin doux naturel; or dry, perfumed Viognier or Australian Marsanne.

Minestrone Red: Chianti, Zinfandel, Rhône Syrah, etc. Or fino.

Omelettes See Eggs.

Oysters Raw White: NV Champagne, Chablis Premier Cru, Muscadet, white Graves, Sancerre or Guinness.
Cooked Puligny-Montrachet, or good New World Chardonnay. Champagne is good with both.

Pasta Red or white according to the sauce or trimmings:
cream sauce Orvieto, Frascati, Alto Adige Chardonnay.
meat sauce Montepulciano d'Abruzzo, Salice Salentino, Merlot.
pesto (basil) sauce Barbera, Ligurian Vermentino, NZ Sauv Bl, Hungarian Hárslevelü or Furmint
seafood sauce (eg vongole) Verdicchio, Soave, top white Rioja, Cirò, Sauvignon Blanc.
tomato sauce Sauv Bl, Barbera, S Italian red, Zin, S Australian Grenache.

Pâté
chicken livers Call for pungent white (Alsace Pinot Gris or Marsanne), a smooth red like a light Pomerol or Volnay, or even amontillado sherry.

Pâté de campagne A dry white **: Good vin de pays, Graves, Fumé Blanc.
with duck pâté Ch'neuf-du-Pape, Cornas, Chianti Classico, Franciacorta.
fish pâté Muscadet, Mâcon-Villages, Australian Chard (unoaked).

Peperonata Dry Australian Ries, WA Sem or NZ Sauv Bl. Tempranillo
or Beaujolais.

Pipérade Navarra rosado, Provence or S'th'n French rosés. Or dry
Australian Ries.

Pimentos, roasted NZ Sauvignon, Spanish Chardonnay, or Valdepeñas.

Pizza Any dry Italian red ** or Rioja, Australian Shiraz or California
Sangiovese. Corbières, Coteaux d'Aix-en-Provence or red Bairrada.

Prawns, shrimps or langoustines Fine dry white: burgundy, Graves, NZ
Chard, Washington Riesling – even fine mature Champagne.
Indian-, Thai- or Chinese-style rich Australian Hunter Valley
Chardonnay. ('Cocktail sauce' kills wine, and in time, people.)

Prosciutto (also with melon, pears or figs) Full dry or medium white:
Orvieto, Lugana, Sauv Bl, Grüner Veltliner, Tokay Furmint, w Rioja,
Australian Sem or Jurançon Sec.

Quiches Dry full-bodied white: Alsace, Graves, Sauv, dry Rheingau; or
young red (Beauj-Villages, Chilean Pinot N), according to ingredients.

Risotto Pinot Gr from Friuli, Gavi, youngish Sém, Dolcetto or Barbera
d'Alba.
with mushrooms Cahors, Madiran, Barbera or New World Pinot Noir.
with fungi porcini Finest mature Barolo or Barbaresco

Ravioli See Pasta.
with wild mushrooms Dolcetto or Nebbiolo d'Alba, Oregon Pinot N,
red Rioja crianza.

Salade niçoise Very dry, **, not too light or flowery white or rosé:
Provençal, Rhône or Corsican; Catalan white; Fernão Pires, Sauv Bl
or Hungarian dry white.

Salads As a first course, especially with blue cheese dressing, any dry
and appetizing white wine.
NB Vinegar in salad dressings destroys the flavour of wine. If you want
salad at a meal with fine wine, dress the salad with wine or a little
lemon juice instead of vinegar.

Salami Barbera, top Valpolicella, genuine Lambrusco, young Zinfandel,
Tavel or Ajaccio rosé, Vacqueyras, young Bordeaux, Chilean Cab S or
New World Gamay.

Salmon, smoked A dry but pungent white: fino sherry, Alsace Pinot Gris,
Chablis Grand Cru, Pouilly-Fumé, Pfalz Ries Spätlese, vintage
Champagne. If you must have red try a lighter one such as Barbera.
Vodka, schnapps or akvavit.

Seafood salad Fresh N Italian Chard or Pinot Grigio. Australian Verdelho
or Clare Ries.

Shark's fin soup Add a teaspoon of Cognac. Sip amontillado.

Shrimps, potted Fino sherry, Chablis, white Rioja or Long Island Chard.

Soufflés As show dishes these deserve wines.
fish Dry white: *** burgundy, Bordeaux, Alsace, Chardonnay, etc.
cheese Red burgundy or B'dx, Cab S (not Chilean or Australian), etc.
spinach (tougher on wine) Mâcon-Villages, St-Véran, Valpolicella.
Champagne can also be good with all textures of soufflé.

Spinach A challenge here. Can make reds taste of rust. Good Cabs usually survive, as do neutral whites like unoaked Chard.

Tapenade Manzanilla or fino, or any sharpish dry white or rosé.

Taramasalata A rustic southern white with personality; not necessarily Retsina. Fino sherry works well. Try white Rioja or a Rhône Marsanne. The bland supermarket version goes well with fine delicate whites or Champagne.

Terrine As for pâté, or similar r: Mercurey, St-Amour or Beaujolais-Villages, youngish St-Emilion, Calif Syrah, Sangiovese; Bulgarian or Chilean Cab.

Tortilla Rioja crianza, fino sherry or white Mâcon-Villages.

Trout, smoked Sancerre, California or S African Sauv Bl. Rully or Bourgogne Aligoté, Chablis or Champagne.

Vegetable terrine Not a great help to fine wine, but California, Chilean or S African Chards make a fashionable marriage, Chenin Blanc such as Vouvray a lasting one.

Whitebait Crisp dry whites: Muscadet, Touraine Sauvignon Bl, Verdicchio or fino sherry.

Fish

Abalone Dry or medium w: Sauvignon Blanc, Côte de Beaune blanc, Pinot Grigio, Muscadet sur lie. Chinese style: vintage Champagne.

Anchovies A robust wine: red, white or rosé – try Rioja. Or Muscadet.

Bass, sea Weissburgunder from Baden or Pfalz. Vg for any fine/delicate white, eg Coonawarra dry Riesling, Chablis, white Châteauneuf-du-Pape.

Beurre blanc, fish with A top-notch Muscadet sur lie, a Sauvignon/Sémillon blend, Chablis Premier Cru, Vouvray or a Rheingau Charta wine.

Brandade Chablis Premier Cru or Sancerre Rouge.

Bream (esp baked in a salt crust) Full-bodied white or rosé; Rioja, Albariño, Costières de Nîmes, Côte de Lubéron or Minervois.

Brill Very delicate: hence a top fish for fine old Puligny and the like.

Carpaccio of salmon or tuna See also First courses. Puligny-Montrachet, Condrieu, California Chardonnay or NZ Sauvignon Blanc.

Cod If roast, a good neutral background for fine dry/medium whites: Chablis, Meursault, Corton-Charlemagne, cru classé Graves, top Muscadet; German Kabinett or dry Spätlesen, or a gd light red, eg Beaune.

Crab, cioppino Sauv Bl; but West Coast friends say Zinfandel. Also California sp wine.

cold, with salad Alsace or Rhine Riesling, dry California or Australian Riesling, or Condrieu.

softshell Chardonnay or top-quality German Riesling Spätlese.

Chinese, baked with ginger and onion German Riesling Kabinett or Spätlese Halbtrocken. Tokay Furmint, Gewürz.

with Black Bean sauce A big Barossa Shiraz or Syrah.

Eel, jellied NV Champagne or a nice cup of (Ceylon) tea.

smoked Strong/sharp wine: fino sherry, Bourgogne Aligoté. Schnapps.

Fish and chips, fritto misto (or tempura) Chablis, white Bordeaux, Sauv Bl, Pinot Blanc, Gavi, Fino, Montilla, Koshu (?), tea or NV Champ and Cava.

Fish pie (with creamy sauce) Albariño, Soave Classico, Pinot Gr d'Alsace.

Haddock Rich dr w: Meursault, Calif or NZ Chard, Marsanne or Albariño.

Hake Sauv Bl or any freshly fruity white: Pacherenc, Tursan, white Navarra.

Halibut As turbot.

Herrings Need a white with some acidity to cut their richness. Rully, Bourgogne Aligoté, Gros Plant from Brittany, dry Sauvignon Bl. Or cider.

Kedgeree Full white, still or sparkling: Mâcon-Villages, South African Chard or (at breakfast) Champagne.

Kippers A good cup of tea, preferably Ceylon (milk, no sugar). Scotch? Dry oloroso sherry is surprisingly good.

Lamproie à la Bordelaise 5-yr-old St-Emilion or Fronsac. Or Esparão or Bairrada with Portuguese lampreys.

Lobster, richly sauced Vintage Champagne, fine white burgundy, cru classé Graves, California Chard or Australian Ries, Pfalz Spätlese.

salad White: NV Champagne, Alsace Riesling, Chablis Premier Cru, Condrieu, Mosel Spätlese, Penedès Chard or Cava.

Mackerel Hard or sharp white: Sauvignon Blanc from Touraine, Gaillac, Gros Plant, Vinho Verde, white Rioja, English white wine. Or Guinness.

Monkfish Often roasted, which suggests fuller rather than leaner wines. Try NZ Chard or NZ/Oregon Pinot Noir, Chilean Merlot.

Mullet, red A chameleon, adaptable to good white or red, esp Pinot N.

Mussels Muscadet sur lie, Chablis Premier Cru, Chardonnay.

stuffed, with garlic See Escargots.

Perch, sandre Exquisite fishes for finest wines: top white burgundy, Alsace Riesling Grand Cru or noble Mosels. Or try top Swiss Fendant or Johannisberg.

Salmon, seared or grilled Fine white burgundy: Puligny- or Chassagne-Montrachet, Meursault, Corton-Charlemagne, Chablis Grand Cru; Condrieu, California, Idaho or NZ Chard, Rheingau Kabinett/Spätlese, Australian Ries. Young Pinot N can be good, too — Merlot or light claret not bad. Salmon fishcakes call for similar, but less grand, wines.

Sand-dabs This sublime fish can handle your fullest Chardonnay (but not oaky).

Sardines, fresh grilled Very dry white: Vinho Verde, Soave, Muscadet, modern Greek.

Sashimi If you are prepared to forego the wasabi, sp wines will go, or Washington or Tasmanian Chard, Chablis Grand Cru, Rheingau Riesling Halbtrocken, English Seyval Bl. Otherwise, iced sake, fino sherry or beer. Recent trials have matched 5-putt Tokáji with fat tuna, sea urchin, and anago (eel).

Scallops An inherently slightly sweet dish, best with med-dry whites.
in cream sauces German Spätlese, Montrachet, or top Australian Chard.
grilled or seared Hermitage Blanc, Grüner Veltliner, Entre-Deux-Mers, vintage Champagne or Pinot Noir.
with Asian seasoning NZ, S Africa Sauv Bl, Verdelho, Australian Ries, Gewürz.

Shellfish Dry white with plain boiled shellfish, richer wines with richer sauces. Crab and Riesling are part of the Creator's plan. With plateaux de fruits de mer: Muscadet, Picpoul de Pinet.

Skate with brown butter White with some pungency (eg Pinot Gris d'Alsace), or a clean straightforward one like Muscadet or Verdicchio.

Snapper Sauvignon Blanc if cooked with oriental flavours, white Rhône with Mediterranean flavours.

Sole, plaice, etc: plain, grilled or fried Perfect with fine wines: white burgundy, or its equivalent.
with sauce Depending on the ingredients: sharp dry wine for tomato sauce, fairly rich for sole véronique, etc.

Sushi Hot wasabi is usually hidden in every piece. German QbA trocken wines or simple Chablis or NV brut Champ. Or, of course, sake or beer.

Swordfish Full-bodied dry white of the country. Nothing grand.

Trout Delicate white wine, eg Mosel (especially Saar or Ruwer), Alsace Pinot Blanc.
smoked See First courses.

Tuna, grilled or seared White, red or rosé of fairly fruity character; a top St-Véran or white Hermitage, or Côtes du Rhône would be fine. Pinot Noir and Merlot are the best reds to try.

Turbot Your best rich dry white: Meursault or Chassagne-Montrachet, mature Chablis or its California, Australian or NZ equivalent. Condrieu. Mature Rheingau, Mosel or Nahe Spätlese or Auslese (not trocken).

Meat, poultry, etc

Barbecues Red with a slight rasp, therefore young: Shiraz, Chianti, Navarra, Zinfandel, Turkish Buzbag (?). Bandol for a real treat.

Beef, boiled Red: Bordeaux (Bourg or Fronsac), Roussillon, Gevrey-Chambertin, Côte-Rôtie. Medium-ranking white Burgundy is good, eg. Auxey-Duresses. Or top-notch beer.
roast An ideal partner for fine red wine of any kind.

Beef stew Sturdy red: Pomerol or St-Emilion, Hermitage, Cornas, Barbera, Shiraz, Napa Cabernet, Torres Gran Coronas.

Beef Stroganoff Dramatic red: Barolo, Valpolicella Amarone, Cahors, Hermitage, late-harvest Zin – even Moldovan Negru de Purkar.

Boudin Blanc Loire Chenin Bl esp when served with apples: dry Vouvray, Saumur, Savennières. Mature red Côtes de Beaune, if without apple.

Cabbage, stuffed Hungarian Cab Franc/Kadarka; village Rhônes; Salice Salentino and other spicy S Italian reds. Or Argentine Malbec.

Cajun food Fleurie, Brouilly, or Sauv Bl. With gumbo: amontillado or Mexican beer.

Cassoulet Red from SW France (Gaillac, Minervois, Corbières, St-Chinian or Fitou), or Shiraz. But best of all Beaujolais Cru or young red Navarra.

Chicken/turkey/guinea fowl, roast Virtually any wine, incl very best bottles of dry/med white and finest old reds (esp burgundy). The meat of fowl can be adapted with sauces to match almost any fine wine (eg coq au vin with red or white burgundy). Try sparkling Shiraz with strong, sweet or spicy stuffings and trimmings.

Chicken Kiev Alsace Riesling, Collio, Chardonnay, Bergerac Rouge.

Chilli con carne Young red: Beauj, Navarra, Zinfandel, Argentine Malbec.

Chinese food, Canton or Peking style Dry to med-dry white – Mosel Ries Kabinett or Spätlese trocken – can be good throughout a Chinese banquet. Gewürz, often suggested but rarely works yet Chasselas and Pinot Gris are attractive alternatives. Dry or off-dry sparkling (esp cava) cuts the oil and matches sweetness. Eschew sweet/ sour dishes but try St-Emilion ** (or Le Pin?), New World Pinot N, or Châteauneuf-du-Pape with duck. I often serve both white and red wines concurrently during Chinese meals.

Szechuan style Muscadet, Alsace Pinot Blanc or v cold beer.

Choucroute garni Alsace, Pinot Blanc, Pinot Gris or Riesling or beer.

Cold meats Generally better with full-flavoured white than red. Mosel Spätlese or Hochheimer and Côte Chalonnaise are very good. And so is Beaujolais.

Confit d'oie/de canard Young tannic red B'x Cru Bourgeois California Cab and Merlot, and Priorato help cut richness. Alsace Pinot Gris or Gewürz matches it.

Coq au vin Red burgundy. In an ideal world, one bottle of Chambertin in the dish, two on the table.

Curry see Indian food

Duck or goose Rather rich white: Pfalz Spätlese or Alsace réserve exceptionelle; or mature gamey red: Morey-St-Denis or Côte-Rôtie or Bordeaux or burgundy. With oranges or peaches, the Sauternais propose drinking Sauternes, others Monbazillac or Riesling Auslese.

Peking See Chinese food.

wild duck Big-scale red: Hermitage, Bandol, California or S African Cab, Australian Shiraz – Grange if you can find it.

with olives Top-notch Chianti or Tuscan VdT.

Frankfurters German, NY Riesling, Beaujolais, light Pinot Noir. Or Budweiser (Budwar).

Game birds, young birds plain-roasted The best red wine you can afford.

older birds in casseroles Red (Gevrey-Chambertin, Pommard, Santenay or Grand Cru St-Emilion, Napa Valley Cabernet or Rhône).

well-hung game Vega Sicilia, great red Rhône, Château Musar.

cold game Mature vintage Champagne.

Game pie
hot Red: Oregon Pinot Noir.
cold Good quality white Burgundy, cru Beaujolais or Champagne.

Goulash Flavoursome young red: Zinfandel, Bulgarian Cabernet or Mavrud, Hungarian Kadarka, young Australian Shiraz.

Grouse See Game birds – but push the boat right out.

Haggis Fruity red, eg young claret, New World Cabernet or Châteauneuf-du-Pape. Or of course malt whisky.

Ham Softer red burgundles: Volnay, Savigny, Beaune; Chinon or Bourgueil; slightly sweet German white (Rhine Spätlese); Czech Frankova; lightish Cabernet (eg Chilean), or California Pinot Noir. And don't forget the heaven-made match of ham and sherry (or ham and Chablis).

Hamburger Young red: Beaujolais or Bulgarian Cabernet, Chianti, Zinfandel. Or Coke or Pepsi (not 'Diet', but 'Max').

Hare Jugged hare calls for flavourful red: not-too-old burgundy or Bordeaux, Rhône (eg Gigondas), Bandol, Barbaresco, Rib del Duero, Rioja Reserva. The same for saddle. Australia's Grange would be an experience.

Indian food Medium-sw w, very cold: Orvieto abboccato, California Chenin Bl, Slovenian Traminer, Indian sp, cava and NV Champagne. Or emphasize the heat with a tannic Barolo or Barbaresco, or deep-flavoured reds such as Chât'neuf-du-Pape, Cornas, Shiraz-Cab or Valpolicella Amarone.

Kebabs Vigorous red: Greek Nemea or Naoussa, Corbières, Chilean Cabernet, Zinfandel or Barossa Shiraz. Sauvignon Blanc, if cooked with lots of garlic.

Kidneys Red: St-Emilion or Fronsac: Nuits-St-Georges, Cornas, Barbaresco, Rioja, Spanish or Australian Cabernet, Portuguese Bairrada.

Lamb, cutlets or chops As for roast lamb, but a little less grand.
roast One of the traditional and best partners for very good red Bordeaux – or its Cabernet equivalents from the New World. In Spain, the partner of the finest old Rioja and Ribera del Duero Reservas.

Liver Young red: Beaujolais-Villages, St-Joseph, Médoc, Italian Merlot, Breganze Cabernet, Zinfandel, Portuguese Bairrada.
Calf's Red Rioja crianza, Salice Salentino Riserva, Fleurie.

Meatballs Tangy medium-bodied red: Mercurey, Crozes-Hermitage, Madiran, Rubesco, Dão, Zinfandel or Cabernet.
Spicy Middle-Eastern style Simple, crisp dry white or rustic red.

Moussaka Red or rosé: Naoussa from Greece, Chianti, Corbières, Côtes de Provence, Ajaccio, Chilean Pinot Noir.

Osso buco Low tannin, supple red, eg Dolcetto d'Alba, Pinot Noir; dry Italian white such as Soave, Lugana.

Oxtail Rather rich red: St-Emilion, Pomerol, Pommard, Nuits-St-Georges, Barolo or Rioja Reserva, California or Coonawarra Cabernet, Châteauneuf-du-Pape.

Paella Young Spanish red, dry white or rosé: Penedès, Somontano, Navarra or Rioja.

Pigeons Lively reds: Savigny, Chambolle-Musigny; Crozes-Hermitage, Chianti Classico or California Pinot. Or try Franken Silvaner Spätlese.

Pork, roast A good rich neutral background to a fairly light red or rich white. It deserves treatment – Médoc is fine. Portugal's famous sucking pig is eaten with Bairrada Garrafeira, Chinese is good with Pinot Noir.

Pot au feu, bollito misto, cocido Rustic red wines from the region of origin; Sangiovese di Romagna, Chusclan, Lirac, Rasteau, Portuguese Alentejo and Yecla and Jumilla from Spain.

Quail As for squab. Carmignano, Rioja Reserva, mature claret, Pinot N.

Rabbit Lively medium-bodied young Italian red or Aglianico del Vulture or Chiroubles, Chinon, Saumur-Champigny or Rhône rosé.

Satay Australia's McLaren Vale Shiraz or Alsace or NZ Gewürztraminer.

Sauerkraut (German) Lager or Pils. (But see also Choucroute garni.)

Sausages See also Frankfurters, Salami. The British banger requires a young Malbec from Argentina (a red wine, anyway), or a traditional British ale.

Shepherd's pie Rough-and-ready red seems most appropriate, eg Barbera, but beer or dry cider is the real McCoy.

Squab Fine white or red Burgundy, Alsace Ries Grand Cru or mature claret.

Steak, au poivre A fairly young Rhône red or Cabernet.
tartare Vodka or light young red: Beaujolais, Bergerac, Valpolicella.
Korean Yuk Whe (the world's best steak tartare) Sake.
filet or tournedos Any red (but not old wines with
Béarnaise sauce: top Californian Chard is better).
T-bone Reds of similar bone structure: Barolo, Hermitage, Australian Cabernet or Shiraz.
fiorentina (bistecca) Chianti Classico Riserva or Brunello.

Steak and kidney pie or pudding Red Rioja Reserva Dão or Bairrada or mature Bordeaux.

Stews and casseroles Burgundy such as Chambolle-Musigny or Bonnes-Mares if fairly simple; otherwise lusty full-flavoured red: young Côtes du Rhône, Toro, Corbières, Barbera, Shiraz, Zinfandel, etc.

Sweetbreads A grand dish, so grand wine: Rhine Ries or Franken Silvaner Spätlese, Alsace Grand Cru Pinot Gr, or Condrieu, depending on sauce.

Tandoori chicken Sauvignon Blanc, or young red Bordeaux or light N Italian red served cool. Also cava and NV Champagne.

Thai food Ginger and lemongrass call for pungent Sauvignon Bl (Loire, Australia, NZ, South Africa) or Riesling (Spätlese or Australian).
coconut milk Hunter Valley and other ripe, oaked Chards; Alsace Pinot Bl for refreshment; Gewürz or Verdelho. And of course cava or NV Champagne.

Tongue Good for any red or white of abundant character, esp Italian. Also Beaujolais, Loire reds and full dry rosés.

Tripe Red, eg Corbières, Roussillon or rather sweet white (eg German Spätlese). Better: W Australian Sem-Chard, or cut with pungent dry white such as Pouilly-Fumé or fresh red eg Saumur-Champigny.

Veal, roast A good neutral background dish for any fine old red which may have faded with age (eg a Rioja Reserva) or a German or Austrian Riesling or Vouvray or Alsace Pinot Gris.

Venison Big-scale red incl Mourvèdre (Mataro) solo as in Bandol, or in blends, Rhône, Bordeaux or California Cab of a mature vintage; or rather rich white (Pfalz Spätlese or Alsace Pinot Gr).

Vitello tonnato Full-bodied white esp Chard; light red (eg Valpolicella) served cool.

Vegetarian dishes

Baked pasta dishes Pasticcio, lasagne and cannelloni with elaborate vegetarian fillings and sauces: an occasion to show off a grand wine esp finest Tuscan vdt, but also Claret and Burgundy. Also Gavi from Italy.

Bubble-and-squeak Beer, stout, or Beaujolais Nouveau.

Cauliflower cheese Crisp aromatic white: Sancerre, Ries Spätlese, Muscat, English Seyval Bl or Schönburger

Couscous with vegetables Young red with a bite: Shiraz, Corbières, Minervois or well chilled rosé from Navarra or Somontano, or a robust Moroccan red.

Fennel-based dishes Sauv Bl: Pouilly-Fumé or one from NZ; English Schönburger or Seyval Blanc or a Beaujolais.

Grilled Mediterranean vegetables Brouilly, Barbera, or Cab-Shiraz.

'Meaty' aubergine, lentil or mushroom bakes Corbières, Zinfandel, Shiraz-Cabernet.

Mezze Hot and cold vegetable dishes. Cava is a good all-purpose choice as is rosé from Languedoc or Provence.

Mushrooms (in most contexts) Fleshy red; eg Pomerol, California Merlot, Rioja Reserva, top Burgundy or Vega Sicilia.
on toast Your best claret.
wild mushroom risotto (ceps/porcinis are best for wine) Ribera del Duero, Barolo or Chianti Rufina, or top claret: Pauillac or St-Estèphe.

Onion/leek tart Fruity off-dry or dry w: Alsace Pinot Gr or Gewürz, Canadian Ries, English Whites, Jurançon, Australian Ries. Or Beaujolais or Loire red.

Peppers or aubergines (eggplant), stuffed Vigorous red wine: Nemea, Italian Chianti or Dolcetto, California Zinfandel, Bandol, Vacqueyras.

Pies Depending on filling, lighter styles of Chard or Côtes du Rhône.

Pumpkin/Squash ravioli or risotto Full-bodied fruity dry or off-dry white: white Rhône (Viognier or Marsanne); demi-sec Vouvray, Gavi, or South African Chenin.

Ratatouille Vigorous young red: Chianti, Bulgarian Cabernet or Merlot; young red Bordeaux or Gigondas or Coteaux du Languedoc.

Spiced vegetarian dishes See under Indian food, Thai Food.

Spinach, ricotta and pasta bake/Spanacopitta Valpolicella (its bitterness helps); Greco di Molise, or w Sicilian/Sardinian.

Desserts

Apple pie, strudel or tarts Sweet German, Austrian, Loire white, Tokáji Aszú or Canadian Ice Wine.

Apples, Cox's Orange Pippins Vintage port (55 60 63 66 70 75 82 +?).

Bread-and-butter pudding Fine 10-yr-old Barsac, Tokáji Azsú or Australian botrytized Sem.

Cakes and gâteaux see also Chocolate, Coffee, Ginger, Rum. Bual or Malmsey Madeira, oloroso or cream sherry.

Cheesecake Sweet white: Vouvray or Anjou or fizz, refreshing but nothing special.

Chocolate flavours Generally only powerful flavours can compete. Bual, California orange Muscat, Tokay Azsú, Australian liqueur Muscat, 10-yr-old tawny port; Asti for light, fluffy mousses. Experiment with rich, ripe reds: Syrah, Zinfandel even sparkling Shiraz. Banyuls for a weightier partnership. Or a tot of good rum.

Christmas pudding, mince pies Tawny port, cream sherry, or liquid Christmas pudding itself, Pedro Ximénez sherry. Asti or Banyuls.

Coffee flavours Sw Muscat incl Australia liqueur Muscats or Tokáji Aszú.

Creams, custards, fools, syllabubs see also Chocolate, Coffee, Ginger, Rum. Sauternes, Loupiac, Ste-Croix-du-Mont, Monbazillac.

Crème brûlée Sauternes or Rhine Beerenauslese, best Madeira or Tokáji. (With concealed fruit, a more modest sweet wine.)

Crêpes Suzette Sweet Champagne, Orange Muscat or Asti spumante.

Fruit
fresh Sweet Coteaux du Layon, light sweet Muscat.
poached, ie apricots, pears, etc Sweet Muscatel: try Muscat de Beaumes-de-Venise, Moscato di Pantelleria or Spanish dessert Tarragona.
dried fruit (and compotes) Banyuls, Rivesaltes, Maury.
flans and tarts Sauternes, Monbazillac or sweet Vouvray or Anjou.
salads, orange salad A fine sweet sherry, or any Muscat-based wine.

Ginger flavours Sweet Muscats, New World botrytized Ries and Sém.

Ice-cream and sorbet Fortified wine (Australian liqueur Muscat, Banyuls); sweet Asti spumante or sparkling Moscato. Amaretto liqueur with vanilla; rum with chocolate.

Lemon flavours For dishes like Tarte au Citron, try sw Riesling from Germany or Austria, or Tokay Aszú; very sw if lemon is very tart.

Meringues Recioto di Soave, Asti or Champagne doux.

Mille-feuille Delicate sweet sparkling white, eg Moscato d'Asti, demi-sec Champagne.

Nuts Finest oloroso sherry, Madeira, vintage or tawny port (nature's match for walnuts), Vin Santo, Setúbal Moscatel.

Orange flavours Experiment with old Sauternes, Tokáji Aszú or California Orange Muscat.

Panettone Jurançon moelleux, late-harvest Riesling, Barsac, Tokáji Aszú.

Pears in red wine A pause before the port. Or try Rivesaltes, Banyuls or Ries Beerenauslese.

Pecan pie Orange Muscat or liqueur Muscat.

Raspberries (no cream, little sugar) Excellent with fine reds that themselves taste of raspberries: young Juliénas, Regnié.

Rum flavours (baba, mousses, ice-cream) Muscat – from Asti to Australian liqueur, according to weight of dish.

Strawberries, wild (no cream) Serve with red Bordeaux (most exquisitely Margaux) poured over.

Strawberries and cream Sauternes or similar sweet Bordeaux, Vouvray Moelleux (90) or Jurançon Vendange Tardive.

Summer pudding Fairly young Sauternes of a good vintage (83 85 86 88 89 90).

Sweet soufflés Sauternes or Vouvray moelleux. Sw (or rich) Champagne.

Tiramisú Vin Santo, young tawny port, Beaumes-de-Venise or Sauternes and Australian liqueur muscats.

Trifle Should be sufficiently vibrant with its internal sherry.

Zabaglione Light-gold Marsala or Australian botrytized Semillon or Asti.

Wine & cheese

The notion that wine and cheese were married in heaven is not born out by experience. Fine red wines are slaughtered by strong cheeses: only sharp or sweet white wines survive.

Principles to remember, despite exceptions, are first: the harder the cheese the more tannin the wine can have. And the creamier it is the more acidity is needed in the wine. The main exception constitutes a third principle: wines and cheeses of a region usually sympathize.

Cheese is classified by its texture and the nature of its rind, so its appearance is a guide to the type of wine to match it. Individual cheeses mentioned below are only examples taken from the hundreds sold in good cheese shops.

Fresh, no rind – cream cheese, crème fraîche, Mozzarella Light crisp white – Côtes de Duras, Bergerac, Vinho Verde, English unoaked whites; or pink – Anjou, Rhône; or very light, v young, v fresh red Bordeaux, Bardolino or Beaujolais.

Hard cheeses, waxed or oiled, often showing marks from cheesecloth – Gruyère family, Manchego and other Spanish cheeses, Parmesan, Cantal, Comté, old Gouda, Cheddar and most 'traditional' English cheeses Particularly hard to generalize here; Gouda, Gruyère, some Spanish, and a few English cheeses complement fine claret or Cab and great Shiraz/Syrah wines, but strong cheeses need less refined wines, preferably local. Sugary, granular old Dutch red Mimolette or Beaufort are good for finest mature Bordeaux. Also for Tokáji Aszú.

Blue cheeses Roquefort can be wonderful with Sauternes, but don't extend the idea to other blues. It is the sweetness of Sauternes, especially old, which complements the saltiness. Stilton and port, preferably tawny, is a classic. Intensely flavoured old oloroso, amontillado, Madeira, Marsala, and other fortified wines go with most blues.

Natural rind (mostly goat's cheese) with bluish-grey mould (the rind becomes wrinkled when mature), s'times dusted with ash – St-Marcellin
Sancerre, Valençay, light fresh Sauvignon, Jurançon, Savoie, Soave, Italian Chard, lightly oaked English whites.

Bloomy rind soft cheeses, pure white rind if pasteurized, or dotted with red: Brie, Camembert, Chaource, Bougon (goat's milk 'Camembert')
Full dry white burgundy or Rhône if cheese is white, immature; powerful, fruity St-Emilion, E European Pinot, young Australian (or Rhône) Shiraz/ Syrah if mature.

Washed-rind soft cheeses, with rather sticky orange-red rind – Langres, mature Epoisses, Maroilles, Carré de l'Est, Milleens, Munster
Local reds, especially for Burgundy cheeses; vigorous Languedoc, Cahors, Côtes du Frontonnais, Corsican, southern Italian, Sicilian, Bairrada. Also powerful whites, esp Alsace Gewurztraminer and Muscat.

Semi-soft cheeses, grey-pink thickish rind – Livarot, Pont l'Evêque, Reblochon, Tomme de Savoie, St-Nectaire
Powerful w Bordeaux, Chard, Alsace Pinot G, dryish Riesling, southern Italian and Sicilian w, aged w Rioja, dry oloroso sherry. But the strongest of these cheeses kill most wines.

Food & finest wine

With very special bottles, the wine sometimes guides the choice of food rather than the usual way around. The following suggestions are based largely on the gastronomic conventions of the wine regions producing these treasures, plus much diligent research. They should help bring out the best in your best wines.

Red wines

Red Bordeaux and other Cabernet Sauvignon-based wines
(very old, light and delicate: eg pre-59, with exceptions such as 45)
Leg or rack of young lamb, roast with a hint of herbs (but not garlic); entrecôte; roast partridge or grouse, sweetbreads; or cheese soufflé after the meat has been served.

Fully mature great vintages (eg Bordeaux 59 61) Shoulder or saddle of lamb, roast with a touch of garlic, roast ribs or grilled rump of beef.

Mature but still vigorous (eg 82 70 66) Shoulder or saddle of lamb (incl kidneys) with rich sauce. Fillet of beef marchand de vin (with wine and bone-marrow). Avoid Beef Wellington: pastry dulls the palate.

Merlot-based Bordeaux (Pomerol, St-Emilion) Beef as above (fillet is richest) or venison.

Côte d'Or red burgundy (Consider the weight and texture, which grow lighter/more velvety with age. Also the character of the wine: Nuits is earthy, Musigny flowery, great Romanées can be exotic, Pommard renowned for its four-squareness, etc.) Roast chicken, or better, capon, is a safe standard with red burgundy; guinea-fowl for slightly stronger wines, then partridge, grouse or woodcock for those progressively more rich and pungent. Hare and venison (chevreuil) are alternatives.
Great old reds The classic Burgundian formula is cheese: Epoisses (unfermented). A fabulous cheese but a terrible waste of fine old wines.
Vigorous younger burgundy Duck or goose roasted to minimize fat.

Great Syrahs: Hermitage, Côte-Rôtie, Grange; or Vega Sicilia
Beef, venison, well-hung game; bone-marrow on toast; English cheese (esp best farm Cheddar) but also the newer hard goat's milk and ewe's milk cheese such as Berkswell and Ticklemore.

Rioja Gran Reserva, Pesquera... Richly flavoured roasts: wild boar, mutton, saddle of hare, whole suckling pig.

Barolo, Barbaresco Risotto with white truffles; pasta with game sauce (eg pappardelle alle lepre); porcini mushrooms; Parmesan.

White wines

Very good Chablis, white burgundy, other top quality Chardonnays
White fish simply grilled or meunière. Dover sole, turbot, halibut are best; brill, drenched in butter, can be excellent. (Sea-bass is too delicate; salmon passes but does little for the finest wine.)

Supreme white burgundy (Le Montrachet, Corton-Charlemagne) or equivalent Graves Roast veal, organic chicken stuffed with truffles or herbs under the skin, or sweetbreads; richly sauced white fish or scallops as above. Or lobster or wild salmon.

Condrieu, Château-Grillet or Hermitage Blanc Very light pasta scented with herbs and tiny peas or broad beans.

Grand Cru Alsace, Riesling Truite au bleu, smoked salmon or choucroute garni.
Pinot Gris Roast or grilled veal.
Gewurztraminer Cheese soufflé (Münster cheese).
Vendange Tardive Foie gras or Tarte Tatin.

Sauternes Simple crisp buttery biscuits (eg Langue-de-Chat), white peaches, nectarines, strawberries (without cream). Not tropical fruit. Pan- seared foie-gras. Experiment with blue(?) cheeses.

Supreme Vouvray moelleux, etc Buttery biscuits, apples, apple tart.

Beerenauslese/TBA Biscuits, peaches, greengages. Desserts made from rhubarb, gooseberries, quince or apples.

Tokay Aszú (4–6 putts) Foie gras is thoroughly recommended. Fruit desserts, cream desserts, even chocolate can be wonderful.

Great vintage port or Madeira Walnuts or pecans. A Cox's Orange Pippin and a digestive biscuit is a classic English accompaniment.

Old vintage Champagne (not Blanc de Blancs) As an aperitif, or with cold partridge, grouse or woodcock.

France

More heavily shaded areas
are the wine growing regions

The following abbreviations
of regional names
are used in the text:

Al	Alsace
Beauj	Beaujolais
Burg	Burgundy
B'x	Bordeaux
Champ	Champagne
Lo	Loire
Prov	Provence
Pyr	Pyrenees
N/S Rh	North/South Rhône
SW	Southwest

Le Havre

Caen

Brest

LOIRE

Loire

Nantes

Anjou-
Muscadet Saumur

La Rochelle

BORDE

Médoc

Bordeaux Pomer
St-Em
Ent
Graves De
Sauternes

Côtes du B
Marmandai
Tursan Côte
St-M
Biarritz Mad
Jurançon

France is beginning to realize that she can afford to rest on her laurels no longer. It is not just Australia she has to watch but Chile, Argentina, New Zealand, the USA, and South Africa. Quality and value are uppermost in the mind of the 21st century wine consumer. Former loyalties cannot be relied upon.

The New World emulates the best of France at almost all levels. However sublime her best wines, the *fonctionnaires* who run the system of Appellations Contrôlées must abandon nit-picking restrictions and apply their minds to quality. The danger of fossilization combined with commercialization is a sombre prospect. The French genius for taste and style is on trial.

Appellations remain the key to French wine. An appellation defines a type. It may apply to a single small vineyard or to a large district.

Burgundy, on the whole, has the most precise and smallest appellations, Bordeaux the widest and most general. An appellation is the first thing to look for on a label, but more important still is the name of the winemaker. The best growers' and merchants' names are a vital ingredient of these pages. Regions without the overall quality and traditions required for an appellation can be ranked as *vins délimités de qualité supérieure* (VDQS), a shrinking category as its members gain AC status. Their place is being taken by the relatively new and highly successful *vins de pays. Vins de pays* are almost always worth trying. They include some brilliant originals and often offer France's best value for money – which still, despite all the competition, can mean the world's.

Recent vintages of the French classics

Red Bordeaux

Médoc/red Graves For some wines bottle-age is optional: for these it is indispensable. Minor châteaux from light vintages need only 2 or 3 yrs, but even modest wines of great years can improve for 15 or so, and the great châteaux of these years need double that time.

2001 A cool September and rain at vintage meant Cabernet Sauvignon had difficulty in ripening fully. Some good wines but overall quality variable.

2000 Late flowering and a somewhat damp start to the summer looked worrying but the final product is outstanding – superb wines throughout. Keep.

1999 Vintage rain again diluted ripe juice, useful wines to drink 2004-2015.

1998 Rain at vintage *again*. But August heat ripened (even roasted) grapes. Good to very good. 2006-2015.

1997 Uneven flowering and summer rain were a double challenge. Cabernet Sauvignon ripened best. Some good wines for the canny. Now–2015.

1996 Cool summer, fine harvest, esp Cabernet. Good to excellent. Now–2020.

1995 Heatwave and drought; saved by rain. Good to excellent. Now–2020+.

1994 Hopes of a supreme year; then heavy vintage rain. The best very good, but be careful. Now–2010.

1993 Ripe grapes but a wet vintage. Generally disappointing. Now 2010.

1992 Rain at flowering, in August and at vintage. A huge crop; light wines, but some easy-drinking. Now–2005.

1991 Frost in April halved crop and rain interrupted vintage. The northern Médoc did best. Drink soon. Now–2010?

1990 A paradox: a drought year with a threat of over-production. Self-discipline was essential. Its results are magnificent. To 2020+.

1989 Early spring, splendid summer. The top wines will be classics of the ripe, dark kind with elegance and length. Small ch'x are uneven. To 2020.

1988 Generally vg; tannic, balanced, beginning to open, keep top wines. To 2015.

1987 Much more enjoyable than seemed likely. Drink up.

1986 Another splendid, huge, heatwave harvest. Better than 85 in Pauillac and St-Julien; a long-term prospect. Now–2020.

1985 Vg vintage, in a heatwave. V fine wines now accessible. Now–2010.

1984 Poor. Originally overpriced. Avoid.

1983 A classic vintage, esp in Margaux: abundant tannin with fruit to balance it. But many wines need drinking. To 2010 for the best.

1982 Made in a heatwave. Huge, rich, strong wines which promise a long life but are developing unevenly. Top châteaux will run to 2015.

1981 Admirable despite rain. Not rich, now a touch austere. Now–2005.

1980 Small late harvest: ripe but rained-on. Drink up.

1979 Abundant harvest of above-average quality. Drink now.

1978 A miracle vintage: magnificent long warm autumn. Now at full stretch.

Older fine vintages: 75 70 66 62 61 59 55 53 49 48 47 45 29 28.

St-Emilion/Pomerol

2001 Less rain than Médoc during vintage. Some powerful Merlot but variable.

2000 Similar conditions to Médoc less kind to Merlot but still a v gd vintage.

1999 Careful, lucky growers made excellent wines but rain was again a problem.

1998 Earlier ripening Merlot largely escaped the rain. Some excellent wines.

1997 The Merlot vintage suffered in the rain. But growers are getting better at handling problems. Good for supple wines. Now–2010.

1996 Cool, fine summer. Vintage rain on Merlot. Less consistent than Médoc. Now–2020.

1995 Perhaps even better than Médoc/Graves. Now–2015.
1994 Less compromised by rain than Médoc. Vg, esp Pomerol. Now–2015.
1993 As Médoc, but better, esp in Pomerol; gd despite terrible vintage weather.
1992 Very dilute but some charming wines to drink quickly. Drink up.
1991 A sad story. Many wines not released.
1990 Another chance to make great wine or a lot of wine. Now–2020.
1989 Large, ripe, early harvest; an overall triumph. To 2020.
1988 Generally excellent; ideal conditions. But some chx over-produced. Pomerol best. Now–2005.
1987 Some v adequate wines (esp in Pomerol). Drink up.
1986 A prolific vintage; but top St-Emilions have long life ahead.
1985 One of the great yrs, with a long future. To 2010+.
1984 A sad story. Most of the crop wiped out in spring. Avoid.
1983 Less impressive than it seemed. Drink soon.
1982 Enormously rich and concentrated wines, most excellent. Now–2005.
1981 A vg vintage, though not as great as it first seemed. Now or soon.
1979 A rival to 78, but not developing as well as hoped. Drink now.
1978 Fine wines, but some lack flesh. Drink soon.
1976 V hot, dry summer, but vintage rain. Fine, tannic. Drink soon.
Older fine vintages: 71 70 67 66 64 61 59 53 52 49 47 45.

Red burgundy

Côte d'Or Côte de Beaune reds generally mature sooner than the bigger wines of the Côte de Nuits. Earliest drinking dates are for lighter commune wines, eg Volnay, Beaune; latest for the biggest wines of eg Chambertin, Romanée. But even the best burgundies are much more attractive young than the equivalent red Bordeaux.

2001 A cool damp September took the edge off; should still be good though.
2000 Difficult. Fragile grapes in Côte de Beaune. Much better in Côte de Nuits.
1999 Big ripe vintage; good colour, bags of fruit, silky tannins. Wines to keep.
1998 Wet Sept could have diluted a v ripe harvest, but now wines look luscious.
1997 Again the gods smiled. Very ripe grapes, with low acidity the main potential problem. Lovely wines for medium term, to 2010+.
1996 Fine summer and vintage. Fine ripe wines for keeping. Now–2020.
1995 Small, excellent crop, despite vintage rains. Grapes were very ripe.
1994 Compromised by vintage rain. Generally lean, but exceptions in Côte de Nuits. Drink soon.
1993 An excellent vintage – concentrated. Now–2010.
1992 Ripe, plump, pleasing. No great concentration. Drink up.
1991 Very small harvest; some wines v tannic. Côte de Nuits best. Now–2010.
1990 Great vintage: perfect weather compromised only by touches of drought and some over-production. Long life ahead but start to enjoy. To 2020.
1989 A year of great charm, not necessarily for very long maturing. Now–2010.
1988 Very good but tannic. Now–2015 (but only the best).
1987 Small crop with ripe fruit flavours, esp in Côte de Beaune. Drink up.
Older fine vintages: 78 71 69 66 64 62 61 59 (all mature).

White burgundy

Côte de Beaune Well-made wines of good vintages with plenty of acidity as well as fruit will improve and gain depth and richness for some years – anything up to 10. Lesser wines from lighter vintages are ready for drinking after 2 or 3 years.

2001 Generally good results despite lower sugar levels.
2000 Looks very exciting. A big crop of ripe, healthy grapes.
1999 A generous vintage of good, fresh, well-balanced wines.

1998 Difficult year for white. Chassagne was successful.

1997 Overall excellent: it will be a joy to compare these to 96 and 95.

1996 A great vintage to lay down top wines. Now–2015.

1995 A potentially great vintage, diluted in places. Now–2010.

1994 Patchy; top growers: v fine potent wines but not for keeping. Now or soon.

1993 Sept rain on under-ripe grapes. Easy & pleasant; far behind reds. Soon.

1992 Ripe, aromatic and charming. Mostly ready. Now–2005.

1991 Mostly lack substance. Frost problems. For early drinking. Now.

1990 Very good, even great, but with a tendency to fatness. Now–2005.

1989 At best ripe, tense, structured, and long. Now–2010.

1988 Some v gd wines; others seem out of balance. Drink soon.

The white wines of the Mâconnais (Pouilly-Fuissé, St-Véran, Mâcon-Villages) follow a similar pattern, but do not last as long. They are more appreciated for their freshness than their richness.

Chablis Grand cru Chablis of vintages with both strength and acidity can age superbly for up to 10 years; Premiers crus proportionately less.

2001 Smaller crop should provide decent wines.

2000 Fine weather for harvesting ripe grapes – excellent.

1999 Another ripe vintage, some of it compromised by rain.

1998 Cool weather and some hail. Wines fair to good: not for long keeping.

1997 Another fine vintage; perhaps drink before the 96s.

1996 Ideal harvest but hail on top v'yds. Classic keeping Chablis. Now–2010.

1995 Very good to very, very good. Now–2006.

1994 Downpours on a ripe vintage. Easy wines; drink up.

1993 Fair to good quality; nothing great. Drink up.

1992 Ripe and charming wines. Grands crus splendid. Now–2005 at least.

1991 Generally better than Côte d'Or. Useful wines. Now.

1990 Grands crus magnificent; others lack intensity and acidity. Now–2005.

1989 Excellent vintage of potent character. Soon.

Beaujolais 01: vg if if picked before the rain 00: excellent. 99: splendid, rich and deep. 98: v gd, if patchy. Best Crus will keep. 97: excellent and will keep. 95: excellent. Older wines should be finished.

Southwest France

2001 Hot summer & perfect vintage conditions. Perhaps too much sugar/alcohol.

2000 Mixed quality, due to heavy rain in Sept. Those who picked early will be gd but probably not for keeping. Better wines should keep.

1999 Patchy weather spoiled the vintage for some, but not disastrous.

1998 Outstanding everywhere. The reds should be at peak in 03.

1997 Dismally wet, but sweet whites excellent after brilliant autumn. Otherwise patchy.

1996 Good "commercial year" in most areas. Madirans will still keep.

1995 Outstanding everywhere. Hard to come by, but worth finding.

1990 Fabulous for long-lived reds – Cahors, Pécharmants, Madirans.

The Midi

2001 Quantity lower than average. Quality generally very good with a hot summer making for ripe concentrated wines.

2000 A warm summer throughout giving ripe fruity wines in Roussillon and Provence, and healthy grapes and balanced wines in Languedoc.

1999 Bad weather failed to ruin vintage in Roussillon, patchy in Languedoc (gd in La Clape – not in Pic St Loup). Gd weather & results in Provence.

1998 Drought in Roussillon meant small crop of conc'd wines. Wonderful vintage in Languedoc made ripe, fruity wines with great potential. Well-balanced fruity wines in Provence.

1997 Problematic in Roussillon and Languedoc – light but fruity wines. Small crop in Provence with concentration and ageing potential. To drink.

1996 Rain diluted the crop in Roussillon and Languedoc – light wines. In Provence, good fruit but reds benefit from bottle-age. To drink.

Northern Rhône

2001 Good, lively year if picked before September rain. Fresh fruit, good acidity. Traditional Côte-Rôties very good. Whites successful.

2000 Gd density and tannic structure. Wines are warm and rich. Hermitage will age well, more tannin there.

1999 V successful. Full, ripe fruit. Delicious, likely to live long. More balance than the '98s. Harmony a key word. Ace Côte-Rôties. Sound whites.

1998 V gd. Big, notably robust vintage. More overt tannins than '99. Will need time to soften. From 2006–10. Good Marsanne-based whites.

1997 Gd/v gd. Fat, fleshy wines that will evolve fast. Lower acidity means rich, smooth flavours. Drinking well now. Good vintage for restaurants.

1996 Potential if left to age. Early discord with fruit, tannin, acidity. Can be complex – track progress for right moment. Drink top wines 2006–08.

1995 Lots of full, ample flavour. Lesser names like Crozes delicious now. Top names need more time, maybe 2004–06. Some have firm tannins.

1994 Gd in general, v gd in Côte-Rôtie. Well-framed wines with sound core. More mineral than the '95s. Top wines will show well around 2002.

1992 Easy fruit, rather cooked at times. A mid-weight vintage, with not too many hidden corners. Drinking fine now.

1991 V gd in Côte-Rôtie, gd in Hermitage. Underestimated due to typical unfair linking with other parts of France. V gd whites.

Southern Rhône

2001 Smaller crop than 2000. Uneven due to September rain, Good density from most careful domaines. Top names are the safest bet.

2000 Tasty wines, led by fruit, juicy and fat. Not a very long-lived year. Go for leading names. Gigondas may edge Châteauneuf in quality.

1999 V gd overall. Ripe, open fruit with correct structure in the best wines. Châteauneuf: Gd harmony 2007+. Vacqueyras: V gd. Lirac: Gd form.

1998 Excellent. A triumph for Grenache. Warm wines which hide their true power and tannin. Some can be too potent, fiery.

1997 Undemanding. Fruit can be cooked, rather jammy. Drink within max 10 years, unless top name and low yields. Some whites interesting.

1996 Uneven. Tannins are brusque. The best will age for 10+ years.

1995 Sweet, succulent, fruity wines. Evolving with speed, esp if growers went for extreme ripeness. The best will live to 2010–14.

1994 Good at Châteauneuf. Good extract with noticeable tannins. Good at Lirac as well. Gigondas showing well now.

1993 Difficult ripening, uneven quality. Lack of acidity, but careful selection made interesting, drier-toned wines for a 10–12 year life.

Champagne

2001 Heavy rain dashed hopes of a possible vintage. Though short of natural alcohol, some respectable wines especially from Chardonnay.

2000 The sun shone through harvest to produce wines of good natural sugar and acidity. Likely to be a vintage year for all producers.

1999 Sporadic rain at harvest changed a great vintage into a good one. Some ripe expressive wines from Chardonnay.

1998 Well constituted, sound wines from both Pinot Noir and Chardonnay. A possible vintage mainly for growers rather than houses.

1997 Brilliant Sept weather saved vintage. Ripe, low-acid wines for easy early drinking. Could be declared before the 96s.

1996 Champagnes of monumental structure, high in alcohol and acidity, needing more time to reach maturity. Growers compare this to 1928.

1995 Classic, finely balanced wines; a Chardonnay year *par excellence*. For most producers the current available vintage.

1993 The best vintage in the lean period 1991–5. Aromatic, delicate, and clean flavours. Excellent wines from Pol Roger and Jacquesson.

1990 One of the greatest recent vintages, best wines are rich, slow maturing, high quality. Varied in quality. Some Blanc de blancs already taste tired.

The Loire

2001 Warm, wet winter left soils gorged with water. Best wines are from those who harvested late. But Muscadet perfect. Taste before buying.

2000 Warm rainy year, with lack of sunshine. Muscadet, Sancerre, and Touraine – satisfactory to gd. The Cab F wines are deeply coloured but not rich. Drink within 6 years. Vouvray: good for sec and demi-sec.

1999 Looked to rival the great 89 when the rains came. Cab F marked by musky "animal" aromas. Vouvray: gd for secs and demi-secs

1998 End of the Loire's luck. Episodes of frost, hail, drought, and heavy rain during harvest. Wines are light, some Cab-based reds are overly tannic.

1997 Warm and sunny with a beautiful "arrière saison". The third excellent vintage. Supple reds and dry whites, and spectacular sweet wines.

1996 Excellent, though not as "flattering" as the 97s. The Cab-based reds need time but will age beautifully (ultimately surpassing the 97s).

1995 An excellent vintage across the board. Long-lived, well-structured, delicious wines in every appellation.

1994 A poor vintage throughout but a handful of growers in the Coteaux deLayon made extremely rich, heavily botrytized wines.

Alsace

2001 After very unsettled weather in Sept, vintage was saved by an Indian Summer. Generally well-balanced wines, good but not great.

2000 Superb – probably best since 90. V gd for Vendanges Tardives and Sélections des Grains Nobles.

1999 A difficult growing season saved by dry, sunny period mid-Aug to mid-Sept. Growers who kept yields down made gd, well-balanced wines.

1998 Unusually the 4th fine vintage in a row. Gd wines despite heatwave Aug – mid-Sept and harvest rain. More Gewürz than previous years.

1997 Almost perfect growing season ending with dry sunny conditions produced concentrated dry wines and outstanding sweet ones.

1996 Harsh winter and late spring followed by hot July and Aug. Ideal conditions in Oct gave a ripe harvest. Fine dry wines, little Gewürz.

1995 Thanks to an Indian summer the late ripening varieties were particularly successful (Pinot Gr, Gewürz, and esp Riesling). Gd sweet wines too.

1994 Superb summer spoiled by wet Sept. A patchy year in which timing was all. Oct sunshine made some Vendanges Tardives possible.

To decipher codes, please refer to "Key to symbols" on front flap of jacket, or to "How to use this book" on page 6.

Abelé Small Reims CHAMPAGNE house with vg NV.

Abel-Lepitre Middle-rank CHAMP house linked with Philipponnat.

Abymes Savoie w ★ DYA Hilly area nr Chambéry; light, mild Vin de Savoie AC from Jacquère grape has alpine charm. SAVOIE has many such crus for local pleasure.

Agenais SW France r p (w) ► DYA VDP of Lot-et-Garonne, mostly from coops at Goulens, Donzac, Monflanquin and Mézin. Also from Marmandais coops.

Ajaccio Corsica r p w ★→★★ 95 96 97 **98 99** 00 01 The capital of CORSICA. AC for some vg Sciacarello reds. Top grower: Peraldi (try his Vermentino). Also Clos Capitoro, Jean Courrèges (Dom de Pratavone).

Aligoté Second-rank burgundy white grape and its wine. Should be pleasantly tart and fruity with local character when young. BOUZERON is the one commune to have an all-Aligoté appellation. The shining example is de Villaine's, but try others from good growers. NB PERNAND-VERGELESSES.

Alliet, Philippe Lo r ★★★ 85 86 87 **88 89 90 93** 95 96 **97 98 99 00** 01 Top-notch producer of long-lived, barrel-aged Chinons: particularly Ch du Noire CUVÉE.

Aloxe-Corton Burg r w ★★→★★★ 78' 85' 88' 89' 90' 91 92 93' 94 95 96' 97 98 99' 00 Village at N end of CÔTE DE BEAUNE famous for two GRANDS CRUS: CORTON (red), CORTON-CHARLEMAGNE (white). Village wines are lighter but to try.

Alsace Al w (r sp) ★★→★★★ **88** 90' **93 95 96 97 98** 99 00 01 Region comprising eastern foothills of Vosges mountains, esp Strasbourg–Mulhouse. Unique wines: aromatic, fruity, full-strength, usually dry and expressive of grape variety, but often sweeter these days. See Vendange Tardive, Sélection des Grains Nobles. Mostly sold by grape variety (PINOT Bl, Ries, GEWURZT etc). Matures well (except Pinot Bl, MUSCAT) up to 5, even 10 yrs; GRAND CRU even longer. Good-quality and value CREMANT. PINOT N can have good varietal character but is not widely sold outside the region.

Alsace Grand Cru w ★★★ →★★★★ **76 85 88 89' 90 93 95** 96 97 98 99 00 01 AC restricted to 50 of the best named v'yds (approx 4,000 acres, 2025 in production) and four noble grapes (Ries, PINOT Gr, GEWURZ, MUSCAT) mainly dry, some sw. Not without controversy but generally vg and expressive of terroir.

Ampeau, Robert Burg ★★★ Exceptional grower and specialist in MEURSAULT & VOLNAY; also POMMARD. Perhaps unique in releasing only long-matured bottles.

Alsace: Wines to look for in 2003

Muscat (always dry in Alsace) DYA. Either the supremely elegant Côte de Rouffach from René Muré or the slightly fuller Muscat from Albert Mann.

Pinot Blanc (The Alsace alternative to Chardonnay) Domaine Mittnach 2000 is full of fruit, Josmeyer's Mise du Printemps 2000 is superb!

Riesling (greatest Alsacien variety) Jean Becker's Kronenbourg LD 98, Leon Beyer's Les Ecaillers 1997 or for a special treat René Muré's Clos St. Landelin 98.

Pinot Gris (Sometimes called Tokay-P-G) Paul Zinck's 99 Prestige, Albert Mann's Grand Cru Furstentum 1999 or Josmeyer's 1854 Foundation vintage 97.

Gewürztraminer (V aromatic and spicy) Dopff & Irion's Les Sorcières 1998, Paul Blanck's Altenbourg 1999 at a higher level Kuentz-Bas's Grand Cru Eichberg 1998 and Willm's Clos Gaensbroennel.

André, Pierre Burg ★★ NEGOCIANT at Ch Corton-André, ALOXE-CORTON; 95 acres of v'yds in CORTON (Gd. C-Charlemagne, Corton Blanc), SAVIGNY, GEVREY-CHAMBERTIN, etc. Also owns REINE PEDAUQUE.

d'Angerville, Marquis Burg ★★★ Top grower with immaculate 35-acre estate all in VOLNAY. Top wines: Champans and intense, potent CLOS des Ducs.

Anjou Lo p r w (sw dr sp) ★→★★★★ Both region and Loire AC. Wide spectrum of styles: light reds incl AC Anjou GAMAY; improving dry whites. Gd red (CAB) ANJOU-VILLAGES; strong dry SAVENNIERES; luscious COTEAUX DU LAYON whites of CHENIN BLANC.

Anjou-Coteaux de la Loire Lo w s/sw sw ★★→★★★ 89' 90' 93 94 95' 96 97 98 99 00 01 Tiny AC for forceful CHENIN whites. DEMI-SEC or sw not as rich as COTEAUX DU LAYON, esp Musset-Roullier, Ch de Putille, Doms du Fresche, de Putille.

Anjou-Villages Lo r ★→★★★ 89 90 93 95 96 97 98 99 00 01 Superior central ANJOU AC for r's (mainly CAB F, some CAB S). Juicy, tannic young; gd value esp Bablut, RICHOU, Rochelles, PIERRE-BISE, Ogereau, Montigilet, Ch'x de Coulaine, de Tigné (Gérard Dépardieu's domaine). New sub-AC to watch: Anjou-Villages-Brissac.

Appellation Contrôlée (AC or AOC) Government control of origin and production (*not* quality) of all the best French wines (see Introduction).

Apremont Savoie w ★★ DYA One of the best villages of SAVOIE for pale, delicate whites, mainly from Jacquère grapes, but recently incl CHARD.

Arbin Savoie r ★★ Deep-coloured lively red from MONDEUSE grapes, rather like a good Loire CABERNET. Ideal après-ski. Drink at 1–2 yrs.

Arbois Jura r p w (sp) ★★→★★★ Various good and original light but tasty wines; speciality is VIN JAUNE. On the whole, DYA except excellent Vin Jaune.

l'Ardèche, Coteaux de Central France r p (w) ★→★★ DYA Area W of Rhône given impetus by G DUBOEUF of BEAUJOLAIS. Bargain fresh country reds; best from pure SYRAH, GAMAY, CAB (NB Serret). Powerful, almost burgundian CHARD "Ardèche" by LOUIS LATOUR (keep 1–2 yrs); Grand Ardèche is v oaked. Also Dom du Colombier.

Ariège SW. Watch out for new vin de pays from 1998 plantings of Cabernet, Merlot, Cot etc. under leadership of DOM. DE RIBONNET.

l'Arlot, Domaine de ★★★ Outstanding producer of excellent NUITS-ST-GEORGES, esp CLOS de l'Arlot, red and white. Owned by AXA Insurance.

Armagnac SW The alternative brandy; more tasty, rustic, and peppery than COGNAC. Table wines: COTES DE GASCOGNE, GERS, TERROIRS LANDAIS.

Armand, Comte Burg ★★★ Excellent POMMARD wines, esp Clos des Epéneaux.

Aube Southern extension of CHAMP. Now known as Côte des Bar.

Aujoux, J-M Beauj Substantial grower/merchant of BEAUJOLAIS. Swiss-owned.

Auxey-Duresses Burg r w ★★→★★★ 90' 91 92 93 95 96' 97 98 99 2nd-rank (but v pretty) COTE DE BEAUNE village: affinities with VOLNAY, MEURSAULT. Best estates: Diconne, HOSPICES DE BEAUNE (Cuvée Boillot), LEROY, M Prunier, R Thévenin. Drink whites in 3–4 yrs. Top white: Leroy's Les Boutonniers.

Avize Champ One of the top Côte des Blancs villages. All CHARDONNAY.

Aÿ Champ. One of the best PINOT N-growing villages of CHAMP.

Ayala Once-famous AY-based old-style CHAMP firm. Deserves more notice for its Pinot-based blends (not its BLANC de BLANCS).

Bahuaud, Donatien ★★ Leading Loire wine merchant. Le Master de Donatien is the top MUSCADET. Ch de la Cassemichère also good.

Bandol Prov r p (w) ★★★ 85' 86 87 88 89 90 91 92 93 94 95 96 97 98 99 00 01 Little coastal region near Toulon producing Provence's best wines; splendid, vigorous, tannic reds predominantly from MOURVEDRE; esp Dom de Pibarnon, Ch Pradeaux, Mas de la Rouvière, DOM TEMPIER.

Banyuls Pyr br sw ★★→★★★ One of best VINS DOUX NATURELS, chiefly from GRENACHE (Banyuls GRAND CRU: over 75% Grenache, aged for 2 yrs+): a distant relation of port. The best are RANCIOS, eg those from Doms la Rectorie, du Mas Blanc (★★★), Vial Magnères, at 10–15 yrs old. Cheap NV wines end up in bars.

Barancourt One of many CHAMP marques bought by the acquisitive Paul-François VRANKEN. PINOT N-led Champagnes, esp Cuvée des Fondateurs. Gd BOUZY ROUGE.

Barrique The Bordeaux (and Cognac) term for an oak barrel holding 225l (300 bottles). Barrique-ageing to flavour almost any wine with oak was craze of late '80s, with some sad results. Current price of oak should enjoin discretion.

Barsac B'x w sw ★★→★★★★ 70 71' 75 76' 79' 81 83' 85 86' 88' 89' 90' 95 96 97 98 99 01' Neighbour of SAUTERNES with similar superb golden wines from different soil; generally less rich and more racy. Richly repays long ageing. Top ch'x: CLIMENS, COUTET, DOISY-DAENE, DOISY-VEDRINES.

Barthod-Noëllat, Ghislaine Burg ★★★ Impressive range of CHAMBOLLE-MUSIGNY.

Barton & Guestier BORDEAUX shipper since 18th C, now owned by Seagram.

Bâtard-Montrachet Burg w ★★★★ 79 85 86' 88 89' 90' 92 93 94 95 96' 97' 98 99 00 Larger (55-acre) n'bour of M'RACHET. Should be v long-lived: intense flavours, rich texture. Bienvenues-B-M: separate adjacent 9-acre GRAND CRU, 15 owners, thus no substantial bottlings; v rare. Seek out: BOUCHARD PERE, J-M BOILLOT, CARILLON, DROUHIN, Gagnard, L LATOUR, LEFLAIVE, MOREY, Pernot, RAMONET, SAUZET.

Baudry, Domaine Bernard Lo r p w ★★★ 85 86 87 88 89 90 93 95 96 97 98 99 00 01 Impeccable CHINONS in a range of styles from CHENIN-based whites to rosés to several excellent cuvées of red, including Les Grezeaux, Clos Guillot, and Les Croix Boissées.

Baumard, Domaine des Lo ★★→★★★★ 75 76 78 81 85 86 88 89 90 93 94 95 96 97 98 99 00 01 Leading grower of ANJOU wine, esp SAVENNIERES, COTEAUX DU LAYON (CLOS Ste-Catherine), and QUARTS DE CHAUME. Baumard is making a tasty vin de table from VERDELHO. Get it while it lasts.

Baux-en-Provence, Coteaux des Prov r p ★→★★★ 95 96 97 98 99 00 01 Formerly joined with COTEAUX D'AIX, now AC in its own right for r and p, but not w. Best wine: DOM DE TREVALLON (CAB-SYRAH) is VDP: no GRENACHE in v'yd so doesn't conform to AC (!) Also Mas Gourmonnier, Romanin, Mas Ste Berthe, Dom Hauvette.

Béarn SW France r p w ★→★★ w p DYA r 98 00 01 Low-key Basque AC centred on coop at Bellocq. Also ★★ Dom de Guilhémas. JURANCON red (esp Dom Nigri) and MADIRAN rosé must be sold as Béarn or VDP PYRENEES-ATLANTIQUES.

Beaujolais Beauj r (p w) ★ DYA Simple AC of the v big Beaujolais region: light short-lived fruity red of GAMAY grapes. Beaujolais Supérieur is little different.

Beaujolais de l'année The BEAUJOLAIS of the latest vintage, until the next.

Beaujolais Primeur (or Nouveau) Same as above, made in a hurry (often only 4–5 days fermenting) for release at midnight on the third Wednesday in November. Ideally soft, pungent, fruity and tempting; too often crude, sharp, too alcoholic. BEAUJ-VILLAGES should be a better bet.

Beaujolais-Villages Beauj r ★★ 99 00 01 Wines from better (N) half of BEAUJOLAIS; should be much tastier than plain BEAUJOLAIS. The 10 (easily) best "villages" are the "CRUS": FLEURIE, etc (see box above). Of the 30 others the best lie around Beaujeu. Crus cannot be released EN PRIMEUR before December 15th. Best kept until spring (or considerably longer).

Beaumes-de-Venise S Rh br (r p) ★★→★★★ DYA Widely regarded as France's best dessert MUSCAT, from S COTES DU RHONE; can be highly flavoured, subtle, lingering (eg from Ch Saint Sauveur, Dom de Coyeux, Dom Durban, JABOULET, VIDAL-FLEURY). Mid weight reds (Ch Redortier, Dom du Fenouillet, Cassan, coop) also gd.

Beaune Burg r (w) ★★★ 88 89' 90' 91 93' 95 96' 97 98 99 Historic wine capital of Burgundy: walled town hollow with cellars. Wines: classic burgundy – but no GRAND CRU. Many fine growers. NEGOCIANTS' CLOS wines (usually PREMIER CRU) often best; eg DROUHIN's superb Clos des Mouches (esp white), JADOT's Clos des Ursules. Beaune du Château is a BOUCHARD PERE brand. Best v'yds: Bressandes, Fèves, Grèves, Marconnets, Teurons.

Becker, Caves J Proud old family firm at Zellenberg, ALSACE now making even finer wines. Classic RIESLING Hagenschlauf and GRAND CRU Froehn MUSCAT. Second label: Gaston Beck.

Bellet Prov p r w ★★★ Fashionable, much-above-average local (Rolle grape) wines from Nice. Serious producers: Ch de Bellet, Dom de la Source. Pricey.

Bergerac Dordogne r w p dr sw ★★ (r) 90 95 96 99 00 (01) Effectively, but not politically, an eastward extension of B'X with no clear break in style/quality. Top properties incl La Tour des Gendres ★★★, Dom l'Ancienne Cure, de Gouyat,

Ch'x de la Colline, Grinou, de la Jaubertie, du Constant, les Eyssards, de la Mallevieille, les Marais, le Paradis, le Raz, la Tour de Grangemont Vari; and CLOS des Verdots; brand-named Julien de Savignac dry whites from Bélingard-Chayne. See also MONBAZILLAC, ROSETTE, SAUSSIGNAC and PECHARMANT.

Besserat de Bellefon Champ Grande Tradition NV; Cuvée des Moines Brut and Rosé NV; Grande Cuvée NV; Brut and Rosé **90 95** Now in Epernay, CHAMP house known for lightish wines, not to keep. Owned by MARNE ET CHAMPAGNE.

Beyer, Léon Ancient ALSACE family firm at Eguisheim. Forceful dry wines needing 5–10 yrs, esp Comtes d'Eguisheim GEWURZ, Comtes d'Eguisheim RIES from GRAND CRU Pfersigberg. Beyer is militant against GRAND CRU restrictions.

Bichot, Maison Albert Burg One of BEAUNE's lgst growers/merchants. V'yds (32-acre Dom du CLOS Frantin (★★): excellent): CHAMBERTIN, RICHEBOURG, CLOS DE VOUGEOT; Dom Long-Depaquit (★★) in CHABLIS; also many other brand names.

Billecart-Salmon NV; Rosé NV; Nicolas François Billecart (**88 90 95** 96 97); Bl de Blancs (**90 95** 96 97); Elizabeth Salmon Rosé (**95** 96 97); Grande Cuvée (**90** 95 96) One of the best CHAMP houses, founded in 1818, still family-owned. Exquisite fresh-flavoured wines age beautifully. Part oak-fermented vintages from 2000. A new single v'yd Clos St-Hilaire (BLANC DE NOIRS: **95**) available mid 2003.

Bize, Simon Burg ★★★ Admirable red burgundy grower with 35 acres at SAVIGNY-LES-BEAUNE. Usually model wines in the racy and elegant Savigny style.

Blagny Burg r w ★★→★★★ (w) **89** 90' **92 95** 96' **97 99** 00 01 Hamlet between MEURSAULT and PULIGNY-M'RACHET: whites have affinities with both (and sold under both ACS); reds with VOLNAY (sold as AC Blagny). Good ones need age; esp AMPEAU, JOBARD, LATOUR, LEFLAIVE, MATROT, G Thomas.

Blanc de Blancs Any white wine made from white grapes only, esp CHAMP. Not an indication of quality but should be of style.

Blanc de Noirs White (or slightly pink or "blush") wine from red grapes.

Blanck, Paul et Fils Versatile ALSACE grower at Kientzheim. Good PINOT Bl, and GRANDS CRUS Furstentum (GEWURZ, Pinot Gr, esp RIES), SCHLOSSBERG (Ries).

Blanquette de Limoux Midi w sp ★★ **98** 99 **00 01** Gd-value fizz from nr Carcassonne with long local history. V dry, clean, increasingly tasty: CHARD and Chenin added to basic Mauzac, esp in newer AC CREMANT de Limoux.

Blaye B'x r w ★ **88 89** 90 94 95 **96** 98 00 Your daily BORDEAUX from E of the Gironde. PREMIERES COTES DE BLAYE is the AC of the better wines.

Boillot, J-M ★★★ POMMARD-based domaine: though best known for v fine, oaky whites from PULIGNY-M'RACHET, BATARD and remarkable MONTAGNY.

Boisset, Jean-Claude Burg Far and away the biggest burgundy merchant based in NUITS-ST-GEORGES. Owner of Bouchard-Aîné, Lionel Bruck, F Chauvenet, Delaunay, Jaffelin, Morin Père et Fils, de Marcilly, Pierre Ponnelle, Thomas-Bassot, Vienot, CELLIER DES SAMSONS (BEAUJOLAIS), MOREAU (CHABLIS) and a share in MOMMESSIN. Predictable commercial standards. From '99 own v'yds separated as Dom de la Vougeraie (★★★). Potentially vg.

Boizel Quality Epernay family CHAMP house; brilliant, aged BLANC DE BLANCS NV and prestige Joyau de France (90 **91 95**) at keen prices. Part of Boizel Chanoine.

Bollinger NV 'Special Cuvée'; Grande Année **82 85** 88 **95** 96; Rosé **85 88 90 95** 96 Top CHAMP house, at AY with a distinct, winey style. Luxury wines: RD (**73 75 76 79 81** 82 **85** 88), VIEILLES VIGNES Françaises (**75 79** 82 85 88 **90** 95 96) from ungrafted Pinot vines. Pioneered Charter of Quality ('91).

Bonneau du Martray, Domaine Burg ★★★★ (w) ★★ (r) Biggest grower (22 acres) of CORTON-CHARLEMAGNE of highest quality; also red GRAND CRU CORTON all on a high since '90. Cellars at PERNAND-VERGELESSES. White have often outlived reds.

Bonnes-Mares Burg r ★★★→★★★★ 78' 85' **87 88'** 89 **90' 91** 92 **93** 95 96' 97 98 99' 00 01 37-acre GRAND CRU between CHAMBOLLE-MUSIGNY and MOREY-ST-DENIS.

V sturdy long-lived wines, less fragrant than MUSIGNY; can rival CHAMBERTIN. Top growers: DUJAC, GROFFIER, JADOT, ROUMIER, DOM DES VAROILLES, DE VOGUE, VOUGERAIE.

Bonnezeaux Lo w sw ★★★→★★★★ 76' 78 **85' 86 88' 89' 90' 93' 94** 95' 96 **97 98 99 00** 01 Velvety, structured, complex sw CHENIN, potentially best of CTX DU LAYON. Esp Angeli, Ch de Fesles, Dom du Petit Val. Ages well, but v tempting young.

Bordeaux B'x r w (p) ★→★★ **90 94 95 96 98** 00' (for ch'x see pages 80–105) Catch-all AC for low-strength B'x. Often despised: it may be light but it still cannot be imitated. If I had to choose one simple daily wine, gd B'x would be it.

Bordeaux Supérieur ★→★★ As above, with more alcohol and ageing potential.

Borie-Manoux Admirable B'x shipper, château-owner owned by Castéja family. Ch'x incl BATAILLEY, BEAU-SITE, DOM DE L'EGLISE, HAUT-BAGES-MONPELOU, TROTTEVIEILLE.

Bouchard Père et Fils Important burgundy shipper (est 1731) and grower; excellent v'yds (232 acres), mainly COTE DE BEAUNE; cellars at Ch de Beaune. Fine quality since 1995: often poor before.

Bouches-du-Rhône Prov r p w ★ VINS DE PAYS from Marseille environs. Warming reds from southern varieties, plus CAB S, SYRAH and Merlot.

Bourg B'x r (w) ★★ **86' 88' 89' 90'** 94 95 **96** 98 99 00' Un-fancy claret from E of the Gironde. For ch'x see Côtes de Bourg.

Bourgeois, Henri Lo **89 90 93** 95 96 97 **98 99 00 01** Leading SANCERRE grower/merchant in Chavignol; also owns Laporte. Also POUILLY-FUME, MENETOU-SALON, and QUINCY. Top wines incl: Etienne Henri, MD de Bourgeois, La Bourgeoise, D'Antan Sancerrois, Sancerre Jadis. Recently bought a v'yd in New Zealand.

Bourgogne is the generic word for the cheaper end of Burgundy. As well as some indifferent mass-produced wines, it also covers out-lying areas which have their own subdivisions within the AC Bourgogne.
Coulanges-la-Vineuse, Epineuil, and Vézélay (Yonne département)
Hautes Côtes de Beaune and Hautes Côtes de Nuits (Côte d'Or)
Côte Chalonnaise and Couchois (Saône et Loire).
The best tip is to buy Bourgogne Rouge or Blanc from good growers in the famous villages of the Côted'Or – they will be delicious simple wines.

Bourgogne Burg r w (p) ★→ 97 **98** 99' 00 01 Catch-all Burgundy AC, with higher standards than basic B'x. Light often gd flavour, best at 2–4 yrs. Top growers make bargain beauties from fringes of COTE D'OR villages; do not despise. BEAUJOLAIS CRUS can also be labelled Bourgogne.

Bourgogne Grand Ordinaire Burg r (w) ★ DYA Lowest B'y AC, also allowing GAMAY. Rare. White may incl ALIGOTE, PINOT Bl, Melon de Bourgogne.

Bourgogne Passe-Tout-Grains Burg r (p) ★ Age 1–2 yrs, junior burgundy: min 33% PINOT N, the balance GAMAY, mixed in vat. Often enjoyable. Not as heady as BEAUJ.

Bourgueil Lo r (p) ★★→★★★(★) 76' 85 86' 88 **89'** 90' **95' 96** 97 98 **99** 01 Relatively brawny, fruity TOURAINE red (mainly CAB F). Deep-flavoured, ageing like B'x in top yrs. ST-NICOLAS-DE-B'GUEIL often lighter. Esp from Amirault, Audebert, Billet, Breton, Caslot, Cognard, Delaunay, Druet, Gambier, Lamé-Delisle-Boucard, Mailloches.

Bouvet-Ladubay Lo ★→★★★ Major sp SAUMUR house, TAITTINGER-controlled. Wines incl vintage BRUT Saphir, CREMANT Excellence, oak-fermented deluxe Trésor (white, rosé), with 2 yrs age, and Instinct. Also still wines (Les Nonpareils); gd sw Grand Vin de Dessert. CUVÉES: Brut Zero, Trésor Rouge.

Bouzeron Burg w ★ COTE CHALONNAISE AC specifically for ALIGOTE. Age 1–2 years. Top grower: de Villaine. Also NB BOUCHARD pere.

Bouzy Rouge Champ r ★★★ **89 90** 95 96 **97** 98 99 Still red of famous CHAMP PINOT village. Like v light burgundy, but can last well in sunny vintages.

Brana, Domaine 94 95' 96 (98') Pioneering IROULEGUY property high above St-Jean-Pied-du-Port. Excellent eaux-de-vie.

FRANCE

Brand ALSACE GRAND CRU hot spot nr Turkheim. PINOT Gris does extremely well here; also excellent GEWURZ from ZIND-HUMBRECHT.

Brédif, Marc Lo ★★→★★★ One of the most important growers and traders of VOUVRAY, esp sp (METHODE TRADITIONELLE and PETILLANT). Owned by LADOUCETTE.

Bricout BRUT NV (Rés, Prestige, CUVÉE Spéciale Arthur Bricout **90 95**); Rosé NV; Brut **90 95** 96 97AVIZE CHAMP house bought by P Martin and O Giraudière in '99. First-rate CUVÉE Prestige.

Brocard, J-M Burg ★★ CHABLIS grower to note for fine value, crisp and typical wines, incl Montmains, Montée de Tonnerre. Expanding into new terroir.

Brouilly Beauj r ★★ **98 99 00 01** Biggest of the 10 CRUS of BEAUJOLAIS: fruity, round, refreshing wine, can age 3–4 yrs. CH DE LA CHAIZE is largest estate. Top growers: Michaud, Dom de Combillaty, Dom des Grandes Vignes.

Brumont, Alain SW Best known producer in MADIRAN and one of the first to introduce oak-ageing & 100% Tannat wines. Adopted the Coop at Castelnau-Rivière-Basse. Flagship wines: Ch MONTUS, Dom Bouscassé, and gd-value MADIRAN Domaine Meinjarre. Varietals interesting but not in same class.

Brut Term for the dry classic wines of CHAMP. Brut Ultra/Zéro: for bone-dry wines.

Buisse, Paul ★★ Quality Montrichard merchant: range of Loire, esp TOURAINE wines.

Bugey Savoie r p w sp ★→★★ DYA VDQS for light sparkling, still or half-sparkling wines from Roussette (or Altesse) and CHARDONNAY (gd). Best from Montagnieu; also Rosé de Cerdon, mainly GAMAY.

Burguet, Alain Burg ★★→★★★ Superb GEVREY-CHAMB; esp VIEILLES VIGNES village wine.

Buxy Burg w Village in AC MONTAGNY with good coop for CHARD & PINOT.

Buzet SW France r (w p) ★★ **98' 99 00** (01) Region SE of B'DX; similar wines, s'times a bit pruney. Dynamic co-op has bulk of production, including some single properties (eg Châteaux de Gueyze, Mazelières). More local character from (independent) Dom de Pech, Ch'x du Frandat, Sauvagnères and Tournelles.

Cabardès Midi r (p w) ★→★★ **95 96 97** 98 99 00 New AC NW of Carcassonne. MIDI and B'X grapes show promise at Ch Pennautier, Ch des Hautes-Caunettes, Ch Ventenac, Dom de Cabrol, Co-op de Conques sur Orbiel.

Cabernet See Grapes for red wine (pages 11–13).

Cabernet d'Anjou Lo p s/sw ★→★★ DYA Delicate, grapey, med-sw rosé. Traditionally sw, age-worthy; a few venerable bottles survive. Esp from Bablut, Genaiserie.

Leading Cahors Producers

CLOS DE GAMOT, Coutale, Reysséguier. Ch'x du Cayrou, La Coustarelle, La Caminade, Garinet, Lamartine, La Hauts d'Aglan, Pech de Jammes, La Reyne, du Cèdre, Les Ifs, Latuc, De Lauze, Les Rigalets. Doms de la Bérangeraie, Paillas, Pineraie, Savarines, Eugénie, Bateliers, Manoir du Rouergou.

Cabrières Midi p (r) ★★ DYA COTEAUX DU LANGUEDOC.

Cahors SW France r ★→★★★ **85 89 90' 95 98** (99) (00) Historically "black" and tannic wines, mostly from Malbec (here Auxerrois). Now range from conc, tannic, to quick-drinking.

Cairanne S Rh r p w ★★ **89 90' 94 95' 96' 97** 98' 99' **00'** One of best COTES DU RHONE-VILLAGES: solid, robust esp from Doms Alary, Ameillaud, Brusset, l'Oratoire St-Martin, Rabasse-Charavin, Richaud. Some improving whites.

Canard-Duchêne CHAMP house connected with VEUVE CLICQUOT. Fair prices for lively, PINOT-tasting wines. Improved quality recently. Good Charles VII prestige CUVÉE both BRUT and ROSÉ.

Canon-Fronsac B'x r ★★→★★★ **85' 86 88 89' 90' 94 95** 96 97 98 00' Full tannic reds of increasing quality from small area W of POMEROL. Need less age than formerly. Eg Ch'x: Barrabaque, CANON, CANON-DE-BREM, CANON-MOUEIX, Cassagne

Haut-Canon, Croix Canyon, La Fleur Caillou, Grand-Renouil, Mazeris, Moulin-Pey-Labrie, Vraye-Canon-Boyer. See also Fronsac.

Cantenac B'x r ★★★ Village of HAUT-MEDOC entitled to the AC MARGAUX. Top ch'x include BRANE-CANTENAC, PALMER, etc.

Cap Corse Corsica w br ★★ →★★★ CORSICA'S wild N cape. Splendid MUSCAT from CLOS Nicrosi (Rogliano), & rare, soft, dry Vermentino w. Vaut le détour, if not le voyage.

Caramany Pyr r (w) ★ 95 96 97 **98 99** 00 01 Notionally superior AC for single-village COTES DU ROUSSILLON-VILLAGES.

Carillon, Louis Burg ★★★ Leading PULIGNY-M domaine now in top league. Esp PREMIER CRU Referts, Perrières and tiny amount of GRAND CRU Bienvenues-Bâtard.

Cassis Prov w (r p) ★★ DYA Seaside village E of Marseille known for dry white wines with a certain character, drunk with bouillabaisse (eg Dom de la Ferme Blanche, Clos Ste Magdeleine, Clos d'Albizzi). Not to be confused with cassis: blackcurrant liqueur made in Dijon.

Cave Cellar, or any wine establishment.

Cave coopérative Wine-growers' co-op winery; over ½ of all French production. Usually well-run, well-equipped and their wine reasonable value for money.

Cellier des Samsons ★ BEAUJOLAIS/MACONNAIS co-op at Quincié with 2,000 grower-members. Wines widely distributed; now owned by BOISSET.

Cépage Variety of vine, eg CHARD, Merlot.

Cérons B'x w dr sw ★★ 83' 85' 86' 88' 89' 90 95 96 97 98 99 01 Neighbour of SAUTERNES with some gd, sweet wine, eg Ch'x de Cérons et de Calvimont, Chantegrine, Grand Enclos. Ch Archambeau makes vg dry GRAVES.

Chablis

There is no better expression of the all-conquering Chardonnay than the full but tense, limpid but stony wines it makes on the heavy limestone soils of Chablis. Chablis terroir divides into 3 quality levels (4 including Petit Chablis) with great consistency. Best makers use little or no new oak to mask the precise definition of variety and terroir. They incl: Barat, Bessin*, Billaud-Simon, Boudin*, J-M Brocard, J Collet *, D Dampt, R & V Dauvissat*, J Dauvissat*, B, D et E, and J Defaix, Droin, Drouhin*, Durup, Fèvre, Geoffroy, J-P Grossot*, Laroche, Long-Depaquit, Dom des Malandes, L Michel*, Picq*, Pupillon, Raveneau*, G Robin*, Servin, Tribut, Vocoret. Simple unqualified "Chablis" may be thin; best is premier or grand cru (see below). The co-op, La Chablisienne, has high standards (esp Grenouille*) and many different labels (it makes 1 in every 3 bottles). (* = outstanding)

Chablis Burg w ★★→★★★ 95 **96' 97 99** 00' 01 Unique, flavoursome, dry minerally wine of N Burgundy, CHARD only; a total of 10,000 acres for all levels.

Chablis Grand Cru Burg w ★★★→★★★★ 83 85 86 **88 89 90'** 92 **93 95'** 96' 97 98 99 00' 01 In maturity a match for great w burgundy: often dumb in youth, at best with age combines mineral "cut" with hint of SAUTERNES. 7 v'yds: Blanchots, Bougros, CLOS, Grenouilles, Preuses, Valmur, Vaudésir. See also MOUTONNE.

Chablis Premier Cru Burg w ★★★ 85 86 **88 89** 90 92 93 95' **96'** 97 98 99 00' 01 Technically second-rank but at best excellent, more typical of CHABLIS than its GRANDS CRUS. Can outclass more expensive MEURSAULT and other COTE DE BEAUNE. Best vineyards incl Côte de Léchet, Fourchaume, Mont de Milieu, Montée de Tonnerre, Montmains, Vaillons. See above for producers.

Chai Building for storing and maturing wine, esp in BORDEAUX.

Chambertin Burg r ★★★★ 78' 85' **87 88** 89 **90' 91 92 93** 95 96' 97 98 99' 00 01 32-acre GRAND CRU; some of the meatiest, most enduring, best red burgundy, 20 growers, including BOUCHARD, Charlopin, Damoy, DROUHIN, LEROY, MORTET, PONSOT, Rebourseau, Rossignol-Trapet, ROUSSEAU, Trapet.

FRANCE

Chambertin-Clos de Bèze Burg r ★★★★ 78' 85 **87 88** 89 **90' 91 92 93** 95 96' 97 98 99' 00 01 37-acre neighbour of CHAMBERTIN. Similarly splendid wines. May legally be sold as Chambertin. 15 growers, incl B CLAIR, Damoy, DROUHIN, Drouhin-Laroze, FAIVELEY, GROFFIER, JADOT, ROUSSEAU.

Chambolle-Musigny Burg r ★★★→★★★★ **78'** 85' **87 88** 89 **90'** 91 92 93 95 96' **97** 98 99 00 420-acre COTE DE NUITS village: fabulously fragrant, complex, but never heavy wine. Best vineyards: Les Amoureuses, part of BONNES-MARES, Les Charmes, MUSIGNY. Growers to note: BARTHOD-NOELLAT, DROUHIN, FAIVELEY, GROFFIER, HUDELOT-NOELLAT, JADOT, MUGNERET, MUGNIER, RION, ROUMIER, Serveau, DE VOGUE.

> ### Champagne: a handful of good small houses
> **Alain Robert** – perfectionist Le Mesnil grower-maker; superlative Cuvée Mesnil Sélection and Tête de Cuvée.
> **Beaumont des Crayères** – small outstanding cooperative at Mardeuil. Exceptional Meunier-led Grande Réserve NV.
> **Richard Cheurlin** – one of best grower/winemakers of the Aube. Rich but balanced Carte d'Or and vintage-dated Cuvée Jeanne.
> **Egly-Ouriet** first-rate grower/winemaker in Ambonnay. Superb expressions of great Pinot, esp. Blanc de Noirs Vielles Vignes.
> **Jacques Selosse** – Pre-eminent Avize domaine; natural non-interventionist methods; superb barrique-fermented all Chardonnay Cuvée Substance.
> **René Geoffroy** – grower-maker at Cumières; vibrant, fruity NV, vg oak-fermented vintages and Cumières rouge.
> **Pierre Gimmonet** – leading Côte des Blancs grower at Cuis. Delicate, dry Cuvée Gastronome is ideal with oysters.
> **Henri Mandois** – Pierry. Elegant wines from Meunier and Chard blends.
> **Larmandier-Bernier** – Vertus; top-flight Blanc de Blancs grower-maker, esp Cramant Grand Cru.
> **A R Lenoble** – tiny low-key house at Damery. V gd quality, esp Chard-led cuvées.
> **Jean-Marie Tarlant** – great grower in Marne valley at Oeuilly. Excellent vintage wines (esp. 95) and outstanding Krug-like Cuvée Louis fermented in oak.

Champagne Sparkling wine of PINOTS Noir and Meunier and/or CHARD, and its region (70,000⁺ acres 90 miles E of Paris); made by METHODE TRADITIONELLE. Bubbles from elsewhere, however good, cannot be Champagne.

Champy Père et Cie Burg ★★→★★★ Oldest NEGOCIANT, in BEAUNE, rejuvenated by Meurgey family (also brokers "DIVA"). Range of very well-chosen wines.

Chandon de Briailles, Domaine Burg ★★★ Small burgundy estate at SAVIGNY. Makes wonderful CORTON (and Corton Blanc) and vg PERNAND-VERGELESSES.

Chanson Père et Fils Burg ★→★★★ Old grower-NEGOCIANT at BEAUNE (110 acres), now owned by BOLLINGER. Esp BEAUNE CLOS des Fèves, SAVIGNY, PERNAND-VERGELESSES, CORTON. Expect better quality now.

Chapelle-Chambertin Burg r ★★★ 85 87 88 89' **90'** 91 **92 93** 95 96' 97 98 99' 00 01 13-acre neighbour of CHAMBERTIN. Wine more "nervous", not so meaty. Top producers: Damoy, JADOT, Rossignol-Trapet, Trapet.

Chapoutier Rh Long-est'd grower and trader of full Rhônes; bio-dynamic principles. Best: special CUVEES CH'NEUF Barbe Rac (GRENACHE), HERMITAGE: L'Hermité, Le Pavillon (red), and Cuvée d'Orée (white, late-picked Marsanne), also CROZES red Les Varonniers. New holdings in BANYULS, COLLIOURE, CTX DU TRICASTIN, and CTX D'AIX-EN-PROVENCE promising.

Chardonnay See Grapes for white wine (pages 12–16). Also the name of a MACON-VILLAGES commune. Hence Mâcon-Chardonnay.

Charlopin, Philippe Burg ★★★ Perfectionist GEVREY-CHAMBERTIN estate. To watch.

Charmes-Chambertin Burg r ★★★ 85' 87 88 89' 90' 91 92 93 95 96' 97 98 99' 00 01 CHAMBERTIN n'bour, incl AC MAZOYERES-C. "Suppler", rounder wines; esp Bachelet, Dugat, DROUHIN, DUJAC, LEROY, Perrot-Minot, ROTY, ROUMIER, ROUSSEAU, Vougeraie.

Chassagne-Montrachet Burg w r ★★★→★★★★ r (★★★) 85 88 89 90' 91 93 95 96' 97 98 99; w 85 86 88 89' 90 92 94 95 96' 97 98 99 00 01 750-acre COTE DE BEAUNE village. Sterling hefty r; excellent rich dry w rarely with quite the finesse of PULIGNY next door but often costs less. Best vineyards incl part of M'RACHET, BATARD-M, Boudriottes (r w), Caillerets, CRIOTS-BATARD-M, Morgeot (r w), Ruchottes, CLOS ST-JEAN (r). Growers incl Amiot-Bonfils, Blain-Gagnard, COLIN-DELEGER, DROUHIN, Fontaine-Gagnard, J N Gagnard, GAGNARD-DELAGRANGE, Lamy-Pillot, Ch de la Maltroye, MOREY, Niellon, Pillot, RAMONET.

Château d'Arlay Major JURA estate; 160 acres in skilful hands with wines inc very good VIN JAUNE, VIN DE PAILLE, PINOT N and MACVIN.

Château de Beaucastel S Rh r w ★★★ 78' 79 81' 83 85 86' 88 89' 90' 92 93' 94' 95' 96' 98' 99' 00' One of biggest, best-run CH'NEUF-DU-PAPE estates. Deep-hued, complex wines; unusual varietal mix incl ⅓ MOURVEDRE. Drink well young, too. Sm amount of wonderful Roussanne w: keep 5–14 yrs. Also leading COTES DU RHONE Coudoulet de Beaucastel (r and w – part Viognier); excellent Ch du Grand Prébois. Solid NEG Perrin wines. Also Tablas Creek, Paso Robles, Calif.

Château de la Chaize Beauj r ★★★ 96 97 98 99 00 01 Best-known BROUILLY estate.

Château Fortia Rh r (w) ★★★ 78' 81' 83 85 86 88 90 95' 96' 97 98' 99 00' Trad 72-acre CHATEAUNEUF property. Owner's father, Baron Le Roy, also fathered the AC system in '20s. Not at top form, but signs of revival, inc whites.

Château Fuissé Burg w ★★→★★★ Now being challenged as the top estate in Pouilly-Fuissé. Numerous cuvées, made to mature more rapidly than before.

Château de Meursault Burg r w ★★★ 150-acre estate owned by PATRIARCHE, with good v'yds and wines in BEAUNE, MEURSAULT, POMMARD, VOLNAY. Splendid cellars open to the public for tasting.

Château de Mont-Redon S Rh r w ★★★ 78 86 88 89 90' 93' 94' 95' 97' 98' 99' 01 Outstanding CH'NEUF-DU-PAPE estate. Fine complex r; vg aromatic, s'times substantial w (eg 94/96). Also gd wines from Cantegril v'yd (LIRAC).

Château de Montaigne Dordogne w (sw) ★★ Home of great philosopher Michel de M, now making sw COTES DE MONTRAVEL; part-owns CH PALMER (MARGAUX).

Château Montus ★★★ SW France 89 90' 94 95 96 97 98 (99) Top MADIRAN estate. Some wines 100% Tannat, long vinification, slow-maturing. Owner: A BRUMONT.

Château La Nerthe S Rh r (w) ★★★ 78' 81' 85 86 88 89' 90' 93 94 95' 96' 97 98' 99' 00 Renowned 222-acre CHATEAUNEUF estate. Solid modern-style wines, esp special CUVEES Cadettes (r) and oaked Beauvenir (w). Take 5 yrs to show.

Château de Pierre-Bise Loire r w ★★★→★★★★ 85 86 88 89 90 93 95 96 97 98 99

> ## Château
> Means an estate, big or small, good or indifferent, particularly in Bordeaux (see pages 80–105). Elsewhere in France château tends to mean, literally, castle or great house, as in most of the following entries. In Burgundy, "domaine" is the usual term.

00 01 Superb producer of ANJOU, partic COTEAUX DE LAYON, incl QUARTS DE CHAUME, vinified and bottled by terroir. Also SAVENNIERES under label Clos de Coulaine.

Château Rayas S Rh r (w) ★★★ 78' 79 81' 83 85 86 88' 89 90' 93 94' 95' 96' 98 99 Famous old-style 37–acre estate in CH'NEUF. Conc'd wines entirely GRENACHE, yet age superbly. Trad w Rayas can be vg. Pignan is gd value 2nd label. Vg Ch Fonsalette, COTES DU RHONE (NB CUVEE SYRAH & w). All benefit from decanting.

Château Routas Prov r p w ★★ Estate making its mark in COTEAUX VAROIS. Wines including SYRAH, CAB S, CHARD-Viognier, both AC and VDP.

Château de Selle Prov r p w ★★→★★★ 100-acre estate of OTT family nr Cotignac, Var. The original pace-setters for PROVENCE. Cuvée Spéciale is largely CAB S.

Château Simone Prov r p w ★★→★★★ Age 2–6 yrs or longer. Famous old property synonymous with AC PALETTE, nr Aix-en-Provence. The red is best: smooth but herby and spicy. White is good too and repays bottle age.

Château de Villeneuve Loire r w ★★★→★★★★ 89 90 93 94 95 96 97 98 99 00 01 Dynamic SAUMUR estate. Exciting SAUMUR Blanc (especially Les Cormiers) and S-CHAMPIGNY (esp VIEILLES VIGNES, Grand Clos).

Château-Chalon Jura w ★★★ Not a CHATEAU but AC and village. Unique dry yellow sherry-like wine (Savagnin grape). Develops flor while ageing in barrels for min 6 yrs. Ready to drink when when bottled (62cl "Clavelin" bottle), but ages forever. A curiosity.

Château-Grillet N Rh w ★★★★ 94' 95 96 98 99 9-acre terraced vineyard of Viognier; one of France's smallest ACS. Absurdly over-expensive, but shows signs of revival. Always cask-reared. Less floral aromas than CONDRIEU. Drink young – or drink Condrieu.

Châteaumeillant Lo r p ★→★★ DYA A tiny VDQS area nearr SANCERRE. GAMAY and PINOT NOIR for light reds and rosés. Top producers: Lanoix and Cave des Vins de Châteaumeillant.

Châteauneuf-du-Pape S Rh r (w) ★★★ 78' 79 80 81' 83 85 86 88 89' 90' 93 94 95' 96 98' 99' 00' 8,200 acres near Avignon with core of 30 or so domaines for v fine wines (quality more variable over remaining 90). Mix of up to 13 varieties led by GRENACHE, SYRAH, MOURVEDRE. The best are dark, strong, exceptionally long-lived. Whites either fruity and zesty or rather heavy: many now "DYA". Top growers incl Ch'x DE BEAUCASTEL, FORTIA, Gardine, MONT REDON, LA NERTHE, RAYAS; Doms de Beaurenard, Bosquet des Papes, Les Caillous, Font-de-Michelle, Grand Tinel, Pegaü, VIEUX TELEGRAPHE, Villeneuve, Henri Bonneau, Clos du Mont-Olivet, CLOS DES PAPES, Clos St-Jean, Vieux Donjon, etc.

Châtillon-en-Diois Rh r p w ★ DYA Small AC of mid-Rhône. Adequate largely GAMAY reds; white (some ALIGOTE) mostly made into CLAIRETTE DE DIE.

Chave, Gérard Rh To many the superstar grower (with his son Jean-Louis) of HERMITAGE, with 25 acres red, 12 acres white – spread over 9 hillside v'yds. Fleshy, v long-lived red and white (inc good red ST-JOSEPH), and also VIN DE PAILLE. Interesting new J L Chave brand St-Joseph bought from growers.

Chavignol SANCERRE village with famous v'yd, Les Monts Damnés. Chalky soil gives vivid wines that age 4–5 yrs (or longer); esp from BOURGEOIS and Cotat.

Chénas Beauj r ★★★ 96 97 98 99 00 01 Smallest BEAUJOLAIS CRU and one of the weightiest; n'bour to MOULIN-A-VENT and JULIENAS. Growers incl Benon, Champagnon, Charvet, Ch Chèvres, DUBOEUF, Lapierre, Robin, Trichard, co-op.

Chenin Blanc See Grapes for white wine (pages 10–16).

Chenonceau, Ch de Lo ★→★★ DYA Architectural jewel of Loire makes gd to v gd AC TOURAINE SAUV BL, CAB and CHENIN, still and sparkling. See vintages for CHEVERNY.

Chéreau-Carré ★★★ 85 87 88 89 90 93 95 96 97 98 99 00 01 Makers of some of top domaine MUSCADETS (esp Ch'x du Chasseloir, du Coing, Comte Leloup de Chasseloir). A name to follow.

Chevalier-Montrachet Burg w ★★★★ 78 85' 86 88 89' 90 92 93 95 96' 97 98 99 00 01 17-acre neighbour of M'RACHET making similar luxurious wine, perhaps less powerful. Incl 2.5-acre Les Demoiselles. Growers incl LATOUR, JADOT, BOUCHARD PERE, CHARTRON, COLIN-DELEGER, LEFLAIVE, Niellon, PRIEUR.

Cheverny Lo r p w ★→★★ 95 96 97 98 99 00 01 Loire AC nr Chambord. Dry crisp whites from SAUV BL and CHARD. Also GAMAY, PINOT N or CAB; usually light but tasty. "Cour-Cheverny" uses the local Romorantin grape. Sp wines use CREMANT DE LOIRE and TOURAINE AC. Esp Cazin, Clos Tue-Boeuf, Huards, OISLY ET THESEE, Dom de la Desoucherie, Domaine du Moulin (Herve Villemade).

Chevillon, R ★★★ 32-acre estate at NUITS-ST-GEORGES; soft and juicy wines.

Chignin Savoie w ★ DYA Light, soft white from Jacquère grapes for alpine summers. Chignin-Bergeron (with Roussanne grapes) is best and liveliest.

Chinon Lo r (p w) ★★→★★★ 85 86' 87 88 89' 90' 93' 95' 96 97 98 99 00 01 Juicy, variably rich TOURAINE CAB F. Drink cool, young; treat very good yrs like B'x. Sml quantity crisp dry CHENIN. Top growers: Bernard Baudry, Alliet, Crespin, Ch de Coulaine, COULY-DUTHEIL (CLOS de l'Echo), Druet, Ch Grille, Joguet, Lambert, Loup, Raffault.

Chiroubles Beauj r ★★★ 98 99 00 01 Good but tiny BEAUJOLAIS CRU next to FLEURIE; freshly fruity silky wine for early drinking (1–3 years). Growers incl Bouillard, Cheysson, DUBOEUF, Fourneau, Passot, Raousset, co-op.

Chorey-lès-Beaune Burg r (w) ★★ 90' 93 95 96' 97 98 99' 01 Minor AC N of BEAUNE. 3 fine growers: Arnoux, Germain (Ch de Chorey), esp TOLLOT-BEAUT.

Chusclan S Rh r p w ★→★★ 95' 96' 98' 99' 00' COTES DU RHONE-VILLAGES with able co-op. Soft reds. Labels incl Cuvée de Marcoule, Les Genets, Seigneurie de Gicon. Also Dom de Lindas and special CUVEES from André Roux. Drink young.

Cissac HAUT-MEDOC village just west of PAUILLAC.

Clair, Bruno Burg ★★→★★★ Leading MARSANNAY estate. Vg wines from there and GEVREY-CHAMBERTIN (esp CLOS DE BEZE), FIXIN, MOREY-ST-DENIS, SAVIGNY.

Clairet Very light red wine, almost rosé. Bordeaux Clairet is an AC.

Clairette Traditional white grape of the MIDI. Its low-acid wine was a vermouth base. Revival by Terrasses de Landoc is full and zesty.

Clairette de Bellegarde Midi w ★ DYA Small AC nr Nîmes: plain neutral white.

Clairette de Die Rh w dr s/sw sp ★★ NV Popular dry or (better) semi-sweet MUSCAT-flavoured sparkling wine from pre-Alps in E Rhône; or straight dry CLAIRETTE white, surprisingly ageing well 3–4 yrs. Worth trying.

Clairette du Languedoc Midi w ★ DYA Nr Montpellier. Neutral dry white AC, more interest for late-harvest grapes, barrel ageing. Ch'x La Condamine Bertrand, St-André, and Cave d'Adissan looking good.

Clape, La Midi r p w ★→★★ CRU to note of AC COTEAUX DU LANGUEDOC. Full-bodied wines from limestone hills between Narbonne and sea. Red gains character after 2–3 yrs, whites can last even longer. Especially from Châteaux Rouquette-sur-Mer, Mire l'Etang, Pech-Céléyran, Pech-Redon, Dom de l'Hospitalet.

Claret Traditional English term for all red BORDEAUX.

Climat Burgundian word for individually named v'yd, eg BEAUNE Grèves.

Clos A term carrying some prestige, reserved for distinct (walled) v'yds, often in one ownership (esp Burgundy and ALSACE). Les Clos is CHABLIS' Grandest Cru.

Clos de Bèze See Chambertin-Clos de Bèze.

Clos de Gamot SW France ★★★ 82 83' 85 89 90' 95 96 98 (oo) One of the most famous CAHORS estates. Ultra-traditional, long-lived benchmark wines. New top Cuvée "Clos St. Jean" outstanding.

Clos des Lambrays Burg r ★★★ 15-acre GRAND CRU vineyard at MOREY-ST-DENIS. Great potential here, now at last being realized.

Clos des Mouches Burg r w ★★★ Splendid PREMIER CRU BEAUNE v'yd, largely owned by DROUHIN. White and red wines, spicy and memorable – and consistent.

Clos de la Roche Burg r ★★★ 78' 85' 87 88 89' 90 91 92 93' 95 96' 97 98 99' 00 01 MOREY-ST-DENIS GRAND CRU (38-acres). Powerful and complex like CHAMBERTIN. Esp Amiot, BOUCHARD PERE, Bourée, DUJAC, LEROY, G. Lignier, PONSOT, REMY, ROUSSEAU.

Clos des Papes S Rh r w Immaculate 79-acre (18 plots) CH'NEUF estate. Long-lived, stylish reds (mainly GRENACHE, MOURVEDRE) and whites (5–10 yrs).

Clos du Roi Burg r ★★★ Part of GRAND CRU CORTON. Also a BEAUNE PREMIER CRU.

France entries also cross-refer to Châteaux of Bordeaux section, pages 80–105.

FRANCE

Clos Rougeard Lo r (sw) ★★★→★★★★ 85 86 87 88 89 90 93 94 96 97 98 99 00 01 Controversial SAUMUR-CHAMPIGNY; cult following. Intense wines aged in new (or nearly new) B'X barrels. Also tiny amount of luscious COTEAUX DE SAUMUR.

Clos St-Denis Burg r ★★★ 78 85' 87 88 89' 90' 91 92 93' 95 96' 97 98 99' 00 01 16-acre GRAND CRU at MOREY-ST-DENIS. Splendid sturdy wine growing silky with age. Growers incl Bertagna, DUJAC, G. Lignier, PONSOT.

Clos Ste-Hune Al w ★★★★ V fine austere RIES from TRIMBACH; perhaps ALSACE's best. Needs 5[+] yrs age; doesn't need GRAND CRU status.

Clos St-Jacques Burg r ★★★ 78' 85' 88 89' 90' 91 93' 95 96' 97 98 99' 00 01 17-acre GEVREY-CHAMBERTIN PREMIER CRU. Excellent powerful velvety long-ager, often better (and dearer) than some GRANDS CRUS, esp by ESMONIN and ROUSSEAU.

Clos St-Jean Burg r ★★★ 85' 88 89' 90' 91 93 95 96' 97 98 99' 01 36-acre PREMIER CRU of CHASSAGNE-M. Vg red, more solid than subtle, eg Ch de la Maltroye. NB RAMONET.

Clos de Tart Burg r ★★★ 85' 88' 89' 90' 93 95 96' 97 98 99' 00 01 GRAND CRU at MOREY-ST-DENIS, owned by MOMMESSIN. At best wonderfully fragrant, young or old.

Clos de Vougeot Burg r ★★★ 78 85' 88 89' 90' 91 92 93' 95 96' 97 98 99' 00 01 124-acre COTE DE NUITS GRAND CRU with many owners. Variable, occasionally sublime. Maturity depends on the grower's philosophy, technique, and position. Top growers incl CH DE LA TOUR, DROUHIN, ENGEL, FAIVELEY, GRIVOT, GROS, HUDELOT-NOELLAT, JADOT, LEROY, Chantal Lescure, MEO-CAMUZET, MUGNERET, VOUGERAIE.

Coche-Dury Burg ★★★★ 21-acre MEURSAULT dom (& 1 acre+ of CORTON-CHARLEMAGNE) with high reputation for oak-perfumed wines. Also vg ALIGOTE reds.

Cognac Town and region of the Charentes, W France, and its brandy.

Colin-Deléger Burg ★★★ Leading CHASSAGNE-MONTRACHET estate. Superb, but rare PULIGNY-MONTRACHET Les Caillerets.

Collines Rhodaniennes S Rh w p ★ Popular, lively Rhône VDP. Also young vine CÔTE-RÔTIE Mainly reds: Merlot, SYRAH, GAMAY. Some Viognier & CHARD.

Collioure Pyr r ★★ 95 96 97 98 99 00 01 Strong dry red from BANYULS area. Tiny production. Top growers incl Le CLOS des Paulilles, Doms du Mas Blanc, de la Rectorie, La Tour Vieille, Vial-Magnères.

Comté Tolosan SW r p w ★ DYA Vin de Pays. Covers multitude of sins and whole of southwest. Mostly co-op wines. Pioneering ★★ DOM DE RIBONNET (Christian Gerber, S of Toulouse) for range of varietal wines, some long keepers.

Condrieu N Rh w ★★★ 99' 00 01 DYA Soft fragrant white of great character (and price) from Viognier. Can be outstanding but rapid growth of v'yd (now 250 acres worked by 90 growers) has made quality more variable. Increased use of young oak (eg GUIGAL's Doriane CUVEE, Cuilleron, Villard) is a doubtful move. Best growers: Y Cuilleron, DELAS, Gangloff, GUIGAL, JABOULET, André Perret, Niéro-Pinchon, Vernay (esp Coteau de Vernon), Verzier. CHATEAU-GRILLET: similar. Don't even try ageing it. Dubious move to VENDANGE TARDIVE by some growers.

Confuron, Jean-Jacques ★★★ Tiny NUITS-ST-GEORGES estate to follow closely.

Corbières Midi r (p w) ★★→★★★ 90 91 92 93 94 95 96 97 98 99 00 01 Vigorous bargain reds. Best growers: Ch'x Aiguilloux, Lastours, des Ollieux, Les Palais, de la Voulte Gasparet, Doms de Fontsainte, du Vieux Parc, de Villemajou, and coops de Embrès et Castelmaure, Camplong, St-Laurent-Cabrerisse.

Cordier, Ets D Important BORDEAUX shipper and château-owner with wonderful track-record, now owned by Groupe Val d'Orbieu-Listel. Over 600 acres. Incl Ch'x CANTEMERLE, LAFAURIE-PEYRAGUEY, MEYNEY, etc.

Cornas N Rh r ★★→★★★ 83' 85' 86 88' 89' 90' 91' 93 94' 95' 96' 97' 98' 99' 00' 01' Sturdy v dark SYRAH wine from 215-acre steep granite v'yds S of HERMITAGE. Needs to age 5–15 yrs but always keeps its rustic character. Top: Allemand, Colombo (beware: new oak), Clape, Courbis, DELAS, Dumien-Serrette, Juge, Lionnet, JABOULET (esp St-Pierre CUVEE), Tardieu-Laurent (modern), N Verset, Voge.

Corrèze Dordogne r ✶ DYA VDP from Co-op de Branceilles, between Brive and Beaulieu. Also Dom de la Mégénie.

Corsica (Corse) Strong wines of all colours. ACS are: AJACCIO and PATRIMONIO and better crus Cap Corse and Calvi. VIN DE PAYS: ILE DE BEAUTE.

Corton Burg r ★★★→★★★★ 78' 85' 88 89' 90' **91 92 93** 95 96' 97 98 99' 00 01 The only GRAND CRU red of the CÔTE DE BEAUNE. 200 acres in ALOXE-C incl CLOS DU ROI, Les Bressandes. Rich & powerful, should age well. Many good growers.

Corton-Charlemagne Burg w ★★★★ 78' 85' **86 88** 89' 90' 92' **94** 95 96' 97 98 99 00' 01 White section (½) of CORTON. Rich, spicy, lingering, the Grand Cru Chablis of the Côte d'Or; ages like a red. Top growers: BONNEAU DU MARTRAY, Chapuis, COCHE-DURY, Delarche, Dubreuil-Fontaine, FAIVELEY, HOSPICES DE BEAUNE, JADOT, LATOUR, Rapet, P André.

> **Côte(s)** Means hillside; generally a superior v'yd to those on the plain.
> Many ACs are prefixed by "Côtes" or "Coteaux", meaning the same.
> In St-Emilion, distinguishes valley slopes from higher plateaus.

Costières de Nîmes S Rh r p w ✶→✶✶ 95 96 97 **98' 99'** 00' 01 Rhône delta AC; fast-improving quality, from best names (best reds: 4-6 yrs). Formerly Costières du Gard. Fast improving quality from best wines: Ch'x de Campuget, Grande Cassagne, Mourgues du Grès, de Nages (esp Joseph Torres), de la Tuilerie, Mas des Bressades, Dom du Vieux Relais.

Côte de Beaune Burg r w ★★→★★★★ Used geographically: the southern half of the CÔTE D'OR. Applies as an AC only to parts of BEAUNE itself.

Côte de Beaune-Villages Burg r ★★ 90' 95 96' 97 98 99' 01 Regional APPELLATION for lesser wines of classic area. Cannot be labelled "Côte de Beaune" without either "-Villages" or village name added.

Côte de Brouilly Beauj r ★★ **98** 99 00 01 Fruity rich BEAUJ CRU. One of best. Esp from: Dom de Chavanne, G Cotton, Ch Delachanel, J-C Nesme, Ch Thivin.

Côte Chalonnaise Burg r w sp ★★ V'yd area between BEAUNE and MACON. See also BOUZERON, GIVRY, MERCUREY, MONTAGNY, RULLY. Alias "Région de Mercurey".

Côte de Nuits Burg r (w) ★★→★★★★ N half of CÔTE D'OR. Mostly red wine.

Côte de Nuits-Villages Burg r (w) ★★ 90' **93** 95 96' **97** 98 99' 00 01 A junior AC for extreme N and S ends of CÔTE DE N; well worth investigating for bargains.

Côte d'Or Département name applied to the central and principal Burgundy v'yd slopes: CÔTE DE BEAUNE and CÔTE DE NUITS. The name is not used on labels.

Côte Roannaise Central France r p ✶→★★ 95 96 97 98 99 **00 01** AC W of Lyon. Silky, focused GAMAY. Doms Demon, Lapandéry, du Pavillon, des Millets.

Côte-Rôtie N Rh r ★★★→★★★★ 78' 83' 85' 88' **89'** 90' **91' 94'** 95' 96' 97 98' 99' 00' 01' Finest Rhône red, from S of Vienne, mainly SYRAH; can achieve rich, complex softness and finesse with age (esp 5 to 10⁺ years). Top growers including Barge, Bernard, Burgaud, Champet, CHAPOUTIER, Clusel-Roch (improving fast), DELAS, Gaillard, J-M Gérin, GUIGAL (long oak-ageing, different and fuller), JABOULET, Jamet, Jasmin, Ogier, ROSTAING (oak here, too), VIDAL-FLEURY.

Coteaux d'Affreux Aspiring to VDP status. Should perhaps use grapes as base.

Coteaux d'Aix-en-Provence Prov r p w ✶→★★★ AC on the move. Top properties incl Ch'x Revelette, Calissanne and Domaine des Béates (CHAPOUTIER-owned). See also Baux-en-Provence.

Coteaux d'Ancenis Lo r p w (sw) ✶ DYA VDQS E Of Nantes. Light GAMAY r's and p's, sharpish dry w's (CHENIN). Semi-sw from Malvoisie (ages well) – esp Guindon.

Coteaux de l'Ardèche See l'Ardèche.

Coteaux de l'Aubance Lo w sw ★★→★★★★ 88' 89' 90' **93' 94' 95'** 96 97 **98 99** 00 01 Similar to C'X DU LAYON, nervy sw wines from CHENIN. A few SELECTION DES GRAINS NOBLES. Esp from Bablut, Haute-Perche, Montgilet, RICHOU, Rochelles.

Coteaux des Baronnies S Rh r p w ★ DYA Rhône VIN DE PAYS near Nyons. SYRAH, Merlot, CAB S, CHARD, plus trad grapes. Promising. Dom du Rieu-Frais (incl gd Viognier) and Dom Rosière (incl gd Syrah) worth noting.

Côteaux de Chalosse SW France r p w ★ DYA. Good country wines from co-op at Mugron (Landes).

Coteaux Champenois Champ r w (p) ★★★ DYA (whites) AC for non-sp CHAMP. Vintages (if mentioned) follow those for Champ. Not worth inflated prices.

Coteaux du Giennois Lo r p w ★ DYA Sm area N of POUILLY promoted to AC in '98. Light red: blend of GAMAY and PINOT; SAUV à la SANCERRE. Top grower: Paulat.

Coteaux de Glanes SW France r ★ DYA Lively VDP from nr Bretenoux (Lot). Co-op only producer. Mostly drunk in local restaurants.

Coteaux du Languedoc Midi r p w ★★→★★★ 95 96 97 98 99 00 01 Scattered well-above-ordinary MIDI AC areas. Best reds (eg LA CLAPE, FAUGERES, St-Georges-d'Orques, Quatourze, ST-CHINIAN, Montpeyroux, PIC ST-LOUP) age for 2–4 yrs. Now also some good whites. Standards rising dizzily.

Coteaux du Layon Lo w s/sw sw ★★→★★★★ 75 76 85' 86 88' 89' 90' 93' 94 95 96 97 98 99 00 01 The heart of ANJOU, S of Angers: sw CHENIN; admirable acidity, ageing forever. New SELECTION DES GRAINS NOBLES; cf ALSACE. 7 villages can add name to AC. Top ACs: BONNEZEAUX, C du Layon-Chaume, QUARTS DE CHAUME. Growers incl BAUMARD, Dme de la Bergerie, Cady, Delhumeau (Dme de Brize) Delesvaux, des Forges, Dme de Juchepie, Ogereau, Papin (CH DE PIERRE-BISE), Jo Pithon, Yves Soulez (Genaiserie), P-Y Tijou (Soucherie), du Breuil.

Coteaux du Loir Lo r p w dr sw ★→★★★ 76 85 88' 89' 90' 92 93' 95 96 97 98 99 00 01 Small region N of Tours, incl JASNIERES. Sometimes fine CHENIN, GAMAY, Pineau d'Aunis, CAB. Top growers: de Rycke, Fresneau, Gigou, Nicolas. A tributary of the Loire.

Coteaux de la Loire See Anjou-Coteaux de la Loire.

Coteaux du Lyonnais Beauj r p (w) ★ DYA Junior BEAUJOLAIS. Best EN PRIMEUR.

Coteaux de Peyriac Midi r p ★ DYA One of the most-used VIN DE PAYS names of the Aude département. Huge quantities.

Coteaux de Pierrevert S Rh r p w sp ★ DYA Gd, early drinking co-op reds, rosés, fresh whites from nr Manosque. Ch Régusse fuller reds. Promoted to AC '98.

Coteaux du Quercy SW France r ★→★★ 95 96 98 99 (00) S of CAHORS promoted to VDQS. Private growers working alongside vg co-op near Monpezat incl Doms de la Combarade, la Garde, d'Aries, de Guyot, de Lafage, de Merchien.

Coteaux de Saumur Lo w sw ★★→★★★ 89 90 93 95' 96 97 98 99 Rare potentially fine s/sw CHENIN. VOUVRAY-like sw (MOELLEUX) best. Esp CLOS ROUGEARD, Lavigne, Legrand.

Coteaux et Terrasses de Montauban SW France r p ★→★★ Dominated by co-op at LAVILLEDIEU-LE-TEMPLE. Better from Doms de Biarnès and de Montels.

Coteaux du Tricastin S Rh r p w ★★ 90' 95' 97 98' 99' 00' Fringe RHONE AC of increasing quality. Attractively spiced red can age 8 yrs. Dom de Grangeneuve, Dom de Montine, Dom St-Luc, Ch La Décelle among best.

Coteaux Varois Prov r p w ★→★★ Substantial new AC zone: California-style Dom de St-Jean de Villecroze makes vg red, also CHX ROUTAS, la Calisse, Doms les Alysses, du Deffends.

Coteaux du Vendômois Lo r p w ★→★★ DYA Fringe Loire VDQS west of Vendôme. Pineau d'Aunis is the key grape alone or with others, in rosés and reds and with CHENIN in whites. Promoted to AC in 2000. Producers incl Dom du Four à Chaux, Cave du Vendôme-Villiers, Patrice Colin.

Côtes d'Auvergne Central Fr r p (w) ★→★★ DYA Flourishing small VDQS. Mainly GAMAY; also PINOT NOIR, CHARDONNAY. Producers include Boulin-Constant, Bellard, Cave St-Verny.

Côtes de Blaye B'x w ★ DYA Run-of-the-mill B'x white from BLAYE.

Côtes de Bordeaux St-Macaire B'x w dr sw ★ DYA From E of SAUTERNES.

Côtes de Bourg B'x r ★→★★ 89' 9 94 95 96 98 99 00' APPELLATION used for many of the better reds of BOURG. Ch'x incl DE BARBE, DU BOUSQUET, Brûlesécaille, Bujan, Falfas, Fougas, Grand-Jour, Guerry, Haut-Guirand, Haut-Maco, Haut-Mondésir, Mercier, Nodoz, Peychaud, Roc de Cambes, Rousset, Sociondo, Tayac.

Côtes du Brulhois SW France r p (w) ★→★★ 98 99 Nr Agen. Mostly centred on Goulens and Donzac coops. Also Dom de Coujétou-Peyret.

Côtes de Castillon B'x r ★→★★ 89 90' 94 95' 96' 98 99 00' Flourishing region just E of ST-EMILION; similar, often lighter wines. Best CHX incl de l'A, d'Aiguilhe, de Belcier, Cap de Faugères, La Clarière-Laithwaite, Clos l'Eglise, PITRAY, Robin, Ste-Colombe, Vieux Château Champs de Mars.

Côtes de Duras Dordogne r w p ★→★★ 98 99 00 (01) B'x satellite; mostly lighter wines. Top producers incl Doms de Laulan (gd SAUV), de Durand (bio), de la Solle, du Vieux Bourg, Amblard, Petit Malrome, Clos du Cadaret, and Ch La Grave Béchade. Good co-op.

Côtes de Forez Lo r p (sp) ★ DYA Uppermost Loire VDQS (GAMAY), around Boën, N of St-Etienne. Promoted to AC '00, but hardly worth bothering with.

Côtes de Francs B'x r w ★★ 89' 90' 94 95 96 97 98 00' Fringe BORDEAUX from E of ST-EMILION. Increasingly attractive tasty wines, esp from Ch'x Charmes-Godard, Laclaverie, de Francs, Lauriol, PUYGUERAUD, La Prade.

Côtes du Frontonnais SW France r p ★★ 98 99 00 (01) S'times called the "BEAUJOLAIS of Toulouse". DYA but reds with CAB need longer. Gd growers Doms de Caze, Joliet, du Roc, and Ch'x Bellevue-la-Forêt, Boujac, Bouissel, Cahuzac, Coutinel, Plaisance, and St-Guilhem give the gd co-op a hard time keeping up.

Côtes de Gascogne SW w (r p) ★ DYA VIN DE PAYS branch of ARMAGNAC. Remarkably popular, led by Plaimont co-op and Grassa family (Ch de Tariquet etc). Best-known for fresh fruity whites based on the Colombard grape, often with some Gros Manseng. Also Domaines de Papolle, Bergerayre, Maubet, Sancet, and Château Monluc.

Côtes du Jura r p w (sp) ★ DYA Many light tints/tastes. ARBOIS more substantial.

Côtes du Lubéron Prov r p w sp ★→★★ 95' 96 97 98' 99' 00' 01 Spectacularly improved country wines from N PROVENCE. Actors and media-magnates among owners. Star is Ch de la Canorgue, with vg largely SYRAH red, and whites (esp Viognier) as well. Others incl Ch Val-Joanis, de l'Isolette, Vieille Ferme (white) and Cellier de Marrenon a reliable co-op.

Côtes de la Malepère Midi r ★ DYA Rising star VDQS on frontier of MIDI and SW, nr Limoux using grape varieties from both. Watch for fresh eager reds.

Côtes du Marmandais Dordogne r p w ★→★★ 98 99 00 (01) Mostly light wines. Cocumont co-op better than Beaupuy. Chante Coucou Clos Bacqueys, La Verrerie, Ch de Beaulieu, and Dom des Geais better still and weightier.

Côtes de Montravel Dordogne w dr sw ★★ dr DYA sw 97 98 99 00 (01) Part of BERGERAC; traditionally med-sw, now often drier. Gd from Ch'x de Montaigne, Pique-Sègue, La Raye, La Resssaudie, Doms de Golse, de Perreau. Montravel SEC is dry, HAUT-MONTRAVEL SW.

Côtes de Provence Prov r p w ★→★★★ Wines of Provence; revolutionized by new attitudes and investment. Castel Roubine, Commanderie de Peyrassol, Doms Bernarde, de la Courtade, OTT, des Planes, Rabiéga, Richeaume, Ch Ste Rosaline are leaders. 75% rosé, 20% red, 5% white. See also Coteaux d'Aix, Côtes de Lubéron, Bandol, etc.

Côtes du Rhône S Rh r p w ★ 95' 96 98' 99 00' Basic Rhône AC. Best drunk young – even as PRIMEUR. Wide variations of quality: some heavy over-production. Look for estate bottlings. See Côtes du Rhône-Villages.

Côtes du Rhône-Villages S Rh r p w ★→★★ 89' 90' 95' 96' 97' **98'** 99' 00' Wine of the 17 best S Rhône villages. Substantial and mainly reliable; s'times delicious. Red base is GRENACHE; but more SYRAH and MOURVEDRE now used. Growing white quality, often with Viognier, Roussanne. See Beaumes-de-Venise, Cairanne, Chusclan, Laudun, Rasteau, Sablet, Séguret, St-Gervais, etc. Sub-category with non-specified village name: gd value eg Ch. Signac, Doms Cabotte, Montbayon, Rabasse-Charavin, Renjarde, Romarins, Ste-Anne.

Côtes du Roussillon Pyr r p w ★→★★ 95 96 97 **98** 99 00 01 E Pyrenees AC. Hefty Carignan r best, can be v tasty (eg Gauby). Some w: sharp VINS VERTS.

Côtes du Roussillon-Villages Pyr r ★★ 95 96 97 **98** 99 00 01 Region's best reds, 28 communes incl CARAMANY, LATOUR DE FRANCE, LESQUERDE, Tautavel. Best labels: Co-op Baixas, Cazes Frères, Doms des Chênes, la Cazenove, Gauby (incl full, exotic white), Ch de Jau, Co-op Lesquerde, Dom Piquemal, Co-op Les

> Top Côtes du Rhône producers: Ch'x Courac, La Courançonne, l'Estagnol, Fonsalette, Hugues, Montfaucon, St-Esteve and Trignon (incl Viognier white); Clos Simian; Co-ops Chantecotes (Ste-Cécile-les-Vignes), Villedieu (esp white); Doms La Bouvade ,Charvin, Coudoulet de Beaucastel (red and white), Cros de la Mûre, Gourget, Gramenon (Grenache, Viognier), Janasse, Jaume, Perrin, Réméjeanne, St-Georges, Vieille Julienne, Vieux Chêne; Guigal, Jaboulet.

Vignerons Catalans. Some now renounce AC status and make varietal VDP'S.

Côtes de St-Mont SW France r w p ★★ (r) **98 99** (00) Highly successful Gers VDQS seeking AC status, imitating MADIRAN, PACHERENC. Co-op Plaimont all-powerful (Hauts de Bergelle range and Ch de Sabazan) sw Cuvée Saint-Albert (★★★) outstanding. Private growers incl Ch de Bergalasse and Dom. de Bartat.

Côtes du Tarn SW France VDP r p w ★ DYA overlaps GAILLAC; from same growers esp co-ops, Ch de Vigné-Lourac, Doms de Labarthe and d'Escausses.

Côtes de Thongue Midi r w ★ DYA Popular VDP from the HERAULT. Some gd wines esp Doms Arjolle, les Chemins de Bassac, COUSSERGUES, Croix Belle, Montmarin.

Côtes de Toul E France p r w ★ DYA V light wines from Lorraine; mainly VIN GRIS (rosé). Promoted to AC '98.

Côtes du Ventoux S Rh r p (w) ★★ 95' 96 97 98' 99' 00' Booming (15,000-acre) AC between the Rhône and PROVENCE for tasty reds (from café-style to much deeper flavours), easy rosés, and some decent domaine whites. La Vieille Ferme, owned by J-P Perrin of CH DE BEAUCASTEL, is top producer; Co-op Goult, St-Didier, Domaine Anges, Brusset, Fondrèche, Font-Sane, Murmuriem, Verrière, Ch'x Pesquié, Valcombe, and PAUL JABOULET are gd too.

Côtes du Vivarais S Rh r p w ★ 98' **99'** 00 DYA 2,500 acres across several villages W of Montélimar; promoted to AC '99. Improving simple CUVEES; more substantial oak-aged reds. Best producers: Boulle, Gallety, Dom de Belvezet.

Coulée de Serrant Lo w dr sw ★★★★ 76' 78 79' 81 82 83' 85' **86 88 89' 90'** 91 92 **93** 95' 96 97 98 99 00 01 16-acre CHENIN v'yd on Loire's N bank at SAVENNIERES run on ferociously organic principles. Intense strong fruity/sharp wine, good aperitif and with fish. Ages almost for ever.

Couly-Dutheil Lo r p w ★★→★★★ 85 86 87 **88 89 90 93** 95 96 97 98 99 00 01 Major CHINON grower/merchant; range of reliable wines – CLOS d'Olive and l'Echo: top wines. New CUVEE, Crescendo (oak-aged).

Courcel, Dom de Mme de ★★★ Leading POMMARD estate – top PREMIER CRU Rugiens.

Coussergues, Domaine de Midi r w p ★ DYA Large estate with Australian winemakers nr Beziers. CHARD, SYRAH, etc: bargains.

Crémant In CHAMP meant "creaming" (half-sparkling). Since 75, an AC for quality classic-method sparkling from ALSACE, Loire, BOURGOGNE and most recently LIMOUX – often a bargain. Term no longer used in Champagne.

Crémant de Loire Lo w sp ★★–★★★★ NV High quality sp, esp SAUMUR and TOURAINE. Esp BAUMARD Berger, Delhumeau (Dme de Brizel), LANGLOIS-CHATEAU, Nerleux, OISLY ET THESEE, Passavant.

Crépy Savoie w ★★ DYA Light, soft, Swiss-style white from S shore of Lake Geneva. "Crépitant" has been coined for its faint fizz.

Criots-Bâtard-Montrachet Burg w ★★★ 78' 79 85 86 88 89' 90 92 94 95' 96' 97 98 99 00' 01 4-acre neighbour to BATARD-MONTRACHET. Similar without the extreme pungency. Fontaine-Gagnard, Blein-Gagnard

Crozes-Hermitage N Rh r (w) ★★ 85' 88 89' 90' 91' 94 95' 96' 97' 98' 99' 00' Nr HERMITAGE: larger v'yds, SYRAH wine with fewer dimensions. Some is fruity, early-drinking (2⁺ yrs); some cask-aged (wait 4–8 yrs). Gd examples from Belle, Ch Curson, Desmeure, Doms du Colombier, des Entrefaux, du Pavillon-Mercurol, de Thalabert of JABOULET, CHAPOUTIER, Fayolle et Fils, Alain Graillot. Drink whites (mostly Marsanne) young.

Cruse et Fils Frères Historic BORDEAUX shipper. Now owned by Pernod-Ricard. The Cruse family (not the company) owns CH D'ISSAN.

Cunac SW France ★ r DYA Part of GAILLAC area. Light, fruity, quaffable reds.

Cussac Village S of ST-JULIEN. (AC HAUT-MEDOC.) Top ch'x: BEAUMONT, LANESSAN.

Cuve Close Short-cut method of making sparkling wine in a tank. Sparkle dies away in glass much quicker than with METHODE TRADITIONELLE wine.

Cuvée Wine contained in a cuve, or vat. A word of many uses, incl synonym for "blend" and first-press wines (as in CHAMPAGNE); in Burgundy interchangeable with "cru". Often just refers to a "lot" of wine.

Dagueneau, Didier Lo ★★★ 85 86 88 89 90 91 92 93 94 95 96 97 98 99 00 01 Top POUILLY-FUME producer. Pouilly's *enfant terrible* has created new benchmarks for the AC and for SAUV. Top CUVEE is barrel-fermented Silex. Serge D, another top producer, is Didier's uncle.

Daumas Gassac See Mas de Daumas Gassac.

De Castellane Brut NV; Blanc de Blancs; Brut 89 90 93 95; Cuvée Commodore Brut 85 88 89 90 95; Prestige Florens de Castellane 88 90 95. Trad Epernay CHAMP house linked with LAURENT-P. Best for v'tage wines; esp Commodore.

Degré alcoolique Degrees of alcohol, ie percent by volume.

Deiss, Domaine Marcel Fine ALSACE grower at Bergheim with 50 acres, wide range incl splendid RIES (GRAND CRU Schoenenberg), GEWURZ (Altenburg de Bergheim), good SELECTION DES GRAINS NOBLES and VIN DE PAILLE.

Delamotte Brut; Bl de Blancs (90 95 96 97); Cuvée Nicolas Delamotte Fine sml CHARDY-dominated CHAMPAGNE house at Le Mesnil, owned by LAURENT-PERRIER.

Delas Frères Old and worthy firm of Rhône wine specialists with vineyards at CONDRIEU, COTE-ROTIE, HERMITAGE. Top wines: Condrieu, Marquise de Tourette Hermitage (red and white). Owned by ROEDERER. Quality on the rise.

Delbeck Small fine CHAMP house revitalized by Martin/Giraudière partners since 95. Plenty of PINOT N in blend. Excellent vintage wines (85 90 95 96) and Grand Cru Ay, Cramant and Bouzy. Also owns Bricout.

Delorme, André ★★ Leading COTE CHALONNAISE merchants and growers. Specialists in vg CREMANT DE BOURGOGNE and excellent RULLY, etc.

Demi-Sec Half-dry: in practice more than half sweet (eg of CHAMP).

Des Guelasses, Dom Restaurant house wine, mostly in pubs and theatre bars.

Deutz Brut Classic NV; Rosé NV; Brut 82 85 88 90 93 95 96 97; Rosé 88 90; Bl de Bls 88 89 90 95 96 97 One of top sm CHAMP houses, ROEDERER-owned. V dry, classic wines. Superb CUVEE William Deutz (88 90 95).

Dirler, J-P ALSACE producer of GRAND CRUS Kessler, Saering. Spiegel; esp for RIES.

Dom Pérignon, Cuvée 73 75' 76 78 80 82 85 90 92 93 95 96; Rosé 88 90 95 Luxury CUVEE of MOET & CHANDON (launched 1936), named after the legendary abbey cellarmaster who first blended CHAMP. Astonishing

FRANCE

consistent quality and creamy character, esp with 10–15 yrs bottle-age. New limited release of five recently disgorged vintages (93 85 80 73).

Domaine Property, particularly in Burgundy and rural France.

Dopff & Irion Famous Riquewihr (ALSACE) business. Esp MUSCAT les Amandiers, RIES Les Murailles, GEWURZ Les Sorcières, PINOT Gr Les Maquisards: long-lived. Good CREMANT d'Alsace. Now part of PFAFFENHEIM co-op.

Dopff au Moulin Ancient top-class family wine house at Riquewihr, ALSACE. Best: GEWURZ: GRAND CRUS BRAND and Sporen, RIES SCHOENENBOURG, Sylvaner de Riquewihr. Pioneers of Alsace sp wine; good CUVEES: Bartholdi and Julien.

Dourthe Frères B'X merchant with wide range: good CRUS BOURGEOIS, incl BELGRAVE, MAUCAILLOU, TRONQUOY-LALANDE. Beau-Mayne is well-made brand.

Doux Sweet.

Drappier, André Leading AUBE region CHAMP house (esp). Family-run. Vinous NV, Brut Zéro, Rosé Saignée, Carte d'Or 90 **93** 95 **96** 97, Signature Bl de Bl **93** 95 **96** 97, Sumptuous prestige CUVEE Grande Sendrée **90** 95 96.

DRC See Romanée-Conti, Domaine de la.

Drouhin, J & Cie Burg ★★★ Deservedly prestigious grower (150 acres) and merchant with highest standards. Cellars in BEAUNE; v'yds in Beaune, CHABLIS, CLOS DE VOUGEOT, MUSIGNY, etc, and Oregon, USA. Top wines incl (esp) (w) BEAUNE-CLOS DES MOUCHES, CHABLIS LES CLOS, CORTON-CHARLEMAGNE, Les Folatières (r) GRIOTTE-CHAMBERTIN, MUSIGNY, PULIGNY-M'RACHET. Majority share now held by a Tokyo co.

Duboeuf, Georges ★★→★★★ The Grand Fromage of BEAUJOLAIS. Top-class merchant at Romanèche-Thorin. Region's leader in every sense; huge range of admirable wines. Also MOULIN-A-VENT atypically aged in new oak, white MACONNAIS, etc.

Dubos High-level BORDEAUX NEGOCIANT.

Duclot BORDEAUX NEGOCIANT; top-growth specialist. Linked with J-P MOUEIX.

Dugat Burg ★★★ Cousins Claude and Bernard both make excellent, deep coloured wines in GEVREY CHAMBERTIN under their respective labels.

Dujac, Domaine ★★★ Burg grower (Jacques Seysses) at MOREY-ST-DENIS with v'yds in that village and BONNES-MARES, ECHEZEAUX, GEVREY-CHAMBERTIN, etc. Splendidly vivid and long-lived wines. Now also buying grapes in MEURSAULT, and venture with other grapes in COTEAUX VAROIS.

Dulong Highly competent BORDEAUX merchant. Breaking all the rules with unorthodox Rebelle blends. Also VINS DE PAYS.

Durup, Jean Burg ★★ One of the biggest CHABLIS growers with 375 acres, including Domaine de l'Eglantière and admirable Ch de Maligny.

Duval-Leroy Fleur de Champagne Brut NV and Rosé NV; Extra Brut; Brut **90** 95; Bl de Bls 95 **96**; Prestige Cuvée des Rois 88 **90** 95; Cuvée Spéciale "Fin de Siècle". Rising Côte des Bl house; fine quality, gd value. Many other labels.

Echézeaux Burg r ★★★ 78' 85' 88 89' 90' 91 93 95 96' 97 98 99' 00 01 74-acre GRAND CRU between VOSNE-ROMANEE and CLOS DE VOUGEOT. Can be superlative, fragrant, without great weight, eg Confuron-Cotetidot, DUJAC ENGEL, Gouroux, GRIVOT, A F GROS, MUGNERET, DRC, RION, ROUGET.

Ecu, Dom de l' Lo dr w r ★★★ 81 85 86 87 88 89 90 93 95 96 97 98 99 00 01 Outstanding producer of Muscadet de Sevre et Maine as well as delicious Gros Plant du Pays Nantais. The Cabernet rivals many Saumur-Champigny. Viticulture is biodynamic.

Edelzwicker Alsace w ★ DYA Modest blended light white.

Eguisheim, Cave Vinicole d' Very good ALSACE co-op: fine GRAND CRUS Hatschbourg, Hengst, Ollwiller and Spiegel. Owns Willm. Top label: WOLFBERGER (65% of production). Best ranges: Grande Réserve, Sigillé and Armorié. Good CREMANT and PINOT.

Eichberg Eguisheim (ALSACE) GRAND CRU. A warm patch, with the lowest rainfall in Colmar area: Famed for GERWURZ esp vg KUENTZ-BAS VENDANGE TARDIVE.

Engel, R ★★★ Top-class grower of CL DE VOUGEOT, ECHEZEAUX, GRANDS-ECH'X, VOSNE-ROM.

Entraygues SW France r p w DYA ★ Fragrant country VDQS. Esp F Avallon's dry w.

Entre-Deux-Mers B'x w ★→★★ DYA Improving dry white B'x from between Rivers Garonne and Dordogne (aka E-2-M). Esp Ch'x BONNET, Fontenille, Moulin de Launay, Sainte-Marie, Tour de Mirambeau, Toutigeac, Turcaud, etc.

Esmonin, Sylvie Burg ★★★ V classy GEVREY-CHAMBERTIN esp CLOS ST-JACQUES.

Estaing SW France r p w ★ DYA Neighbour of ENTRAYGUES and similar in style.

L'Estandon Brand name of everyday wine of Nice (AC COTES DE PROVENCE): all colours.

l'Etoile Jura w dr sp (sw) ★★ Subregion of the JURA known for stylish whites, incl VIN JAUNE, similar to CHATEAU-CHALON; good sparkling.

Faiveley, J Burg ★★→★★★★ Family-owned growers and merchants at NUITS-ST-GEORGES, with v'yds (270 acres) in CHAMBERTIN-CLOS DE BEZE, CHAMBOLLE-MUSIGNY, CORTON, MERCUREY, NUITS (74 acres). Consistent high quality (rather than charm).

Faller, Théo/Domaine Weinbach Top ALSACE grower (Kaysersberg) run by Mme Colette Faller and her two daughters. Concentrated wines needing long ageing, up to 10 yrs. Esp GRAND CRUS SCHLOSSBERG (RIES), Furstentum (GEWURZ).

Faugères Midi r (p w) ★★ 95 96 97 **98** 99 00 01 Isolated COTEAUX DU LANGUEDOC village with above-average wine and exceptional terroir. Gained AC status 82. Esp Dom Alquier, Dom des Estanilles, Ch La Liquière.

Fesles, de Lo r w sw p ★★→★★★ **93 94** 95 96 **97 98 00** Historic estate in Bonnezeaux producing the entire range of Anjou wines. Encompasses Coteaux de Layon Chateau la Guimonière and la Roulerie.

Fessy, Sylvain Beauj ★★ Dynamic BEAUJOLAIS merchant with wide range.

Fèvre, William Burg ★★★ CHABLIS grower with the biggest GRAND CRU holding, Dom de la Maladière (45 acres). Bought 98 by HENRIOT, with immediate improvement.

Fiefs Vendéens Lo r p w ★ DYA Up-and-coming VDQS for light wines from the Vendée, just S of MUSCADET on the Atlantic coast. Wines from CHARD, CHENIN, Colombard, Grolleau, Melon (whites), CAB, PINOT N and GAMAY for reds and rosés. Esp Coirier, Ferme des Ardillers, Michon.

Filliatreau, Domaine Lo r ★★→★★★ 89 **90** 93 95 96 **97** 98 00 01 Paul Filliatreau put SAUMUR-CHAMPIGNY on map and in Paris restaurants. Supple, fruity, drinkable Jeunes Vignes. Other CUVEES aged 2–5 yrs (Vieille Vignes & La Grande Vignolle).

Fitou Midi r ★★ 95 96 97 **98** 99 00 01 Superior CORBIERES-style red wines; powerful, ageing well. Best from co-ops at Cascastel, Paziols and Tuchan. Interesting experiments with MOURVEDRE grapes in Leucate. Good estates, incl Ch Nouvelles, Dom Lérys, Rolland.

Fixin Burg r ★★★ 89' 90' 91 **92 93 95 96' 97** 98 99 Worthy and under-valued northern neighbour of GEVREY-CHAMBERTIN. Often splendid reds. Best v'yds: CLOS du Chapitre, Les Hervelets, Clos Napoléon. Growers incl Bertheau, R Bouvier, CLAIR, FAIVELEY, Gelin, Gelin-Molin, Guyard.

Fleurie Beauj r ★★★ **98 99 00 01** The epitome of a BEAUJOLAIS CRU: fruity, scented, silky, racy wines. Esp from Chapelle des Bois, Chignard, Depardon, Després, DUBOEUF, de Fleurie, Métrat, the co-op.

Floc de Gascogne SW France r p w ARMAGNAC'S answer to PINEAU DES CHARENTES. Aperitif from unfermented grape juice blended with Armagnac.

Fortant de France Midi r p w ★→★★ VDP D'OC brand (dressed to kill) of remarkable quality single-grape wines from Sète neighbourhood. See Skalli.

Frais Fresh or cool.

Frappé Ice-cold.

Froid Cold.

Fronsac B'x r ★→★★★ **85' 86' 88'** 89' 90' **94 95** 96 97 98 00' Picturesque area; increasingly fine, often tannic r just W of ST-EM. Ch'x incl de Carles, DALEM, LA DAUPHINE, Fontenil, La Grave, Mayne-Vieil, Moulin-Haut-Laroque, LA RIVIERE, La Rousselle, La Vieille Cure, Villars. Give them time. See also Canon-Fronsac.

FRANCE

Frontignan Midi golden sw ★★ NV Strong, sweet, liquorous MUSCAT of ancient repute. Quality steadily improving, esp from Ch'x Stony and La Peyrade.

Gagnard, Jean-Noel Burg ★★★ Jean Noel's daughter, Caroline l'Estimé, has pushed this domaine to the top of the Gagnard clan. Beautifully expressive GRAND CRU, PREMIER CRU, and village wines in CHASSAGNE-MONTRACHET.

A Guide to Gaillac

Good all-rounders Mas Pignou, Mas d'Aurel, Doms de Barreau, Labarthe, and d'Escausses, Ch de Mayragues, co-op at Técou (esp. "Passion" range).

Reds Doms. Larroque, Pialentou, Salvy and La Chanade, Ch Raynal, d'Arlus.

Local varieties Robert Plageoles, Doms de Ramaye, Causse-Marines (all good).

Sweet whites Doms de Causse-Marines, Rotier, Long Pech, Mas de Bicary.

Dry whites Dom des Perches, Ch Vigné-Lourac.

Sparkling Doms Réné Rieux, La Tronque and Canto Perlic.

Vins de pays Ch Vigné-Lourac, Dom Borie-Vieille (muscadelle)

Gagnard-Delagrange, Jacques Burg ★★★ Estimable small (12-acre) grower of CHASSAGNE-MONTRACHET, including some MONTRACHET. Look out also for his daughters' estates, Blain-Gagnard and Fontaine-Gagnard.

Gaillac SW France r p w dr sw sp ★→★★ Mostly DYA except oaked reds **95** 98 99 (00), sw whites (97' 98 **99** 00' 01').

Gamay See Grapes for red wine (pages 10-12).

Garage Not a french term, but expressive of trend for pricey mini-châteaux.

Gard, Vin de Pays du Languedoc ★ The Gard département at the mouth of the Rhône is a centre of gd VDP production, incl Coteaux Flaviens, Pont du Gard, Cévennes, SABLES DU GOLFE DU LION, Salavès, Uzège and Vaunage.

Gers r w p ★ DYA Indistinguishable from nearby COTES DE GASCOGNE.

Gevrey-Chambertin Burg r ★★★ 85' 88 89' 90' 91 93 95 96' 97 98 99' 00 01 Village containing the great CHAMBERTIN, its GRAND CRU cousins and many other noble vineyards (eg PREMIERS CRUS Cazetiers, Combe aux Moines, CLOS ST-JACQUES, Clos des Varoilles), as well as much more commonplace land. Growers include Bachelet, L. Boillot, Damoy, DROUHIN, DUGAT, Esmonin, FAIVELEY, Harmand-Geoffroy, JADOT, Leclerc, LEROY, MORTET, ROTY, ROUSSEAU, Serafin, TRAPET, VAROILLES.

Gewurztraminer Speciality grape of ALSACE: one of 4 allowed for specified GRAND CRU wines. The most aromatic of Alsace grapes: at best like rose-petals to smell, grapefruit and/or lychees to taste.

Gigondas S Rh r p ★★→★★★ 78 81' 83 85 86 88 **89' 90' 93 94** 95' 96 97 98' 99' 00' 01 Worthy neighbour to CH'NEUF-DU-PAPE. Strong, full-bodied, s'times peppery, largely GRENACHE; eg Ch de Montmirail, Redortier, Saint-Cosme, Clos du Joncuas, Dom du Cayron, Font-Sane, Goubert, Gour de Chaulé, Grapillon d'Or, Les Hauts de Montmirail, Pesquier, les Pallières, Raspail-Äy, Sta-Duc, St-Gayan, des Travers, du Trignon.

Ginestet Long-established B'X NEGOCIANT now owned by Bernard Taillan, said to be second in turnover.

Girardin, Vincent Burg r w ★★→★★★ Quality grower in SANTENAY has become dynamic merchant, specializing in C' DE BEAUNE ACs. Modern, oak and fruit style.

Gisselbrecht, Louis High-quality ALSACE growers and merchants at Dambach-la-Ville. RIES and GEWURZ best. Cousin Willy Gisselbrecht's wines are v competitive.

Givry Burg r w ★★ **93** 95 96' 97 98 99 00 Underrated COTE CHALONNAISE village: light but tasty and typical burgundy from eg DELORME, Dom Joblot, L LATOUR, T Lespinasse, CLOS Salomon, Sarrazin, BARON THENARD.

Gorges et Côtes de Millau SW France r p w ★ DYA Locally popular country wines. Reds best. Co-op at Aguessac dominant .

Gosset V old small CHAMP house at AY. Excellent full-bodied wine (esp Grand Millésime 96). Gosset Celebris (90 95) is prestige CUVÉE, with Celebris Rosé (95 96), launched '95 by ambitious new owners, Cointreau family of COGNAC Frapin.

Gouges, Henri ★★★ Reinvigorated estate for rich, complex NUITS-ST-GEORGES.

Goût Taste, eg goût anglais: as the English like it (ie dry, or, for CHAMP, well-aged).

Grand Cru One of top Burgundy v'yds with its own APPELLATION CONTROLEE. In ALSACE one of the 50 top v'yds covered by Alsace Grand Cru AC, but more vague elsewhere. In ST-EMILION the third rank of ch'x, incl about 200 properties.

Grande Champagne The AC of the best area of COGNAC. Nothing fizzy about it.

Grande Rue, La Burg r ★★★ 89' 90' **91 93** 95 96' 97 98 99' 00 01 VOSNE-R GRAND CRU, neighbour to ROMANEE-CONTI. Owned by Dom Lamarche.

Grands-Echézeaux Burg r ★★★★ 78' 85' 88' 89' 90' 91' **92 93** 95 96' 97 98 99' 00 01 Superlative 22-acre GRAND CRU next to CLOS DE VOUGEOT. Wines not weighty but aromatic. Viz: DROUHIN, ENGEL, DRC, GROS.

Gratien, Alfred and Gratien & Meyer Brut NV; Brut 91 **95 96**; Prestige Cuvée Paradis Rosé (96). Excellent smaller family CHAMP house with top traditional standards. Fine, v dry, long-lasting wine is still fermented in barrels. Gratien & Meyer is counterpart at SAUMUR. (Vg Cuvée Flamme.)

Graves B'x r w ★★→★★★ Region S of B'DX city with excellent soft earthy reds, dry whites (SAUV–Sém) reasserting star status. PESSAC-LEOGNAN is inner zone.

Graves de Vayres B'x r w ★ 95 96 98 99 00' DYA ENTRE-D-M; no special character.

Grenache See grapes for red and white wine (pages 10–16).

Griotte-Chambertin Burg r ★★★★ 85' 88' 89' **90'** 91 **92 93** 95 96' 97 98 99' 00 01 14-acre GRAND CRU adjoining CHAMBERTIN. Similar wine, but less masculine, more "tender". Growers incl DUGAT, DROUHIN, PONSOT.

Grivot, Jean Burg ★★★→★★★★ 35-acre COTE DE NUITS domaine, in 5 ACS incl RICHEBOURG, Nuits PREMIERS CRUS, VOSNE-ROMANEE, CLOS DE VOUGEOT. Top quality.

Groffier, Robert Burg ★★★ Pure, elegant GEVREY-CHAMBERTIN, CHAMBOLLE-MUSIGNY, esp Les Amoureuses.

Gros, Domaines Burg ★★★→★★★★ An excellent family of vignerons in VOSNE-ROMANEE comprising (at least) Domaines Jean, Michel, Anne et François, Anne-François Gros and Gros Frère et Soeur.

Gros Plant du Pays Nantais Lo w ★ DYA Junior VDQS cousin of MUSCADET, sharper, lighter; from the COGNAC grape, aka Folle Blanche, Ugni Bl, etc.

Guffens-Heynen Burg ★★★ Belgian POUILLY-FUISSE grower. Tiny quantity, top quality. Heady GAMAY and COTE D'OR wines (bought-in grapes) – also VERGET.

Guigal, Ets E Celebrated grower (22 ha COTE-ROTIE) Hermitage, St-Joseph, and merchant of CONDRIEU, Côte-Rôtie, HERMITAGE. Since '85 owner of VIDAL-FLEURY. 01 of de Vallouit & Dom J-L Grippat. By ageing single-v'yd Côte-Rôtie (La Mouline, La Landonne and La Turque) for 42 months in new oak, Guigal (plus Ch d'Ampuis: 38 months oak since 95) breaks local tradition to please (esp) American palates. His standard wines are gd value and reliable, esp the red COTES DU RHONE. Special CONDRIEU CUVEE La Doriane (since 95) – full, oaky.

Guy Saget Lo ★ A family firm with v'yds in the Pouilly-Fume and Pouilly sur Loire appellations (Domaine Saget), gradually buying up estates throughout the Loire to become one of the region's biggest proprietors. Saget's negociant line accounts for half the firm's annual production of 5 million bottles.

Haut-Poitou Lo w r ★→★★ DYA Up-and-coming VDQS S of ANJOU. Vg whites (CHARD, SAUV, CHENIN) from CAVE linked with DUBOEUF. Reds: GAMAY, CAB, best age 4–5 yrs. Has rejected restrictions of AC status for freedom of choice.

Haut-Benauge B'x w ★ DYA AC for a limited area in ENTRE-DEUX-MERS.

Haut-Médoc B'x r ★★→★★★ 82' 83' 85' 86' 88' 89' 90' **93 94 95 96** 98 00' Big AC incl best parts of MEDOC. Most of zone has communal ACS (eg MARGAUX, PAUILLAC). Some excellent ch'x (eg LA LAGUNE): simply AC HAUT-MEDOC.

Haut-Montravel Dordogne w sw ★★ 90' 94 95' 96 97' 98 (99) Rare MONTAVEL sw white; rather like MONBAZILLAC. Look for Ch'x Le Bondieu, Moulin Caresse, Puy-Servain-Terrement, Roque-Peyre, also Dom de Libarde and Dom. de Grouyat.

Hautes-Côtes de Beaune Burg r w ★★ 95 96' 97 98 99' 00 01 AC for a dozen villages in the hills behind the COTE DE BEAUNE. Light wines, worth investigating. Top growers: Cornu, Deverey, Jacob Mazilly.

Hautes-Côtes de Nuits Burg r w ★★ 95 96' 97 98 99' 00 01 As above, for COTE DE NUITS. An area on the way up. Top growers: Duband, C Cornu, Jayer-Gilles, M GROS. Also has large BEAUNE co-op.

Heidsieck, Charles Brut Réserve NV; Brut 85 90 95 96; Rosé 90 95 96 Major Reims CHAMP house, now controlled by Rémy Martin Bl des Millénaires (90 95). Fine quality recently esp new BRUT Exceptional, innovative Brut Réserve Mis en Cave range created by the late Daniel Thibault (died 2002). NV: real bargain. See also Piper-Heidsèck.

Heidsieck, Monopole Brut NV Blue Top; Red Top; Gold Top (96). Once illustrious CHAMP house now owned by VRANKEN group. Red Top CUVEE virtually BL DE NOIRS. Luxury brand Diamant Bleu (85 90 95) is excellent.

Hengst Wintzenheim (ALSACE) GRAND CRU. Excels with top-notch GEWURZ from Albert Mann; also Pinot-Auxerrois, Chasselas (esp JOSMEYER'S) and PINOT Noir (esp A Mann's) with no GRAND CRU status.

Henriot Brut Souverain NV; Blanc de Blancs de CHARD NV; Brut 85 88 90 95 96; Brut Rosé 88 90 95 96; Luxury Cuvée: Cuvée des Enchanteleurs 85 88 90 Old family CHAMP house; regained independence in '94. Very fine, fresh, creamy style. Joseph H. also owns BOUCHARD PERE (since 95) and FEVRE.

Hérault Midi Biggest v'yd département: 980,000 acres of vines. Some vg AC COTEAUX DU LANGUEDOC and pioneering VDP de l'Hérault, as well as VIN DE TABLE.

Hermitage N Rh r w ★★★→★★★★ 61' 66 72 78' 79 82 83' 85' 88 89' 90' 91' 94 95' 96' 97' 98' 99' 00' 01' By tradition, the 'manliest' wine of France: dark, powerful and profound. Truest example of SYRAH from 309 hillside acres on E bank of Rhône, granite plus clay-chalk. Needs long ageing. White (Marsanne, some Roussanne) is heady and golden; now usually made for early drinking, though best wines mature for up to 25 yrs; can be better than red (eg 93). Top makers: Belle, CHAPOUTIER, CHAVE, DELAS, Desmeure, Faurie, GUIGAL, JABOULET, Sorrel, Tardieu-Laurent. TAIN co-op also useful and improving.

Hospices de Beaune Burg Historic hospital and charitable institution in BEAUNE, with excellent v'yds (known by "CUVEE" names) in BEAUNE, CORTON, MEURSAULT, POMMARD, VOLNAY. Wines are auctioned on the third Sunday of each November.

Hudelot-Noëllat, Alain ★★★ Under-appreciated VOUGEOT estate producing some excellent wines, in a light but fine style.

Huët L'Echansonne Lo ★★→★★★★ 47' 59' 76' 85' 88' 89' 90' 93 95' 96 97 98 99 00 01 (SEC and DEMI-SEC) Leading top-quality estate in VOUVRAY, run on biodynamic principles. Wines for long ageing. Single-v'yard wines best: Le Haut Lieu, Le Mont, Clos du Bourg, Le Vodanis.

Hugel et Fils The best-known ALSACE co; founded at Riquewihr in 1639 and still in the family. "Johnny" H (ret'd '97) is the region's beloved spokesman (Jean-Philippe and Etienne are in charge with Marc as winemaker). Quality escalates with Tradition and Jubilee ranges. Hugels are militantly against Alsace GRAND CRU system. SELECTIONS DES GRAINS NOBLES: Hugel pioneered this style and still makes some of finest examples. Also occasionally VIN DE PAILLE.

Ile de Beauté Name given to VINS DE PAYS from CORSICA. Mostly red.

Impériale BORDEAUX bottle holding 8.5 normal bottles (6.4 litres).

Irancy ('Bourgogne Irancy') Burg r (p) ★★ 96' 97 98 99' 00 Good light red made nr CHABLIS from PINOT N and the local César. The best vintages mature well. To watch. Growers incl Colinot.

Irouléguy SW France r p (w) ★★ **95' 96** 97 **98 99** (01') Local wines of Basque country with a rustic twang. Was mainly rosé, but now dark dense Tannat/CAB reds to keep 5 yrs⁺. Gd from Doms Ilarria, BRANA, Arretxea, Etchegaraya and Abotia and co-op. A future MADIRAN?

Jaboulet Aîné, Paul Old family firm at TAIN, leading grower of HERMITAGE (esp La Chapelle ★★★★), CORNAS St-Pierre, CROZES Thalabert (vg value), Roure; merchant of other Rhône wines – esp COTES DU RHONE Parallèle 45, COTES DU VENTOUX. Whites now more fat than before.

Jacquart Brut NV, Brut Rosé NV (Carte Blanche and Cuvée Spéciale); Brut **90** 95 96 Relatively new ('62) co-op-based CHAMP marque; in quantity the sixth-largest. Fair quality. Luxury brands: CUVEE Nominée Blanc **88** 90, 95, CN Rosé **95 96** Vg Mosaïque BL DE BLANCS **92** 95 96 Mosaïque Rosé 95

Jacquesson Excellent small Dizy CHAMP house. Vg vintage BL DE BLANCS (**93** 95); exquisite barrel-fermented "Grand Vin" luxury CUVEES: both w (88 **93** 95) and rosé (90 93). Also Dégorgement Tardif (75 85) and Vigneron de L'Année 2002 (gde des Sommeliers).

Jadot, Louis Burg ★★→★★★★ Top-quality merchant house with v'yds (155 acres) in BEAUNE, CORTON, Magenta, Ch des Jacques (MOULIN A VENT), etc. Wines to bank on.

Jardin de la France Lo w r p DYA One of France's four regional VINS DE PAYS. Covers Loire Valley: mostly single grape (esp CHARD, GAMAY, SAUV).

Jasnières Lo w dr (sw) ★★★ 76 78 79 83 85 86 88' **89' 90' 93' 95' 96** 97 98 **99 00 01** Rare and almost immortal dry VOUVRAY-like wine (CHENIN) of N TOURAINE. Esp Aubert la Chapelle, Gigou, Nicolas.

Jayer, Henri Near-legendary Burgundy figure. See Rouget, Emmanuel.

Jeroboam In BORDEAUX, a 6-bottle bottle (holding 4.5 litres) or triple MAGNUM; in CHAMP, a double magnum.

Jobard, François Burg ★★★ Small MEURSAULT domaine; classic, slow-evolving wines. Look out also for nephew Remi Jobard's more modern-style wines.

Joliver, Pascal Lo ★★→★★★★ Considerable producer of good Sancerre and Pouilly-Fumé at several levels.

Joseph Perrier CUVEE Royale BRUT NV; Cuvée Royale Bl de Blancs NV; Cuvée Royale Rosé NV; Brut **85 90** 95 96 Family-run CHAMP house at Chalons with good v'yds in Marne Valley. Supple fruity style; vg prestige Cuvée Joséphine, mainly CHARD **85 90** 95. Part-owned since 98 by ALAIN THIENOT.

Josmeyer Family house at Wintzenheim, ALSACE. Vg long-ageing wines, esp GEWURZ and Pinot Bl. Fine RIES from GRAND CRU Hengst. Wide range.

Juliénas Beauj r ★★★ **98 99 00 01** Leading CRU of BEAUJOLAIS: vigorous fruity wine to keep 2–3 yrs. Growers incl Ch'x du Bois de la Salle, des Capitans, de Juliénas, des Vignes; Doms Bottière, R Monnet, Michel Tête, co-op.

Jura See Côtes du Jura.

Jurançon SW France w sw dr ★★→★★★ **89' 90' 94** 95' 96 97' 98 00 (01') Highly flavoured long-lived speciality of Pau in Pyrenean foothills, at best like wildflower SAUTERNES. Not to be missed. Both sw and dr should age. Top growers: Dom du Bellegarde, Barrère, Bordenave, du Cinquau, Dom Cauhapé, Gaillot, Guirouilh, Jolys, Lamouroux, Lapeyre, Larredya, Nigri, de Rousse, Uroulat, Bousquet, and (esp dry) Bellevue, Cabarrouy. Also co-op's dry Grain Sauvage, BRUT d'Ocean and Peyre d'Or.

Kaefferkopf Alsace w dr sw ★★★ Ammerschwihr v'yd famous for blends rather than single-variety wines and denied GRAND CRU status for this reason.

Kientzheim-Kayserberg, Cave Vinicole de Important ALSACE co-op now returning to top quality. Esp GEWURZ, RIES GRAND CRU Schlossberg and CREMANT.

Kientzler, André ALSACE RIES specialist in Geisburg GRAND CRU, esp VENDANGE TARDIVE and SGN. Equally gd from GCs Kirchberg de Ribeauvillé for GEWURZ, Osterberg for occasional "vins de glaces" (Eisweins). Also vg Auxerrois, Chasselas.

Kreydenweiss Marc Fine ALSACE grower: 30 acres at Andlau, esp for PINOT Gr (vg GRAND CRU Moenchberg), Pinot Bl and RIES. Top wine: Grand Cru Kastelberg (Ries ages 20 yrs); also fine Auxerrois "Kritt Klevner" and gd VENDANGE TARDIVE. One of first in Alsace to use new oak. Good Ries-Pinot Gr blend "Clos du Val d'Eléon". Great believer in terroir and in biodynamic viticulture.

Kriter Popular sparkler processed in Burgundy by PATRIARCHE. See the fountain on the Autoroute du Soleil.

Krug Grande CUVÉE; Vintage **82** 85 88 90 95 96; Rosé; CLOS du Mesnil (BL DE BLANCS) **82** 85 88 90 95 96; Krug Collection **62 64 66 69 71 73** 76 79 Small and supremely prestigious CHAMP house. Dense full-bodied v dry wines: long ageing, superlative quality. Owned since 99 by MOET-Hennessy.

Kuentz-Bas Top-quality ALSACE grower/merchant at Husseren-les-Châteaux, esp for PINOT Gr, GEWURZ. Also good VENDANGES TARDIVES.

Labouré-Roi Burg ★★→★★★ Reliable, dynamic merchant at NUITS. Mostly whites. Many fine dom wines, esp René Manuel's MEURSAULT, Chantal Lescure's Nuits.

Ladoix-Serrigny Burg r (w) ★★ **95** 96' 97 98 99' 01 Northernmost village of COTE DE BEAUNE below hills of CORTON. To watch for bargains.

Ladoucette, de ★★→★★★ 89 90 93 94 95 **96** 97 **98 99 00 01** Leading producer of POUILLY-FUME, based at Ch de Nozet. Luxury brand Baron de L can be wonderful (but at a price). Also SANCERRE Comte Lafond and La Poussie (and PIC, CHABLIS).

Lafarge, Michel ★★★★ 25-acre COTE DE BEAUNE estate with excellent VOLNAYS.

Lafon, Domaine des Comtes ★★★★ 34-acre top burgundy estate in MEURSAULT, LE M'RACHET, VOLNAY. Glorious intense whites; extraordinary dark reds.

Laguiche, Marquis de Burg ★★★★ Largest owner of LE MONTRACHET. Superb DROUHIN-made wines.

Lalande de Pomerol B'x r ★★→★★★ 88' 89' 90' 94 95 **96** 98 00' Neighbour to POMEROL. Wines similar, but less mellow. Top ch'x: Les Annereaux, DE BEL-AIR, Belles-Graves, Bertineau-St-Vincent, La Croix-St-André, La Fleur de Boüard, Garraud, Haut-Chaigneau, Hauts-Conseillants, SIAURAC, TOURNEFEUILLE. To try.

Langlois-Château Lo ★→★★★One of top SAUMUR sp houses (esp CREMANT). Controlled by BOLLINGER. Also range of still wines, esp Saumur Bl VIEILLES VIGNES.

Lanson Père & Fils Black Label NV; Rosé NV; BRUT **90 93** 95 96 Imp't improving CHAMP house; cellars at Reims. Long-lived luxury brand: Noble CUVEE (85 **88 90**) Black Label reliable, sharp, appley NV. New cuvée: BL DE BLS **90** 95.

Laroche ★★→★★★★ Important grower (190 acres) and dynamic CHABLIS merchant, incl Domaines La Jouchère and Laroche. Top wines: Blanchots (esp Réserve de l'Obédiencerie ★★★) and CLOS VIEILLE VIGNES. Also blends gd non-regional CHARD and now ambitious MIDI range, Dom La Chevalière.

Latour, Louis Burg ★★→★★★★ Famous merchant and grower with v'yds (120 acres) in BEAUNE, CORTON, etc. Among the v best for white: CHEVALIER-M'RACHET Les Demoiselles, CORTON-CHARLEMAGNE, M'RACHET, gd-value MONTAGNY and ARDECHE CHARD etc. Ch de Corton Grancey. Also PINOT N Valmoissine from the Var.

Latour de France r (w) ★→★★ **95** 96 97 **98 99** 00 01 Supposedly superior village in AC COTES DE ROUSSILLON-VILLAGES.

Latricières-Chambertin Burg r ★★★ 85' **88'** 89' **90'** 91 **92 93** 95 96' 97 98 99' 00 01 17-acre GRAND CRU neighbour of CHAMBERTIN. Similar wine but lighter and "prettier", eg from FAIVELEY, LEROY, PONSOT, TRAPET.

Laudun S Rh w r p ★ Village of COTES DU RHONE-VILLAGES (west bank). Red style is soft. Attractive wines from Serre de Bernon co-op incl fresh whites. Dom Pelaquié is best, esp white, also Ch. Courac, Duseigneur, Prieuré St-Pierre.

Laurent-Perrier BRUT NV; Rosé NV; Brut **88 90** 93 95 Dynamic highly successful family-owned CHAMP house at Tours-sur-Marne. Steady NV; excellent luxury brands: CUVEE Grand Siècle (NV and 90 95 96), CGS Alexandra Brut Rosé (85 90). Also Ultra Brut. Owns SALON, DELAMOTTE, DE CASTELLANE.

Lavilledieu-du-Temple SW France r p w ★ DYA Fruity wines from co-op nr Montauban. Also VDP from COTEAUX DU QUERCY, COTEAUX ET TERRASSES DE MONTAUBAN.

Leflaive, Domaine Burg ★★★★ Once again among the best w burgundy growers, at PULIGNY-M. Best v'yds: Bienvenues-, Chevalier-M, Clavoillons, Pucelles and (since 91) Le M'rachet. Ever-finer wines on biodynamic principles.

Leflaive, Olivier Burg ★★★ High-quality NEGOCIANT at PULIGNY-M'RACHET, cousin of the above. Reliable wines, mostly white.

Léognan B'x r w ★★★→★★★★ Top village of GRAVES with its own AC: PESSAC-LEOGNAN. Best ch'x: DOM DE CHEVALIER, HAUT-BAILLY.

Leroy, Domaine Burg ★★★★ Domaine built around purchase of Dom Noellat in VOSNE ROMANEE in 1988 & Leroy family holdings (known as Dom d'Auvenay). Extraordinary quality from tiny yields; equally extraordinary prices.

Leroy, Maison Burg ★★★★ The ultimate NEGOCIANT-ELEVEUR at AUXEY-DURESSES with sky-high standards and the finest stocks of expensive old wine in Burgundy.

Lesquerde ★★ 95 96 97 98 99 00 New superior AC village of COTES DU ROUSSILLON-VILLAGES.

Lichine, Alexis & Cie BORDEAUX merchants (once of the late Alexis Lichine). No connection with CH PRIEURE-LICHINE.

Lie, sur On the lees. MUSCADET is often bottled straight from the vat, for maximum zest and character.

Limoux Pyr r w ★★ Burgeoning AC for sp BLANQUETTE DE LIMOUX or better CREMANT de Limoux, oak-aged CHARD for Limoux AC and PINOT N for VDP as well as traditional grapes. Growers incl Doms de Fourn , des Martinolles; gd co-op.

Liquoreux Term for a very sweet wine: eg SAUTERNES, top VOUVRAY, JURANCON, etc.

Lirac S Rh r p w ★★ 89' 90' 94' 95' 96 98' 99' 00' Next to TAVEL. Approachable often soft r (can age 5+ yrs). Red overtaking rosé, esp Doms Cantegril, Devoy-Martine, Maby (Fermade), André Méjan, de la Mordorée, Sabon, Ch d'Aquéria, de Bouchassy, Ségriès. Greater use of MOURVEDRE firming some reds. Gd whites.

Listel Midi r p w ★→★★ DYA Vast (4,000-acre[+]) historic estate on sandy beaches of Golfe du Lion. Owned by VAL D'ORBIEU. Pleasant light "vins des sables" incl sp. Dom du Bosquet-Canet: fruity CAB; Dom de Villeroy: fresh BLANC DE BLANCS SUR LIE; rosé Gris de Gris; and CHARD. Also fruity, almost non-alcoholic PETILLANT, Ch de Malijay: COTES DU RHONE; Abbaye de Ste-Hilaire: CTX VAROIS; Ch La Gordonne: COTES DE PROVENCE.

Listrac-Médoc B'x r ★★→★★★ 90' 95 96 98 00' Village of HAUT-MEDOC next to MOULIS. Grown-up clarets with tannic grip Best ch'x: CLARKE, FONREAUD, FOURCAS-DUPRE, FOURCAS-HOSTEN, Mayne-Lalande, and good co-op.

Livinière, La See Minervois-La Livinière.

Long-Depaquit Burg Vg CHABLIS domaine (esp MOUTONNE), owned by BICHOT.

Lorentz, Gustave ALSACE grower and merchant at Bergheim. Esp GEWURZ, RIES from GRAND CRUS Altenberg de Bergheim, Kanzlerberg. Also owns Jerome Lorentz.

Loron & Fils Big-scale grower and merchant at Pontanevaux; specialist in BEAUJOLAIS and sound VINS DE TABLE.

Loupiac B'x w sw ★★ 85 86' 88' 89 90 95 96 97 98 99 01' Across River Garonne from SAUTERNES and by no means to be despised. Top ch'x: CLOS-Jean, LOUPIAC-GAUDIET, Mémoires, Noble, RICAUD, Les Roques.

Lugny See Mâcon-Lugny.

Lussac-St-Emilion B'x r ★★ 85 86' 88' 89' 90' 94 95 96 98 01' NE neighbour to ST-EMILION. Top ch'x incl Barbe Blanche, BEL AIR, Bellevue, de la Grenière, Mayne-Blanc, DU LYONNAT, Co-op (at PUISSEGUIN) makes pleasant Roc de Lussac.

Macération carbonique Traditional fermentation technique: whole bunches of unbroken grapes in a closed vat. Fermentation inside each grape eventually bursts it, giving vivid fruity mild wine, not for ageing. Esp in BEAUJOLAIS; now much used in the MIDI and elsewhere, even CHATEAUNEUF-DU-PAPE.

FRANCE

Mâcon Burg r w (p) DYA oo Sound, usually unremarkable reds (GAMAY best), tasty dry (CHARD) whites. Also Macon Superieur (similar).

Mâcon-Lugny Burg r w sp ★★ 99 00' 01 Village next to VIRE with huge and vg co-op (4M bottles). Les Genevrières is sold by LOUIS LATOUR.

Mâcon-Villages Burg w ★★-★★★ 99 00' 01 Increasingly well-made typical w burgundies (when not over-produced). Named for their villages, eg M-Lugny, -Prissé, -Uchizy. Best co-op Prissé, Lugny. Top growers: Vincent (Fuissé), THEVENET, Bonhomme, Merlin (La Roche Vineuse). See Viré-Clessé.

> **The Mâconnais**
> The hilly zone just north of Beaujolais has outcrops of limestone where Chardonnay gives full, if not often fine, wines. The village of Chardonnay here may (or may not) be the home of the variety. Granite soils give light Gamay reds. The top Mâconnais AC is Pouilly-Fuissé, followed by Pouilly Vinzelles, St Véran and Viré-Clessé, then Mâcon-Villages with a village name. The potential is here to produce lower-priced, richly typical Chardonnays to out-do the New World (and indeed the S of France). Currently, most wines are less than extraordinary but things are looking up.

Macvin Jura w sw ★★ AC for "traditional" MARC and grape-juice aperitif.

Madiran SW France r ★★-★★★★ 89' 90' 94 95' 96 97 98' (99) Dark vigorous red from S of ARMAGNAC, like tough fruity MEDOC with a fluid elegance of its own. Needs age. Try ch'x MONTUS, Bouscassé, (Ch d'Aydie), Chapelle Lenclos, Labranche-Laffont, Peyros, Pichard, Laffitte-Teston, Capmartin, Good co-op's Crouseilles, Plaimont, Castelnau-Rivière-Baise. White is AC PACHERENC DU VIC BILH.

Magnum A double bottle (1.5 litres).

Mähler-Besse First-class Dutch NEGOCIANT in B'X. Has share in CH PALMER and owns Ch Michel de Montaigne. Brands incl Cheval Noir. (Total: 250 acres.)

Mailly-Champagne Top CHAMP co-op. Luxury wine: CUVEE des Echansons.

Maire, Henri The biggest grower/merchant of JURA wines, with half of the entire AC. Some top wines, many cheerfully commercial. Fun to visit.

Maranges Burg r (w) ★★ 96 97 98 99' 01 AC for 600-odd acres of S COTE DE BEAUNE, beyond SANTENAY: one-third PREMIER CRU. Top NEGOCIATORS: DROUHIN, Jaffelin.

Marc Grape skins after pressing; also the strong-smelling brandy made from them (the equivalent of Italian "Grappa").

Marcillac SW France r p ★-★★★ DYA Became AC in '90. Violet-hued with grassy red-fruit character. Gd if rustic from Valady co-op, J-L Matha, Doms du Cros, Laurens.

Margaux B'x r ★★★-★★★★★ 78 81 82' 83' 85 86' 87 88' 89 90' 93 94 95 96 98 99 00' Village of HAUT-MEDOC. Some of most "elegant" and fragrant red BORDEAUX. AC incl CANTENAC and several other villages. Top ch'x incl MARGAUX, RAUZAN-SEGLA, BRANE-CANTENAC etc.

Marionnet, Henry Lo ★-★★★★ 89 90 93 95 96 97 98 99 00 01 Leading TOURAINE property specializing in GAMAY and SAUV. Top CUVEE Le M de Marionnet. Other cuvées include Première Vendange, Vinifera, Cepages Oubliés, Provignage.

Marne et Champagne Recent but huge-scale CHAMP house, owner (since 91) of LANSON and many smaller brands, incl BESSERAT DE BELLEFON. Alfred Rothschild brand v gd CHARD-based wines.

Marque déposée Trademark.

Marsannay Burg r p (w) ★★★ 95 96' 97 98 99' 00 01 (rosé DYA) Village with fine light red and delicate PINOT N rosé. Incl villages of Chenôve, Couchey. Growers: Charlopin, CLAIR, Dijon University, JADOT, ROTY, TRAPET.

Mas de Daumas Gassac Midi r w p ★★★ 82 93 94' 95 96 97 98 99 00 01 The one "first-growth" estate of the LANGUEDOC, producing potent largely CAB S on apparently unique soil. Extraordinary quality. Also Rosé Frisant and a rich fragrant white of blended CHARD, Viognier, Petit Manseng etc to drink at 2–3 yrs. Also quick-drinking red, Les Terrasses de Guilhem, from nearby co-op and trad Languedoc varietals (Clairette, Cinsaut, Aramon etc) from old vines under Terrasses de Landoc label. VIN DE PAYS status. From 98 intriguing new sw wine: Vin de Laurence (Sém, Muscats and Sercial!).

Maury Pyr r sw ★★ NV Red VIN DOUX NATUREL of GRENACHE from ROUSSILLON. Taste the terroir. Much recent improvement, esp at Mas Amiel.

Mazis (or Mazy) Chambertin Burg r ★★★ 78' 85' 88' 89' 90' 91 92 93 95 96' 97 98 99' 00 01 30-acre GRAND CRU neighbour of CHAMBERTIN, s'times equally potent. Best from FAIVELEY, HOSPICES DE BEAUNE, LEROY, Maume, ROTY.

Mazoyères-Chambertin See Charmes-Chambertin.

Médoc B'x r ★★ 85 86' 88' 89' 90' 94 95 96 98 00' AC for reds of the less-good (northern) part of BORDEAUX's biggest top-quality district. Flavours tend to earthiness. HAUT-MEDOC is much better. Top ch'x include LA CARDONNE, GREYSAC, LOUDENNE, LES ORMES-SORBET, POTENSAC, LA TOUR-DE-BY.

Meffre, Gabriel The biggest S Rhône estate, based at GIGONDAS. Variable quality, recent progress. Often in French supermarkets. Also bottles and sells for small CHATEAUNEUF-DU-PAPE domaines, eg Guy Jullian, Dom de Baban.

Mellot, Alphonse Lo ★★→★★★ 88 89 90 91 92 93 94 95 96 97 98 99 00 01 Leading SANCERRE grower and merchant. Especially for La Moussière and wood-aged CUVEE Edmond, Génération XIX; also MENETOU-SALON.

Menetou-Salon Lo r p w ★★(★) DYA Highly attractive similar wines from W of SANCERRE: SAUV BL white full of charm, PINOT N light red. Top growers: Henri Pellé, Jean-Max Roger. Reds from Clément can age.

Méo-Camuzet ★★★★ V fine domaine in CLOS DE VOUGEOT, NUITS-ST-GEORGES, RICHEBOURG, VOSNE-ROMANEE. HENRI JAYER inspired. Esp V-R Cros Parantoux.

Mercier & Cie, Champagne BRUT NV; Brut Rosé NV; Brut 90 93 95 96 97 One of biggest CHAMP houses at Epernay. Controlled by MOET & CHANDON. Gd commercial quality, sold mainly in France. Good powerful PINOT-led CUVEE du Fondateur and rich, supple BLANC DE NOIRS (95 96).

Mercurey Burg r w ★★ ·★★★ 90' 93 95 96' 97 98 99' 01 (Vintages are for reds). Leading red- wine village of COTE CHALONNAISE. Gd middle-rank burgundy incl improving w's. Try Ch de Chamirey, FAIVELEY, M Juillot, Lorenzon, Raquillet, Dom de Suremain.

Mercurey, Région de The up-to-date name for the COTE CHALONNAISE.

Mérode, Domaine Prince de ★★★ A top domaine for CORTON and POMMARD.

Mesnil-sur-Oger, Le Champ ★★★★ One of top Côte des Blancs villages; Structured CHARD for v long ageing.

Métaireau, Louis Loire w ★★→★★★ 87 88 89 90 91 92 93 94 95 96 97 98 99 00 01 A key figure in the MUSCADET quality revolution. Expensive well-finished wines: Number One, CUVEES Grand Mouton, and LM.

Méthode champenoise Traditional laborious method of putting bubbles into CHAMP by refermenting wine in its bottle. Must use terms "classic method" or "méthode traditionnelle" outside region. Not mentioned on Champ labels.

Méthode traditionnelle See entry above.

Meursault Burg w (r) ★★★→★★★★★ 89' 90 91 92 95 96' 97 99 00' 01 COTE DE BEAUNE village with some of world's greatest w's: savoury, dry but nutty and mellow. Best v'yds: Charmes, Genevrières, Perrières; also: Goutte d'Or, Meursault-Blagny, Poruzots, Narvaux, Tesson, Tillets. Producers incl AMPEAU, J-M BOILLOT, M Bouzereau, Boyer-Martenot, CH DE MEURSAULT, COCHE-DURY, Ente, Fichet, Grivault, P Javillier, JOBARD, LAFON, LATOUR, O LEFLAIVE, LEROY, Manuel, Matrot, Michelot-Buisson, P MOREY, G ROULOT. See also neighbouring Blagny.

Meursault-Blagny See Blagny.

Michel, Louis ★★★ CHABLIS domaine with model unoaked, v long-lived wines, incl superb LES CLOS, vg Montmains, MONTEE DE TONNERRE.

Midi General term for S of Fr, W of Rhône delta. Improving reputation; brilliant promise. Top wines often based on variety rather than AC. A melting-pot.

Minervois Midi r (p w) br sw ★→★★ **90 91 92 93 94 95 96 97 98 99** 00 01 Hilly AC region; good, lively wines, esp Ch du Donjon, Fabas, Dom Laurent Fabre, co-ops LA LIVINIERE, de Peyriac, Pouzols; La Tour Boisée, de Violet, CLOS Centeilles. Sw Minervois Noble being developed. See St-Jean de Minervois.

Minervois-La Livinière, La Midi r (p w) ★→★★ Quality village (see last entry) the only sub-appellation in Minervois. Best growers: Abbaye de Tholomies, Combe Blanche, Ch de Gourgazaud, Clos Centeilles, Laville-Bertrou, Doms Maris, Ste-Eulalie, Vallière, Co-op La Livinière.

Mis en bouteille au château/domaine Bottled at the CHATEAU, property or estate. NB "dans nos caves" (in our cellars) or "dans la région de production" (in the area of production) are often used but mean little.

Moelleux "With marrow": creamy sweet. ie. sw wines of VOUVRAY, COT' DU LAYON.

Moët & Chandon Brut NV; Rosé **90 92 93** 95 96; Brut Imperial **85 88 90 92 93 95** 96 97 Much the biggest CHAMP merchant and grower with cellars in Epernay; branches in Argentina, Australia, Brazil, California, Germany, Spain. Consistent high quality, esp in vintage wines. Coteaux Champenois Saran: still wine. Prestige CUVEE: DOM PERIGNON. Impressive multi-vintage Esprit du Siècle. Links with CLICQUOT, MERCIER, POMMERY, RUINART and since 99 KRUG.

Moillard Burg ★★→★★★★ Big family firm (Domaine Thomas-Moillard) in NUITS-ST-GEORGES, making full range, incl dark and v tasty wines.

Mommessin, J Major BEAUJOLAIS merchant, merged with THORIN, now owned by BOISSET. Owner of CLOS DE TART. White wines less successful than red.

Monbazillac Dordogne w sw ★★→★★★ 76' 85' 89 90' 94 95' 97' 98 99' (00') Golden SAUTERNES-style wine from BERGERAC, now back on top form. Can age well. Wines like fine Sauternes as at Tirecul-la-Gravière. Top producers: L'Ancienne Cure, Ch'x de Belingard-Chayne, Bellevue, La Borderie, Treuil-de-Nailhac, Le Fagé, Haut-Bernasse, Petit Paris, Poulvère, Theulet, Dom de la Haute-Brie et du Caillou, Clos Fontindoule and La Grande Maison stand out among 120 growers. Also Co-op de Monbazillac (Ch'x de Monbazillac & Septy).

Mondeuse Savoie r ★★ DYA Red grape of SAVOIE. Potentially good vigorous deep-coloured wine. The same as NE Italy's Refosco. Don't miss a chance.

Monopole V'yd under single ownership.

Montagne-St-Emilion B'x r ★★ 85 86' 88' **89'** 90' 94 95 96 98 00' North East neighbour and largest "satellite" of ST-EMILION: similar wines and APPELLATION regulations; becoming more important each year. Top ch'x: Calon, Faizeau, Maison Blanche, Montaiguillon, Roudier, Teyssier, DES TOURS, VIEUX-CH-ST-ANDRE.

Montagny Burg w (r) ★★ 96' **97** 99' **00** 01 COTE CHALONNAISE village. Between MACON and MEURSAULT, both geographically and gastronomically. Top producers: Aladame, J-M BOILLOT, Cave de Buxy, LOUIS , Michel, Ch de la Saule.

Montée de Tonnerre Burg w ★★★ **90** 93 95 96' **97 98 99** 00' 01 Famous excellent CHABLIS 1ER CRU. Esp BROCARD, Duplessis, L MICHEL, Raveneau, Robin.

Monthelie Burg r (w) ★★→★★★ **93** 95 96' **97** 98 99' 00 01Little-known VOLNAY neighbour, s'times almost equal. Excellent fragrant reds, esp BOUCHARD PERE, COCHE-DURY, LAFON, DROUHIN, Garaudet, Ch de Monthelie (Suremain).

Montille, Hubert de Burg ★★★ VOLNAY and POMMARD domaine to note.

Montlouis Lo w dr sw (sp) ★★→★★★★ 85' 88' **89 90' 93' 95' 96 97 98 99** 00 01 (sec) Neighbour of VOUVRAY. Similar sweet, or long-lived dry wines; also sparkling. Top growers: Berger, Chidaine, Deletang, Moyer, Taille aux Loups.

Montrachet Burg w ★★★★ 78 79 82 85' 86 88 89' 90 91 92' 93 94 95 96' 97 98 99 00' 00 (Both 't's in the name are silent.) 19-acre GRAND CRU v'yd in both PULIGNY- and CHASSAGNE-M'RACHET. Potentially the greatest white burgundy: strong, perfumed, intense, dry yet luscious. Top wines from LAFON, LAGUICHE (DROUHIN), LEFLAIVE, RAMONET, DOM DE LA ROMANEE-CONTI, THENARD.

Montravel Dordogne ★★ p dr w DYA r oo (01) Now AC for all three colours. Similar to BERGERAC. Good examples from Doms de Krevel, Gouyat, Perreau, ch'x du Fouga, Masburel, Péchaurieux, Pique-Sègue. Separate ACS for semi-sw COTES DE MONTRAVEL and sw HAUT-MONTRAVEL.

Moreau & Fils Burg ★→★★ CHABLIS merchant and grower with 100 acres. Also major table wine producer. Best wine: CLOS DES HOSPICES (GRAND CRU).

Morey, Domaines Burg ★★★ 50 acres in CHASSAGNE-M'RACHET. Vg wines made by family members, esp Bernard, incl BATARD-M'RACHET. Also Pierre M in MEURSAULT.

Morey-St-Denis Burg r ★★★ 85' 88 89' 90' **91 93** 95 96' **97** 98 99' oo 01 Small village with four GRANDS CRUS between GEVREY-CHAMBERTIN and CHAMBOLLE-MUSIGNY. Glorious wine often overlooked. Incl Amiot, DUJAC, Lignier, Moillard-Grivot, Perrot-Minot, PONSOT, ROUMIER ROUSSEAU, Serveau.

Morgon Beauj r ★★★ **95 96 97 98** 99 oo 01 The "firmest" cru of BEAUJOLAIS, needing time to develop its rich savoury flavour. Growers incl Aucoeur, Ch de Bellevue, Desvignes, J Foillard, Lapièrre, Ch de Pizay. DUBOEUF excellent.

Mortet, Denis ★★★ Splendid perfectionist GEVREY domaine. Super wines since 93, incl a range of village Gevreys and excellent 1ER CRU Lavaux St-Jacques.

Moueix, J-P et Cie B'x Legendary proprietor and merchant of ST-EM and POM Ch'x incl LA FLEUR-PETRUS, MAGDELAINE and PETRUS. Also in Calif: see Dominus.

Moulin-à-Vent Beauj r ★★★ **91 93** 95 96' **97** 98 99 oo 01The "biggest" and potentially best wine of BEAUJOLAIS; can be powerful, meaty, and long-lived, eventually can even taste like fine Rhône or burgundy. Many good growers, esp Ch du Moulin-à-Vent, Ch des Jacques, Dom des Hospices, Janodet.

Moulis B'x r ★★→★★★ **90 94 95** 96 98 oo' H-MEDOC village with several Crus Exceptionnels: CHASSE-SPLEEN, MAUCAILLOU, POUJEAUX (THEIL). Gd hunting ground.

Mourvèdre See Grapes for red wine pages 10–12.

Mousseux Sparkling.

Mouton Cadet Popular brand of blended red and white BORDEAUX.

Moutonne ★★★ CHABLIS GRAND CRU honoris causa (between VAUDESIR and Preuses), owned by BICHOT.

Mugneret/Mugneret-Gibourg Burg ★★★ Superb reds from top COTE DE NUITS sites.

Mugnier, J-F Burg ★★★ 10-acre Ch de Chambolle estate with first-class delicate CHAMBOLLE-MUSIGNY Les Amoureuses and MUSIGNY. Also BONNES-MARES.

Mumm, G H & Cie Cordon Rouge NV; Mumm de Cramant NV; Cordon Rouge **90** 95 96; Rosé NV Major CHAMP grower and merchant. NV much improved by new winemaker; v fair vintages. Luxury brands: René Lalou (**85** 90 95), Grand Cordon (90 95). Also in Napa, Calif; Chile, Argentina, S Africa ("Cape Mumm").

Muré, Clos St-Landelin V. fine ALSACE grower and merchant at Rouffach with v'yds in GRAND CRU Vorbourg. Full-bodied wines: ripe (unusual) PINOT N, big RIES and MUSCAT VENDANGES TARDIVES.

Muscadet Lo w ★★→★★★ DYA (but see below) Popular, good-value, often delicious very dry wine from near Nantes at the mouth of the Loire. Should never be sharp but should have a faint iodine tang. Perfect with fish and seafood. Best are from zonal ACS: COTEAUX DE LA LOIRE, M COTES DE GRAND LIEU, SEVRE-ET-MAINE. Choose a SUR LIE.

Muscadet Côtes de Grand Lieu ★→★★★ 88 89 90 93 95 96 97 98 99 oo **01** Recent zonal AC ('95) for MUSCADET around the eponymous lake. Best are SUR LIE, from eg Bâtard, Luc Choblet, Malidain.

Muscadet Coteaux de la Loire Lo w ★→★★★ 88 89 90 93 95 96 97 98 99 oo **01** Small MUSCADET zone E of Nantes, best are SUR LIE, esp Guindon, Luneau-Papin, Les Vignerons de la Noëlle.

Muscadet de Sèvre-et-Maine ★→★★★ 88 89 90 93 95 96 97 98 99 00 01 Wine from central (best) part of area. Top growers incl Guy Bossard (DME DE L'ECU), CHEREAU-CARRE, Bruno Cormerai, Dom de la Haute Fevrie, Douillard, Landron, Luneau-Papin, METAIREAU. 2001 vintage can be perfection.

Muscat Distinctively perfumed grape and its (usually sweet) wine, often fortified as VIN DOUX NATUREL. Made dry and not fortified in ALSACE.

Muscat de Beaumes-de-Venise See Beaumes-de-Venise.

Muscat de Frontignan See Frontignan.

Muscat de Lunel Midi golden sw ★★ NV Ditto. A small area but good, making real recent progress. Look for Dom CLOS Bellevue, Lacoste.

Muscat de Mireval Midi golden sw ★★ NV Ditto, from nr Montpellier.

Muscat de Rivesaltes Midi golden sw ★★ NV Sweet MUSCAT wine from large zone near Perpignan. Especially good from Cazes Frères, CH de Jau.

Musigny Burg r (w) ★★★★ 85' 88' 89' 90' 91 **92 93** 95 96' 97 98 99 00 01 25-acre GRAND CRU in CHAMBOLLE-MUSIGNY. Can be the most beautiful, if not the most powerful, of all red burgundies (and a little white). Best growers: DROUHIN, JADOT, LEROY, MUGNIER, PRIEUR, ROUMIER, DE VOGUE, Vougeraie.

Napoléon Brand name of family-owned Prieur CHAMPAGNE house at Vertus. Excellent Carte d'Or NV and first-rate vintages, esp 95.

Nature Natural or unprocessed – esp of still CHAMP.

Négociant-éleveur Merchant who "brings up" (ie matures) the wine.

Nicolas, Ets Paris-based wholesale and retail wine merchant controlled by Castel Frères. One of the biggest in France and one of the best.

Nuits-St-Georges Burg r ★★→★★★★ 85' 88' 89' 90' 91 93 95 96' 97 98 99' 00 01 Important wine town: wines of all qualities, typically sturdy, tannic, needing time. Name often shortened to "Nuits". Best v'yds incl Les Cailles, CLOS des Corvées, Les Pruliers, Les St-Georges, Vaucrains, etc. Many growers and merchants esp DOM DE L'ARLOT, Ambroise, J Chauvenet, R. Chevillon, CONFURON, FAIVELEY, GOUGES, GRIVOT, Lechéneaut, LEROY, Machard de Gramont, Michelot, RION, THOMAS-MOILLARD.

d'Oc (Vin de Pays d'Oc) Midi r p w ★→★★ Regional VIN DE PAYS for Languedoc and ROUSSILLON. Esp single-grape wines and VINS DE PAYS PRIMEURS. Tremendous technical advances recently. Top producers: VAL D'ORBIEU, SKALLI, Jeanjean and numerous small growers.

Oisly & Thesée, Vignerons de ★★ 89 90 93 95 96 97 98 99 00 01 Go-ahead co-op in E TOURAINE (Loire), with gd SAUV BL (esp Cuvée Excellence), CAB, GAMAY, Cot, and CHARD. Blends labelled Baronnie d'Aignan and gd domaine wines. Value.

Orléanais, Vin de l' Lo r p w ★ DYA Small VDQS for light but fruity wines, based on Pinots Meunier and Noir, CAB and CHARD. Esp CLOS St-Fiacre.

Ostertag Sm ALSACE domaine at Epfig. Uses new oak for gd PINOT N; best RIES, Pinot Gr of GRAND CRU Muenchberg. GEWURZ from lieu-dit Fronholz worth ageing.

Ott, Domaines Top high-quality producer of PROVENCE, incl CH DE SELLE (rosé, red), CLOS Mireille (white), BANDOL CH de Romassan.

Pacherenc du Vic-Bilh SW Fr w dr sw ★★→★★★ The white wine of MADIRAN Dry DYA and sw (age up to 5 yrs for oaked versions). For growers see Madiran.

Paillard, Bruno Brut Première Cuvée NV; Rosé Première Cuvée; CHARD Réserve Privée, Brut **85** 90 95 Superb Nec Plus Ultra Prestige Cuvée (90). Small prestigious young CHAMP house; very high standard. Also owns Château de Sarrin in Provence.

Palette Prov r p w ★★ Near Aix-en-Provence. Full reds, solid rosés, fragrant whites from CH SIMONE.

Pasquier-Desvignes Beauj ★→★★ V old firm of BEAUJ merchants nr BROUILLY.

Patriarche Burg ★→★★ One of the bigger burgundy merchants. Cellars in BEAUNE; also owns CH DE MEURSAULT (150 acres), sparkling KRITER etc.

Patrimonio Corsica r w p ★★→★★★ 95 **96 97 98** 99 00 Wide range from dramatic chalk hills in N CORSICA. Corsica's best. Fragrant reds from Nielluccio, crisp whites. Top growers: Gentile, Leccia, Arena.

Pauillac B'x r ★★★→★★★★★ 66' 70' 75 78' 79 81' 82' 83' 85' 86' 88' 89' 90' 93 94 95' 96' 98 99 00' B'x (HAUT-MEDOC) village with 3 first growths (LAFITE, LATOUR, MOUTON) and many other fine CHT'X, famous for high flavour; varied in style.

Pécharmant Dordogne r ★★ 90' 95' 98 99 Inner AC for top BERGERAC r, for ageing. Best: La Métairie, Doms du Haut-Pécharmant, des Costes des Bertranoux; CHX Champarel, Terre Vieille, Les Grangettes, and de Tiregand. Also (from Bergerac co-op) Doms Brisseau-Belloc, du Vieux Sapin, Ch le Charmeil. To watch.

Pelure d'oignon "Onion skin" – tawny tint of certain rosés.

Perlant or Perlé Very slightly sparkling.

Pernand-Vergelesses Burg r (w) ★★★ 90 **93 95 96' 97** 98 99' 00 01 Village next to ALOXE-CORTON containing part of the great CORTON and C-CHARLEMAGNE v'yds and one other top v'yd: Ile des Vergelesses. Growers incl CHANDON DE BRIAILLES, CHANSON, Delarche, Dubreuil-Fontaine, JADOT, LATOUR, Rapet.

Perrier-Jouët Brut NV; Blason de France NV; Blason de France Rosé NV; BRUT 82 85 88 90 95 96 Excellent CHAMP grower at Epernay, the first to make dry Champagne and once the smartest name of all; now best for vintage wines. Luxury brands: Belle Epoque (85 88 90 95) in a painted bottle. Also Belle Epoque Rosé (85 88 90 95).

Pessac-Léognan B'x r w ★★★→★★★★ 90' 95 96 98 99 00' AC for the best part of N GRAVES, incl the area of most of the GRANDS CRUS, HAUT-BRION, PAPE CLÉMENT etc.

Pétillant Normally means slightly sparkling; but half-sparkling speciality in TOURAINE esp VOUVRAY and MONTLOUIS.

Petit Chablis Burg w ★ DYA Wine from fourth-rank CHABLIS v'yds. Not much character but can be pleasantly fresh. Best: co-op La Chablisienne.

Pfaffenheim Top ALSACE co-op with 580 acres. Strongly individual wines incl good Sylvaner and vg PINOTS (N, Gr, Bl). GRANDS CRUS: Goldert, Steinert and Hatschbourg. Hartenberger CREMANT d'Alsace is vg. Also owns DOPFF & IRION.

Pfersigberg Eguisheim (ALSACE) GRAND CRU with two parcels; v aromatic wines. GEWURZ does v well. RIES esp Paul Ginglinger, BRUNO SORG and LEON BEYER Comtes d'Eguisheim. Top grower: KUENTZ-BAS.

Philipponnat NV; Rosé NV; Réserve Spéciale 88 90 95; Grand Blanc Vintage 76 81 82 88 89 90 95; CLOS des Goisses 76 78 79 82 85 88 89 90 95 Small family-run CHAMP house producing well-structured wines, esp remarkable single-v'yd CLOS des Goisses and charming rosé. Also Le Reflet BRUT NV.

Piat Père & Fils ★ Big-scale merchant of BEAUJ and MACON, controlled by Diageo.

Pic St-Loup Midi ★→★★ r (p) Notable COTEAUX DU LAN'DOC commune. Top growers: Ch'x de Cazeneuve, de Lancyre, Lascaux, Mas Bruguière, Dom de l'Hortus.

Picpoul de Pinet Midi w ★→★★ Improving AC exclusively for the old variety Picpoul. Best growers: Dom Gaujal, Co-op Pomérols, Félines-Jourdan.

Pineau des Charentes Strong sweet aperitif: white grape juice and COGNAC.

Pinot See Grapes for white and red wine (pages 10–16).

Piper-Heidsieck BRUT NV; Brut Rosé NV; Brut 90 95 CHAMP-makers of old repute at Reims. Rare (85 90 95) and Brut Sauvage (90 95 96) are best, but non-vintage CUVEES much improved. See also Piper Sonoma, California.

Plageoles, Robert The arch-priest of GAILLAC and defender of the lost grape varieties of the Tarn. Amazingly eccentric wines include a *vin jaune* which is left to oxidize like sherry, and an ultra sweet dessert wine from Ondenc grapes left to dry in the sun. Other oddities include a 100% Muscadelle.

Pol Roger BRUT White Foil NV; Brut 82 85 88 90 93 95 96; Rosé 82 85 88 90; Blanc de CHARD 88 90 93 95 96 Top-ranking family-owned CHAMP house at Epernay, much loved in Britain. Esp gd silky NV White Foil, Rosé, Réserve PR

(88) and CHARD. Sumptuous CUVEE: Sir Winston Churchill (82 85 **88 90** 93 95 96). New chef de CAVES Dominique Petit, ex KRUG.

Pomerol B'x r ★★★→★★★★ 70 75' **81'** 82' 83 85 86 88 **89'** 90' 94 95 96 98' 00' Next village to ST-EM: similar but more plummy, creamy wines, often maturing sooner, reliable, delicious. Top ch'x incl: CERTAN-DE-MAY, L'EVANGILE, LA FLEUR, LA FLEUR-PETRUS, LATOUR-A-POMEROL, PETRUS, LE PIN, TROTANOY, VIEUX CH CERTAN etc.

Pommard Burg r ★★★ 85' **88'** 89' 90 91 **93** 95 96' 97 98 99' 00 01 The biggest COTE D'OR village. Few superlative wines, but many potent and often tannic ones to age 10 yrs[+]. Best v'yds: Epenots, HOSPICES DE BEAUNE CUVEES, Rugiens. Growers incl COMTE ARMAND, Billard-Gonnet, J-M BOILLOT, DE COURCEL, Gaunoux, LEROY, Machard de Gramont, DE MONTILLE, Ch de Pommard, Pothier-Rieusset.

Pommery Brut NV; Rosé NV; Brut **82 85 87** 90' **91** 95 96 V big CHAMP house at Reims, much improved. Sold to VRANKEN 02. Wines much improved. Outstanding luxury CUVEE Louise (82 85 90). Cuvée Louise Rosé (85 **87 88** 99). Also Flacons d'Exception, late-disgorged vintages in MAGNUM (79).

Ponsot, J M ★★★★ 25-acre MOREY-ST-DENIS estate. Many high-quality GRANDS CRUS, incl CHAMBERTIN, CHAPELLE-C, CLOS DE LA ROCHE, CLOS ST-DENIS.

Potel, Nicolas Burg ★★→★★★★ M. Potel founded a small négociant after his father's DOM DE LA POUSSE D'OR was sold. Impressive reds, especially BOURGOGNE ROUGE, VOLNAY, NUITS-ST-GEORGES.

Pouilly-Fuissé Burg w ★★→★★★ 90 **92'** 95 96 97 98 99 00 01 The best white of the MACON region, potent and dense. At its best (eg Ch Fuissé VIEILLES VIGNES) outstanding, but usually over-priced compared with (eg) CHABLIS. Top growers: Ferret, Forest, VERGET, Luquet, Merlin, Noblet, Valette, Vincent.

Pouilly-Fumé Lo w ★★→★★★★★ 90' 91' 92' 93' 94 95' 96 97 98 99 **00 01** "Gunflinty", fruity, often sharp white from upper Loire, nr SANCERRE. Grapes must be SAUV BL. Best CUVEES can improve 5–6 yrs. Top growers incl Cailbourin, Chatelain, DAGUENEAU, Ch de Favray, Edmond and André Figeat, LADOUCETTE, Masson-Blondelet, Ch de Tracy, Tinel Blondelet, CAVE de Pouilly-sur-Loire.

Pouilly-Loché Burg w ★★ **96 97** 99 00' 01 POUILLY-FUISSE's neighbour. Similar, cheaper; scarce. Can be sold as POUILLY-VINZELLES.

Pouilly-sur-Loire Lo w ★ DYA Neutral wine from the same v'yds as POUILLY-FUME but different grapes (Chasselas). Rarely seen today.

Pouilly-Vinzelles Burg w ★★ **95 96 97** 98 99 **00'** 01 Neighbour of POUILLY-FUISSE. Similar wine, worth looking for. Value. Best: Soufrandière.

Pousse d'Or, Domaine de la Burg ★★★ 32-acre estate in POMMARD, SANTENAY and esp VOLNAY, where its MONOPOLES Bousse d'Or and CLOS des 60 Ouvrées are powerful, tannic, and were justly famous under Gérard Potel (manager 1964-96).. Unproven under new ownership.

Premier Cru First growth in B'x; second rank of v'yds (after GRAND CRU) in Burgundy.

Premières Côtes de Blaye B'x r w ★→★★ 88' 89' 90' **93 94** 95 **96** 98 00' Restricted AC for better BLAYE wines; greater emphasis on r. Ch'x incl, Bel Air la Royère, Bertinerie, Côtes de Bourg Charron, Haut-Sociando, Jonqueyres, Loumède, Segonzac, des Toutes, La Tonnelle.

Premières Côtes de Bordeaux B'x r w (p) dr sw ★→★★ **94 95 96** 98 00' Large hilly area east of GRAVES across the River Garonne: gd bet for quality and value, upgrading sharply. Largely Merlot. Ch'x incl Carignan, Carsin, Chelivette, Fayau, Grand-Mouëys, du Juge, Lamothe de Haux, Plaisance, Puy Bardens, REYNON, Suau, Tanesse. To watch, esp in gd vintages.

Prieur, Domaine Jacques Burg ★★★ Splendid 40-acre estate all in top Burgundy sites, incl PREMIER CRU MEURSAULT, VOLNAY, PULIGNY- and even LE M'RACHET. Now 50% owned by RODET. Quality could still improve.

Primeur "Early" wine for refreshment and uplift; esp from BEAUJOLAIS; VINS DE PAYS too. Wine sold "En Primeur" is still in barrel for delivery when bottled.

Prissé See Mâcon-Villages.

Propriétaire-récoltant Owner-manager.

Provence See Côtes de Provence.

Puisseguin St-Emilion B'x r ★★ 88' 89' 90' **94 95 96** 98 00' "Satellite" neighbour of ST-EMILION; wines similar – not so fine or weighty but often value. Ch'x incl Bel Air, Durand-Laplagne, Fongaban, LAURETS, Soleil, Vieux-Ch-Guibeau. Also Roc de Puisseguin from co-operative.

Puligny-Montrachet Burg w (r) ★★★★ 89' **90' 92 95 96' 97 99** 00 01 Smaller neighbour of CHASSAGNE-M: potentially even finer, more vital and complex rich, dry wine. (But apparent finesse can be result of over-production.) Best v'yds: BATARD-M, Bienvenues-Bâtard-M, Caillerets, CHEVALIER-M, Clavoillon, Les Combettes, M'RACHET, Pucelles etc. Top growers incl AMPEAU, J-M BOILLOT, BOUCHARD PERE, L CARILLON, CHARTRON, Chavy, DROUHIN, JADOT, LATOUR, DOM LEFLAIVE, O LEFLAIVE, Pernot, SAUZET.

Pyrénées-Atlantiques SW France DYA VDP for wines not qualifying for local ACS MADIRAN, PACHERENC DU VIC BILH or JURANCON.

Quarts de Chaume Lo w sw ★★★→★★★★ 75 76 78' 79' 82 **85' 86 88'** 89' **90' 91 92 93' 94** 95 96 **97** 98 99 00 01 Famous COTEAUX DU LAYON plot. CHENIN grapes grown for immensely long-lived intense rich golden wine. Esp from BAUMARD, Bellerive, Claude Papin (CH DE PIERRE-BISE), Suronde.

Quatourze Midi r w (p) ★ **95** 96 **97** 98 99 00 Minor cru of COTEAUX DE LANGUEDOC. Best wines from Dom Notre Dame du Quatourze.

Quincy Lo w ★→★★ DYA Sml area: v dry SANCERRE-style SAUV BL. Worth trying. Growers: Domaine Mardon, Sorbe, Domaine de Silice (whose wines can age).

Ramonet, Domaine Burg ★★★ Leading (indeed legendary) estate in CHASSAGNE-M'RACHET with 42 acres, incl some M'RACHET. Vg whites, & red CLOS ST-JEAN.

Rancio The delicious nutty tang of brown wood-aged fortified wine eg VDN, esp BANYULS. Indicates exposure to oxygen and/or heat: a fault in table wine.

Rangen V high-class ALSACE GRAND CRU in Thann and Vieux Thann. Owes much of its reputation to ZIND-HUMBRECHT. Esp for PINOT Gr, GEWURZ, RIES.

Rasteau S Rh r br sw (p w dr) ★★ 89 90' **94** 95' **96 98'** 99' 00' Village for sound, robust reds, especially Beaurenard, CAVE des Vignerons, CH du Trignon, Doms Didier Charavin, Rabasse-Charavin, Girasols, Gourt de Mautens, St-Gayan, Soumade. Strong sweet GRENACHE dessert wine is (declining) speciality.

Ratafia de Champagne Sweet aperitif made in CHAMP of 67% grape juice and 33% brandy. Not unlike PINEAU DES CHARENTES.

Récolte Crop or vintage.

Regnié Beauj r ★★ **98 99 00** 01 Village between MORGON and BROUILLY, promoted to cru in '88. About 1,800 acres. Try DUBOEUF, Aucoeur, or Rampon.

Reine Pédauque, La Burg ★ Long-est'd grower-merchant at ALOXE-CORTON. V'yds in ALOXE-CORTON, SAVIGNY, etc, and COTES DU RHONE. Owned by PIERRE ANDRE.

Remoissenet Père & Fils Burg ★★ Fine merchant (esp for whites and THENARD wines) with a tiny BEAUNE estate (5 acres). Give red time. Also broker for NICOLAS.

Rémy Pannier Important Loire wine merchant at SAUMUR.

Reuilly Lo w (r p) ★★ N'bour of QUINCY. Similar whites; rising reputation. Also rosés (PINOTS N, Gr), reds (PN). Esp Claude Lafond, Beurdin, Sorbe, Vincent.

Ribonnet, Domaine de SW France ★★ Christian Gerber makes pioneering range of varietals (r p w) without benefit of APPELLATION; S of Toulouse.

Riceys, Rosé des Champ p ★★★ DYA Minute AC in AUBE for a notable PINOT N rosé. Principal producers: A Bonnet, Jacques Defrance.

Richeaume, Domaine Côte de Prov r ★★ Notable Cab/Syrah; organic; a model.

Richebourg Burg r ★★★★ 78' 85' **88' 89' 90' 91 92 93'** 95 96' 97 98 99' 00 01 19-acre VOSNE-ROMANEE GRAND CRU. Powerful, perfumed, fabulously expensive wine, among Burg's best. Top growers: GRIVOT, J GROS, A GROS, LEROY, MEO-CAMUZET, DRC.

Richou, Dom Lo ★→★★★★ 88 **89** 90 **95 96** 97 **98 99** 00 01 Long-est'd, quality ANJOU estate for wide range of wines, esp ANJOU-VILLAGES VIEILLES VIGNES, COTEAUX DE L'AUBANCE Les Trois Demoiselles.

Riesling See Grapes for white wine (pages 12–16).

Rion, Daniel et Fils Burg ★★★ 48-acre domaine in Prémeaux (NUITS). Excellent VOSNE-ROMANEE (Les Chaumes, Les Beaumonts), Nuits PREMIER CRU Les Vignes Rondes and CHAMBOLLE-MUSIGNY-Les Charmes. Former winemaker Patrice Rion now has his own domaine and négociant label.

Rivesaltes Midi r w br dr sw ★★ NV Fortified wine of east Pyrenees. A tradition v much alive, if struggling these days. Top producers: Doms Cazes, Sarda-Malet, Vaquer, des Schistes, CH de Jau. See Muscat de Rivesaltes.

Roche-aux-Moines, La Lo w sw ★★★ 76' 78 79 82 **83** 85 86 88' 89' 90' **93' 94** 95' 96 **97** 98 99 00 01 Sixty-acre v'yd in SAVENNIERES, ANJOU. Intense strong fruity/sharp wine, needs long ageing or drinking fresh.

Rodet, Antonin Burg ★★→★★★ Substantial quality merchant with large (332-acre) estate, esp in MERCUREY (Ch de Chamirey). See also Prieur.

Roederer, Louis Brut Premier NV; Rich NV; BRUT **75 76 79 83 85** 90 93 95 96 97; BLANC DE BLANCS 91 93 95 96; Brut Rosé 88 91 95 96 Top-drawer family-owned CHAMP-grower and merchant at Reims. Vanilla-rich NV with plenty of flavour. Sumptuous Cristal may be greatest of all prestige CUVEES (79 82 83 85 **88 89** 90 94 95 96) and Cristal Rosé (82 88 90 95 96). Also owns Champ house DEUTZ and CH DE PEZ in B'DX. See also Roederer Estate, California.

Rolly Gassmann Distinguished ALSACE grower at Rorschwihr, esp for Auxerrois and MUSCAT from lieu-dit Moenchreben. House style is usually off-dry.

Romanée, La Burg r ★★★★ 78' 85' 88' 89' **90' 91** 93 95 96' 97 98 99' 00 01 2-acre GRAND CRU in VOSNE-ROMANEE, just uphill from ROMANEE-CONTI. MONOPOLE of Liger-Belair, sold by BOUCHARD PERE.

Romanée-Conti Burg r ★★★★ 66' 76 78' 80' 82 83 85' **88' 89' 90' 91** 93' 95 96' 97 98 99' 00 01 4.3-acre MONOPOLE GRAND CRU in VOSNE-ROMANEE; 450 cases per annum. The most celebrated and expensive red wine in the world, with reserves of flavour beyond imagination. See next entry.

> **Rhône for 2002 – Vacqueyras**
>
> It is time to take seriously the young AC of Vacqueyras. More confident growers are using fruit from mature vineyards. Moving away from the shadow of Gigondas, Vacqueyras wines have a refined, peppered aspect, taken as they are off the stony garrigue plateau. Their young fruit is more red-berried and overt than the darker style of Gigondas.
>
> Power and elegance comes through in the best domaines. These reds can live for 12 -15 years.
>
> Look for 1998 and 1999 vintages from: Serge Ferigoule's Le Sang des Cailloux ("blood of the stones", what imagery!), Le Grapillon d'Or, Charbonnière.

Romanée-Conti, Domaine de la (DRC) Burg ★★★★ The grandest estate in Burgundy. Incl the whole of ROMANEE-C and LA TACHE and major parts of ECHEZEAUX, GRANDS ECH'X, RICHEBOURG and ROMANEE-ST-VIVANT. Also tiny part of M'RACHET. Crown-jewel prices (if you can buy them at all). Keep top DRC vintages for decades.

Romanée-St-Vivant Burg r ★★★★ 85' 88' 89' 90' **91 92 93'** 95 96' 97 98 99' 00 01 23-acre GRAND CRU in VOSNE-ROMANEE. Similar to ROMANEE-CONTI but lighter and less sumptuous. Top growers: DRC, DROUHIN, HUDELOT-NÖELLAT, LEROY.

Rosé d'Anjou Lo p ★ DYA Pale slightly sw rosé. CAB D'ANJOU should be better.

Rosé de Loire Lo p ★→★★ DYA Wide-ranging AC for dr Loire rosé (ANJOU is sw).

Rosette Dordogne w s/sw ★★ DYA Pocket-sized AC for charming aperitif wines, eg CLOS Romain, CH Puypezat-Rosette and Dom de la Cardinolle.

Rostaing, René Rh Growing COTE-ROTIE estate with prime plots, notably La Blonde (soft, elegant wines) & fuller, firmer La Viaillère and La Landonne (15–20 years). Style is normally polished, accomplished, some new oak. CONDRIEU also.

Roty, Joseph Burg ★★★ Small grower of classic GEVREY-CHAMBERTIN, esp CHARMES- and MAZIS-CHAMBERTIN. Long-lived wines.

Rouget, Emmanuel Burg ★★★★ Inheritor of the legendary estate of Henri Jayer in ECHEZEAUX, NUITS-ST-G, and VOSNE-ROMANEE. Top wine: Vosne-R-Cros Parantoux.

Roulot, Domaine G Burg ★★★ Excellent range of 7 (2 1ER CRU) distinctive MEURSAULTS.

Roumier, Georges Burg ★★★★ Christophe R makes exceptional long-lived wines in BONNES-MARES, CHAMBOLLE-MUSIGNY-Amoureuses, MUSIGNY etc. V high standards.

Rousseau, Domaine A Burg ★★★★ Major grower famous for CHAMBERTIN etc, of v highest quality. Wines are intense, long-lived and mostly GRAND CRU.

Roussette de Savoie w ★★ DYA The tastiest fresh white from S of Lake Geneva.

Roussillon Midi Top region for VINS DOUX NATURELS (eg MAURY, RIVESALTES, BANYULS). Lighter MUSCATS are taking over from darker heavier wines. See Côtes du Roussillon for table wines.

Ruchottes-Chambertin Burg r ★★★★ 85' 88' 89' 90' 91 92 93' 95 96' 97 98 99' 00 01 7.5-acre GRAND CRU neighbour of CHAMBERTIN. Similar splendid lasting wine of great finesse. Top growers: LEROY, MUGNERET, ROUMIER, ROUSSEAU.

Ruinart Père & Fils "R" de Ruinart BRUT NV; "R" de Ruinart Rosé NV; "R" de Ruinart Brut 88 90 95 96 Oldest CHAMP house, owned by MOET-Hennessy, with elegant yet vinous wines. Top luxury brands: Dom Ruinart BLANC DE BLANCS (85 88 90 95 96), Dom Ruinart Rosé (88 90 95 96). Also new mineral-fresh Bl de Bls NV.

Rully Burg r w (sp) ★★ (r) 98 99 01 (w) 99 00 01 COTE CHALONNAISE village. Still white and red are light but tasty, good value, esp whites. Growers incl DELORME, FAIVELEY, Dom de la Folie, Jacquesson, A RODET.

Sables du Golfe du Lion Midi p r w ★ DYA VIN DE PAYS from Mediterranean sand-dunes: esp Gris de Gris from Carignan, GRENACHE, Cinsault. Dominated by LISTEL.

Sablet S Rh r w (p) ★★ 90' 94 95' 96 98' 99' 00 Admirable, improving COTES DU RHONE village, esp Dom de Boisson, Les Goubert, Piaugier, CH du Trignon, Dom de Verquière. Nicely full whites to try, too.

St-Amour Beauj r ★★ 98 99 00 01 Northernmost CRU of BEAUJOLAIS: light, fruity, irresistible (esp. on Feb 14th?). Growers to try: Janin, Patissier, Revillon.

St-Aubin Burg w r ★★★ (w) 96' 97 99 00 01 (r) 95 96' 97 98 99' 01 Understated n'bour of CHASSAGNE-M, up a side-valley. Several PREMIERS CRUS: light firm quite stylish wines; fair prices. Also sold as COTE DE BEAUNE-VILLAGES. Top growers incl JADOT, J Lamy, Lamy-Pillot, H Prudhon, RAMONET, Roux, Thomas.

St-Bris Burg w (r) ★ DYA Village west of CHABLIS known for fruity ALIGOTE, but chiefly for SAUVIGNON DE ST-BRIS. Also good CREMANT. Goisot is best grower.

St-Chinian Midi r ★→★★ 95 96 97 98 99 00 Hilly area of growing reputation in COTEAUX DU LANGUEDOC. AC since 82. Tasty southern reds, esp at Berlou and Roquebrun, and from CHX de Viranel, Coujan.

St-Emilion B'x r ★★→★★★★ 70' 75 79' 81 82' 83' 85' 86' 88 89' 90' 94 95 96 98 99 00' The biggest top-quality BORDEAUX district (13,300 acres); solid rich tasty wines from hundreds of CHX, incl AUSONE, CANON, CHEVAL BLANC, FIGEAC, MAGDELAINE, etc. Also a gd co-op.

St-Estèphe B'x r ★★→★★★★ 78' 81 82' 83' 85' 86 88' 89' 90' 94 95' 96 98 99 00' N village of HAUT-MEDOC. Solid, structured, sometimes superlative wines. Top CHX: COS D'ESTOURNEL, MONTROSE, CALON-SEGUR, etc, and more notable CRUS BOURGEOIS than any other HAUT-MEDOC commune.

St-Gall BRUT NV; Extra Brut NV; Brut BLANC DE BLANCS NV; Brut Rosé NV; Brut Blanc de Blancs 90 95 96; CUVEE Orpale Blanc de Blancs 88 90 95 96 Brand name used by Union-Champagne: top CHAMP growers' co-op at AVIZE. Cuvée Orpale exceptionally gd value.

St-Georges-St-Emilion B'x r ★★ **82 83' 85'** 86' 88' 89' 90' **94 95 96** 98 99 00' Part of MONTAGNE-ST-EM with high standards. Best ch'x: Belair-Montaiguillon, Maquin-St-G, ST-GEORGES, Tour du Pas-St-G.

St-Gervais S Rh r (w) ★ West bank S Rhône village. Sound co-op, excellent Dom Ste-Anne reds (marked MOURVEDRE flavours); whites incl a Viognier.

St-Jean de Minervois Min w sw ★★ Perhaps top French MUSCAT: sw and fine. Much recent progress esp Dom de Barroubio, Michel Sigé, co-op.

St-Joseph N Rh r w ★★ **88' 89 90' 91 94'** 95' 96 97' 98' 99' 00' 01 AC stretching whole length of N Rhône (40 miles). Delicious, fruit-packed wines at its core, around Tournon; elsewhere quality variable. Often better, more structure than CROZES-HERMITAGE, esp from CHAPOUTIER (Les Granits) B Gripa, Guigal's Grippat; also CHAVE, Chèze, Coursodon, Faury, Gaillard, Gonon, JABOULET, Marsanne, Paret, Perret (esp Grisières), Trollat. Gd aromatic whites, too (mainly Marsanne grape).

St-Julien B'x r ★★★→★★★★ **70' 75** 78' 81' 82' **83'** 85' 86' **88' 89' 90'** 93 **94** 95' 96 97 98 99 00' Mid-MEDOC village with a dozen of BORDEAUX's best ch'x, incl three LEOVILLES, BEYCHEVELLE, DUCRU-BEAUCAILLOU, GRUAUD-LAROSE, etc. The epitome of harmonious, fragrant and savoury red wine.

St-Nicolas-de-Bourgueil Lo r p ★★→★★★ 85' 86 88 **89'** 90' **95'** 96 97 98 00 01 The next village to BOURGUEIL: the same lively and fruity CAB F red. Top growers: Amirault, Cognard, Mabileau, Taluau.

St-Péray N Rh w sp ★★ 99' 00 01' W Rhône (mainly Marsanne grape), some of it sp. Curiosity worth trying. Top names: S Chaboud, B Gripa, Lionnet, J-L Thiers, TAIN co-op. Jaboulet planting here. Also a négoce wine.

St-Pourçain-sur-Sioule Central France r p w ★→★★ DYA Niche wine of the centre of France. Light red and rosé from GAMAY and/or PINOT NOIR, white from Tressalier and/or CHARDONNAY (increasingly popular) or SAUVIGNON BLANC. Recent vintages improved. Growers include: Ray, Dom de Bellevue, Pétillat, and good co-operative.

St-Romain Burg w r ★★ (w) 96' 97 **98 99 00** 01 Overlooked village just behind COTE DE BEAUNE. Value, esp for firm fresh whites. Reds have a clean "cut". Top growers: De Chassorney, FEVRE, Jean Germain, Gras, LATOUR, LEROY.

St-Véran Burg w ★★ **99 00'** 01 Next door AC to POUILLY-FUISSE. Best nearly as good; others on unsuitable soil. Try DUBOEUF, Doms Corsin, des Deux Roches, des Valanges, Demessey, CH FUISSE.

Ste-Croix-du-Mont B'x w sw ★★ **83** 86' 88' 89 90 **95'** 96 97 98 99 Neighbour to SAUTERNES with similar golden wine. No superlatives but well worth trying, esp CH Loubens, Ch Lousteau Vieil, Ch du Mont. Often a bargain, esp with age.

Salon 71 73 76 82 83 85 88 90 The original BLANC DE BLANCS CHAMP, from Le Mesnil in the Côte des Blancs. Intense v dry wine with long keeping qualities. Tiny quantities. Bought in '88 by LAURENT-PERRIER.

Sancerre Lo w (r p) ★★→★★★ 89 90' 93' 95' **96 97 98 99 00 01** The world's model for fragrant SAUV BL, almost indistinguishable from POUILLY-FUME, its neighbour across River Loire. Top wines can age 5 yrs[+]. Also generally light PINOT N red (best drunk at 2–3 yrs) and rosé (do not over-chill). Occasional vg VENDANGES TARDIVES. Top growers incl BOURGEOIS, Cotat Frères, Lucien Crochet, André Dezat, Jolivet, MELLOT, Vincent Pinard, Roger, Vacheron.

Santenay Burg r (w) ★★★ **88' 89'** 90 93 95 96' 97 98 **99'** 01 Sturdy reds from village S of CHASSAGNE. Best v'yds: La Comme, Les Gravières, CLOS de Tavannes. Top growers: Girardin, Lequin-Roussot, Muzard POUSSE D'OR.

Saumur Lo r w p sp ★→★★★ 89 90 93 **95 97 98 00 01** Fresh fruity whites plus a few more serious, vg CREMANT and Saumur MOUSSEUX (producers incl BOUVET-LADUBAY, CAVE des Vignerons de Saumur, GRATIEN ET MEYER, LANGLOIS-CHATEAU), pale rosés and increasingly good CAB F (see next entry).

Saumur-Champigny Lo r ★★→★★★ **82** 85 86' 88 **89'** 90' 93' 95' 96 97 98 00 01 Flourishing 9-commune AC for fresh CAB F ageing remarkably in sunny years. Look for CH DU HUREAU, CH DE VILLENEUVE, domaines FILLIATREAU, Legrand, Nerleux, Roches Neuves, Val Brun, CLOS ROUGEARD, co-op St-Cyr.

Saussignac Dordogne w sw ★★→★★★ 95' 96 97' 98 99 (00) MONBAZILLAC-style age-worthy wines. Producers of new ultra-sw style incl Dom de Richard, CHX les Miaudoux, Tourmentine, le Payral, le Chabrier and Clos d'Yvigne.

Sauternes B'x w sw ★★→★★★★ 67' 71' 75 76' **78** 79' **80** 81 **82** 83' 85 86' **88'** 89' 90' 95' 96 97 98 99 01' District of 5 villages (incl BARSAC) which make France's best sw wine, strong (14%+ alcohol), luscious and golden, demanding to be aged 10 yrs. Top CHX are D'YQUEM, CLIMENS, COUTET, GIRAUD, SUDUIRAUT, etc. Dry wines cannot be sold as Sauternes.

Sauvignon Blanc See Grapes for white wine (pages 12–16).

Sauvignon de St-Bris Burg w ★★ DYA A new AC, cousin of SANCERRE, from nr CHABLIS. To try. "Dom Saint Prix" from Dom Bersan is good. Goisot best.

Sauzet, Etienne Burg ★★★ Top-quality white burgundy estate at PULIGNY-M'RACHET. Clearly-defined, well-bred wines, at best superb.

Savennières Lo w dr sw ★★★→★★★★ 75 76' 78' 82 83 **85** 86' 88 **89'** 90' 93 95' **96** 97 98 99 00 01 Small ANJOU district of pungent long-lived whites, incl Baumard, CH de Chamboureau, Ch de Coulaine, Closel, Ch d'Epiré. Top sites: COULEE DE SERRANT, ROCHE-AUX-MOINES, CLOS du Papillon.

Savigny-lès-Beaune Burg r (w) ★★★ **89'** 90' 93 95 **96'** 97 98 99' 00 01 Important village next to BEAUNE; similar balanced mid-weight wines, often deliciously lively, fruity. Top v'yds: Dominode, Les Guettes, Lavières, Marconnets, Vergelesses; growers: BIZE, Camus, CHANDON DE BRIAILLES, CLAIR, Ecard, Girard, LEROY, Pavelot, TOLLOT-BEAUT.

Savoie E France r w sp ★★ DYA Alpine area with light dry wines like some Swiss or minor Loires. APREMONT, CREPY and SEYSSEL are best-known whites, ROUSSETTE is more interesting. Also good MONDEUSE reds.

Schaller, Edgard ALSACE grower (dry-style wines) in Mandelburg GRAND CRU, Mittelwihr; esp for RIES "Mandelberg VIELLES VIGNES" (needs time) and "Les Amandiers" (younger-drinking).

Schlossberg V successful ALSACE GRAND CRU for RIES in two parts: Kientzheim and small section at Kaysersberg. Top growers: FALLER/DOM WEINBACH & PAUL BLANCK.

Schlumberger, Domaines ALSACE growers at Guebwiller and lgst v'yd owners in region. Unusually rich wines incl luscious GEWURZ GRAND CRUS Kessler and Kitterlé (also SGN and VT). Fine RIES from GRAND CRUS Kitterlé, Saering. Also gd PINOT GR.

Schlumberger, Robert de Lo SAUMUR sparkling wine made by Austrian method: fruity and delicate.

Schoffit, Domaine Colmar ALSACE house with GRAND CRU RANGEN PINOT Gr, GEWURZ of top-quality. Chasselas is unusual everyday delight.

Schröder & Schÿler Old BORDEAUX merchant, co-owner of CH KIRWAN.

Schoenenbourg V rich successful Riquewihr GRAND CRU (ALSACE): RIES, Tokay-PINOT Gr, v fine VT and SGN. Esp from MARCEL DEISS and DOPFF AU MOULIN. Also vg MUSCAT.

Sciacarello Original grape of CORSICA for red and rosé, eg AJACCIO, Sartène.

Sec Literally means dry, though CHAMP so-called is medium-sweet (and better at breakfast, tea-time, and weddings than BRUT).

Séguret S Rh r w ★ Good S Rhône village nr GIGONDAS. Peppery, quite full red; rounded clean white. Esp CH La Courançonne, Dom de Cabasse, Mourchon.

Sélection des Grains Nobles (SGN) Term coined by HUGEL for ALSACE equivalent to German Beerenauslese. Grains nobles are individual grapes with "noble rot".

Serafin Burg ★★★ Christian S has gained a cult following for his intense GEVREY CHAMBERTIN VIEILLES VIGNES and CHARMES CHAMBERTIN GRAND CRU.

Sèvre-et-Maine The delimited zone containing the best v'yds of MUSCADET.

Seyssel Savoie w sp ★★ NV Delicate pale dry Alpine white, v pleasant sp.

Sichel & Co One of B'x most respected merchant houses. Peter A Sichel died in '98; his five sons continue with the family's interests in CHX D'ANGLUDET and PALMER, in CORBIERES, and as B'x merchants.

Silvaner See Grapes for white wine (pages 12–16).

Sipp, Jean and Louis ALSACE growers in Ribeauvillé (Louis is also a NEGOCIANT). Both produce vg RIES GRAND CRU Kirchberg. Jean's: youthful elegance (smaller v'yd, own vines only); Louis': firmer when mature. Louis also makes vg GEWURZ, esp Grand Cru Osterberg.

Sirius Serious oak-aged blended BORDEAUX from Maison SICHEL.

Skalli Revolutionary producer of VINS DE PAYS D'OC from CAB S, Merlot, CHARD etc, at Sète in the LANGUEDOC, inspired by Mondavi. FORTANT DE FRANCE is standard brand. Style and value. Watch this name.

Sorg, Bruno First-class small ALSACE grower at Eguisheim for GRAND CRUS Florimont (RIES) and PFERSIGBERG (MUSCAT). Also v good Auxerrois.

Sparr, Pierre Important old-established ALSACE grower, at Sigolsheim famed for rich GRAND CRUS but slightly less impressive lately.

Sur Lie See Lie and Muscadet.

Syrah See Grapes for red wine (pages 10–12).

Tâche, La Burg r ★★★★ 78' 80' 85' 88' 89' 90' 93' 95 96' 97 98 99' 00 **01** 15-acre (1,500-case) GRAND CRU of VOSNE-ROMANEE and one of best v'yds on earth: big perfumed luxurious wine. See DOMAINE DE LA ROMANEE-CONTI.

Tain, Cave Co-opérative de, 425-members in N Rhône ACS; owns ¼ HERMITAGE. Making increasingly gd red Hermitage since 91 & sound Crozes. Good value.

Taittinger BRUT NV; Rosé NV; Brut **82 85** 88 **89** 90 95 96; Collection Brut **78 81 82 83 85 86 88** 90 Fashionable (and excellent) Reims CHAMP grower and merchant; wines have distinctive silky flowery touch. Luxury brand: Comtes de Champagne BLANC DE BLANCS (**79 81** 82 85 88 90 **91 94** 95 96), also vg rich Pinot Prestige Rosé NV. See also Domaine Carneros, California.

Tastevin, Confrèrie des Chevaliers du Burgundy's cheerful and colourful promotion society. Wine with the Tastevinage label has been approved by it and is usually of a fair standard. A "tastevin" is the traditional shallow silver wine-tasting cup of Burgundy.

Tavel Rh p ★★★ DYA France's most famous, though not her best, rosé: strong, very full, & dry. Best growers: CH d'Aquéria, Dom Corne-Loup, GUIGAL, Maby, Dom de la Mordorée, Prieuré de Montézargues, Lafond, Ch de Trinquevedel.

Tempier, Domaine ★★★★ The top grower of BANDOL: noble reds & also rosé.

Terroirs Landais Gascony r p w ★ VDP an extension in the département of Landes of the COTES DE GASCOGNE. Domaine de Laballe is most seen example.

Thénard, Domaine Burg The major grower of the GIVRY appellation, but best known for his substantial portion (4⁺ acres) of LE MONTRACHET. Could still try harder with this jewel.

Thevenet, Jean Burg ★★★ Dom de la Bongran at Clessé stands out for rich concentrated (even sweet!) white MACON.

Thézac-Perricard SW Fr r p ★ 98' 99 (00) VDP W of CAHORS. Same grapes but lighter style. Made by co-op at Thézac. Incl 100% Malbec multi-prizewinner.

Thiénot, Alain Broker-turned-merchant; dynamic force for gd in CHAMP. Grande Cuvée **85 88** 90 95: could become one of best luxury CUVEES. Also owns Marie Stuart CHAMP, Ch Ricaud in LOUPIAC.

Thomas-Moillard Burg ★★★ Underrated NUITS-ST-GEORGES estate for slow-emerging wines; sister co is Moillard-Grivot NEGOCIANT house.

Thorin, J Beauj ★ Grower and major merchant of BEAUJOLAIS.

Thouarsais, Vin de Lo w r p ★ DYA Light CHENIN (20% CHARD permitted), GAMAY and CAB from tiny VDQS S of SAUMUR. Esp Gigon.

Tokay d'Alsace Old name for PINOT Gris in ALSACE in imitation of Hungarian Tokay. Now changed to Tokay-Pinot-Gris. Will soon be just Pinot Gris.

Tollot-Beaut ★★★ Stylish and consistent burgundy grower with 50 acres in the COTE DE BEAUNE, including v'yds at Beaune Grèves, CORTON, SAVIGNY- (Les Champs Chevrey) and at his CHOREY-LES-BEAUNE base.

Touraine Lo r p w dr sw sp ★-★★★ 88 89 90 93 **94** 95 **96** 97 **98** 99 00 01 Big mid-Loire region; immense range, incl dry white SAUVIGNON BLANC, dry and sweet CHENIN (eg VOUVRAY), red CHINON and BOURGUEIL. Also large AC with light CABERNET FRANC, GAMAYS, gutsy Cot, or increasingly a blend of these; grassy Sauvignon Blanc and MOUSSEUX; often bargains. Producers MARIONNET, Dehelly, Puzelat/Clos de Tue-Boeuf, Courtois, Oisly-Thesée, Ch de Petit Thouars, Jacky Marteau, Dom des Corbillieres, Clos Roche Blanche, Dom de la Presle.

Touraine-Amboise Lo r w p ★-★★ Touraine subappellation. "François Ler" is engaging local blend of GAMAY, Cot (MALBEC), & CAB F. Dutertre, Xavier Frissant.

Touraine-Azay-le-Rideau Lo dr w p ★-★★ CHENIN-based dry & off-dry whites, Grolleau-dominated rosés. Ch de la Roche, James Paget, Pibaleau Pere et Fils.

Touraine-Mesland Lo r w p ★-★★ Best represented by its user-friendly red blends (Gamay, Cot, and Cab F). Ch Gaillard, Clos de la Briderie.

Touraine-Noble Joué Loire p ★-★★ DYA Ancient but recently revived rosé from three PINOTS (Gris, Meunier, Noir) just S of Tours. Esp from Rousseau and Sard. Granted AOC status (Touraine-Noble Joué) in 2000.

Trévallon, Domaine de Provence r w ★★★ 88 89 90 91 92 **93 94** 95 **96'** 97 98 99 00 Highly fashionable estate at Les Baux. Rich intense CABERNET-SYRAH blend to age.

Trimbach, F E Al ★★★ Distinguished ALSACE grower/merchant at Ribeauvillé; supremely elegant if at times austere house style. Best wines incl RIES CLOS STE-HUNE, CUVEE Frédéric-Emile (grapes mostly from GRAND CRU Osterberg). Also GEWURZ. Opposed to GRAND CRU system like HUGEL.

Turckheim, Cave Vinicole de Important co-op in ALSACE. Large range of wines, incl GRANDS CRUS from 790 acres. Less exciting recently.

Tursan SW France r p w ★★★ VDQS aspiring to AOC. Easy drinking holiday-style wines. Mostly from co-operative at Geaune, but Château de Bachen (★★★) belongs to master-chef Michel Guérard. The white is excellent; super-ripe oak-aged Sauvignon Blanc. Also Domaine de Perchade-Pourrouchet (recent investment).

Vacqueyras S Rh r ★★ 88' 89' **90'** 93 94 **95'** **96'** **97** 98' 99' 00' Full, peppery GRENACHE-based neighbour to GIGONDAS – finer structure and often cheaper. Try JABOULET'S, Armouriers, Château de Montmirail, Château des Tours, Domaine Archimbaud-Vache, Charbonnière, Le Couroulu, La Fourmone, Garrigue, Grapillon d'Or, Montvac, Pascal Frères, Le Sang des Cailloux.

Val d'Orbieu, Vignerons du Association of some 200 top growers and co-ops in CORBIERES, COTEAUX DU LANGUEDOC, MINERVOIS, ROUSSILLON etc, marketing a first-class range of selected MIDI AC and VDP wines.

Valençay Lo r p w ★ DYA VDQS in eastern TOURAINE, south of Cher; light easy-drinking sometimes sharp wines from similar range of grapes as Touraine, especially SAUVIGNON BLANC.

Vallée du Paradis Midi r w p ★ Popular VDP of local red varieties in CORBIERES.

Valmagne, Abbaye de Glorious Cistercian abbey nr Sète (Hérault) converted to cellar. Wines to try.

Valréas S Rh r (p w) ★★ 90' 95' 96 97 **98'** 99 00 COTES DU RHONE village with big co-op. Gd mid-weight reds (more sap than CAIRANNE, RASTEAU), improving whites. Esp Emmanuel Bouchard, Dom des Grands Devers, Ch la Décelle.

Varichon & Clerc Principal makers and shippers of SAVOIE sparkling wines.

Vaudésir Burg w ★★★★ 85' **86 88** 89' 90 **92 93 95** 96' 97 98 99 00' 01
Arguably the best of seven CHABLIS GRANDS CRUS (but then so are the others).

VDQS Vin Délimité de Qualité Supérieure (see page 33).

Vendange Harvest.

Vendange Tardive Late harvest. ALSACE equivalent to German Auslese, but
usually higher alcohol.

Verget Burg ★★–★★★ The NEGOCIANT business of J-M GUFFENS-HEYNEN with mixed
range from MACON to MONTRACHET. Intense wines, often models, bought-in grapes.
Chablis, too oaky. New Lubéron venture: Verget du Sud. Follow v closely.

Veuve Clicquot Yellow label Non Vintage; White Label DEMI-SEC Non Vintage;
Gold Label 59 75 (since 1985 called Vintage Réserve: 85 **90** 93 95); Rosé
Reserve 85 90 95 Historic CHAMPAGNE house of highest standing, now
owned by LVMH. Full-bodied, almost rich: one of Champagne surest things.
Cellars at Reims. Luxury brands: La Grande Dame (**79 83** 85 90 **95**), new
Rich Réserve (**89**) released '95 and La Grande Dame Rosé (90) in 97.

Veuve Devaux Premium CHAMP of powerful Union Auboise co-op in Bar-sur-Seine.
Vg aged Grande Réserve NV, Oeil de Perdrix Rosé, and new Prestige Cuvée D.

Vidal-Fleury, J Rh Long-established GUIGAL-owned shipper of top Rhône wines
and grower of COTE-ROTIE. Steady quality. La Chatillonne top Côte-Rôtie.

Vieille Ferme, La S Rh r w Vg brand of COTES DU VENTOUX (red) and COTES
DU LUBERON (white) made by the Perrins, owners of CH DE BEAUCASTEL Reliable.

Vieilles Vignes Old vines – therefore the best wine. Used by many, esp by
BOLLINGER, DE VOGUE and CH FUISSE.

Vieux Télégraphe, Domaine du S Rh r w ★★★ 78' 79 **81'** 83 85 86 **88** 89' 90 93
94' 95' 96' 97 98' 99' 00 A leader in fine, vigorous, modern red CHATEAUNEUF-
DU-PAPE, and tasty whites (fuller style since late 90s), which age well in lesser
yrs. New second wine: Vieux Mas des Papes. Second dom: de la Roquette.

The vin de pays revolution

The junior rank of country wines. No one should overlook this category, the
most dynamic in France today. More than 140 vins de pays names have
come into active use in the past few years, mainly in the Midi. They fall into
three categories: regional (eg Vin de Pays d'Oc for the whole Midi);
departmental (eg Vin de Pays du Gard for the Gard département near the
mouth of the Rhône), and vins de pays de zone, the most precise, usually
with the highest standards. Varietal vins de pays and vins de pays primeurs
(reds and whites, all released on the third Thursday in November) are esp
popular. Well-known zonal vins de pays include Coteaux de l'Uzège, Côtes
de Gascogne, Val d'Orbieu. Don't hesitate to try them. There are some real
gems among them, and a great many charming trinkets.

Owns GIGONDAS Dom des Pallières with US importer Kermit Lynch.

Vigne or vignoble Vineyard, vineyards.

Vigneron Vinegrower.

Vin de l'année This year's wine. See Beaujolais, Beaujolais-Villages.

Vin Doux Naturel (VDN) Sweet wine fortified with wine alcohol, so the sweetness
is "natural", not the strength. The speciality of ROUSSILLON. based on GRENACHE
or MUSCAT. A staple in French bars, but the top wines can be remarkable.

Vin de garde Wine that will improve with keeping. The serious stuff.

Vin Gris "Grey" wine is very pale pink, made of red grapes pressed before
fermentation begins – unlike rosé, which ferments briefly before pressing.
Oeil de Perdrix means much the same; so does "blush".

Vin Jaune Jura w ★★★ Speciality of ARBOIS: odd yellow wine like fino sherry.
Normally ready when bottled (after at least 6 yrs). Best is CH-CHALON.

Vin Nouveau See Beaujolais Nouveau.

Vin de Paille Wine from grapes dried on straw mats, consequently v sweet, like Italian passito. Esp in the JURA. See also Chave.

Vin de Table Standard everyday table wine, not subject to particular regulations about grapes and origin. Choose VINS DE PAYS instead.

Vinsobres S Rh r (p w) ★★ 95' 96 97 **98' 99'** 00 Contradictory name of gd S Rhône village. Potentially substantial reds, rounded and fruity, but many ordinary. Best producers incl Doms les Aussellons, Bicarelle, Charme-Armaud, Jaume, du Moulin.

Viré-Clessé Burg w ★★ 98 99 00' 01 New AC based around two of the best white-wine villages of MACON. Esp A Bonhomme, CLOS du Chapitre, JADOT, Château de Viré, Merlin, and co-op.

Visan S Rh r p w ★★ 95' 96 97 **98' 99** 00 RHONE village for far better medium-weight reds than whites. Note: Dom des Grands Devers.

Viticulteur Wine-grower.

Vogüé, Comte Georges de ("Dom les Musigny") ★★★★ First-class 30-acre BONNES-MARES and MUSIGNY domaine at CHAMBOLLE-MUSIGNY. At best, esp since 90, the ultimate examples. Avoid most of the '80s.

Volnay Burg r ★★★→★★★★ 85' 88' 89' 90' 91 93 **95** 96' **97** 98 99' 00 01 Village between POMMARD and MEURSAULT: often the best reds of the COTE DE BEAUNE, not dark or heavy but structured and silky. Best v'yds: Caillerets, Champans, CLOS des Chênes, Santenots, Taillepieds, etc. Best growers: D'ANGERVILLE, J M BOILLOT, HOSPICES DE BEAUNE, LAFARGE, LAFON, DE MONTILLE, POUSSE D'OR.

Volnay-Santenots Burg r ★★★ Excellent red wine from MEURSAULT is sold under this name. Indistinguishable from other PREMIER CRU VOLNAY. Best growers: AMPEAU, LAFON, LEROY.

Vosne-Romanée Burg r ★★★→★★★★ 85' 88' 89' 90' 91 9̶2̶ 93 95 96' **97** 98 99' 00 01 Village with Burgundy's GRANDEST CRUS (ROMANEE-CONTI, LA TACHE etc). There are (or should be) no common wines in Vosne. Many good growers include Arnoux, Chevigny, DRC, ENGEL, GRIVOT, GROS, JAYER, LATOUR, LEROY, MEO-CAMUZET, Mongeard-Mugneret, Mugneret, RION.

Vougeot Burg r w ★★★ 90' **91** 93 95' 96' **97** 98 99' 00 01 Some village and premier cru red (and white) wines. See Clos de Vougeot. Exceptional Clos Blanc de Vougeot, white since 12th Century.

Vougeraie, Dom de la Burg r ★★→★★★ DOMAINE uniting all BOISSET's v'yd holdings. Good-value BOURGOGNE ROUGE up to exceptional MUSIGNY GRAND CRU.

Vouvray Lo w dr sw sp ★★→★★★★ 76' 79 82 83 85' 86 88' 89' 90' 93 95' 96' 97 98 99 00 01 (SEC and DEMI-SEC) 4,350-acre AC just E of Tours: v variable wines, increasingly gd, reliable. Demi-sec is classic style but in great years MOELLEUX can be intensely sw, almost immortal. Gd, dry sp – look out for PETILLANT. Best producers: Allias, Champalou, Foreau, Fouquet, Ch Gaudrelle, HUET, Pinon, Poniatowski, Vigneau-Chevreau.

Vranken, Champagne Ever more powerful CHAMP group created in 76 by Belgian marketing man. CHARD-led wines of gd quality. Leading brand Demoiselle. Acquired HEIDSIECK MONOPOLE in 96. Now Pommery, too.

Wolfberger Principal label of Eguisheim co-op. Exceptional quality for such a large-scale producer. V. important for CREMANT.

"Y" (pron: "ygrec") B'x 78' 79' 80' 85 86 88 94 96 Intense dry wine produced occasionally at CH D'YQUEM. Most interesting with age.

Zind-Humbrecht, Domaine Outstanding 99-acre ALSACE estate in Wintzenheim, Thann, Turckheim. First-rate, single-vineyard wines (especially CLOS St-Urbain), and very fine from GRANDS CRUS.

France entries also cross-refer to Châteaux of Bordeaux section, pages 80-105.

Châteaux of Bordeaux

The following abbreviations
of regional names
are used in the text:

B'x	Bordeaux
E-Deux-Mers	Entre-Deux-Mers
H-Méd	Haut-Médoc
Mar	Margaux
Méd	Médoc
Pau	Pauillac
Pessac-L	Pessac-Léognan
Pom	Pomerol
St-Em	St-Emilion
St-Est	St-Estèphe
St-Jul	St-Julien
Saut	Sauternes

Heavier shaded
areas are the wine
growing regions.

Gironde

MEDOC

St-Estèphe

Pauillac

St-Julien

Côtes de Blaye

Listrac

Moulis

Margaux

Côtes de Bourg

Dronne

Isle

POMEROL

Fronsac

Lalande de Pomerol

○ Libourne

St-Emilion Satellites

Côtes de Castillon

ST-EMILION

Dordogne

HAUT-MEDOC

Bordeaux

Premières Côtes de Bordeaux

Ste-Foy-Bordeaux

PESSAC-LEOGNAN

Garonne

ENTRE-DEUX-MERS

GRAVES

Loupiac

Cérons

Côtes de Bordeaux/St-Macaire

BARSAC

Ste-Croix-du-Mont

SAUTERNES

○ Langon

Which Bordeaux vintages to drink now, and which to keep? There is little need or temptation to stock up on the most recent vintages now, either for drinking or investment – except for the more modest chateaux of 2000, which are consistently ripe and pleasing without inflated prices. There is plenty of wine to enjoy at all stages of maturity at similar or lower prices in the pipeline.

Anything older than 1982 is speculative: storage conditions will be decisive to its state of health. But 1982, a great vintage all round, does not look overpriced today. Nor do 1985 and 86 – a classic Cabernet vintage and still a keeper for Médocs of quality. 1988 is relatively undervalued; 1989 fully valued but excellent for drinking or keeping. 1990 is a banker; an easy choice. No need to buy anything from 1991 to 1994, but 95 is an all-rounder beginning to be splendid drinking. Buy 1996s from the northern Médoc, 1997 all round for pleasant drinking soon, 1998s from the Right Bank, and 2000s as you need them. Leave "garage" wines to boy racers.

In case of doubt the term Left Bank is wine trade short-hand for the Médoc and Graves, lying on the west side of the north-flowing river Garonne and its estuary the Gironde. Right Bank means St. Emilion, Pomerol, Fronsac, and vineyards to the east.

In this listing we have picked out in colour the vintages which proprietors themselves may be serving this year as their first choices: their own wines in the state of maturity they prefer. Their choices, for older or younger wines or both, remind us that there are no absolutes – least of all in the glorious diversity of Bordeaux.

d'Agassac H-Méd r ★★ 82' **85' 86 88** 89' **90** 93 94 **95 96** 98 99 00' Sleeping Beauty 14th-C moated fort. 86 acres v nr Bordeaux suburbs. Wine popular in Holland. New owners since '96.

Andron-Blanquet St-Est r ★★ 82 85' **86** 88 89' **90** 91 93 **94 95** 96 **97** 98' 99 00'. Sister château to COS-LABORY. 40 acres. Toughish wines showing more charm lately.

Angélus St-Em r ★★★★ 85' 86 **87 88** 89' **90'** 92' 93 **94** 95 96 **97** 98' 99 00' 57-acre classed-growth on ST-EMILION COTES. A current star with some sumptuous wines. Promoted to Premier Grand Cru Classé status in '96.

d'Angludet Cantenac-Mar r ★★★ 82 83' 85 86 88' 89' 90 94 95 96' 97' 98' 99 00 75-acre CRU EXCEPTIONNEL of classed-growth quality run by Benjamin SICHEL. Lively long-living MARGAUX of great style popular in Britain. Good value.

Archambeau Graves r w dr (sw) ★★ (r) 85 86 88 89 90 93 **94 95 96 97** 98 99 00 (w) **95 96 97** 98 99 00 Up-to-date 54-acre property at Illats. Vg fruity dry white; fragrant barrel-aged reds (¾ of v'yd).

d'Arche Saut w sw ★★ 83' 85 86' **88' 89'** 90 95 96 97 98 99 01' Classed-growth of 88 acres rejuvenated since '80. Modern methods. Rich juicy wines to follow with pleasure.

d'Arcins H-Méd r ★★ 90 **94 95 96** 98 99 00 185-acre Castel family property (Castelvin: famous VIN DE TABLE). Sister to n'bour Barreyres (160 acres).

Vintages shown in light type should only be opened now out of curiosity to gauge their future. Vintages shown in bold type are deemed (usually by their makers) to be ready for drinking. Remember though that the French tend to enjoy the vigour of young wines, and that many 88s, 89s, and 90s have at least another decade of development in front of them. Vintages marked thus' are regarded as particularly successful for the property in question. Vintages in colour are the first choice for 2002.

d'Armailhac Pau r ✩✩✩ 82' **85** 86' **88**' 89 **90**' 93 **94** 95' 96' **97** 98 99 (00) Formerly CH MOUTON BARONNE PHILIPPE. Substantial fifth-growth nurtured by the late Baron Philippe de Rothschild. 125 acres: wine much less rich and luscious than MOUTON ROTHSCHILD, but outstanding in its class.

l'Arrosée St-Em r ✩✩✩ 82 83 85' **86**' 88 89' **90**' **92 93 94**' 95 96 **97** 98' 99 00 24-acre CÔTES estate. Name means diluted, but wine is top-flight: opulent, structured. 100% new barrels.

Ausone St-Em r ✩✩✩✩ 75 76 78' **79 82**' 83' **85** 86' **88 89 90 93** 94 95' 96' 97' 98' 99 00' Illustrious first-growth with 17 acres (about 2,500 cases); best position on the CÔTES with famous rock-hewn cellars. Priciest ST-EMILION, but for a long time behind CHEVAL BLANC or FIGEAC in performance. Second wine: La Chapelle d'Ausone. Now superb.

Bahans-Haut-Brion Pessac-L r ✩✩✩ NV and **82 85** 86' **88** 89' 90 **93 94 95** 96' 97 98 99 00 The second-quality wine of CH HAUT-BRION. Worthy of its noble origin; softly earthy yet intense.

Balestard-la-Tonnelle St-Em r ✩✩ **85** 86' **88**' **89 90**' 93 **94 95 96 97** 98' 99 00' Historic 30-acre classed-growth on the plateau. Big flavour and finesse.

de Barbe Côtes de Bourg r (w) ✩✩ **90 94** 95 **96** 97 98 99 00 The biggest (148 acres), best-known château of BOURG. Light fruity Merlot.

Barde-Haut St-Em r ✩✩ 98 99 00 42-acre sister-property of CLOS L'EGLISE and HAUT-BERGEY. VALANDRAUD influence: opulent.

Baret Pessac-L r w ✩✩ (r) **85 86 88** 89' **90' 95** 96 98 99 00 Famous name recovered from a lull. Now run by BORIE-MANOUX. White well-made too.

Bastor-Lamontagne Saut w sw ✩✩ **85 86** 88' 89' **90**' 95 96' 97 98' 99 01 Large Bourgeois Preignac sister-château to CH BEAUREGARD. Classed-growth quality; excellent rich wines. Second label: Les Remparts de Bastor. Also Ch St-Robert at Pujols: red and white GRAVES. 10,000 cases.

Batailley Pau r ✩✩✩ **82**' **83**' 85' 86 **88**' 89' 90' 93 94 95 96 97 99 00 The bigger of the famous pair of fifth-growths (with HAUT-BATAILLEY) on the borders of PAUILLAC and ST-JULIEN. 110 acres. Fine, firm, strong-flavoured, and good value Pauillac, to age. Home of the Castéja family of BORIE-MANOUX.

Beaumont Cussac (Haut-Méd) r ✩✩ **82 85** 86' **88 89**' 90' 93' 94 95 **96** 97 98' 99 200-acre+ CRU BOURGEOIS, well known in France for easily enjoyable wines from maturing vines. Second label: Ch Moulin d'Arvigny. 35,000 cases. In the same hands as CH BEYCHEVELLE.

Beauregard Pom r ✩✩✩ **85 86 88 89**' **90**' **94**' 95' 96' 97 98' 99 00' 42-acre vineyard; fine 17th century château near LA CONSEILLANTE. Top-rank rich wines. Advice from consultant Michel Rolland. Second label: Benjamin de Beauregard.

Beau-Séjour Bécot St-Em r ✩✩✩ **82**' 85 86' **88**' 89' 90' **94** 95' 96 97 98' 99 00' Other half of BEAUSEJOUR-DUFFAU; 45 acres. Controversially demoted in class in '85 but properly re-promoted to 1er Grand Cru Classé in '96. The Bécots also own GRAND-PONTET. Now also la Gomerie: 1,000 cases, 100% Merlot.

Beau-Site St-Est r ✩✩ 82 85 86' **88 89**' 90 **94 95 96 97** 98 00 55-acre CRU BOURGEOIS EXCEPTIONNEL in same hands as CH BATAILLEY etc. Recent wines rather "easy" for ST-ESTEPHE.

Beauséjour-Duffau St-Em r ✩✩✩ 82 83 85 **86** 88 89' 90' 93' **94 95** 96 **97**' 98 99 00 Part of the old Beau-Séjour Premier Grand Cru estate on W slope of the CÔTES. 17 acres in old family hands; only 2,000+ cases of firm-structured, concentrated, even hedonistic wine.

de Bel-Air Lalande de Pom r ✩✩ **82**' 85 86 88' 89' 90 **94**' 95 96 98 99 00 The best-known estate of Lalande de Pomerol, just north of POMEROL. Similar wine. 37 acres.

Bel-Air Marquis d'Aligre Soussans-Mar r ★★ 82' 85 86 88 89 90 95 96 97 98' 00 Organically run CRU EXCEPTIONNEL with 42 acres of old vines giving only 3,500 cases. Concentrated but supple; a sleeper.

Bel-Orme-Tronquoy-de-Lalande St-Seurin-de-Cadourne (H-Méd) r ★★ 85 86 88 89 90 94 95 96 97' 98' 99 00 60-acre CRU BOURGEOIS north of ST-ESTEPHE. Old vineyard previously known for tannic wines. More tempting since new management in 1997.

Belair St-Em r ★★★ 82' 83' 85' 86' 87 88' 89' 90' 94 95' 96 97 98 99 00' Neighbour of AUSONE. Fine wine but simpler; less tightly wound. Also NV Roc-Blanquant (magnums only). Biodynamic approach since '98.

Belgrave St-Laurent r ★★ 82 85 86' 88 89 90' 94 95 96' 98' 99 00' Fifth-growth well-managed by DOURTHE in ST-JULIEN'S back-country. 107 acres. Second label: Diane de Belgrave.

Bellegrave Listrac r ★★ 82 85 86 88 89 90 95 96 97 98 99 00 38-acre CRU BOURGEOIS making full-flavoured wine with help and advice from PICHON-LALANDE.

Belles-Graves Lalande de P r ★★ 82 85 86 88 93 94 95 96 97 98 99 00 Confusing name, but one of the reasons to watch LALANDE DE POMEROL.

Berliquet St-Em r ★★ 86 88 89' 90 91 93 94 95 96 97 98' 99 00' 23-acre Grand Cru Classé recently v well run.

Bernadotte H-Méd-r ★★ 98 99 00' Small château managed by PICHON-LALANDE. One to watch.

Bertineau St-Vincent Lalande de P r ★★ 98 99 00' 10 acres owned by top oenologist Michel Rolland (see also LE BON PASTEUR).

Beychevelle St-Jul r ★★★ 82' 85 86' 88 89' 90' 93 94' 95 96 97 98 99 00 170-acre fourth-growth with historic mansion, owned by an insurance company; now also Suntory. Wine should have elegance and power, just below top-flight ST-JULIEN. Second wine: Amiral de Beychevelle.

Biston-Brillette Moulis r ★★ 95 97 98 00 Another attractive MOULIS wine. Making 7,000 cases.

le Bon Pasteur Pom r ★★★ 82' 85 86' 88 89' 90' 93' 94' 95 96' 97 98' 99 00 Excellent small property on ST-EMILION boundary, owned by consultant oenologist Michel Rolland. Concentrated, even creamy wines can be virtually guaranteed.

Bonalgue Pom r ★★ 89 90 93 94 95 96' 97 98' 99 00 Ambitious little estate recently off-form. Les Hautes-Tuileries is sister château. Also manages CLOS DU CLOCHER in POMEROL.

Bonnet E-Deux-Mers r w ★★ (r) 90 94 95 96 97 98' 99 00 (w) DYA Owned by Lurton family. Big producer (600 acres!) of some of the best ENTRE-DEUX-MERS. Watch out for new Cuvée Prestige "Dominus" (2000).

le Boscq St-Est r ★★ 85 86 88 89' 90 93 95' 96' 97' 98 99 00 Leading CRU BOURGEOIS giving excellent value in tasty ST-EST.

le Bourdieu Vertheuil H-Méd r ★★ 82 85 86 88 89 90' 94 95 96 97 98 00 Vertheuil CRU BOURGEOIS with sister château Victoria (134 acres in all); ST-ESTEPHE-style wines.

Bourgneuf-Vayron Pom r ★★ 85' 86 88 89' 90 94 95' 96' 97 98' 99 00 22-acre v'yd on sandy gravel soil, its best wines with typically plummy POMEROL perfume. 5,000 cases.

Bouscaut Pessac-L r w ★★ (r) 82' 85 86' 88 89 90 94 95 96 98 99 00 (w) 96 97 98 99 00 Underperforming classed-growth at Cadaujac bought in '80 by Lucien Lurton of BRANE-CANTENAC etc. 75 acres red (largely Merlot); 15 white. Sophie Lurton is making steady improvements.

du Bousquet Côtes de Bourg r ★★ 85 86 88 89 90' 95 96 98 99 00 Reliable estate with 148 acres making attractive solid wine.

Boyd-Cantenac Mar r ✶✶✶ 82' 85 86' 88 89 90 94' 95 96' 98' 99 00 44-acre third-growth often producing attractive wine, full of flavour, if not of third-growth class. Wines now aged in 50% new oak. Second wine: Jacques Boyd. See also CH POUGET.

Branaire St-Jul r ✶✶✶ 82' 85 86 88 89' 90' 93' 94 95 96 97 98 99 00 4-growth of 125 acres. Reliable source of smooth, typical ST-JULIEN. Second label: Duluc.

Brane-Cantenac Cantenac-Mar r ✶✶✶ 82' 85 86' 88 89 90 95 96 97 98 99 00 01' Big (211-acre) second-growth. At (rare) best rich, even gamey wines of strong character. Also owned by the Lurton family. Second label: Baron de Brane. To watch.

du Breuil Cissac (H-Méd) r ✶✶ 89 90 93 94 95 96 98 99 00 Historic château being restored by CISSAC's owners.

Brillette Moulis r ✶✶ 85' 86 88 89' 90 95 96 97 98 99 00 70-acre CRU BOURGEOIS. Reliable and attractive. Second label: Berthault Brillette.

la Cabanne Pom r ✶✶ 82' 88' 89' 90' 94' 95 96 98' 99 00 Well-regarded 25-acre property nr the great TROTANOY. Recently modernized. Second wine: Dom de Compostelle. See also CH HAUT-MAILLET.

Cadet-Piola St-Em r ✶✶ 82 85' 86 88 89' 90 93' 94' 95 96 97 98 99 00 Distinguished sm property (17.5 acres) north of ST-EMILION town. 3,000 cases of tannic wine. FAURIE-DE-SOUCHARD: same owner; less robust.

Caillou Saut w sw ✶✶ 75 76 79 81 83 85 86 87 88' 89' 90' 95 96 97 98 99 01 Well-run second-rank 37-acre BARSAC vineyard for firm fruity wine. Private CUVÉE (86 88 89' 97) is a top selection.

Calon-Ségur St-Est r ✶✶✶ 82' 85 86' 88' 89' 90' 93 94 95 96' 97 98 99 00' Big (123-acre) third-growth; great historic reputation. Greater consistency since 1995. Second label: Marquis de Ségur.

Cambon La Pelouse H-Méd r ✶✶ 94 95 96' 97 98' 99 00 Big accessible CRU BOURGEOIS, near GISCOURS. A sure bet for rich typical MEDOC.

Camensac St-Laurent (H-Méd) r ✶✶ 82' 85 86' 88 89 90 95 96' 97' 98' 99 00 149-acre fifth-growth. Quite lively if not exactly classic wines. Second label: La Closerie de Camensac.

Canon Canon-Fronsac r ✶✶→✶✶✶ 82 85 86' 88 89' 90 93 94 95 96 97 98' 99 Tiny property owned until '00 by CHRISTIAN MOUEIX. Long-ageing wine.

Canon St-Em r ✶✶✶ 82' 85' 86 88' 89' 90' 93' 94 95 96 97 98' 99 00 Famous first-classed-growth with 44⁺ acres on plateau west of the town bought in 1996 by (Chanel) owners of RAUZAN-SEGLA. Conservative methods, Vineyard being restructured. Not yet at very best. Second label Clos J Kanon.

Canon-de-Brem Canon-Fronsac r ✶✶ 82' 85 86 88 89' 90 94 95 96 97 98 99 One of the top FRONSAC v'yds for vigorous wine.

Canon La Gaffelière St-Em r ✶✶✶ 82 85 86' 88' 89' 90' 93' 94' 95 96 97 98' 99 00 47-acre classed-growth on lower slopes of COTES. Same ownership as CLOS DE L'ORATOIRE and LA MONDOTTE. Stylish, upfront impressive wines.

Canon-Moueix Canon-Fronsac r ✶✶ 82 86 88 89' 90 95 96 97 98 99 00 Owned until 2000 by MOUEIX. V stylish wine. NB also sister chx CANON-DE-BREM, CANON (Canon-Fronsac).

Cantegril Graves r ✶✶ 94 95 96 97 98 99 Gd earthy red from CH DOISY-DAENE.

Cantemerle Macau (H-Méd) r ✶✶✶ 82 85 88 89' 90 95 96' 97 98' 99 00 Romantic southern MEDOC estate, a château in a wood (sadly battered in 99 gales) with 150 acres of vines. Fifth-growth capable of great things. Second label: Les Allées de Cantemerle.

Cantenac-Brown Cantenac-Mar r ✶✶→✶✶✶ 82 85 86' 88 89 90' 94 95 96 97 98 99 Formerly old-fashioned 77-acre third-growth. Now owned by AXA Millésimes (same as PICHON-LONGUEVILLE) heir investment is starting to pay off. Tannic wines. 2nd label: Canuet.

Cap de Mourlin St-Em r ★★ 82' 85 86 88 89 90 93 94 95 96 97 98' 99 00 Well-known 37-acre property of Cap-de-Mourlin family, owners of CH BALESTARD and Château Roudier, MONTAGNE-ST-EMILION. Should be a rich tasty ST-EMILION.

Capbern-Gasqueton St-Est r ★★ 86 88 89 90 94 95 96 98 99 00 Good 85-acre CRU BOURGEOIS; same owner as CALON-SEGUR.

Carbonnieux Pessac-L r w ★★★ 82 85 86' 88 89' 90' 93 94 95 96 97 98 99 00 Historic estate at LEOGNAN for sterling red and white. The whites, 65% sauv (eg 92' 94' 95 96 97 98 00), can have the structure to age 10 yrs. Ch'x Le Pape and Le Sartre are also in the family. Second label: La Tour-Léognan.

de Cardaillan Graves r ★★ 94 95 96 98 99 00 The trusty red wine of the distinguished CHATEAU DE MALLE (SAUTERNES).

la Cardonne Blaignan (Méd) r ★★→★★★ 94 95 96 97 98 99 00 Fairly large (125 acre) CRU BOURGEOIS of northern MEDOC.

de Carles Fronsac r ★★ 86 88 89 90 94 95 96 97' 98 99 00 Ancient château (named after Charlemagne). Steadily well-made quite juicy FRONSACS. Haut Carles is the top selection.

les Carmes-Haut-Brion Pessac-L r ★★★ 85 86 88' 89 90' 93' 94 95 96 97 98 99 00 Small (11-acre) neighbour of HAUT-BRION with classed-growth standards. Old vintages show its potential. Produces 2,000 cases.

Caronne-Ste-Gemme St-Laurent (H-Méd) r ★★→★★★ 83 85 86 89' 90 94' 95 96' 98 99 00 CRU BOURGEOIS EXCEPTIONNEL (100 acres). Steady stylish quality repays patience. At minor CRU CLASSE level (esp 96).

Carsin Premières Côtes r w ★★ (r) 94 95 96 97 98' 99 00 (w) 95 96 97 98 99 00 Ambitious enterprise: Finnish-owned, Australian winemaker. Very attractive (especially "CUVEE Prestige" and whtie "Etiquette Grise"). To follow.

Carteau Côtes-Daugay St-Em r ★★ 85 88 89 90 94 95 96' 97 98' 99 00 Emerging 5,000-case GRAND CRU; full-flavoured wines maturing fairly early.

Certan-Guiraud Pom r ★★ 82 83' 85 86 88 89' 90' 93' 94 95 96 97 98 99 00 Small (17-acre) property next to PETRUS. Has underperformed but was bought in '99 by J-P MOUEIX. Renamed Ch. Hosanna in 2000.

Certan-de-May Pom r ★★ 82' 83' 85' 86 87 88' 89' 90' 94 95 96' 98 99 00' Neighbour of VIEUX-CHATEAU-CERTAN. Tiny property (1,800 cases) with full-bodied, rich, tannic wine.

Chambert-Marbuzet St-Est r ★★→★★★ 82 85 86 88 89' 90' 93 94' 95 96 97' 98 99 00 HAUT-MARBUZET's tiny (20-acre) sister château. V gd predominantly Cabernet, aged in new oak. M Duboscq likes his wine well hung.

Chantegrive Graves r w ★★→★★★ 88 89 90 94 95 96 98' 99' 00 215-acre estate, half white, half red; modern GRAVES of very fair quality. CUVEE Caroline is top white selection (93 94 95 96 97 98' 99 00); top reds (85 88 89 90 94 95 96 98 99 00). Other labels incl Mayne-Lévêque, Mayne-d'Anice, Bon-Dieu-des-Vignes.

Chasse-Spleen Moulis r ★★★ 78' 82' 83' 85 86 88 89' 90' 93 94 95 96 97 00 180-acre CRU EXCEPTIONNEL at classed-growth level. Consistently good, often outstanding (eg 90'), long-maturing wine. Second label: Ermitage de C-S. One of the surest things in Bordeaux. See also LA GURGUE and HAUT-BAGES-LIBÉRAL.

Chauvin St Em r ★★ 88 89 90 93 94 95 96 97 98' 99 00 Steady performer; increasingly serious stuff. New vineyards purhased '98.

Cheval Blanc St-Em r ★★★★ 75' 76 78 79 82' 83' 85' 86 88 89 90' 93 94 95 96' 97 98' 99 00' This and AUSONE are the "first-growths" of ST-EMILION. Until recent vintages, Cheval Blanc has been consistently richer, more full-blooded, intensely vigorous,and perfumed, from 100 acres. Delicious young; lasts a generation. For many *the* first choice in Bordeaux. Second wine: Le Petit Cheval.

Chevalier, Domaine de Pessac-L r w ★★★ 79'83' 85 86' 88' 89' 90' 93 94' 95' 96' 97 98' 99 00' Superb estate of 94 acres at LEOGNAN. The red is stern at first, softly earthy with age. The white matures slowly to rich flavours (83' 85' 87' 88 89 90' 92 93 94 95 96' 97 98' 99 00). Second wine: Esprit de Chevalier. Also look out for Domaine de la Solitude, PESSAC-LEOGNAN.

Cissac Cissac-Médoc r ★★ 82' 83' 85 86' 88 89 90 93 94' 95 96' 97 98 99 00 Pillar of the bourgeoisie. 80-acre CRU GRAND BOURGEOIS EXCEPTIONNEL: steady record for tasty, very long-lived wine. New winery '00. Second wine: Les Reflets du Ch Cissac. Also, since 1987, CH DU BREUIL.

Citran Avensan (H-Méd) r ★★ 82 85 86 88 89' 90' 94' 95 96 97 98 99 00 CRU EXCEPTIONNEL of 178 acres, back in the possession of Villars-Merlaut family since 1996 after a Japanese interlude of dark, tannic wines. Much of the vineyard was replanted in 1999. Second label: Moulins de Citran. This is one to watch.

Clarke Listrac r (p w) ★★ 82 85' 86' 88 89' 90' 95 96' 97 98' 99 00 Huge (350-acre) CRU BOURGEOIS Rothschild development, incl visitor facilities and neighbouring Ch'x Malmaison and Peyrelebade. Also a dry white "Le Merle Blanc du Ch Clarke".

Clerc Milon Pau r ★★★ 82' 85 86' 88 89' 90' 93 94 95 96' 97 98' 99 00 Once-forgotten fifth-growth bought by the late Baron Philippe de Rothschild in '70. Now 73 acres and a top performer, weightier than ARMAILHAC.

Climens Saut w sw ★★★★ 71' 75' 76 78 79 80' 83' 85' 86' 88' 89 90' 95 96 97' 98 99 01' 74-acre BARSAC classed-growth making some of the world's most stylish wine (but not v sweetest) for a good 10 yrs' maturing. (Occasional) second label: Les Cyprès. Owned by Berenice Lurton.

Clinet Pom r ★★★★ 82 83 85 86 88' 89' 90' 93' 94 95 96 97' 98' 99 00 17-acre property in central POMEROL making intense sumptuous wines from old vines. Since '88 one of the models for Pomerol. Since '98 owned by Groupe Jean Louis Laborde. 2nd label: Fleur de Clinet

Clos l'Eglise Pom r ★★★ 85 86 88 89 90' 93 94 95 96 97 98 99 00' 15-acre v'yd on one of the best sites in POMEROL. Fine wine with more depth since '98. M Rolland consults. The same family owns CH HAUT-BERGEY.

Clos Floridène Graves r w ★★ (r) 95 96 97 98' 99 00 (w) 93 94 95 96' 97 98' 99 00 A sure thing from one of B'dx's best white winemakers, Denis Dubourdieu. Oak-fermented Sauv-Sém to keep 5 years; fruity red. See also CH REYNON. New winery 2000.

Clos Fourtet St-Em r ★★★ 82' 83 85 86 88 89 90 94 95 96 97 98 99 00 Well-placed 42-acre first-growth on the plateau, cellars almost in town. Back on form after a middling patch: Acquired by Philippe Cuvelier in January 2001. Second label: Dom de Martialis.

Clos Haut-Peyraguey Saut w sw ★★ 75 76 79 82 83' 85 86' 88' 89 90' 95' 96 97 98 99 00 Tiny production of excellent medium-rich wine. Haut-Bommes is the second label.

Clos des Jacobins St-Em r ★★ 82' 83' 85 86 88 89' 90' 94 95 96 97 98 99 00 Well-known and well-run little (18-acre) classed-growth. New ownership from 2001; new creamy style. To watch.

Clos du Marquis St-Jul r ★★ ·★★★ 82 85 86' 88 89' 90 94 95 96 97 98 99 00 The second wine of LEOVILLE-LAS-CASES, cut from the same cloth and regularly a match for many highly classed growths.

Clos de l'Oratoire St-Em r ★★ 90 94 95 96 97 98 99 00 Serious performer on the NE slopes of ST-EM. Same stable as CANON-LA-GAFFELIÈRE and LA MONDOTTE.

Clos René Pom r ★★ 82' 85 86 88 89 90 94 95 96 97 98 99 Leading château west of POMEROL. 38 acres. Increasingly concentrated wines. Alias Ch Moulinet-Lasserre.

Clos Toumilon Pessac-L r w ★★ 96 97 98 99 00 Little château in St-Pierre-de-Mons to note. Fresh and charming red and white.

la Closerie du Grand-Poujeaux Moulis r ★★ 85 86 88 **89 90 94'** 95 96 98' 99 00 Small but respected middle-MEDOC property with emphatic wines. Also owners of neighbouring Ch'x Bel-Air-Lagrave and Haut-Franquet.

la Clotte St-Em r ★★ 82 83' **85 86 88 89 90' 93' 94** 95' 96' 97 98' 99 00' Tiny COTES GRAND CRU CLASSÉ: pungent supple wine. Drink at owners' restaurant, Logis de la Cadène in ST-EM. Second label: Clos Bergat Bosson.

Colombier-Monpelou Pau r ★★ 86' 88 89 90' 94 95 96 97 98 99 00 Reliable small CRU BOURGEOIS; fair standard.

la Conseillante Pom r ★★★★ 70' 75' 81' 82' 83 85 86 87 88 89 90' **93 94** 95' 96' 97 98' 99 00 29-acre historic property on the plateau between PETRUS and CHEVAL BLANC. Some of the noblest and most fragrant POMEROL, worthy of its superb position; drinks well young or old.

Corbin St-Em r ★★ 82' 83 85 86 **88 89 90' 95 96 97** 98 99 00 28-acre classed-growth in N ST-EMILION where a cluster of Corbins occupy the plateau edge. Top vintages are very rich.

Corbin-Michotte St-Em r ★★ 82 85 88 89' 90 93 94' 95 96 97 98' 99 00 Well-run modernized 19-acre property; "generous" POMEROL-like wine. In same hands as Chx Calon, Cantelauze.

Cordeillan-Bages Pau r ★★ A mere 1,000 cases of rather lean PAUILLAC. Better known as a luxury health-spa for wealthy wine writers.

Cos d'Estournel St-Est r ★★★★ 82' 85' 86' 87 88' 89' 90' 93' 94 95 96' 97' 98' 99 00 140-acre second-growth with eccentric chinoiserie tower overlooking CHÂTEAU LAFITE. Most refined ST-EST and regularly one of best wines of the MEDOC. Second label: Les Pagodes de Cos. Managed by Jean-Guillaume Prats.

Cos-Labory St-Est r ★★ 82 85 86 87 **88 89' 90'** 93 94 95 96' **97'** 98' 99 00 Little-known fifth-growth neighbour of COS-D'ESTOURNEL with 37 acres. Efforts since 1985 have raised it steadily to classed-growth form (especially since 1990). ANDRON-BLANQUET is sister château.

Coufran St-Seurin-de-Cadourne (H-Méd) r ★★ 82' 85 86' 88 89 90 94 95 96' 97 98 99 00 Coufran and CH VERDIGNAN, in the extreme N of the HAUT-MEDOC, are co-owned. Coufran is mainly Merlot for supple wine. 148 acres. CH SOUDARS is another, smaller sister.

Couhins-Lurton Graves w ★★→★★★ 93 94 **95** 96 **97' 98'** 99 00 Tiny quantity of fine oaky Sauvignon Blanc. Classed-growth château.

la Couspaude St Em r ★★★ **89 90** 93 94 95 96 97 98 99 00 Another to watch closely. Modern methods and full-flavoured wine.

Coutet Saut w sw ★★★ 71' 75' 76 79 81' **83' 85** 85 86' 88' 89' **90'** (no 93 94) 95 96 97 98' 99 01' Traditional rival to CH CLIMENS; 91 acres in BARSAC. Usually slightly less rich; at its best equally fine. CUVEE Madame is a v rich selection in the best vintages. A dry GRAVES is sold under the same name.

Couvent des Jacobins St-Em r ★★ 82' **85 86 87 88 89 90** 94 95 96' **97** 98' 99 00 Well-known 22-acre vineyard on east edge of town. Among the best of its kind. Splendid cellars. Second label: Ch Beau-Mayne.

le Crock St-Est r ★★ 82 85 86 **88 89 90' 93 95** 96 97 98 99 00 Outstanding CRU BOURGEOIS of 74 acres in the same family as CH LEOVILLE-POYFERRE. Among the best Crus Bourgeois of the commune.

La Croix Pom r ★★ 83 85' 86 88 89 90 **93 94 95** 96 **97** 98 99 00 Well-reputed property of 32 acres. Appealing plummy POMEROL. Also La C-St-Georges, La C-Toulifaut, Castelot, Clos des Litanies, and HAUT-SARPE (St-Em).

To decipher codes, please refer to "Key to symbols" on front flap of jacket, or to "How to use this book" on page 6.

la Croix-de-Gay Pom r ★★★ 85 86 88' **89 90** 93 94' 95 96 **97** 98 99 00 30 acres in best part of the commune. Recently on fine form. Has underground cellars (rare in POMEROL). LA FLEUR-DE-GAY is the best selection.

la Croix du Casse Pom r ★★ 89 90 **93 94** 95 96 **97** 98 99 00 Up-and-coming property to look out for. Same owner as CLINET.

Croizet-Bages Pau r ★★ **82' 85** 86 88 89 **90' 95** 96' 98' 99 00 52-acre fifth-growth (lacking a château or a reputation). Same owners as CH RAUZAN-GASSIES. The '98 may indicate better things to come.

Croque-Michotte St-Em r ★★ **82' 83** 85 86 88 89' 90' **94 95** 96 98 99 00 35-acre Grand Cru on the POMEROL border. Good steady wines but not grand enough to be classé.

de Cruzeau Pessac-L s r w ★★ (r) **86 88 89 90** 94 **95** 96 97 99 00 100-acre PESSAC-LEOGNAN v'yd recently developed by André Lurton of LA LOUVIERE etc. To try. Oak-fermented white keeps 2–5 years.

Curé-Bon St-Em r ★★ **82' 85 86 88 89 90** 93 94 95 96 97 98 99' 00 Tiny little-known (12-acre) GRAND CRU CLASSE between AUSONE and CANON. Sold in June '00 to CANON into which it will be integrated.

Dalem Fronsac r ★★ **85 86 88 89 90 94** 95 96' **97** 98' 99 00 Leading full-blooded FRONSAC. 36 acres: 85% Merlot.

Dassault St-Em r ★★ 82 **85 86** 88 **89** 90 94 **95 96** 97 98' 99 00 A consistent, early-maturing middle-weight GRAND CRU CLASSE. 58 acres. Could be more exciting.

de la Dauphine Fronsac r ★★ **85 86 88 89' 90'** 94 95 **96 97** 98' 99 00 Old star rejuvenated by J-P MOUEIX and sold '00. No need to keep very long, though you can.

Dauzac Labarde-Mar r ★★→★★★ **82' 85 86** 88' 89' 90' **93' 94 95** 96 **97** 98' 99 00 120-acre fifth-growth nr the river south of MARGAUX; underachiever for many years. New owner (insurance company) in '89; began to achieve in the '90s. Second wine: La Bastide Dauzac.

Desmirail Mar r ★★→★★★ 82 **85 86 88 89** 90 94 95' 96' 97 98 99 00 3rd-growth, now 45 acres. Wines for drinking fairly young, but higher ambitions.

Doisy-Daëne Barsac w (r) sw dr ★★★ 76' 80 82 83 85 86 88' 89' 90' **95** 96 97 98' 99 01 Forward-looking, even experimental, 34-acre estate for crisp oaky dry white and red CH CANTEGRIL, but above all notably fine (and long-lived) sweet BARSAC. L'Extravagance (**90** 96 97) is a super-CUVEE.

Doisy-Dubroca Barsac w sw ★★ 75' 76 **78 79** 83 **85 86 88' 89 90' 95** 96 97 99 00 Tiny (8.5-acre) BARSAC classed-growth allied to CH CLIMENS.

Doisy-Védrines Saut w sw ★★★ 75' 76' 79 80 83' 85 86 88' 89' **90 95** 96 97 98' 99 01 50-acre classed-growth at BARSAC, near CLIMENS and COUTET. Delicious, sturdy, rich: for keeping. A sure thing for many years.

la Dominique St-Em r ★★★ 79 81 82' **83** 86' **87** 88' 89' 90' 93 94 95 96 **97** 98 99 00 45-acre classed-growth next to CHÂTEAU CHEVAL BLANC for fruity, nose-catching wines. Second label: St Paul de Dominique.

Ducluzeau Listrac r ★★ **82 85 86 88 89 90** 94 95 96' 97 99 00 Tiny sister property of DUCRU-BEAUCAILLOU. 10 acres, unusually 90% Merlot.

Ducru-Beaucaillou St-Jul r ★★★★ 61 66' 70' 75' 78' **81 82' 83' 85' 86' 89 90 93** 94 95 96' 97 98 99 00' Outstanding second-growth on excellent form; 120 acres overlooking the river. Classic cedar-scented claret for long ageing. The devoted J-E Borie died in '98; family goes on. See also Grand-Puy-Lacoste, HAUT-BATAILLEY, LALANDE-BORIE.

Duhart-Milon Rothschild Pau r ★★★ 82' 85 **86 88 89 90** 93 **94** 95 96' **97** 98 99 00' Fourth-growth neighbour of LAFITE, under same management. Maturing vines; increasingly fine quality and reputation. 2000 is the best yet. 110 acres. Second label: Moulin de Duhart.

Duplessis Moulis r ✭✭ **82 85 86 88'** 89 90 93 95 96 97 98 99 00 CRU BOURGEOIS run by Marie Laure Lurton-Roux. Wines typical of MOULIS. See also VILLEGEORGE.

Durfort-Vivens Mar r ✭✭✭ **82' 85' 86 88' 89' 90** 94 95 96 **97** 98 99 00 Relatively small (49-acre) second-growth owned by Gonzague Lurton. Recent wines have structure (lots of Cabernet S) and class.

Dutruch Grand-Poujeaux Moulis r ✭✭ **82' 85 86 88 89 90 93** 94 95 96' 97 98' 99 00 One of the leaders of MOULIS making full-bodied and tannic wines.

de l'Eglise, Domaine Pom r ✭✭ **82'** 85 86 **88 89 90 95** 96 **97** 98 99 00 Small property: stylish resonant wine distributed by BORIE-MANOUX.

l'Eglise-Clinet Pom r ✭✭✭✭ **82' 83' 84** 85' 86 88' **89** 90' 93' **94** 95 96 97' 98' 99 00 11 acres. Ranked very near top; full, concentrated, fleshy wine. A château to follow but is expensive. 1,700 cases produced. Second label: La Petite Eglise.

l'Enclos Pom r ✭✭✭ **82' 85 86 88** 89' 90' 93 94 **95** 96 **97** 98 99 00 Excellent 26-acre property on west side of POMEROL, nr CLOS RENE. Usually big well-made long-flavoured wine.

l'Evangile Pom r ✭✭✭✭ 75' **82' 83' 85'** 86 87 88' 89' 90' 93 **95'** 96' 97 98' 99 00 33 acres between PETRUS and CHEVAL BLANC. Deep-veined but elegant style in a POMEROL classic. In the same area and class as LA CONSEILLANTE. Bought in '90 by Domaines (LAFITE) Rothschild. New equipment '00.

de Fargues Saut w sw ✭✭✭ 70' 71' 75' 76' 78 79 81 83 85' 86 88 89 90 95 96 97 98 99' 25-acre v'yd by ruined château owned by Luc-Saluces of YQUEM fame. Fruity and extremely elegant wines, maturing earlier than Yquem.

Faurie-de-Souchard St-Em r ✭✭ 85 86 88 89 90 93 94 95 96 97 98' 99 00 Small GRAND CRU CLASSE on the COTES. See also CH CADET-PIOLA.

de Ferrand St-Em r ✭✭→✭✭✭ 85 86 88 89 90' 93' 94 95 96 **97** 98 99 00 Big (75-acre) plateau estate. Rich oaky wines, with plenty of tannin.

Ferrande Graves r (w) ✭✭ **95** 96 98 00 Major estate at Castres: 100⁺ acres. Easy enjoyable red and good white wine, at their best at 1–4 yrs.

Ferrière Mar r ✭✭ **89 90** 93 94 **95** 96 **97'** 98 99 00 In same capable hands as CHASSE-SPLEEN, LA GURGUE and HAUT-BAGES-LIBERAL. New equipment '00.

Feytit-Clinet Pom r ✭✭ **82' 85' 86 90'** 94 95 96 97' 98 99 00 Little property nr LATOUR-A-POM. At best fine lightish wines. '00 owning Chasseuil family took back management from J-P MOUEIX.

Fieuzal Pessac-L r (w) ✭✭✭ **82' 85' 86' 88 89 90' 93 94** 95 96' 97 98' 99 00 75-acre classed-growth at LEOGNAN. Finely made, memorable wines of both colours. Classic whites since '85 are 4–10-yr keepers. Ch Le Bonnat is sister château vinified at FIEUZAL.

Figeac St-Em r ✭✭✭✭ 70' 75 82' 83 85' 86' 88 89' 90' **94' 95'** 96 **97** 98 99 00 First-growth neighbour of CHEVAL BLANC. 98-acre gravelly vineyard gives one of Bordeaux's most stylish, rich but elegant wines, lovely to drink relatively quickly but lasting indefinitely. Second label: Grangeneuve.

Filhot Saut w sw dr ✭✭ 82' 83' 85 86' **88' 88** 90 95 **96** 97 98 99 (01) Second-rank classed-growth with splendid château, 148-acre vineyard. Lightish and rather simple (Sauvignon) sweet wines for fairly early drinking, a little dry, and red. Very good "Crème de Tête" (**90** extremely rich).

la Fleur St-Em r ✭✭ **82' 85 86 88** 89' 90' 94 95 96 97 98 99 00 16-acre COTES estate; deliciously fruity wines. Managed by J-P MOUEIX.

la Fleur-de-Gay Pom r ✭✭✭ 1,000-case super-CUVEE of CH LA CROIX DE GAY.

la Fleur-Pétrus Pom r ✭✭✭✭ 82 83' 85 86 87 88' 89' 90' 93 94 **95** 96' 97 98 99 00 32-acre vineyard flanking PETRUS with the same management. Exceedingly fine densely plummy wines; POMEROL at its most stylish (and expensive).

Fombrauge St-Em r ★★ 88' 89 90 **94' 95 96 97** 98 99 00 120 acres at St-Christophe-des-Bardes, east of ST-EM; Mainstream St-Em making great efforts. Second label: Château Maurens. Magrez-Fombrauge is its "GARAGE" wine.

Fonbadet Pau r ★★ **85 86 88 89 90'** 94 95 96' 97 98' 00 CRU BOURGEOIS of solid reputation. 50 acres next to PONTET-CANET. Old vines; wine needs long bottle-age. Value.

Fonplégade St-Em r ★★ 82' 85 86 88 89 90' 94 95 96 97 98 00 48-acre GRAND CRU CLASSE on the COTES W of ST-EMILION. At best firm and long-lasting.

Fonréaud Listrac r ★★ 82' 83 85' 86' 88 89 90 **94** 95 96 98 00 One of the bigger (96 acres) and better CRUS BOURGEOIS of its area. Investment in 1998 and onwards. 5 acres of white: Le Cygne, barrel-fermented. See also CHÂTEAU LESTAGE.

Fonroque St-Em r ★★★ 75' 78 82 83' 85' 86 87 88 89' 90' 94 95 96 98 00 48 acres on the plateau N of ST-EMILION. WAS J-P MOUEIX property until '00, now Alain Moueix. Major investment and organic ideas. Big deep dark wine: drink or (better) keep.

Fontenil Fronsac r ★★★ 88 89 90 **94** 95 96 97 98 99' 00 A new FRONSAC leader started by Michel Rolland in '86. Dense, oaky, new-style.

Fontmarty Pom r ★★ **82 83 85 86 88' 89 90** 94 95' 96 98' 00 Small property owned by Bernard Moueix group (also TAILLEFER); 1,500 cases.

Forts de Latour Pau r ★★★ 70' 78' 81 82' 83 85 86 87 88 89' 90' 93 94 95' 96' **97** 98 99 00 The (worthy) second wine of CH LATOUR; the authentic flavour in (slightly) lighter format. Until 1990 unique in being bottle-aged at least three years before release; now offered EN PRIMEUR.

Fourcas-Dupré Listrac r ★★ 82' 83' 85' 86' 88 89' 90 94 95 96' 97 98' 99 00 Top-class 100-acre CRU BOURGEOIS EXCEPTIONNEL making consistent wine in the tight LISTRAC style. To follow. Second label: Château Bellevue-Laffont. Complete renovation 2000.

Fourcas-Hosten Listrac r ★★→★★★ 82' 83' 85 86' 87 88 89' 90' 94 **95' 96'** 97 98' 99 00 96-acre CRU BOURGEOIS often the best of its (underestimated) commune. Firm wine with a long life. New gear '98.

Franc-Mayne St-Em r ★★ 85 86 88 89' 90' 94 95 96 97 98' 99 00 18 acre-GRAND CRU CLASSE. Ambitious new owners 1996. Michel Rolland consults. To watch. Continuing renovation started '98.

de France Pessac-L r w ★★ (r) 89 **90'** 95' 96' 97 **98** 99 00 (w) **95 96 97** 98 99 Well-known GRAVES property (the name helps) with Michel Rolland consulting. Try a top vintage.

la Gaffelière St-Em r ★★★ 82' 83' 85 86' 88' **89' 90' 94** 95 96 **97** 98' 99 00 61-acre first-growth at the foot of the COTES below CH BELAIR. Elegant, not rich wines. Re-equipped and improved since 1998.

Galius St-Em r ★★ 95 96 98 00 Oak-aged selection from ST-EMILION cooperative, to a high standard. Formerly Haut Quercus.

La Garde Pessac-L r w ★★ 90 **94** 95' 96' 97' 98' 99 00 Substantial property of 120 acres owned by negociant CVBG-Dourthe; reliable red and improving. More Merlot planted 2000.

le Gay Pom r ★★★ 75' 76' 82' 83' 85 86 88 89' 90' 95 96 97 98 99 00 Fine 14-acre vineyard on north edge of POMEROL. Same owner as CH LAFLEUR; under J-P MOUEIX management since '85. Usually impressive tannic wines.

Gazin Pom r ★★★ 82 85 86 87' 88 89' 90' 94' 95 96 **97** 98' 99 00 Large property (for POMEROL): 58 acres alongside PETRUS recently shining. Second label: l'Hospitalet de Gazin.

NB The vintages printed in colour are the ones you should choose first for drinking in 2002.

Gilette Saut w sw ★★★ 49 53 **55 59 61 67 70** 75 76 78 79 81 Extraordinary small Preignac château stores its sumptuous wines in concrete vats to a great age. Only about 5,000 bottles of each. Château Les Justices is the sister château (96 97 99).

Giscours Labarde-Mar r ★★★ **70 75' 78' 82 85 88** 89' 90 **94 95** 96' **97** 98 99 00 Splendid 182-acre third-growth property south of CANTENAC. Excellent vigorous wine in '70s; '80s very wobbly; some revival during '90s esp under new owner since 1995, but should do better. Second labels: Château Cantelaude, Grand Goucsirs (!) and La Sirène de Giscours. Ch La Houringue is its baby sister.

du Glana St-Jul r ★★ **89 90 94** 95 96 97' 98 99 00 Big CRU BOURGEOIS. Undemanding; undramatic; value. Second wine: Château Sirène.

Gloria St-Jul r ★★ →★★★ **82 85 86 88 89 90 94** 95' 96 **97** 98 99 00 CRU BOURGEOIS with wine of vigour. 110 acres. Recent return to long-maturing style. Second label: Peymartin.

la Gomerie See BEAUSÉJOUR-BÉCOT.

Grand Barrail Lamarzelle Figeac St-Em r ★★ **85 86 88 89 90 94** 95 96 97 98 00 48-acre property south of FIGEAC. Well-reputed and popular, if scarcely exciting.

Grand-Corbin-Despagne St-Em r ★★→★★★ 82' 83 85 **88** 89 90' 93 94 95 96 **97** 98 99 00 One of the bigger and better GRANDS CRUS on CORBIN plateau. New generation (of the founding Despagnes, since 1812) in '93. Now fashionably thick wines. Also Ch Maison Blanche, MONTAGNE ST-EM.

Grand-Mayne St-Em r ★★★ 82 85 86 **88 89' 90' 94** 95 96 **97** 98 99 00 40-acre GRAND CRU CLASSE on W COTES. Noble old château with wonderfully rich tasty wines recently.

Grand-Pontet St-Em r ★★★ 82' 86' **88** 89 **90' 93 94 95'** 96 **97** 98' 99 00 35 acres beside CH BEAU-SEJOUR-BECOT; both have been revitalized since '85. Quality improving.

Grand-Puy-Ducasse Pau r ★★★ 82' 85 86 **88** 89' 90 94 95 96' 98' 99 00 Fifth-growth enlarged to 90 acres under expert management, but lacks the vigour of the next entry. Second label: Ch Artiges-Arnaud.

Grand-Puy-Lacoste Pau r ★★★ 70' 75 78' 79' 81' 82' 83 85' 86' 88' 89' 90' 93 94 95 96' **97** 98 99 00 Leading fifth-growth famous for excellent full-bodied vigorous examples of PAUILLAC. 110 acres among the "Bages" châteaux, owned by the Borie family (see Ducru-Beaucaillou). Second label: Lacoste-Borie.

Gravas Saut w sw ★★ 96 97 Small BARSAC property; impressive firm sweet NB CUVÉE Spéciale.

La Grave à Pomerol Pom r ★★★ 82' 85 86' **88** 89' 90 **93 94** 95 96 97 98' 99 00 Verdant château with small but first-class v'yd owned by CHRISTIAN MOUEIX. Beautifully structured POMEROL of medium richness.

Gressier-Grand-Poujeaux Moulis r ★★→★★★ 82 83' **85** 86 **88 89 90** 94 95 96 97 98 99 00 Vg CRU BOURGEOIS, neighbour of CHASSE-SPLEEN. Fine firm wine with good track record. Repays patient cellaring.

Greysac Méd r ★★ 95 96 00 Elegant 140-acre property. Easy, early maturing wines popular in US.

Gruaud-Larose St-Jul r ★★★ 61 70 75 78' 82' 83' 85 86' **88' 89 90' 93** 95 96 98 99 00 One of the biggest and best-loved second-growths. 189 acres. Smooth rich stylish claret, year after year; ages for 20+ years. Owned by Societé Bernard Taillan since 1997. Very good second wine: Sarget de Gruaud-Larose.

Guadet-St-Julien St-Em r ★★ 82 85 86 **88** 89 90' **94** 95 96' **97** 98 99 00 Extremely well-made wines from v small GRAND CRU CLASSE.

BORDEAUX

Guiraud Saut w (r) sw (dr) ★★★ **79 81** 83' **85** 86' 88' **89' 90'** 95 96' 97' 98 99 01' Restored classed-growth of top quality. 250+ acres. At best excellent sweet wine of great finesse; also small amount of red and dry white.

la Gurgue Mar r ★★ **82 83' 85' 86 87 88 89' 90 93 94** 95' 96' **97'** 98 99 00 Small, well-placed 25-acre property, for MARGAUX of the fruitier sort. From owners of CHASSE-SPLEEN and HAUT-BAGES-LIBERAL. Winery renovated '00.

Hanteillan Cissac r ★★ **95 96** 98 00 Huge vineyard: very fair CRU BOURGEOIS, conscientiously made. Ch Laborde is the second label.

Haut-Bages Averous Pau r ★★ 82' 85' 86 88 89' 90 94 **95** 96 **97** 98 99 (00) The second wine of CH LYNCH BAGES. Should be tasty drinking.

Haut-Bages-Libéral Pau r ★★★ **82' 85 88 89** 90' **93 94'** 95 96' **97'** 98 99 00 Lesser-known fifth-growth of 70 acres (next to LATOUR) in same stable as CHASSE-SPLEEN. Results are excellent, full of PAUILLAC vitality.

Haut-Bages-Monpelou Pauillac r ★★ **85 86 88** 89' 90 **94** 95 96 **97** 98 99 00 25-acre CRU BOURGEOIS stable-mate of CH BATAILLEY on former DUHART-MILON land. Good minor PAUILLAC.

Haut-Bailly Graves r ★★★ 82 83 85' **86 88' 89'** 90' 92 **93' 94 95** 96 97 98' 99' 00 70-acres+ at LEOGNAN American-owned since '98, but old family still directing. Since '79 some of the best savoury, round, intelligently made red GRAVES have regularly come from this château. Second label is La Parde de Haut-Bailly.

Haut-Batailley Pau r ★★★ **70'** 75' **78 82' 83 85 86 88 89' 90'** 95 96' **97** 98 99 00 Smaller part of divided fifth-growth BATAILLEY: 49 acres. Gentler than sister château GRAND-PUY-LACOSTE. Second wine: La Tour-d'Aspic.

Haut-Beauséjour St-Est r ★★ **95 97** 98 99 00 Another CRU BOURGEOIS performing well. Owned by CHAMPAGNE house ROEDERER.

Haut-Bergey Pessac-L r ★★ 98 99 00 65 acres, largely Cab; fragrant delicate GRAVES. Also a little dry white. Completely renovated in the '90s.

Haut Bommes See Clos Haut-Peyraguey.

Haut-Brion Pessac (Graves) r (w) ★★★★ **59' 61' 66' 70' 71' 75' 76 78'** 79' 81 82' **83'** 85' 86' **87** 88' 89' 90' **91 92 93** 94 95 96' 97 98' 99 00. The oldest great château of BORDEAUX and the only non-MEDOC first-growth of 1855. 108 acres. Deeply harmonious, never-aggressive wine with endless, honeyed, earthy complexity. Consistently great (and modestly priced) since '75. A little full dry white in 82 83 85 87 **88 89'** 90 **91 92 93 94 95** 96 97 98 99 00. See Bahans Haut-Brion, La Mission Haut-Brion.

Haut-Condissas Méd r ★★ 99 00 Aspiring new cru at Bégadan. To watch.

Haut Carles See CH. DE CARLES.

Why do the Châteaux of Bordeaux have such a large section of this book devoted to them? Wine-lovers love to snipe at them and complain about their prices, but collectively they form by far the largest supply of high-quality wine on earth. A single typical Médoc château with 150 acres (some have far more) makes approximately 26,000 dozen bottles of identifiable wine each year – the production of two or three California "boutique" wineries. Moreover, between the extremes of plummy Pomerol, grainy Graves and tight, restrained Médocs – not to mention crisp dry whites and unctuous golden ones – Bordeaux offers a wider range of tastes than any other homogenous region.

The tendency over the last two decades has been to buy more land. Many classed-growths have expanded quite considerably since their classification in 1855. The majority have also raised their sights and invested their recent profits in better technology.

Haut-Maillet Pom r ★★ 98' 00 12-acre sister château of LA CABANNE. Well-made gentle wines.

Haut-Marbuzet St-Est r ★★ →★★★ 82' 85' 86' 88 89' 90' 91 93' 94 95 96' 97 98 99 00 The best of many good ST-ESTEPHE CRUS BOURGEOIS. Monsieur Dubosq has reassembled the ancient Dom de Marbuzet, in total 175 acres. Haut-M is 60% Merlot. Also owns CHAMBERT-MARBUZET, MACCARTHY, Tour de Marbuzet. New oak gives them a distinctive, if not subtle, style of great appeal.

Haut-Pontet St-Em r ★★ 98 00 Reliable 12-acre v'yd of the COTES deserving its GRAND CRU status. 2,500 cases.

Haut-Sarpe St-Em r ★★ 82 83' 85 86 88 89 90' 93 94 95 96 97 98 99 00 GRAND CRU CLASSE (6,000 cases) with elegant château and park, 70% Merlot. Same owner as CH LA CROIX, POMEROL.

Hortevie St-Jul r ★★ 90 95 96 98 00 One of the few ST-JULIEN CRUS BOURGEOIS. This tiny v'yd and its bigger sister TERREY-GROS-CAILLOU are shining examples. Now hand-harvesting only.

Hosanna Pom r ★★★★ 00 The new name for Moueix-owned CERTAN-GUIRAUD. Stellar ambitions.

Houissant St-Est r ★★ 90 95 96 98 00 Typical robust well-balanced ST-ESTEPHE CRU BOURGEOIS also called Ch Leyssac; well-known in Denmark.

d'Issan Cantenac-Mar r ★★★ 85 86 88 89 90' 95 96' 97 98 99 00 Beautifully restored moated château nr the Gironde with 75-acre 3rd-growth v'yd; lightish, fragrant wines. 2nd label: Ch de Candale.

Kirwan Cantenac-Mar r ★★★ 82' 85 86 88 89' 90' 93' 94 95 96 97 98 99 00 86-acre third-growth; from '97 majority owned by SCHRODER & SCHYLER. Michel Rolland advises. Mature vineyards now giving classy wines.

Labégorce Mar r ★★ 82' 85 86 88 89' 90' 94 95 96 97 98 99 00 Substantial 95-acre property N of MARGAUX; long-lived wines of true Margaux quality. Recent investment. Making every effort.

Labégorce-Zédé Mar r ★★ →★★★ 82' 83' 85 86' 88 89' 90' 93 94 95 96' 97 98 99 00 CRU BOURGEOIS on road N from MARGAUX. 62 acres. Typically delicate, fragrant classic Same family as VIEUX-CH-CERTAN. Second label: Dom Zédé. Also 23 acres of AC Bordeaux: "Z".

Lacoste-Borie The second wine of CH GRAND-PUY-LACOSTE.

Lafaurie-Peyraguey Saut w sw ★★★ 78 82 83' 85 86' 88 89' 90' 95 96' 97 98 99 01 Fine classed-growth of only 49 acres at Bommes, belonging to CORDIER. Now one of best buys in SAUTERNES. 2nd wine: La Chapelle de Lafaurie.

Lafite Rothschild Pau r ★★★★ 59 76' 78 79 81' 82' 83 85 86' 87 88' 89' 90' 91 93 94 95 96' 97 98 99 00' First-growth of famous elusive perfume and style in its great vintages, which keep for decades. Recent vintages are well up to form. Amazing circular cellars. Joint ventures in Chile ('88), California ('89), Portugal ('92). Second wine: Carruades de Lafite. 225 acres. Also owns CH'X DUHART-MILON, L'EVANGILE, RIEUSSEC.

Lafleur Pom r ★★★★ 70' 75' 79' 82' 83 85' 86' 88' 89' 90' 93 94 95 96 97 98 99 00' Superb 12-acre property just N of PETRUS. Resounding wine of the turbo-charged, tannic, less "fleshy" kind for long maturing and investment. Same owner as LE GAY. Second wine: Les Pensées de Lafleur.

Lafleur-Gazin Pom r ★★ 82' 83 85' 86 88' 89 90 93 94 95 96 97 98 99 00 Distinguished small J-P MOUEIX estate on the NE border of POMEROL.

Lafon-Rochet St-Est r ★★★ 70' 78 82 83' 85 86 88' 89' 90' 94 95 96' 97 98 00 Fourth-growth n'bour of COS D'ESTOURNEL, 110 acres. Gd hard full-bodied ST-ESTEPHE, slow to "give". Same owner as CH PONTET-CANET. New equipment '98. Second label: Numéro 2. Renovation '00.

Lagrange Pom r ★★ **82' 83 85' 86 88** 89' 90' 94 95 96 97 98 99 00 20-acre vineyard in the centre of POMEROL run by the ubiquitous house of J-P MOUEIX. Rising profile for flavour/value.

Lagrange St-Jul r ★★★ 82 85' **86' 88' 89' 90'** 93 94 95 96 **97** 98 99 00 Formerly neglected third-growth inland from ST-JULIEN, bought by Suntory ('83). 280 acres now in tiptop condition with wines to match (and lots of oak). Second wine: Les Fiefs de Lagrange.

la Lagune Ludon (H-Méd) r ★★★ 82' **83' 85** 86' 88' **89'** 90' **94** 95 96' 98 99 00 Ultra-modern 160-acre third-growth in southernmost MEDOC. Rich wines with marked oak and steady, high quality. Owned by CHAMPAGNE AYALA.

Lalande-Borie St-Jul r ★★ A baby brother of the great DUCRU-BEAUCAILLOU created from part of the former vineyard of CHÂTEAU LAGRANGE. Gracious, easy drinking wine.

de Lamarque Lamarque (H-Méd) r ★★ **82 85 86' 88 89** 90' **94** 95 96 97 98 99 00 Splendid medieval fortress in central MEDOC. 113 acres giving admirable wine of high BOURGEOIS standard. Second wine: Donjon de L.

Lamothe Bergeron H-Méd r ★★ **88 89 90 93 94** 95 96' 97 98' 99 00 150 acres at CUSSAC making 25,000 cases of reliable claret. Run by GRAND-PUY-DUCASSE.

Lanessan Cussac (H-Méd) r ★★★ **78' 81 82 83 85 86' 88' 89' 90'** 93 94 95 96' 97 98 99 00 Distinguished 108-acre CRU BOURGEOIS EXCEPTIONNEL just S of ST-JULIEN. Fine rather than burly but ages well. Same family owns Châteaux de Ste-Gemme, Lachesnaye, La Providence.

Langoa Barton St-Jul r ★★★ 78' **82'** 83 85 **86' 88' 89' 90' 93 94'** 95 96 98 99 00 49-acre third-growth sister château to LEOVILLE-BARTON. V old Barton-family estate with impeccable standards and generous value. Second wine: Réserve de Léoville-Barton

Larcis-Ducasse St-Em r ★★ 85 86 **88' 89' 90'** 94 95 96 98' 00 Top property of St-Laurent, eastern neighbour of ST-EMILION, on COTES next to CH PAVIE. 30 acres in a fine situation; wines could be better.

Larmande St-Em r ★★★ 82 **83' 85 86 88' 89'** 90' 93 94 95' 96 **97** 98' 00 Substantial 60-acre property. Replanted, re-equipped, and now making rich strikingly scented wine, silky in time. Second label: Ch des Templiers.

Laroque St-Em r ★★→★★★ **82' 85 86 88** 89 90 **94** 95 96 97 98 99 00 Important 108-acre v'yd on the ST-EMILION COTES in St-Christophe. Promoted to GRAND CRU CLASSE in '96.

Larose-Trintaudon St-Laurent (H-Méd) r ★★ 89 90' **94'** 95 96' 97 98 99 00 The biggest v'yd in the MEDOC: 425 acres. Modern methods make reliable fruity and charming CRU BOURGEOIS wine to drink young. Second label: Larose St-Laurent. Special CUVÉE: Larose Perganson.

Laroze St-Em r ★★ 90' **94** 95 **96'** 98' 99 00 Large v'yd (74 acres) on western COTES. Fairly light wines from sandy soils, more depth from '98; approachable when young.

Larrivet-Haut-Brion Pessac-L r (w) ★★ **82'** 83 **85 86 87 88 89 90 94** 95 96' **97** 98' 99 00 LEOGNAN property with perfectionist standards; M Rolland consulting. Also 500 cases of fine, barrel-fermented white (**93 94 95** 96' **97 98'** 99 00). New plantings '99.

Lascombes Mar r (p) ★★★ **70'** 82 83' **85 86 88' 89'** 90' 95 96' 98' 99 00 240-acre second-growth owned since '01 by an American pension fund. Wines have been wobbly but improvements in recent vintages. Second label: Ch Segonnes.

Latour Pau r ★★★★ 49 59 **61 62 64** 66 70' **75' 78'** 79 81 82' **83** 85 **86' 87 88' 89' 90' 91' 92** 93' 94' 95' 96' 97 98 99 00 First-growth considered the grandest statement of the MEDOC. Profound, intense, almost immortal wines in great yrs; even weaker vintages have the characteristic note of terroir and run for many years. 150 acres sloping to R Gironde. Latour always needs 10 yrs to show its hand. British-owned from '63 to '93, now again in (private) French hands. Radical rebuilding in 2000/01. 2nd wine: LES FORTS DE LATOUR; 3rd, PAUILLAC.

Latour-Martillac Pessac-L r w ★★ (r) **82' 85' 86 88' 89** 90 93 94 95 96 **97** 98' 99 00 Small but serious property at Martillac. 10 acres of white grapes; 37 of black. The white can age admirably (94' **95** 96 97 98' 99 00).

Latour-à-Pomerol Pom r ★★★ **61' 70'** 82 **83** 85' **86 87** 88' 89' 90' 93 94 95 96 97 98' 99 00 Top growth of 19 acres under MOUEIX management. POMEROL of great power and perfume, yet also ravishing finesse.

des Laurets St-Em r ★★ **89' 90'** 94 95 **96** 97 98 **99** 00 Major property in PUISSEGUIN-ST-EMILION and MONTAGNE-ST-EMILION (to the east) with 160 acres of v'yd on the COTES (40,000 cases). Sterling wines sold by J-P MOUEIX.

Laville-Haut-Brion Pessac-L w ★★★★ **85' 86 88** 89' **90 92 93' 94** 95' 96 97 98 99 00 A tiny production of the v best white GRAVES for long succulent maturing, made at CH LA MISSION-HAUT-BRION. The 89, 95, 96 are off the dial.

Léoville Barton St-Jul r ★★★→★★★★ 78 **82'** 83 85' **86' 88' 89'** 90' **93'** 94' 95 96' 97 98 99 00 The 90-acre portion of the great second-growth LEOVILLE vineyard in Anglo-Irish hands of the Barton family for over 150 years. Powerful classic claret; traditional methods, very fair prices. Major investment raised already high standards to "super-second". See also Langoa-Barton.

Léoville Las Cases St-Jul r ★★★★ 66' 75' 78' 79 81' **82' 83'** 84 85' 86' 87 88 89' 90' **91** 93' 94 95 96 97 98 99 00 The largest LEOVILLE. Next to LATOUR; 210 acres with daunting reputation. Elegant complex powerful austere wines, for immortality. Second label CLOS DU MARQUIS also outstanding.

Médoc: the class system

The Médoc has 60 crus classés, ranked in 1855 in five classes. In a separate classification it has 18 Crus Grands Bourgeois Exceptionnels, 41 Crus Grands Bourgeois (which must age their wine in barrels), and 68 Crus Bourgeois. This classification is presently being revised.

Apart from the first-growths, the five classes of 1855 are now hopelessly jumbled in quality, with some second-growths at fifth-growth level and vice versa. They also overlap in quality with the Crus Exceptionnels. (Besides the official 18, another 13 châteaux are unofficially acknowledged as belonging to this category.) The French always do things logically.

Léoville Poyferré St-Jul r ★★★ 82' 83' **85 86' 88** 89' 90' 94 95 96 98 99 00 For years the least outstanding of the LEOVILLES; high potential rarely realised. Michel Rolland now makes the wine; things should be better. 156 acres. Second label: Ch Moulin-Riche .

Lestage Listrac r ★★ 86' 88 89' 90' 95 96 98 99 00 130-acre CRU BOURGEOIS in same hands as CH FONREAUD. Light stylish wine, oak-aged since '85. Second wine: Ch Caroline. Also La Mouette (white).

Lilian Ladouys St-Est r ★★ 89 90 **94** 95 96 97 98 99 00 Created in the '80s: a 50-acre CRU BOURGEOIS with high ambitions and early promise. There have been problems, but early and recent wines are looking good.

Liot Barsac w sw ★★ 75' 76 82 83 85 86 88 89' 90' 95 96 97 98 99 01 Consistent fairly light golden wines from 50 acres. How they last!

Liversan St-Sauveur (H-Méd) r ★★ **82' 85 86'** 88' 89' 90' **93** 94 95 96 **97** 98 99 00 116-acre GRAND CRU BOURGEOIS inland from PAUILLAC. The Polignac family have had steadily high standards. Same owners as of PATACHE D'AUX. Second wine: Ch Fonpiqueyre.

Livran Méd r ★★ **82' 86** 88' 89' 90' **94' 95** 96 97 98 00 Big CRU BOURGEOIS at St-Germain in the N MEDOC. Consistent round wines (half Merlot).

Loudenne St-Yzans (Méd) r ★★ **82' 85 86' 88 89' 90 94 95** 96' 97 98 99 00 Beautiful riverside château owned by Gilbeys 1975–2000. New owners, so watch this space. Well-made CRU BOURGEOIS red and Sauvignon Blanc white from 155 acres. The new oak-scented white is best at 2–4 yrs (**95 96 97 98 99' 00**).

Loupiac-Gaudiet Loupiac w SW ★★ **85 86 88 89 90** 95 96 97 98' 99 01 A reliable source of good-value "almost-SAUTERNES", just across River Garonne.

la Louvière Pessac-L r w ★★★ (r) **82' 85 86'** 88' 89' 90' **94' 95** 96' 97 98' 99 00 (w) **93' 94 95' 96' 97' 98' 99** 00 135-acre LEOGNAN estate with classical mansion restored by ubiquitous Lurton family. Excellent white and red of classed-growth standard.

de Lussc St-Em r ★★ **85 86 88 89' 90 94 95** 96 97 98 99 00 One of the best estates in LUSSAC-ST-EMILION (to the NE). New technical methods '00.

Lynch-Bages Pau r (w) ★★★→★★★★ 59 61 70 **79** 82' **83' 84** 85' 86' 88' **89'** 90' **91 94** 95 96 97 98 99 00 Always popular, now a regular star. 200 acres. Rich robust wine: deliciously dense, brambly; aspiring to greatness. See also Haut-Bages-Averous. From '90, intense oaky white – Blanc de Lynch-Bages. Same owners (Cazes family) as LES ORMES-DE-PEZ.

Lynch-Moussas Pau r ★★ **89** 90' **94 95'** 96' **97 98** 99 00 Fifth-growth restored by the director of CH BATAILLEY. Now 60⁺, but scarcely classed-growth standard.

Lyonnat Lussac-St-Em r ★★ 95 96 98 99 00 120-acre estate; well-distributed reliable wine.

MacCarthy St-Est r ★★ The second label of CH CHAMBERT-MARBUZET.

Macquin-St-Georges St-Em r ★★ **89** 90' **94 95 96 97** 98 99 00 Steady producer of delicious, not weighty, "satellite" ST-EMILION at ST-GEORGES.

Magdelaine St-Em r ★★★ 82' 83' **85 86** 88 89' 90' 93 94 **95** 96 **97** 98' 99 00 Leading COTES first-growth: 28 acres next to AUSONE owned by J-P MOUEIX. Top-notch, Merlot-led wine; recently powerful and fine.

Magence Graves r w ★★ (r) 90 94 95 96 98 00 (w) 96 97 **98** 00 Go-ahead 93-acre property in S GRAVES. Sauv Bl-flavoured dry white and fruity red. Both age well 2–6 yrs.

Malartic-Lagravière Pessac-L r (w) ★★★ (r) **82' 85 86'** 88 89 90' **94** 95 96 **97** 98 99 00 (w) **93 94 95 96 97 98** 99 00 LEOGNAN classed-growth of 53 acres. Rather hard red wine and a little long-ageing Sauv Bl white. New Belgian owner ('96) M Rolland and D Dubourdieu now consulting. To watch.

Malescasse Lamarque (H-Méd) r ★★ **82 85 86 88 89 90** 93' 94 **95'** 96' **97** 98 99 00 Renovated CRU BOURGEOIS with 100 well-situated acres. Second label: Le Tana de M. Wines steadily improving.

Malescot-St-Exupéry Mar r ★★★ 61 70 **82' 83' 86 88 89** 90' **94** 95 96 **97** 98' 99 00 Third-growth of 59 acres returned to fine form in the '90s. Can be tough when young, eventually fragrant MARGAUX.

de Malle Saut w r sw dr ★★★ (w sw) **75 76 78 79 81' 82' 83 85 86' 88 89'** 90' **94 95** 96' 97 98' 99 01 Beautiful Preignac château. 124 acres. Very good SAUTERNES; also M de Malle dr w **95 96 97 98 99** 00). See also Château du Cardaillan.

Marbuzet St-Est r ★★ **85 86 88** 89 90 **93 94** 95' 96' **97** 98 99 00 Second label of COS-D'ESTOURNEL until '94 when it became a CRU BOURGEOIS in its own right.

Margaux Mar r (w) ★★★★ 53 61' **78' 79** 80 81' **82' 83' 84** 85' 86' 87 88' **89'** 90' 91 93' 94 95' 96' **97'** 98' 99 00' First-growth (209 acres), the most seductive and fabulously perfumed of all in its frequent top vintages. Pavillon Rouge **86 88 89** 90' **93 94 95** 96 97 98 99 00) is second wine. Pavillon Blanc is best white (Sauv) of MEDOC: keep 5 yrs plus (**88 89 90 91 93 94 95 96 97** 98 99 00).

Marojallia Mar r ★★★ 99 00 New micro-château with 5 acres, looking for big prices for big wines. 2nd wine Clos Margalaine.

Marquis-d'Alesme-Becker Mar r ★★ 85 86 88' 89 90 94 95 96 97 98 99 00 Tiny (17-acre) third-growth. A lost CRU CLASSE, once highly regarded. Potential here for classic MARGAUX.

Marquis de St-Estèphe St-Est r ★ The growers' coop; bigger but not as interesting as formerly.

Marquis-de-Terme Mar r ★★–★★★ 82 83' 85 86' 88' 89' 90' 95 96 97 98 99 00 Renovated fourth-growth of 84 acres. Fragrant lean style has developed since '85, with more Cab S and more flesh.

Martinens Mar r ★★ 86 88 89 90 93 94' 95 96 97 98 99 (00) Worthy 75-acre CRU BOURGEOIS of the mayor of CANTENAC.

Maucaillou Moulis r ★★ 82 83' 85' 86' 88' 89' 90' 93 94' 95 96 97 98' 99 00 130-acre CRU BOURGEOIS with high standards, property of DOURTHE family. Richly fruity Cap de Haut-Maucaillou is second wine.

Mazeyres Pom r ★★ 95 96' 97' 98' 99 00 Consistent, if not exciting lesser POMEROL. Better since '96. 50 acres.

Méaume B'x Supérieur r ★★ 90 96 98 00 An Englishman's domaine, N of POMEROL. Solid reputation for vg daily claret to age 4–5 yrs. 7,500 cases.

Meyney St-Est r ★★–★★★ 82' 85 86' 88' 89' 90' 93 94 95 96 97 98 99 00 Big (125-acre) riverside neighbour to CH MONTROSE in a superb situation; among many steady long-lived CRUS BOURGEOIS in ST-ESTEPHE. Owned by CORDIER. Second label: Prieur de Meyney.

Millet Graves r w (p) ★★ 98 00 Useful GRAVES. Second label, Clos Renon: drink young. Cuvée Henri: oak-aged white.

la Mission-Haut-Brion Pessac-L r ★★★★ 59' 61' 66' 75' 78' 82' 83 85' 86 88 89' 90' 93' 94' 95 96' 97 98' 99 00 N'bour and long-time rival to CH HAUT-BRION; since '84 in same hands. Consistently grand-scale full-blooded long maturing wine; even "bigger" than H-B and sometimes more impressive. 30 acres. 2nd label is La Chapelle de la Mission. White is LAVILLE-H-B.

Monbousquet St-Em r (w) ★★★ 82 85' 86 88' 89' 90' 93 94 95 96 97 98 99 00. A familiar old property on gravel revolutionized by new owner. Now super-rich, conc'd, and voluptuous wines. New owners also acquired PAVIE and PAVIE-DECESSE in '98.

Monbrison Arsac-Mar r ★★–★★★ 82 83 85 86 88' 89' 90 93 94 95 96' 97 98 99 00 A name to follow. High standards (lavish with new oak) make it Margaux's most modish CRU BOURGEOIS. 4,000 cases and 2,000 of second label, Ch Cordet.

la Mondotte St-Em r ★★★–★★★★ 96' 97' 98 99 (00) Intense wines from micro-property owned by Comte Stephen Von Neipperg (CANON-LA GAFFELIERE, CLOS DE L'ORATOIRE).

Montrose St-Est r ★★★–★★★★ 61 70' 75' 82' 85 86' 88 89' 90' 91 93 94 95 96' 97 98 99 00 158-acre family-run second-growth famous for deeply coloured forceful old-style claret. Vintages '79–'85 (except '82) were lighter, but recent Montrose is almost ST-EST's answer to LATOUR. Second wine: La Dame de Montrose.

Moulin du Cadet St-Em r p ★★ 89' 90' 94 95 96 97 98 00 Little vineyard on the COTES, owned by J-P MOUEIX. Fragrant medium-bodied wines.

Moulin de la Rose St-Julien r ★★ 95 96 98 00 Tiny CRU BOURGEOIS; high standards. To watch.

Moulin Pey-Labrie Canon-Fronsac r ★★ 89 90 94 95 96 97 98' 99 00 Increasingly well-made drinker-friendly FRONSAC. To follow.

Moulin-St-Georges St-Em r 95 96 97 98 99 00 ★★ A satellite of AUSONE. Stylish and rich wine.

Moulin-à-Vent Moulis r ★★ **82' 85' 86 88 89 90' 94 95** 96' 98 99 60-acre property in the forefront of this booming AC. Lively forceful wine. LA TOUR-BLANCHE (MEDOC) has the same owners.

Moulinet Pom r ★★ **85 88 89' 90 95 96** 98 99 00 One of POMEROL's bigger châteaux; 45 acres on lightish soil, wine lightish too.

Mouton Baronne Philippe See D'ARMAILHAC.

Mouton Rothschild Pau r (w) ★★★★ **59 61 62' 66' 70' 75' 76 78 81 82' 83' 85' 86' 88' 89' 90' 91 93' 94 95' 96 97 98' 99 00** Officially a first-growth since '73, though in reality far longer. 175 acres (87% Cab S) can make majestic rich wine, often MEDOC's most opulent (also, from '91, white Aile d'Argent). Artists' labels and the world's greatest museum of art relating to wine. Baron Philippe, the foremost champion of the MEDOC, died in '88. His daughter Philippine now reigns. See also Opus One, California.

Nairac Saut w sw ★★ **76' 82 83' 85 86' 88 89 90' 95' 96** 97 98 99 01 Perfectionist BARSAC classed-growth. 2,000 cases of oak-fermented and – scented wine to lay down for a decade.

Nenin Pom r ★★ **82 85' 86 88' 89 90** 94' 95 **96** 97 98 99 00 Well-known 66-acre estate, one of POMEROL's biggest; on a (v necessary) but slow upswing since '85. CH LEOVILLE-LAS-CASES involvement since 1997.

Olivier Graves r w ★★★ (r) **82 86 88 89' 90' 95 96 97** 98 00 (w) **93 94 95 96 97 98'** 99 00 90-acre classed-growth, surrounding a moated castle at LEOGNAN. 9,000 cases oaky red, 6,000 oaky white. 95 seems to promise more charm.

les Ormes-de-Pez St-Est r ★★→★★★ **82' 85 86' 88 89' 90' 93 94 95 96 97** 98 99 00 Outstanding 72-acre CRU BOURGEOIS owned by CH LYNCH-BAGES. Consistently one of the most likeable ST-ESTEPHES.

les Ormes-Sorbet Méd r ★★ **82' 85' 86' 88 89 90' 94 95 96 97** 98' 99 00 10,000-case Couquèques producer of gd stylish r aged in new oak. A leader in N MEDOC. Second label: Ch de Conques.

Palmer Cantenac-Mar r ★★★★ **61' 62 66' 70 71' 75' 76 78' 79' 81 82 83' 85 86' 87 88' 89 90 93 94** 95 96' 97 98' 99 00. The star of CANTENAC: a third-growth occasionally outshining first-growths. Wine of power, flesh, delicacy, and much Merlot. 110 acres with Dutch, British (the SICHEL family), and French owners. Second wine: Alter Ego de Palmer (a steal for early drinking).

Pape Clément Pessac-L r (w) ★★★→★★★★ **70 75' 83 85 86' 88' 89' 90' 93'** 94' 95 96 **97** 98 99' 00 Ancient PESSAC v'yd; record of seductive, scented, not ponderous reds. Early '80s not so gd: dramatic quality (and more white) since '85. Watch very closely. Also Ch Poumey at Gradignan.

de Parenchère r (w) ★★ **98** 99 00 Steady supply of useful AC Ste-Foy Bordeaux and AC Bordeaux Supérieur from handsome château with 125 acres.

Patache d'Aux Bégadan (Méd) r ★★ **89' 90' 95 96 97** 98 99 00 90-acre CRU BOURGEOIS of the N MEDOC. Fragrant largely Cabernet wine with the earthy quality of its area. See also Ch Liversan.

Paveil-de-Luze Mar r ★★ **82' 85 86' 88' 89' 90 95** 96' **97** 98 99 00 Old family estate at Soussans. Small but highly regarded. Investment '00.

Pavie St-Em r ★★★ **82' 83' 85 86' 88' 89' 90' 94 95 96'** 98 99 00 Splendidly sited first-growth; 92 acres mid-slope on the COTES. Great old track record. Bought by owners of CHÂTEAU MONBOUSQUET, along with adjacent PAVIE-DECESSE and La Clusière. This is new-wave St-Emilion. Thick, intense, sweet, Mid-Atlantic.

Pavie-Decesse St-Em r ★★ **82 86 88 89 90 94** 95 96 97 98 99' 24 acres. Brother to the above and on form since '98.

Pavie-Macquin St-Em r ★★★ **85' 86 88 89' 90' 93 94 95** 96' **97** 98' 99 00' Another PAVIE; this time the neighbours up the hill. 25-acre COTES vineyard East of ST-EMILION. Steadily fine organic winemaking by Nicolas Thienpont of CHÂTEAU PUYGUERAUD. Second label: Les Chênes.

Pavillon Rouge (Blanc) du Château Margaux See Ch Margaux.

Pedesclaux Pau r ★★ 82' 85 86 88 89' 90' 94 95' 96 97 98' 99 00 50-acre fifth-growth on the level of a CRU BOURGEOIS. Wines mostly go to Belgium. Second labels: Bellerose, Grand-Duroc-Milon.

Petit-Village Pom r ★★★ 75' 82' 83 85' 86 88 89' 90' 91 93 94' 95 96 97 98' 99 00 Top property revived. 26 acres next to VIEUX-CHATEAU-CERTAN, same owner (AXA) as CH PICHON-LONGUEVILLE since '89. Powerful plummy wine. Second wine: Le Jardin de Petit-Village.

Pétrus Pom r ★★★★ 61 62 64 66 67 70' 71' 73 75' 76 78 79' 81 82' 83 84 85' 86 87 88' 89' 90 93' 94 95' 96 97 98' 99 00 The (unofficial) first-growth of POMEROL: Merlot solo in excelsis. 28 acres of gravelly clay giving 5,000 cases of massively rich and concentrated wine, on allocation to the world's millionaires. Each vintage adds lustre (NB no 1991 produced).

Peyrabon St-Sauveur (H-Méd) r ★★ 00 Serious 132-acre CRU BOURGEOIS popular in the Low Countries. Also La Fleur-Peyrabon (only 12 acres).

Peyre-Labade Listrac r p ★ Second label of CH CLARKE. Investment '00.

Peyreau St-Em r ★★ 90 94 95 96 97 98 99' 00 Sister-château of CLOS DE L'ORATOIRE.

de Pez St-Est r ★★→★★★ 82' 85 86' 88 89 90' 93' 94 95' 96' 97 98' 99 00 Outstanding CRU BOURGEOIS of 60 acres. As reliable as any of the classed-growths of the village, though not so fine. Bought in 1995 by CHAMPAGNE house ROEDERER.

Phélan-Ségur St-Est r ★★→★★★ 88' 89' 90' 94 95 96' 97 98 99 00 Big and important CRU BOURGEOIS (125 acres): rivals the last as one of ST-ESTEPHE's best. From '86 has built up a strong reputation.

Pibran Pau r ★★ 88 89' 90' 94 95 96 97 98 99 (00) Small CRU BOURGEOIS allied to PICHON-LONGUEVILLE. Should be classy wine with PAUILLAC drive.

Pichon-Longueville Comtesse de Lalande Pau r ★★★★ 61 62 66 70' 75' 76 78' 79' 80 81 82' 83 85' 86' 88' 89' 90' 93 94 95 96 97 98 99 00 "Super-second"-growth neighbour to CH LATOUR. 148 acres. Consistently among v top performers; long-lived wine of fabulous breed for those who like it lusciously, even in lesser yrs. Second wine: Réserve de la Comtesse. Rivalry across the road (next entry)worth watching. Other property Ch Bernadotte.

Pichon-Longueville (formerly Baron de Pichon-Longueville) Pau r ★★★★ 82' 83 85 86' 88' 89' 90' 93 94' 95 96 97 98 99 77-acre second- growth. Since 1987 owned by AXA Insurance. Revitalized winemaking matches aggressive new buildings. Second label: Les Tourelles de Longueville

le Pin Pom r ★★★★ 82 83 85 86 88 89 90 94 95 96 97 98 00 The first of the new Bordeaux cult mini-crus. A mere 500 cases of Merlot, with same owners as VIEUX-CHATEAU-CERTAN (a much better buy). Almost as rich as its drinkers, but prices well beyond PETRUS are ridiculous.

de Pitray Castillon r ★★ 85 86 88 89 90 94 95 96' 98' 99 00 Large (77-acre) vineyard on COTES DE CASTILLON E of ST-EM. Flavoursome wines, once the best-known of the APPELLATION.

Plince Pom r ★★ 82 85 86 88 89' 90 93 94 95 96 98' 99 00 Reliable 20-acre property nr Libourne. Lightish wine from sandy soil.

la Pointe Pom r ★★→★★★ 89' 90' 94 95 96 97 98 99 00 Prominent 63-acre estate; wines recently plumper and more pleasing. LA SERRE is in same hands.

Pontac-Monplaisi Pessec-L r (w) ★★ 90 94 95 96 97 98' 99 00 Offers useful white and fragrant light red.

Pontet-Canet Pau r ★★★ 82' 85 86' 88 89' 90 93 94' 95 96' 97 98 99 00 182-acre neighbour to MOUTON-ROTHSCHILD. Dragged its feet for many yrs. Owners (same as LAFON-ROCHET) have done better since '86. Should make v fine wines, but hardness is an old problem. Vintages since 1994 promise better things. Second label: Les Hauts de Pontet.

Potensac Méd r ★★ 82' 85' 86 88 89' 90' **94 95** 96 **97** 98 99 00 Biggest and best-known CRU BOURGEOIS of N MEDOC. N'bouring Ch'x Lassalle, Gallais-Bellevue and super-second LEOVILLE-LAS-CASES all owned by Delon family. Class shows.

Pouget Mar r ★★ 82' 85 86 88 89 90 94 95 96 98' 99 00 27-acre fourth-growth attached to BOYD-CANTENAC. Similar wines. New CHAI '00.

Poujeaux (Theil) Moulis r ★★ 82' 85' 86 88' 89' 90' 93' 94' 95' 96' 97 98 99 00 Family-run CRU EXCEPTIONNEL of 120 acres with CHASSE-SPLEEN and MAUCAILLOU the high-point of Moulis. 20,000-odd cases of characterful tannic and concentrated wine for a long life, year after year. Second label: La Salle de Poujeaux. Also Ch Arnauld.

Prieuré-Lichine Cantenac-Mar r ★★★ 82' 83' 85 86' 88 89' **90'** 94' 95 96 97 98' 99 00 143-acre fourth-growth brought to the fore by the late Alexis Lichine, now owned by the Ballande Group and advised by Michel Rolland. Stéphane Derenoncourt winemaker – to watch. Fragrant MARGAUX currently on fair form. Second wine: Clairefont. A good Bordeaux Blanc, too.

Puy-Blanquet St-Em r ★★ 82' 85 86 88 89' 90' 94 95 96 98 99 00 A major property in St-Etienne-de-Lisse, E of ST-EMILION, with 50 acres.

Smaller Bordeaux châteaux to watch for:

The detailed list of ch'x on these pages is limited to the prestigious classified parts of the Bordeaux region. But this huge v'yd by the Atlantic works on many levels. Standard Bordeaux AC wine is claret at its most basic – but it is still recognizable. The areas and representative châteaux listed below are an important resource; they are potentially distinct and worthwhile variations on the claret theme to be investigated and enjoyed.

Bordeaux Supérieur Ch Mouton, Penin, Bouillerot, de Seguin, Trocard

Canon-Fronsac Chx Barrabaque, Cassagne-Haut-Canon (La Truffière), Croix Canon, La Fleur Caillou, Grand Renouil, Vrai Canon-Bouché, Vraye-Canon-Boyer

Côtes de Bourg Chx Bujan, Brûlesécaille, Falfas, Fougas, Guerry, Haut-Maco, Mercier, Nodoz, Roc de Cambes, Rousset, Tayac Cuvée Prestige

Côtes de Castillon Chx d'Aiguilhe, de Belcier, Cap de Faugères, Cantegrive, La Clarière-Laithwaite,Clos l'Eglise, Côte Montpezat, Lapeyronie, Peyrou Robin, Roque le Mayne, Ste-Colombe, Vieux Château Champs de Mars

Côtes de Francs Chx Les Charmes Godard, de Francs, Laclaverie, Lauriol, Marsau, La Prade, Puygueraud

Entre-Deux-Mers Chx de Fontenille, Launay, Moulin de Launay, Nardique la Gravière, Sainte-Marie, Tour de Mirambeau, Toutigeac, Turcaud

Fronsac Chx Dalem, Fontenil, Mayne-Vieil, Moulin-Haut-Laroque, La Rousselle, Tour du Moulin, Les Trois Croix, La Vieille Cure, Villars.

Lalande de Pomerol Chx Les Annereaux, La Croix-St-André, La Fleur de Boüard, Garraud Grand Ormeau, Haut Chaigneau, Les Hauts Conseillants aka Les Hauts-Tuileries, Sergant, de Viaud

Lussac St-Emilion Chx de la Grenière, Mayne-Blanc

Montagne St-Emilion Chx Calon, Faizeau, Maison Blanche, Roudier

Premières Côtes de Blaye Chx Bel Air la Royère, Bertinerie, Charron, Haut-Sociando, Jonqueyres, Loumède, Prieuré Malesan (formerly Pérenne), Roland-la-Garde, Segonzac, La Tonnelle, des Tourtes

Premières Côtes de Bordeaux Chx Carignan, Chelivette, Clos Ste-Anne, Fayau, Grand-Mouëys, Haux, du Juge, Jonchet, Lamothe de Haux, Pic, Plaisance, Puy Bardens, Reynon, Suau, Tanesse

Ste-Croix du Mont Chx Loubens, Lousteau-Vieil, du Mont, Pavillon, La Rame

Puygueraud Côtes de Francs r ★★ 88 **89'** 90 **95' 96 97'** 98 99 00 Leading château of this tiny AC. Wood-aged wines of surprising class. Château Laclaverie and Les Charmes-Godard follow the same lines. Same winemaker as CH PAVIE-MACQUIN (ST-EM).

Rabaud-Promis Saut w sw ★★→★★★ 83' 85 86' 87 **88' 89'** 90 94 95 96 97 98 99 01 74-acre classed-growth at Bommes. Since 1986 it has been near top rank. Rich stuff.

Rahoul Graves r w ★★ (r) 82 85 86 88 **89'** 90' 94 **95 96 97** 98' 99 00 37-acre vineyard at Portets is still a sleeper despite long record of good red (80%) and very good (Sémillon) white (**94 95 96 97** 98 99 00).

Ramage-la-Bâtisse H-Méd r ★★ 89' 90 **95** 96' **97** 98 99 00 Potentially outstanding CRU BOURGEOIS; 130 acres at ST-SAUVEUR, NORHT of PAUILLAC. Château Tourteran: second wine.

Rauzan-Gassies Mar r ★★ 88 89' 90' 95 96 98 99 00 75-acre second-growth neighbour of the next with little to report for two decades. But '96 could be the new leaf.

Rauzan-Ségla Mar r ★★★★ 70' 82 83' 85 86' 88' 89' 90' 94' 95 96 **97** 98 99 00 106-acre second-growth famous for its fragrance; a great MEDOC name back at the top. New owners in '94 (Chanel) have rebuilt the château and CHAIS. Second wine: Ségla. This should be the top second-growth of all. Ancient vintages can be superb and latest ones are splendid.

Raymond-Lafon Saut w sw ★★★ 75' 76 79 80' 82 83' 85 86' **88 89' 90' 95 96' 97** 98 99 (01) Serio
s little SAUTERNES estate (44 acres) owned by YQUEM ex-manager. Splendid wines for ageing. Ranks among the very top Sauternes.

Rayne Vigneau Saut w sw ★★★ 76' 83 85 86' 88' 89 90' 95 96 97 98 99 01 164-acre classed-growth at Bommes. V gd. Sweet wine and dry Rayne SEC.

Respide Médeville Graves w (r) ★★ (w) 90 **92' 93** 94 95' 96' 99 00 One of the better unclassified properties but current whites disappointing. Should be full-flavoured wines for ageing. (NB CUVEE Kauffman.) Drink the reds at 4–6 years – longer for the better vintages.

Reynon Premières Côtes r w ★★ 100 acres for fragrant white from old Sauv vines (VIEILLES VIGNES) (**98' 99** 00); also serious red (**88' 89** 90 94 95 **96 97** 98 99 00). Second wine (red): Ch Reynon-Peyrat. From '96 very good Ch Reynon Cadillac liquoreux, too. See also CLOS FLORIDÈNE.

Reysson Vertheuil (H-Méd) r ★★ 95 96 00 Recently replanted 120-acre CRU BOURGEOIS; same owners as GRAND-PUY-DUCASSE.

Ricaud Loupiac w sw (r dr) ★★ 95 96 97 99 Substantial grower of SAUTERNES-like age-worthy wine just across the river.

Rieussec Saut w sw ★★★★ 67 71' 75' 79 82 83' 85 86' 88' 89' 90' 95 96' 97' 98' 99 01 Worthy neighbour of CH D'YQUEM with 136 acres in Fargues, bought in '84 by the (LAFITE) Rothschilds. Vinified in oak since '96. Fabulous opulent wine. Also dry "R" and super-wine Crème de Tête.

Ripeau St-Em r ★★ 95 98 **99** 00 Steady GRAND CRU CLASSÉ with the right idea in the centre of the plateau. 40 acres.

de la Rivière Fronsac r ★★ 85' 86 88' 89 90 **94 95 96'** 97 98' 99 00 The biggest and most impressive FRONSAC property, with a Wagnerian castle and cellars. Formerly big tannic wines seem to have lightened recently.

de Rochemorin Pessac-L r (w) ★★→★★★ 89' 90' 93 94 95 96 97 98' 99 00 An important restoration at Martillac by the Lurtons of CH LA LOUVIERE: 165 acres of maturing vines. Oaky whites to keep 4–5 yrs.

Rol Valentin St-Em r ★★★ 95 96 97 98 **99** 00 New 10-acre estate going for modestly massive style (and price).

Rouet Fronsac r ★★ **90** 95 96 98 **99** 00 Well-made, full of life and fruit.

Rouget Pom r ★★ 85' 86 88 89' 90 **93 94 95 96** 97 98' **99** 00 Attractive old estate on the N edge of POMEROL. New owners are doing well. Track-record is for solid long-agers. To watch.

Royal St-Emilion Brand name of important, dynamic growers' coop. See Galius.

Ruat-Petit-Poujeaux Moulis r ★★ **95** 96 98 00 45-acre vineyard with local reputation for vigorous wine, keep for 5–6 years.

St-André-Corbin St-Em r ★★ **95 96 97** 98' **99** 00 54-acre estate in MONTAGNE- and ST-GEORGES-ST-EMILION: above-average wines.

St-Georges St-Georges-St-Em r ★★ 88' 89' 90' 94 95' 96' **97 98' 99** 00 Noble 18th-C château overlooking the ST-EMILION plateau from the hill to the north. 125 acres. Very good wine sold direct to the public.

St-Georges-Côte-Pavie St-Em r ★★ 82 85' **86** 88' 89' 90' **94 95** 96' **97'** 98' **99** 00 Perfectly placed little vineyard on the COTES. Run with dedication.

St-Pierre St-Jul r ★★★ 82' 85 86' 88' 89' 90' **93 94 95'** 96' **97** 98 99 00 Small (42-acre) fourth-growth. Very stylish and consistent classic ST-JULIEN.

de Sales Pom r ★★★ 82' 85 86 88 89' **90' 94 95 97** 98 00 Biggest v'yd of POMEROL (116 acres), attached to grandest château. Never poetry: recently below form. Second labels: ch'x Chantalouette, du Delias.

Sansonnet St-Em r ★★ **99** 00 17 acres ambitiously run in the new St-Em style (rich, fat) since 1999.

Saransot-Dupré Listrac r (w) ★★ **86 88 89** 90 95 96' **97** 98' 99 00 Small property performing well since 1986. Also one of LISTRAC's little band of whites.

Sénéjac H-Méd r (w) ★★ 82' 85 86' 88 89' 90' **94 95** 96 97 98 99 00 60-acre CRU BOURGEOIS in S MEDOC recently bought by the same family as CH TALBOT. Tannic reds to age and unusual all-Sém white, also to age (**93 94 95 96 97** 98 99 00). Second label: Artigue de Sénéjac.

la Serre St-Em r ★★ 82 85 86 **88'** 89 90 **94** 95 96 98 99 00 Small GRAND CRU, same owner as LA POINTE. Pleasant stylish wines.

St-Emilion: the class system

St-Emilion has its own class system, revised every ten years, the last in 1996. At the top are two Premiers Grands Crus Classés "A": Châteaux Ausone and Cheval Blanc. Then come 11 Premiers Grands Crus Classés "B". 55 châteaux were elected as Grands Crus Classés. To be considered for classification the ch'x must have obtained the AC St. Emilion Grand Cru certificate which is renewable every year.

Sigalas-Rabaud Saut w sw ★★★ 75 76' 80 82 83 85 86 88 89' **90' 95' 96'** 97' 98 99 01 The smaller part of the former RABAUD estate: 34 acres in Bommes run by CORDIER. At best very fragrant and lovely. Since '95 second wine: Le Cadet de Sigalas Rabaud.

Siran Labarde-Mar r ★★→★★★ 82' **83 85** 86 **88** 89' 90' **95** 96 **97** 98 99 (00) 77-acre property of passionate owner who resents lack of CLASSE rank. To follow for full-flavoured wines to age. Property is continually striving.

Smith-Haut-Lafitte Graves r (w p) ★★★ (red) 82' 85 86 89' 90' 94 95 96 97 98 99 00, (white) **93 94** 95 96 97 98 99' 00 Classed-growth at Martillac: 122 acres (14 acres white). Ambitious owners (since '90) continue to spend hugely to spectacular effect incl a luxurious wine therapy (external!) clinic. Second label: Les Hauts de Smith.

Sociando-Mallet H-Méd r ★★★ 82' 85' 86' 88' **89'** 90' **94** 95 96' **97** 98 99 00 Splendid, widely followed CRU GRAND BOURGEOIS at St-Seurin. 65 acres. Conservative big-boned wines to lay down for years. Second wine: Demoiselles de Sociando.

Soudars H-Méd r ★★ **86 89 90 94 95 96' 98** 99 00 Sister to COUFRAN; recent CRU BOURGEOIS doing pretty well.

Soutard St-Em r ★★★ **82' 85' 86 88' 89' 90'** 93 94 95 **96 97 98'** 99 00 Potentially excellent 48-acre classed-growth, 70% Merlot. Potent wines: long-lived for Anglo-Saxon drinking; exciting young to French palates. Forward-thinking viticultural practices. 2ⁿᵈ label: Clos de la Tonnelle.

Suduiraut Saut w sw ★★★★ 67 75 76' **78 79' 81** 82 83 **85 86 88'** 89' 90' 95 96 97 98 99 01 One of the best SAUTERNES, in its best vintages supremely luscious. 173 acres potentially are of top class. See Pichon-Longueville.

du Tailhas Pom r ★★ **89 90 94 95 96' 98' 99** 00 5,000 cases. POMEROL of the lighter kind, near FIGEAC.

Taillefer Pom r ★★ **82 85 86 88' 89 90** 94 95' **96 98' 99** 00 28-acres on the edge of POMEROL in the Bernard Moueix family (see also FONTMARTY).

Talbot St-Jul r (w) ★★★ **78' 82' 83' 85' 86' 88'** 89' 90 94 95 96' **97'** 98' 99 00 Important 240-acre fourth-growth, for many years younger sister to GRUAUD-LAROSE. Wine similarly attractive: rich, consummately charming, reliable; gd value. Very good second label: Connétable Talbot. White: "Caillou Blanc". Oenologist also oversees TOUR DE MONS.

Tayac Soussans-Mar r ★★ **95 96 98** 00 MARGAUX's biggest CRU BOURG. Reliable if not noteworthy.

de Terrefort-Quancard B'x r w ★ **98 99** 00 Huge producer of good-value wines at ST-ANDRE-DE-CUBZAC on the road to Paris. Very drinkable quality. 33,000 cases. Also Bordeaux Supérior: Ch Canada.

Terrey-Gros-Caillou St-Jul r ★★ **82' 86' 88 89 90 94 95 96 97** 98 99 00 Sister château to HORTEVIE; at best, equally noteworthy and stylish.

du Tertre Arsac-Mar r ★★★ **82' 83' 85 86 88' 89' 90' 94** 95 **96' 98'** 99 00 Fifth-growth isolated S of MARGAUX. History of undervalued fragrant and fruity wines. Since '97, same owner as CH GISCOURS. To watch. New techniques and investment '00 have produced a really conc'd wine.

Tertre Daugay St-Em r ★★★ 82' 83' 85 86 88' 89' 90' 94 95 96 **97** 98 **99** 00 Sml, spectacularly sited GRAND CRU. Currently being restored to gd order. Potent and stylish wines. Same owner as CH LA GAFFELIÈRE.

Tertre-Rôteboeuf St-Em r ★★★★ 85 86 **88' 89' 90' 93** 94 95 96 **97** 98' 99 (00) A cult star making concentrated, even dramatic, largely Merlot wine since '83. The prices are frightening. The "roast beef" of the name gives the right idea. Also COTE DE BOURG property, Roc de Cambes.

Thieuley E-Deux-Mers r p w ★★ Supplier of consistent quality red and white AC Bordeaux; fruity CLAIRET; oak-aged red and white cuvée Francis Courselle. Also owns Clos Ste-Anne in Premières Côtes de Bordeaux.

la Tour-Blanche Saut w (r) sw ★★★ 83' 85 **86 88' 89' 90'** 95 96 97 98 99 01 Historic leader of SAUTERNES, now a gov't wine college. Coasted in '70s; hit historic form again in '88.

La Tour-de-By Bégadan (Méd) r ★★ **82' 85' 86 88' 89' 90' 94 95'** 96' 98 99 00 V well-run 182-acre CRU BOURGEOIS in N MEDOC with a name for the most attractive sturdy wines of the area.

la Tour-Carnet St-Laurent (H-Méd) r ★★ **82 85 86 89'** 90 **94'** 95 **96 97** 98 99 00 4th-growth with medieval fortress, long neglected. More charming than exciting; slight upswing. 2nd wine: Sire de Comin.

la Tour Figeac St-Em r ★★ **82' 83 85 86 88 89'** 90 **94' 95** 96' **97'** 98' **99** 00 36-acre GRAND CRU CLASSE between CH FIGEAC, POMEROL. California-style ideas since '94. Keep an eye on this.

la Tour Haut Brion Graves r ★★★ 85 **88 89 90** 94 95 96' **97** 98' 99 00 Formerly second label of CH LA MISSION-HAUT-BRION. Up to '83, a plainer, v tannic wine. Now a separate 12-acre vineyard: wines stylish, to keep.

Tour Haut-Caussan Méd r ★★ **95 96 98** oo Ambitious 40-acre estate at Blaignan to watch for full firm wines.

Tour-du-Haut-Moulin Cussac (H-Méd) r ★★ **82' 85' 86' 88' 89' 90' 94 95** 96 98 99 (oo) Conservative grower: intense CRU BOURGEOIS to mature.

la Tour de Mons Soussans-Mar r ★★ **82' 83 85 86 88** 89 90' **94** 95 96' 98' 99 (oo) Famous CRU BOURGEOIS of 87 acres, 3 centuries in the same family. A long dull patch but new ('95) TALBOT-influence is returning to the old fragrant, vigorous, age-worthy style.

Tour-du-Pas-St-Georges St-Em r ★★ 86 88 **89 90 94** 95 **96 97** 98 **99** oo Wine from 40 acres of ST-GEORGES-ST-EMILION made by BELAIR winemaker.

la Tour-du-Pin-Figeac St-Emilion r ★★ 98 oo 26-acre GRAND CRU CLASSÉ worthy of restoration.

la Tour du Pin Figeac Moueix St-Em r ★★ 82 83 85 86 88' 89' 90' **94** 95 96 98 99 Another 26-acre section of the same old property, owned by the Armand Moueix family. Splendid site; should be powerful wines.

Tour-St-Bonnet Méd r ★★ 86 89' 90' **95 96 97** 98 99 oo Consistently well-made potent N MEDOC from St-Christoly. 100 acres.

Tournefeuille Lalande de Pom r ★★ **82' 83' 85 86 88 88** 89 90' **94 95' 96** 97 98' 99 oo Well-known Néac château. 43 acres; gd near-POMEROL. Also Ch de Bourg.

des Tours Mont-St-Em r ★★ 98 **99** oo Spectacular château – modern 170-acre vineyard. Sound, easy wine.

Tronquoy-Lalande St-Est r ★★ **82'** 85 86 88 89 90' **94 95** 96 **97** 98 99 oo 40-acre CRU BOURGEOIS: high-coloured wines to age, but no thrills. DOURTHE-distributed.

Troplong-Mondot St-Em r ★★★ 82' 83 85' 86 88' 89' 90' **94'** 95 96' **97** 98' **99** oo' 75 acres well-sited on the COTES above CH PAVIE. One of ST-EM's hottest things. Second wine: Mondot.

Trotanoy Pom r ★★★★ 61' 70' 71' 75' 81 82' 85' 88 89 90' 93 94 95 96 97 98' 99 oo Potentially the second POMEROL, after PETRUS, from the same stable. Only 27 acres; but at best (eg **82**) a glorious fleshy perfumed wine. Ten wobbly years since; now resurgence under J-P MOUEIX control.

Trottevieille St-Em r ★★★ 82' 85 86 89' **90 94** 95 96 98 99 oo GRAND CRU of 27 acres on the COTES. Dragged its feet for yrs. Same owners as BATAILLEY have raised their game.

le Tuquet Graves r w ★★ (r) **95 96'** 98' **99** oo (w) **93 94 95 96 97 98'** 99 oo Big estate at Beautiran. Light fruity red; the white is better. (CUVEE Spéciale oak-aged.)

de Valandraud St-Em r ★★★★ 92 **93 94** 95 96 97 98 99 oo Leader among "garagiste" micro-château fulfilling aspirations to glory. But silly prices for the sort of thick, vanilla-scented wine California can make. Vineyards expanded '98. Second and third wines available in even smaller quantities: Virginie and Axelle.

Valrose St-Est r ★★ A newcomer since '99, co-owned with CLINET. To watch.

Verdignan Méd r ★★ 86 89' **90 94 95' 96 97 98** 99 oo Substantial Bourgeois sister to CH COUFRAN. More Cabernet than Coufran. Second label: Ch Plantey de la Croix.

la Vieille Cure Fronsac r ★★ **94 95** 96 **97** 98 99 oo 50-acre property, US-owned, leading the commune.

Vieux-Château-Certan Pom r ★★★★ 78 79 81 82' 83' 85 86' 88' 89 90' 93 94 95' 96' 97 98' 99 oo Traditionally rated close to PETRUS in quality, but totally different in style; almost HAUT-BRION build. 34 acres. Same (Belgian) family owns LABEGORCE-ZEDE and tiny LE PIN.

Vieux Château St-André St-Em r ★★ 82' 85' 86 88' 89' 90' 93' 94' 95 97 98 99 oo Sml v'yd in MONTAGNE-ST-EM owned by winemaker of PETRUS. To follow. 2,500 cases.

Villegeorge Avensan (H-Méd) r ★★ 82 85 **86 88** 89 90 **94 95** 96' 97 98' 99 00 24-acre CRU BOURGEOIS north of MARGAUX. Enjoyable rather tannic wine. Sister-château: DUPLESSIS.

Villemaurine St-Em r ★★ **82' 85' 86** 88 89 90 95 96 **97** 98 99 00 Small GRAND CRU with splendid cellars well-sited on the COTES by the town. Firm wine with a high proportion of Cab. Also Chx du Cartillon, Timberlay.

Vray Croix de Gay Pom r ★★ **82' 85 86** 88 89 **90 95** 96 98 00 Very small but ideally situated vineyard in the best part of POMEROL. Could do a lot better.

Yon-Figeac St-Em r ★★ **85 86 88 89** 90 95 96 97 98 **99** 00 59-acre GRAND CRU for savoury supple wine at best.

d'Yquem Saut w sw (dr) ★★★★ **67' 70 71' 75'** 76' 79 80' **81' 83'** 85 86' **88'** 89' 90' 93 94 95' The world's most famous sweet-wine estate. 250 acres; only 500 bottles per acre of very strong intense, luscious wine, kept four years in barrel. Most vintages improve for 15 years[+]; some live 100 years[+] in transcendent splendour. Sadly, after centuries in the Lur-Saluces family, in 1998 they surrendered control to Bernard Arnault of LVMH (see Cheval Blanc). Also makes dry YGREC ("Y").

Vins de garage

The concept of "garage" wine started in B'dx as a joke; the name at least: production was so small that a garage was big enough to make it in. With small production went rarity; hence the chance of a high price. It is now stylistic. Garage wines are made with v small crops, preferably from old vines, and have the dark colour, thick texture, rich mouthfeel, and coffee/vanilla/chocolate flavours associated with toasted new oak. The current runners are massively concentrated in St-Emilion, where the stylistic change is becoming widely influential. Not all are over-priced. In **St Emilion** Andréas, Barde Haut, Clos Badon-Thunévin, Croix de Labrie, Clos St Martin, Le Fer, Ferrand-Lartigue, Magrez-Fombrauge, Gracia, Péby-Fombrauge, Quinault-l'Enclos, Rol Valentin; in **Pomerol** Beau Soleil; in **Graves** Branon; in **Margaux** Marojallia; in **Côtes de Castillon** Domaine de l'A; in **Premières Côtes de Blaye** Gigault-Cuvée Viva; in **Entre-Deux-Mers** Balestard.

Italy

More heavily shaded areas
are the wine growing regions

The following abbreviations
are used in the text:

Ab	Abruzzi	Pie	Piedmont
Ap	Apulia	Sar	Sardinia
Bas	Basilicata	Si	Sicily
Cal	Calabria	T-AA	Trentino-
Cam	Campania		Alto Adige
E-R	Emilia-Romagna	Tus	Tuscany
F-VG	Friuli-	Umb	Umbria
	Venezia Giulia	VdA	Valle d'Aosta
Lat	Latium	Ven	Veneto
Lig	Liguria		
Lom	Lombardy	fz	frizzante
Mar	Marches	pa	passito

VALLE
D'AOSTA

L Como

L Maggiore

Milan

Turin

PIEDMONT

LOMBAR

Genoa

PO

LIGURIA

Ligurian Sea

Wine is central to the Italian way of life. The vine is cultivated in almost every region and province and there are few Italians who are not linked in some way to viticulture and winemaking. Until recently in Italy, a meal without wine was virtually unthinkable.

Italy produces a massive 55 million hectolitres each year, making it, along with France, the dominant player on the world wine stage. Italians are now drinking less than they used to, but the wine they do drink is of higher quality. The long conflict in the national psyche between wine as a basic essential and as a pleasurable choice is resolving itself in favour of the latter. But tension remains, and nowhere so visibly as in the proliferation of wines with indecipherable names and few clear links to their *terroir*. Often of excellent quality and having a lasting impact on their region, they have generated constant complaint about the confusion they create.

The first Italian appellations (DOCs) were created in the 1960s. They were not designed to assure quality, simply to protect "tradition" – yields, varieties, viticulture, and ageing practices were absurdly proscriptive. Houses with greater ambition were forced to operate outside their appellations, thereby creating the parallel production system which exists to this day. If consumers are fazed when presented by the challenge of a very long list of names to memorize, there may be some consolation in the fact that never before have so many fantastic choices been available.

Italy's two most important regions, Piemonte and Tuscany, have long produced wines with unambiguous links to precise, easily identifiable zones. This is where the quality revolution began. Now it is spreading to other parts of the country: first to Soave and Friuli-Venezia Giulia, where an excessively technological approach had led to a dull standardization in white wines. But no longer. Central Italy – Umbria,

then the Marches – was next to feel the winds of change, as has Emilia-Romagna, once known only for its abundance. And perhaps the most encouraging sign of all in the 1990s has been the coming of quality and character to the south and the islands.

Italy, after a brief flirtation with international varieties, is also returning to its native grapes. They include many original, ancient, and individual kinds that have never, before the advent of modern winemaking, had the airing they deserve.

Recent Vintages in Tuscany

2001 A scorching August, unusually cool in early Sept, then humid when warm weather returned. Some excellent wines but much irregularity.

2000 Very hot, dry, late summer/early autumn, one of earliest vintages in memory. Full, alcoholic wines, impressive but not always balanced.

1999 Warm, dry August and September, early harvest, shaping up as an excellent vintage in all major zones.

1998 Excessively hot and dry in August, stressed vines, then early October rains. Very good along the coast, irregular elsewhere.

1997 Virtually perfect summer and the early autumn weather; rich, round, full wines, one of the outstanding vintages of the entire post-war period.

Recent Vintages in Piemonte

2001 Hot and dry in August, a damp early Sept. Classy and firm Nebbiolo and Barbera, less successful for other grapes.

2000 Very warm late August and September. Excellent Barolo, Barbaresco, Barbera. Fifth highly positive vintage in a row.

1999 Balanced and elegant Barbaresco and Barolo, Barbera more spotty due to irregular end-of-season weather, lovely Dolcetto.

1998 Very good whites, excellent reds. For Barolo and Barbaresco, third fine vintage in a row after difficulties in 91, 92, and 94.

1997 Hot, dry summer and early autumn. Superlative Barbera; rich, round, and alcoholic; very good Barolo and Barbaresco with unusually soft tannins. Less positive for whites and Dolcetto.

Abbazia Sant'Anastasia ★★→★★★ New Sicilian producer of excellent reds.

Abboccato Semi-sweet.

Aglianico del Vulture Bas DOC r dr (s/sw sp) ★★★ 90' 93' 94' 95 97' 98 99 00 01 Among the best wines of S Italy. Ages well to rich aromas. Called VECCHIO after three years, RISERVA after five years. Top growers: D'ANGELO (also makes very good pure Aglianico IGT Canneto), Elena Fucci, Torre degli Svevi, PATERNOSTER, Basilium, and Cantina del Notaio.

Alba Major wine city of PIEMONTE, on River Tanaro, SE of Turin.

Albana di Romagna E-R DOCG w dr s/sw (sp) ★★→★★★ DYA Italy's first DOCG for white wine, though it was hard to see why. Albana is the (undistinguished) grape. AMABILE is usually better than dry. ZERBINA's botrytis-sweet PASSITO (Scacco Matto) is outstanding.

Alcamo Si DOC w ★ Soft, neutral whites. Rapitalà is the best brand.

Aleatico Interesting red Muscat-flavoured grape for sweet, aromatic, often fortified wines, chiefly in the S Aleatico di Puglia DOC (best grower is CANDIDO) is better and more famous than Aleatico di Gradoli (Latium) DOC. ELBA makes a little. Try it where you find it.

Alessandria Gianfranco ★★★ Small producer of high-level ALBA wines at Monteforte d'Alba, esp BAROLO San Giovanni, BARBERA Vittoria, DOLCETTO.

Alezio Ap DOC p (r) ★★. Salento DOC especially for full, flavourful reds and delicate rosés. The top growers are Guiseppe Calò with fine, barrel-aged NEGROAMARO Portulan and Michele Calò with Negroamaro IGT Spano.

Allegrini ★★★ Top-quality Veronese producer; outstanding single-vineyard IGT wines (Palazzo della Torre, Grola, and Poja), AMARONE, and RECIOTO.

Altare, Elio ★★★ Small producer of good, very modern BAROLO. Look for Barolo Arborina, LANGHE DOC Larigi (Barbera), La Villa (NEBBIOLO-Barbera), VDT L'Insieme (native PIEMONTE grapes plus Cab).

Alto Adige T-AA DOC r p w dr sw sp ★→★★★ Alto Adige or SÜDTIROL DOC includes almost 50 types of wines: different grapes of different zones (incl varietals of VALLE ISARCO/EISACKTAL, TERLANO/TERLANER, Val Venosta/Vinschgau, AA STA MAGDALENA, AA Bozner Leiten, AA MERANESE DI COLLINA/Meraner).

Ama, Castello di, (Fattoria di Ama) ★★★→★★★★ One of the best, most consistent modern CHIANTI CLASSICO estates, near Gaiole. La Casuccia and Bellavista: top single-v'yd wines. Gd IGTS, CHARD, MERLOT (Vigna L'Apparita), PINOT N (Il Chiuso).

Amabile Means semi-sweet, but usually sweeter than ABBOCCATO.

Amaro Bitter. When prominent on label, contents are not wine but "bitters".

A Barole of honour
The classic style: Borgogno, Brovia, Cavallotto, Aldo Conterno, Giovanni Conterno, Paolo Conterno, Fontanafredda, Bruno Giacosa, Bartolo Mascarello, Giuseppe Mascarello, Massolino, Prunotto, Renato Ratti, Giuseppe Rinaldi, Vietti. A promising new generation: Gianfranco Alessandria, Altare, Boglietti, Cabutto, Cappellano, M Chiarlo, Elvio Cogno, Damilano, Conterno Fantino, Cordero di Montezemolo, Corino, Clerico, Ettore Germano, Elio Grasso, Silvio Grasso, Giovanni Manzone, Molino, Oberto, Parusso, Luigi Pira, Principiano, Rocche Costamagna, Rocche dei Manzoni, Revello, Sandrone, Scavino, Fratelli Seghesio, Vajra, Gianni Voerzio, Roberto Voerzio, and many others.

Amarone della Valpolicella (formerly Recioto della Valpolicella Amarone) Ven DOC r ★★★ 83' 85' 86 88' 90' 93 94 95' 97' 98' 00 Dry version of RECIOTO DELLA V: from air-dried VALPOLICELLA grapes; concentrated, long-lived, v impressive from: Stefano Accordini, Serègo Alegheri, Alighieri, ALLEGRINI, Begali, BERTANI, BOSCAINI, BRUNELLI, BUSSOLA, Campagnola, CS Valpolicella, DAL FORNO, Guerrieri-Rizzardi, LE SALETTE, MASI, Mazzi, Novaia, QUINTARELLI, LE RAGOSE Villa Monteleone, Speri, TEDESCHI, Trabucchi, Viviani, ZENATO.

Ambra, Fattoria di Top CARMIGNANO (Tusc) producer with two very good single-vineyard DOCG wines, Elzana and Vigne Alte.

Angelini, Tenimenti ★★→★★★ Owner of Val di Suga BRUNELLO estate in MONTALCINO, Tre Rose in MONTEPULCIANO, and San Leonino in CHIANTI CLASSICO.

Anselmi, Roberto ★★★ A leader in SOAVE with his single-vineyard Capitel Foscarino and exceptional sweet dessert RECIOTO i Capitelli, now both IGT.

Antinori, Marchesi L & P ★★→★★★★ V influential, long-est'd Florentine house of highest repute, owned by Piero A, sharing mng't with oenologist Renzo Cotarella. Famous for 1st-rate CHIANTI CLASSICO (esp, Tenute Marchese Antinori & Badia a Passignano), Umbrian (CASTELLO DELLA SALA) & PIEDMONT (PRUNOTTO) wines. Pioneer of new IGT, eg TIGNANELLO, SOLAIA (TOSCANA), CERVARO DELLA SALA (Umbria). Marchese Piero A was the "Voice of Italy" in wine circles in 70s & 80s. Expanding into S Tuscan MAREMMA, MONTEPULCIANO (La Braccesca), MONTALCINO, Pitigliano, in PIEDMONT, in ASTI (for BARBERA), in FRANCIACORTA (Lombardy) & in APULIA ("Vigneti del Sud"). Very good DOC BOLGHERI Guardo al Tasso (Cab-Merlot). See Prunotto.

Apulia Puglia. Italy's heel, producing almost a 6th of Italian wine, mostly bottled in N Italy/France. Region to follow in increasing quality/value. Best DOC: CASTEL DEL MONTE, MANDURIA (PRIMITIVO DI), SALICE SALENTO. Prods: ANTINORI, Botromagno, CANDIDO, Castel di Selva, Co-op Copertino, Co-op Due Palme, Conti Zecca, La Corte, D'Alfonso del Sordo, Fatalone, Felline, I Pástini, LEONE DE CASTRIS, Masseria Monaci, Masseria Pepe, Michele Calò, Pasquale Petrera, Pervini, RIVERA, Rubino, ROSA DEL GOLFO, Santa Lucia, Sinfarosa, TAURINO, Valle dell'Asso, VALLONE.

Aquileia F-VG DOC r w ★→★★ (r) 95 96 97 99' 00 12 single-grape wines from around the town of Aquileia. Gd REFOSCO, SAUVIGNON. Denis Montanara is one to watch.

Argiolas, Antonio ★★→★★★ Important SARDINIAN producer. High-level CANNONAU, NURAGUS, VERMENTINO, Bovale, and red IGT Turriga (★★★).

Arneis Pie w ★★ DYA Fairly gd white from BAROLO country: the revival of an ancient grape to make fragrant, light wine. DOC: ROERO Arneis, a zone N of ALBA, and LANGHE Arneis. Gd from Almondo, Ca' du Russ, Cascina Chicco, Correggia, Deltetto, BRUNO GIACOSA, Malvirà, Monchiero-Carbone, PRUNOTTO.

Assisi Umb r (w) ★→★★ DYA IGT ROSSO and BIANCO di Assisi: v attractive. Try cool.

Asti Major wine centre of PIEDMONT.

Asti (Spumante) Pie DOCG w sw sp ★→★★ NV Unfortunately, the big Asti houses are not remotely interested in making production of 80 million bottles better than routine. Despite its unique potential, Asti is a cheap, fairly proper product for supermarket shelves. Few producers care: WALTER BERA, Dogliotti-Caudrina, CASCINA FONDA, Vignaioli di Santo Stefano (see also Moscato d'Asti).

Avignonesi ★★★ Noble MONTEPULCIANO house; highly ambitious and v fine range: VINO NOBILE, blended red Grifi, CHARD, superlative VIN SANTO (★★★★).

Azienda agricola/agraria A farm producing crops, often incl wine.

Azienda/casa vinicola Wine firm using bought-in grapes and/or wines.

Azienda vitivinicola A (specialized) wine estate.

Badia a Coltibuono ★★★ Fine CHIANTI-maker in lovely old abbey at Gaiole with a restaurant and collection of old vintages. Best wine: IGT SANGIOVETO.

Badia di Morrona ★★→★★★ Nr Pisa (Tus). Gd CHIANTI, outstanding IGT N'Antia (Cab S-SANGIO), and IGT Vigna Alta (Sangio-Canaiolo).

Banfi (Castello or Villa) ★★★ Space-age CANTINA of biggest US importer of Italian wine. Huge plantings at MONTALCINO, mostly SANGIO; also Syrah, PINOT N, Cab S, CHARD, SAUV, etc: part of a drive for quality plus quantity. BRUNELLO gd but "Poggio all'Oro" is ★★★. Centine is ROSSO DI M. In PIEMONTE also produces gd Banfi Brut, GAVI, BRACCHETO D'ACQUI, PINOT GR. See also Eastern States US.

Barbaresco Pie DOCG r ★★→★★★★ 88' 89' 90' 93 95' 96' 97' 98' 99' 00 01 Neighbour of BAROLO; other great NEBBIOLO wine. Perhaps marginally less sturdy. At best palate-cleansing, deep, subtle, fine. At four years becomes RISERVA. Producers include Antichi PODERI di Gallina, Ca' del Baio, Piero Busso, Cascina Luisin, CERETTO, CIGLIUTI, Cortese, Fontanabianca, GAJA, BRUNO GIACOSA, MARCHESI DI GRESY, La Contea, MOCCAGATTA, Fiorenzo Nada, Giorgio Pelissero, Paitin, PIO CESARE, PRODUTTORI DEL B, PRUNOTTO, Roagna, Albino Rocca, BRUNO ROCCA, RIVETTI, Ronchi, Sottimano, Varaldo.

Barbatella, Cascina La ★★★ Top producer of BARBERA D'ASTI: excellent single-v'yard. VIGNA dell'Angelo and MONFERRATO Rosso Sonvico (Barbera-Cab).

Barbera d'Alba Pie DOC r ★★→★★★ 95' 96 97' 98' 99 00 01 Tasty, fragrant red. Best age up to 7 years. Many excellent wines, often from fine producers of BAROLO and BARBARESCO. Top producers: Gianfranco Alessandria, Almondo, Cascina Chicco, ALDO CONTERNO, Giovanni CONTERNO, Corino, Correggia, Ghisolfi, ELIO GRASSO, Silvio Grasso, MANZONE, Massolino, OBERTO, PARUSSO, Pelissero, Gianmatteo Pira, Principiano, PRUNOTTO, Rivetti, Albino Rocca, RouccHE Costamagna, SCAVINO, Vajra, VIETTI, ROBERTO VOERZIO.

Barbera d'Asti Pie DOC r ★★→★★★ 95' 96 97 98' 99 00 For real BARBERA-lovers: Barbera alone, tangy and appetizing, drunk young or aged up to 7–10 years or longer. Top growers: LA BARBATELLA, BAVA, BERA, Berta, BERTELLI, Alfiero Boffa, BRAIDA, Brema, Cantina Sociale Vinchio e Vaglio, MICHELE CHIARLO, Contratto, COPPO, HASTAE, Hohler, La Lune del Rospo, L'Arbiola, La Tenaglia, Marchesi Alfieri, Martinetti, La Morandina, PRUNOTTO, RIVETTI, Scrimaglio, Scagliola, VIETTI.

Barbera del Monferrato Pie DOC r ★→★★ DYA Easy-drinking Barbera from Alessandria and ASTI. Pleasant, slightly fizzy, sometimes sweetish. Delimited area is almost identical to BARBERA D'ASTI but style is simpler, less ambitious.

Barco Reale Tus DOC r ★★ 97 98 99 00 DOC for junior wine of CARMIGNANO; using the same grapes.

Bardolino Ven DOC r (p) ★→★★ DYA Pale, summery, sl bitter red from E shore of Lake Garda. Bardolino CHIARETTO: paler and lighter. Top makers: Cavalchina, Guerrieri-Rizzardi, MONTRESOR, Le Vigne di San Pietro, ZENATO, Zeni.

Barolo Pie DOCG r ★★★→★★★★ 88' 89' 90' 93' 95' 96' 97' 98' 99' 00 01 Sml area S of ALBA with one of Italy's supreme reds: rich, tannic, alcoholic (min 13%), dry but wonderfully deep and fragrant (also crisp and clean) in the mouth. From NEBBIOLO grapes. Ages for up to 20–25 yrs (RISERVA after 5).

Barolo Chinato A dessert wine made from BAROLO DOCG, alcohol, sugar, herbs, spices, and Peruvian bark. Producers: Guilio Cocchi, Cappellano.

Basciano ★★ Producer of good DOCG CHIANTI RUFINA and IGT wines.

Bava ★★→★★★ Producer of very good BARBERA D'ASTI Stradivarius, MONFERRATO BIANCO, BAROLO CHINATO; the Bava family controls the old firm Guilio Cocchi in Asti where they produce good sparkling METODO CLASSICO.

Bellavista ★★★ FRANCIACORTA estate with brisk SPUMANTE (Gran Cuvée Franciacorta is top). Also Satèn (a crémant-style sparkler). Terre di Franciacorta DOC and Sebino IGT Solesine (both Cab-MERLOT blends).

Bera, Walter ★★→★★★ Small estate nr BARBARESCO. V gd MOSCATO D'ASTI, ASTI, BARBERA D'ASTI, and LANGHE NEBBIOLO .

Berlucchi, Guido Italy's biggest producer of sparkling METODO CLASSICO.

Bersano Historic wine house in Nizza MONFERRATO with most of the PIEMONTE DOC wines incl BAROLO, BARBARESCO, BARBERA D'ASTI, sp MOSCATO.

Bertani ★★→★★★ Well-known, good-quality wines from VERONA, especially old-style AMARONE.

Bertelli ★★★ Superb wines from a family of medical researchers near ASTI, especially BARBERA D'ASTI, CHARD, Cabernet; very interesting experiments with SAUVIGNON, Sémillon, Syrah, Marsanne-Roussanne.

Bianco White.

Bianco di Custoza Ven DOC w (sp) ★→★★ DYA Twin of SOAVE from VERONA'S other side (W). Corte Sant'Arcadio, Le Tende, Le VIGNE di San Pietro, MONTRESOR all good.

Bianco di Pitigliano Tus DOC w ★ DYA A dry white from extreme S of TOSCANA.

Biondi-Santi ★★★★ The original producer of BRUNELLO DI MONTALCINO, from 45-acre Il Greppo estate. Absurd prices, but occasional old vintages are v fine.

Boca Pie DOC r ★★ 90' 91' **95 96' 97'** 98' 99 00 Another NEBBIOLO from N of PIEMONTE. Look for Poderi ai Valloni (Vigneto Cristiana ★★★).

Boccadigabbia ★★★ Top Marche producer of IGT wines: SANGIO, Cab, PINOT N, CHARD. Proprietor Elvidio Alessandri also owns fine Villamagna estate in Rosso Piceno DOC.

Bolgheri Tus DOC r p w (sw) ★★→★★★★ On the coast S of Livorno. Incl 7 types of wine: BIANCO, VERMENTINO, SAUVIGNON BLANC, ROSSO, ROSATO, VIN SANTO and Occhio di Pernice, plus top IGTS. Newish DOC Bolgheri Rosso: Cab-MERLOT-SANGIO blend. Top producers: Caccia al Piano: DOC Levia Gravia; Giovanni Chiapinni: DOC Guado de Gemoli; Enrico Santini: DOC Montepergoli; Le Macchiole: DOC Paleo, TOSCANA IGTS Scrio (Syrah), Messorio (MERLOT); ORNELLAIA: DOC Ornellaia, Toscana IGT Masseto (Merlot); SAN GUIDO: DOC SASSICAIA; ANTINORI: DOC Guado al Tasso; Meletti-Cavallari: DOC Grattamacco; Michele Satta: DOC Piastraia, Toscana IGT VIGNA al Cavaliere (SANGIO). Much new investment and forthcoming wines from GAJA and Ambrogio Folonari.

Bolla ★★ Famous VERONA firm for VALPOLICELLA, AMARONE, SOAVE, etc. Top wines: Castellaro, Creso (red and white), Jago. And RECIOTO.

Bonarda Minor red grape (alias Croatina) widely grown in PIEDMONT, Lombardy, Emilia-Romagna, and blended with BARBERA.

Bonarda Lom DOC r ★★ **95 97** 98 00 Soft, fresh FRIZZANTE from S of Pavia.

Borgo del Tiglio ★★★ FRIULI estate for one of NE Italy's top MERLOTS, ROSSO della Centa; also superior COLLIO CHARD, TOCAI, and BIANCO.

Boscaini Ven ★★ VERONA producer of VALPOLICELLA, AMARONE, SOAVE.

Boscarelli, Poderi ★★★ Small estate with very good VINO NOBILE DI MONTEPULCIANO, barrel-aged IGT Boscarelli, and good ROSSO DI M.

Brachetto d'Acqui Pie DOCG r sw (sp) ★★ DYA Sweet, sparkling red with enticing Muscat scent. Can be much better than it sounds. Or dire.

Braida ★★★ The late Giacomo Bologna's estate; for top BARBERA D'ASTI (BRICCO dell'Uccellone, Bricco della Bigotta, Ai Suma).

Bramaterra Pie DOC r ★★ 95' 96 97' 98' 99' 00 01 Neighbour to GATTINARA. NEBBIOLO grapes predominate in a blend. Good producer: SELLA.

Breganze Ven DOC ★→★★★ (r) 95' 96 97' 98 00 01 Catch-all for many varieties nr Vicenza. Cab and CHARD are best. Top producers: MACULAN, Miotti, Zonta.

Bricco Term for a hilltop (and by implication very good) vineyard in PIEMONTE.

Brindisi Ap DOC r ★★ 94 95 97 99 00 Strong NEGROAMARO, especially from Vallone, Due Palme.

Brolio, Castello di ★★→★★★ After a sad period under foreign ownership, the RICASOLI family has taken this legendary 900-yr-old estate in hand again. Results are heartening. Very good CHIANTI CLASSICO & IGT Casalferro (SANGIOVESE-Cab-MERLOT).

Brunelli ★★→★★★ Vg quality of AMARONE and RECIOTO.

Brunello di Montalcino Tus DOCG r ★★★→★★★★★ 88' 90' 93 95' 97' With BAROLO, Italy's most celebrated red: strong, full-bodied, high-flavoured, tannic, and long-lived. Four years' ageing; after five becomes RISERVA. Quality ever-improving. Montalcino is 25 miles S of Siena.

> **Brunello di Montalcino to buy**
>
> Altesino, Argiano, Banfi, Barbi, Biondi-Santi, Campogiovanni, Canalicchio di Sopra, Caparzo, Casanova di Neri, Case Basse, Castelgiocondo, Castella di Argiano, Cerbaiona, Col d'Orcia, Costanti, Eredi Fuligni, Fanti-San Filippo, Gorelli, La Campana, La Fuga, La Gerla, Lambardi, La Serena, Lisini, Marroneto, Mastrojanni, Siro Pacenti, Franco Pacenti, Ciacci Piccolomini, Pieve di Santa Restituta, La Poderina, Poggio Antico, Poggione, Salvioni-Cerbaiola, Scopetone, Sesta, Talenti, Tiezzi, La Rasina, La Torre, Valdicava, and Vitanza.

Bussola, Tommaso ★★★ Emerging leading prod of AMARONE & RECIOTO in VALPOLICELLA.

Ca' dei Frati ★★→★★★ One of best producers of DOC LUGANA: and v gd, dry w IGT Pratto (Sauv Bl/CHARD), sw Tre Filer, and r IGT Ronchedone (Cab-MERL).

Ca' del Bosco ★★★ FRANCIACORTA estate; some of Italy's best sparklers (outstanding DOCG Annamaria Clementi ★★★★), vg CHARD, and excellent reds: a Cab blend (Maurizio Zanella), PINOT N (Pinèro).

Cacchiano, Castello di ★★★ First-rate CHIANTI CLASSICO estate at Gaiole, owned by Barone Giovanni RICASOLI-Firidolfi, cousin of the Brolio Ricasolis.

Cafaggio, Villa ★★★ Very reliable CHIANTI CLASSICO estate with excellent IGTS San Martino (SANGIO) and Cortaccio (Cab).

Calatrasi SI ★★→★★★ Good producer of r and w IGT labels, esp D'Istinto line of better wines (Syrah, Nero d'Avola, SANGIO-MERLOT, Magnifico red blend).

Caldaro (Lago di Caldaro) T-AA DOC r ★ DYA Alias KALTERERSEE. Light, soft, bitter-almond red from SCHIAVA grapes. From a huge area. CLASSICO from a smaller area is better.

Candido, F ★★★ Top grower of Salento, APULIA; gd reds: Duca d'Aragona, Cappello i Prete, SALICE SALENTINO; also gd dessert wine: ALEATICO DI PUGLIA.

Cannonau di Sardegna Sar DOC r (p) dr s/sw ★★ 95 96 97 98 99 00 01 Cannonau (Grenache) is S's basic red grape. Ranges from v potent to fine and mellow: ARGIOLAS, CS di Jerzu, Giuseppe Gabbas, SELLA & MOSCA.

Cantalupo, Antichi Vigneti di ★★→★★★ Top GHEMME wines – especially single-vineyard Breclemae and Carellae.

Cantina Cellar or winery.

Cantina Sociale (CS) Growers' cooperative.

Capannelle ★★★ Gd producer of IGT (formerly CHIANTI CLASSICO), nr Gaiole.

Capezzana, Tenuta di (or Villa) ★★★ The TUSCAN estate (W of Florence) of the Contini Bonacossi family. Gd CHIANTI Montalbano, excellent CARMIGNANO (esp Villa Capezzagna, Villa Tefiano). Also vg B'dx-style red, Ghiaie Della Furba.

Capichera ★★★ No 1 producer of VERMENTINO DI GALLURA, esp VENDEMMIA Tardiva.

Caprai ★★★ Widely copied, superb DOCG SAGRANTINO, very good DOC ROSSO DI MONTEFALCO. Highly rated.

Capri Cam DOC r p w ★→★★ Legendary island with widely abused name. Only interesting wines are from La Caprense.

Cartizze Famous, frequently too expensive, and too sweet DOC PROSECCO of top sub-zone of Valdobbiadene.

Carema Pie DOC r ★★→★★★ 89' 90' 91 93 **95** 96' 97' 98 99' 00 01 Old speciality of N PIEDMONT. Best from Luigi Ferrando (or the CANTINA SOCIALE).

Carignano del Sulcis Sar DOC r p ★★→★★★ 90 91 93 **94 95 96 97** 98 99 00 01 Well-structured, age-worthy red. Best are Terre Brune and Rocca Rubia from CANTINA SOCIALE di SANTADI.

Carmignano Tus DOCG r ★★★ 90' 92' 93 **94 95 96** 97' 98 99' 00 01 Region W of Florence. CHIANTI grapes plus 15% Cab S makes distinctive, reliable, even excellent rs. Best incl AMBRA, CAPEZZANA, Farnete, La Piaggia, Lo Locco.

Carpenè Malvolti Leading producer of classic PROSECCO and other sp wines at Conegliano, Veneto. Seen everywhere in Venice.

Carso F-VG DOC r w ★★→★★★ (r) 90 91' 93 **94 97'** 99' 00 01 DOC nr Trieste incl good MALVASIA. Terrano del C is a REFOSCO red. Top grower: EDI KANTE.

Casa fondata nel... Firm founded in...

Casanova di Neri ★★★ BRUNELLO DI MONTALCINO (and vg ROSSO DI M) from Neri family.

Cascina Fonda ★★★ Brothers Marco & Massimo Barbero have risen to top in MOSCATO D'ASTI DOC: look for VENDEMMIA Tardiva & METODO CLASSICO ASTI SPUMANTE.

Case Basse ★★★★ Pace-setter at MONTALCINO with sublime BRUNELLO and single-vineyard Brunello Intistieti.

Castel del Monte Ap DOC r p w ★★→★★★ (r) 93' 94 **95 96** 97' 98 99 00 01 Dry, fresh, well-balanced southern wines. The red is RISERVA after 3 yrs. Rosé most widely known. RIVERA'S Il Falcone and Santa Lucia Riserva outstanding.

Castelgiocondo ★★★ FRESCOBALDI estate in MONTALCINO: very good BRUNELLO and IGT MERLOT Lamaïone.

Castell' in Villa ★★★ Very good CHIANTI CLASSICO estate. Also VIN SANTO.

Castellare ★★→★★★ Small but admired CHIANTI CLASSICO producer. First-rate SANGIO IGT I Sodi di San Niccoló and sprightly GOVERNO di Castellare: old-style CHIANTI updated. Also CHARD and Cab.

Castello Castle. (See under name: eg Albola, Castello d'.)

Castello della Sala See Antinori.

Castello di Albola See Zonin.

Castelluccio ★★→★★★ Pioneering producer of quality SANGIO of Romagna: IGT RONCO dei Ciliegi and Ronco della Simia.

Caudrina-Dogliotti Romano ★★★ Top MOSCATO D'ASTI: La Galeisa and Caudrina.

Cavalleri ★★★ Vg reliable FRANCIACORTA producer. Esp sparkling.

Cavicchioli Large Emilia-Romagna producer of LAMBRUSCO and other sparkling: Lambrusco di Sorbara Vigna del Cristo is best. Also TERRE DI FRANCIACORTA.

Ca'Vit (Cantina Viticoltori) Group of quality co-ops nr Trento. Wines incl MARZEMINO, Cab, PINOTS N, BL, GR, NOSIOLA. Top wines: Brune di Monte (r & w) & sp Graal.

Cecchi Large-scale producer and bottler of TUSCAN wines.

Cerasuolo Ab DOC p ★★ The ROSATO version of MONTEPULCIANO D'ABRUZZO.

Cerasuolo di Vittoria Si DOC p ★★★ **97 98** 99 oo Garnet, full-bodied, aromatic (Frappato and Nero d'Avola grapes); can be interesting, esp from Valle dell'Acate and COS.

Ceretto ★★★ Very good grower of BARBARESCO (BRICCO Asili), BAROLO (Bricco Rocche, Brunate, Prapò), LANGHE Rosso Monsordo, CHARD (La Bernardina), and ARNEIS. Also vg METODO CLASSICO SPUMANTE La Bernardina.

Cervaro See Castello della Sala.

Chardonnay Permitted for several northern DOCS (eg T-AA, FRANCIACORTA, F-VG, PIEDMONT). Some of the best (eg from ANTINORI, CAPANNELLE, BOCCADIGABBIA, and REGALEALI) are still only IGT. Now being tried almost everywhere.

Chianti Tus DOCG r ★→★★★ **95' 97'** 99' oo o1 Chianti Annata DYA The lively local wine of Florence and Siena. At best fresh, fruity, and tangy. Of the subdistricts, RUFINA (★★→★★★) and COLLI Fiorentini (★→★★★) can make CLASSICO-style RISERVAS. Montalbano, COLLI Senesi, Aretini, and Pisani: lighter wines. New subdistrict since 97 is Chianti Montespertoli; wines similar to Colli Fiorentini.

Chianti Classico Tus DOCG r ★★→★★★★ 95' **97'** 99' oo o1 (Riserva and single-v'yd) **88' 90' 93 95 97'** 99 oo Senior CHIANTI from central area. Its old, pale style is now rarer as top estates opt for darker, richer, firmer wines. Some are among the best wines of Italy, but too much Cabernet can spoil the style. Members of the CONSORZIO use the badge of a black rooster, but not all top firms belong.

Chiarlo, Michele ★★→★★★ Good PIEDMONT producer. (BAROLOS Cerequio and Cannubi, BARBERA D'ASTI, LANGHE, and MONFERRATO Rosso). Also BARBARESCO.

Chiaretto Rosé (the word means "claret") produced esp around Lake Garda. See Bardolino, Riviera del Garda.

Chionetti ★★→★★★ Makes top DOLCETTO di Dogliani (look for Briccolero).

Cigliuti, Renato ★★★ Small, high-quality estate for BARBARESCO and BARBERA D'ALBA.

Cinqueterre Lig DOC w dr sw pa ★★ Fragrant, fruity white from precipitous coast nr La Spezia. PASSITO is known as SCIACCHETRA (★★→★★★). Good from De Batte, Co-op Agricola di Cinqueterre, Forlini & Cappellini.

Cinzano Major Vermouth co also known for its ASTI. Now owned by Campari.

Who makes really good Chianti Classico?
AMA, ANTINORI, Castello di Brolio, Cacchiano, Carobbio, Casa Emma, Casale dello Sparviero, Casaloste, Castel Ruggero, CASTELLARE, CASTELL'IN VILLA, Le Cinciole, Collelungo, Colombaio di Cencio, COLTIBUONO, Le Corti, Felsina, Le Filigare, FONTERUTOLI, FONTODI, ISOLE E OLENA, LILLIANO, La Massa, Le Masse di San Leolino, Monsanto, Giovanna Morganti, Nittardi, Palazzino, Paneretta, Petroio-Lenzi, Poggerino, Poggiolino, Poggio al Sole, Querceto, Querciabella, Rampolla, Riecine, Rocca di Montegrossi, Rodano, San Felice, San Giusto, Valtellina, Vecchie Terre di Montefili, Verrazzano, Villa Cafaggio, Volpaia.

Cirò Cal DOC r (p w) ★→★★★ 93 **94' 95 96** 97 98 99 oo o1 V strong r from Gaglioppo grapes; light, fruity w (DYA). Best: LIBRANDI (Duca San Felice ★★★), San Francesco (Donna Madda, RONCO dei Quattroventi), Caparra & Siciliani.

CIV & CIV ★ Large co-op: over 8o million bottles, mainly Lambrusco of fair quality.

Classico Term for wines from a restricted area within the limits of a DOC. By implication, and often in practice, the best of the district. Applied to sparkling wines it denotes the classic method (as for Champagne).

Clerico, Domenico ★★★ Constantly evolving PIEDMONT wines; the aim is for international flavour. Especially good for BAROLO.

Col d'Orcia ★★★ Top MONTALCINO estate; interesting IGTS. Best wine: BRUNELLO.

Colli Hills. Occurs in many wine names.

Colli Berici Ven DOC r p w ★★ **95 97** 99 00 01 Hills S of Vicenza. Cab: best wine. Top producer: Villa Dal Ferro.

Colli Bolognesi E-R DOC r w ★★SW of Bologna, 8 wines, 5 varieties. TERRE ROSSE: the pioneer, now joined by Bonzara (★★★), Santarosa, Vallona.

Colli del Trasimeno Um DOC r w ★→★★★ (r) **97 98** 99' 00 01 Lively white wines from near Perugia, but now more important reds as well. Best: Duca della Corgna, La Fioraia, Marella, Pieve del Vescovo.

Colli Euganei Ven DOC r w dr s/sw (sp) ★→★★★ DYA DOC SW of Padua for 7 wines. Adequate r; w, sp soft, pleasant. Best producers: Vignalta, Ca' Lustra.

Colli Orientali del Friuli F-VG DOC r w dr sw ★★→★★★★ (r) **94 95 97** 99' 00 01 Hills E of Udine. 20 wines (18 named after their grapes). Both w and r can be vg. Top growers: Castello di Buttrio, DORIGO, Dri, Fiore dei Liberi, Le Due Terre, Le Viarte, LE VIGNE DI ZAMÒ, LIVIO FELLUGA, Meroi, Miani, Moschioni, Rosa Bosco, Rocca Bernarda, Ronchi di Manzano, Ronchi di Cialla, RONCO DEL GNEMIZ, SCHIOPETTO, Scubla, Specogna, Torre Rosazzo, Volpe Pasini, WALTER FILIPUTTI, Zof.

Colli Piacentini E-R DOC r p w ★→★★ DYA DOC incl traditional GUTTURNIO and Monterosso Val d'Arda among 11 types grown S of Piacenza. Good, fizzy MALVASIA. Most wines FRIZZANTE. New French and local reds: La Stoppa, La Tosa, Montesissa, Mossi, Romagnoli, Solenghi.

Colline Novaresi Pie DOC r w ★→★★ DYA New DOC for old region in Novara province. 7 different wines: BIANCO, ROSSO, NEBBIOLO, BONARDA, Vespolina, Croatina, and BARBERA. Incl declassified BOCA, GHEMME, FARA, and SIZZANO.

Collio F-VG DOC r w ★★→★★★★ **97 98** 99' 00 01 19 wines, 17 named after their grapes, nr Slovenian border. Vg whites, esp SAUV, PINOTS B and GR from: BORGO DEL TIGLIO, CASTELLO di Spessa, Damijan, Edi Keber, MARCO FELLUGA, Fiegl, GRAVNER, La Castellada, LIVON, Primosic, Princic, Renato Keber, RONCO dei Tassi, RUSSIZ SUPERIORE, SCHIOPETTO, Aldo Polencic. Tercic, Terpin, Venica & Venica, VILLA RUSSIZ.

Colterenzio CS (or Schreckbichl) T-AA ★★→★★★ No 1 ALTO ADIGE cooperative. Look for Cornell line of selections (CHARD, Gewürz, LAGREIN, PINOT NOIR. Schwarzhaus), Lafoa Cab S and Sauv Bl, Cornelius red and white blends.

Consorzio In Italy there are 2 types of association recognized by wine law. One is dedicated to the observance of DOC regulations (eg Consorzio Tutela del CHIANTI CLASSICO). The 2nd is to promote the wines of their members (eg Consorzio del Marchio Storico di Chianti Classico, previously Gallo Nero).

Conterno, Aldo ★★★★ Legendary grower of BAROLO, etc, at Monforte d'Alba. Good CHARD Printanier and Bussia d'Oro, BARBERA D'ASTI Conca Tre Pile. Best BAROLOS: Gran Bussia, Cicala, and Colonello. Barrel-aged NEBBIOLO VDT Favot vg.

Conterno, Giacomo ★★★★ Top grower of BAROLO, etc, at Monforte d'Alba. Monfortino BAROLO is long-aged, rare, outstanding.

Conterno-Fantino ★★★ 2 young families for vg BAROLO, etc, at Monforte d'Alba.

Contini, Attilio ★→★★★ Famous producer of VERNACCIA DI ORISTANO; best is vintge blend "Antico Gregori".

Contratto ★★ At Canelli (owned by GRAPPA-producing family Bocchino), produces very good BARBERA D'ASTI, SPUMANTE, ASTI (De Miranda), MOSCATO D'ASTI.

Copertino Ap DOC r (p) ★★ **95 97** 99 00 01 Savoury, age-able, strong red of NEGROAMARO from the heel of Italy. Look for CANTINA SOCIALE'S RISERVA and Masseria Monaci.

Coppo ★★ ⋅★★★ Ambitious producers of BARBERA D'ASTI (eg "Pomorosso").

Cordero di Montezemolo-Monfalletto ★★→★★★ Historic maker of gd BAROLO.

Cortese di Gavi See Gavi. (Cortese is the grape.)

Corzano & Paterno, Fattoria di ★★★ Dynamic CHIANTI COLLI Fiorentini estate. Very good RISERVA, red IGT Corzano, and outstanding VIN SANTO.

COS ★★★ Small estate: 3 friends making top Sicilian wines.

D'Ambra ★★ Top producer of ISCHIA wines, especially red Dedicato a Mario D'Ambra, w IGT Frassitelli, and Piellero.

D'Angelo ★★→★★★ Leading prod of admirable DOC AGLIANICO DEL VULTURE. Barrel-aged AGLIANICO IGT Canneto, Aglianico-MERLOT IGT Serra delle Querce also vg.

Dal Forno, Romano ★★★★ Very high-quality VALPOLICELLA, AMARONE, and RECIOTO from perfectionist grower, bottling only best: 14,000 bottles from 20 acres.

Darmagi Pie r ★★★★ 85 88 89 **93 95** 96 97 98 99 00 01 Cabernet S from GAJA in BARBARESCO is one of PIEMONTE'S most discussed (and expensive) reds. Born as a VDT, now DOC LANGHE.

Decugnano dei Barbi ★★ Good ORVIETO estate with an ABBOCCATO known as "Pourriture Noble", and a good red IGT.

Del Cerro, Fattoria ★★★ Estate with vg DOCG VINO NOBILE DI MONTEPULCIANO (especially RISERVA and Antica Chiusina, red IGTS Manero (SANGIO) and Poggio Golo (MERLOT). Controlled by insurance co SAI. Also owns: La Poderina (BRUNELLO DI MONTALCINO), Colpetrone (MONTEFALCO SAGRANTINO).

Denominazione di Origine Controllata (DOC) Means much the same as Appellation d'Origine Contrôlée (qv France).

Denominazione di Origine Controllata e Garantita (DOCG) Like DOC but with an official "guarantee" of origin shown by an officially numbered neck-label on the bottle indicating limited production.

Di Majo Norante ★★→★★★ Lone star of Molise south of Abruzzo with vg Biferno ROSSO DOC (esp Don Luigi), IGT AGLIANICO, and white IGT blends of Falanghina-Fiano, Falanghina-Greco.

DOC, DOCG See Denominazione di Origine Controllata (e Garantita).

Dogliotti Romano See Caudrina.

Dolce Sweet.

Dolceacqua See Rossese di Dolceacqua.

Dolcetto ★→★★★ PIEMONTE'S earliest-ripening grape, for very attractive everyday wines: dry, youthful, fruity, and fresh with deep-purple colour. Gives its name to several DOCS: D d'Acqui, D d'Asti, D delle Langhe Monregalesi (look for Barome Ricatti), D di Diano d'Alba (also Diano DOC), esp Alari and Bricco Maiolica. D di Dogliani (esp from CHIONETTI, San Fereolo, San Romano, Poderi Luigi Einaudi, Pecchenino, M & E Abbona, Gillardi), and D di Ovada (best from La Guardia, Rossi Contini). D d'Alba: ALESSANDRIA, ALTARE, AZELIA, Baudana, Brovia, Cabutto, Ca' Viola, CLERICO, ALDO CONTERNO, CONTERNO-FANTINO, Corino, Gastaldi, Germano, GRESY, MANZONE, GIUSEPPE MASCARELLO, Massolino, Mossio, OBERTO, Luigi Pira, Gianmatteo Pira, PRUNOTTO, Rocche Costamanga, Sandrone, SCAVINO, Schiavenza, Fratelli Seghesio, VAJRA, ROBERTO VOERIO.

Donnafugata Si r w ★★→★★★ Zesty Sicilian whites (best from VIGNA di Gabri). Also solid, improving reds, especially Tancredi and IGT Mille e Una Notte. Was VDT, now in DOC Contessa Entellina.

Dorigo, Girolamo ★★→★★★ G COLLI ORIENTALI producer for white Ronc di Juri VDT, CHARDONNAY, dessert PICOLIT, red Pignolo (★★★), REFOSCO, Schioppettino, and Monsclapade (Cab-MERLOT).

Duca Enrico See Duca di Salaparuta.

Duca di Salaparuta ★★ (Elsewhere in Aka) Vini Corvo. Popular Sicilian wines. Sound, dry reds; pleasant, soft whites. Excellent Duca Enrico (★★★) is one of Sicily's best reds. Valguarnera is premium oak-aged white.

Elba Tus r w (sp) ★→★★ DYA The island's white is very drinkable with fish. Try Acquabona. Napoléon in exile here loved the sweet red ALEATICO. Me too.

Enoteca Wine library; also wine shop or restaurant with extensive wine list. There are many, the impressive original being the Enoteca Italiana of Siena. Also used for wine shops or restaurants.

Eredi Fulighi ★★★ Vg producer of BRUNELLO and ROSSO DI MONTALCINO.

Est! Est!! Est!!! Lat DOC w dr s/sw ★ DYA Unextraordinary white from Montefiascone, N of Rome. Trades on its oddball name. See FALESCO.

Etna Si DOC r p w ★★ (r) 93 94 **95 96 97** 98 99 00 Wine from volcanic slopes. Good producers: Benanti, Cambria, Bonaccorsi.

Falchini ★★★ Producer of good DOCG VERNACCIA DI SAN GIMIGNANO and some of the best reds of the area, eg VDT Campora (★★★) and BIANCO Selva d' Oro.

Falerno del Massico ★★→★★★ Cam DOC r w ★★ (r) 90 93 **94 95 97'** 98 99 00 As in Falernum, the best-known wine of ancient times. Times change. Elegant red from AGLIANICO, fruity white from Falanghina. Vg producer: VILLA MATILDE.

Falesco ★★→★★★ Latium estate, very good MERLOT Montiano (★★★), red IGT Vitiano, Cab Marciliano, good DOC EST! EST!! EST!!!

Fara Pie DOC r ★★ 90 **95' 96' 97** 98 99 00 01 Good NEBBIOLO from Novara, N PIEMONTE. Fragrant; worth ageing; esp Dessilani's Caramino.

Italy's DOCG wines: the complete list

Albana di Romagna, Asti and Moscato d'Asti, Barbaresco, Barolo, Brachetto d'Acqui, Brunello di Montalcino, Carmignano, Chianti, Chianti Classico, Franciacorta, Gattinara, Gavi, Ghemme, Montefalco Sagrantino, Soave Recioto, Taurasi, Torgiano Rosso Riserva, Valtellina Superiore, Vermentino di Gallura, Vernaccia di San Gimignano, and Vino Nobile di Montepulciano.

Farneta, Tenuta ★★→★★★ Nr Siena but outside CHIANTI CLASSICO, an estate for pure SANGIO VDT: eg Bongoverno (★★→★★★) and Bentivoglio.

Farnetella, Castello di ★★→★★★ Estate near MONTEPULCIANO where Giuseppe Mazzocolin of FELSINA makes gd SAUV and CHIANTI COLLI Senesi. Also vg PINOT N "Nero di Nubi" and Poggio Granoni (SANGIO-Syrah-Cab-MERLOT blend).

Faro Si DOC r ★★ **95 96 97** 98 99 00 01 Quite interesting, full-bodied red from Messina. Gd producer: Palari.

Fattoria TUSCAN term for a wine-growing property, traditionally noble.

Fazi-Battaglia ★★ Well-known prod of VERDICCHIO, etc. Le Moie & San Sisto are best Verdicchio selections. Owns Fassati (prod of VINO NOBILE DI MONTEPULCIANO).

Felluga, Livio ★★★ Substantial estate, consistently fine COLLI ORIENTALI DEL FRIULI wines, esp PINOT GR, SAUVIGNON, TOCAI, MERLOT, REFOSCO, PICOLIT.

Felluga, Marco Brother of LIVIO FELLUGA, owns *négociant* house bearing own name plus RUSSIZ SUPERIORE in COLLIO DOC, Castello di Buttrio in COLLI ORIENTALI DOC.

Felsina-Berardenga ★★★ CHIANTI CLASSICO estate; famous RISERVA VIGNA Rancia, VDT Fontalloro; the regular Chianti Classico and RISERVA, although less fashionable and less expensive, are more traditional.

Ferrari ★★→★★★ Cellars making dry sparkling wines nr Trento DOC, TRENTINO-ALTO ADIGE. Giulio Ferrari RISERVA is best.

Feudi di San Gregorio ★★★ Top DOCG TAURASI DOC FIANO r IGT Serpico and Patrio (MERLOT), w IGTs Campanaro and Idem.

Fiano di Avellino Cam w ★★→★★★ (DYA) Considered the best w of Campania, Can be intense, slightly honeyed, memorable. Best producers: COLLI di Lapio, FUEDI DI SAN GREGORIO, MASTROBERARDINO, Terradora, Valdiaperti.

Filiputti, Walter ★★→★★★ Since 1997, tenant of the vineyards of Abbazia di Rosazzo (owned by bishopric of Udine) again. Produces very good white and red COLLI ORIENTALI wines under the label "Walter Filiputti".

Florio The major volume producer of MARSALA, controlled by Illva-Saronno.

Folonari Large, run-of-the-mill merchant of Lombardy. See also GIV.

Folonari Ambrogio Folonari & son Giovanni have split off from RUFFINO to create own house. Will continue to make w and r Cabreo (a CHARD and a SANGIO-Cab), wines of NOZZOLE (incl Cab Pareto), VINO NOBILE DI MONTEPULCIANO Gracciano, new offerings from BOLGHERI and COLLI ORIENTALI DEL FRIULI.

Fontana Candida ★→★★ One of the biggest producers of FRASCATI. Single-v'yd Santa Teresa stands out. See also GIV.

Fontanafredda ★★→★★★ Historic prod of PIEDM wines on former royal estates, incl single-v'yd BAROLOS & range of ALBA DOCS. Vg SPUMANTE Brut (esp ★★★ GATTINARA).

Fonterutoli ★★★ Historic CHIANTI CLASSICO estate of the Mazzei family at Castellina. Noted new RISERVA CASTELLO di Fonterutoli (dark, oaky, fashionable Chianti), IGT Siepi (SANGIO-MERLOT). Mazzei also own Tenuta di Belguardo in MAREMMA, good MORELLINO DI SCANSANO.

Fontodi ★★★ Top Panzano CHIANTI CLASSICO estate for Chianti and RISERVA, (esp Riserva del Sorbo) vg red IGT Fontalloro, Case Via Pinot Nero, Case Va Syrah.

Foradori ★★★ Elizabetta F makes v best TEROLDEGO. Also oak-aged Teroldego Granato, red IGT Karanar, white IGT Myrto.

Forteto della Luja ★★★ Number 1 for LOAZZOLO; vg BARBERA-PINOT N "Le Grive".

Fossi Enrico ★★★ High-level small estate in Signa, west of Florence, very fine SANGIOVESE, Cabernet, Syrah, CHARDONNAY.

Franciacorta Lom DOCG w (p) sp ★★→★★★★ Small sp wine centre fast growing in quality and renown. Wines exclusively bottle-fermented. Top producers: BELLAVISTA, CA' DEL BOSCO, CAVALLERI, Gatti, UBERTI, Vezzoli, VILLA; also vg: Contadi Gastaldi, Cornaleto, Il Mosnel, Monte Rossa, Castellino, La Montina, Majolini, Monzio Compagnoni, Ricci Curbastri. For w and r, see Terre di Franciacorta.

Frascati Lat DOC w dr s/sw sw (sp) ★→★★ DYA Best-known wine of Roman hills: should be soft, limpid, golden, tasting of whole grapes. Most is disappointingly neutral today: look for Conte Zandotti, Villa Simone, or Santa Teresa from FONTANA CANDIDA. Sweet is known as Cannellino. The best place to drink it is from the jug in a *trattoria* in Trastevere, Rome.

Freisa Pie r dr s/sw sw (sp) ★★ DYA Usually v dry (except nr Turin), often FRIZZANTE red, said to taste of raspberries and roses. With enough acidity it can be highly appetizing, esp with salami. Gd wines from CIGLIUTI, Clerico, CONTERNO, COPPO, PARUSSO, Pecchenino, Pelissero, Sebaste, Trinchero, VAJRA, and VOERZIO.

Frescobaldi ★★→★★★ Ancient noble family, leading CHIANTI RUFINA pioneers at NIPOZZANO, E of Florence. Also w POMINO & Cab (Mormoreto). See also Montesodi. Owners of Castelgiocondo (★★★), big estate for BRUNELLO DI M & vg IGT MERLOT Lamaïone. From 97: joint TUSCAN venture with Mondavi of Calif nr MONTALCINO producing LUCE & Lucente. New vineyards in COLLIO DOC.

Friuli-Venezia Giulia The NE region on the Slovenian border. Many wines: the DOCS COLLIO and COLLI ORIENTALI include most of the best.

Frizzante (fz) Semi-sparkling. Used to describe wines such as LAMBRUSCO.

Gaja ★★★★ Old family firm at BARBARESCO under meteoric direction of Angelo G. Top-quality – and price – wines, especially BARBARESCO (single v'yds SORI Tildin, Sorì San Lorenzo, Costa Russi), BAROLO Sperss. Trend-setting, excellent CHARD (Gaia & Rey), CAB DARMAGI. Latest acquisition: Marengo-Marenda estate (BAROLO), commercial Gromis label, PIEVE DI SANTA RESTITUTA (BRUNELLO); recently planted v'yd at BOLGHERI. Single-v'yd BARBARESCOS & BAROLO now marked LANGHE DOC.

Galardi ★★★→★★★★ Producer of Terra di Lavoro, mind-boggling blend of AGLIANICO and Piedirosso, in northern Campania near FALERNO DEL MASSICO DOC.

Galestro Tus w ★ V light white from eponymous shaley soil in CHIANTI country.

Gambellara Ven DOC w dr s/sw (sp) ★ DYA Neighbour of SOAVE. Dry wine similar. Sweet (RECIOTO DI G), nicely fruity. Top producer: La Biancara.

Gancia Famous ASTI house also producing dry sparkling.

Garganega Principal white grape of SOAVE and GAMBELLARA.

Garofoli ★★→★★★ One of quality leaders in the Marches (nr Ancona). Notable style in VERDICCHIO Podium, Macrina, & Serra Fiorese. ROSSO CONERO Piancarda and very good Grosso Agontano.

Gattinara Pie DOCG r ★★★ 89' 90' **93 95 96'** 97' 98 99' 00 01 Very tasty BAROLO-type red (from NEBBIOLO, locally known as Spanna). Best are TRAVAGLINI (RISERVA), Antoniolo (single-v'yd wines). Others incl Bianchi, Nervi, SERGIO GATTINARA.

Gavi Pie DOCG w ★→★★★ DYA At (rare) best, subtle, dry white of CORTESE grapes. LA SCOLCA is best-known, g from BANFI (esp Vigna Regale), Castellari Bergaglio, TERRE DA VINO. CASTELLO di Tassarolo, Villa Sparina, CHIARLO, PODERE Saulino, Cascina degli Ulivi, Broglia, La Giustiniana are also fair.

Geografico ★★ Co-op with rising-quality CHIANTI CLASSICO; gd RISERVA "Montegiachi".

Ghemme Pie DOCG r ★★★ 89 90' **93 95 96** 97' 98 01 Neighbour of GATTINARA but not as good. Best is Antichi Vigneti di Cantalupo.

Ghizzano See Venerosi Pesciolini.

Giacosa, Bruno ★★★★ Inspired loner: outstanding BARBARESCO, BAROLO, and PIEMONTE wines at Neive. Remarkable ARNEIS white and PINOT N sparkling.

Goldmuskateller Aromatic ALTO ADIGE grape made into irresistible dry white, esp LAGEDER, CS CALDARO.

Governo Old TUSCAN custom, enjoying mild revival, in which dried grapes or must are added to young wine to induce second fermentation and give a slight prickle – sometimes instead of using must concentrate to increase alcohol.

Gradi Degrees (of alcohol), ie per cent by volume.

Grappa Pungent and potent spirit made from grape pomace (skins, etc, after pressing), sometimes excellent. Best grappa comes from PIEMONTE (Ugo Marolo, Paolo Marolo, Distilleria Astigiana, Berta), Trentino (POJER & SANDRI, Pilzer, Giovanni Poli), Friuli (Nonino), Veneto (Carlo Gobetti, Vittorio Capovilla, Jacopo Poli), Toscana (Nannoni), Sicily (Giovi).

Grasso, Elio ★★★ Vg BAROLO (look for Gavarini and Casa Maté), full, barrel-aged BARBERA D'ALBA VIGNA Martina, DOLCETTO D'ALBA, and CHARD Educato, etc.

Grattamacco ★★→★★★ Pioneering producer near BOLGHERI, on TUSCAN coast. Very good DOC BOLGHERI red.

Grave del Friuli F-VG DOC r w ★★ (r) **94 95 97** 99 00 01 DOC covering 15 different wines, 14 named after their grapes, from central part of region. Good REFOSCO, MERLOT, and Cabernet. Best producers: Borgo Magredo, Di Leonardo, Le Fredis, Le Monde, Plozner, Vicentini-Orgnani, Villa Chiopris.

Gravner, Josko ★★★ Visionary COLLIO prod, leading drive for low yields, oak-ageing, age-worthy wines. Tirelessly self-critical in search of new concepts & methods.

Grechetto W grape, more flavour than ubiquitous TREBBIANO, increasingly in Umbria.

Greco di Bianco Cal DOC w sw ★★ **97** 98 99 00 Original, smooth, & fragrant sw wine from Italy's toe; worth ageing. Best from Ceratti. See Mantonico.

Greco di Tufo Cam DOC w (sp) ★★→★★★ (DYA) One the best w from the S: fruity and slightly wild in flavour. Vg examples from Benito Ferrara, Feudi di San Gregorio, MASTROBERARDINO (Nuovaserra & Vignadangelo), Terradora, Vadiaperti.

Gresy, Marchesi de (Cisa Asinari) ★★★ Consistent LANGHE producer of fine BARBARESCO. Also vg Langhe Rosso, SAUV, CHARD, and MOSCATO D'ASTI.

Grevepesa CHIANTI CLASSICO Co-op.

Grignolino d'Asti Pie DOC r ★ DYA Lively, standard, light red of PIEMONTE IGT.

Gruppo Italiano Vini (GIV) Complex of co-ops and wineries incl BIGI, Conti Serristori, FOLONARI, FONTANA CANDIDA, LAMBERTI, Macchiavelli, MELINI, Negri, Santi and since 1997 controls Ca' Bianca (PIEMONTE) and Vignaioli di San Floriano (FRIULI). Now moving into south: recent investments in Sicily and Basilicata.

Guerrieri-Gonzaga ★★★ Top TRENTINO estate; esp ★★★San Leonardo (Cab-MERLOT).

Gutturnio dei Colli Piacentini E-R DOC r dr ★→★★ DYA BARBERA-BONARDA blend from the hills of Piacenza, often FRIZZANTE.

Haas, Franz ★★★ Very good ALTO ADIGE PINOT N, LAGREIN, IGT r and w blends.

Hastae ★★★ New Super-BARBERA from ASTI from group of producers: BRAIDA, CHIARLO, COPPO, PRUNOTTO, VIETTI.

Hofstätter ★★★ ALTO ADIGE producer of top PINOT NOIR. (look for S Urbano), LAGREIN, Cab-MERL, Gewürztraminer.

IGT (Indicazione Geografica Tipica) New category for wines heading for DOC status or higher; replaces the anomaly of glamorous VDTS.

Ischia Cam DOC w (r) ★→★★ DYA Wine of the island off Naples. Top producer D'AMBRA makes good DOC red Dedicato a Mario D'Ambra, IGT red Tenuta Montecorvo, IGT white Tenuta Frassitelli, and Piellero.

Isole e Olena ★★★→★★★★ Top CHIANTI CLASSICO estate of great beauty with fine red VDT Cepparello. Very good VIN SANTO, Cab, CHARD, and L'Eremo Syrah.

An Italian choice for 2002

Barbaresco Asili Bruno Giacosa (Piemonte)
Barolo Bussia Vigna Cicala Aldo Conterno (Piemonte)
Barbera d'Asti Superiore Rivetti (Piemonte)
Collio Bianco Studio Bianco Borgo di Tiglio (Friuli-Venezia Giulia)
Colli Orientali del Friuli Refosco Livio Felluga (Friuli-Venezia Giulia)
Rosso Conero Visions of J Le Terrazze (Marches)
Chianti Classico Riserva Badia a Passignano Antinori (Toscana)
Brunello di Montalcino Riserva Col d'Orcia (Toscana)
Vigna Camarato Villa Matilda (Campania)
Villa Fidelia Rosso Sportoletti (Umbria)

Isonzo F-VG DOC r w ★★★ (r) **94 95** 97' 98 99 **00** 01 DOC covering 19 wines (17 varietals) in NE. Best white and MERLOT compare to COLLIO wines. Esp from Masut da Rive, LIS NERIS-PECORARI, Pierpaolo Pecorari, RONCO del Gelso, Borgo San Daniele, VIE DI ROMANS.

Jermann, Silvio ★★★ Family estate with vineyards in COLLIO & ISONZO: top white VDT, include white blend VINTAGE TUNINA oak-aged Capo Martino and CHARD "WHERE THE DREAMS NOW IS JUST WINE …" (sic).

Kalterersee German (and local) name for LAGO DI CALDARO.

Kante, Edi ★★★ Lone star of CARSO; outstanding DOC CHARD, SAUV, MALVASIA; very good red Terrano.

Klosterkellerei Muri-Gries See Muri Gries.

Lacryma (or Lacrima) Christi del Vesuvio Cam r p w dr (sw fz) ★→★★ DYA Famous but ordinary wines in great variety from Vesuvius. (DOC Vesuvio.) MASTROBERARDINO: the only good example.

Lageder, Alois ★★→★★★ Exciting wines, include oak-aged CHARDONNAY and Cabernet Löwengang and Römigberg. Single-vineyard SAUV is Lehenhof, PINOT GRIGIO Benefizium Porer, PINOT NOIR. Krafuss, Lagrein Lindenberg, TERLANO Tannhammer. Also owns Cason Hirschprunn for very good IGT red and white blends.

Lago di Caldaro See Caldaro.

Lagrein, Südtiroler T-AA DOC r p ★★→★★★ **95' 96** 97' 98 99 00 01 A Tyrolean grape with a bitter twist. Good, fruity wine – at best very appetizing. The rosé: "Kretzer", the dark: "Dunkel". Best from Colterenzio co-op, Gries, HAAS, HOFSTÄTTER, LAGEDER, Laimburg, Josephus Mayr, Thomas Mayr, Muri Gries, NIEDERMAYR, Gojer, Niedrist estates, TERLANO co-op, St Magdalena.

La Massa ★★★ Highly rated new producer; vg CHIANTI CLASSICO; best: Giorgio Primo.

Lamberti ★★ Large producers of SOAVE, VALPOLICELLA, BARDOLINO, etc, at Lazise on the E shore of Lake Garda.

Lambrusco E-R DOC (or not) r p dr s/sw ★→★★ DYA Popular fizzy red, best-known in industrial s/sw version. Best is SECCO, traditional with second fermentation in bottle (with sediment). DOCS: L Grasparossa di Castelvetro, L Salamino di Santa Croce, L di Sorbara. Best from: Bellei, Caprari, Casali,

CAVICCHIOLI, Graziano, Lini Oreste, Medici Ermete (especially Concerto), Rinaldo Rinaldini, Venturini Baldini.

La Morandina ★★★ Small family estate with top MOSCATO and BARBERA D'ASTI.

Langhe The hills of central PIEMONTE, home of BAROLO, BARBARESCO, etc. Has become name for recent DOC (r w ★★→★★★) for 8 different wines: ROSSO, BIANCO, NEBBIOLO, DOLCETTO, FREISA, ARNEIS, Favorita, and CHARDONNAY. Barolo and Barbaresco can now be declassified to DOC Langhe Nebbiolo.

La Scolca ★★ Famous GAVI estate for good Gavi and SPUMANTE.

Latisana F-VG DOC r w ★→★★ (r) **97' 99** 00 DOC for 13 varietal wines from 50 miles NE of Venice. Best wine is TOCAI FRIULANO.

Le Cinciole ★★★ Tiny prod of DOCG CHIANTI CLASSICO (best is RISERVA "Valle del Pozzo").

Le Fonti ★★★ Very good CHIANTI CLASSICO house in Poggibonsi; look for RISERVA and IGT Vito Arturo (SANGIO).

Le Macchiole ★★★ Outstanding red DOC BOLGHERI Paleo, TOSCANA IGTS Messorio (MERLOT), and Scrio (Syrah).

Le Pupille ★★★ Top producer of MORELLINO DI SCANSANO (look for RISERVA, Poggia Valente), excellent IGT. Cab-MERLOT blend Saffredi.

Le Salette ★★→★★★ Small VALPOLICELLA producer: look for very good AMARONE Pergole Vece and RECIOTO Le Traversagne.

Le Vigne di Zamò ★★★ First-class FRIULI estate for PINOT BLANC, TOCAI, Pignolo, Cabernet, and MERLOT from vineyards in three areas of COLLI PRIENTALI DEL FRIULI DOC: Buttrio, MANZANO, Premariacco.

Leone de Castris ★★ Large, reliable producer to follow for APULIAN wines. Estate at SALICE SALENTO, near Lecce.

Lessona Pie DOC r ★★ **94 95 96' 97'** 98 99 00 01 Soft, dry claret-like wine from Vercelli province. NEBBIOLO, Vespolina, BONARDA grapes. Best producer: SELLA.

Librandi ★★★ Top Calabria prod. Vg red CIRO (RISERVA Duca San Felice is ★★★) IGT Gravello (Cab-Gaglioppo blend), & VDT Magno Megonio from Magliocco grape.

Liquoroso Means strong, usually sweet and always fortified.

Lis Neris ★★★ Alvaro Pecorari's top ISONZO estate with bevy of high-quality wines: CHARD, PINOT GR, SAUV, a MERLOT-based red, and lovely VDT dessert VERDUZZO.

Lisini ★★★ Historic small estate for some of the finest BRUNELLO.

Livon ★★→★★★ Substantial COLLIO producer, also some COLLI ORIENTALI wines like VERDUZZO. Expanded into the CHIANTI CLASSICO and Montefalco DOCGS.

Loazzolo Pie DOC w sw ★★★ **90 91 93 94 95 96' 97'** 98' 99' 00 01 New DOC for MOSCATO dessert wine from botrytized, air-dried grapes: expensive and sweet. Especially from Forteto della Luja.

Locorotondo Ap DOC w (sp) ★→★★ DYA Pleasantly fresh southern white.

Lugana Lom and Ven DOC w (sp) ★→★★ DYA Whites of S Lake Garda: can be fragrant, smooth, full of body and flavour. Good from CA' DEI FRATI, ZENATO.

Luce ★★★ Typically ambitious Mondavi (cf California) joint venture (launched 98) with FRESCOBALDI. SANGIO-MERLOT blend. Could become Italy's Opus One.

Lungarotti ★★→★★★ Leading prod of TORGIANO, with cellars, hotel, & museum nr Perugia. Gd IGT Sangiorgio (SANGIO-Cab), Il Vessillo, & Giubilante. See Torgiano.

Macchiavelli See Gruppo Italiano Vini.

Maculan ★★★ Excellent Cab (Fratta, Ferrata), CHARD (Ferrata), MERLOT (Marchesante), Torcolato (esp RISERVA Acininobili).

Malvasia Widely planted grape; chameleon-like: w or r, sp or still, strong or mild, sweet or dry, aromatic or rather neutral, often IGT, sometimes DOC.

Manduria (Primitivo di) Ap DOC r s/sw ★★→★★★ **95 96 97'** 98 99 00 01 Dark red, naturally strong, sometimes sweet from nr Taranto. Good producers: Felline, Pervini, Sinfarosa.

Mantonico Cal w dr sw fz ★★ **95** 97 99 00 01 Fruity, deep-amber sw wine from Reggio Calabria. Can age remarkably well. Ceratti's is gd. See Greco di Bianco.

Manzone, Giovanni ★★★ Vg ALBA wines of much personality from Ciabot del Preve estate nr Manforte d'Alba, esp single-v'yard BAROLOS, BARBERA D'ALBA, DOLCETTO.

Marchesi di Barolo ★★ Important ALBA house: BAROLO, BARBARESCO, DOLCETTO D'ALBA, BARBERA, FREISA D'ASTI, and GAVI.

Maremma Southern coastal area of TOSCANA in provinces of Livorno & Grosseto. DOCS incl BOLGHERI & VAL DI CORNIA (Livorno), MONTEREGIO, MORELLINO DI SCANSANO, PARRINA, SOVANA (Grosseto). Now attracting much interest and new investments for high quality potential demonstrated by wines.

Marino Lat DOC w dr s/sw (sp) ★→★★ DYA A neighbour of FRASCATI with similar wine; often a better buy. Look for Di Mauro.

Marroneto, Il ★★→★★★ Sml estate; v mild, fruity, burgundy-like DOCG BRUNELLO DI M.

Marsala Si DOC br dr s/sw sw fz ★→★★★ NV Sicily's sherry-type wine, invented by the Woodhouse Bros from Liverpool in 1773; excellent apéritif or for dessert, but mostly used in the kitchen for zabaglione, etc. The dry ("virgin"), s'times made by the *solera* system, must be 5 yrs old. Top producers: FLORIO, Pellegrino, Rallo, VECCHIO SAMPERI. Very special old vintages ★★★★.

Martini & Rossi Vermouth and sparkling-wine house now controlled by Bacardi group. (Has a fine wine-history museum in Pessione, nr Turin.)

Marzemino (Trentino) T-AA DOC r ★→★★ 97 98' 99 00 01 Pleasant local red. Fruity, slightly bitter. Especially from Bossi Fedrigotti, CA'VIT, De Tarczal, E Spagnolli, Gaierhof, Longariva, Letrari, Simoncelli, Vallarom.

Mascarello The name of two top producers of BAROLO, etc: Bartolo M and Giuseppe M & Figli. Look for the latter's supreme BAROLO Monprivato.

Masi ★→★★★ Well-known, conscientious, reliable VALPOLICELLA, AMARONE, RECIOTO, SOAVE, etc, incl fine r Campo Fiorin. Also excellent barrel-aged r IGT Toar.

Mastroberardino ★★→★★★ Campania's historic house has split into two parts: M and Terredora , but with very few changes. Wines incl FIANO DI AVELLINO, GRECO DI TUFO, LACRYMA CHRISTI, TAURASI (look for Radici), IGT Historia Naturalis, new top blend of AGLIANICO and Piedirosso.

Melini ★★ Long-est'd producers of CHIANTI CLASSICO at Poggibonsi. Good quality/price; look for single-v'yd C Classico Selvanella. Look for RISERVAS La Selvanella and Masovecchio.

Meranese di Collina T-AA DOC r ★ DYA Light red of Merano, known in German as Meraner Hügel.

Merlot Adaptable red B'x grape widely grown in N (esp) and central Italy. Merlot DOCS: abundant. Best producers: BORGO DEL TIGLIO, LIVIO FELLUGA (Sossò), Miani, Radikon, VILLA RUSSIZ (De la Tour) in F-VG; Bonzara (Rocca di Bonacciara) in Emilia-Romagna; FALESCO (Montiano) in Latium; PLANETA in Sicily; and TUSCAN Super-IGTS AMA (L'Apparita), Casa Emma (Soloio), FRESCOBALDI (Lampione), Ghizzano (Nambrot), La Braccesca, Macchiole (Messorio), ORNELLAIA (Masseto), Petrolo (Galatrona), RODANO (Lazzicante), Tua Rita (Redigaffi).

Metodo classico or tradizionale Now mandatory terms to identify classic method sparkling wines. "Metodo Champenois" banned since 94 and now illegal. (See also Classico.)

Mezzacorona Huge TRENTINO co-op with gd DOC TEROLDEGO and MC sp Rotari.

Moccagatta ★★→★★★ Specialist in impressive single-v'yd BARBARESCO: Basarin, Bric Balin (★★★) and Vigna Cole. Also BARBERA D'ALBA and LANGHE.

Molino ★★★ Talented producer of elegant ALBA wines at La Morra; look for BAROLOS Gancia and Conca, BARBERA Gattere, DOLCETTO, and CHARD.

Monacesca, La ★★→★★★ Fine producer of VERDICCHIO DI MATELICA. Top wine: Mirus.

Moncaro Marches co-op: good VERDICCHIO DEI CASTELLI DI JESI.

Monferrato Pie DOC r w sw p ★★ Hills between River Po and Apennines and name of a new DOC; incl ROSSO, BIANCO, CHIARETTO, DOLCETTO, Casalese, FREISA CORTESE.

Monica di Sardegna Sar DOC r ★→★★ DYA Monica is the grape of light, dry red.

Monsanto ★★→★★★ Esteemed CHIANTI CLASSICO estate, especially for Il Poggio vineyard and IGTS Fabrizio Bianchi (SANGIO) and Nemo (Cabernet).

Montalcino Small town in province of Siena (TOSCANA), famous for concentrated, very expensive BRUNELLO and more approachable, better-value ROSSO DI M.

Montevertine ★★★ Radda estate and a leading force in renaissance of TUSCAN wine in the 1970s and 1980s. IGT Le Pergole Torte a pioneering example of small barrel-aged SANGIO. Also Sodaccio (Sangio plus Canaiolo).

Montecarlo Tus DOC w r ★★ DYA (w) White-wine area nr Lucca in N TOSCANA: smooth, neutral blend of TREBBIANO with range of better grapes. Applies to CHIANTI-style red, too. Good prods: Buonamico (r IGTS Cercatoja Rosso & Fortino), CARMIGNANI (vg r IGT "For Duke"), r IGT's of La Torre, Montechiari, Wandanna.

Montefalco (Rosso di) Umb DOC r ★★→★★★ 93 94 95 96 97' 98 99' 00 SANGIO-TREBBIANO-SAGRANTINO blend. For gd producers, see Montefalco Sagrantino.

Montefalco Sagrantino Umb DOCG r dr (sw) ★★★→★★★★ 90 91 93 94 95' 96 97' 98 99' 00 Strong, v interesting SECCO or sw PASSITO r from Sagrantino grapes only. Good from CAPRAI, Colpetrone, Rocca di Fabbri, CASTELLO di Antignana.

Montellori, Fattoria di ★★→★★★ TUSCAN producer making SANGIO-Cab IGT blend Castelrapiti, Cab-MERLOT blend Salamartano, white IGTs Montecupoli, a blend, and Sant'Amato (SAUV), MC SPUMANTE.

Montepulciano An important red grape of central-east Italy as well as the famous TUSCAN town (see next entries).

Montepulciano d'Abruzzo Ab DOC r p ★→★★★ 90 91 92 93 94 95 97' 98' 00 01 At best, one of Italy's tastiest reds, full of flavour and warmth, from Adriatic coast near Pescara. Best: VALENTINI, Barone Cornacchia, Nestore Bosco, Cataldi-Madonna, Filomusi-Guelfi, Illuminati, Masciarelli, Montori, Nicodemi, Orlandi Contucci Ponno, Terre d'Aligi, Torre dei Beati, and La Valentina. Farnese is the big-value brand. See also Cerasuolo.

Montepulciano, Vino Nobile di See Vino Nobile di Montepulciano.

Monteregio Emerging DOC zone near Massa Marittima in MAREMMA, high-level SANGIO and Cabernet wines from MORIS FARMS, Massa Vecchia. New investors (incl ANTINORI) flocking in.

Montescudaio Tus DOC r w ★★ 95 97 98 99 00 DOC between Pisa & Livorno; best are SANGIO or Sangio-Cab blends. Try Merlini, Poggio Gagliardo, Sorbaiano.

Montesodi Tus r ★★★ 90 93 95 97 99 00 Tip-top CHIANTI RUFINA RISERVA from FRESCOBALDI.

Montevetrano ★★★ Tiny Campania producer; superb IGT Montevetrano (Cabernet S- MERLOT-AGLIANICO).

Montresor ★★ VERONA wine house: good LUGANA, BIANCO DI CUSTOZA, VALPOLICELLA.

Morellino di Scansano Tus DOC r ★→★★★ 90' 93 94 95 97 98 99' 00 01 Local SANGIO of the MAREMMA, the S TUSCAN coast. Cherry-red, should be lively and tasty young or matured. Fattorie LE PUPILLE, MORIS FARMS, Mantellasi, Lhosa, Banti, Poggio Argentiera, Poggiolungo, Malfatti, Scansano Cantina, and Belguardo are producers to try. Avoid oaky Riservas.

Moris Farms ★★★ Top producer of MORELLINO DI SCANSANO nr Grosseto; look for RISERVA and IGT Avvoltore, a rich SANGIO-Cab-Syrah blend.

Moscadello di Montalcino Tus DOC w sw (sp) ★★ DYA. Revived traditional wine of MONTALCINO, once more important than BRUNELLO. Sweet, white fizz and sweet to high-octane MOSCATO PASSITO. Best producers: COL D'ORCIA, La Poderina, Poggio Salvi.

Moscato Fruitily fragrant ubiquitous grape for a diverse range of wines: sparkling or still, light or full-bodied, but always sweet.

Moscato d'Asti Pie DOCG w sp sw ★★→★★★ DYA Similar to DOCG ASTI, but usually from better grapes; lower in alcohol, sweeter & fruitier, usually from small producers. Best DOCG MOSCATO from Bera Walter, CASCINA FONDA,

ITALY

Caudrina, Il Falcheto, La Morandina, Perrone, Rivetti, Saracco, Scagliola, Vignaioli di Sante Stefano.

Müller-Thurgau Makes wine to be reckoned with in TRENTINO-ALTO ADIGE, Lavis, LAGEDER, POJER & SANDRI, Zeni, and FRIULI.

Murana, Salvatore ★★★ Vg MOSCATO di PANTELLERIA and PASSITO di P.

Muri Gries, Klosterkellerei ★★→★★★ Very good producer of DOC ALTO ADIGE, best is DOC LAGREIN.

Nada, Fiorenzo ★★★ Vg producer of v smooth DOCG BARBARESCO.

Nebbiolo The best red grape of PIEMONTE. Also the grape of VALTELLINA (Lombardy).

Nebbiolo d'Alba Pie DOC r dr (s/sw sp) ★★ 95 **96 97** 98 99 00 01 From ALBA (but not BAROLO, BARBARESCO). Often like lighter Barolo but more approachable. Best from Alario, BRICCO Maiolica, Cascina Chicco Correggia, De Marie, GIACOSA, Hillberg, MASCARELLO, PRUNOTTO, SANDRONE, VAL DI PRETE. See also Roero.

Negri See Gruppo Italiano Vini.

Negroamaro Literally "black bitter"; APULIAN red grape with high quality potential. See Copertino and Salice Salentino.

Niedermayr ★★★ Vg DOC ALTO ADIGE, esp LAGREIN, PINOT N. Gewürztraminer, SAUVIGNON, and IGT Euforius (LAGREIN-Cab) and Aureus (sweet white blend).

Niedrist, Ignaz ★★★ Small, gifted producer of white and red ALTO ADIGE wines (esp LAGREIN, PINOT NOIR, PINOT BLANC, RIESLING).

Nipozzano, Castello di ★★★ FRESCOBALDI estate in RUFINA east of Florence making MONTESODI CHIANTI. The most important outside the CLASSICO zone.

Nittardi ★★→★★★ Up-and-coming little CHIANTI CLASSICO estate.

Nosiola (Trentino) T-AA DOC w dr sw ★★ DYA Light, fruity white from dried Nosiola grapes. Also good VIN SANTO. Best from Pravis: Castel Noarna, POJER & SANDRI, Giovanni Poli, Zeni.

Nozzole ★★→★★★ Famous estate now owned by AMBROGIO FOLONARI, in heart of CHIANTI CLASSICO, N of Greve. Also very good CABERNET Pareto.

Nuragus di Cagliari Sar DOC w ★ DYA Lively Sardinian white.

Oberto, Andrea ★★→★★★ Small La Morra prod: top BAROLO and BARBERA D'ALBA.

Oddero Pie ★★★ Well-known, reliable La Morra estate producing excellent BAROLO (look for Mondocco di Bussia, Rocche di Castiglione, and VIGNA Rionda).

Oltrepò Pavese Lom DOC r w dr sw sp ★→★★★ DOC applicable to 14 wines from Pavia province, mostly named after grapes. Sometimes very good PINOT NOIR & M-C-SPUMANTE. Top growers incl Anteo, Barbacarlo, Casa Re, Frecciarossa, Le Fracce, La Versa co-op, Monsupello, Mazzolino, Ruiz de Cardenas, Travaglino, Vercesi del Castellazzo.

Ornellaia Tus ★★★★ Lodovico ANTINORI's prestigious 200-acre estate nr BOLGHERI on the TUSCAN coast. Watch for very good Bolgheri DOC ORNELLAIA (Cab-MERLOT), excellent IGT Masseto (Merlot), Le Volte (SANGIO-Cab).

Orvieto Umb DOC w dr s/sw ★→★★★ DYA The classical Umbrian golden white: smooth and substantial; formerly very dull but recently more interesting, esp in sweet versions. Orvieto CLASSICO is better. Only the finest examples (eg Barberani, Co.Vi.O, DECUGNANO DEI BARBI, La Carraia, Palazzone, Vi.C.Or) age well. But see Castello della Sala.

Pacenti, Siro ★★★ Very international BRUNELLO and ROSSO DI MONTALCINO.

Pagadebit di Romagna E-R DOC w dr s/sw ★ DYA Pleasant, traditional "payer of debts" from around Bertinoro.

Palazzino, Podere Il ★★★ Small estate with admirable CHIANTI CLASSICO and IGT Grosso Sanese.

Paneretta, Castello della ★★★ To follow for very fine CHIANTI CLASSICO, IGTS Quattrocentenario, terrine.

Pancrazi, Marchese ★★→★★★ Estate nr Florence: some of Italy's top PINOT N.

Panizzi ★★→★★★ Makes top VERNACCIA DI SAN GIMIGNANO. Also CHIANTI COLLI Senesi.

Pantelleria See Moscato.

Paradiso, Fattoria ★★ Old family estate near Bertinoro (E-R). Good ALBANA and SANGIO, unique Barbarossa. Also TREBBIANO di Romagna.

Parrina Tus DOC r w ★★ Grand estate near the classy resorts of Argentario. Good w Ansonica, improving red (SANGIO-Cab) from MAREMMA.

Parusso ★★★ Marco and Tiziana Parusso make fine BAROLO (eg single-vineyard Bussia VIGNA Rocche and Bussia Vigna Munie), BARBERA D'ALBA and DOLCETTO, W LANGHE (SAUVIGNON).

Pasolini Dall'Onda ★★ Noble family with estates in CHIANTI COLLI Fiorentini and Romagna, producing traditional-style wines.

Pasqua, Fratelli ★★ Good-level producer and bottler of VERONA wines: VALPOLICELLA, AMARONE, SOAVE. Also BARDOLINO and RECIOTO.

Passito (pa) Strong, mostly sw wine from grapes dried on the vine or indoors.

Paternoster ★★★ Top AGLIANICO DEL V producer.

Patriglione ★★★ Dense, strong r (NEGROAMARO-MALVASIA Nera). See Taurino.

Per'e Palummo Cam r ★ Appetizing, light red from island of ISCHIA.

Piave Ven DOC r w ★→★★ (r) **95 97** 99' 00 01 (w) DYA Flourishing DOC NW of Venice covering 8 wines, 4 red and 4 white, named after their grapes. Cabernet, MERLOT, and RABOSO reds can all age. Good examples from Molon, Loredan Gasparini.

Picolit (Colli Orientali del Friuli) F-VG DOC w s/sw sw ★★→★★★★ **95 97** 98 Delicate, sw wine; exaggerated reputation. A little like France's Jurançon. Ages up to 6 yrs, but v overpriced. Best: DORIGO, FELLUGA, Meroi, Specogna, VILLA RUSSIZ.

Piemonte (Piedmont) With TUSCANY, the most important Italian region for top-quality wine. Turin is the capital, ASTI and ALBA the wine centres. See Barbaresco, Barbera, Barolo, Dolcetto, Grignolino, Moscato, etc.

Piemonte Pie DOC r w p (sp) ★→★★ New all-PIEMONTE blanket-DOC incl BARBERA, BONARDA, BRACHETTO, CORTESE, GRIGNOLINO, CHARD, SPUMANTE, MOSCATO.

Pieropan ★★★ Outstanding SOAVE and RECIOTO: for once, deserving its fame, esp Soave La Rocca and Calvarino, sweet PASSITO della ROCCA.

Pieve di Santa Restituta ★★★ Estate for admirable BRUNELLO DI MONTALCINO, esp Sugarile. Owned by GAJA.

Pigato Lig DOC w ★★ DOC under Riviera Ligure di Ponente. Often out-classes VERMENTINO as Liguria's finest white, with rich texture and structure. Good from: Bruna, COLLE dei Bardellini, Durin, Feipu, Foresti, Lupi, TERRE ROSSE, Vio.

Pighin, Fratelli ★★ One of Friuli producers. Reliable COLLIO, Goriziano, Friuli, and GRAVE reds and whites.

Pinot Bianco (Pinot Bl) Popular grape in NE for many DOC wines, generally bland and dry. Best from ALTO ADIGE ★★ (top growers: CS SAN MICHELE, Colterenzio, HOFSTÄTTER, NIEDRIST), COLLIO ★★→★★★ (very good from Renato Keber, Aldo Polencic, RUSSIZ SUPERIORE, SCHIOPETTO, VILLA RUSSIZ), and COLLI ORIENTALI ★★→★★★ (best from Zamò & Zamò). ISONZO ★★ (from Masut da Rive).

Pinot Grigio (Pinot Gr) Tasty, low-acid white grape popular in NE. Best from DOCS ALTO ADIGE (SAN MICHELE APPIANO, Schwanburg) and COLLIO (Renato Keber, LIVON, Aldo Polencic, RUSSIZ SUPERIORE, Tercic, Terpin, Venica, VILLA RUSSIZ, SCHIOPETTO) COLLI ORIENTALI (LIVIO FELLUGA), and ISONZO (Borgo San Daniele, LIS NERIS, Masut da Rive, Pierpaolo Pecorari, VIE DI ROMANS).

Pinot Nero (Pinot Noir) Planted in much of NE Italy. DOC status in ALTO ADIGE (HAAS, Haderburg, Laimburg, NIEDERMAYR, Termeno co-op, Colterenzio co-op SAN MICHELE APPIANO CO-OP, Niedrist, HOFSTÄTTER, co-op Cortaccia, co-op Caldaro, NIEDERMAYR, LAGEDER) and in OLTREPO PAVESE (Frecciarossa, Ruiz de Cardenas). Promising trials elsewhere eg TOSCANA (Ama, FARNETELLA, FONTODI, Pancranzi). Also fine from several regions: TRENTINO (Lunelli, Maso Cantanghel, POJER & SANDRI), Lombardy (CA' DEL BOSCO), Umbria (ANTINORI), Marches (BOCCADIGABBIA).

Pio Cesare ★★→★★★ Long-est'd ALBA producer, esp for BAROLO, BARBARESCO.

Planeta ★★★ Top Sicilian estate featuring Segreta Bianco (Grecanico, Catarratto, CHARDONNAY), Segreta ROSSO (Nero d'Avola-MERLOT); outstanding Chardonnay, Cabernet, Cometa (Fiano) Merlot, Santa Cecilia (Nero d'Avola).

Podere TUSCAN term for a wine-farm; smaller than a FATTORIA.

Poggio Antico (Montalcino) ★★★ Admirably consistent, top-level BRUNELLO.

Poggione, Tenuta Il ★★★ Very reliable estate for BRUNELLO, ROSSO DI MONTALCINO.

Pojer & Sandri ★★★ Top TRENTINO producers: reds and whites, incl SPUMANTE.

Poliziano ★★★→★★★★ Montepulciano estate. Federico Carletti makes superior VINO NOBILE (especially Asinine), and superb IGT Le Stanze (Cab-MERLOT).

Pomino Tus DOC w r ★★★ r 93 94 95 97 98 99' Fine white, partly CHARD (esp Il Benefizio), a SANGIO-Cab-MERLOT-PINOT N blend. Esp from FRESCOBALDI & SELVAPIANA.

Primitivo Vg r grape of far S, identified with Calif's Zin. Few prods. See Manduria.

Produttori del Barbaresco ★★→★★★ Co-op & one of DOCG's most reliable producers. Often outstanding single-v'yd wines (Asili, Montestefano, Ovello, etc).

Prosecco W grape making light very dry sp wine popular in Venice. The name is widely used by consumers to mean any dry Italian fizz. Next is better.

Prosecco di Conegliano-Valdobbiàdene Ven DOC w s/sw sp (dr) ★★ DYA Slight fruity bouquet, the dry, pleasantly bitter, the sweet fruity; the sweetest (most expensive) are known as Superiore di Cartizze. CARPENE-MALVOLTI is best-known producer, now challenged by Adami, Bisol, Bortolin, Canevel, Case Bianche, Le Colture, Col Salice, Col Vetoraz, Gregoletto, Nino Franco, Ruggeri, Zardetto.

Prunotto, Alfredo ★★★→★★★★ Very serious ALBA company with top BARBARESCO, BAROLO, NEBBIOLO, BARBERA D'ALBA, etc. Since 1999 Prunotto (now controlled by ANTINORI) also produces BARBERA D'ASTI (look for Costamiole).

Puglia See Apulia

Puiatti ★★ Reliable, important producer of COLLIO; also METODO CLASSICO SPUMANTE. Puiatti also owns a FATTORIA in CHIANTI CLASSICO (Casavecchia).

Querciabella ★★★→★★★★ Leader in CHIANTI CLASSICO with fine RISERVA, excellent IGT Camartina (SANGIO-Cab), and barrel-fermented white Batàr.

Quintarelli, Giuseppe ★★★★ True artisan producer of VALPOLICELLA, RECIOTO, and AMARONE, at the top in both quality and price.

Raboso del Piave (now DOC) Ven r ★★ 93 94 95 97 99' 00 01 Powerful, sharp, interesting country red; needs age. Look for Molon.

Ragose, Le ★★→★★★ Family estate, one of VALPOLICELLA'S best. AMARONE and RECIOTO top quality; Cabernet and VALPOLICELLA very good, too.

Ramandolo See Verduzzo Colli Orientali del Friuli.

Ramitello See Di Majo Norante.

Rampolla, Castello dei ★★★ Fine estate in Panzano in CHIANTI CLASSICO, notable Cabernet-based wines Sammarco and VIGNA di Alceo.

Recioto

Wine made of half-dried grapes. Speciality of Veneto since the days of the Venetian empire; has roots in classical Roman wine, Raeticus. Always sw; s'times sp (drink young). Sweet, concentrated, can be kept for a long time.

Recioto di Gambellara Ven DOC w sw (sp s/sw DYA) ★ Mostly half-sparkling and industrial. Best is strong and sweet. Look for La Biancara.

Recioto di Soave Ven DOCG w s/sw (sp) ★★★ 90 91 92 93 94 95 97 98 99 00 01 SOAVE made from selected half-dried grapes: sweet, fruity, slightly almondy; high alcohol. Outstanding from ANSELMI, Gini, Tamellini, and PIEROPAN.

Recioto della Valpolicella Ven DOC r s/sw (sp) ★★→★★★ 95 97 98 00 Strong, sometimes sparkling red. Very good from ALLEGRINI, Baltieri, BOLLA,

BRUNELLI, BUSSOLA, Castellani, DAL FORNO, LE RAGOSE, LE SALETTE, QUINTARELLI, Serègo Alighieri, Speri, Stefano Accordini, TEDESCHI, Trabucchi, CS Valpolicella, Villa Bellini, Villa Monteleone, and Viviani.

Recioto della Valpolicella Amarone See Amarone.

Refosco r ★★→★★★ 90 93 94 **95 96 97'** 99' 00 Interesting, full, dark, tannic red for ageing. The same grape as the Mondeuse of Savoie. Best comes from F-VG DOC COLLI ORIENTALI, Dorigo, Denis Montanara, and CARSO (where known as Terrano). Vg from LIVIO FELLUGA, LIVON, Miani, Moschioni, Ronchi di Manzano, Venica. Often value.

Regaleali ★★★ Perhaps best Sicilian producer owned by noble family of Tasca d'Almerita (between Palermo and Caltanissetta to the SE). Vg IGT red, white, and p Regaleali, red Ross Also very impressive CHARD.

Ribolla (Colli Orientali del Friuli and Collio) F-VG DOC w ★→★★★ DYA Thin NE white. The best comes from COLLIO. Top estates: La Castellada, Damijan, Fliegl, GRAVNER, Il Carpino, Primosic, Radikon.

Ricasoli Famous TUSCAN family, "inventors" of CHIANTI, whose C CLASSICO is named after their BROLIO estate and castle.

Riecine r (w) ★★★ First-class CHIANTI CLASSICO estate at Gaiole, created by its former English owner, John Dunkley. Also fine IGT La Gioia SANGIO.

Riesling Formerly used to mean Italian Ries (Ries Italico or Welschriesling). German (Rhine) Ries, now ascendant. Best: DOC ALTO ADIGE ★★ (esp, HOFSTÄTTER, Ignaz Niedrist, Kuenhof, co-op La Vis, Unterortl) and DOC OLTREPO PAVESE LOM ★★ (Brega, Frecciarossa, Le Fracce), also excellent from RONCO del Gelso (DOC ISONZO). Also vg from Le Vigne di San Pietro (Ven), JERMANN, Vajra (Pie).

Ripasso VALPOLICELLA re-fermented on AMARONE grape skins to make a more complex, longer-lived, and fuller wine. First-class is MASI's Campo Fiorin.

Riserva Wine aged for a statutory period, usually in barrels.

Riunite One of the world's largest co-op cellars, nr Reggio Emilia, producing huge quantities of LAMBRUSCO and other wines.

Rivera ★★→★★★ Reliable winemakers at Andria, near Bari (APULIA), with very good red Il Falcone (★★★) and CASTEL DEL MONTE. Also VIGNA al Monte label.

Rivetti, Giorgio (La Spinetta) ★★★→★★★★ Fine MOSCATO d'Asti, excellent BARBERA, interesting IGT Pin, series of top single-vineyard BARBARESCOS. Now owner of v'yards both in the BAROLO and the CHIANTI Colline Pisane DOCGS.

Riviera del Garda Bresciano Lom DOC w p r (sp) ★→★★ r **97** 99 00 01 Simple, sometimes charming cherry-pink CHIARETTO, neutral white from SW Garda. Esp from: Ca' dei Frati, Comincioli, Costaripa, Monte Cigogna.

Rocca, Bruno ★★★ Young producer with admirable BARBARESCO (Rabajà).

Rocca delle Macìe ★★ Large CHIANTI CLASSICO winemaker near Castellina.

Rocche dei Manzoni, Valentino ★★★ Modernist estate at Monforte d'Alba. Vg oaky BAROLO (esp VIGNA Big, Vigna d'la Roul, Cappella di Santo Stefano), BRICCO Manzoni (pioneering BARBERA-NEBBIOLO blend), Valentino Brut.

Rodano ★★→★★★ Pozzesi family makes typical CHIANTI, both Annata and RISERVA, at Castellina and new, very good IGT Lazzicante (MERLOT).

Roero Pie DOC r ★★ **95 96 97'** 98' 99' 00 01 Evolving former drink-me-quick NEBBIOLO from Roeri hills nr ALBA. Can be delicious. Best: Almondo, Ca' Rossa, Cascina Chicco, Correggia, Funtanin, Malvirà, Monchiero-Carbone, Taliano.

Roero Arneis See Arneis.

Ronco Term for a hillside vineyard in N Italy, esp FRIULI-VENEZIA GIULIA.

Ronco del Gnemiz ★★★ Small estate, very fine COLLI ORIENTALI DEL FRIULI.

Rosa del Golfo ★★→★★★ ROSATO DEL SALENTO: one of best. Also vg red VDT Portulano.

Rosato Rosé.

Rosato del Salento Ap p ★★ DYA From near BRINDISI; can be strong, but often really juicy and good. See Copertino, Salice Salento for producers.

Rossese di Dolceacqua Lig DOC r ★★ DYA Quite rare, fragrant, light red of the Riviera. Good from Foresti, Giuncheo, Guglielmi, Lupi.

Rosso Red.

Rosso Cònero Mar DOC r ★★→★★★ 90' **93 94 95** 97' 98 00 01 Some of the best MONTEPULCIANO (varietal) reds of Italy, eg GAROFOLI'S Grosso Agontano, Moroder's RC Dorico, and Le Terrazze's Sassi Neri, Visioni of J. Also very good from Lanari, Leopardi Dittajuti, Malacari, Poggio Morelli.

Rosso di Montalcino Tus DOC r ★★→★★★ **97' 98'** 99' 00 DOC for younger wines from BRUNELLO grapes. For growers see Brunello di Montalcino.

Rosso di Montepulciano Tus DOC r ★★ **97' 98'** 99' 00 Equivalent of the last for jnr VINO NOBILE. For growers see Vino Nobile di M. While ROSSO DI MONTALCINO is increasingly expensive, Rosso di Montepulciano stills offers value.

Rosso Piceno Mar DOC r ★★ **95 97'** 98' 00 01 Stylish Marches red from MONTEPULCIANO-SANGIO, SUPERIORE from classic zone nr Ascoli: Best incl: Bucci, COLLI Ripani, Fonte della Luna, Forano, Le Caniette, Saladini Pilastri, Velenosi Ercole, Villamagna.

Rubesco ★★ The excellent popular red of LUNGAROTTI; see Torgiano.

Ruchè (also Rouchè or Rouchet) A rare old grape (French origin); fruity, fresh, rich-bouqueted red wine (s/sw). Ruchè di Castagnole Monferrato: recent DOC; look for Crivelli, Garetto. SCARPA'S Rouchet Briccorosa: dr, excellent (★★★).

Ruffino ★→★★★ Outstanding CHIANTI merchant at Pontassieve, E of Florence. RISERVA Ducale & Santedame: best. Gd IGT CHARD Solatia, SANGIO-Cab Modus. Owns Lodola Nuova in MONTEPULCIANO for VINO NOBILE DI M, & Greppone Mazzi in MONTALCINO for BRUNELLO DI M. Excellent new SANGIO-Colorino blend Romitorio from Santedame estate. Recent purchase: Borgo Conventi estate in F-VG.

Rufina ★★★ Important subregion of CHIANTI in the hills E of Florence. Best wines from Basciano, CASTELLO del Trebbio, CASTELLO DI NIPOZZANO (FRESCOBALDI), Colognole, SELVAPIANA, Tenuta Bossi, Travignoli.

Russiz Superiore (Collio) See Felluga, Marco.

Sagrantino di Montefalco See Montefalco.

Sala, Castello della ★★→★★★ ANTINORI estate at ORVIETO, Campogrande is the regular white. Top wine is Cervaro della Sala, oak-aged CHARD and GRECHETTO. Muffato della Sala is one of Italy's best botrytis wines. PINOT N also good.

Salice Salento Ap DOC r ★★→★★★ **93 94' 95** 97' **97'** 99 00 Resonant but clean and quenching red from NEGROAMARO grapes. RISERVA after 2 years. Top makers: CANDIDO, De Castris, Due Palme, TAURINO, VALLONE, Valle dell'Asso.

San Felice ★★★ Fine CLASSICO RISERVA Poggio Rosso. Also red IGT Vigorello (SANGIO-Cab), BRUNELLO DI MONTALCINO Campogiovanni.

San Gimignano Famous TUSCAN city of towers & its dry w VERNACCIA. Also v fine r wines: Cesani, Cusona, FALCHINI, La Rampa di Fugnano, PARADISO, Le Calcinaie.

San Giusto a Rentennano ★★★→★★★★ One of the best CHIANTI CLASSICO prods (★★★). Delicious but v rare VIN SANTO. Superb SANGIO IGT Percarlo (★★★★).

San Guido, Tenuta See Sassicaia.

San Leonardo ★★★ Top estate in TRENTINO with outstanding San Leonardo (Cabernet S) and good Trentino DOC MERLOT.

San Michele Appiano Top ALTO ADIGE co-op, look for Sanct Valentin (★★★) selections: CHADONNAY, PINOT GR, SAUV, Cabernet, PINOT N, Gewürztraminer.

Sandrone, Luciano ★★★ Exponent of new-style BAROLO vogue with vg Barolo Cannubi Boschi, Le Vigne, DOLCETTO, BARBERA D'ALBA, and NEBBIOLO D'ALBA.

Sangiovese (Sangioveto) Principal red grape of central Italy. Top performance only in TOSCANA, where many forms incl CHIANTI, VINO NOBILE, BRUNELLO, MORELLINO, etc. V popular: S di Romagna (Emilia-Romagna DOC), a pleasant standard red. Very good from Drei Donà, Madonia, La Berta, Berti, Calonga, San Patrignano, Tre Monti, Zerbina, IGT RONCO dell Ginestre, Ronco della Simia from CASTELLUCCIO. Very good MONTEFALCO ROSSO & TORGIANO (Umbria), sometimes good from ROSSO PICENO (Marches).

Santa Maddalena (or St-Magdalener) T-AA DOC r ★→★★ DYA Typical SCHIAVA AA red, s'times lightish with bitter aftertaste or warm, smooth, & fruity esp: CANTINA SOCIALE St-Magdalena (eg Huck am Bach), Gojer, Hans Rottensteiner (Premstallerhof), Heinrich Rottensteiner, Georg Ramoser-Josephus Mayr.

Santa Margherita Large Veneto (Portogruaro) merchants: Veneto (Torresella), A-A (Kettmeir), TUSCAN (Lamole di Lamole, Vistarenni), Lombardy (CA' DEL BOSCO).

Santadi ★★★ Consistently fine wines from SARDINIAN co-op, esp DOC CARIGNANO DEL SULCIS TERRE BRUNE, ROCCA Rubia and IGT Baie Rosse (Carignano), Villa di Chiesa (VERMENTINO-CHARDONNAY).

Santi See Gruppo Italiano Vini.

Saracco, Paolo ★★★ Small estate with top MOSCATO D'ASTI.

Sardinia (Sardegna). Major potential, at times evidenced in excellent wines, eg TERRE BRUNE from SANTADI CO-OP, Turriga from ARGIOLAS, Arbeskia from Gabbas, VERMENTINO of CAPICHERA, CANNONAU RISERVAS of Jerzu co-op.

Sartarelli ★★★ One of top VERDICCHIO DEI CASTELLI DI JESI producers, (Tralivio), outstanding, rare Verdicchio VENDEMMIA Tardiva (Contrada Balciana).

Sassicaia Tus r ★★★★ 85' 88' 90' 93 95' 96 97' 98 99' 01 Pioneering Cabernet, outstanding in 70s and 80s & extraordinarily influential, from the Tenuta San Guido of the Incisa della Rocchetta family at BOLGHERI. Promoted from SUPER TUSCAN VDT to special sub-zone status in the Bolgheri DOC in 1994.

Satta, Michele ★★★ Vg DOC BOLGHERI, IGT red blend Piastraia.

Sauvignon Sauvignon Blanc is working very well in the northeast, best from DOCS ALTO ADIGE, COLLIO, COLLI ORIENTALI, ISONZO.

Savuto Cal DOC r p ★★ 93 94 95 97' 98 99 00 01 Fragrant, juicy wine from the provinces of Cosenza and Catanzaro. Best producer is Odoardi.

Scarpa ★★→★★★ Old-fashioned house with BARBERA D'ASTI (La Bogliona), rare Rouchet (RUCHE), vg DOLCETTO, BAROLO, BARBARESCO.

Scavino, Paolo ★★★ Successful, modern-style BAROLO producer. Sought-after single-v'yd wines: Bric del Fiasc and Cannubi; also oak-aged BARBERA.

Schiava High-yielding red grape of TRENTINO-ALTO ADIGE, used for light reds such as LAGO DI CALDARO, SANTA MADDALENA, etc.

Schiopetto, Mario ★★★→★★★★ Legendary COLLIO pioneer with brand-new 25,000-case winery; vg DOC SAUV, PINOT BL, TOCAI, IGT blend Bl de Rosis, etc.

Sciacchetrà See Cinqueterre.

Secco Dry.

Sella & Mosca ★★ Major SARDINIAN grower & merchant with very pleasant white TORBATO & light, fruity VERMENTINO Cala Viola (DYA), g Alghero DOC Marchese di Villamarina (Cabernet Sauvignon) & Tanca Farrà (CANNONAU-Cab), interesting port-like Anghelu Ruju.

Selvapiana ★★★ Top CHIANTI RUFINA estate. Best wines are RISERVA Bucerchiale and Riserva Fornace. Also fine red DOC POMINO.

Sforzato See Valtellina.

Sizzano Pie DOC r ★★ 90 93 95 96' 97' 98 99' 00 01 Full-bodied r from Sizzano, (Novara); mostly NEBBIOLO. Ages up to 10 years. Esp from: Bianchi, Dessilani.

Soave Ven DOC w ★→★★★ DYA Famous Veronese white, widely available. Should be fresh with smooth, limpid texture. Standards rising (at last). Soave CLASSICO: better, more restricted. Especially from PIEROPAN; also La Cappuccina, Fattori and Graney, Gini, Guerrieri-Rizzardi, Inama, Portinari, Tamellini, TEDESCHI, Ca' Rugate.

Solaia Tus r ★★★★ 85 86 88 90 91 93 94 95 96 97 98 99 00 01 V fine Bordeaux-style VDT of Cabernet Sauvignon and a little SANGIO from ANTINORI; first made in 78. Italy's best Cabernet in the 1990s and great wine by any standards.

Solopaca Cam DOC r w ★★ **94 95 97** 99 00 Rather sharp red; soft, dry white from near Benevento. Some promise: especially Antica Masseria Venditti.

Sorì Term for a high S-, SE- or SW-oriented vineyard in PIEMONTE.

Sovana New MAREMMA DOC; inland from coast nr Pitigliano, look for SANGIO, Ciliegiolo from Tenuta Roccaccia, Ripa, Sassotondo, forthcoming Cab from ANTINORI.

Spanna Local name for NEBBIOLO in a variety of N PIEMONTE zones (BOCA, BRAMATERRA, FARA, GATTINARA, GHEMME, LESSONA, SIZZANO).

Sportoletti ★★★ Very good wines from Spello, near ASSISI in Umbria, esp Villa Fidelia BIANCO (CHARD-GRECHETTO) and Villa Fidelia ROSSO (MERLOT-Cab).

Spumante Sparkling, as in sweet ASTI or many gd dry wines, incl both METODO CLASSICO (best from TRENTINO, A ADIGE, FRANCIACORTA, PIEMONTE, OLTREPO PAVESE, some very good also from FRIULI and Veneto) and tank-made cheapos.

Stravecchio Very old.

Südtirol The local name of German-speaking ALTO ADIGE.

Supertuscans Term coined for innovative wines from TOSCANA, often involving pure SANGIOVESE or international varieties, barriques, and elevated prices.

Superiore Wine that has undergone more ageing than normal DOC and contains 0.5–1% more alcohol.

Talento ★★→★★★ Consorzio of producers of METODO CLASSICO SPUMANTE of northern Italy (FRANCIACORTA does not belong, nor do other important producers).

Tasca d'Almerita See Regaleali.

Taurasi Cam DOCG r ★★★ **90' 93' 94' 95** 97' 99 00 01 The best Campanian red. Tannic when young. RISERVA after four years. Radici is MASTROBERARDINO's top bottling. Also gd from FEUDI DI SAN GREGORIO, Gaggiano, Molettieri, Terredora.

Taurino, Cosimo ★★★ Tip-top producer of Salento-APULIA, vg SALICE SALENTO, VDT Notarpanoro, and PATRIGLIONE ROSSO.

Tedeschi, Fratelli ★★★ V reliable and vg producer of VALPOLICELLA, AMARONE, RECIOTO. Good Capitel San ROCCO red IGT.

Terlano T-AA w ★★→★★★ DYA Terlano DOC recently incorporated into ALTO ADIGE. AA Terlano DOC is applicable to 8 varietal whites, especially SAUV. Terlaner in German. Esp from CS Terlan, LAGEDER, NIEDERMAYR, NIEDRIST.

Teroldego Rotaliano T-AA DOC r p ★★→★★★ **95 97** 98 00 01 Attractive, blackberry-scented r; slightly bitter aftertaste; can age v well. Esp FORADORI's. Also good from CA'VIT, Dorigati, Endrizzi, MEZZACORONA's RISERVA, & Zeni.

Terre Brune Sard r ★★★ Splendid Carignano-Boveladda from the CS SANTADI, exemplary in its indication of the potential of SARDINIA.

Terre di Franciacorta Lom DOC r w ★★ **97** 98 99 00 01 Usually pleasant reds (blends of Cab, BARBERA, NEBBIOLO, MERLOT); quite fruity and balanced whites (CHARD, PINOTS). Best producers: see Franciacorta DOCG.

Terre Rosse ★★ Pioneering small estate nr Bologna. Its Cab, CHARD, PINOT BL, RIES, even Viognier were trail-blazing wines for the region.

Terre da Vino ★→★★★ Association of 27 PIEMONTE co-ops and private estates incl most local DOCS. Best: Barbaresco La Casa in Collina, Barolo Podere Parussi, Barbera d'Asti La Luna e I Falò.

Terriccio ★★★→★★★★ Estate south of Livorno with excellent IGT Lupicaia, vg IGT Tassinaia both Cab-MERLOT blends.

Tignanello Tus r ★★★→★★★★ **88 90 91 93 94 95** 96 97 98 99 00 01 Pioneer and leader of new international-style TUSCAN r's, made by ANTINORI. Needs bottle-age.

Tocai Mild, smooth w (no relation of Hungarian Tokay) of NE. DOC also in Ven and Lom (★→★★), but producers are most proud of it in F-VG (esp COLLIO and COLLI ORIENTALI): (★★→★★★). Best prods: Aldo Polencic, BORGO DEL TIGLIO, Borgo san Daniele, LE VIGNE DI ZAMO, LIVIO FELLUGA, Masut da Rive, Renato Keber, RONCO del Gelso, RONCO DI GNEMIZ, RUSSIZ SUPERIORE, SCHIOPETTO, Venica and Venica, VILLA RUSSIZ.

Torbato di Alghero Sar w ★→★★ DYA Good, fresh, white N Sardinian table wine. Leading brand is SELLA & MOSCA.

Torgiano Umb DOC r w p (sp) ★★ and **Torgiano , Rosso Riserva** Umb DOCG r ★★→★★★ 90 93 **94 95 97** 00. Good red from Umbria, resembles CHIANTI CL in style. RUBESCO: standard. RISERVA VIGNA Montecchi has been outstanding in vintages such as 75, 79, 85; keeps for many years.

Toscana (Tuscany) Italy's central wine region, incl DOCS CHIANTI, MONTALCINO, MONTEPULCIANO, etc, regional IGT Toscana and of course "SUPERTUSCANS".

Traminer Aromatico T-AA DOC w ★★→★★★ DYA (German: Gewürztraminer) Delicate, aromatic, soft. Best from: various co-ops (Caldaro, Colterenzio, Prima & Nuova, SAN MICHELE APPIANO, TERLANO, Termeno) plus Abbazia di Novacella, HAAS, HOFSTÄTTER, Kuenhof, LAGEDER, Laimberg, NIEDERMAYR.

Trebbiano Principal white grape of TOSCANA, found all over Italy. Ugni Blanc in French. Sadly, a waste of good vineyard space, with very rare exceptions.

Trebbiano d'Abruzzo Ab DOC w ★→★★ DYA Gentle, neutral, slightly tannic white from Pescara. Best producer: VALENTINI (also MONTEPULCIANO D'A), but challenged by Masciarelli; Valentina very good as well.

Trentino T-AA DOC r w dr sw ★→★★★ DOC for as many as 20 different wines, mostly named after their grapes. Best are CHARDONNAY, PINOT BLANC, MARZEMINO, TEROLDEGO. The region's capital is Trento.

Triacca ★★→★★★ Very good producer of VALTELLINA; also owns estates in TOSCANA (CHIANTI CLASSICO: La Madonnina; MONTEPULCIANO: Santavenere. All ★★).

Trinoro, Tenuta di ★★★ Tus DOC Isolated and exceptional red wine estate (B'x varieties) in DOC Val d'Orcia between MONTEPULCIANO and MONTALCINO. Early wines jaw-dropping. TRINORO: Cab-MERLOT, Palazzi: Merlot-Cab, both IGT..

Uberti ★★→★★★ Vg prod of DOCG FRANCIACORTA, good white Terre di Franciacorta.

Umani Ronchi ★→★★★ Leading Marche merchant and grower, good quality, esp for VERDICCHIO (Casal di Serra, Plenio), ROSSO CONERO Cumaro white IGT Le Busche (Verdicchio-Chard), red IGT Pelago (Cab-MONTEPULCIANO-MERLOT).

Vajra, Giuseppe Domenico ★★★ Vg consistent BAROLO producer, especially for Barbera, BAROLO, DOLCETTO, LANGHE, etc. Also an interesting (not fizzy) FREISA.

Valcalepio Lom DOC r w ★→★★ From nr Bergamo. Pleasant red; lightly scented, fresh white. Good from Brugherata, CASTELLO di Grumello, Monzio.

Val di Cornia Tus DOC r p w ★★→★★★ 95 97 98 99 00 01 New DOC nr Livorno, now competing in quality with BOLGHERI with many vg wines from SANGIO, Cabernet, MERLOT, MONTEPULCIANO. Look for: Jacopo Banti, Botrona, Bulichella, Il Bruschello, Incontri, Tua Rita (Redigaffi), Montepeloso (Gabbro, Nardo), Ambrosini, Petra, Russo, San Giusto, San Luigi, San Michele, Suveraia, Tenuta Vignale.

Valdadige T-AA DOC r w dr s/sw ★ Name for the simple wines of the ADIGE Valley – in German "Etschtaler".

Valentini, Edoardo ★★★ The grand tradition and the best maker of MONTEPULCIANO and TREBBIANO D'ABRUZZO.

Valgella See Valtellina.

Valle d'Aosta VdA DOC Regional DOC for more than 20 Alpine wines including Premetta, Fumin, Blanc de Morgex et de La Salle, Chambave, Nus Malvoisie, Arnad Montjovet, Torrette, Donnas, Enfer d'Arvier.

Valle Isarco (Eisacktal) T-AA DOC w ★★ DYA Recently this DOC was incorporated into ALTO ADIGE DOC. AA Valle Isarco DOC is applicable to 7 varietal wines made NE of Bolzano. Good Gewürztraminer, MULLER-T, RIESLING, SILVANER. Top producers: CS Eisacktaler, Abbasid di Novacella, and Kuenhof.

Vallone ★★→★★★ Always better DOC BRINDISI DOC SALICE SALENTO; outstanding, very concentrated red IGT from dried NEGROAMARO grapes (Gratticaia).

Valpolicella Ven DOC r ★→★★★ (Superiore) 93 94 95 **97 98** 00 01 (others) DYA Attractive r from nr VERONA; best young. Recent quality improvement. V best can be concentrated, complex and merit higher prices. Delicate nutty scent, slightly bitter taste, (none true of junk sold in big bottles). CLASSICO more restricted; SUPERIORE has 12% alcohol and 1 yr of age. Good esp from Stefano Accordino, Bertani, Brunelli, Guerrieri-Rizzardi, LE RAGOSE, LE SALETTE, MASI, Michele Castellani, Sant' Antonio, Speri, TEDESCHI, Tommasi, Tommaso Bussola, CS VALPOLICELLA Villa Monteleone, ZENATO. DAL FORNO and QUINTARELLI make the best (★★★). Interesting IGTS on the way to a new Valpolicella style: MASI'S Toar and Osar, ALLEGRINI'S La Grola, La Poja, Palazzo della Torre (★★★).

Valtellina Lom DOC r ★★→★★★ 89 90 94 **95 96 97** 98 99' 00 01 DOC for tannic wines: mainly from Chiavennasca (NEBBIOLO) grapes in Alpine Sondrio province, N Lombardy. Vg SUPERIORE (since 1998 DOCG) from Grumello, Inferno, Sassella, Valgella vineyards. Best from: Conti Sertoli-Salis, Fay, TRIACCA, Nera, Nino Negri, Rainoldi. Sforzato is most conc'd type of Valtellina; similar to AMARONE.

Vecchio Old.

Vecchio Samperi Si ★★★ MARSALA-like VDT from outstanding estate. Best is barrel-aged 30 years, not unlike amontillado sherry. The owner, Marco De Bartoli, also makes the best DOC Marsalas.

Vendemmia Harvest or vintage.

Venerosi Pesciolini, Tenuta di Ghizzano ★★★ Producer of excellent IGT Veneroso (SANGIOVESE, Cab S) and IGT Nambrot (MERLOT) nr Pisa.

Verdicchio dei Castelli di Jesi Mar DOC w (sp) ★★→★★★ DYA Ancient, fresh, pale w from nr Ancona. Current revivial; result: fruity, well-structured, good-value wines. Also CLASSICO. Especially from Bonci-Vallerosa, Brunori, Bucci, Casalfarneto, Cimarelli, Colonnara, Coroncino, Fonte della Luna, GAROFOLI, Lucangeli Aymerich di Laconi, Mancinelli, Sta Barbara, SARTARELLI, UMANI RONCHI, Zaccagnini; also FAZI-BATTAGLIA.

Verdicchio di Matelica Mar DOC w (sp) ★★→★★★ DYA Similar to the above, smaller, less well-known but longer lasting. Especially from Belisario, Bisci, San Biagio, and La Monacesca.

Verduno Pie DOC r ★★ (DYA) Pale red with spicy perfume, from Pelaverga grape. Good producers: Alessandria, Castello di Verduno.

Verduzzo (Colli Orientali del Friuli) F-VG DOC w dr s/sw sw ★★→★★★ Full-bodied w from a native grape. Ramandolo: highly regarded sub-zone. Top makers: Dario Coos, DORIGO, Giovanni Dri. Superb sw VDT from LIS NERIS in ISONZO.

Verduzzo (del Piave) Ven DOC w ★ DYA A dull little white wine.

Vermentino Lig w ★★ DYA Best seafood white wine of Italian Riviera: esp from Pietra Ligure and San Remo. DOC is Riviera Ligure di Ponente. See Pigato. Particularly good from Colle dei Bardellini, Durin, Lambruschi, La Rocca di San Niccolao, Lunae Bosoni, Lupi, Picedi Benettini, ANTINORI'S from BOLGHERI.

Vermentino di Gallura Sar DOCG w ★★→★★★ DYA Soft, dry, strong white of N Sardinia. Especially from CS di Gallura, CS Del Vermentino, Capichera.

Vernaccia di Oristano Sar DOC w dr (sw fz) ★→★★★ **71' 80'** 85' 86' 87 88 90' 91' 93' 94' 95' 97' 98 99 00 01 Sardinian speciality, like light sherry, a touch bitter, full-bodied, and interesting. SUPERIORE with 15.5% alcohol and 3 yrs of age. Top producer: CONTINI.

Vernaccia di San Gimignano Tus DOCG w ★→★★ DYA A Renaissance favourite, then ordinary tourist wine. Much recent improvement, now newly DOCG with tougher production laws. Best: Cusona, Cesani, FALCHINI, Fontaleoni, Le Calcinaie, Il Paradiso, Montenidoli, PANIZZI, Rampa di Fugnano, TERUZZI, PUTHOD.

Verona Capital of the Veneto region (home of VALPOLICELLA, BARDOLINO, SOAVE, etc) and seat of Italy's splendid annual April Wine fair "Vinitaly".

Verrazzano, Castello di ★★→★★★ Vg CHIANTI CLASSICO estate near Greve.

Vicchiomaggio ★★→★★★ CHIANTI CLASSICO estate near Greve.

VIDE Assoc of Italian prods for marketing estate wines from many parts of Italy.

Vie di Romans ★★★→★★★★ Gifted young producer Gianfranco Gallo has built up his father's ISONZO estate to top FRIULI status within a few years. Excellent Isonzo CHARD and SAUV; excellent TOCAI and PINOT GR.

Vietti ★★★ Exemplary producer of characterful PIEMONTE wines, incl BAROLO and BARBARESCO and BARBERA D'ALBA, at Castiglione Falletto in Barolo region.

Vigna or vigneto A single vineyard (but unlike elsewhere, higher quality than that for generic DOC is not required in Italy).

Vignalta ★★→★★★ Top producer in COLLI EUGANEI near Padova (Veneto); very good COLLI Euganei Cab RISERVA and MERLOT-Cab "Gemola".

Vignamaggio ★★→★★★ Historic, beautiful, vg CHIANTI CLASSICO estate nr Greve.

Villa ★★★ Top producer of DOCG FRANCIACORTA, also very good red DOC TERRE DI FRANCIACORTA (Gradoni).

Villa Matilde ★★★ Top Campania producer of VDT VIGNA Camarato, Falerno ROSSO and BIANCO (Vigna Caracci).

Villa Russiz ★★★ Impressive white DOC COLLIO Goriziano from Gianni Menotti: vg SAUV and MERLOT (esp "de la Tour" selections), PINOT BL, PINOT GR, TOCAI, CHARD.

Vin Santo or Vinsanto, Vin(o) Santo Term for certain strong, sweet wines esp, in TOSCANA: usually PASSITO. Can be very fine both in Toscana and TRENTINO.

Vin Santo Toscano Tus w s/sw ★→★★★ Aromatic, rich, & smooth. Aged in very small barrels called *caratelli*. Can be as astonishing as expensive, but a good one is very rare and top producers are always short of it. Best from AVIGNONESI, CAPEZZANA, CORZANO & PATERNO, FELSINA, ISOLE E OLENA, SAN GIUSTO A RENTENNANO, SELVAPIANA.

Vino da arrosto "Wine for roast meat" – ie, good, robust, dry red.

Vino Nobile di Montepulciano Tus DOCG r ★★★ 90 91 93 95' 96' 97' 98 99 00 01 Impressive SANGIO r with bouquet & style but often v. tannic, now making its name & fortune. RISERVA after 3 yrs. Best estates incl AVIGNONESI, Bindella, BOSCARELLI, Canneto, Le Casalte, Fattoria del Cerro, Contucci, Dei, Fassati. La Bracesca, La Ciarliana, Macchione, Nottola, Paterno, POLIZIANO, Romeo, Salcheto, Trerose, Valdipiatta, & Vecchia Cantina (look for Briareo), Villa Sant'Anna. So far reasonably priced.

Vino novello Italy's equivalent of France's *primeurs* (as in Beaujolais).

Vino da tavola (vdt) "Table wine": the humblest class of Italian wine, with no specific geographical or other claim to fame. See IGT.

Vintage Tunina F-VG w ★★★ A notable blended white from JERMANN estate.

Vivaldi-Arunda ★★→★★★ Winemaker Josef Reiterer makes top SUDTIROL sp. Best: Extra Brut RISERVA, Cuvée Marianna.

Voerzio, Roberto ★★★→★★★★ Young BAROLO pace-setter. Excellent single v'yd BAROLOS: Brunate, Cerequio, Serra; also impressive BARBERA D'ALBA.

Volpaia, Castello di ★★→★★★ First-class CHIANTI CLASSICO estate at Radda. Elegant, rather light Chianti, IGT r Coltassala (SANGIO) & Balifico (Sangio-Cab).

VQPRD Often found on the labels of DOC wines to signify "Vini di Qualità Prodotti in Regione Delimitata".

"Where the Dreams now is just wine"... ★★★. JERMANN's high-level VDT CHARD.

Zanella, Maurizio Creator of CA' DEL BOSCO. His name is on his top Cab-MERLOT blend, one of Italy's best.

Zenato Ven ★★→★★★ V reliable estate for VALPOLICELLA, SOAVE, AMARONE.

Zerbina, Fattoria ★★★ New leader in Romagna; best ALBANA DOCG to date (rich PASSITO: Scacco Matto), gd SANGIO; barrique-aged Sangio-Cab IGT "Marzieno".

Zibibbo Si w sw ★★ Fashionable MOSCATO from PANTELLERIA island. Gd prod: Murana.

Zonin ★→★★★ One of Italy's biggest privately owned estates and wineries, based at GAMBELLARA, with DOC and DOCG VALPOLICELLA, etc. Others are at ASTI and in CHIANTI CLASSICO (Castello di Albola), SAN GIMIGNANO, FRIULI, now in Sicily and throughout Italy. Also at Barboursville, Virginia (USA).

ITALY

Germany

More heavily shaded areas are the wine growing regions

North Sea

The following abbreviations of regional names are used in the text:

Bad	Baden
Frank	Franken
M-M	Mittelmosel
M-S-R	Mosel-Saar-Ruwer
Na	Nahe
Rhg	Rheingau
Rhh	Rheinhessen
Pfz	Pfalz
Würt	Württemberg

German wines should be enjoying a worldwide boom today. New ideas, easier labelling on many wines, reasonable prices, and an unprecedented string of fourteen good-to-great vintages are all in their favour. Yet outside Germany they are still a hard sell. What is wrong? Pure, penetrating flavours and low-to-moderate alcohol should be ideal for modern tastes. Instead, Germany has everyone confused: there are too many variations on the theme; producers make too many styles. Kabinett, Spätlese, and Auslese might all be sweet, dry, or in the middle. Their appellations might mean single vineyards, whole communes, or entire regions.

This is a pivotal time in the politics of German wine. With the 2000 vintage, two new designations were introduced on a national level. "Classic" denotes dry wines intended for good, everyday drinking from a single variety. Each region has put together its own list of eligible varieties. There is no limit on yield, but the vineyards must be identified in the spring before the harvest. "Selection" is intended as the top designation for dry wines; a limited selection of varieties is allowed and the rules include a maximum yield and blind tasting test. But the international impact of these new categories has been almost zero. The new German craze for dry wines is not shared by the cognoscenti abroad.

Other German wines are still classified according to grape ripeness levels. Most wines (like most from France) need sugar added before fermentation to make up for missing sunshine. But unlike in France, German wine from grapes ripe enough not to need extra sugar is made and sold as a separate product: *Qualitätswein mit Prädikat*, or QmP. Within this top category, natural sugar content is expressed by traditional terms in ascending order of ripeness: *Kabinett, Spätlese, Auslese, Eiswein, Beerenauslese, Trockenbeerenauslese*.

QbA (*Qualitätswein bestimmter Anbaugebiete*), the second level, is for wines that needed additional sugar. The third level, *Tafelwein*, like Italian *vino da tavola*, is free of restraints. Officially it is the lowest grade, but impatience with the outdated law can make it the logical resort for innovative producers who set their own high standards.

Though there is much more detail in the laws, this is the gist of the quality grading. It differs completely from other countries' systems in ignoring geographical differences. In theory, all any German vineyard has to do to make the best wine is to grow the ripest grapes – even of inferior varieties – which is patent nonsense.

The law does distinguish between degrees of geographical exactness – but in a way that just leads to confusion. In labelling "quality" wine, growers or merchants are given a choice. They can (and generally do) label their best wines with the name of a single vineyard or *Einzellage*. Germany has about 2,600 *Einzellage* names. Obviously, only a relative few are famous enough to help sell the wine, so the 1971 law created a second class of vineyard name: the *Grosslage*. A *Grosslage* is a group of *Einzellagen* of supposedly similar character. Because there are fewer *Grosslage* names, and far more wine from each, they have the advantage of familiarity – a poor substitute for hard-earned fame. This is another law that must change.

Thirdly, growers or merchants may choose to sell their wine under a *Bereich* or regional name. To cope with demand for "Bernkasteler", "Niersteiner" or "Johannisberger" these famous names were made legal for large districts. "Bereich Johannisberg" covers the entire Rheingau: another avenue to consumer disappointment that must be closed.

Leading growers are now simplifying labels to avoid confusion and clutter. Many use the village name only, or indeed sell top wines under a brand name alone, as in Italy. Whatever they do, the consumer remains confused because the law is framed to protect the producer – and sadly, not the quality producer.

Nonetheless, make a vow to drink a fine German wine once a month (at least). It will change your perception of purity and finesse (and make most Chardonnay taste gross).

Recent vintages

Mosel-Saar-Ruwer

Mosels (including Saar and Ruwer wines) are so attractive young that their keeping qualities are not often enough explored, and wines older than about 8 years are unusual. But well-made Riesling wines of *Kabinett* class gain from at least 5 years in bottle (often much more), *Spätlese* from 10 to 20, and *Auslese* and *Beerenauslese* anything from 10 to 30 years.

As a rule, in poor years the Saar and Ruwer make sharp, lean wines, but in the best years, above all with botrytis, they can surpass the whole world for elegance and thrilling, steely "breed".

2001 A golden October resulted in the best Mosel Riesling since 1990. Saar and Ruwer less exciting but still perfect balance. (Lots of Spätlesen & Auslesee.)

2000 Riesling stood up to harvest rain here better than most other places. Dominated by gd QbA and Kabinett. Auslesen rarer, but exciting.

1999 Excellent in Saar and Ruwer, lots of Auslesen; generally only good in the Mosel due to high yields. Best wines will drink well young and age.

1998 Riesling grapes came through rainy autumn to give astonishingly good results in the Middle Mosel; Saar and Ruwer less lucky with most QbA. Plenty of Eiswein.

1997 A generous vintage of consistently fruity, elegant wines for the entire region. In the Saar and Ruwer marvellous Auslesen.

1996 A very variable vintage with fine Spätlesen and Auslesen from top sites, but only QbA and Tafelwein elsewhere. Many excellent Eisweins.

1995 Excellent vintage, mainly of Spätlesen and Auslesen of firm structure and long ageing potential. Try to resist drinking too early.

1994 Another vg vintage, mostly QmP with unexceptional QbA and Kabinett, but many Auslesen, BA, and TBA. Rich fruit and high acidity. Drinking well now but will keep.

1993 Small excellent vintage: lots of Auslesen/botrytis; nr perfect harmony. Ready to drink except top Auslesen.

1992 A very large crop. Mostly good QbA, but 30% QmP. To drink soon.

1991 A mixed vintage. Bad frost damage in the Saar and Ruwer, many tart QbA wines but also fine Spätlesen. To drink soon.

1990 Superb vintage, though small. Many QmP wines were the finest for 20 years. Try to resist drinking them all too soon.

1989 Large and often outstanding, with noble rot giving many Auslesen, etc. Saar wines best; the Mittelmosel overproduced, causing some dilution. Except for top Auslesen, ready to drink.

1988 Excellent vintage. Much ripe QmP, esp in the Mittelmosel. For long keeping. Lovely now but no hurry.

1976 Vg small vintage, with some superlative sweet wines and almost no dry. Most wines ready; only the best will keep.

Older fine vintages: 71 69 64 59 53 49 45 37 34 21.

Rheinhessen, Nahe, Pfalz, Rheingau

Even the best wines can be drunk with pleasure when young, but Kabinett, Spätlese, and Auslese Riesling gain enormously in character by keeping for longer. Rheingau wines tend to be longest-lived, improving for 15 years or more, but best wines from the Nahe and Pfalz can last as long. Rheinhessen wines usually mature sooner, and dry Franken and Baden wines are generally best at 3–6 years. Rheingau and Nahe are the longest-living.

2001 Though more erratic than in the Mosel, here, too, this was often an exciting vintage for both dry and classic styles, excellent balance.

2000 The further south, the more difficult the harvest was, the Pfalz catching worst of harvest rain. However, in all regions are islands of excellence.

1999 Average quality where yields were high, but for top growers an excellent vintage of rich, aromatic wines with lots of charm.

1998 An excellent vintage of rich, balanced wines giving many good Spätlesen and Auslesen with excellent ageing potential. They look better as they age. Very closed at present.

1997 Very clean, ripe grapes gave excellent QbA, Kabinett, Spätlese in dry and classic styles. Rare botrytis means Auslese and higher qualities rare.

1996 An excellent vintage, particularly in the Pfalz and the Rheingau with many fine Spätlesen that will benefit from long ageing. Great Eiswein.

1995 Rather variable, but some excellent Spätlesen and Auslesen maturing well – like the 90s. Weak in the Pfalz due to harvest rain.

1994 Good vintage, mostly QmP, with abundant fruit and firm structure. Some superb Auslesen, BA and TBA. Except for them, beginning to drink

1993 A small vintage of v good to excellent quality. Plenty of rich Spätlesen and Auslesen, which are just beginning to reach their peak.

1992 Very large vintage, would have been great but for October cold and rain. A third QmP wines of rich, stylish quality. Most drinking well now.

1991 A good middling vintage, though light soils in the Pfalz suffered from drought. Some fine wines are emerging. Beginning to drink well.

1990 Small but exceptionally fine. High percentage of QmP will keep many years. Try to resist drinking too soon.

1989 Summer storms reduced crop in Rheingau. Vg quality elsewhere, up to Auslese level. Maturing more quickly than expected. Soonish.

1983 Vg Rieslings, esp in the Rheingau and central Nahe. Generally about half QbA, but plenty of Spätlesen, now excellent to drink.

1976 The richest vintage since '21 in places. Very few dry wines. Apart from BA/TBA, most wines fully mature now.

NB On the German vintage notation

Vintage notes after entries in the German section are given in a different form from those elsewhere, to show the style of the vintage as well as its quality. Three styles are indicated:

Bold type (eg **93**) indicates classic, super-ripe vintages with a high proportion of natural (QmP) wines, including Spätlesen and Auslesen.

Normal type (eg 92) indicates "normal" successful vintages with plenty of good wine but no great preponderance of sweeter wines.

Italic type (eg *91*) indicates cool vintages with generally poor ripeness but a fair proportion of reasonably successful wines, tending to be over-acidic. Few or no QmP wines, but correspondingly more selection in the QbA category. Such wines sometimes mature more favourably than expected.

Where no mention is made, the vintage is generally not recommended, or most of its wines have passed maturity.

GERMANY

Achkarren Bad w (r) ★★ Village on the KAISERSTUHL, known esp for GRAUBURGUNDER. First Class vineyard: Schlossberg. Wines generally best drunk during first five years. Good wines: DR HEGER and co-op (WG).

Ahr Ahr r ★→★★ 90 *91 92* **93 94 95** 96 **97** 98 **99** 00 01 Traditional specialized red-wine area, south of Bonn. Light, at best elegant SPÄTBURGUNDER, esp from Adeneuer, Deutzerhof, Kreuzberg, MEYER-NAKEL, Nelles, Stodden.

Amtliche Prüfungsnummer See Prüfungsnummer.

Anheuser, Paul Well-known NAHE grower (★) at BAD KREUZNACH.

APNr Abbreviation of AMTLICHE PRÜFUNGSNUMMER.

Assmannshausen Rhg r ★→★★★ 76 89 90 *92* **93** 94 **95** 96 **97** 98 **99** 00 01 RHEINGAU village known for its usually pale, light SPÄTBURGUNDERS. Top wines: Spätlese Trocken. First Class vineyard: Höllenberg. Grosslagen: Steil and Burgweg. Growers including AUGUST KESSELER, Robert König, Hotel Krone, Von Mumm, and the STATE DOMAIN.

Auslese Wines from selective harvest of super-ripe grapes, the best affected by "noble rot" (*Edelfäule*) and correspondingly unctuous in flavour. Dry Auslesen are usually too alcoholic and clumsy for me.

Avelsbach M-S-R (Ruwer) w ★★★ 71 75 76 83 85 88 **89 90** *91 92* **93** 94 **95** 96 97 *98* **99** 00 01 Village near TRIER. At (rare) best, lovely, delicate wines. Esp BISCHÖFLICHE WEINGÜTER, STAATLICHE WEINBAUDOMÄNE (see Staatsweingut). Grosslage: Römerlay.

Ayl M-S-R (Saar) w ★★★ 71 75 76 83 85 88 **89 90** 91 *92* **93** 94 **95** 96 **97** *98* **99** 00 01 One of the best villages of the SAAR. First Class v'yd: Kupp. Grosslage: SCHARZBERG. Growers incl BISCHÖFLICHE WEINGÜTER, Lauer, DR WAGNER.

Bacchus Modern, perfumed, often kitsch, grape. Best for KABINETT wines.

Bacharach ★→★★★ 83 88 **89 90** *91 92* **93** 94 95 96 97 **98** 99 00 **01** Principal wine town of MITTELRHEIN just downstream from RHEINGAU. Now part of the new BEREICH LORELEY. Racy, austere RIESLINGS, some v fine. First Class v'yards: Hahn, Posten, Wolfshöhle. Growers include FRITZ BASTIAN, TONI JOST, Randolph Kauer, Helmut Mades, RATZENBERGER.

Bad Dürkheim Pfz w (r) ★★→★★★ 76 88 **89 90** *91* 92 **93** 94 95 **96 97** 98 99 00 01 Main town of MITTELHAARDT, with the world's biggest barrel (kitsch) and an ancient September wine festival, the characterful *Würstmarkt* (sausage market). First Class v'yds: Michelsberg, Spielberg. Grosslagen: Feuerberg, Hochmess, Schenkenböhl. Growers: Kurt Darting, Fitz-Ritter, Karst, Pflüger, Karl Schäfer.

Bad Kreuznach Nahe w ★★→★★★ 76 79 **83 85** 86 88 **89 90** *91 92* **93** 94 95 96 **97** 98 99 00 01 Pleasant spa town with fine vineyards. First Class: Brückes, Kahlenberg and Krötenpfuhl. Grosslage: Kronenberg. Growers incl ANHEUSER, Anton Finkenauer, Carl Finkenauer, VON PLETTENBERG.

Baden Huge SW area of scattered v'yds but rapidly growing reputation for substantial, generally dry but supple wines for dining table. Fine Pinots, SPÄTBURGUNDER, RIES, GEWÜRZ. Best areas: KAISERSTUHL, ORTENAU.

Badische Bergstrasse/Kraichgau (Bereich) Widespread district of N BADEN. WEISSBURGUNDER and GRAUBURGUNDER make best wines.

Badischer Winzerkeller Germany's (and Europe's) biggest co-op, at BREISACH; 25,000 members with 12,000 acres, producing almost half of BADEN'S wine: dependably unambitious.

Badisches Frankenland See Tauberfranken.

Barriques Small, new-oak casks arrived tentatively in Germany 20 years ago. Results are still rather mixed. Oak aromatics can add substance to the white Pinots, SPÄTBURGUNDER and LEMBERGER. But they ruin RIESLING.

Bassermann-Jordan ★★★ 76 79 81 83 86 88 **89** 90 **96** 97 **98 99** 00 01 104-acre MITTELHAARDT family estate with many of the best v'yds in DEIDESHEIM, FORST,

RUPPERTSBERG, etc. New winemaker Ulrich Mell has put this historic estate back on top since 1996. Now one of the most dependable large estates.

Bastian, Weingut Fritz ★★ 14-acre BACHARACH estate. Racy, austere RIESLINGS with MOSEL-like delicacy, best from the First Class Posten v'yd.

Becker, J B ★★→★★★ Dedicated family estate and brokerage house at WALLUF. 30 acres in ELTVILLE, MARTINSTHAL, Walluf. Specialist in dry RIESLING.

Beerenauslese Luscious sweet wine from exceptionally ripe individual berries (sugar and flavour usually concentrated by "noble rot"). Rare, expensive.

Bensheim See Hessische Bergstrasse.

Bercher ★★★ KAISERSTUHL estate; 40 acres of white and red Pinots at Burkheim. Excellent Chardonnay, etc, and some of Germany's best SPÄTBURGUNDER.

Bernkastel M-M w ★→★★★★ 71 75 **76** 83 85 86 **88** 89 **90** 91 92 **93** 94 95 96 **97** 98 **99** 00 **01** Top wine town of the MITTELMOSEL; the epitome of RIES. Great First Class vineyard: Doctor, 8 acres; First Class v'yds: Graben, Lay. Grosslagen: Badstube, Kurfürstlay. Top growers incl HERIBERT KERPEN, DR LOOSEN, Markus Molitor, DR PAULY-BERGWEILER, J J PRÜM, Studert-Prüm, THANISCH, WEGELER.

Bernkastel (Bereich) Wide area of deplorably dim quality and superficial flowery character. Mostly MÜLLER-T. Includes all the MITTELMOSEL. Avoid.

GERMANY

Biffar, Josef ★★ Important DEIDESHEIM estate. 40 acres (also WACHENHEIM) of RIES. Dependable classic wines.

Bingen Rhh w ★→★★★ **76** 83 85 **89 90** 91 92 **93** 94 95 96 **97** 98 99 Rhine/NAHE town; fine v'yds: First Class: Scharlachberg. Grosslage: St-Rochuskapelle. Best grower: Villa Sachsen.

The Mosel-Saar-Ruwer, Germany's most dynamic region

Nowhere else in Germany are there so many exciting new producers to be discovered as in the Mosel-Saar-Ruwer. Perhaps this is the result of the special mentality of the *Moselaner* as much as the international interest in the elegant and subtly aromatic Rieslings that this archetypal cool-climate region produces. These are four names to watch for:

Clemens Busch Clemens and Rita Busch's organic estate in Pünderich is situated in one of the least well-known sections of the Mosel Valley and produces unusually powerful, dry Rieslings as well as great Auslese.

Martin Müllen Finally, the historic Mosel town of Traben-Trarbach has a producer whose wines live up to its architecture. Using 19th-century winemaking technology Müllen produces powerful and expressive wines.

Daniel Vollenweider A young Swiss who bought vines in the forgotten Mosel top site of Wolfer Goldgrube in 2000 and specializes in classic-style Spätlese and Auslese inspired by famous names of Middle Mosel.

Dr Wehrheim An historic Saar estate brought back to life by owner Roman Niewodniczanski and winemaker Gernot Kollmann. Good, classic Kabinett and Spätlese, but it is the v'yard-designated dry wines that stand out.

Bingen (Bereich) District name for northwest RHEINHESSEN.

Bischöfliche Weingüter ★★→★★★ Famous Mosel-Saar-Ruwer estate at TRIER, a union of the cathedral property with two other famous charities, the Bischöfliches (Dom) Priesterseminar and the Bischöfliches Konvikt. 240 acres of top vineyards, especially in SAAR and RUWER. Recent vintages returning to former fine form.

Bocksbeutel Flask-shaped bottle used for FRANKEN wines.

Bodensee (Bereich) Idyllic district of S BADEN, on Lake Constance. Dry wines are best drunk within 5 years. Riesling-like MÜLLER-THURGAU a speciality.

Boppard ★→★★★ **76** 83 88 **90** 91 92 **93** 94 **95** 96 97 **98** 99 00 **01** Important wine town of MITTELRHEIN where quality is rapidly improving. Best sites all

> **Warning notice:** *Bereich*
> District within an *Anbaugebiet* (region). The word on a label should be treated as a flashing red light. Do not buy. See Introduction and under Bereich names, eg Bernkastel (Bereich).

belong to amphitheatre of vines called Bopparder Hamm. Growers: Heinrich Müller, August Perll, Weingart. Unbeatable value for money.

Braun, Weingut Heinrich ★★ 60-acre NIERSTEIN estate. Dry and sweet RIESLING of variable quality, the best from First Class v'yds in Nierstein, esp Pettenthal.

Brauneberg M-M w ★★★★ 71 75 76 83 85 87 **88** 89 **90** 91 **92 93** 94 **95** 96 **97** 98 99 00 **01** Top M-S-R village nr BERNKASTEL (750 acres), unbroken tradition for excellent, full-flavoured RIES – Grand Cru if anything on the Mosel is. Great First Class vineyard: Juffer-SONNENUHR. First Class v'yd is Juffer. Grosslage: Kurfürstlay. Growers: Bastgen, FRITZ HAAG, WILLI HAAG, Paulinshof, M F RICHTER.

Breisach Frontier town on Rhine near KAISERSTUHL. Seat of the largest German co-op, the BADISCHER WINZERKELLER.

Breisgau (Bereich) Little-known BADEN district. Good reds and pink WEISSHERBST.

Breuer, Weingut Georg ★★★ Family estate of 36 acres in RUDESHEIM, a CHARTA leader: 6 acres of Berg Schlossberg, also 12.5-acre monopole RAUENTHALER Nonnenberg. Both have given superb quality, full-bodied, dry Ries in recent years. Also excellent Auslesen, BA,TBA since 1995.

Buhl, Reichsrat von ★★ Historic PFALZ family estate, returning to historic form as of '94. 160 acres (DEIDESHEIM, FORST, RUPPERTSBERG...). Leased by Japanese firm.

Bundesweinprämierung The German State Wine Award, organized by DLG (see below): gives great (grosse), silver or bronze medallion labels.

Bürgerspital zum Heiligen Geist ★★★ Ancient charitable WURZBURG estate. 275 acres: W'bg, RANDERSACKER etc. Rich, dry wines, esp SILVANER, RIES; can be vg.

Bürklin-Wolf, Dr ★★★ Famous PFALZ family estate. 234 acres in FORST, DEIDESHEIM, RUPPERTSBERG and WACHENHEIM including many First Class sites. The full-bodied, dry wines from these are often spectacular, but avoid the 99s.

Castell'sches Fürstlich Domänenamt ★→★★★ Historic 142-acre princely estate in STEIGERWALD. SILVANER, RIESLANER. Back on form since 1999.

Chardonnay Can now be grown legally throughout Germany but total planted area remains less than 300 acres. A few good wines from recent vintages. Best growers: K H Johner, Rebholz.

Charta Organization of top RHEINGAU estates making forceful, dry RIES to far higher standards than dismally permissive laws require.

Christmann ★★★ 35-acre estate in Gimmeldingen (PFALZ) making rich, dry RIES from First Class v'yds, notably Königsbacher Idig. Impressive quality since 95.

Christoffel, J J ★★★ Tiny domain in ERDEN, URZIG. Polished, elegant RIESLING.

Clevner (or Klevner) Synonym in WURTTEMBERG for Blauer Frühburgunder red grape, a mutation of Pinot Noir or Italian Chiavenna (early ripening black Pinot). Confusingly also ORTENAU (BADEN) synonym for TRAMINER.

Crusius ★★★ 33-acre family estate at TRAISEN, NAHE. Vivid RIES from Bastei and Rotenfels of Traisen and SCHLOSSBÖCKELHEIM. Top wines age v well. Also good SEKT and freshly fruity SPÄTBURGUNDER dry rosé.

Deidesheim Pfz w (r) ★★→★★★★ 71 76 83 85 **88** 89 **90** 91 **92** 93 94 95 **96** 97 **98** 99 00 01 Lgst top-quality village of the PFALZ (1,000 acres). Richly flavoured lively wines. Also SEKT. First Class vineyards: Grainhübel, Hohenmorgen, Kalkofen, Kieselberg, Langenmorgen, Leinhöhle. Grosslagen: Mariengarten, Hofstück. Esp BASSERMANN-JORDAN, BIFFAR, V BUHL, BÜRKLIN-WOLF, DEINHARD, WOLF.

Deinhard In 97 the Wegeler family sold the 200-yr-old merchant house and SEKT prod Deinhard to sp-wine giant Henkell-Söhnlein of Schierstein on the Rhine. But the splendid Deinhard estates remain in family ownership (see WEGELER).

Deinhard, Dr ★★ Fine 74-acre family estate: some of DEIDESHEIM's best v'yds.

Deutscher Tafelwein Officially the term for very humble German wines. Now, confusingly, the flag of convenience for some costly novelties as well (eg BARRIQUE wines). As in Italy, the law will have to change.

Deutsches Weinsiegel A quality seal (ie neck label) for wines which have passed a statutory tasting test. Seals are: yellow for dry, green for medium-dry, red for medium-sweet. Means little; proves nothing.

Diel, Schlossgut ★★★ Fashionable 30-acre NAHE estate; made its name by ageing GRAUBURGUNDER and WEISSBURGUNDER in French BARRIQUES. But today its traditional RIESLING is among finest Nahe wines. Stunning AUSLESE and EISWEIN.

DLG (Deutsche Landwirtschaftgesellschaft) The German Agricultural Society at Frankfurt. Awards national medals for quality – far too generously.

Domäne German for "domain" or "estate". Sometimes used alone to mean the "State domain" (STAATSWEINGUT or Staatliche Weinbaudomäne).

Dönnhoff, Weingut Hermann ★★★★ 88 **89** 90 91 92 93 94 **95** 96 97 **98** 99 00 01 31½-acre leading NAHE estate with exceptionally fine RIES from NIEDERHAUSEN, Oberhausen, SCHLOSSBÖCKELHEIM. Some of Germany's greatest wines.

Dornfelder New red grape making deep-coloured, rustic wines in the PFALZ.

Durbach Baden w (r) ★★→★★★ **76** 90 **93** 94 **95** 96 97 **98** 99 00 01 Village with 775 acres of vineyards incl a handful of First Class sites. Top growers: A LAIBLE, H Männle, SCHLOSS STAUFENBERG, WOLFF METTERNICH. Choose their KLINGELBERGERS (RIESLING) and CLEVNERS (TRAMINER). Grosslage: Fürsteneck.

Edel Means "noble". *Edelfäule* means "noble rot".

Egon Müller zu Scharzhof ★★★★ 75 76 *77* 78 **79** 80 81 82 **83** 84 85 86 *87* 88 **89** 90 91 *92* **93** 94 **95** 96 **97** 98 **99** 00 **01** Top SAAR estate of 30 acres at WILTINGEN. Its rich and racy SCHARZHOFBERGER RIESLING in AUSLESEN vintages is among the world's greatest wines; best are given gold capsules. 93s, 95s, 97s, and 99s are sublime, honeyed, immortal. Le Gallais is a second estate in WILTINGER Braune Kupp.

Eiswein Dessert wine made from frozen grapes with the ice (ie water content) discarded, thus very concentrated in flavour, acidity and sugar – of BEERENAUSLESE ripeness or more. Alcohol content can be as low as 5.5%. Very expensive. S'times made as late as Jan/Feb of following year.

Eitelsbach M-S-R (Ruwer) w ★★→★★★★ 71 75 **76** 83 **85** 88 **89** 90 *91* 92 **93** 94 **95** *96* **97** 98 **99** 00 01 RUWER village now part of TRIER, incl superb Great First Class KARTHAUSERHOFBERG vineyard site. Grosslage: Römerlay.

Elbe Important wine-river of eastern Germany. See Sachsen.

Elbling Grape introduced by the Romans, widely grown on upper MOSEL. Can be sharp and tasteless, but capable of real freshness and vitality in the best conditions (eg at Nittel or SCHLOSS THORN in the OBERMOSEL).

Eltville Rhg w ★★→★★★ **71** 76 **83** 88 **89** 90 *91* 92 **93** 94 **95** 96 **97** 98 **99** 00 01 Major wine town with cellars of RHEINGAU STATE DOMAIN, FISCHER and VON SIMMERN estates. First Class v'yd: Sonnenberg. Grosslage: Steinmächer.

Enkirch M-M w ★★→★★★ **71** 76 **85** 88 **89** 90 *91* **93** 94 **95** *96* **97** 98 **99** 00 **01** Little-known MITTELMOSEL village, often overlooked but with lovely, light, tasty wine. The best grower is Immich-Batterieberg.

Erbach Rhg w ★★★ **71** 76 **83** 85 86 88 **89** 90 *91* 92 **93** 94 **95** 96 **97** 98 **99** 00 01 RHG area: big, perfumed, age-worthy wines, including First Class vineyards Hohenrain, MARCOBRUNN, Siegelsberg, Steinmorgen, Schlossberg. Major estates: SCHLOSS REINHARTSHAUSEN, Schloss, SCHÖNBORN. Also BECKER, JAKOB JUNG, KNYPHAUSEN, VON SIMMERN, etc. Not as good as it once was.

GERMANY

Erben Word meaning "heirs", often used on old-established estate labels.

Erden M-M w ★★★ 71 75 76 83 85 88 89 90 91 92 93 94 95 96 97 98 99 00 01
Village between Urzig and Kröv: noble, full-flavoured, vigorous wine (More herbal and mineral than the wines of nearby BERNKASTEL and WEHLEN but equally long-living). Great First Class v'yds: Prälat, Treppchen. Grosslage: Schwarzlay. Growers incl BISCHÖFLICHE WEINGÜTER, J J CHRISTOFFEL, DR LOOSEN, Meulenhof, Mönchhof, Peter Nicolay.

Erstes Gewächs Literally translates as "first growth". See box on p.152.

Germany's quality levels

The official range of qualities in ascending order are as follows:

1 Deutscher Tafelwein: sweetish light wine of no specified character. (From certain producers, can be very special.)
2 Landwein: dryish Tafelwein with some regional style.
3 Qualitätswein: dry or sweetish wine with sugar added before fermentation to increase its strength, but tested for quality and with distinct local and grape character.
4 Kabinett: dry or dryish natural (unsugared) wine of distinct personality and distinguishing lightness. Can be very sublime.
5 Spätlese: stronger, often sweeter than Kabinett. Full-bodied. Today many top Spätlesen are *trocken* or completely dry.
6 Auslese: sweeter, sometimes stronger than Spätlese, often with honey-like flavours, intense and long. Occasionally dry and weighty.
7 Beerenauslese: v sweet and usually strong, intense; can be superb.
8 Eiswein: (Beeren- or Trockenbeerenauslese) concentrated, sharpish, and very sweet. Can be v fine or too extreme, unharmonious.
9 Trockenbeerenauslese: intensely sweet and aromatic; alcohol slight. Extraordinary and everlasting.

Erzeugerabfüllung Bottled by producer. Being replaced by "GUTSABFÜLLUNG". NB: only the estates will make this switch. Co-ops will continue with Erzeugerabfüllung.

Escherndorf Frank w ★★→★★★ 76 83 88 89 90 91 92 93 94 95 96 97 98 99 00 01 Important wine town near WURZBURG. Similar, tasty dry wine. First Class vineyard: Lump. Grosslage: Kirchberg. Growers incl JULIUSSPITAL, Egon Schäffer, Horst Sauer.

Eser, Weingut August ★★ 20-acre RHEINGAU estate at OESTRICH. V'yds also in Hallgarten, RAUENTHAL (esp Gehrn, Rothenberg), WINKEL. Variable wines.

Faul, Fritz Prolific producer of MÜLLER-THURGAU under fashionable BEREICH label.

Filzen M-S-R (Saar) w ★★→★★★ 76 83 88 89 90 92 93 94 95 96 97 98 99 00 Sml SAAR village nr WILTINGEN. First Class v'yd: Pulchen. Grower to note: Piedmont.

Fischer Erben, Weingut ★★★ 18-acre RHEINGAU estate at ELTVILLE with high traditional standards. Long-lived, classic wines.

Forschungsanstalt Geisenheim See Hessische Forschungsanstalt.

Forst Pfz w ★★→★★★★ 71 76 83 89 90 91 92 93 94 95 96 97 98 99 00 01 MITTELHAARDT village with 500 acres of Germany's best v'yds. Ripe, richly fragrant, full-bodied but subtle wines. First Class vineyards: Jesuitengarten, Kirchenstück, FREUNDSTÜCK, Pechstein, Ungeheuer. Grosslagen: Mariengarten, Schnep-fenflug. Top growers incl BASSERMANN-JORDAN, BURKLIN-WOLF, DR DEINHARD, G MOSBACHER, Eugen Müller, H Spindler, Werlé, J L WOLF.

Franken Franconia Region of excellent, distinctive, dry wines, esp SILVANER, always bottled in round-bellied flasks (BOCKSBEUTEL). The centre is WURZBURG. Bereich names: MAINDREIECK, STEIGERWALD. Top producers: BURGERSPITAL, CASTELL'SCHES, FÜRST RUDOLF, JULIUSSPITAL, LÖWENSTEIN, Horst Sauer, WIRSCHING, etc.

Freiburg Baden w (r) ★→★★ DYA Wine centre in BREISGAU, N of MARKGRÄFLERLAND. Good GUTEDEL.

Friedrich-Wilhelm Gymnasium ★★ Important 82-acre charitable estate based in TRIER with v'yds in BERNKASTEL, GRAACH, OCKFEN, TRITTENHEIM, ZELTINGEN, etc, all M-S-R. Since 95 much improved after poor patch.

Fuhrmann See Pfeffingen.

Fürst Rudolf ★★★ Small estate in Bürgstadt making some of the best wines in FRANKEN, particularly Burgundian SPÄTBURGUNDER and oak-aged WEISSBURGUNDER.

Gallais Le See Egon Müller.

Geisenheim Rhg w ★★→★★★ **71 76 85** 88 **89 90** 91 92 **93** 94 95 **96** 97 98 **99** 00 01 Village famous for Germany's best-known wine school and vg aromatic wines. First Class v'yds: Kläuserweg, Rothenberg. Grosslagen: Burgweg, Erntebringer. Top growers: JOHANNISHOF, SCHLOSS SCHÖNBORN, WEGELER, VON ZWIERLEIN.

Gemeinde A commune or parish.

Gewürztraminer (or Traminer) "Spicy" grape, speciality of Alsace, also giving some impressive wines in Germany, esp in PFALZ, BADEN and WÜRTTEMBERG.

Gimmeldingen Pfz w ★★ **76 85** 88 **89 90** 91 92 **93** 94 95 **96** 97 **98** 99 00 **01** Village just South of MITTELHAARDT. At best, rich, succulent wines. Grosslage: Meerspinne. Growers incl: CHRISTMANN, MÜLLER-CATOIR.

Graach M-M w ★★★ **71** 75 76 **83** 85 **88 89 90** 91 92 **93** 94 95 **96** 97 **98** 99 00 01 Small village between BERNKASTEL and WEHLEN. First Class v'yds: Domprobst, Himmelreich, Josephshofer. Grosslage: Münzlay. Many top growers: VON KESSELSTATT, DR LOOSEN, J J PRÜM, WILLI SCHAEFER, SELBACH-OSTER, DR WEINS-PRÜM.

Grans-Fassian ★★ Fine 25-acre MOSEL estate at Leiwen. V'yds there and in TRITTENHEIM. EISWEIN a speciality. Dependable high quality since 95.

Grauburgunder Synonym of RULÄNDER or Pinot Gris: grape giving soft, full-bodied wine. Best in BADEN and southern PFALZ.

Grosser Ring Group of top (VDP) MOSEL-SAAR-RUWER estates, whose annual September auction regularly sets world-record prices.

Grosslage See Introduction, pages 133–134.

Gunderloch ★★★★ 88 **89 90** 91 92 **93** 94 95 **96 97 98** 99 00 **01** 30-acre NACKENHEIM estate making some of the finest RIES on the entire Rhine, including spectacular BA/TBA. The undisputed number one in RHEINHESSEN. Owns well-known Balbach estate in NIERSTEIN.

Guntrum, Louis ★★ Large (67-acre) family estate in NIERSTEIN, OPPENHEIM, etc. Good SILVANER and GEWÜRZTRAMINER as well as RIESLING.

Gutedel German name for the ancient Chasselas grape, used in S BADEN.

Gutsabfüllung Estate-bottled. Term for genuinely estate-bottled wines.

Gutsverwaltung Estate administration.

Haag, Weingut Fritz ★★★★ **69** 70 **71** 72 73 74 **75 76** 77 78 **79** 80 81 82 **83** 84 **85** 86 87 **88** 89 **90** 91 92 93 94 **95** 96 97 98 99 00 **01** Top estate in BRAUNEBERG run by Wilhelm Haag, president of GROSSER RING. MOSEL RIES of crystalline purity & racy brilliance for long ageing. Haag's son runs the SCHLOSS LIESER estate.

Haag, Weingut Willi ★★ 7-acre BRAUNEBERG estate. Full, "old-style" RIES. Some fine AUSLESE. Improving quality since 95.

Haart, Reinhold ★★★ The best estate in PIESPORT, and growing in repute. Refined, aromatic wines, capable of long ageing.

Halbtrocken Medium-dry (literally "semi-dry"). Containing fewer than 18 but more than 9 grams per litre unfermented sugar. Popular category of wine intended for mealtimes, usually better balanced than TROCKEN.

GERMANY

Remember that vintage information for German wines is given in a different form from the ready/not ready distinction applying to other countries. Read the explanation at the bottom of page 137.

Hattenheim Rhg w ★★→★★★★ 71 76 83 89 90 91 **92 93** 94 **95 96** 97 98 **99** 00 01 Superlative 500-acre wine town. The First Class vineyards are Engelmannsberg, Mannberg, Pfaffenberg, Nussbrunnen, Wisselbrunnen, and most famously STEINBERG (ORTSTEIL). Grosslage: Deutelsberg. MARCOBRUNN: on ERBACH boundary. Estates include KNYPHAUSEN, RESS, SCHLOSS SCHÖNBORN, VON SIMMERN, STATE DOMAIN, etc.

Heldenmut, Weingut Ideal VDP member; organic PRÄDIKAT wines only.

Henkell See Deinhard.

Heger, Dr ★★★ Leading estate of BADEN with excellent, dry WEISSBURGUNDER, GRAUBURGUNDER and powerful oak-aged SPÄTBURGUNDER reds.

Heilbronn Würt w r ★→★★ **89 90 93** 94 **96 97** 98 99 00 01 Wine town with many small growers and a good co-op. Best wines are RIES and LEMBERGERS. Seat of DLG competition. Top growers: Amalienhof, Drautz-Able, Heinrich.

Hessen, Prinz von ★★→★★★ Famous 75-acre estate in JOHANNISBERG, KIEDRICH, and WINKEL. Rapidly improving quality since 95 vintage.

Hessische Bergstrasse w ★★→★★★ **90** 91 **92 93** 94 95 96 **97** 98 **99** 00 01 Smallest wine region in western Germany (1,000 acres), N of Heidelberg. Pleasant RIES from STATE DOMAIN v'yds at BENSHEIM, Bergstrasser co-op, Heppenheim, Simon-Bürkle, and Stadt Bensheim.

Hessische Forschungsanstalt für Wein-Obst & Gartenbau Famous wine school and research establishment at GEISENHEIM, RHEINGAU. Good wines incl reds. The name on the label is Forschungsanstalt.

Heyl zu Herrnsheim ★★★ Leading 92-acre NIERSTEIN estate, 60% RIES. Since fine 96 v'tge owned by Ahr family. Dry RIES, SILVANER, W'BURGUNDER of classical elegance.

Heymann-Löwenstein ★★★ Young estate in Lower or "Terrace Mosel" with most consistent dry RIESLING in MOSEL-SAAR-RUWER and some remarkable AUSLESE and TBA. A rapidly rising star!

Hochgewächs Supposedly superior level of QBA RIES, esp in MOSEL-SAAR-RUWER.

Hochheim Rhg w ★★→★★★★ **71** 75 76 79 **83 85** 86 **88 89** 90 91 **92 93** 94 95 **96 97 98** 99 00 **01** 600-acre wine town 15 miles E of main RHEINGAU area, once thought of as best on Rhine. RHEINGAU-like wines with an earthy intensity and fragrance of their own. First Class vineyards: Domdechaney, Hölle, Kirchenstück, Königin Viktoria Berg (12-acre monopoly of Hupfeld of OESTRICH). Grosslage: Daubhaus. Growers incl Hupfeld, FRANZ KUNSTLER, WJ SCHAEFER, SCHLOSS SCHÖNBORN, STAATSWEINGUT, WERNER.

Hock Traditional English term for Rhine wine, derived from HOCHHEIM.

Hoensbroech, Weingut Reichsgraf zu ★★ Top KRAICHGAU estate. 37 acres. Dry WEISSBURGUNDER, GRAUBURGUNDER, SILVANER, eg Michelfelder Himmelberg.

Hohenlohe-Oehringen, Weingut Fürst zu ★★ Noble 47-acre estate in Oehringen and WURTTEMBERG. Earthy, bone-dry RIESLING and powerful reds from SPÄTBURGUNDER and LEMBERGER grapes.

Hövel, Weingut von ★★★ Very fine SAAR estate at OBERMOSEL (Hütte is 12-acre monopoly) and in SCHARZHOFBERG. Superb wines since 93.

Huber, Bernard ★★★ Rising star of Breisgau area of BADEN with powerful, oak-aged SPÄTBURGUNDER reds and Burgundian-style WEISSBURGUNDER, CHARDONNAY.

Huxelrebe Modern, aromatic grape variety, best for dessert wines.

Ihringen Bad r w ★→★★★ **86** 88 **89 90** 91 92 **93** 94 95 **96 97 98 99** 00 01 One of the best villages of the KAISERSTUHL, BADEN. Proud of its SPÄTBURGUNDER red, WEISSHERBST, and GRAUBURGUNDER. Top growers: DR HEGER, Stigler.

Ilbesheim Deutsches Weintor Pfz w (r) ★→★★ **90 93** 94 95 **96 97** 98 99 00 01 Vast growers co-op with solid reputation for quality.

Ingelheim Rhh r w ★★ **90** 92 **93** 94 95 96 **97** 98 **99** 00 Town opposite RHEINGAU historically known for its SPÄTBURGUNDER. Sadly, few wines today live up to reputation. Top v'yds are Horn, Pares, Sonnenberg and Steinacker.

Iphofen Frank w ★★→★★★ 76 79 83 85 *87* 88 *89* 90 *91 92* **93** 94 *95* 96 **97** 98 **99** 00 01 Village nr WURZBURG. Superb First Class v'yds: Julius-Echter-Berg, Kalb. Grosslage: Burgweg. Growers: JULIUSSPITAL, Ruck, WIRSCHING.

Jahrgang Year – as in "vintage".

Johannisberg Rhg w ★★→★★★★ 71 75 76 83 85 86 88 **89 90** 91 92 **93** 94 **95 96 97** 98 *99* 00 **01** 260-acre classic RHEINGAU village with superlative, subtle RIES. First Class v'yds: Hölle, Klaus, SCHLOSS JOHANNISBERG. Grosslage: Erntebringer. Top growers: JOHANNISHOF, SCHLOSS JOHANNISBERG.

Johannisberg (Bereich) District name for the entire RHEINGAU. Avoid.

Johannishof ★★★ JOHANNISBERG family estate, aka HH Eser. 45 acres. RIESLINGS that justify the great Johannisberg name. Since 96 also RÜDESHEIM wines.

Johner, Karl-Heinz ★★★ Small BADEN estate at Bischoffingen, in the front line for New World Style SPÄTBURGUNDER and oak-aged WEISSBURGUNDER.

Josephshöfer First Class v'yd at GRAACH, the sole property of VON KESSELSTATT.

Jost, Toni ★★★ Perhaps the top estate of the MITTELRHEIN. 25 acres, mainly RIES, in BACHARACH and also in the RHEINGAU.

Juliusspital ★★★ Ancient WÜRZBURG religious charity with 374 acres of top FRANKEN v'yds and many top wines. Look for its dry SILVANERS and RIES.

Kabinett The term for the lightest category of natural, unsugared (QMP) wines. Low in alcohol (RIES averages 7–9%) but capable of sublime finesse. Drink young or with several yrs' age.

Kaiserstuhl (Bereich) One of the top BADEN districts, with notably warm climate and volcanic soil. Villages incl ACHKARREN, IHRINGEN. Grosslage: Vulkanfelsen.

Kallfelz, Albert ★★ Useful producer of fresh MOSELS at ZELL and Merl.

Kallstadt Pfz w (r) ★★→★★★ 76 83 85 88 89 90 92 **93** 94 **95 96** 97 **98** 99 00 01 Village of N MITTELHAARDT. Often underrated fine, rich, dry Riesling and Pinot. First Class vineyard: Saumagen. Grosslagen: Feuerberg, Kobnert. Growers incl Henninger, KOEHLER-RUPRECHT, Schüster.

Kammerpreismünze See Landespreismünze.

Kanzem M-S-R (Saar) w ★★★ 71 76 88 89 90 91 92 **93** 94 **95 96 97** *98* **99** 00 01 Small neighbour of WILTINGEN. First Class vineyard: Altenberg. Grosslage: SCHARZBERG. Growers incl Othegraven, Reverchon, J P Reinert.

Karlsmühle ★★★ Small estate with Lorenshofer monopoly site in RUWER making classic Ruwer RIES, also wines from First Class KASEL v'yds sold under Patheiger label. Consistently excellent quality since 94.

Karthäuserhofberg ★★★★ Top RUWER estate of 46 acres at Eitelsbach. Easily recognized by bottles with only a neck-label. Since 1993, estate has been back on top form. Also good TROCKEN wines.

Kasel M-S-R (Ruwer) w ★★→★★★ 71 76 83 85 88 89 90 91 92 **93** 94 **95** 96 **97** *98* **99** 00 01 Stunning, flowery Römerlay wines. First Class v'yds: Kehrnagel, Nies'chen. Top growers: KARLSMUHLE, VON KESSELSTATT, WEGELER.

Keller Wine cellar. **Kellerei** Winery (ie a big commercial bottler).

Kerner Modern aromatic grape variety, earlier ripening than RIES, of fair quality but without Riesling's inbuilt grace and harmony. Best in SACHSEN.

Kerpen, Weingut Heribert ★★ Small good estate in BERNKASTEL, GRAACH, WEHLEN.

Kesseler, Weingut August ★★★ 35-acre estate making the best SPÄTBURGUNDER reds in ASSMANNSHAUSEN. Also very good, classic-style RIES.

Kesselstatt, von ★★★ The lgst private MOSEL estate, 650 yrs old. Now belonging to Reh family. Some 150 acres in GRAACH, KASEL, PIESPORT, WILTINGEN, etc, producing aromatic, generously fruity MOSELS. Consistent high quality, often magnificent wines from JOSEPHSHÖFER monopoly v'yd and SCHARZHOFBERG.

Kesten M-M w ★→★★★ 71 76 83 88 89 **90** 91 92 **93** 94 **95** 96 **97** 98 **99** 00 01 Neighbour of BRAUNEBERG. Best wines (from Paulinshofberg v'yd) similar. Grosslage: Kurfürstlay. Top growers: Bastgen, Kees-Kieren, PAULINSHOF.

Kiedrich Rhg w ★★→★★★★ 71 76 83 89 90 91 92 93 94 95 96 97 98 99 00 01 Neighbour of RAUENTHAL; equally splendid and high-flavoured. First Class v'yds: Gräfenberg, Wasseros. Grosslage: Heiligenstock. Growers incl FISCHER, KNYPHAUSEN, Speicher-Schuth. R WEIL now top estate.

Klingelberger ORTENAU (BADEN) term for RIESLING, esp at DURBACH.

Kloster Eberbach Glorious 12th-C Cistercian abbey in HATTENHEIM forest. Monks planted STEINBERG, Germany's Clos de Vougeot. Now STATE DOMAIN-owned; HQ of German Wine Academy.

Klüsserath M-M w ★→★★★ 76 83 88 90 91 92 93 94 95 96 97 98 99 00 01 Little-known MOSEL village whose winegrowers have joined forces to classify its top site, Brüderschaft. Growers: Bernhard Kirsten, FRIEDRICH-WILHELM-GYMNASIUM, Regnery.

Knyphausen, Weingut Freiherr zu ★★★ Noble 54-acre estate on former Cistercian land (see Kloster Eberbach) in ELTVILLE, ERBACH, HATTENHEIM, KIEDRICH and MARCOBRUNN. Classic RHEINGAU wines, many dry.

Koehler-Ruprecht ★★★★ 76 77 78 79 80 81 82 83 84 85 86 87 88 89 90 91 92 93 94 95 96 97 98 99 00 01 Highly rated estate (25-acre) going from strength to strength; top KALLSTADT grower. V traditional winemaking; v long-lived, memorable, dry RIES from K Saumagen. Since 91 outstanding SPÄTBURGUNDER.

Kraichgau Small BADEN region S of Heidelberg. Top grower: HOENSBROECH.

Kröv M-M w ★→★★★ 88 90 91 92 93 94 95 96 97 98 99 00 01 Popular tourist resort famous for its Grosslage name: Nacktarsch, or "bare bottom". Be very careful. Best grower: Martin Müllen.

Künstler, Franz ★★★★ HOCHHEIM estate expanded in 1996 to 50 acres by purchase of well-known Aschrott estate. Superb dry RIESLING, esp from First Class Domdechaney, H Hölle, and Kirchenstück, also excellent AUSLESE.

Kuntz, Sybille ★★★ M-S-R Successful protagonist of untypical, dry MOSEL RIESLING of AUSLESE strength.

Laible, Weingut Andreas ★★★ 10-acre DURBACH estate. Fine, sweet and dry RIES, SCHEUREBE, GEWÜRZ (First Class Plauelrain vineyard). "Klingelberger" can be utter joy. Superb quality since 1997.

Landespreismünze Prizes for quality at state, rather than national, level.

Landwein A category of better-quality TAFELWEIN (the grapes must be slightly riper) from 20 designated regions. It must be TROCKEN or HALBTROCKEN. Similar in intention to France's *vin de pays* but without the buzz.

Leitz, J ★★★ Fine little RÜDESHEIM family estate for elegant, dry RIES. A rising star.

Lemberger Red variety imported from Austria where it is known as Blaufränkisch. Deep-coloured, moderately tannic wines; can be excellent. Or rosé.

Liebfrauenstift 26-acre v'yd in city of Worms; origin of "LIEBFRAUMILCH".

Lieser M-M w ★★ 71 76 83 88 89 90 91 92 93 94 95 96 97 98 99 00 01 Little-known neighbour of BERNKASTEL. Lighter wines. First Class v'yd: Niederberg-Helden. Grosslage: Kurfürstlay. Top grower: SCHLOSS LIESER.

Lingenfelder, Weingut ★★ Small, innovative Grosskarlbach (PFALZ) estate: good dry and sweet SCHEUREBE, full-bodied RIES, etc.

Loewen, Carl ★★★ Top grower of Leiwen on MOSEL making ravishing AUSLESE from town's First Class Laurentiuslay site. Also fine EISWEIN.

Loosen, Weingut Dr ★★★★ 71 72 73 74 75 76 77 78 79 80 81 82 83 84 85 86 87 88 89 90 91 92 93 94 95 96 97 98 99 00 01 Dynamic 24-acre St-Johannishof estate in BERNKASTEL, ERDEN, GRAACH, URZIG, WEHLEN. Deep, intense RIESLINGS from old vines in great First Class vineyards. Also JL Wolf in the Pfalz since 1996. Superlative quality since 1990. Joint-venture Riesling in Washington State with Ch Ste Michele: Eroica (dry) first vintage 1999.

Lorch Rhg w (r) ★→★★ 71 76 83 85 88 89 90 92 93 94 95 96 97 98 99 00 01
Extreme W of RHEINGAU. Some fine MITTELRHEIN-like RIESL. Best grower: von Kanitz.

Loreley (Bereich) New BEREICH name for RHEINBURGENGAU and BACHARACH.

Löwenstein, Fürst ★★★ Top FRANKEN estate. 66 acres. Intense, savoury SILVANER
from Homberger Kallmuth, one of Germany's most dramatic slopes. Also 45-
acre Hallgarten estate long rented by SCHLOSS VOLLRADS, independent since 97.

Maindreieck (Bereich) District name for central FRANKEN, incl WÜRZBURG.

Marcobrunn Historic RHEINGAU v'yd; one of Germany's very best. See Erbach.

Markgräflerland (Bereich) District S of FREIBURG, BADEN. Typical GUTEDEL wine can
be delicious refreshment when drunk very young, but best wines are the -
BURGUNDERS: WEISS-, GRAU- and SPÄT-. Also SEKT.

> ### Liebfraumilch
> Much-abused name, once accounting for 50% of all German wine exports –
> to the detriment of Germany's better products. Legally defined as a QBA "of
> pleasant character" from RHEINHESSEN, PFALZ, NAHE, or RHEINGAU, of a blend with
> at least 51% RIESLING, SILVANER, KERNER, or MÜLLER-T. Most is mild, semi-sweet
> wine from Rheinhessen and the Pfalz. Rules now say it must have more
> than 18 grams per litre unfermented sugar. Its definition makes a mockery
> of the legal term "Quality Wine". With sales falling fast everywhere, this
> category is in the process of disappearing.

GERMANY

Maximin Grünhaus M-S-R (Ruwer) w ★★★★ 71 75 76 79 83 85 86 88 89 90 91
92 93 94 95 96 97 98 99 00 01 Supreme RUWER estate of 80 acres at
Mertesdorf. Wines of firm elegance and great subtlety to mature 20 yrs+.

Meyer-Näkel, Weingut ★★★ 15-acre AHR estate. Fine SPÄTBURGUNDERS in Dernau
and Bad Neuenahr exemplify modern, oak-aged German reds.

Mittelhaardt The north-central and best part of the PFALZ, incl DEIDESHEIM, FORST,
RUPPERTSBERG, WACHENHEIM, largely planted with RIESLING.

Mittelhaardt-Deutsche Weinstrasse (Bereich) District name for the northern and
central parts of the PFALZ.

Mittelmosel The central and best part of the MOSEL, incl BERNKASTEL, PIESPORT,
WEHLEN, etc. Its top sites are (or should be) entirely RIESLING.

Mittelrhein Northern Rhine area of domestic importance (and great beauty),
incl BACHARACH and BOPPARD. Some attractive, steely RIESLING.

Morio-Muskat Stridently aromatic grape variety now on the decline.

Mosbacher, Weingut ★★★ Fine 23-acre estate for some of best dry and sweet
RIES of FORST. Best wines are Grosses Gewächs.

Mosel The TAFELWEIN name of the area. All quality wines from the Mosel must be
labelled MOSEL-SAAR-RUWER. (Moselle is the French – and English – spelling.)

Mosel-Saar-Ruwer (M-S-R) 26,000 acre QUALITÄTSWEIN region between TRIER and
Koblenz; incl MITTELMOSEL, RUWER, and SAAR. The natural home of RIESLING.

Moselland, Winzergenossenschaft Huge M-S-R co-op, at BERNKASTEL, incl Saar-
Winzerverein at WILTINGEN. Its 5,200 members produce 25% of M-S-R wines
(incl classic method SEKT), but little above average.

Müller zu Scharzhof, Egon See Egon Müller.

Müller-Catoir, Weingut ★★★★ 76 77 78 79 80 81 82 83 84 85 86 87 88 89 90
91 92 93 94 95 96 97 98 99 00 01 Outstanding 40-acre NEUSTADT estate.
V aromatic, powerful wines (RIESLING, SCHEUREBE, RIESLANER, GEWÜRZ,
WEISSBURGUNDER, GRAUBURGUNDER, and MUSKATELLER). Consistent quality & gd
value; dry/sweet equally impressive.

Müller-Thurgau Fruity, early ripening, usually low-acid grape; most common in PFALZ, RHEINHESSEN, NAHE, BADEN, and FRANKEN; increasingly planted in all areas, incl MOSEL. Should be banned from all top v'yds by law.

Münster Nahe w ★→★★★ 71 75 76 83 88 **89 90** 91 92 **93** 94 95 **96** 97 **98** 99 00 **01** Best N NAHE village; fine, delicate wines. First Class vineyards: Dautenpflänzer, Kapellenberg, Pittersberg. Grosslage: Schlosskapelle. Top growers: Kruger-Rumpf, Göttelmann.

Muskateller Ancient aromatic white grape with crisp acidity. A rarity in the PFALZ, BADEN, and WÜRTTEMBERG, where it is mostly made dry.

Nackenheim Rhh w ★→★★★★ **76** 83 **89 90** 91 92 **93** 94 95 **96 97 98** 99 00 NIERSTEIN n'bour also with top Rhine *terroir*; similar best wines (esp 1st-class Rothenberg). Grosslagen: Spiegelberg, Gutes Domtal. Top grower: GUNDERLOCH.

Nahe Tributary of the Rhine and high-quality wine region. Balanced, fresh, clean but full-bodied, even minerally wines; RIES best. BEREICH: NAHETAL.

Nahetal (Bereich) BEREICH name for amalgamated BAD KREUZNACH and SCHLOSS-BÖCKELHEIM districts.

Neckar The river with many of WÜRTTEMBERG'S finest v'yds, mainly between STUTTGART and HEILBRONN.

Neef M-S-R w ★★ 71 76 83 **89 90** 91 92 **93** 94 95 96 **97** 98 99 00 **01** Village of lower MOSEL with one fine v'yd: Frauenberg.

Neipperg, Graf von ★★★ Noble 70-acre estate in Schwaigern, WÜRTTEMBERG: elegant dry RIES and TRAMINER, and good reds, esp from LEMBERGER.

Neumagen-Dhron M-M w ★★ Neighbour of PIESPORT: fine but sadly neglected.

Neustadt Central town of PFALZ with a famous wine school. Top growers: MÜLLER-CATOIR, Weegmüller.

Niederhausen Nahe w ★★→★★★★ 71 75 76 83 85 86 87 88 **89 90** 91 **93** 94 **95 96** 97 **98** 99 **00** 01 Neighbour of SCHLOSSBÖCKELHEIM. Graceful, powerful wines. First Class vineyards incl Felsensteyer, Gutsverwaltung, Hermannsberg, Hermannshöhle, Niederhausen-SCHLOSSBÖCKELHEIM. Grosslage: Burgweg. Esp from CRUSIUS, DONNHOFF, Hehner-Kilz.

Nierstein Rhh w ★→★★★★ 71 75 **76** 83 85 86 **88 89 90** 91 92 **93** 94 95 **96** 97 **98** 99 00 **01** Famous but treacherous village name. 1,300 acres. Superb First-Class vineyards: Brüderberg, Glöck, Heiligenbaum, Hipping, Oelberg, Orbel, Pettenthal. Grosslagen: Auflangen, Rehbach, Spiegelberg. Ripe, aromatic, elegant wines. Beware Grosslage Gutes Domtal: a supermarket deception now disappearing from shelves. Try GUNDERLOCH, GUNTRUM, HEYL ZU HERRNSHEIM, ST-ANTONY, GA Schneider, Strub, Wehrheim.

Nierstein (Bereich) Large E RHEINHESSEN district of ordinary quality.

Nierstein Winzergenossenschaft ★→★★ The leading NIERSTEIN CO-OP, with above-average standards. (Formerly traded under the name Rheinfront.)

Nobling New white grape: light, fresh wine in BADEN, esp MARKGRÄFLERLAND.

Norheim Nahe w ★★→★★★ 71 76 79 83 88 **89 90** 91 92 93 94 **95** 96 **97 98** 99 00 **01** Neighbour of NIEDERHAUSEN. First Class v'yds: Dellchen, Kafels, Kirschheck. Grosslage: Burgweg. Growers: DONNHOFF, CRUSIUS, Mathern.

Oberemmel M-S-R (Saar) w ★★→★★★ 71 75 **76** 83 85 88 **89 90** 91 92 **93** 94 95 96 **97** 98 **99** 00 01 Next village to WILTINGEN. Very fine wines from First Class vineyard Hütte, etc. Grosslage: SCHARZBERG. Top growers: VON HOVEL and VON KESSELSTATT.

Obermosel (Bereich) District name for the upper MOSEL above TRIER. Generally uninspiring wines from the ELBLING grape, unless very young.

Ockfen M-S-R (Saar) w ★★→★★★ 71 75 **76** 83 85 86 87 **88 89 90** 91 92 93 94 **95** 96 **97** 98 **99** 00 01 Superb, fragrant, austere wines. 1st-class vineyard: Bockstein. Grosslage: SCHARZBERG. Growers: DR FISCHER, WAGNER, ZILLIKEN.

Oechsle Scale for sugar content of grape juice (see page 272).

Oestrich Rhg w ★★→★★★ 71 75 76 83 88 89 90 *91* 92 93 94 95 96 97 98 99 00 01 Big village; variable but some splendid RIES esp AUSLESE. 1st-class vineyards: Doosberg, Lenchen. Grosslage: Gottesthal. Top growers: AUGUST ESER, PETER JAKOB KÜHN, QUERBACH, SPREITZER, WEGELER.

Offene weine Wine by the glass: the way to order it in wine villages.

Oppenheim Rhh w ★→★★★ 76 83 88 89 90 *91* 92 93 94 95 96 **97** 98 99 00 01 Town S of NIERSTEIN; spectacular 13th-C church. 1st-class Herrenberg and Sackträger v'yds: top wines. Grosslagen: Guldenmorgen, Krötenbrunnen. Growers including GUNTRUM, C Koch, Kühling-Gillot. None of these, though, are realizing the full potential of these sites.

Ortenau (Bereich) District just South of Baden-Baden. Good KLINGELBERGER (RIES), SPÄTBURGUNDER and RULÄNDER. Top village: DURBACH.

Ortsteil Independent part of a community allowed to use its estate vineyard name without the village name, e.g. SCHLOSS JOHANNISBERG, STEINBERG.

Palatinate English for PFALZ.

Paulinshof See Brauneberg.

Pauly-Bergweiler, Dr ★★ Fine 31-acre BERNKASTEL estate. V'yds there and in WEHLEN, etc. Peter Nicolay wines from URZIG and ERDEN are usually best.

Perlwein Semi-sparkling wine.

Pfalz 56,000-acre v'yd region S of RHEINHESSEN (see Mittelhaardt and Südliche Weinstrasse). Warm climate: grapes ripen fully. The classics are rich wines, with TROCKEN and HALBTROCKEN increasingly fashionable and well-made. Biggest RIES area after M-S-R. Formerly known as the Rheinpfalz.

Pfeffingen, Weingut ★★★ Messrs Fuhrmann and Eymael make very good RIES and SCHEUREBE on 26 acres of UNGSTEIN. Back on fine form since 1999.

Piesport M-M w ★→★★★★ 71 75 76 83 88 89 90 91 92 93 94 95 96 **97** 98 99 00 **01** Tiny village with famous vine amphitheatre: at best glorious, rich, aromatic RIES. Great First Class v'yds: Goldtröpfchen & Domherr. Treppchen far inferior. Grosslage: Michelsberg (mainly MÜLLER-T; avoid). Esp Grans Fassian R HAART, KESSELSTATT, St Urbanshof, Weller-Lehnert.

Plettenberg, von ★★→★★★ 100-acre estate at BAD KREUZNACH. Mixed quality.

Portugieser Second-rate red-wine grape now often used for WEISSHERBST.

Prädikat Special attributes or qualities. See QmP.

Prinz, Fred Rhg w ★★ Best RIESLING in the village of Hallgarten.

Prüfungsnummer The official identifying test-number of a quality wine.

Prüm, J J ★★★★ 69 *70* 71 *72* 73 *74* 75 76 *77* 78 **79** 80 81 82 **83** *84* 85 **86** 87 **88** **89** 90 *91* 92 *93* 94 **95** 96 **97** 98 **99** 00 01 Superlative and legendary 34-acre MOSEL estate in BERNKASTEL, GRAACH, WEHLEN, ZELTINGEN. Delicate but long-lived wines, especially in Wehlener SONNENUHR: 81 KABINETT is *still* young. Plain Prüm RIESLING is a bargain.

Qualitätswein bestimmter Anbaugebiete (QbA) The middle quality of German wine, with sugar added before fermentation (as in French "chaptalization"), but controlled as to areas, grapes, etc.

Qualitätswein mit Prädikat (QmP) Top category, for all wines ripe enough to be unsugared (KABINETT to TROCKENBEERENAUSLESE). See pages 133 and 141.

Randersacker Frank w ★★→★★★ 76 83 88 89 90 91 92 **93** 94 **95** 96 **97** **98** 99 00 **01** Leading village for distinctive dry wine. First Class v'yds: Marsberg, Pfülben, Sonnenstuhl. Grosslage: Ewig Leben. Growers incl BURGERSPITAL, STAATLICHER HOFKELLER, JULIUSSPITAL, Robert Schmitt, Schmitt's Kinder.

Ratzenberger, Jochen ★★ 20-acre estate making racy, dry and off-dry RIES in BACHARACH; best from First Class Posten and Steeger St-Jost v'yds.

Rauenthal Rhg w ★★★→★★★★ 71 75 76 83 88 89 90 *91* 92 93 94 95 96 **97** 98 99 00 **01** Supreme village: spicy, complex wine. First Class v'yds: Baiken, Gehrn, Nonnenberg, Rothenberg, Wülfen. Grosslage: Steinmächer. Top grower: BREUER.

GERMANY

Rebholz ★★★ Top SÜDLICHE WEINSTRASSE estate for 50 years. Many varieties on 25 acres. Makes the best MUSKATELLER, GEWÜRZTRAMINER, CHARDONNAY (Burgundian style), and SPÄTBURGUNDER in Pfalz.

Ress, Balthasar ★★ R'GAU estate (74 good acres), cellars in HATTENHEIM. Also runs SCHLOSS REICHARTSHAUSEN. Variable quality; original artists' labels.

Restsüsse Unfermented grape sugar remaining in (or in cheap wines added to) wine to give it sweetness. TROCKEN wines have very little, if any.

Rheinburgengau (Bereich) District name for MITTELRHEIN v'yds around the Rhine Gorge. Wines with "steely" acidity needing time to mature.

Rheingau Best v'yd region of Rhine, W of Wiesbaden. 7,000 acres. Classic, substantial but subtle RIES, yet on the whole recently eclipsed by brilliance elsewhere. BEREICH name for whole region: JOHANNISBERG.

Rheinhessen Vast region (61,000 acres of v'yds) between Mainz and Worms, bordered by River NAHE, mostly second-rate, but includes top RIESLINGS from NACKENHEIM, NIERSTEIN, OPPENHEIM, etc.

Rheinhessen Silvaner (RS) New uniform label for earthy, dry wines from SILVANER – designed to give a modern quality image to the region.

Rheinpfalz See Pfalz.

Rhodt SÜDLICHE WEINSTRASSE village: esp Rietburg co-op; agreeable fruity wines.

Richter, Weingut Max Ferd ★★★ Top 37-acre MITTELMOSEL family estate, based at Mülheim. Fine, barrel-aged RIESLING from First Class v'yds: BRAUNEBERG Juffer-SONNENUHR, GRAACH Domprobst, Mülheim (Helenenkloster), WEHLEN Sonnenuhr.

Regions to watch out for in the early 2000s

Mittlerhein had a string of poor vintages to contend with, but with 2001 it proves that it is capable of producing great classic Rieslings.

Rheinhessen is producing a wave of new-style, clean, harmonious dry white wines that are often excellent value for money.

Saale-Unstrut has finally shaken off the legacy of its communist past and is starting to make some surprisingly full-bodied, supple, dry whites.

Sachsen, too, has overcome the same problems and is making sleeker and more aromatic dry whites than Saale-Unstrut.

Rieslaner Cross between SILVANER and RIES; makes fine AUSLESEN in FRANKEN, where most is grown. Also superb from MÜLLER-CATOIR.

Riesling The best German grape: fine, fragrant, fruity, long-lived. Only CHARDONNAY can compete as the world's best white grape.

Rosswein Rosé wine made from red grapes fermented without their skins.

Rüdesheim Rhg w ★★→★★★★ 71 75 76 79 81 82 83 84 85 86 87 88 89 90 91 92 93 94 95 96 97 98 99 00 01 Rhine resort with First Class vineyards; the three best are called Rüdesheimer Berg–. Full-bodied wines, fine-flavoured, often remarkable in "off" years. Grosslage: Burgweg. Many of the top RHEINGAU estates own some Rüdesheim vineyards. Best growers: G BREUER, JOHANNISHOF, August Kesseler, J LEITZ, SCHLOSS SCHONBORN, STATE DOMAIN.

Ruländer Pinot Gris: now more commonly known as GRAUBURGUNDER.

Ruppertsberg Pfz w ★★→★★★ 89 90 91 92 93 94 95 96 97 98 99 00 01 Southern village of MITTELHAARDT. First Class vineyards incl Hoheburg, Linsenbusch, Nussbein, Reiterpfad, Spiess. Grosslage: Hofstück. Growers incl BASSERMANN-JORDAN, BIFFAR, VON BUHL, BÜRKLIN-WOLF, DEINHARD.

Ruwer 76 83 88 89 90 91 92 93 94 95 96 97 98 99 00 01 Tributary of MOSEL nr TRIER. V fine, delicate but highly aromatic and well-balanced wines. Villages incl EITELSBACH, KASEL, MERTESDORF.

Saale-Unstrut 92 93 94 95 *96* **97** 98 99 **00 01** Region in former East Germany, 1,300 acres around confluence of these two rivers at Naumburg, near Leipzig. The terraced vineyards of WEISSBURGUNDER, SILVANER, RIESLING, GEWURZTRAMINER, etc, and red PORTUGIESER have Cistercian origins. Quality leaders: Lützkendorf, Landesweingut Kloster Pforta.

Saar 75 *76 77 78* 79 80 81 82 **83** *84* 85 86 *87* 88 **89 90** 91 *92* **93** 94 **95** *96* **97** *98* **99** 00 01 Hill-lined tributary of MOSEL S of RUWER. The most brilliant, austere, "steely" RIESLING of all. Villages include AYL, OCKFEN, Saarburg, SERRIG, WILTINGEN (SCHARZHOFBERG). Grosslage: SCHARZBERG. Many fine estates.

Saar-Ruwer (Bereich) District covering these 2 regions.

Sachsen 93 94 *95 96* 97 98 99 **00** 01 Former E-German region (900 acres) in ELBE Valley around Dresden and Meissen. MÜLLER-T dominant, but WEISSBURGUNDER, GRAUBURGUNDER, TRAMINER, RIES give dry wines with real character. Best growers: SCHLOSS PROSCHWITZ, Vincenz Richter, Klaus Seifert, Schloss Wackerbarth, Klaus Zimmerling.

St-Antony, Weingut ★★★ Excellent 57-acre estate. Rich, intense, dry and off-dry RIES from First Class v'yds of NIERSTEIN.

St-Ursula Well-known merchants at BINGEN.

Salm, Prinz zu Owner of SCHLOSS WALLHAUSEN in NAHE and Villa Sachsen in RHEINHESSEN. President of VDP.

Salwey, Weingut ★★★ Leading BADEN estate at Oberrotweil, especially for RIESLING, WEISSBURGUNDER and RULÄNDER.

Samtrot Red WÜRTTEMBERG grape. Makes Germany's closest shot at Beaujolais.

Schaefer, Willi ★★★ The finest grower of GRAACH (but only 5 acres).

Scharzberg Grosslage name of WILTINGEN and neighbours.

Scharzhofberg M-S-R (Saar) w ★★★★ 71 *75* 76 **83** 88 **89** 90 91 *92* **93** 94 **95** *96* **97** 98 **99** 00 01 Superlative 67-acre SAAR v'yd: austerely beautiful wines, the perfection of RIESLING, best in AUSLESEN. Do not confuse with the previous entry. Top estates: BISCHÖFLICHE WEINGÜTER, EGON MULLER, VON HOVEL, VON KESSELSTATT, Van Volxem.

Schaumwein Sparkling wine.

Scheurebe Aromatic grape of high quality (and RIESLING parentage), esp used in PFALZ. Excellent for botrytis wine (BA, TBA).

Schillerwein Light red or rosé QBA; speciality of WÜRTTEMBERG (only).

Schloss Johannisberg Rhg w ★★★★ 76 79 **83** 85 86 **88 89** 90 91 92 93 94 95 *96* 97 98 **99** 00 **01** Famous R'GAU estate of 86 acres owned by Princess Metternich and the Oetker family. The original Rhine "first growth". Wines incl fine SPÄTLESE, KABINETT TROCKEN. Since 96 there has been a dramatic return to form.

Schloss Lieser ★★★ Small estate run by Thomas Haag, from FRITZ HAAG estate, making pure, racy RIESLINGS from underrated v'yds of Lieser.

Schloss Proschwitz ★★ Resurrected princely estate at Meissen, leading former E Germany in quality, esp with dry WEISSBURGUNDER and GRAUBURGUNDER.

Schloss Reichartshausen 10-acre HATTENHEIM v'yd run by RESS.

Schloss Reinhartshausen ★★★ Fine 250-acre estate in ERBACH, HATTENHEIM, KIEDRICH, etc. Originally property of Prussian royal family, now in private hands. Model RHEINGAU RIESLING. The mansion beside the Rhine is now a luxury hotel. The last couple of vintages were nothing special.

Schloss Schönborn ★★★ One of biggest RHEINGAU estates, based at HATTENHEIM. Full-flavoured wines, variable, at best excellent. Also vg SEKT.

Schloss Neuweier ★★★ Leading producer of dry Riesling in Baden.

Schloss Thorn Ancient OBERMOSEL estate, remarkable ELBLING, RIES and castle.

Schloss Vollrads Rhg w ★★★ 71 *76* **83** 85 88 **89** 90 *91 92* 93 94 95 *96* 97 **98 99** 00 01 Since the sudden death of owner Erwein Count Matuschka in August 97, is owned by a bank. Since 98 vintage quality is much improved.

Schloss Wallhausen ★★★ The 25-acre NAHE estate of the Prinz Zu Salm, one of Germany's oldest. 65% RIES. Vg TROCKEN. Very good quality since 97.

Schlossböckelheim Nahe w ★★→★★★★ 71 75 76 79 **83 85** 86 88 **89 90** 91 92 **93** 94 **95** 96 **97 98** 99 00 01 Village with top NAHE v'yds, including First Class Felsenberg, In den Felsen, Königsfels, Kupfergrube. Firm yet delicate wine. Grosslage: Burgweg. Top growers: CRUSIUS, DONNHOF, GUTSVERWALTUNG NIEDERHAUSEN-SCHLOSSBÖCKELHEIM.

Schneider, Weingut Georg Albrecht ★★ Impeccably run 32-acre estate. Classic off-dry and sweet RIES IN NIERSTEIN, the best from First Class Hipping.

Schoppenwein Café (or bar) wine: ie wine by the glass.

Erstes Gewächs

From 1st September 2000, the Rheingau's vineyard classification came into force and with it the designation "Erstes Gewächs" or "First Growth". It applies to wines produced according to strict rules (incl max yield and blind-tasting test). The weakness of the classification takes in just over 35% of the region's vineyards including some rather flat sites. The scheme is open for Spätburgunder and Riesling, which may be dry or sweet. So far, few Erstes Gewächs wines have been released.

Schubert, von Owner of MAXIMIN GRUNHAUS.

Schwarzer Adler, Weingut ★★★ Franz Keller and his son make top BADEN dry GRAU-, WEISS-, and SPÄTBURGUNDER on 35 acres at Oberbergen.

Schweigen Pfz w r ★★ **89 90** 91 **92 93** 94 95 **96 97 98** 99 00 01 Southern PFALZ village. Grosslage: Guttenberg. Best growers: Fritz Becker, especially for SPÄTBURGUNDER, Bernhart.

Sekt German (QBA) sparkling wine, best when the label specifies RIESLING, WEISS-BURGUNDER, or SPATBURGUNDER. Sekt BA is the same but comes from a specified area.

Selbach-Oster ★★★ 26-acre ZELTINGEN estate among MITTELMOSEL leaders.

Serrig M-S-R (Saar) w ★★→★★★ 71 75 76 83 **85 88 89 90** 91 **93** 94 95 96 **97** 98 99 00 01 Village for "steely" wines, excellent in sunny years. First Class vineyards: Herrenburg, Saarstein, WÜRZBERG. Grosslage: SCHARZBERG. Top grower: SCHLOSS SAARSTEIN.

Silvaner Third most-planted German white grape variety, generally underrated; best examples in FRANKEN. The closest thing to Chablis in Germany. Worth looking for in RHEINHESSEN and KAISERSTUHL too.

Simmern, Langwerth von ★★★ Famous ELTVILLE family estate. Famous v'yds: Baiken, Mannberg, MARCOBRUNN. After disappointing quality during the 90s some improvement with 99.

Sonnenuhr Sundial. Name of several vineyards, esp First Class one at WEHLEN.

Spätburgunder Pinot Noir: the best red-wine grape in Germany – esp in BADEN and WÜRTTEMBERG and, increasingly, PFALZ – generally improving quality, but most still underflavoured in spite of improved colour.

Spätlese Late harvest. One better (stronger, usually sweeter) than KABINETT. Good examples age at least 5 years, often longer. TROCKEN Spätlesen can be very fine with food.

Staatlicher Hofkeller ★★★ The Bavarian STATE DOMAIN. 370 acres of the finest FRANKEN vineyards with spectacular cellars under the great baroque Residenz at WÜRZBURG.

Staatsweingut (or Staatliche Weinbaudomäne) The state wine estates or domains; esp KLOSTER EBERBACH, TRIER.

State Domain See Staatsweingut.

Steigerwald (Bereich) District name for E part of FRANKEN.

Steinberg Rhg w ★★★ **71 75 76** 79 **83** 86 88 89 **90** 91 92 **93** 94 **95** 96 97 98 **99** 00 **01** Famous 79-acre HATTENHEIM walled v'yd, planted by Cistercians 700 yrs ago. Now owned by STATE DOMAIN, ELTVILLE. Some glorious wines; some feeble.

Steinwein Wine from WÜRZBURG's best v'yd, Stein.

Südliche Weinstrasse (Bereich) District name for S PFALZ. Quality improved tremendously in last 25 yrs. See Ilbesheim, Rebholz, Schweigen.

Tafelwein Table wine. The *vin ordinaire* of Germany. Frequently blended with other EU wines. But DEUTSCHER TAFELWEIN must come from Germany alone and may be excellent. (See also LANDWEIN.)

Tauberfranken (Bereich) New name for minor Badisches Frankenland BEREICH of N BADEN: FRANKEN-style wines.

Thanisch, Weingut Dr H ★★ BERNKASTEL estate, includes part of the Doctor vineyard.

Traben-Trarbach M-M w ★★ **76 83 88 89 90 93** 94 **95** 96 **97** 98 99 00 **01** Major wine town of 800 acres, 87% of it RIESLING. Top vineyards: Ungsberg, Würzgarten. Grosslage: Schwarzlay. Top growers: Martin Müller and MAX FERD RICHTER.

Traisen Nahe w ★★★ **71 75 76** 79 **83** 85 86 87 **88 89 90** 91 92 **93** 94 **95 96** 97 98 99 00 **01** Small village incl First Class Bastei and Rotenfels v'yds, capable of making RIES of concentration and class. Top grower: CRUSIUS.

Traminer See Gewürztraminer.

Trier M-S-R w ★★→★★★ Great wine city of Roman origin, on MOSEL, nr RUWER, now also incl AVELSBACH and EITELSBACH. Grosslage: Römerlay. Big Mosel charitable estates have cellars here among imposing Roman ruins.

Trittenheim M-M w ★★ **71 75 76** 85 **89 90** 91 92 **93** 94 **95** 96 97 98 99 00 **01** Attractive S MITTELMOSEL light wines. Top v'yds were Altärchen, Apotheke, but now incl second-rate flat land: First Class v'yds are Felsenkopf, Leiterchen. Grosslage: Michelsberg (avoid). Growers incl E Clüsserath, Clüsserath-Weiler, GRANS-FASSIAN, Milz.

Trocken "Dry". By law, *trocken* means max 9 grams per litre unfermented sugar. Some are highly austere, others (better) have more body & alcohol.

Trockenbeerenauslese Sweetest, most expensive category of German wine, extremely rare, with concentrated honey flavour. Made from selected shrivelled grapes affected by "noble rot" (botrytis). TBA for short. See also Edel. *Edelbeerenauslese* would be a less confusing name.

Trollinger Common (pale) red grape of WÜRTTEMBERG; locally v popular.

Ungstein Pfz w ★★→★★★ **71 76 83 85 88 89 90** 91 92 **93** 94 95 **96** 97 98 **99 00 01** MITTELHAARDT village with fine, harmonious wines. First Class v'yds: Herrenberg, Weilberg. Top growers: Darting, FITZ-RITTER, PFEFFINGEN, Pflüger, Karl Schäfer. Grosslagen: Honigsäckel, Kobnert.

Urzig M-M w ★★★★ **71 75 76 83 88 89 90** 91 92 **93** 94 **95** 96 **97** 98 **99** 00 00 Village on red sandstone and red slate foundation for firm, full, spicy wine unlike other MOSELS. First Class v'yd: Würzgarten. Grosslage: Schwarzlay. Growers incl J J CHRISTOFFEL, DR LOOSEN, Mönchhof, WEINS-PRUM.

Valckenberg, P J Major merchants and growers at Worms, with Madonna LIEBFRAUMILCH. Also dry RIES.

VDP Verband Deutscher Prädikats und Qualitätsweingüter. The pace-making association of premium growers. Look for their eagle insignia. President: Prinz Zu Salm.

Vereinigte Hospitien ★★→★★★ "United Hospices". Ancient charity at TRIER with large holdings in PIESPORT, SERRIG, TRIER, WILTINGEN, etc; wines recently well below their wonderful potential.

Verwaltung Administration (of property/estate etc).

Wachenheim Pfz w ★★★→★★★★ **71 76 83** 88 **89 90** *91* 92 **93** 94 95 **96** 97 **98** 99 00 01 840 acres, including exceptionally fine RIESLING. First Class v'yds: Belz, Gerümpel, Goldbächel, Rechbächel, etc. Top growers: BURKLIN-WOLF, BIFFAR, WOLF. Grosslagen: Mariengarten, Schenkenböhl, Schnepfenflug.

Wagner, Dr ★★★ Saarburg estate. 20 acres of RIES. Fine wines incl TROCKEN.

Walluf Rhg w ★★★ **75 76** 79 **83 88 89 90 92** 93 94 95 96 **97** 98 **99** 00 01 Neighbour of ELTVILLE; formerly Nieder- & Ober-Walluf. Underrated wines. First Class vineyard: Walkenberg. Grosslage: Steinmächer. Growers include BECKER, TONI JOST.

Walporzheim Ahrtal (Bereich) District name for the whole AHR Valley.

Wawern M-S-R (Saar) w ★★→★★★ **71 75 76 83** 85 88 **89 90** *91* 92 **93** 94 **95** 96 **97** 98 **99** 00 01 Small village, fine RIESLING. First Class vineyard: Herrenberg. Grosslage: SCHARZBERG.

Wegeler ★★★ Important family estates in OESTRICH, MITTELHARDT, and BERNKASTEL. The Wegelers owned the merchants Deinhard until 1997.

Wehlen M-M w ★★★→★★★★ **71 75 76 83** 85 86 **88 89** 90 91 92 **93** 94 **95** 96 **97** 98 **99** 00 **01** Neighbour of BERNKASTEL with equally fine, somewhat richer wine. Location of great First Class vineyard: SONNENUHR. Grosslage: Münzlay. The top growers are: Meribent Kenjsen, DR LOOSEN, J J PRÜM, S A Prüm, Studert-Prüm, WEGELER, and WEINS-PRÜM.

Weil, Weingut Robert ★★★★ *71* 76 83 84 85 *86 87* 88 89 **90** 91 92 93 **94** 95 **96** 97 98 **99** 00 **01** Outstanding 145-acre estate in KIEDRICH; now owned by Suntory of Japan. Superb QMP, EISWEIN, BA, TBA; standard wines also vg since 92. Widely considered RHEINGAU'S No 1.

Weinbaugebiet Viticultural region. For TAFELWEIN (eg MOSEL, RHEIN, SAAR).

Weingut Wine estate.

Weinkellerei Wine cellars or winery. See Keller.

Weins-Prüm, Dr ★★→★★★ Classic MITTELMOSEL estate; 12 acres at Wehlen. WEHLENER SONNENUHR is top wine.

Weinstrasse Wine road. Scenic route through v'yds. Germany has several.

Weintor, Deutsches See Schweigen.

Weissburgunder Pinot Blanc. Most reliable grape for TROCKEN wines: low acidity, high extract. Also much used for SEKT.

Weissherbst Usually a pale pink wine of QBA standard or above, from a single variety, occasionally BEERENAUSLESE; it is the speciality of BADEN, PFALZ, and WÜRTTEMBERG.

Werner, Domdechant ★★★ Erratic family estate on best HOCHHEIM slopes.

Wiltingen M-S-R (Saar) w ★★→★★★★ **71 75 76 83** 85 86 **88 89 90** 91 92 **93** 94 **95** 96 **97** 98 **99** 00 01 The centre of the SAAR. 790 acres. Beautifully subtle, austere wine. Great First Class v'yd is SCHARZHOFBERG (ORTSTEIL); and First Class are Braune Kupp, Hölle. Grosslage (for the whole SAAR): SCHARZBERG. Top growers: EGON MÜLLER, LE GALLAIS, VON KESSELSTATT, Von Volxem, etc.

Winkel Rhg w ★★★ **71 75 76 83 88 89 90** *91* 92 **93** 94 95 **96** 97 98 **99** 00 01 Village famous for full fragrant wine. First Class vineyards incl Hasensprung, Jesuitengarten, SCHLOSS VOLLRADS, Schlossberg. Grosslagen: Erntebringer, Honigberg. Growers incl PRINZ VON HESSEN, Johannish of Wegelen, Von Mumm, BALTHASAR RESS, SCHLOSS SCHÖNBORN, etc.

Winningen M-S-R w ★★ Lower MOSEL town near Koblenz: unusually full RIES for region. First Class v'yds: Röttgen, Uhlen. Top grower: Heymann-Löwenstein, Knebel, Richard Richter.

Wintrich M-M w ★★→★★★ **71 76 83 88 89 90** 91 **92 93** 94 **95** *96* **97** 98 99 00 01 Neighbour of PIESPORT; similar wines. First Class vineyards: Ohligsberg. Grosslage: Kurfürstlay. Top grower: REINHOLD HAART.

Winzergenossenschaft (WG) Wine-growers' co-operative, often making sound and reasonably priced wine. Referred to in this text as "co-op".

Winzerverein The same as the above.

Wirsching, Hans ★★★ Estate in IPHOFEN and FRANKEN. Wines can be firm, elegant, and dry but quality is variable. 170 acres in 1st-class vineyards: Julius-Echter-Berg, Kalb, etc.

Wonnegau (Bereich) District name for S RHEINHESSEN.

Wolf ★★★ Run-down estate in WACHENHEIM acquired by Ernst Loosen (see Dr Loosen) of Bernkastel. From first vintage (1996) PFALZ wines with a Mosel-like delicacy. Superb quality since 1998.

Wolff Metternich ★★ Noble DURBACH estate: some good RIESLING.

Württemberg 83 *84* 85 86 *87* 88 **89 90** *91* 92 **93** 94 *95* 96 **97** 98 **99** 00 01 Vast S area, little known for wine outside Germany despite some very good RIES (esp NECKAR Valley) and frequently unrealized potential to make good reds: LEMBERGER, TROLLINGER, SAMTROT.

Würzburg Frank ★★→★★★★ 71 76 **81 83** 85 86 **88 89 90** *91* 92 **93** 94 96 **97** 98 99 00 01 Great baroque city on the Main, centre of FRANKEN wine: fine, full-bodied, dry. 1st-class v'yds: Abtsleite, Innere, Leiste, Stein. No Grosslage. See Maindreieck. Growers: BURGERSPITAL, JULIUSSPITAL, STAATLICHER HOFKELLER.

Zell M-S-R w ★→★★★ **76 83 88** 89 **90 93** 94 **95** 96 **97** 98 99 *00* 01 The best-known lower MOSEL village, especially for its awful Grosslage: Schwarze Katz ("Black Cat"). RIESLING on steep slate gives aromatic wines. Top grower: KALLFELZ.

Zell (Bereich) District name for whole lower MOSEL from Zell to Koblenz.

Zeltingen M-M w ★★→★★★★ **71 75 76** 79 **83 85** 86 **88 89 90** *91* 92 **93** 94 **95** 96 **97 98** 99 00 **01** Top MOSEL village near WEHLEN. Lively, crisp RIESLING. First Class vineyard: SONNENUHR. Grosslage: Münzlay. Top growers: Markus Molitor, J J PRÜM, and SELBACH-OSTER.

Zilliken, Forstmeister Geltz ★★★ Former estate of Prussian royal forester with 25 acres at Saarburg and OCKFEN, SAAR. Racy, minerally RIESLINGS, incl superb AUSLESE, EISWEIN with excellent ageing potential.

Zwierlein, Freiherr von ★★ 55-acre family estate in GEISENHEIM. 100% RIES.

Luxembourg

Luxembourg has 3,285 acres of v'yds on limestone soils on the Moselle's left bank. High-yielding Elbling and Rivaner (Müller-T) vines dominate, but there are also significant acreages of Ries, Gewürz and (usually best) Auxerrois, Pinot Bl and Pinot Gr. These give light to medium-bodied (10.5–11.5%), dry, Alsace-like wines. the Vins Moselle co-op makes 70% of the total. Domaine et Tradition estates association, founded in '88, promotes quality from noble varieties. The following vintages were all good: 89 90 92 95; 97 outstanding, 98 average, 99 similar but softer, 00 poor, 2001 much better. Best from: Aly Duhr et Fils, M Bastian, Caves Gales, Bernard Massard (surprisingly good Cuvée de l'Ecusson classic method sparkling), Clos Mon Vieux Moulin, Ch de Schengen, Sunnen-Hoffmann.

Spain & Portugal

More heavily shaded areas
are the wine growing regions

The following abbreviations are used in the text:

Amp	Ampurdán-Costa Brava
Alen	Alentejo
Bair	Bairrada
Bul	Bullas
Cos del S	Costers del Segre
El B	El Bierzo
Est	Estremadura
La M	La Mancha
Mont-M	Montilla-Moriles
Nav	Navarra
Pen	Penedès
Pri	Priorato
Rib del D	Ribera del Duero
Rib del G	Ribera del Guadiana
R Ala	Rioja Alavesa
R Alt	Rioja Alta
RB	Rioja Baja
Som	Somontano
Set	Setúbal
U-R	Utiel-Requena
VV	Vinhos Verdes
g	vino generoso
res	reserva

MADEIRA (off west coast of Africa)

Funchal

Santiago de Compostela

El Bierzo

Rias Ribeiro
Baixas Monterrei Valdeorras

RIOS DO MINHO TRAS-
OS-MONTES

Vinhos Douro
Verdes

Porto Douro

BEIRA
Bairrada Dao

Mondego

Tagus

ESTREMADURA

BAIRADEIO

Bucelas
Colares Lisbon
Carcavelos Setúbal Ribera d

ALENTEJO

TERRAS
DO SADO

ALGARVE
Lagoa Tavira Condado
Lagos Faro de Huelva
Portimão Jerez de la F rontera
Cádiz

Seville

Spain and Portugal joined the EU (and, as far as most of their wine is concerned, the 20th century) only 16 years ago. Both made rapid progress, Euro-grants allowing massive re-equipping. Ferment continues: splendid new wines continue to appear. But some makers are asking (and indeed getting) silly prices.

Currently in Spain (apart from sherry country), the north, Rioja, Navarra, Galicia, Rueda, Catalonia, and Ribera del Duero hold most interest; those in Portugal (apart from the port vineyards and Madeira) are the Douro, Ribatejo, Alentejo, the central coast, and the north. In Portugal especially, newly delimited areas have successfully challenged old, traditional appellations. Portugal is now concentrating on its huge range of indigenous grape varieties, especially Touriga Nacional, Tinta Roriz, and Trincadeira. Still largely unknown elsewhere, they are one of Portugal's greatest strengths.

The following list includes the best and most interesting makers, types, and regions of each country, whether legally delimited or not. Geographical references (see map above) are to demarcated regions (DOs and DOCs), autonomies, and provinces.

Bay of Biscay

Bilbao

Logroño O *Ebro* Navarra

Somontano

Ampurdán-
Costa Brava

Rioja

ales Campo de Borja

Costers del Segre

Conca de
Barbera

Valladolid *Duero*

Alella

Ribera del
Duero

Calatayud Cariñena Priorato

O Barcelona

Rueda

Penedès
Tarragona

Madrid O

Vinos de
Madrid

Mentrida

Utiel-
Requena

Valencia

Binassalem

La Mancha

O Valencia

Palma

Almansa Valencia

Valdepeñas Jumilla Alicante

adalquivir

Bullas Yecla

O Alicante

ontilla Moriles

alaga

O
Málaga

Mediterranean Sea

SPAIN

Sherry, Port and Madeira have a chapter each on pages 176 and 179.

Spain

Recent vintages of the Spanish classics
Rioja

2001 Smaller harvest and good-quality fruit. Excellent potential.

2000 Generally favourable conditions. Huge harvest, but abnormally high summer
and autumn temperatures led to uneven quality.

1999 The worst April frost in memory delayed maturation, and summer rain resulted
in mildew. Average.

1998 Biggest-ever vintage. Lack of sun and rain in the autumn delayed picking. V gd.

1997 Given little sun & much rain, the vintage was lge and patchy. Average/poor.

1996 An unusually cold spring and cool summer resulted in well-structured but fairly
immediate wines. Very good.

1995 Favourable weather conditions throughout. Good alcoholic strength and
acidity. Excellent.

1994 Textbook weather produced colour, backbone, and intensity but wines are thinning out earlier than expected. Excellent.

1993 Few sunny days and little rain. Wines thin and short-lived. Poor.

1992 Rainiest October in 50 yrs produced great contrasts in quality according to date of picking. Attractive but immediate. Good.

1991 Generally cold and rainy with hot, dry summer. Medium-intensity wines, now mostly beyond their best.

Ribera del Duero

2001 Although an April frost severely reduced the crop, it was otherwise an almost perfect growing season and quality is outstanding.

2000 Very lge harvest but because of sporadic weather, ripening was uneven. Some *bodegas* made spectacular wines; in general, good.

1999 Almost perfect weather and bumper harvest, but rainfall around harvest time resulted in lack of acidity. Very good.

1998 Torrential rain in early autumn and record grape prices. Good.

1997 Cool and wet with spring and summer frosts. Poor.

1996 Splendid spring and dry summer and autumn resulted in good acidity and long-lived *reservas*. Excellent.

1995 Devastating April frost presaged catastrophe, but later sun and warmth resulted in rich, structured wines. Excellent.

1994 Frost-free benevolent year, but crop small. Very good.

1993 Dank and sodden. Most appalling vintage of the decade. Poor.

1992 Fertile year, but rain at harvest. Decent but short-lived wines. Gd.

1991 Sunny summer and warm September produced substantial wines with great ageing potential. Excellent.

Navarra

2001 This promises to be an excellent year with big, ripe, well-balanced wines.

2000 Very dry year of prolific yields, calling for rigorous selection. Best wines are big and fleshy, with gd potential for ageing. Very gd.

1999 Most frost-afflicted vintage of decade with soaring grape prices. Wines promise to be well-structured and long-ageing. Excellent.

1998 Spring frosts but dry, hot summer. Well-structured wines with excellent colour and elegant aromas. Very good.

1997 Dank, overcast summer. Short-lived wines. Poor.

1996 Cold, wet summer. Wines spare, but notably fresh and aromatic with adequate acidity and concentration. Good.

1995 Very small crop due to major frost in April. Wines similar to those of 94, but longer-lived because of superior acidity. Excellent.

1994 Frost and snow in March, exceptionally hot, dry summer. Wines, with structure, colour, tannins, and acidity, mostly peaked. V gd.

1993 Late, patchy harvest. Light wines for consumption now. Avge.

1992 Uniformly hot and dry. Textbook maturation with excellent alcohol-acid-colour balance. Good wines in their day.

1991 Late harvest following a cold winter. Healthy grapes resulted in substantial wines that developed well. Good.

Penedès

2001 April frosts reduced the yield but warm, dry summer produced v good wines.

2000 Dry winter, some spring rain, and very dry summer. Perfect ripening of the grapes gave well-balanced wines. Very good.

1999 Mild winter and spring and dry, warm summer contributed to an abundant harvest. Very good.

1998 Low winter temperatures and rainy spring. Good ripening of grapes. Very good whites and excellent reds.

1997 Mild and humid winter. Good flowering with abundant rains. Large harvest. Good white wines and very good reds.

1996 Cold, frosty winter and wet, mild spring. Heavy August rains resulted in a prolific harvest. Very good.

1995 Dry, windy, and mild winter. Vines budded thanks to water from previous year. Summer alternately wet and hot. Very good.

1994 A very dry year with minimal and irregular rain resulted in a scant harvest with small, slow-ripening grapes. Very good.

1993 The driest of recent years. Vineyards survived thanks to rain accumulated earlier; harvest was scarce but good quality. V gd.

1992 Exceptionally wet during the vegetal period. Slow and deficient ripening, but acceptable harvest. Good.

1991 Great contrasts between heavy rains and high temperatures led to a bumper harvest. Good.

Abadia Retuerta Castilla y León r ★★★ 96 97 98 **99** One of the most modern BODEGAS in Spain. Non-DO, but with top Bordeaux help is making exceptional Temp, Cab S, and Merlot with prices to match. Esp El Campanario 96.

Agapito Rico Jumilla r ★★★ 94 96 99 oo Young BODEGA making some of Spain's best VINOS JOVENES in the unlikely region of JUMILLA, esp 98 99 Carchelo wines (Syrah, Merlot, or Monastrell with Temp and Merlot) Also excellent CRIANZA.

Agramont See Príncipe de Viana, Bodegas.

Agrícola Falset-Marca Tarragona r ★→★★ 98 Co-op bordering PRIORATO, making intensely fruity Castel de Falset. Avoid the fiercely astringent younger wines.

Albariño High-quality, aromatic white grape of GALICIA and its wine, now perhaps Spain's most highly regarded white. See Rías Baixas, Cervera, Gran Bazán, Pazo de Barrantes.

Alella r (p) dr sw 91 93 94 95 96 97 98 ★★ Sml, demarcated region North of Barcelona. Pleasantly fruity wines. (See Marfil, Marqués de Alella, Parxet.)

Alicante r (w) ★ DO. Most wines still earthy and over-strong.

Alión Rib del D r ★★★ 95 96' 98 99' oo Since discontinuing the 3-yr-old VALBUENA, VEGA SICILIA has acquired this second BODEGA to make 100% Tempranillo CRIANZAS; impressive results. Vigorous; gd short- to mid-term keeping.

Allende, Finca R Ala r ★★★→★★★★★ 96 97 98' 99 oo Much-praised newish (94) BODEGA: elegan, oak-aged Tempranillos. Vastly expensive Aurus (98'): and single-estate Calvario (99').

Almendralejo E Spain r w ★ Wine centre of Extremadura. Makes the spirit for fortifying sherry. See Lar de Lares.

Alvaro Palacios Pri r ★★★★ 93 94 95 96 98 99 Gifted emigré from RIOJA making some of the most expensive and fashionable red wine in Spain, incl Finca Dofi (98'), L'Ermita (95), Les Terrasses. One of the few PRIORATOS to repay bottle-age.

Ampurdán, Cavas del Amp r w p ★→★★ Big-selling w Pescador, r Cazador.

Ampurdán-Costa Brava Amp r w p ★→★★ Demarcated region abutting Pyrenees. Mainly co-op-made rosés, reds. See also last entry.

Año Year: 4° Año (or Años) means 4 yrs old when bottled. Was common on labels, now largely discontinued in favour of vintages, or terms such as CRIANZA.

Arco Bodegas Unidas See Berberana, Bodegas.

Artadi See Cosecheros Alaveses.

Arzuaga, Bodegas Ribera del Duero r ★★★ 94 95 96 97 98 Architecturally spectacular new BODEGA with 370 acres aiming for luscious, modern wines.

Bach, Masía Pen r w p dr sw res ★★→★★★ 92 **94 95 96** 97 98 Stately villa-winery nr SAN SADURNÍ DE NOYA, owned by CODORNÍU. Speciality is white Extrísimo, both sweet and oaky, and dry. Also good red RESERVAS.

Barbier, René Pen r w res ★★ **91** 96 **97** Owned by FREIXENET, known for fresh white Kraliner, red RB RESERVAS.

Barón de Ley RB r (w) res ★★★ 94 **95 96 97 98** Newish RIOJA BODEGA linked with EL COTO: good single-estate wines.

Barril, Masía Pri r br res ★★★ 87 95 Hard to find, old-fashioned, tarry reds and unusual herbalized RANCIO. Bought in 1998 by CAVAS HILL and renamed Mas d'en Gil. New, more modern styles imminent.

Baso r w ★★ Brand name for reliable Garnacha from NAVARRA made by young winemaker Telmo Rodríguez, formerly of LA GRANJA REMELLURI.

Berberana, Bodegas R Alt r (w) res ★★→★★★ 90 91 **96** 98 Now part of ARCO BODEGAS UNIDAS, incorporating BERBERANA, MARQUÉS DE GRIÑON, MARQUES DE MONISTROL, MARQUÉS DE CACERES Lagunilla, Vinícola del Mediterraneo, and Bodegas Hispano Argentinas. Fruity, full-bodied reds, but Berberana is increasingly selling its best wines as MARQUÉS DE GRIÑON.

Berceo, Bodegas R Alt r w p res ★★→★★★ 87 **93** 94 **97** 98 Cellar in HARO with good Gonzalo de Berceo GRAN RESERVA.

Beronia, Bodegas R Alt r w res ★★→★★★ 94 95 **97** Small, modern BODEGA making reds in traditional, oaky style and fresh, "modern" whites. Owned by González-Byass (see page 179).

Bilbaínas, Bodegas R Alt r w (p) dr sw sp res ★★ 90 91 **93** 94 95 Long-established makers of traditional Viña Pomal, lighter Viña Zaco, and Vendimia Especial RESERVAS. New owners CODORNÍU are introducing less-oaky, modern-style wines, eg. La Vicalanda RESERVA (**95**). White Monopole is a national standard. Good Royal Carlton CAVA.

Binissalem r w ★★ Best-known MALLORCA DO. See also Franja Roja.

Blanco White.

Bodega Spanish term for (i) a wineshop; (ii) a concern occupied in the making, blending and/or shipping of wine; and (iii) a cellar.

Bodegas de Crianza Castilla la Vieja Rueda w dr sp ★★→★★★ The Sanz family produce some of RUEDA's liveliest whites under a variety of labels (eg PALACIO DE BORNOS and CON CLASS) using Verdejo, Viura, and Sauv B. Reds include concentrated, oaky Almirantazgo de Castilla from VT. Medina del Campo and wines from new BODEGA in DO TORO.

Bodegas y Bebidas Part of Allied-Domecq, owns wineries all over Spain. Mainly mid-market brands. Also controls various prestigious firms, eg AGE, CAMPO VIEJO, MARQUÉS DEL PUERTO.

Over-hyped Priorato?

With their deep, black hues and bewitching nose, some new releases from this DO initially promised structural immortality with their use of oak and French varieties. But after a relatively short time in bottle, many have proved to be disappointing. Priorato's neighbour, Tarragona, offers more affordable alternatives

---

Bodegas y Viñedos del Jalón Calatayud r (w dr p) ★★ **99 00** 01 Leading brands are the very drinkable Castillo Maluenda and Marqués de Aragón. Value. Scotswoman Pamela Geddes is making sophisticated Poema Garnacha and Garnacha Syrah wines and, on her own account, Spain's first sparkling red from Murcian Monastrell, La Pamelita.

Bornos, Palacio de Bornos Rueda w sp ★★★ 99 00 01 First-rate Sauv Bl and Verdejo wines. See BODEGAS DE CRIANZA CASTILLA LA VIEJA.

Bretón, Bodegas R Alt r res ★★★ 90 91 94 95 96 Respected Loriñon range & little-seen, expensive, conc'd Dominio de Conté 90 91 94 95 **96** (compares to CONTINO).

Calatayud ★→★★ **94** 97 98 99 Aragón DO (of 4): especially Garnacha. VINOS Y VIÑEDOS DE JALON holds sway.

Campillo, Bodegas R Ala r (p) res ★★★ 89 **91 92** 94 95 96 **97** Affiliated with FAUSTINO MARTÍNEZ, a young BODEGA with good wines.

Campo Viejo, Bodegas R Alt r (w) res ★→★★★ 91 94 95 96 **97** 98 00 100% Tempranillo Alcorta; big, fruity red RESERVAS, esp Marqués de Villamagna. See Bodegas y Bebidas.

Can Rafols dels Caus Pen r p w ★★ 94 96 **97** 98 Young, small PENEDÈS BODEGA: own-estate, fruity Cabernet, pleasant Chard-Xarel-lo-Chenin; Gran Caus and less, expensive Petit Caus ranges. Best red is Caus Lubis 100% Merlot. Avoid the 95.

Canary Islands (Islas) r w p g ★→★★ Until recently, there were few wines of any quality other than dessert Malvasías (BODEGAS El Grifo and Bodegas Mozaga on Lanzarote). No fewer than 8 DOs have now been created, and modernized bodegas esp on TENERIFE are making better and lighter wines. The tourist trade may keep prices high, but the flavours have real interest. To investigate.

Caralt, Cavas Conde de Pen r w sp res ★★→★★★ CAVA wines from outpost of FREIXENET, esp good, vigorous Brut NV; also pleasant, still wines.

Cariñena r (w p) ★ **91 92 93 96 98** Co-op-dominated DO: large-scale supplier of strong, everyday wine. Being invigorated and wines lightened.

Casa Castillo Jumilla r (w p) ★★→★★★ 98 99 Some of the best wines from JUMILLA made by Julia Roch e Hijos, incl fruity Monastrell (**99**), leaner Las Grava (**98**), and deep Pie Franco (**98**) from vines unaffected by phylloxera.

Casa Gualda La Mancha r ★★→★★★ 96 97 Cencibel (Temp), Cab S, Crianza, and young Merlot 99 of unbeatable quality/value from the co-op Nuestra Sra de la Cabeza in Cuenca.

Casa de la Viña Valdepeñas r (w p) ★★ 94 96 **99** BODEGAS Y BEBIDAS-owned estate, since 80s: sound and fruity Cencibel, CRIANZAS, and JOVENES (00).

Castaño, Bodegas Yecla (w dr) r res ★★ 95 96 97 98 **99** 00 Trail-blazer in remote YECLA making sound and pleasant blends of Monastrell with Cab S, Temp and Merlot under the names of Castaño, Colección, Hecula, and Pozuelo.

Castell de Remei Cos de S r w p ★★→★★★ 95 96 97 98 **99** Historic v'yds/winery revived, re-equipped, replanted since 83. Best wines: Gotim Bru (Temp, Cab S, Merlot), new designer-style Oda (**98**), and top 1780.

Castellblanch Pen w sp ★★ PENEDÈS CAVA firm, owned by FREIXENET. Look for Brut Zero and Gran Castell GRAN RESERVAS.

Castillo de Monjardín Nav r w ★★→★★★ 94 97 **98** Newish winery making fragrant, oaky Chard Res (97) and v gd reds, esp blends of Merlot (94).

Castillo de Ygay R Alt r w ★★★★ (r) 25 52 64 68 75 78 82 85 87 **89** A legend. The 64 is still superb. See Marqués de Murrieta.

Castillo del Perelada, Caves Amp r w p res sp ★★→★★★ 92 93 94 95 Large range of both still wines and CAVA, including Chard, Sauv B, Cab S (esp Gran Claustro 94 95 **96**), and sparkling Gran Claustro extra brut.

Cataluña New DO covering the whole Catalan area. Wines may be registered as from one of the existing DOs or from the new global DO, but not from both.

Cava Official term for any classic-method Spanish sparkling wine, and the DO covering the areas up and down Spain where it is made.

Cenalsa See Príncipe de Viana, Bodegas.

Centro Españolas, Bodegas La M r w p ★★ 93 94 95 **97 98 99** 00 Large, modern BODEGA best known for creditable red Allozo, 100% Tempranillo.

Cervera, Lagar de Rías Baixas w ★★★ DYA Maker of one of best Albariños: flowery and intensely fruity with subdued bubbles and a long finish.

Chacolí País Vasco w (r) ★→★★ DYA Alarmingly sharp, often sp wine from Basque coast; 2 DOs for all 395 acres! 9–11% alcohol. Best producers: Txomín Etxaníz (Guetari), Aretxondo (Viscaya).

Chivite, Bodegas Julián Nav r w (p) dr sw res ★★★ 90 92 94 95 96 97 The biggest and best NAVARRA BODEGA. Now some of Spain's top reds, deep-flavoured, v long-lived; flowery, well-balanced white, esp Chivite Colección 125 (99), vg oo rosé and superb Vendemia Tarde Moscatel, the best from Spain. See Gran Feudo.

Cigales r p ★→★★ 99 Recently demarcated region north of Valladolid, esp for light reds (traditionally known as Claretes – a term now banned by the EC).

Clos Mogador Pri r ★★★→★★★★ 94 95 96 97 René Barbier produces first-rate new-wave Clos Mogador PRIORATO.

Codorníu Pen w sp ★★→★★★★ One of the two largest firms in SAN SADURNÍ DE NOYA making good CAVA: v high-tech, 10M bottles ageing in cellars. Mature Non Plus Ultra, fresh Anna de Codorníu or premium Jaume de Codorníu RESERVA. Also owns RAÍMAT, BILBAINAS.

Compañía Vinícola del Norte de España (CVNE) R Alt r w dr (p) ★★→★★★ 89 90 93 94 95 96 97 98 Famous RIOJA BODEGA. In spite of (or because of?) a revolutionary new vinification plant, young wines are less good than formerly, though some of the older Viña Real and Imperial RESERVAS are spectacular. See also CONTINO.

Con Class, Bodegas Rueda w dr ★★→★★★ DYA Despite the dreadful name: exciting Verdejo/Viura and Sauv Bl, esp RUEDA Superior (oo).

Conca de Barberà Pen w (r p) Catalan DO region growing Parellada grapes for making CAVA. Its best wine is TORRES MILMANDA Chard.

Condado de Haza Rib del D r ★★★ 94 95 96 97 98' Pure, oak-aged Tinto Fino. Similar to PESQUERA but more consistent and better value.

Conde de Valdemar See Martínez-Bujanda.

Consejo Regulador Official organization for the control, promotion, and defence of a DENOMINACIÓN DE ORIGEN.

Contino R Ala r res ★★★ 89 91 94 95 96' 97 Very fine single-v'yd red made by a subsidiary of COMPANIA VINICOLA DEL NORTE DE ESPANA. Look for 100% Graciano (94') and new premium Viña del Olivo (96').

Cosecha Crop or vintage.

Cosecheros Alaveses R Ala r (w p) ★★★ 90 92 93 94 95 96 97' Up-and-coming former co-op, esp for gd, young, unoaked red Artadi, and Viñas de Gain, Viña El Pisón, Pagos Viejos RESERVAS.

Costers del Segre Cos del S r w p sp ★★→★★★ 92 95 96 98 Small, demarcated area around the city of Lleida (Lérida), famous for the v'yds of RAÍMAT.

Costers del Siurana Pri r (sw) ★★★→★★★★ A star of Priorato. 94 95 96 97 Carlos Pastrana makes the prestigious Clos de l'Obac, Misere, and Usatges from Garnacha/Cab S, sometimes plus Syrah, Merlot, Tempranillo, and Cariñena. Wonderful sweet Dolç de l'Orbac.

CoViDes Pen r w p sp res ★★→★★★ 93 94 95 97 99 Large former co-op; good Duc de Foix white and Cabernet Sauvignon, Cab Sauvignon-Tempranillo; also first-rate Duc de Foix CAVA.

Criado y embotellado por... Grown and bottled by...

Crianza Literally "nursing"; the ageing of wine. New or unaged wine is "sin crianza" or "joven" (young). Reds labelled "crianza" must be at least two years old (with one year in oak, in some areas six months), and must not be released before the third year.

Cumbrero See Montecillo, Bodegas.

Denominación de Origen (DO) Official wine region (see page 156).

Denominación de Origen Calificada (DOCa) Classification for wines of the highest quality; so far only RIOJA benefits (since 91).

Domecq R Ala r (w) res ★★→★★★ **91 92 93 94 95 96** RIOJA outpost of sherry firm. Inexpensive Viña Eguía CRIANZAS and excellent Marqués de Arienzo RESERVAS, fragrant and medium-bodied.

Don Darias/Don Hugo Alto Ebro r w ★ Huge-selling, modestly priced wines, v like Rioja, from undemarcated BODEGAS Vitorianas. Sound red and white.

A Spanish choice for 2003

González-Byass Apostoles Palo Cortado sherry
Cordorniu Reina Cristina Brut cava
Con Clas Sauvignon Blanc oo Rueda
Castillo de Monjardín Merlot Rosado oo Navarra
Abadía Retuerta Pago Negralada 97 Castilla y León
Torres Grans Muralles 96 Conca de Barberà
Roda Cirsíon 98 Rioja Alta
Riscal Barón de Chirel 95 Rioja Alavesa
Contino Graciano 94 Rioja Alavesa

Dulce Sweet.

El Bierzo El B DO since 90, N of León. See CASAR DE VALDAIGA. **91 92 94 96 98 99** Top wine: Luna Berberida RESERVA (**98**).

El Coto, Bodegas R Ala r (w) res ★★ **91 94 95 96 98** BODEGA best-known for light, soft, red El Coto and Coto de Imaz RESERVAS (**94**).

Elaborado y añejado por... Made and aged by...

Enate Somontano DO r w p res ★★→★★★ **94 95 96 98 99** Good wines from SOMONTANO in the north: light, clean, fruity incl barrel-fermented Chard (**98 99**) and Cab S blends (the CRIANZA is full and juicy). Wonderful **98** Merlot.

Espumoso Sparkling (but see Cava).

Fariña, Bodegas Toro r w res ★★ **94 98 99 00** Best-known BODEGA of newish DO TORO: good, spicy reds. Gran Colegiata is cask-aged; Colegiata not. Young Primero. Recent vintages overpriced and disappointing.

Faustino, Bodegas R Ala r w (p) res ★★→★★★ **91 93 94' 95 96 97** 99 Long-established BODEGA, formerly F Martínez, with good reds. GRAN RESERVA is Faustino I. Top is Faustino de Autor (**94'**)

Fillaboa, Granxa Rías Baixas w ★★★ DYA Small firm; delicately fruity ALBARIÑO.

Franja Roja Majorca r res ★★ **89 91 94 97** Best-known MALLORCA BODEGA at Binissalem making improving José L Ferrer wines.

Freixenet, Cavas Pen w sp ★★→★★★ Huge CAVA firm, rivalling CODORNÍU in size. Good sparklers, notably bargain Cordón Negro in black bottles, Brut Barroco, RESERVA Real, and Premium Cuvée DS. Also owns Gloria Ferrer in California, Champagne Henri Abelé (Reims), and a sparkling-wine plant in Mexico.

Galicia Rainy NW Spain: esp for fresh, aromatic but pricy whites, eg ALBARIÑO.

Generoso (g) Apéritif or dessert wine rich in alcohol.

Granbazán w dr ★★★ DYA Agro de Bazán produces a classic, fragrant ALBARIÑO with mouth-cleansing acidity.

Gran Feudo Nav w res ★★→★★★ **92 93 94 95 96 97** Brand name of fragrant white, refreshing rosé **99**; soft, plummy red; the best-known wines from CHIVITE.

Gran Reserva See Reserva.

Gran Vas Pressurized tanks (French *cuves closes*) for making cheap sparkling wines; also used to describe this type of wine.

Grandes Bodegas Rib del Duero r ★★→★★★ **95 96 97** Reorganized and with own v'yards, this BODEGA (in notoriously highly priced region) makes affordable, unoaked Marqués de Velilla. More intense CRIANZAS and RESERVAS are pricier.

Guelbenzu, Bodegas Nav r (w) res ★★→★★★ **95 96 97 98' 99** 00 Family estate in Navarra making conc, full-bodied reds: Azul, EVO, and top wine Lautus (**96 98'**).

Guitán Godello Valdeorras w ★★★→★★★★ 98 99 Made by BODEGAS Tapada, these splendidly fruity, fragrant, and complex 100% Godello wines, rated among the top whites in Spain, typify renaissance of native grapes in GALICIA. The barrel-fermented type has the edge.

Haro Wine centre of the RIOJA ALTA, a small but stylish old city.

Hill, Cavas Pen w r sp res ★★→★★★ 91 93 95 96 97 98 Old PENEDÈS firm: fresh dry w Blanc Cru, gd Gran Civet, and Gran Toc reds, first-rate young Masía Hill Tempranillo, and delicate RESERVA Oro Brut CAVA.

Iljalba, Viña R Alt r w dr p ★→★★★ 95 96 97 98 99 00 A newish BODEGA with a reputation for organically-made younger wines and a rare 100% Graciano.

Induvasa Jumilla r ★★ Up-and-coming winery making the attractive and attractively priced young Monastrell Taja (**99**).

Josep Anguera Beyme Tarragona r ★★→★★★ 97 **98 99** 00 Small family firm on verges of PRIORATO making superior fruity Finca L'Argata wines from Syrah, Cab S, Garnacha, and Cariñena blends.

Joven (vino) Young, unoaked wine.

Jumilla r (w p) ★→★★★ 91 93 96 98 99 DO in mountains N of Murcia. Its traditionally overstrong wines are being lightened by earlier picking and better winemaking, The Monastrell grape can yield dark and fragrant wines to rival those of RIBERA DEL DUERO. See Agapito Rico and Casa Castillo.

Juvé y Camps Pen w sp ★★★ 97 Family firm. Top-quality CAVA, from free-run juice only, esp RESERVA de la Familia and Gran Juvé y Camps (96).

LAN, Bodegas R Alt r (p w) res ★★→★★★ 91 94 95 96 97 98 00 Huge, modern BODEGA. Recently reorganized; making improved Lan, Lanciano, & premium Culmen de Lan (94').

Lanzarote Canary Island with v fair, dry Malvasía, eg El Grifo.

Lar de Lares Riv del G r res ★★ 93 94 96 98 Meaty GRAN RESERVA from BODEGAS InViOSA, in remote Extremadura (in SW). And younger, lighter Lar de Barros. Also good Bonaval CAVA.

León, Jean Pen r w res ★★★ 82 85 87 90 **91 93** 94 95 96 Small firm; TORRES-owned since 95. Gd, oaky Chard (99). Earlier Cab: was huge, repaid long ageing; lighter since 90. Also outstanding Merlot (97).

Logroño First town of RIOJA region. HARO has more charm (and BODEGAS).

López de Heredia R Alt r w (p) dr sw res ★★→★★★ 42 47 54 57 61 64 68 70 73 78 81 87 93 **94 97** Old-est'd HARO BODEGA: v long-lasting, v trad wines. Best are really old RESERVAS from 54 onwards; marvellous 64S.

Los Llanos Valdepeñas r (p w) res ★★ 92 94 **97 98** One of growing number of VALDEPEÑAS BODEGAS to age wine in oak. RESERVA, GRAN RESERVA; premium Pata Negra Gran Reserva: 100% Cencibel (Tempranillo). Clean, fruity w, Armonioso.

Mallorca Interesting things are happening on the island, incl fresh Chard (better unoaked), Merlot, Syrah, Cab S. Also trad varieties & blends. FRANCA ROJA, Herens de Ribas, Miguel Oliver, Son Bordils, & Jaume Mesquida are leaders.

Mancha, La La M r w ★→★★ **92 93 94 96 97 98 99** Vast demarcated region N and NE of VALDEPEÑAS. Mainly white wines, the reds lack the liveliness of the best Valdepeñas but show signs of improvement. To watch.

Marfil Alella w (p) ★★ Brand of ALELLA Vinícola (oldest-est'd producer in Alella). Means "ivory". Now for lively, rather pricey, new-style dry whites.

Marqués de Alella Alella w (sp) ★★→★★★ 98 99 00 (DYA) Light, fragrant w ALELLA wines from PARXET, some Chard (incl barrel-fermented Allier). Also CAVA.

Marqués de Cáceres, Bodegas R Alt r p w res ★★★ 86 **89 90** 91 92 93 94 95 96 Good r RIOJAS made by modern French methods incl premium Gaudium (94); surprisingly light, fragrant w (DYA), barrel-fermented Antea (98), & sw Santinela.

Marqués de Griñón La M r w ★★★ **94 95** 96 97 98 Enterprising nobleman initiated v fine Cab, delicious new (98) Syrah and Petit Verdot nr Toledo, S of

Madrid, not formerly known for wine. Fruity wines to drink fairly young. Also gd RIOJAS and Durius (**97** 98) r from RIB DEL DUERO area. Owned by ARCO.

Marqués de Monistrol, Bodegas Pen p r sp dr sw res ★★→★★★ **92** 94 95' 98 Old BODEGA now owned by ARCO. Reliable CAVAS. Fresh blends of Cab S, Merlot, and Temp.

Marqués de Murrieta R Ala r p w res ★★★→★★★★ 25 42 50 52 54 60 68 70 75 78 87 89 94 95 96 **97** 99 Historic, revered BODEGA nr LOGRONO, formerly for some of best RIOJAS. Also famous for r CASTILLO DE YGAY and old-style, oaky white. New red Colección 2001 (99).

Marqués de Riscal R Ala r (p w) res ★★★→★★★★ 91 92 94 95 96 97 Best-known RIOJA ALAVESA BODEGA. Fairly light, dry r. Old vintages: v fine, some more recent ones variable; now right back on form. Barón de Chirel, 50% Cab S (94' 95' **96'**) is magnificent. RUEDA w incl Sauv (00), oak-aged RESERVA Limousin (97).

Marqués de Vargas, Bodegas y Viñedos R Aly ★★**92** 93 94 96' Spectacular newcomer making a RESERVA and a Privada (96'), both with magnificent concentration and balance. Avoid the 00.

Marqués del Puerto R Alt r (p w) res ★★→★★★ 85 94 95 **96** 97 Small firm, was BODEGAS López Agos, now owned by Marie Brizard. Reliable.

Martínez-Bujanda R Ala r p w res ★★★ 90 **91** 92 93 94' 95' 96' **97** Refounded (85) family-run RIOJA BODEGA, remarkably equipped. Superb wines, incl fruity sin CRIANZA, irresistible ROSADO; noble Valdemar RESERVAS (95) 100% Garnacha and splendid premium 100% Tempranillo single-v'yd Finca Valpiedra (95 96).

Mascaró, Cavas Pen r p w sp ★★→★★★ **90 91 92 93** Top brandy maker, gd CAVA; fresh, lemony, dry white Viña Franca, and Anima Cab S.

Mas Martinet Pri r ★★★→★★★★ 94' 95' 96 **97** 99 Maker of Clos Martinet and a pioneer of the exclusive boutique PRIORATOS.

Mauro, Bodegas nr Valladolid r ★★→★★★ 95 96 97 98 Young BODEGA in Tudela del Duero; very good, round, fruity TINTO del País (Tempranillo) red and excellent Terrens (96 **98'**). Not DO, as some of the fruit is from outside RIBERA DEL D. Now making excellent TORO San Roman (98).

Milmanda ★★★ See Conca de Barberà, Torres.

Montecillo, Bodegas R Alt r w (p) res ★★ 94 95 96 **97** RIOJA BODEGA owned by OSBORNE. Old GRAN RESERVAS are magnificent. Excellent CRIANZA **96**.

Muga, Bodegas R Alt r (w sp) res ★★★ **89** 91 94 95 96 **97** Small family firm in HARO, known for some of RIOJA's best strictly trad reds. Wines are light but highly aromatic, with long, complex finish. Best is Prado Enea and now extraordinarily concentrated Torre Muga (91 94' 95 96 **98**). Whites and CAVA less good. Fresh white Viura fermented in barrel (00).

Navajas, Bodegas R Alt r w res ★★→★★★ 94 95 **98** 99 00 Small firm: bargain reds, CRIANZAS, RESERVAS. Also excellent oak-aged white Viura 98.

Navarra Nav r p (w) ★★→★★★ **92** 94 95 96 97 98 Demarcated region. Stylish Temp & Cabernet reds, increasingly rivalling RIOJAS in quality and trouncing many in value. See Chivite, Guelbenzu, Palacio de la Vega, Ochoa, Príncipe de Viana.

Nuestro Padre Jésus del Perdón, Co-op de La M r w ★→★★ 91 93 **94** 96 99 00 01 Bargain fresh white Lazarillo and more-than-drinkable Yuntero; 100% Cencibel (alias Tempranillo) and Cencibel-Cab S aged in oak.

Ochoa Nav r p w res ★★→★★★ 87 91 92' 93 94 96 **97** Small family BODEGA; excellent Moscatel (00), but better-known for well-made red and rosés, incl 100% Tempranillo and 100% Merlot (97).

Organic Wines Spain's most prestigious and longstanding producer is Albet i Noya in PENEDÈS, maker of good Chard, Temp, Cab S, and first-rate Syrah (97).

Pago de Carraovejas Rib del D r res ★★→★★★ 98 99 New estate; some of the region's most stylish, densely fruity TINTO Fino/Cabernet in minimal supply after failure of 97 harvest.

Palacio, Bodegas R Ala r p w res ★★★ 90 91 93 94' 95 96 97 98 Good old BODEGA recovered from Seagram ownership. Very sound and typical Cosme Palacio (95) and RESERVA Privada (94).

Palacio de Fefiñanes Rías Baixas w dr ★★★ Oldest-est'd of the BODEGAS in RÍAS BAIXAS, now making excellent, modern-style ALBARIÑOS DYA.

Palacio de la Vega Nav r p w res ★★→★★★ 93 95 96 97 98 00 New BODEGA with juicy Tempranillo JOVEN, Cab S, Merlot, and much promise.

Parxet Alella w p sp ★★→★★★ Excellent fresh, fruity, exuberant CAVA (only one produced in ALELLA): esp Brut Nature. Also elegant w ALELLA: MARQUÉS DE ALELLA.

Paternina, Bodegas R Alt r w (p) dr sw res ★→★★ Known for its standard red brand Banda Azul. Conde de los Andes label was fine, but the famous 78 is strictly for fans of oak/volatile acidity, and recent vintages, as of their other RIOJAS, are disappointing. Most consistent is Banda Dorada white (DYA).

Pazo Ribeiro r p w ★★ DYA Brand name of the RIBEIRO co-op, whose wines are akin to VINHOS VERDES. Rasping red is local favourite. Pleasant, slightly fizzy Pazo whites are safer; white Viña Costeira and Amadeus have quality.

Pazo de Barrantes Rías Baixas w ★★★ DYA New ALBARIÑO from RIAS BAIXAS; estate owned by late Conde de Creixels of MURRIETA. Delicate, exotic, top-quality.

Pazao de Señorans Rías Baixas w dr ★★★ DYA Exceptionally fragrant wines from a BODEGA considered a benchmark of the DO.

Penedès Pen r w sp ★→★★★ 91 93 94 95 96 98 99 Demarcated region including Vilafranca del Penedès and SAN SADURNI DE NOYA. See also TORRES.

Pérez Pascuas Hermanos Rib del D r res ★★★ 91 94 95 96 97 Immaculate, tiny BODEGA. In Spain its fruity & complex r VIÑA Pedrosa rated one of the best.

Pesquera Rib del D r ★★★ 90 91 92 93 94' 95 96' 97 Small quantities of RIBERA DEL D from Alejandro Fernández. Robert Parker once rated it level with finest B'x. Janus (86 94) is special (even more expensive) bottling. Also CONDADO DE HAZA.

Piqueras, Bodegas Almansa r (w dr p) ★★→★★★ 94 95 96 00 Small family BODEGA. Some of LA MANCHA's best reds: Castillo de Almansa CRIANZA, Marius GRAN RESERVA.

Pingus, Dominio de Rib del D r 95 96 97 98 ★★★★ Tempranillo-based (only 450 cases). Winemaker/owner: Peter Sisseck. Spain's answer to B'dx's "garage" wines. Old vines and new oak create conc'd wines. Will they keep?

Pirineos, Bodegas Som w p r ★★ 94 95 96 97 98 99 00 Former co-op and SOMONTANO pioneer. Best: Montesierra range; oak-aged Señorío de Lazán RESERVA.

Príncipe de Viana, Bodegas Nav r w p ★★ 91 94 96 98 99 00 Large firm (formerly "Cenalsa"), blending and maturing co-op wines and shipping a range from NAVARRA, incl flowery, new-style white and fruity red Agramont.

Priorato Pri br r ★★★→★★★★ 92 93 94 95 96 98 99 00 DO enclave of TARRAGONA, traditionally known for alcoholic RANCIO and huge-bodied, almost black r. At its brambly best, one of Spain's triumphs. COSTERS DE SIURANA, MAS MARTINET, and ROTLLAN TORRA rightly rank among Spain's stars. See page 160.

Raïmat Cos del S r w p sp ★★→★★★ (Cab) 90 91 92 94 95 96 97 98 Clean, structured wines from DO nr Lérida, planted by CODORNÍU with Cabernet, Chardonnay, other foreign vines. Good 100% Chardonnay CAVA. Value.

Rancio Describes any maderized (brown) white wine of nutty flavour.

Raventós i Blanc Pen w sp ★★→★★★ Excellent CAVA aimed at top of market, also fresh El Preludi white and 100% Chard.

Remelluri, La Granja R Ala w dr r res ★★★ 94 95 96 98 Small estate (since 70), making very good traditional red RIOJAS but future less certain after departure of Telmo Rodriguez. Avoid the disappointing 97.

Reserva (res) Good-quality wine matured for long periods. Red reservas must spend at least 1 year in cask and 2 in bottle; Gran Reservas 2 in cask and 3 in bottle. Thereafter many continue to mature for years.

> **Important note:**
> Most large Spanish wineries make a range of red, white, and rosé . The
> vintages at the top of an entry refer to the best of a BODEGA's red CRIANZAS
> and RESERVAS and are only a rough guide, since the vintages and degree of
> maturity may well vary from one wine to another. When individual wines
> are named in the text, preferred vintages are given in brackets.

Rías Baixas w ★★→★★★ **95 96 97** DYA NW DO embracing subzones Val do
Salnés, O Rosal, and Condado do Tea, now for some of the best (and
priciest) cold-fermented Spanish whites, mainly from ALBARIÑO grapes.

Ribera del Duero Rib del D **91 94 95 96 98 99** Fashionable, fast-expanding DO
east of Valladolid, (the Duero becomes the Portuguese Douro). Excellent for
TINTO Fino (Temp) rs. Many excellent wines, but high prices. See ARZUAGA, PAGO
DE CARRAOVEJAS, PÉREZ PASCUAS, PESQUERA, TORREMILANOS, VEGA SICILIA. Also MAURO.

Rioja r p w sp ★★→★★★★ **64 70 75 78 81 82 85 89 91 92 94 95 96 98** 00 01 N
upland region along River Ebro for many of Spain's best red table wines in
some 60 BODEGAS *de exportación*. Tempranillo predominates. Other grapes
and/or oak incl depending on fashion and vintage. Subdivided into 3 areas.

Rioja Alavesa N of the R Ebro, produces fine red wines, mostly light in body
and colour but particularly aromatic.

Rioja Alta S of the R Ebro and W of LOGROÑO, grows most of the finest, best-
balanced red and white wines; also some rosé.

Rioja Baja Stretching E from LOGROÑO, makes coarser red wines, high in alcohol,
and often used for blending.

La Rioja Alta, Bodegas R Alt r w (p) (sw) res ★★★ **82 87 88 89 90 91 92 94 95
96** Excellent RIOJAS, esp red RESERVA VIÑA Alberdi, velvety Ardanza RESERVA,
lighter Araña Reserva, splendid Reserva 904, and marvellous Reserva 890
(**82**) – but the wines are not lasting as long as they used to.

Riojanas, Bodegas R Alt r (w p) res ★★→★★★ **88 89 91 92 93 94 95 96 97** Old
BODEGA. Trad VIÑA Albina; big, mellow Monte Real RESERVAS (**96**).

Roda, Bodegas R Alt r ★★★ **92 93 94' 95' 96** 98' Founded in 89 by a Catalan
couple who decided that only in HARO could they make their dream wines.
Superb and costly Roda I (which has the edge) and Roda II. New Cirsión (98').

Rosado Rosé.

Rotllan Torra Pri r (r&w sw) ★★★ **95 96 97 98** 99 Premium Amadis, Balandra,
sweet Amadis Dolç and Moscatel Reserva Especial PRIORATOS.

Rovellats Pen w p sp ★★→★★★ **94 96 97** Small family firm making only good
(and expensive) CAVAS, stocked in some of Spain's best restaurants.

Rueda br w ★★→★★★ **96 97 98 99** Sm, historic DO W of Valladolid. Traditional
FLOR-growing, sherry-like wines up to 17% alcohol; now for fresh whites,
esp MARQUÉS DE RISCAL. Secret weapon is the Verdejo grape.

Ruíz, Santiago Rías Baixas w ★★→★★★ DYA Small, prestigious RIAS BAIXAS co,
now owned by LAN: fresh, lemony ALBARIÑOS, not quite up to former standards.

San Sadurní de Noya Pen w sp ★★→★★★ Town S of Barcelona, hollow with
CAVA cellars. Standards can be v high, though the flavour (of Parellada and
other grapes) never gets close to Champagne.

Sangría Cold-red wine cup traditionally made with citrus fruit, fizzy lemonade,
ice, and brandy. But too often repulsive, commercial fizz.

Sarría, Bodega de Nav r (p w) res ★★→★★★ **94 95 96 97** Quality remains high,
though Duarte family's departure and death of oenologist Francisco
Morriones dimmed this model estate's international reputation.

Scala Dei, Cellers de Pri r w p res ★★→★★★ **91 93 96** 98 Original PRIORATO BODEGA
owned by CODORNIU. Dark, powerful Garnacha. Cartoixa RESERVAS, conc,
blackberry-rich young Negre. Savoury, oak-ferm'd Garnacha Blanca Prior (**99**).

SPAIN

Schenk, Bodegas Valencia r w p ★★ 92 94 97 Decent Estrella Moscatel, good Monastrell/Garnacha "Cavas Murviedro", and Los Monteros. See also below.

Schenk, Bodegas U-R r w p dr ★→★★ 95 98 99 00 Reliable Las Lomas reds and fresh Bobal ROSADO.

Seco Dry.

Segura Viudas, Cavas Pen w sp ★★→★★★ CAVA from SAN SADURNI (FREIXENET-owned). Buy the Brut Vintage 96, Aria 97 or esp RESERVA Heredad 96.

Solís, Félix Valdepeñas w dr p r ★★ 95 96 97 99 00 BODEGA in VALDEPEÑAS making sturdy, oak-aged reds, VIÑA Albali RESERVAS, and fresh white.

Somontano ★★→★★★ 91 94 95 96 98 99 (Som) Fashionable DO in Pyrenean foothills. Given the cool conditions, future could lie with whites and Pinot N. Best-known BODEGAS: old French-est'd Lalanne (esp Viña San Marcos r: Moristel-Tempranillo-Cab S; white Macabeo, Chard), Bodega PIRINEOS, new VIÑAS DEL VERO. Also Viñedos y CRIANZAS del Alto Aragón (excellent ENATE range).

Tarragona r w br dr sw ★→★★★ 95 96 97 98 99 Table wines from demarcated region (DO); previously of little note; now greatly improved and of interest.

Tenerife r w ★→★★ DYA Now 4 DOs; s'times much more than merely drinkable young wines. Best BODEGAS: Flores, Monje, Insulares (VIÑA Norte label).

Tinto Red.

Toro r ★→★★ 90 91 93 94' 95 96 98 99 00 01 This increasingly fashionable DO 150 miles NW of Madrid still produces powerful, fairly basic reds. VEGA SICILIA has now built a BODEGA there; the results should show what the region is capable of. The 01 vintage was tiny but spectacular See BODEGAS FARINA.

Torremilanos Rib del D (p) res ★→★★★ 89 90 91 92 94 95 96 97 99 Label of BODEGAS Peñalba López, a fast-expanding family firm nr Aranda de Duero. TINTO Fino (Tempranillo) is smoother, more RIOJA-like than most.

Torres, Miguel Pen r w p dr s/sw res ★★→★★★★ 87 88 89 90 92 93 94 95 96 97 World-famous family company among the stars of the wine world. Makes most of the best PENEDÈS wines; a flagship for all Spain. Wines are flowery in VIÑA Sol (00), Green Label Fransola Sauv (99), Gran Viña Sol (99) Parellada, MILMANDA oak-fermented Chard (98 99), off-dry aromatic Esmeralda (00), Waltraud Ries (99), red Sangre de Toro (99), Gran Sangre de Toro (96 97), vg Mas la Plana Gran Coronas (Cabernet Sauvignon) RESERVAS (89 93 94 95 96), fresh, soft Atrium Merlot (98 99), and Viña Magdala Pinot. Mas Borrás (96): 100% Pinot Noir. Superb new Grans Muralles (96, 97), full-bodied, made from native grapes including reintroduced Garot, is noble. Also in Chile, California, and China.

Unión de Cosecheros de Labastida R Ala r p w dr ★→★★★ 94 95 96 97 98 99 00 Old-established and first-rate RIOJAN cooperative. Young, juicy Montebuna, good Solagüen CRIANZAS and RESERVAS and top Manuel Qintano reservas (95).

Utiel-Requena U-R r p (w) ★→★★★ 92 93 94 96 97 98 99 Demarcated region W of VALENCIA. Sturdy reds and thick, hyper-tannic wines for blending; also light, fragrant rosé.

Valbuena Rib del D ★★★ 89 90 91 92 94 95' 97 Formerly made with the same grapes as VEGA SICILIA but sold when 5 yrs old. Best at about 10 yrs. Some prefer it to its elder brother. But see Alión.

Valdeorras Gal r w ★→★★★ DO E of Orense. Fresh, dry wines; at best, Godellos are now rated among top white wines in Spain. See GUITÁN GODELLO.

Valdepeñas La M r (w) ★→★★ 90 91 95 96 98 Demarcated region nr Andalucían border. Mainly red wines, high in alcohol but surprisingly soft in flavour. Best wines (eg LOS LLANOS, FELIX SOLIS, and CASA DE LA VIÑA) now oak-matured.

Valdevimbre-Los Oteros r p w ★→★★ 94 95 96 97 N region to watch: fruity, dry, refreshing wines, esp from Vinos de León (aka VILE): young Catedral de Léon, more mature Palacio de los Guzmanes; full-blooded Don Suero RESERVA (96).

Valduero, Bodegas Rib del D r (w p) ★★→★★★ 86 90 91 95 96 97 Now more than 10 yrs old; firm reputation for well-made wine and vg-value RESERVAS.

Valencia r w ★ Demarcated region exporting vast quantities of clean and drinkable table wine; also refreshing whites, esp Moscatel.

Vega Sicilia Rib del D r res ★★★★ 53 60 62 64 66 68 70 73 75 76 80 81 82 83 85 86 90 Top Spanish wine: full, fruity, piquant, rare, and fascinating. Up to 16% alcohol; best at 12-15 yrs. RESERVA Especial: a blend, chiefly of 62 and 79 (!). Also VALBUENA, ALION. Now investing in Tokáji, Hungary.

Vendimia Vintage.

Viña Literally, a vineyard. But wines such as Tondonia (LOPEZ DE HEREDIA) are not necessarily made only with grapes from the v'yd named.

Viña Pedrosa See Pérez Pascuas.

Viñas del Vero Som w p r res ★★→★★★ 91 92 93 94 95 96 97 98 99 SOMONTANO estate. Gd varietal wines: Chard, Ries, Gewürz. Best r Val de Vos Cab (94 96).

Vinícola de Castilla La M r p w ★★ 91 92 94 95 96 98 One of largest LA MANCHA firms. Red and white Castillo de Alhambra are palatable. Top are Cab, Cencibel (Tempranillo), Señorío de Guadianeja GRAN RESERVAS.

Vinícola Navarra Nav r p w dr res ★★ 96 97 98 99 00 Old-est'd firm, now part of BODEGAS Y BEBIDAS, but still thoroughly traditional. Best wines Castillo de Tiebas, Las Campañas.

Vino común/corriente Ordinary wine.

Yecla r w ★→★★ DO north of Murcia. Decent red from BODEGAS CASTAÑO.

> ### Vinos de Alta Expresión
> Within the last few years a new generation of select and very pricey wines has appeared in Spain. The full potential of the grape is realized by using fruit from old vines, picking at the optimum point, hand sorting, and fermenting in small batches. Some examples: from Rioja; ALLENDE Aurus; ARTADI EI PISÓN; MARQUÉS DE RISCAL Barón de Chirel; REMÍREZ DE GANUZA; Roda Cirsión; Musa Torre Muga. From Conca de Barberà: TORRES Grans Muralles. From Priorato: CLOS MOGADOR reserva; ALVARO PALACIO Finca Dolfi. From Navarra: GUELBENZU Lautus. From Ribera del Duero; Dominio de Pingus.

Portugal

Recent vintages

2001 Large vintage throughout. Those producers who undertook careful selection made very good wines.

2000 Sml harvest in fine weather led to ripe-flavoured wines from all regions.

1999 Another small year with prospects dashed by rain during the vintage. Wines from the south better than the north.

1998 Tiny yields, potentially excellent wines in the north diluted by late September rain. Inland areas and the Alentejo fared better.

1997 A good year throughout the country. A healthy crop produced balanced, ripe-flavoured reds. Good red Bairrada.

Abrigada, Quinta da Alenquer r w res ★★ 95 96 97 98 99 Family estate: characterful,j light w, cherry-like PERIQUITA. Best: oaked GARRAFEIRAS.

Adega A cellar or winery.

Alenquer r w ★→★★ Aromatic wines from IPR just North of Lisbon. Good estate wines from QUINTAS DE ABRIGADA, PANCAS, CARNEIRO, and de Monte d'Oiro (Syrah).

Alentejo r (w) ★→★★★ **95 96 97 98 99 00** Vast tract of SE Portugal with only sparse v'yds, over the R Tagus from Lisbon, but rapidly emerging potential for excellent wine. To date the great bulk has been co-op-made. Estate wines from CARTUXA, CORTES DE CIMA, HERDADE DE MOUCHAO, JOÃO RAMOS, JOSE DE SOUSA, QUINTA DO CARMO (part Rothschild-owned), VILA SANTA, and ESPORAO have potency and style. Best co-ops are at BORBA, REDONDO, and REGUENGOS. Now classified as a DOC in its own right with BORBA, REDONDO, REGUENGOS, PORTALEGRE, EVORA, Granja-Amareleja, Vidigueira, and Moura entitled to their own village appellations. Also VINHO REGIONAL Alentejano.

Algarve r w ★ Wines of the holiday area are covered by DOCS Lagos, Tavira, Lagoa, and Portimão. Nothing to write home about.

Aliança, Caves Bair r w sp res ★★ Large BAIRRADA-based firm making classic-method sparkling. Reds and whites incl good Bairrada wines and mature DÃOS. Also interests in ALENTEJO.

Altano Douro **99 00** Good new red from the Symington family (DOW's port). Look out for future releases.

Alvarinho White grape planted in the extreme north of Portugal making floral white wines. Known as ALBARIÑO in neighbouring Galicia.

Ameal, Quinta do VV w ★★★ DYA. One of best VVs available. 100% LOUREIRO.

Aragonez Successful red grape in ALENTEJO for varietal wines. See Tinta Roriz.

Arinto White grape best from central and S Portugal where it retains acidity and produces fragrant, crisp, dry, white wines.

Arruda r w ★ DOC in ESTREMADURA with large co-op.

Aveleda, Quinta da VV w ★★ DYA Reliable VINHO VERDES made on the Aveleda estate of the Guedes family. It is sold dry in Portugal but is slightly sweet for export. There are also gd varietal wines from LOUREIRO, ALVARINHO, and Trajadura. Reds: Charamba (DOURO) and Aveleda (ESTREMADURA).

Azevedo, Quinta do VV w ★★ DYA Superior VINHO VERDE from SOGRAPE. 100% LOUREIRO grapes.

Bacalhoa, Quinta da Set r res ★★★ **97 98 99** Estate nr SETUBAL. Its fruity, reliable, mid-weight Cab is made by J P VINHOS.

Bairrada Bair r w sp ★→★★★ **90' 94 97 98 99** DOC in central Portugal for solid (sometimes astringent) reds from Baga grape. Best wines: CASA DE SAIMA, LUIS PATO, and CAVES SÃO JOÃO will keep for years. Most white used by local sparkling-wine industry.

Barca Velha Douro r res ★★★★ **91'** Portugal's most renowned red, made in very limited quantities in the high Douro by the port firm of FERREIRA (now owned by SOGRAPE). Powerful, resonant wine with deep bouquet, but facing increasing competition from other Douro reds.

Beiras ★→★★ VINHO REGIONAL including DÃO, BAIRRADA, and granite mountain ranges of central Portugal.

Beira Interior ★ DOC incorporating former IPRS of Castelo Rodrigo, Pinhel, and Cova da Beira. Huge potential from old vineyards.

Boavista, Quinta da Est ★★ DYA Large property near ALENQUER making increasingly good range of r and w: Palha Canas, Quinta das Sete Encostas, Espiga, and a Chard, Casa Santos Lima. Winemaker: José Neiva.

Borba Alen r ★→★★ Small DOC in central ALENTEJO; well-managed cooperative producing fruity reds.

Branco White.

Brejoeira, Palácio de VV w (r) ★★ The best-known ALVARINHO fom Portugal, facing increasingly stiff competition from neighbouring VINHO VERDE estates around Monção.

A general rule for Portugal: choose youngest vintages of whites available.

Bright Brothers ★★→★★★ DYA Australian flying winemaker based in Portugal: interests as far-flung as Argentina, Sicily, and Spain. Range of well-made wines from DOURO, RIBATEJO, ESTREMADURA, and BEIRAS. See also Fiuza Bright.

Buçaco Beiras r w (p) res ★★★★ (r) **53 59 62 63 70 78 82 85 89 92** (w) **91 92 93** Recent vintages disappointing. Legendary speciality of the Palace Hotel at Buçaco near Coimbra, not seen elsewhere. An experience worth the journey. So are palace and park.

Bucelas Est w ★★★ Tiny demarcated region North of Lisbon in the hands of 3 producers. QUINTA da Romeira makes attractive wines from the ARINTO grape.

Cadaval, Casa Rib r w ★★ **97 98 99** Good varietal reds especially TRINCADEIRA. Also Pinot Noir and Cabernet Sauvignon.

Camarate, Quinta de Est r ★★★ **97 98 99** Notable red from JOSÉ MARIA DA FONSECA, S of Lisbon, incl detectable proportion of Cab S.

Carcavelos Est br sw ★★★ Normally NV. Minute DOC W of Lisbon. Rare, sweet, apéritif or dessert wines average 19% alcohol and resemble honeyed MADEIRA. The only producer is now Pesos, Caparide.

Carmo, Quinta do Alen r w res ★★★ **87' 93 94 96 97** 98 Beautiful small ALENTEJO ADEGA, partly bought 92 by Rothschilds (Lafite). 125 acres, plus cork forests. Fresh white, red better. 2nd wine: Dom Martinho.

Carneiro, Quinta do Alenquer r ★★ **98 99 00** w DYA New-wave estate; gd, mid-weight reds (PERIQUITA, Trincadeira Preta, TINTA RORIZ, and TOURIGA NACIONAL).

Cartaxo Ribatejo r w ★ District in RIBATEJO N of Lisbon, now a DOC area making everyday wines popular in the capital.

Cartuxa, Herdade de Alen ★★→★★★ r **90 94 96 97** w DYA Vast estate near Evora (500 acres). Big reds especially Pera Manca (**91 94 95**), one of ALENTEJO's best (and most pricey); creamy whites. Also Monte de Pinheiros, Fundacão Eugenio de Almeida.

Carvalhais, Quinta dos Dão ★★★ r **97 98 99** w DYA Excellent single-estate SOGRAPE wine. Gd r varietals (TOURIGA NACIONAL, Alfronchiero Preto) and w Encruzado.

Casal Branco, Quinta de Ribatejo r w ★★ Large family estate making good red and white wines. Best red: Falocoaria (**97 98**).

Casal García VV w ★★ DYA Big-selling VINHO VERDE, made at AVELEDA.

Casal Mendes VV w ★ DYA The VINHO VERDE from CAVES ALIANÇA.

Castelão The official name for PERIQUITA a grape planted throughout southern Portugal, but particularly in TERRAS DO SADO. Makes firm-flavoured, raspberryish reds which take on a tar-like quality with age. Also known as João de Santarem.

Chryseia Douro r ★★★ **00** Bruno Prats from Bordeaux has come together with the Symington family to produce a dense yet elegant wine from vintage-port grapes. A star in the making.

Colares r ★★ Small DOC on the sandy coast W of Lisbon. Its antique-style, dark-red wines, rigid with tannin, are from ungrafted vines. They need ageing, but TOTB (the older the better) no longer. See Paulo da Silva.

Consumo (vinho) Ordinary wine.

Cortes de Cima r ★★★ **98 99** 00 Estate nr Vidigueira (ALENTEJO) owned by Danish family. Gd reds from ARAGONEZ, TRINCADEIRA, PERIQUITA grapes. Chamine: 2nd label. Also Syrah bottled under Incognito label.

Côtto, Quinta do Douro r w res ★★★ r **97 98 99** w DYA Pioneer table wines from port country; vg red Grande Escolha (**87 90 94 95**) and also do Côtto are dense fruity, tannic, wines for long keeping. Also

Crasto, Quinta do Douro r dr sw ★★★ **98 99** 00 01 Top estate nr Pinhão for port and excellent oak-aged reds. Excellent varietal wines (TOURIGA NACIONAL, TINTA RORIZ) and Reserva (**98**). Look out for Vinha do Ponte (**98**) and María Theresa (**98**) made from individual plots of old vines.

Dão r w res ★★→★★★ 96 97 98 **99 00** 01 DOC region round town of Viseu. Too many dull, earthy wines produced in the past but region is improving rapidly with single QUINTAS making headway: solid reds of some subtlety with age; substantial, dry whites. Most sold under brand names. But see Roques, Maias, Saes, Fonte do Ouro, Terras Altas, Porta dos Cavalheiros, Grão Vasco, Duque de Viseu, etc.

DFJ Vinhos r w ★→★★★ DYA Successful partnership making well-priced wines, mainly in RIBATEJO and ESTRAMADURA. Look out for these labels: Ramada (r, w), Segada (r, w), Manta Preta (r), and Grand'Arte (r, w).

DOC (Denominacão de Origem Controlada) Official wine region. There are now 27 in total, a number of mergers having taken place in recent years. See also IPR, Vinho Regional.

Doce (vinho) Sweet (wine).

Douro r w ★★→★★★★ 91 95 96 97 98 99 00 01 N river valley producing port and some of Portugal's most exciting new table wines. Look for BARCA VELHA, QUINTA DO CÔTTO, REDOMA, & Symington's new wines (see ALTANO). Watch this space.

Duas Quintas Douro ★★★ r 97 98 99 00 w DYA Rich red from port shipper RAMOS PINTO. Very good Reserva (**91 92** 94 95 97).

Duque de Viseu Dão ★★★ r 98 99 00 w DYA High quality r DAO from SOGRAPE.

Entre Serras r w ★ DYA BEIRAS. Sound barrel-fermented Chard; soft light reds.

Esporão, Herdade do Alen w DYA r ★★→★★★ 98 99 00 Impressive estate owned by Finagra. Wines made (since 92) by Australian David Baverstock: rich, ripe, gently oaked w; fruity, young r Alandra; superior r Esporão: one of ALENTEJO's best. Also Monte Velho gently oaked r, fruity w. Gd varietals: ARAGONEZ, TRINCADEIRA, Cab S.

Espumante Sparkling.

Esteva Douro r ★ DYA V drinkable DOURO red from port firm FERREIRA.

Estremadura ★ VINHO REGIONAL on Portugal's W coast, s'times called "Oeste". Large co-ops. Alta Mesa, Ramada, Portada: gd, inexpensive wines from local estates and co-ops. IPRS: Encostas d'Aire. DOCS: ALENQUER, ARRUDA, Obidos, TORRES VEDRAS.

Evel Douro r ★★→★★★ 99 00 Much-improved Douro wines from REAL VINICOLA. Worth looking out for the red Grande Escolha.

Fernão Pires White grape making ripe-flavoured, slightly spicy whites in RIBATEJO. (Known as María Gomes in BAIRRADA.)

Ferreirinha, Reserva Douro r ★★★ 89 90 92 Second wine to BARCA VELHA, made in less-than-ideal vintages.

Fojo, Vinha da ★★★ r 96 98 99 Prime DOURO QUINTA; foot-trodden, dense reds.

Fonseca, José María da Est r w dr sw sp res ★★→★★★ Venerable firm in Azeitão nr Lisbon. One of biggest and best ranges in Portugal, incl dry white d'Avillez, Pasmados, and QUINTA DE CAMARATE; red d'Avillez, PERIQUITA, Pasmados, Primum, TERRAS ALTAS, DAO, several GARRAFEIRAS; and famous dessert SETÚBAL. Fonseca also owns JOSÉ DE SOUSA. LANCERS rosé is less distinguished, but Lancers Brut is a drinkable sp wine made by a continuous process of Russian invention.

Fonte do Ouro Dão ★★ r 98 99 00 w DYA Good, balanced red from well-run single estate. Also single QUINTA TOURIGA NATIONAL (**97 98**) under Boas Quintas label. Second wine: Quinta da Giesta.

Foz do Arouce, Quinta da Beiras r ★★ 96 97 98 99 w DYA Big, cask-aged red from heart of BEIRAS.

Franqueira, Quinta da VV w ★★ DYA Typically dry, fragrant VINHO VERDE made by Englishman Piers Gallie.

Fuiza Bright Ribatejo r w ★★ DYA Joint venture with Peter Bright (BRIGHT BROS). Good Chardonnay, Sauvignon Blanc, Merlot, and Cabernet Sauvignon.

Gaivosa, Quinta de Douro r ★ 95 96 97 98 99 Important estate near Regua. Deep, concentrated, cask-aged reds from port grapes. 2nd wine: QUINTA do Vale da Raposa (DYA) is lighter, fruity red. 3rd wine: Quinta da Estação (DYA).

Garrafeira Label term: merchant's "private reserve", aged for minimum of 2 yrs in cask and one in bottle, often much longer. Usually their best, though traditionally often of indeterminate origin. Now has to show origin on label.

Gatão VV w ★ DYA Standard BORGES & IRMÃO VINHO V; fragrant but sweetened.

Gazela VV w ★★ DYA Reliable VINHO VERDE made at Barcelos by SOGRAPE.

Generoso Apéritif or dessert wine rich in alcohol.

Grão Vasco Dão r w ★★ DYA One of the best and largest brands of DÃO, from a new high-tech ADEGA at Viseu. Fine red GARRAFEIRA; fresh, young white. Owned by SOGRAPE.

Portuguese wines to look out for in 2003

Nieport's Redoma and Batuta range
Alentejo reds especially made fom Trincadeira
Single quintas from the Dão: Quinta dos Roques & Quinta de Saes
Quinta do Crasto's Vinha do Ponte and Maria Theresa from old vines
Symington's new Douro red: Chryseia
Varietals Touriga Nac., Tinta Roriz/Aragonez, Tinto Cão, Trincadeira

---

IPR Indicação de Proveniência Regulamentada. See below.

José de Sousa Alen r res ★★→★★★ 98 99 00 Small firm acquired by J M DA FONSECA. The most sophisticated of the full-bodied wines from ALENTEJO (solid, foot-trodden GARRAFEIRAS (**93 94 97 98**), although now slightly lighter in style), fermented in earthenware amphoras and aged in oak.

J P Vinhos Set r w sp res ★→★★★ An enterprising and well-equipped winery making wide range of wines including João Pires Dry Muscat and reds: Meia Pipa, TINTO DA ANFORA, and QUINTA DA BACALHOA. Cova da Ursa is a barrel-fermented Chardonnay.

Lancers Est p w sp ★ Sweet, carbonated rosé and sparkling white extensively shipped to the US by J M DA FONSECA.

Lagoalva, Quinta da r w ★★ 97 98 99 00 Important RIBATEJO property making good reds from local grapes and Syrah. Second label: Monte da Casta. Also good Chardonnay.

Loureiro Best VINHO VERDE grape variety after ALVARINHO: crisp, fragrant whites.

Madeira br dr sw ★★→★★★★ Portugal's Atlantic island making famous fortified dessert and apéritif wines. See pages 176-183.

Maduro (vinho) A mature table wine – as opposed to a VINHO VERDE.

Maias, Quinta das Dão ★★ r 99 00 w DYA New-wave QUINTA: reds to age.

Mateus Rosé Bair p (w) ★ World's biggest-selling, medium-dry, carbonated rosé, from SOGRAPE. Now made at Anadia in BAIRRADA.

Messias r w ★→★★ Large BAIRRADA-based firm; interests in DOURO (incl port). Old-school reds best.

Minho River between Northern Portugal and Spain which lends its name to a VINHO REGIONAL.

Monção N subregion of VINHO VERDE on River Minho: best wines from the ALVARINHO grape. See Palácio de Brejoeira.

Morgadio de Torre VV w ★★ DYA Top VV from SOGRAPE. Largely ALVARINHO.

Mouchão, Herdade de Alen r res ★★★ 82 89 90 91 92 94 95 Perhaps top ALENTEJO estate, ruined in 1974 revolution; since replanted and fully recovered. Good, powerful second wine under the Dom Rafael label.

Mouro, Quinta do Alen r ★★★★ 98 99 Fabulous old-style red. From nr Estremoz.

Palmela Terras do Sado r w Sandy soil IPR. Reds can be long-lived. Now a promising DOC incorporating the limestone hills of the Serra d'Arrabida and the sandy plains around the eponymous town. Reds from PERIQUITA can be long-lived. See Pegos Claros.

Pancas, Quinta das Est r w res ★★ **97** 98 99 00 w DYA Go-ahead estate nr ALENQUER. Dense Cab, balanced, oaked Chard. Outstanding TOURIGA NACIONAL Reserva (**95**) and vg dry white ARINTO: QUINTA de Dom Carlos.

Pato, Luís Bair r sp ★★→★★★ 95 96 97 99 Top estate of BAIRRADA. Tannic reds incl tremendous QUINTA DE RIBEIRINHO and João Pato. 95 reds notable esp Quinta do Ribeirinho Pé Franco. Although still technically within the Bairrada DOC, Pato has declassified all his wines to VINHO REGIONAL BEIRAS after disagreeing with the authorities. Also classic-method sparkling.

Pegos Claros r 95 96 98 99 Solid, traditionally made red from PALMELA area. Proof at last that PERIQUITA can make substantial wine.

Periquita The nickname for the CASTELÃO grape. Periquita is also a brand name for a successful red wine from JOSÉ MARIA DE FONSECA (DYA). Robust, old-style red bottled under Periquita Classico label (94 95).

Pires, João w DYA Fragrant, off-dry, Muscat-based wine from J P VINHOS.

Planalto Douro w ★★ DYA Good white wine from SOGRAPE.

Ponte de Lima, Cooperativa de VV r w ★★ Maker of one of the best bone-dry red VINHOS VERDES, and first-rate dry and fruity white.

Porta dos Cavalheiros Dão ★★→★★★ 97 98 Traditional style red and white DÃO from CAVES SÃO JOÃO. The Reservas (with a cork label) can be exceptional (**85** 95 96).

Portalegre Alen r w ★→★★★ DOC on Spanish border. Strong, fragrant reds with potential to age. Alcoholic whites. Best red wine JOSÉ MARIA DA FONSECA's full flavoured d'Avillez. Promising wines from local co-op.

Quinta Estate.

Ramada See Estremadura.

Ramos, João Portugal Alen r w DYA Vila Santa (**99** 00) and Marqués de Borba. Reservas of the latter fetch a high price.

Raposeira Douro w sp ★★ Well-known fizz made by the classic method at Lamego. Ask for the Bruto.

Real Companhia Vinícola ★★→★★★ Giant of the port trade (see page 181); also produces increasingly good range of DOURO wines: EVEL, QUINTA dos Aciprestes, Quinta de Cidro.

Redoma ★★★ r 98 99 00 w DYA Particularly good DOURO red and white from Port shipper NIEPOORT. Red will age well. Also delicious rosé.

Redondo Alen r w ★ DOC in heart of ALENTEJO with well-managed co-op. Roque Vale: leading estate.

Reguengos Alen r (w) res ★→★★★ Important DOC nr Spanish border. Incl JOSÉ DE SOUSA and ESPORÃO estates, plus large co-op for good reds.

Ribatejo r w The second-largest wine-producing region in Portugal now promoted to DOC with a number of sub-regions entitled to village appellations: ALMEIRIM, CARTAXO, CORUCHE, Chamusca, Tomar, Santarem. Midweight reds include a number made from international grapes: Cabernet Sauvignon, Merlot, Pinot Noir, Chardonnay, and Sauvignon Blanc.

Ribeirinho, Quinta do See Luis Pato.

Roques, Quinta dos Dão r ★ 96 97 98 99 00 w DYA Promising estate for big, solid, oaked reds. Good varietal wines from TOURIGA NATIONAL, TINTA RORIZ, Tinta Cão, and Alfrocherio Preto.

Rosa, Quinta de la Douro r ★★ 97 98 99 00 Firm, oak-aged red from port v'yds. Reserva is especially worthwhile. Amarela: lighter 2nd wine.

Rosado Rosé.

Saes, Quinta de Dão r w ★★★ 97 98 99 00 Sml mountain v'yard making refined wines. QUINTA de Pellada also making gd wines under same ownership.

Saima, Casa de Bair r (w DYA) ★★★ 97 98 99 Small trad estate; big, longlasting, tannic reds (esp GARRAFEIRAS 91 95' 97') & some astounding whites.

Santar, Casa de Dão r ★★★ **98 99 00** Well-established estate now making welcome comeback. Reds much better than old-fashioned whites.

São Domingos, Comp dos Vinhos de Est r w ★ DYA Reds (Espiga, Palha-Canas), from estate managed by José Neiva.

São João, Caves Bair ★★★ r **97 98** Res **95** w DYA Sm, traditional firm making top-class wines the old-fashioned way. Reds can age for decades. BAIRRADA: Frei João; DAO: PORTA DOS CAVALEIROS. Poço do Lobo: well-structured Cab S.

Seco Dry.

Serradayres ★ DYA Everyday red and enjoying something of a comeback having been taken over by CAVES DOM TEODOSIO.

Setúbal Set br (r w) sw (dr) ★★★ Tiny demarcated region South of the River Tagus, where FONSECA makes aromatic, Muscat-based, sweet wine, usually sold at 6 and 20 years old.

Sezim, Casa de VV w ★★ DYA Beautiful estate making very good VINHO VERDES.

Silva, Antonio Bernardino Paulo da Colares r (w) res ★★ **89 90 92** His COLARES Chitas is one of the very few of these classics still made.

Sogrape ★→★★★★ Part-owned by Bacardi. Largest wine concern in the country, making VINHOS VERDES, DAO, BAIRRADA, ALENTEJO, MATEUS ROSE, and now owners of FERREIRA and OFFLEY port.

Tamariz, Quinta do VV w ★ Fragrant VINHO VERDE from LOUREIRO grapes only.

Teodosio, Caves Dom r w Lge producer in the RIBATEJO now making a welcome comeback. Everyday wines under the SERRADAYRES label but delicious red from QUINTA de Almargem made from TRINCADEIRA grape.

Terras Altas Dão r w res ★ DYA Brand of red and white DÃO from JOSÉ MARIA DA FONSECA.

Terras do Sado VINHO REGIONAL covering sandy plains around Sado Estuary.

Tinta Roriz A major port grape (a variant of Tempranillo) making good DOURO table wines. It is increasingly planted for similarly full reds. AKA ARAGONEZ in ALENTEJO.

Tinto Red.

Tinto da Anfora Alen r ★★ **97 98 99 00** New heavyweight red: Tinto da Anfora Grande Escohla. Lighter wines: Montes das Anforas.

Torres Vedras ★ Est r w DOC N of Lisbon famous for Wellington's "lines". Major supplier of bulk wine; one of biggest co-ops in Portugal.

Touriga Nacional Top red grape used for port and DOURO table wines; now increasingly elsewhere, esp DÃO, ALENTEJO, ESTREMADURA.

Trás-os-Montes VINHO REGIONAL covering mountains of NE Portugal. Reds and whites from international grape varieties grown in the DOURO. Also IPRS: Chaves, Mirandes, Valpacos.

Trincadeira Vg red grape in ALENTEJO for spicy, single-varietal wines.

Tuella r w ★★ DYA Good-value DOURO red from COCKBURN.

Vallado ★★ r **97 98 99 00** w DYA Family-owned DOURO estate; vg wines.

Velhas, Caves Bucelas r w res ★ Reds are rather rustic!

Verde Green (see VINHOS VERDES).

Vidigueira Alen w r ★ DOC for traditionally-made unmatured whites from volcanic soils and some plummy reds.

Vinho Regional Larger provincial wine region, with same status as French *vin de pays*: they are: ALGARVE, ALENTEJO, BEIRAS, ESTREMADURA, RIBATEJANO, MINHO, TRÁS-OS-MONTES, TERRAS DO SADO. See also DOC, IPR.

Vinhos Verdes VV w ★→★★★ r ★ DOC between R DOURO and N frontier, for "green wines" (white or red): made from grapes with high acidity and (originally) undergoing a secondary fermentation to leave them slightly sparkling. Today the fizz is usually just added CO_2. Ready for drinking in spring after harvest.

Sherry, Port, & Madeira

Sherry, port, and Madeira are the three classic fortified wines of Spain and Portugal – and the world.

Sherry is the most famous of Spanish wines, and since 1996 its name has been legally recognized as belonging to Spain alone. Like other fortified wines, sherry has suffered a decline in popularity over recent years, but remains an excellent preliminary to a meal and of all thoroughbred wines is perhaps the best value. The continuous blending of wines in a *solera* means that there are no sherry vintages.

The port trade underwent a major restructuring in 2001 leaving three major players (Symingtons, Taylor's, and Sogrape) with ownership of most of the big names. They are reinforced with alcohol up to 15 per cent (for a light sherry) and 22 (for vintage port). Shippers (that is producers, blenders, bottlers) are still far more important than growers in these industries. This section lists types of wines and shippers' names with the names and vintages of their best wines.

The millennium saw the third small vintage in a row for port. Both 1998 and 1999 produced some good single-quinta wines and 2000 is likely to be declared a Vintage across the board.

In Madeira the relatively new *Colheita* or "harvest" wines are now starting to emerge onto the market. Bottled after 6 years in wood (as opposed to the minimum 20 years for "vintage" Madeira) and from a single year, they are intended to be more accessible. Sadly, people used to drinking vintage Madeira will find them pretty simple stuff.

Recent Declared Port Vintages

1997 Fine, potentially long-lasting wines with tannic backbone. Most shippers declared. Drink 2012 onwards.

1994 Outstanding vintage with ripe, fleshy fruit disguising underlying structure at the outset. Universal declaration. Drink 2010-2030.

1987 Dense wines for drinking over the medium-term but only a handful of shippers declared. Drink now – 2015.

1985 Universal declaration which looked good at the outset but has thrown up some disappointments in bottle. Now-2020 for the best wines.

1983 Fine, powerful wines with sinewy tannins. Most shippers declared. Now-2020+ (the best wines need keeping).

1982 Soft, rather simple, early maturing wines declared by a few shippers in preference to 1983. Drink soon.

1980 Lovely fruit-driven wines, perfect to drink now and over the next 15 years. Most shippers declared.

1977 Big, ripe wines declared by all the major shippers except Cockburn, Martinez, and Noval. Drinking now, the best still have a long life ahead.

1975 Soft and early maturing. Drink up.

1970 Classic, tight-knit wines – only just reaching their peak. Now-2020+.

1966 Wines combine power & elegance with the best rivalling 1963. Now-2020+.

1963 Classic vintage, one of the best of the 20th century (with prices to match). Some bottle variation but the wines will last a lifetime.

Abad, Tomás Small sherry BODEGA owned by LUSTAU. Vg light FINO.

Almacenista Individual matured but unblended sherry; usually dark, dry wines for connoisseurs. Often superb quality and value. See LUSTAU.

Alvear Mont-M g Lgst prod of vg sherry-like apéritif & sw wines in MONTILLA.

Barbadillo, Antonio Much the largest SANLÚCAR firm with a wide range of MANZANILLAS and sherries mostly excellent of their type, including Sanlúcar FINO, superb SOLERA manzanilla PASADA, Fino de Balbaina, austere Príncipe dry AMONTILLADO. Beautiful unmanipulated Saca de Invietro Manzanilla. Also young Castillo de San Diego table wines.

Barbeito One of the last independent Madeira shipping firms, now Japanese-controlled. Wines incl rare vintages, eg MALMSEY 1901 and the latest, BUAL 1960.

Barros Almeida Large, family-owned port house with several brands (incl Feist, Feuerheerd, KOPKE): excellent 20-yr-old TAWNY and many COLHEITAS.

Barros e Sousa Tiny, family-owned Madeira producer with old lodges in centre of Funchal. Extremely fine but now rare vintages, plus gd 10-yr-old wines.

Blandy The top name of the MADEIRA WINE CO. Duke of Clarence Rich Madeira is the most famous wine. 10-yr-old reserves (VERDELHO, BUAL, MALMSEY, SERCIAL) are gd. Many glorious old vintages (eg Malmsey 54, Bual 20, Sercial 40), though mostly nowadays at auctions. New COLHEITAS from 94.

Blázquez DOMECQ-owned BODEGA at PUERTO DE S MARIA. Outstanding FINO, Carta Blanca, v old SOLERA OLOROSO Extra; Carta Oro AMONTILLADO *al natural* (unsweetened).

Bobadilla Large JEREZ BODEGA recently bought by OSBORNE and best known for v dry Victoria FINO and Bobadilla 103 brandy, esp among Spanish connoisseurs.

Borges, H M Independent Madeira shipper of old repute.

Bual One of the best grapes of Madeira, making a soft, smoky, sweet wine, usually lighter and not as rich as MALMSEY. (See panel on page 183.)

Burmester Family port house now owned by cork giant Amorim, with fine, soft, sweet 20-yr-old TAWNY; also vg range of COLHEITAS and single-QUINTA: Quinta Nossa Sra do Carmo. Vintages: **70 77 80 85 89** 91 92 94 95 97.

Burdon English-founded sherry BODEGA owned by CABALLERO. Puerto FINO, Don Luis AMONTILLADO, and raisiny Heavenly Cream are top lines.

Caballero Important sherry shipper at PUERTO DE STA MARIA. Pavón FINO, Mayoral Cream OLOROSO, excellent BURDON sherries, PONCHE orange liqueur. Also owns LUSTAU.

Cálem Old Port house; had fine reputation, but recent vintages not as gd. Vtges: **63 66 70 75 77 80 83 85** 91 94 97. Reliable light TAWNY; gd range of COLHEITAS: Sold in 98, but family still owns Quinta da Foz (**84 86 87 88 89 90** 92 95).

Churchill 82 85 91 94 97 Founded as recently as 1981 and already highly respected. Bought their own QUINTA in 99. Vg traditional LBV. Quinta da

---

Sherry Styles

Fino The lightest, finest sherries. Completely dry, v pale, delicate but pungent. Fino should be drunk cool and fresh. Deteriorates rapidly once opened (use ½ bottles if poss). Eg TIO PEPE.

Manzanilla A pale dry wine (not strictly a sherry), often more delicate than a FINO, matured in the cooler maritime conditions of SANLUCAR DE BARRAMEDA (as opposed to JEREZ, which is inland). Eg La Gitana.

Amontillado A FINO aged in cask to become darker, more powerful, and pungent. Naturally dry wines. Eg LUSTAU'S ALMANCENISTAS.

Oloroso Heavier, less brilliant than FINO when young, but matures to greater richness and pungency. Naturally dry, often sweetened for sale. Eg Rio Viejo.

Palo Cortado A rare style close to OLOROSO with some AMONTILLADO character. Dry but rich and soft – worth looking for. Eg DOMECQ'S Sibarita.

Cream Sherry Sweet style from well-aged OLOROSO. Eg Bristol Cream.

Other styles Manzanilla Pasada – half way between a FINO and AMONTILLADO; Pale Cream – sweetened FINO; Amoroso, Brown Sherry, East India Sherry – variations on CREAM SHERRY.

> Top-quality sherry is now the best-value wine in the world. Supreme old dry
> wines cost less than another Chardonnay. With prawns or smoked salmon,
> with soup or a winter picnic, they have few rivals.

Agua Alta and Quinta da Gricha are Churchill's single-QUINTA ports: **83 87**
90 92 95 98.

Cockburn British-owned (Allied-DOMECQ) port shipper with a range of gd wines
incl v popular, fruity Special Res. Fine VINTAGE PORT from v'yds predominantly
in the Douro Superior: sometimes deceptively forward when young but with
great lasting power. Vintages: **63 67 70 75 83 85** 91 94 97.

Colheita Vintage-dated port of a single yr, but aged at least 7 winters in wood:
in effect a vintage TAWNY. The bottling date is also shown on label. Excellent
examples from KOPKE, CALEM, NIEPOORT, Krohn, & C DA SILVA (Dalva). Colheita
now applies to a new category of Madeiras from a single year (see
introductory paragraphs).

Cossart Gordon One-time leading Madeira shipper, founded 1745, with BLANDY
now one of the two top-quality labels of the MADEIRA WINE CO. Wines slightly
less rich than Blandy's. Best-known for Good Company Finest Medium Rich.
Also 5-yr-old reserves, old vintages (latest 74) and SOLERAS (esp BUAL 1845).

Crasto, Quinta do Ports improving in quality, esp LBV. Vtges: **85 87** 91 94 95 97.

Croft One of the oldest firms shipping VINTAGE PORT: since 1678; now owned by
TAYLOR'S. Well-balanced vintage wines tend to mature early (since 66).
Vintages: **63' 66 67 70 75 77 82 85** 91 94; and lighter Quinta da Roeda
vintages in several other years (**78 80 83 87** 95 97). "Distinction": most
popular blend. Morgan: sml separate co (also DELAFORCE). Also produces sherry.

Croft Jerez Founded only in 1970 and recently bought by GONZÁLEZ-BYASS. One of
the most successful sherry firms. Best-known for the sw Croft Original Pale Cream
& drier Croft Particular. Also dry and elegant Delicado FINO and first-rate and
moderately priced PALO CORTADO.

Crusted Term for vintage-style port, usually blended from several vintages
not one. Bottled young, then aged so it forms a "crust". Needs decanting.

Cruz Market leader in France. (French take 40% of port exports.) Standard French-
style TAWNY – not brilliant quality. Owned by La Martiniquaise.

Delaforce Port shipper owned by TAYLOR'S, is best-known in Germany. His
Eminence's Choice is a v pleasant 10-yr-old TAWNY; VINTAGE CHARACTER is also
good. Vintage wines are very fine, among the lighter kind: **55 58 60 63 66
70' 75 77 82 85** 94; Quinta da Côrte in **78 80 84 87** 91 95 97.

Delgado, Zuleta Old-est'd SANLUCAR firm best-known for marvellous La Goya
MANZANILLA PASADA.

Domecq Giant family-run sherry BODEGA at JEREZ, recently merged with Allied-
Domecq, famous also for Fundador and other brandies. Double Century
Original OLOROSO, its biggest brand, recently replaced by Pedro Cream Sherry; La
Ina is excellent FINO. Other famous wines incl Celebration Cream, Botaina (old
AMONTILLADO) and magnificent Rio Viejo (v dry oloroso) and Capuchino (PALO
CORTADO). Recently: a range of wonderful old SOLERA sherries (dry Sibarita,
Amontillado 51-1a, and sw venerable olorosos). Also in RIOJA and Mexico.

Don Zoilo Luxury sherries, including velvety FINO, sold by BODEGAS
INTERNACIONALES to the MEDINA group.

Douro The port country river, known in Spain as the Duero. All the best port
comes from the spectacular Upper Douro.

Dow Brand name of Silva and Cozens, celebrated their bicentenary in 98, now
belonging to the Symington family alongside GRAHAM, WARRE, SMITH WOODHOUSE,
GOULD CAMPBELL, QUARLES HARRIS, and QUINTA DO VESUVIO. Style deliberately slightly
drier than other shippers in group. Vg range of ports incl single-QUINTA Bomfim

(78 79 82 84 86 87 88 89 90 92 95 98) and outstanding vintages: 63 66 70 72 75 77 80 83 85 91 94 97. New v'yd: Quinta da Senhora da Ribeira 98 99.

Duff Gordon Sherry shipper best-known for El Cid AMONTILLADO. Gd FINO Feria; Niña Medium OLOROSO. OSBORNE-owned; name also used as 2nd label for their ports.

Eira Velha, Quinta da Small port estate with old-style vintage wines shipped by MARTINEZ. Vintages: 78 82 87 92 94 95.

Ferreira One of the biggest Portuguese-owned port growers and shippers (since 1751). Largest-selling brand in P. Well-known for old TAWNIES and juicily sweet, relatively light vintages: 63 66 70 75 77 78 80 82 85 87 91 94 95 97. Also Doña Antónia Personal Reserve, splendidly rich tawny Duque de Bragança and single-QUINTA wines Quinta do Seixo and Q da Leda.

Flor A floating yeast peculiar to FINO sherry and certain other wines that oxidize slowly and tastily under its influence.

Fonseca Guimaraens British-owned port shipper with a stellar reputation; connected with TAYLOR'S. Robust, deeply coloured vintage wine, among the v best. Vintages: Fonseca 63' 66' 70 75 77 80 83 85 92 94' 97; Fonseca Guimaraens 76' 78 82 84 86 87 88 91 94 95 98. Quinta do Panascal 78 98 is a single-QUINTA wine. Also delicious VINTAGE CHARACTER Bin 27.

Forrester Port shipper and owner of the famous QUINTA da Boa Vista, now owned by SOGRAPE. The vintage wines tend to be round, "fat", and sweet, good for relatively early drinking. Baron de Forrester is vg TAWNY. Vintages: (Offley Forrester) 63 66 67 70 72 75 77 80 82 83 85 87 89 94 95 97.

Garvey Famous old sherry shipper at JEREZ, now owned by José María Ruiz Mateos. The finest wines are deep-flavoured FINO San Patricio, Tio Guillermo Dry AMONTILLADO, and Ochavico Dry OLOROSO. San Angelo Medium amontillado is the most popular. Also Bicentenary PALE CREAM.

González-Byass Enormous family-run firm shipping the world's most famous and one of v best FINO sherries: TIO PEPE. Brands incl La Concha medium AMONTILLADO, Elegante dry fino, new El Rocío MANZANILLA Fina, San Domingo Pale Cream, Nectar Cream, Alfonso sweet OLOROSO. Amontillado del Duque is on a higher plane, as are Matúsalem OLOROSO & Apóstoles PALO CORTADO. Magnificent Millennium made from the choicest old olorosos. Also makers of top-selling Soberano & exquisite Lepanto brandies.

Gould Campbell Port shipper belonging to the Symington family. Good-value vintage ports 70 77 80 83 85 91 94 97.

Graham 63' 70 Port shipper famous for some of the richest, sweetest, and best of vintage ports, largely from its own Quinta dos Malvedos (76 78 79 80 82 84 86 87 88 90 92 95 98). Also excellent brands, incl Six Grapes RUBY, LBV, and 10- and 20-yr-old TAWNIES. Vintages: 63 66 70 75 77 80 83 85 91 94 97.

Gracia Hermanos Mont-M Firm within the same group as PEREZ BARQUERO and Compañia Vinícola del Sur making gd-quality MONTILLAS. Its labels incl María del Valle FINO, Montearruit AMONTILLADO, OLOROSO CREAM, and Dulce Viejo PX.

Guita, La Famous old SANLÚCAR BODEGA noted for particularly fine MANZANILLA PASADA.

Hartley & Gibson See Valdespino.

Harvey's Important pillar of the Allied-DOMECQ empire, along with TERRY. World-famous Bristol shippers of Bristol Cream and Bristol Milk (sweet), Club AMONTILLADO and Bristol Dry (medium), Luncheon Dry and Bristol FINO (not v dry). More to the point is its v gd "1796" range of high-quality sherries comprising Fine Old Amontillado, PALO CORTADO and Rich Old OLOROSO.

Henriques & Henriques Independent Madeira shipper, with wide range of well-structured, rich wines – 10-yr-olds are medal-winners. Outstanding 15-yr-old wines. Good, extra-dry apéritif Monte Seco, and v fine old reserves & vtges: Bual 54, 57; Malmsey 54; Sercial 44. The joke goes: "There are only 2 names in Madeira ..."

Henriques, Justino The largest Madeira shippers in bulk terms with a modern lodge outside Funchal. Good 10-yr-old and Vintage, eg. 1934 Verdelho.

Hidalgo, Vinícola Old, family firm in SANLUCAR DE BARRAMEDA Excellent pale MANZANILLA La Gitana, fine OLOROSO Seco, lovely soft, deep Jerez Cortado & 1st-rate new Pastrana MANZANILLA PASADA.

Internacionales, Bodegas Once the pride of the now-defunct Rumasa and with such famous houses as BERTOLA, VARELA, and DIEZ-MERITO, the company was taken over by the entrepreneur Marcos Eguizabal and sold on to José Médina.

Jerez de la Frontera Centre of sherry industry, between Cádiz & Seville. "Sherry" is a corruption of the name, pronounced in Spanish "hereth". In French, Xérès.

Kopke The oldest port house, founded by a German in 1638. Now belongs to BARROS ALMEIDA. Fair-quality VINTAGE wines, but some excellent (**70 74 75 77 78 79 80 82 83 85 87 89** 91 94 97) and excellent COLHEITAS.

Krohn. Small family-owned shipper with an excellent range of COLHEITAS, some dating back to the nineteenth century.

Late-bottled vintage (LBV) Port from a single vintage kept in wood for twice as long as VINTAGE PORT (about 5 years), therefore lighter when bottled and ages more quickly. Don't expect miracles "Traditional" (unfiltered) LBV now has to spend an extra 3 yrs in bottle to qualify (WARRE, SMITH WOODHOUSE, NIEPOORT, CHURCHILL, FERREIRA, NOVAL).

Leacock One of the oldest Madeira shippers, now a label of the MADEIRA WINE COMPANY. Basic St-John range is very fair; 10-year-old Special Reserve MALMSEY and 15-year-old BUAL are excellent. Older vintages also available: Bual 34, Verdelho 54.

Lustau One of the largest family-run sherry BODEGAS in JEREZ (now controlled by CABALLERO), making many wines for other shippers, but with a vg Dry Lustau range (esp FINO and OLOROSO) and Jerez Lustau PALO CORTADO. Pioneer shipper of excellent ALMACENISTA and "landed age" wines; AMONTILLADOS and olorosos aged in elegant bottles before shipping. See also Abad.

Macharnudo One of the best parts of the sherry v'yds, N of JEREZ, famous for wines of the highest quality, both FINO and OLOROSO.

Madeira Wine Company Formed in 1913 by two firms as the Madeira Wine Association, subsequently to include all the British Madeira firms (26 in total) amalgamated to survive hard times. Remarkably, three generations later, the wines, though cellared together, preserve their house styles. BLANDY and COSSART GORDON are top labels. Now controlled by the Symington group (see Dow).

Malmsey The sweetest and richest form of Madeira; dark amber, rich, and honeyed yet with Madeira's unique sharp tang. Word is English corruption of "Malvasia" (or the Greek "Monemvasia") qv. See panel on page 183.

Martinez Gassiot Port firm, subsidiary of COCKBURN, known esp for excellent rich, and pungent Directors 20-yr-old TAWNY, CRUSTED, and LBV. Vintages: **63 67 70 75 82 85 87** 91 94 97.

Marqués del Real Tesoro Old firm with a spanking new BODEGA – the first in years. Recently acquired the historic firm of VALDESPINO. Tío Mateo is a very good FINO (now histamine-free!).

Miles Formerly Rutherford & Miles. Madeira shipper famed for Old Trinity House Medium Rich, etc. Latest vintage 73 VERDELHO. Now a MADEIRA WINE COMPANY label.

Medina, José Originally a SANLUCAR BODEGA, now a major exporter, especially to the Low Countries. Now owns BODEGAS INTERNACIONALES and WILLIAMS & HUMBERT, also Pérez Megia and Luis Paez: probably the biggest sherry grower and shipper, with some 25% of total volume.

Montecristo Mont-M Brand of big-selling MONTILLAS by Compañía Vinícola del Sur.

> **Port & Madeira to look out for in 2003**
> **White Port** Churchill
> **Good value Single Quinta Ports** Dow's Quinta do Bomfim 87, Taylor's
> Quinta de Vargellas 87, Martinez Quinta da Eira Velha 92
> **Outstanding Vintage Ports** Croft 63, Fonseca 63, Taylor 63, Dow 66, Fonseca
> 66, Graham 70, W Smith Woodhouse 77, Graham 80
> **Ten-and Fifteen-Year-Old Madeira** from Henriques & Henriques.
> **Vintage Madeiras** Leacock 78 Malvasia, Pereira d'Oliveira Verdelho66,
> Cossart Gordon Bual 58, Justino Henriques Verdelho 34, Justino
> Henriques Malmsey 33, Pereira d'Oliveira Bual 22.

Montilla-Moriles Mont-M DO nr Córdoba. Not sherry, but close. Its soft FINO and AMONTILLADO and luscious PX contain 14–17.5% natural alcohol and remain unfortified. At best, singularly toothsome apéritifs.

Niepoort Sml (Dutch) family-run port house with long record of fine VTGES (**63 66 70 75 77 78 80 82** 83 87 91 92 94 97) & exceptional COLHEITAS. Also produces excellent single-QUINTA port, Quinta do Passadouro (91 92 94 95 97 98).

Noval, Quinta do Historic port house now French (AXA) owned. Intensely fruity, structured, and elegant VINTAGE PORT; a few ungrafted vines at the QUINTA make small quantity of Nacional – extraordinarily dark, full, velvety, slow-maturing. Vg 20-yr-old TAWNY. Vtges: **63 66 67 70 75 78 82** 85 87 91 94 95 97. 2ⁿᵈ label: Silval (98). Also "traditional" (unfiltered) LBV.

Offley Forrester See Forrester.

Osborne Huge Spanish firm producing sherry and quality port, incl FINO QUINTA, Coquinero dr AMONTILLADO, 10 RF (or Res Familiar) med OLOROSO. DUFF GORDON used as 2nd label for Osborne Ports. Declared gd VINTAGE PORTS in 95, 97. NB: range of v fine "Rare" sherries, top-quality numbered bottles.

Paternina, Federico Marcos Eguizabel from RIOJA acquired the sherry firm Diez-Merito, retaining three wines to be marketed under his Paternina label. FINO Imperial, Olorose, Victoria Regina, and Pedro Ximénez Vieja Solera.

Pereira d'Oliveira Vinhos Family-owned Madeira Co est'd 1850. Very good basic range as well as 5-& 10-year-olds; fine old reserve VERDELHO 1890, BUAL 1908, Malvasia 1895.

Pérez Barquero Mont-M. Another firm like GRACIA HERMANOS once part of Rumasa. Its excellent MONTILLAS incl Gran Barquero FINO, AMONTILLADO, and OLOROSO.

Poças Junior Improving family port firm specializing in TAWNIES and COLHEITAS. Good LBV and Vintage (97).

Ponche An aromatic digestif made with old sherry and brandy, flavoured with herbs and presented in eye-catching silvered bottles. See CABALLERO, de SOTO.

Puerto de Santa María 2nd city & former port of sherry, with important BODEGAS.

PX Short for Pedro Ximénez, grape part sun-dried: used in JEREZ for sweetening.

Quarles Harris One of the oldest port houses, since 1680, now owned by the Symingtons (see Dow). Small quantities of LBV, mellow, and well-balanced. Vintages: **63 66 70 75 77 80 83** 85 91 94 97.

Quinta Portuguese for "estate". Also traditionally used to denote VINTAGE PORTS which are usually (legislation says 100%) from estate's vineyards, made in good but not exceptional vintages. Now several excellent QUINTAS produce wines from top vintages in their own right, especially VESUVIO, LA ROSA, Passadouro.

Rainwater A fairly light, medium-dry blend of Madeira – traditional in US.

Ramos-Pinto Dynamic, small port house specializing in single-QUINTA TAWNIES of style and elegance, vintages often on the light side; now owned by Champagne house Louis Roederer.

Real Companhia Vinícola do Norte de Portugal Aka Royal Oporto Wine Co & Real Companhia Velha; large port house, with long political history. Many brands and several QUINTAS, including Quinta dos Carvalhas for TAWNIES and COLHEITAS. VINTAGE PORTS have been dismal, but 97 looks more promising. Some aged tawnies are good.

Rebello Valente See Robertson.

Régua Main town in Douro Valley, centre for port producers and growers.

Robertson Brand owned by SANDEMAN. The name continues to be used for sales to the Netherlands. Rebello Valente: the brand name for vintage ports. These once had a good reputation (63 66 **67** 70) but are now light and early maturing.

Rosa, Quinta de la Fine single-QUINTA port from the Bergqvist family at PINHÃO. Recent return to traditional methods and stone *lagares*. Look for 85 88 90 91 92 94 95 96 97 98 vintages.

Royal Oporto See Real Companhia Vinícola do Norte de Portugal.

Rozès Port shipper owned by Champagne house Vranken. RUBY V popular in France; also TAWNY. Vintages: 63 **66** 67 77 83 85 87 91 94' 95 97.

Ruby Youngest (and cheapest) port style: simple, sweet, and red. The best are vigorous, full of flavour; others can be merely strong and rather thin.

Sanchez Romate Family firm in JEREZ since 1781. Best-known in Spanish-speaking world, especially for brandy Cardenal Mendoza. Good sherry: FINO Cristal, OLOROSO Don Antonio, AMONTILLADO NPU ("Non Plus Ultra").

Sandeman Large firm founded by Scot George Sandeman who set up twin establishments in Oporto and Jerez. Scrupulously-made sherries include Medium AMONTILLADO, Don FINO, and Armada CREAM. Also rare and exceptional Royal Ambrosante PALO CORTADO and dry and sweet Imperial Corregidor and Royal Ambrosante OLOROSOS. Founder's Reserve is their well-known VINTAGE CHARACTER; TAWNIES are much better. Partners' RUBY is new (94). VINTAGE wines have been at least adequate – some of the old vintages were superlative (63 66 70 **75 77 80 82**) but recent vintages are on the light side. 97 was declared as Vau Vintage.

Sanlúcar de Barrameda Historic seaside sherry town (see MANZANILLA).

Sercial Madeira grape for the driest of the island's wines – supreme apéritif (see panel above).

Silva Vinhos New Madeira producer (founded 90) with modern lodges at Estreito de Camara de Lobos. Gd, basic wines from Tinta Negra Mole grapes.

Silva, C da Shipper owned by Ruiz Mateos of GARVEY fame. Mostly inexpensive RUBIES & TAWNIES, but good aged tawnies and outstanding COLHEITAS under Dalva label.

Smith Woodhouse Port firm founded 1784, now owned by Symington's (see Dow). GOULD CAMPBELL is a subsidiary. Relatively light, easy wines including Old Lodge TAWNY, Lodge Res VINTAGE CHARACTER (widely sold in US). Vintages (very fine): 63 66 70 **75** 77' 80 83 85 91 94 97. Single-quinta wine: Madalena (95 98) for secondary vintages.

Solera System used in making sherry. Consists of topping up progressively more mature barrels with slightly younger wine of same sort, the object being to attain continuity in final wine. Most sherries are blends of several solera wines.

Soto, José de Best-known for inventing PONCHE, this family firm, which now belongs to the former owner of Rumasa, José María Ruiz Mateos, also makes a range of gd sherries, esp delicate FINO and fuller-bodied Fino Ranchero.

Tawny Style of port aged for many yrs in wood (VINTAGE PORT is aged in bottle) until tawny in colour. Many of the best are 20 yrs old. Low-price tawnies are blends of red and white ports. Taste the difference.

Since 1993, Madeiras labelled Sercial, Verdelho, Bual, or Malmsey must be at least 85% from that grape variety. The majority, made using the chameleon Tinta Negra Mole grape, which easily imitates each of these grape styles, may only be called Seco (Dry), Meio Seco (Medium Dry), Meio Doce (Medium Rich), or Doce (Rich) respectively. Meanwhile, replanting is building up supplies of the (rare) classic varieties.

Taylor, Fladgate & Yeatman (Taylor's) Often considered the best of the port shippers, especially for full, rich, long-lived VINTAGE wine and TAWNIES of stated age (40-year-old, 20-year-old, etc). Their Vargellas estate is said to give Taylor's distinctive scent of violets. Vintages: 63 66 70 **75** 77 80 83 85 92 94 97. QUINTA DE VARGELLAS is shipped unblended in lesser years (**67 72 74 76 78** 82 84 86 87 88 91 95 98). Also now Terra Feita single-quinta wine (**82** 86 87 88 91 95 96).

Terry, Fernando A de Magnificent BODEGA at PUERTO DE SANTA M, part of Allied-Domecq. Makers of Maruja MANZANILLA & range of popular brandies. Blending & bottling of all HARVEY'S sherries is carried out at the vast modern El Pino plant.

Tío Pepe The most famous of FINO sherries (see González-Byass).

Toro Albalá, Bodegas Mont-M Family firm located in 20s power station & aptly making Eléctrico FINOS, AMONTILLADOS & a PX among the best in MONTILLA & Spain.

Valdespino Famous family BODEGA at JEREZ, recently taken over by José Ertévez of MARQUÉS DEL REAL TESORO. Owner of Inocente v'yd & making excellent aged FINO of that name. Tío Diego is its dry AMONTILLADO, Solera 1842 an OLOROSO, Don Tomás its best AMONTILLADO. Matador is the name of Valdespino's popular range. In US, their sherries rank No 2 in sales volume & are still sold as "Hartley & Gibson".

Verdelho Madeira grape for medium-dry wines, pungent but without the searing austerity of SERCIAL (see panel above). Pleasant apéritif and good, all-purpose Madeira. Some glorious old VINTAGE wines.

Vesúvio, Quinta de Enormous 19th-C FERREIRA estate in the high DOURO. Owned by Symington's. 130 acres planted. Esp **89** 90 91 92 **90 91 92** 94 95 97 98 99.

Vila Nova de Gaia City on the south side of the River Douro from Oporto where the major port shippers mature their wines in "lodges".

Vintage Character Somewhat misleading term used for a gd-quality, full, and meaty port like a premium RUBY. Lacks the splendid "nose" of VINTAGE PORT.

Vintage Port The best port of exceptional vintages is bottled after only 2 yrs in wood and matures very slowly for up to 20 or more in bottle. Always leaves a heavy deposit and therefore needs decanting.

Warre Oldest of British port shippers (since 1670), owned by the Symington family (see DOW) since 1905. Fine, elegant, long-maturing vintage wines, good TAWNY (Nimrod), VINTAGE CHARACTER (Warrior), excellent LBV. Single-vineyard QUINTA da Cavadinha (**78 79 82** 84 86 87 88 89 90 92 95 98). Vintages: 63 66 70' **75** 77' 80 83 85 91 94 97.

White Port Port made of white grapes, golden in colour. Formerly made sweet, now more often dry: NIEPOORT, CHURCHILL, BARROS. Try with tonic water.

Williams & Humbert Famous 1st-class BODEGA, now owned by MEDINA group. a Dry Sack (med AMONTILLADO) is best-seller; Pando is an excellent FINO; Canasta CREAM & Walnut Brown are gd in their class; Dos Cortados is its famous dry, old PALO CORTADO. Also the famous Gran Duque de Alba brandy acquired from DIEZ-MERITO.

Wisdom & Warter Not a magic formula for free wine, but old BODEGA (controlled by GONZÁLEZ-B) with good sherries, esp AMONTILLADO Tizón & v rare SOLERA. Also FINO Olivar.

Switzerland

More heavily shaded areas are the wine growing regions

The high price of living, combined with cost-intensive wine production, means that Switzerland's wines find it difficult to compete on the world market and, in any case, are rarely seen outside the domestic arena. Those areas producing international style wines are Ticino (Merlot), Valais (Pinot Noir, Amigne, Arvigne), and Bündner Herrschaft (Pinot Noir). The most important vineyards (28,550 out of 37,280 acres) are in French-speaking areas: along the south-facing slopes of the upper Rhône Valley (Valais) and Lake Geneva (Vaud). Wines from German- and Italian-speaking zones are treasured and mostly drunk locally. Wines are known by place, grape names, and legally controlled type names and tend to be drunk young. The Swiss cantonal and federal appellation system, set up in 1988, still governs wine production.

Aargau 99 00 01 Wine-growing canton in E Switz (976 acres). Best for fragrant Müller-Thurgau and rich BLAUBURGUNDER.

Aigle Vaud r w ★★→★★★ Well-known for elegant whites and supple reds.

Amigne Trad VALAIS white grape, esp of VETROZ. Full-bodied, tasty, often sweet. Best producer: André Fontannaz ★★ 99 00 01.

Ardon Valais r w ★★→★★★ Wine commune between SION and MARTIGNY.

Arvine Old VALAIS white grape (also "Petite Arvine"): dry and sweet, elegant, long-lasting wines with a characteristic salty finish. Best in SIERRE, SION, Granges, FULLY. Best producer: Benoît Dorsaz ★★ 99 00 01.

Auvernier NE r p w ★★→★★★ Old wine village on Lake NEUCHÂTEL and biggest wine-growing commune of the canton.

Basel Second-largest Swiss town and canton with many vines: divided into Basel-Stadt and Baselland. Best wines: Müller-Thurgau, BLAUBURGUNDER.

Beerliwein Originally wine of destemmed BLAUBURG'R (E). Today name for wine fermented on skins traditionally rather than SÜSSDRUCK. Drink young.

Bern Swiss capital and canton of same name. Vineyards in West (BIELERSEE: CHASSELAS, PINOT NOIR, white SPÉCIALITIÉS) and East (Thunersee: BLAUBURGUNDER, Müller-Thurgau); 648 acres. Prized by Germanic Swiss.

Recent vintages

2001 Low yields but characteristic, full-bodied wines with ageing potential.

2000 4th good vintage in a row. One of the best for reds this century.

1999 Despite difficult weather, quality was vg, with remarkable fruit and colour (red wines). White have gd acidity.

1998 Damp summer, but very warm autumn. High-quality wines. Drink whites now – keep reds for one more year.

Bielersee r p w ★→★★ 99 00 01 Wine region on N shore of the Bielersee (dry light CHASSELAS, PINOT N) and at the foot of Jolimont (SPÉCIALITIÉS).

Blauburgunder German-Swiss name for PINOT N. (Aka Clevner.)

Bündner Herrschaft Grisons r p w ★★→★★★ Best German-Swiss region incl top villages: Fläsch, Jenins, Maienfeld, Malans. Serious BLAUB'R ripens esp well due to warm Föhn wind, cask-aged vg. Also CHARD, Müller-T, SPÉCIALITIÉS. Best producers: Gantenbein ★★★ Davaz ★★, Fromm ★★★ 97 98 99 00 01.

Calamin Vaud w ★★→★★★ LAVAUX v'yds next to DEZALEY: lush, fragrant whites.

Chablais Vaud r w ★★→★★★ 99 00 01 Sunny wine region on right bank of Rhône and upper end of L GENEVA, incl VILLAGES: AIGLE, Bex, Ollon, VILLENEUVE, YVORNE. Robust, full-bodied reds and whites.

Chamoson Valais r w ★★→★★★ Largest VALAIS wine commune, esp for SYLVANER.

Chasselas (Gutedel) French cantons, top w grape: neutral flavour, takes on local character: elegant (GENEVA), refined, full (VAUD), exotic, racy (VALAIS), pétillant (lakes Bienne, NEUCHATEL, Murtensee). Only east of BASEL. Called FENDANT in VALAIS. 37% of Swiss wines are Chasselas.

Completer Native white grape, mostly used in GRISONS making aromatic, generous wines that keep well. Winemakers are increasingly experimenting with this grape. ("Complet" was a monk's final daily prayer, or "nightcap".) Best producer: Adolf Boner, Halans ★★ 99 00.

Cornalin ★★→★★★ 99 00 01 Local VALAIS speciality; dark spicy v strong red. Best: Salgesch, SIERRE, Conthey, Leytron, Leuk.

Côte, La Vaud r p w ★→★★★ Largest VAUD wine area between LAUSANNE and GENEVA (N shore of Lake). Whites with elegant finesse; fruity, harmonious reds. Especially from MONT-SUR-ROLLE, Vinzel, Luins, FECHY, MORGES, etc.

Côtes de l'Orbe Vaud r p w ★→★★ N VAUD appellation between Lake NEUCHATEL and Lake GENEVA esp for light, fruity reds.

Dézaley Vaud w (r) ★★→★★★ Celebrated LAVAUX v'yd on slopes above L GENEVA, once tended by Cistercian monks. Unusually potent CHASSELAS, develops esp after ageing. Red Dézaley is a GAMAY-PINOT N-MERLOT-Syrah rarity.

Dôle Valais r ★★→★★★ Appellation for PINOT N, more often a PINOT-dominated blend of PINOT NOIR and GAMAY (at least 85%) with other red varieties from the VALAIS: full, supple, often very good. Lightly pink Dôle Blanche is pressed immediately after harvest. Eg from MARTIGNY, SIERRE, SION, VETROZ, etc. 99 00 01.

Epesses Vaud w (r) ★★→★★★ 00 01 LAVAUX AC: supple, full-bodied whites.

Ermitage Alias the Marsanne grape; a VALAIS SPÉCIALITÉ. Concentrated, full-bodied dry white, s'times with residual sugar. Esp from FULLY, SION, Noble Contrée.

Féchy Vaud ★★→★★★ Famous appellation of LA CÔTE, esp elegant whites.

Federweisser German-Swiss name for white wine from BLAUBURGUNDER.

Fendant Valais w ★→★★★ VALAIS appellation for CHASSELAS. Wide range of wines. Better ones now use village names only (FULLY, SION, etc.).

Flétri/Mi-flétri Late-harvested grapes for sw/slightly sw wine (respectively).

Fribourg Smallest French-Swiss wine canton (285 acres, nr Jura). Especially for CHASSELAS, PINOT N, GAMAY, SPÉCIALITÉS from VULLY, L Murten, S Lake NEUCHÂTEL.

Fully Valais r w ★★→★★★ Village nr MARTIGNY: excellent ERMITAGE and GAMAY. Best producer: Marie-Thérèse Chappat ★★→★★★ 99 00 01.

Gamay Beaujolais grape; abounds in French cantons. Mainly thin wine used in blends (SALVAGNIN, DÔLE). Gamay: 14% of grapes in Switzerland.

Geneva Capital, and French-Swiss wine canton; the third largest (3,370 acres). Key areas: Mandement, Entre Arve et Rhône, Entre Arve et Lac. Mostly CHASSELAS, GAMAY. Also lately Chard, Cab, PINOT, Muscat, and good Aligote.

Gewürztraminer Grown in Switzerland as a spécialité variety esp in VALAIS. Best producer: Jean-Michel Novelle, Satigny 99 00.

Germanier, Jean-René VETROZ winemaker; Cayas (100% Syrah) ★★★ 96 97 98 99 00; Mitis (sweet) ★★★ 97 98 99.

Glacier, Vin du (Gletscherwein) Fabled oxidized wooded white from rare Rèze grape of Val d'Anniviers; offered by the thimbleful to visiting dignitaries. See also VISPERTERMINEN. Best producer: St Jodern-Kellerei ★ 99 00.

Grand Cru Quality designation. Implication differs by canton: in VALAIS, GENEVA, and VAUD used where set requirements fulfilled.

Grisons (Graubünden) Mountain canton, mainly in German Switz (BÜNDEN HERRSCHAFT, Churer Rheintal; esp BLAUBURGUNDER) and partly S of Alps (Misox, esp MERLOT). 928 acres, primarily red, also Müller-Thurgau & SPÉCIALITIES.

Heida (Païen) Old VALAIS white grape (Jura's Savagnin) for country wine of upper Valais (Visperterminen v'yds 1,000+ m). Successful in lower VALAIS, too. Best producer: Josef-Marie Chanton ★★ 98 99 00 01

Humagne Strong native white grape (VALAIS SPÉCIALITÉ). Humagne Rouge (unrelated, from Aosta Valley) also. Esp from CHAMOSON, LEYTRON, MARTIGNY.

Johannisberg Synomyn for SYLVANER in the VALAIS.

Landwein (Vin de pays) Trad light, easy white and esp red BLAUB'R from east.

Lausanne Capital of VAUD. No longer with v'yds in town area, but long-time owner of classics: Abbaye de Mont, Château Rochefort (LA CÔTE); Clos des Moines, Clos des Abbayes, Dom de Burignon (LAVAUX). Pricey.

Lavaux Vaud w (r) ★→★★★ DYA Scenic region on N shore of L GENEVA between Montreux and LAUSANNE. Delicate, refined whites, gd reds. Best: CALAMIN, Chardonne, DÉZALEY, EPESSES, Lutry, ST-SAPHORIN, VEVEY-MONTREUX, Villette.

Leytron Valais r w ★★→★★★ Commune nr SION/MARTIGNY, esp Le Grand Brûlé.

Malvoisie See Pinot Gris.

Martigny Valais r w ★★ Lower VALAIS commune esp for HUMAGNE ROUGE & Syrah.

Merlot Grown in Italian Switzerland (TICINO) since 1907 (after phylloxera destroyed local varieties): soft to very powerful wines. Also used with Cab.

Mont d'Or, Domaine du Valais w s/sw sw ★★→★★★ 99 00 01 Well-sited property nr SION: rich, conc'd demi-sec and sweet wines, notable SYLVANER.

Mont-sur-Rolle Vaud w (r) ★★ DYA Important appellation within LA COTE.

Morges Vaud r p w ★→★★ DYA Lgst LA CÔTE/VAUD AOC: CHASSELAS, fruity reds.

Neuchâtel City & canton 00 01 V'yds (1,519 acres) from Lake N to BIELERSEE. CHASSELAS: fragrant, lively (sur lie, sp). Gd PINOT N (OEIL DE PERDRIX), PINOT GR, Chard. Best producer: Grillette Domaine de Cressier.

Nostrano Word meaning "ours", applied to red wine of TICINO, made from native and Italian grapes (Bondola, Freisa, Bonarda, etc).

Oeil de Perdrix Pale PINOT rosé. DYA Esp NEUCHÂTEL'S; also VALAIS, VAUD.

Pinot Blanc (Weissburgunder) New variety producing full-bodied, elegant wines.

Pinot Gris (Malvoisie) Widely planted white grape for dry and residually sweet wines. Makes v fine late-gathered wines in VALAIS (called Malvoisie).

Pinot Noir (Blauburgunder) Top red grape (31% of Swiss v'yds). Esp: BÜNDNER H, NEUCHÂTEL, VALAIS, ZÜRICH, THURGAU. Try: Renommée St Pierre ★★ 97 98 99 Pinot Noir (100%) from Mike Favre.

Rauschling Old white ZÜRICH grape; esp for discreet fruit, elegant acidity.

Riesling (Petit Rhin) Mainly in the VALAIS. Excellent botrytis wines.

Riesling-Sylvaner Old name for Müller-THURGAU (top white of E; a SPÉCIALITÉ in W). Typically elegant wines with nutmeg aroma and some acidity. Best producers: Hermann Schwarzenbach, Daniel Marugg, Hans Weisendanger. All: ★★ 00 01.

St-Gallen E wine canton nr L Constance (553 acres). Esp for BLAUBURG'R (full-bodied), Müller-THURGAU, SPÉCIALITÉS. Incl Rhine Valley, Oberland, upper L ZÜRICH.

St-Saphorin Vaud w (r) ★★→★★★ 01 Famous LAVAUX AC for fine, light whites.

Salvagnin Vaud r ★→★★ 00 GAMAY and/or PINOT N appellation. (See also DÔLE.)

Schaffhausen German-Swiss canton and wine town on River Rhine. Esp BLAUBURGUNDER; also some Müller-THURGAU and SPÉCIALITÉS.

Schenk Europe-wide wine giant, founded and based in Rolle (VAUD). Owns firms in Burgundy, Bordeaux, Germany, Italy, Spain.

Sierre Valais r w ★★→★★★ Sunny resort and famous wine town. Known for FENDANT, PINOT N, ERMITAGE, Malvoisie. Very good DÔLE.

Sion Valais r w ★★→★★★ Capital/wine centre of VALAIS. Esp FENDANT de Sion.

Sylvaner (Johannisberg, Gros Rhin) White grape esp in warm VALAIS v'yds. Heady, spicy: some with residual sweetness.

Spécialités (Spezialitäten) Wines of unusual grapes: vanishing local Gwäss, Himbertscha, Bondola, etc, ARVINE and AMIGNE, or modish Chenin Blanc, Sauv, Cabernet, Syrah. Eg VALAIS: 43 of its 47 varieties are considered SPÉCIALITÉS.

Süssdruck Dry rosé/bright-red wine: grapes pressed before fermentation.

Thurgau German-Swiss canton beside Bodensee (678 acres). Wines from Thur Valley: Weinfelden, Seebach, Nussbaum, and Rhine. S shore of the Untersee. Typical: BLAUBURGUNDER, also gd RIES-SYLVANER (aka Müller-Thurgau: Dr Müller was born in the region). SPÉCIALITÉS incl Kerner, PINOT GR, Regent. Best producer: Hans Ulrich Kesselring ★★★ 98 99 00.

Ticino Italian-speaking S Switzerland (with Misox), growing mainly MERLOT (good from mountainous Sopraceneri region) and SPECIALITIES. Trying Cab (oaked B'dx style), Sauv, Sem, Chard, Merlot white, and rosé. (2,347 acres.) Best producers: Guido Brivio, Daniel Huber, Adriano Kaufmann, Christian Zündel. All: ★★★ 96 97 98 99.

Valais (Wallis) Rhône Valley from German-speaking upper-V to French lower-V. Largest and most varied wine canton in French Switz (13,162 acres; source of 30% Swiss wine), now seeing a revival of quality, and ancient grapes. Near-perfect climatic conditions. Wide range: 47 grape varieties incl GAMAY, PINOT N, CHASSELAS, RIES, plus many SPÉCIALITÉS. Esp w; FLETRI/MI-FLETRI wines.

Vaud (Waadt) Fr Switz's 2nd-lgst wine canton (9,591 acres) incl CHABLAIS, LA CÔTE, LAVAUX, BONVILLARS, CÔTES DE L'ORBE, VULLY. CHASSELAS stronghold. Also GAMAY, PINOT N, etc.

Vétroz Valais w r ★★→★★★ Top village nr SION, esp famous for AMIGNE.

Vevey-Montreux Vaud r w ★★ Up-and-coming appellation of LAVAUX. Famous wine festival held about every 30 years.

Villeneuve Vaud w (r) ★★→★★★ Nr L Geneva: powerful yet refined whites.

Visperterminen Valais w (r) ★→★★★ Upper VALAIS vineyards esp for SPÉCIALITÉS.

Vully Vaud w (r) ★→★★ Refreshing white from L Murten/FRIBOURG area.

Yvorne Vaud w (r) ★★★ 00 01 Top CHABLAIS AC for strong, fragrant wines.

Zürich Capital of largest German-speaking wine canton (same name). Mostly BLAUBURGUNDER; also PINOT GR, GEWÜRZ, and esp MÜLLER-T, RAUSCHLING (1,591 acres).

SWITZERLAND

Austria

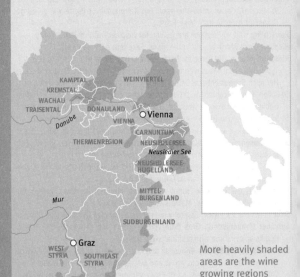

More heavily shaded areas are the wine growing regions

In 17 stirring years Austria has emerged as a vigorous, innovative producer of dry white and dessert wines up to the very finest quality. Here red wines (20 per cent of vineyards) are starting to make an international reputation, too. Strict laws, passed in 1985 and revised for the 1993 vintage, include curbs on yields (Germany: please copy) and impose higher levels of ripeness for each category than their German counterparts. Many regional names, introduced under the 1985 law, are still unfamiliar outside Austria. All are worth trying; there are dramatic discoveries to be made.

Recent vintages

2001 Another top vintage for dry whites and very good for late-harvest wines. Red are more erratic.

2000 V gd vintage in Lower Austria. Mixed in Styria due to harvest rains. In Burgenland, possibly the greatest vintage since 1945

1999 A great vintage whose dry white wines combine concentration and elegance. The best to date for the reds.

1998 A superb vintage for late-harvest wines, a very good one for the dry whites, but rather disappointing for reds.

1997 Very few late-harvest wines (wrong conditions for botrytis), but top dry whites and reds are rich and powerful.

1996 Small crop of variable quality. Generally light and fresh wines for drinking young, but more serious wines from top sites.

1995 Rain threatened to ruin the harvest, but late pickers and dessert winemakers hit the jackpot.

Ausbruch PRÄDIKAT wine (v sweet) between Beerenauslese and Trockenbeerenauslese in quality. Traditionally produced in RUST.

Ausg'steckt ("hung out") HEURIGEN are not open all year. To show potential visitors wine is being served, a green bush is hung up above the door.

Bergwein Legal designation for wines made from grapes grown on slopes with an incline of over 26%.

Blauburger Austrian red grape variety. A cross between BLAUER PORTUGIESER and BLAUFRÄNKISCH. Dark-coloured but light-bodied; simple wines.

Blauer Burgunder (Pinot Noir) A rarity. Vintages fluctuate greatly. Best in BURGENLAND, KAMPTAL and the THERMENREGION (from growers Achs, BRÜNDLMAYER, JOHANNESHOF, STIEGELMAR, IIMATHUM, and WIENINGER).

Blauer Portugieser Light, fruity wines to drink slightly chilled when young. Mostly made for local consumption. Top producers: Fischer, Lust.

Blauer Wildbacher Red grape used to make SCHILCHER wines.

Blauer Zweigelt BLAUFRÄNKISCH-ST-LAURENT cross: high yields and rich colour. Top producers (especially HEINRICH, Nittnaus, Pitnauer, Pöckl, UMATHUM) are making a reputation for it.

Blaufränkisch (Lemberger in Germany, Kékfrankos in Hungary) Austria's red grape variety with the most potential, much planted in MITTELBURGENLAND: wines with good body, peppery acidity, and a fruity taste of cherries. Often blended with CABERNET SAUVIGNON. Best from Gesellmann, HEINRICH, Iby, Igler, Krutzler, Nittnaus, E. TRIEBAUMER.

Bouvier Indigenous grape, generally producing light wines with low acidity but plenty of aroma, esp good for Beeren- and Trockenbeerenauslesen.

Bründlmayer, Willi r w sp ★★★→★★★★ 90 92 93 94 95 97 98 99 00 01 The leading LANGENLOIS-KAMPTAL estate. Very good wines: both local (RIES, GRUNER V) and international styles, incl CHARD and reds. Also Austria's best Sekt.

Burgenland Province and wine area (40,000 acres) in east next to Hungarian border. Warm climate. Ideal conditions, especially for botrytis wines near NEUSIEDLER SEE, also reds. Four wine regions: MITTELBURGENLAND, NEUSIEDLER SEE, NEUSIEDLERSEE-HÜGELLAND and SÜDBURGENLAND.

Buschenschank The same as HEURIGE; often a country cousin.

Cabernet Sauvignon Increasingly cultivated in Austria; used esp in blends.

Carnuntum r w Wine region since 94, E of VIENNA, bordered by the Danube to the north. Best producers: Glatzer, Pitnauer.

Chardonnay Increasingly grown, mainly oaked. Also trad in STYRIA as MORILLON (usually unoaked): strong fruit taste, lively acidity. Esp BRÜNDLMAYER, Loimer, Malat, POLZ, SATTLER, STIEGELMAR, TEMENT, VELICH, WIENINGER.

Deutschkreutz r (w) MITTELBURGENLAND red wine area, esp for BLAUFRÄNKISCH.

Donauland (Danube) w (r) Wine region since 1994, just west of VIENNA. Includes KLOSTERNEUBURG south of Danube and WAGRAM north of the river. Mainly whites, especially GRÜNER VELTLINER. Best producers include: Fritsch, Chorherren Klosterneuburg, Leth, Wimmer-Czerny, R Zimmermann.

Dürnstein w Wine centre of the WACHAU with famous ruined castle. Mainly GRÜNER V, RIES. Top growers: FREIE WEINGÄRTNER WACHAU, KNOLL, PICHLER, Schmidl.

Eisenstadt r w dr sw Capital of BURGENLAND and historic seat of Esterházy family. Major producer: Esterházy.

Falkenstein w Wine centre in the eastern WEINVIERTEL nr Czech border. Good GRÜNER VELTLINER. Best producers: Jauk, Luckner, HEINRICH and Josef Salomon.

Federspiel Medium quality level of the VINEA WACHAU categories, roughly corresponding to Kabinett. Fruity, elegant, dry wines.

Feiler-Artinger r w sw ★★★→★★★★ 91 92 93 94 95 96 97 98 99 00 01 Considered the outstanding RUST estate. Top AUSBRUCH dessert wines since 93. Also good dry whites and increasingly exciting reds.

Freie Weingärtner Wachau w (r) ★★★ 92 93 94 95 96 97 98 99 00 Important and vg growers' cooperative in DÜRNSTEIN. Excellent GRÜNER VELTLINER, RIES.

Gamlitz w Town in southern STYRIA. Growers incl Lackner-Tinnacher, SATTLER.

Gemischter Satz A blend of grapes (mostly white) grown, harvested, and vinified together. Traditional wine, still served in HEURIGEN.

Gobelsburg, Schloss ★★★ Renowned 86-acre estate in KAMPTAL revitalized since 1996, excellent dry RIES and GRÜNER VELTLINER, part-owned by BRÜNDLMAYER.

Gols r w dr sw Largest BURGENLAND wine commune (N shore of NEUSIEDLER SEE). Best producers: Beck, HEINRICH, Leitner, A&H Nittnaus, Renner, STIEGELMAR.

Grüner Veltliner Austria's national white grape (over a third of total v'yd area). Fruity, racy, lively young wines. Distinguished, age-worthy Spätlesen. Best producers: BRÜNDLMAYER, FREIE WEING'R WACHAU, HIRTZBERGER, Högl, KNOLL, MANTLER, NEUMAYER, NIGL, NIKOLAIHOF, PFAFFL, F X PICHLER, PRAGER, Schmelz, Walzer.

G'spritzer Popular refreshing summer drink, usually white-wine-based; made sparkling by adding soda or mineral water. Esp in HEURIGEN.

Gumpoldskirchen w r dr sw Resort village S of VIENNA, famous for HEURIGEN. Centre of THERMENREGION. Distinctive, tasty, often sweet wines from ZIERFANDLER and ROTGIPFLER grapes. Best producers: Biegler, Schellmann.

Heinrich, Gernot r w dr sw ★★→★★★ 92 93 94 96 97 98 99 00 01 Young, modern estate in GOLS with Pannobile and (esp) red Gabarinza labels.

Heurige Wine of the most recent harvest, called "new wine" for one year, then classified as "old". *Heurigen* are wine houses where growers-cum-patrons serve wine by glass/bottle with simple local food – an institution, esp in VIENNA.

Hirtzberger, Franz ★★★★ 90 93 94 95 96 97 98 99 00 01 Leading producer with 22 acres at SPITZ AN DER DONAU, WACHAU. Fine, dry RIES and GRÜNER VELTLINER.

Horitschon MITTELBURGENLAND region for reds. Best: Anton Iby, WIENINGER.

Illmitz w (r) dr sw SEEWINKEL region famous for Beeren- and Trockenbeeren-auslesen. Best from KRACHER, Martin Haider, Helmut Lang, OPITZ.

Jamek, Josef w ★★★ 92 93 94 95 97 98 99 00 01 Well-known estate and restaurant at Joching, WACHAU. Pioneer of dry whites since 50s. Recently back on top form.

Jurtschitsch/Sonnhof w (r) dr (sw) ★→★★ 92 93 94 95 97 98 99 00 01 Domaine run by three brothers: good whites (RIES, GRÜNER VELTLINER, CHARD).

Kamptal r w Wine region since '94, along R Kamp N of WACHAU. Top v'yds: LANGENLOIS, STRASS, Zöbing. Best growers: BRÜNDLMAYER, Dolle, Ehn, Schloss Gobelsburg, Hiedler, Hirsch, JURTSCHITSCH, Loimer, Topf.

Kattus ★→★★ Producer of traditional Sekt in VIENNA.

Kellergassen Picturesque alleyways lined with wine presses and cellars, devoted exclusively to the production, storage, and consumption of wine. Situated outside the town, typical of the WEINVIERTEL region.

Klöch w W STYRIA wine town famous for Traminer. Best from Stürgkh.

Kloster Und Winetasting centre in restored monastery nr KREMS.

Klosterneuburg r w Main wine town of DONAULAND. Rich in tradition with a famous Benedictine monastery and a wine college founded in 1860. Best producers: Chorherren Klosterneuburg, Zimmermann.

KMW Abbreviation for "Klosterneuburger Mostwaage" (must level), the unit used in Austria to measure the sugar content in grape juice.

Knoll, Emmerich w ★★★★ 93 94 95 96 97 98 99 00 01 Traditional, highly regarded estate in LOIBEN, WACHAU, producing showpiece GRÜNER VELTLINER & RIESLING.

Kollwentz-Römerhof w r dr (sw) ★★→★★★ 90 92 93 94 95 96 97 98 99 00 01 Innovative producer in Grosshöflein near EISENSTADT: Sauvignon Blanc, Eiswein and good reds.

Kracher, Alois w (r) dr (sw) ★★★★ 81 89 91 93 94 95 96 97 98 99 00 01 1st-class small ILLMITZ producer; speciality: PRÄDIKATS (dessert wines), some barrique-aged (Nouvelle Vague), others not (Zwischen den Seen), good reds since 97.

Krems w (r) dr (sw) Ancient town, W of VIENNA. Capital of KREMSTAL. Best from Forstreiter, NIGL, SALOMON, Weingut Stadt Krems, Walzer.

Kremstal w (r) Wine region since 94 esp for GRÜNER V and RIES. Top growers: Malat, MANTLER, NIGL, SALOMON, Weingut Stadt KREMS.

Langenlois r w Wine town and region in KAMPTAL with 5,000 acres. Best producers: BRÜNDLMAYER, Ehn, Hiedler, JURTSCHITSCH, Loimer.

Lenz Moser ★★→ Producer nr KREMS. LM III invented high-vine system. Also incl wines from Schlossweingut Malteser Ritterorden (wine estate of Knights of Malta): Mailberg (WEINVIERTEL), Klosterkeller Siegendorf (BURGENLAND).

Loiben w In lower, wider part of Danube Valley (WACHAU). Ideal conditions for RIES and GRÜNER V. Top: Alzinger, FREIE WEINGÄRTNER, KNOLL, F X PICHLER.

Mantler, Josef w ★★→★★★ 90 95 96 97 98 99 00 01 Leading estate in Gedersdorf nr KREMS. Vg trad RIES, GRÜNER V, CHARD, and rare Roter Veltliner (Malvasia).

Mayer, Franz w With 60 acres, the largest producer in VIENNA. Traditional jug wines (at picturesque HEURIGE Beethovenhaus – yes, he drank here), plus in contrast, excellent "older-vintage" (20 yrs) RIESLING and Traminer.

Messwein Mass wine: must have ecclesiastical approval (and natural must).

Mittelburgenland r (w) dr (sw) Wine region on Hungarian border protected by three hill ranges. Makes large quantities of red (especially BLAUFRÄNKISCH). Producers: Gesellmann, HEINRICH, Iby, Igler, P Kerschbaum, WEININGER.

Mörbisch r w dr sw Wine town on the western shore of NEUSIEDLER SEE just north of the Hungarian border. The top grower is Schönberger.

Morillon Name given in STYRIA to CHARDONNAY.

Müller-Thurgau See Riesling-Sylvaner.

Muskat-Ottonel Grape for fragrant, often dry whites, interesting PRÄDIKATS.

Muskateller Rare aromatic grape for dry whites. Best from STYRIA and WACHAU. Top growers: Gross, HIRTZBERGER, Lackner-Tinnacher, F X PICHLER, POLZ, SATTLER.

Neuburger Indigenous white grape: nutty flavour; mainly in the WACHAU (elegant, flowery), in the THERMENREGION (mellow and ample-bodied), and in N BURGENLAND (strong, full). Best from Beck, FREIE WEINGÄRTNER, HIRTZBERGER.

Neumayer ★★★ 94 95 96 97 98 99 00 01 The Neumayer brothers make powerful, pithy, dry GRÜNER VELTLINER and RIESLING at the best estate in the new TRAISENTAL region.

Neusiedler See V shallow (max 1.8m deep) BURGENLAND lake on Hungarian border. Warm temperatures, autumn mists encourage botrytis. Gives name to wine regions of NEUSIEDLERSEE-HÜGELLAND and NEUSIEDLERSEE.

Neusiedlersee r w dr sw Region N and E of NEUSIEDLER SEE. Best growers: Achs, Beck, HEINRICH, KRACHER, Nittnaus, OPITZ, Pöckl, UMATHUM, VELICH.

Neusiedlersee-Hügelland r w dr sw Wine region W of NEUSIEDLER SEE based around OGGAU, RUST, and MORBISCH on the lake shores, and EISENSTADT in the foothills of the Leitha Mts. Best producers: FEILER-ARTINGER, KOLLWENTZ, Mad, Prieler, Schandl, Schönberger, Schröck, ERNST TRIEBAUMER, Wenzel.

Niederösterreich (Lower Austria) With 58% of Austria's v'yds: CARNUNTUM, DONAULAND, KAMPTAL, KREMSTAL, THERMENREGION, TRAISENTAL, WACHAU, WEINVIERTEL.

Nigl ★★★ w 92 93 94 95 96 97 98 99 00 01 Top grower of KREMSTAL making sophisticated, dry RIESLING and GRÜNER VELTLINER capable of long ageing.

Nikolaihof w ★★★ 90 91 92 94 95 97 98 99 00 01 Estate built on Roman foundations. Superb RIESLING from Steiner Hund site, other wines v good and v traditional in style.

Nussdorf VIENNA district famous for HEURIGEN and vg Ried Nussberg.

Oggau Wine region on the W shore of NEUSIEDLER SEE.

Opitz, Willi ★★★ A tiny ILLMITZ estate specializing in late-harvest wines, including "Schilfmandl" and "Opitz One" from grapes dried on reeds from the NEUSIEDLER SEE.

Pfaffl ★★★ 90 93 94 95 96 97 98 99 00 01 WEINVIERTEL estate in Stretten nr VIENNA. Best-known for blended red "Excellence", but racy, dry GRÜNER VELTLINERS are no less impressive. Recently took over nearby Schlossweingut Bockfliess.

Pichler, Franz Xavier w ★★★★ 90 92 93 94 95 96 97 98 99 00 01 Top WACHAU producer with v intense, rich RIES, GRÜNER V (esp Kellerberg), and MUSKATELLER of great breed. Widely recognized as Austria's No 1 grower for dry wines.

Polz, Erich and Walter w ★★★ 92 93 95 96 97 98 99 00 01 S STYRIAN (Weinstrasse) growers; esp Hochgrassnitzberg: Sauv, CHARD, Grauburgunder, WEISSBURGUNDER.

Prädikat, Prädikatswein Quality graded wines from Spätlese upwards (Spätlese, Auslese, Eiswein, Strohwein, Beerenauslese, AUSBRUCH, and Trockenbeerenauslese). See Germany, page 149.

Prager, Franz w ★★★★ 90 91 92 93 94 95 96 97 98 99 00 01 Together with JOSEF JAMEK, pioneer of top-quality WACHAU dry white. Now run by Anton Bodenstein who is introducing new RIESLING clones and making great PRÄDIKAT wines.

Renomierte Weingüter Burgenland Assoc founded 95 by top BURGENLAND producers to promote region's top wines; incl KRACHER, TRIEBAUMER, UMATHUM.

Retz r w Important region in W WEINVIERTEL. Especially Weinbauschule Retz.

Ried Single v'yd.

Riesling On its own always means German RIESLING. WELSCHRIESLING (unrelated) is labelled as such. Top growers: Alzinger, BRÜNDLMAYER, FREIE W WACHAU, HIRTZBERGER, Högl, KNOLL, NIGL, NIKOLAIHOF, PFAFFL, F X PICHLER, PRAGER, SALOMON.

Riesling-Sylvaner Name used for Müller-T (about 10% of Austria's grapes). Best producers: HIRTZBERGER, JURTSCHITSCH.

Rotgipfler Fragrant indigenous grape of THERMENREGION. With ZIERFANDLER, makes lively, interesting wine. Esp Biegler, Schellmann, Stadelmann.

Rust w r dr sw BURGENLAND region, famous since 17th C for dessert AUSBRUCH; now also for r and dry w. Esp from FEILER-ARTINGER, Schandl, Heidi Schröck, ERNST TRIEBAUMER, Paul Triebaumer, Wenzel. The Cercle Ruster Ausbruch is a group of a dozen producers set on re-establishing pre-eminence of their powerful Sauternes-like wines from a wide range of grapes. Standards already v high.

St-Laurent Traditional red-wine grape, potentially very gd, with cherry aroma, believed to be related to Pinot N. Esp from Fischer, Mad, STIEGELMAR, UMATHUM.

Salomon-Undhof w ★★★ Very good producer of RIES, WEISSBURGUNDER, Traminer in KREMS. Excellent quality since 95.

Sattler, Willi w ★★→★★★ 92 93 94 95 96 97 98 99 00 01 Top S STYRIA grower. Esp for Sauv, MORILLON. Recent vintages less oaked, better balanced.

Schilcher Rosé wine from indigenous BLAUER WILDBACHER grapes (sharp, dry: high acidity). Speciality of W STYRIA. Try: Klug, Lukas, Reiterer, Strohmeier.

Schlumberger Largest sparkling winemaker in Austria (VIENNA); wine is bottle-fermented by unique "Méthode Schlumberger". Delicate and fruity.

Seewinkel ("Lake corner") Name given to the part of NEUSIEDLERSEE including Apetlon, ILLMITZ, and Podersdorf. Ideal conditions for botrytis.

Sepp Moser ★★★ 93 94 95 97 98 99 00 01 KREMSTAL estate (Rohrendorf) founded with original LENZ MOSER v'yds. Richly aromatic, elegant, dry RIES, GRÜNER V, CHARD, Sauv. Also good reds from Apetlon in Neusiedlersee region.

Servus w BURGENLAND everyday light and mild, dry white-wine brand.

Smaragd Highest-quality category of VINEA WACHAU, similar to dry Spätlese.

Spätrot-Rotgipfler Typical THERMENREGION (Spätrot and ROTGIPFLER) wine.

Spitz an der Donau w WACHAU cool microclimate: esp from Singerriedel v'yd. Top growers are: HIRTZBERGER, FREIE WEINGARTNER, Högl, Lagler.

Steinfeder VINEA WACHAU quality category for very light, fragrant, dry wines.

Stiegelmar, Georg w r dr sw ★→★★★ 93 95 96 97 98 99 00 01 GOLS grower: CHARD, Sauv Bl, red wine, and unusual specialities. Whites currently dull.

Strass w (r) Centre of KAMPTAL region for gd Qualität w wines. Best prods: Dolle, Topf.

Styria (Steiermark) The southernmost wine region of Austria, bordering Slovenia. Its dry whites are gaining real prestige. Incl SUDSTEIERMARK, SUD-OSTSTEIERMARK and WESTSTEIERMARK (S, SE, and W Styria).

Süd-Oststeiermark (SE Styria) w (r) STYRIAN region with islands of excellent vineyards. Best producers: Neumeister, Winkler-Hermaden.

Südburgenland r w Small S BURGENLAND wine region: good red wines. Best producers: Krutzler, Wachter, Wiesler.

Südsteiermark (S Styria) w Best wine region of STYRIA: makes v popular whites (MORILLON, MUSKATELLER, WELSCHRIESLING, and Sauv Blanc). Top producers: Gross, Lackner-Tinnacher, Muster, POLZ, Prünte, SATTLER, Skoff, TEMENT, Wohlmuth.

Tement, Manfred W ★★★→★★★★ 90 92 93 94 97 98 99 00 01 Renowned estate on S STYRIA Weinstrasse for beautifully made, traditional "Steirisch Klassik" and gently oaked Sauv Bl & MORILLON from Ziereggsite. World-class.

Thermenregion r w dr sw Wine/hot-springs region, south of VIENNA. Indigenous grapes (eg ZIERFANDLER, ROTGIPFLER) and good reds from Baden, GUMPOLDSKIRCHEN Tattendorf, Traiskirchen areas. The top producers are: Alphart, Biegler, Fischer, Johanneshof, Schafler, Schellmann, Stadelmann.

Traditionsweingüter Assoc of KAMPTAL and KREMSTAL wine estates, committed to quality and v'yd classification. Incl BRÜNDLMAYER, Loimer, G Malat, NIGL, SALOMON.

Traisental New region: 1,750 acres just south of KREMS on Danube. Mostly dry whites in style similar to WACHAU. Top producer: NEUMAYER.

Triebaumer, Ernst r (w) dr sw ★★★ 90 92 93 94 95 97 98 99 00 01 RUST producer; some of Austria's best reds: BLAUFRÄNKISCH (Mariental), CAB-Merlot. Vg AUSBRUCH.

Umathum, Josef w r dr sw ★★★ 90 91 92 94 95 97 98 99 00 01 Distinguished NEUSIEDLERSEE producer for vg reds incl BLAUER BURGUNDER; also good whites.

Velich W SW BURGENLAND ★★★ Burgundian-style "Tiglat" CHARDONNAY (99 00) has 22 months in barrel and since 95 some of top PRÄDIKATS in the SEEWINKEL.

Vienna w (r) ("Wien" in German and on labels.) The Austrian capital is a wine region in its own right (1,500 v'yd acres in suburbs). Generally simple, lively wines, served in HEURIGEN: esp Bernreiter, MAYER, Schilling, WIENINGER.

Vinea Wachau WACHAU appellation started by winemakers in 83 with three categories of dry wine: STEINFEDER, FEDERSPIEL, and SMARAGD.

Wachau w Danube wine region W of KREMS: some of Austria's best wines, incl RIES, GRÜNER V. Top producers: Alzinger, FREIE WEINGÄRTNER, HIRTZBERGER, Högl, JAMEK, KNOLL, NIKOLAIHOF, F X PICHLER, PRAGER.

Wagram r w Part of the Donaulano wine region with loess terraces in DONAULAND. Best producers: Fritsch, Leth, Wimmer-Czerny.

Weinviertel "Wine Quarter" w (r) Largest Austrian wine region, between Danube and Czech border. Mostly light, refreshing w, esp from Falkenstein, Poysdorf, RETZ. Best producers: Graf Mardegg, Hardegg, Jauk, Luckner, Lust, Malteser Ritterorden, PFAFFL, Schwarzböck, Taubenschuss, Zull.

Weissburgunder (Pinot Bl) Ubiquitous: good dry wines and PRÄDIKATS. Esp Beck, Fischer, Gross, HEINRICH, HIRTZBERGER, Lackner-Tinnacher, POLZ, TEMENT.

Welschriesling White grape, not related to RIESLING, grown in all wine regions: light, fragrant, young-drinking dry wines, and good PRÄDIKATS.

Weststeiermark (West Styria) p Small Austrian wine region specializing in SCHILCHER. Esp from Klug, Lukas, Reiterer, Strohmeier.

Wien See Vienna.

Wieninger, Fritz w r ★★→★★★★ 92 93 94 95 97 98 99 00 01 Vg VIENNA-Stammersdorf grower: HEURIGE, CHARD, BLAUER BURGUNDER reds; esp gd HUGELLAND V and RIESLING.

Winzer Krems Wine-growers' cooperative in KREMS: dependable, solid whites.

Zierfandler (Spätrot) White variety almost exclusive to the THERMENREGION. Blended with ROTGIPFLER: robust, lively, age-worthy wines. Best producers: Biegler, Schellmann, Stadelmann.

AUSTRIA

Central & Southeast Europe

More heavily shaded
areas are the wine
growing regions

To say that parts of this region are still in transition is an under-statement. But new regional autonomies and new statehoods are being followed in many cases by higher aspirations in winemaking.

In a few much-publicized cases this takes the form of international "flying winemakers" pitching their tents at vintage-time, usually to make wines acceptable to Western supermarkets from predictable grape varieties, occasionally to do far better. This affects indigenous winemaking, too – often with happy results, making fresher and fruitier wines of intriguingly different flavours.

The decade since communism has witnessed the decline of state firms and the emergence of new family- and corporate-owned wineries. These are now establishing their winemaking styles and market positions with either fresh and fruity or more complex, aged wines. So far, Hungary, Bulgaria, Slovenia, and the Czech Republic have taken the lead in what has become an area to follow with fascination. The potential of other ex-communist states has still to emerge, with Romania in particular catching up. But about Greece there is no doubt: the new age of wine has well and truly arrived.

In this section, references are arranged country by country, each shown on the map on this page. Included alongside regions are producers and other terms in the alphabetical listings.

Hungary

Hungary entered the communist era with E Europe's finest and most individual wines. It emerged with traditions battered and modern alternatives still half-baked. The past ten years have been revolutionary. Winemakers have invested capital and earnings into improving cellar equipment and procedures and expanding plantings of international grapes. Very drinkable standard varietals are now easy to find. The initial years of experiment have given way to proven winemaking techniques and definite wine styles. This is especially true for the reds of Villány, Szekszárd (the "z"s are silent), and Eger. Tokay, the one undisputed great wine of Central European history, remains in full renaissance, and native grapes (only white) provide the backbone for the more traditional preference for fiery, hearty, full-bodied wines. 2000 is potentially one of the best vintages in the last 100 years.

Alföld Hungary's Great Plain: much everyday wine (mostly Western grapes) and some better. Incorporates 3 wine districts: HAJÓS-Baja, Csongrád, Kunság.

Aszár-Neszmély W wine district in NW Hung nr Danube. Native & western grapes.

Aszú Botrytis-shrivelled grapes and the sweet wine made from them, similar to Sauternes. Used to designate both wine and shrivelled berries.

Aszú Eszencia Tokaj br sw ★★★★ 57 63 93 Second TOKAJ quality (see Eszencia). 7 PUTTONYOS plus; superb amber elixir, like celestial butterscotch.

Badacsony w dr sw ★★→★★★ Wine district on the N shore of Lake BALATON, home to the native variety KEKNYELU. The basalt soil can give rich, highly flavoured white wines; well-made Rieslings and SZURKEBARAT have fine mineral flavours. The leader is SZEREMLEY's Szent Orbán Winery.

Balaton Hungary's inland sea and Europe's largest (50 miles long) freshwater lake. Many good wines take its name. The ending "i" (eg Balatoni, Egri) is the equivalent of -er in Londoner.

Balatonboglár r w dr sw ★★→★★★ Progressive wine district on S shore of Lake BALATON. Particularly gd whites (Chard, Sémillon, Muscat). Also *cuve close* sp. Also name of large winery with wide range of quality white wines, incl sp. Owned by HUNGAROVIN.

Bátaapáti Kastélyborok Brand name of winery nr SZEKSZARD part-owned by Antinori of Italy. GAL makes vg Sauv Bl, Chard, TRAMINI, KEKFRANKOS, & other reds.

Bikavér Eger r ★ "Bull's Blood", historic red wine of EGER: at best full-b'd & well-balanced, highly variable in export version today. Now under supervision to protect identity & improve quality (see Eger). Mostly 3-variety blend, from KEKFRANKOS, Cab, Kekoporto, & some Merlot. Also made in SZEKSZARD.

Bock, József Family winemaker in VILLANY. Hearty reds, both varietal and blends.

Bodroy-Várhegy French-backed TOKAJI cellar with some delicate wines.

Bodvin Private 16-acre TOKAJ estate in MAD: ASZU and other wines mainly for US.

Bor Wine. Vörös is red, Fehér is white, Asztali is table.

Dégenfeld, Grof Lrge (159 acre, NB Forditas, eight ASZÚ-style.

Disznókő Important 1st-class TOKAJ estate, owned by AXA (French co) since 92, ASZU and other wines should be top-class; 1st vtge (93) v rich with Sauternes touch.

Dusóczky, Tamás An aristocrat of old TOKAJ with small production of wines.

Edes Sweet wine (but not as luscious as ASZU).

Eger Eger district r w dr sw ★→★★★ Best-known red-wine centre of N Hung; Baroque city of cellars full of BIKAVER. Fresh w LEANYKA (perhaps its best product), OLASZRIZLING, Chard, Cab. Top prods: Vilmos Thummerer (consistent Bikaver), TIBOR GAL, Pók Tamás, Ostoros Bor, Béla Vincze, & potentially the huge Egervin.

Eszencia ★★★★ The fabulous quintessence of TOKAJI: intensely sw & aromatic from grapes wizened by botrytis. Properly grape juice of very low, if any, alcoholic strength, reputed to have miraculous properties: its sugar content can be over 750 grams per litre. In commerce, ASZU ESZENCIA takes its place.

Etyek Near Budapest. Source of modern standard wines, esp Chard, Sauv Bl, especially from HUNGAROVIN.

Ezerjó ("Thousand blessings") Widespread traditional variety. At MOR, makes one of Hungary's top dry whites; great potential: fragrant with hint of grapefruit.

François President French-founded (1882) sparkling-wine producer at Budafok, nr Budapest. Vintage wine President is very drinkable.

Furmint The classic grape of TOKAJ, with great flavour, acidity, and fire, also grown for table wine at Lake BALATON and in SOMLO.

Gál, Tibor EGER winemaker for barrique-aged BIKAVER, also oaked GIA Chard.

Gere, Attila Family winemaker in VILLANY with good, forward-looking reds, esp oak-aged Cab S (93). Gere & Wenninger is another label (Cuvée Phoenix).

Hajós Pincék Alföld r ★ Charming village in S Hungary with 1,500 cellars. Mostly traditional, family production. Some quality lighter red wines can be found.

Hárslevelü "Linden-leaved" grape used at Debrö and as 2nd main grape of TOKAJ (cf Sém/Sauv in Sauternes). Gentle, mellow wine with a peach aroma.

Helvécia (Kecskemét) Historic ALFOLD cellars. V'yds ungrafted: phylloxera bugs cannot negotiate sandy soil. Whites and rosés modernist; reds traditional.

Hétszölö Noble first-growth 116-acre TOKAJ estate owned by Grands Millésimes de France and Japanese Suntory. Second label: Dessewffy.

Hilltop Neszmély Winery in ASZAR-NESZMELY; Western-style wines, including Woodcutters White from homegrown Czerszegi Fuszeres hybrid.

Hungarovin Traders/prods with cellars at Budafok nr Budapest: Western varietals, also *cuve close*, transfer, & classic sp. Owner: German Sekt specialist Henkell.

János Arvay TOKAJ family cellar of increasing reputation.

Kadarka Traditional red grape for vast quantities in S, but can produce ample flavour and interesting maturity (eg especially at SZEKSZARD and VILLANY) and considered by some an essential component of BIKAVER.

Kékburgundi German Spätburgunder: Pinot Noir.

Kecskemét Major town of the ALFOLD. Much everyday wine, some better.

Kékfrankos Hungarian for Blaufränkisch; reputedly related to Gamay. Good light or full-bodied reds, esp SOPRON. Used in BIKAVER at EGER.

Kéknyelü ("Blue stalk") High-flavoured, low-yielding white grape making the best and "stiffest" wine of Mt BADACSONY. It should be flowery and spicy stuff. Watch for top producer HUBA SZEREMLEY (aromatic and fruity whites).

Királyudvar Promising new TOKAJ cellar at TARCAL. Directed by ISTVAN SZEPSY.

Kiskunság Largest region in Great Plain. Gd KADARKA esp from Kiskörös.

Különleges Minöség Special quality: highest official grading.

Lauder-Lang Partnership of famous international Hungarians to make TOKAJ at MAD. Also v'yds & cellar at EGER and famous Gundel's restaurant in Budapest.

Leányka ("Little girl") Old Hungarian white grape. Admirable, aromatic, light, dry wine. Királyleányka ("Royal") is a different variety and supposedly superior.

Mád Old commercial centre of the TOKAJ region. Growers incl ROYAL TOKAJI, SZEPSY, József Monyok, Vince Gergely.

Mátraalja w (r) ★★ District in foothills of Mátra range in N, nr Gyöngyös (site of huge modernized winery) incl Debrö, Nagyrede. Promising, dry SZURKEBARAT, Chard, MUSKOTALY, Sauv Bl. French, Australian, and now German investment.

Mecsekalja S Hungary district, known for good whites of PECS, esp sparkling.

Megyer, Château Joint-venture estate between TOKAJ TRADING HOUSE and French investors at Sárospatak. See also Ch Pajzos. Excellent ASZU.

Mézes Mály In TARCAL. This & SZARVAS are historically the greatest v'yds of TOKAJ.

Minöségi Bor Quality wine. Hungary's appellation contrôlée.

Mór N Hungary w ★★→★★★ Region long-famous for fresh, dry EZERJO. Now also Riesling and Sauvignon. Wines now mostly exported.

Muskotály The yellow Muscat. Makes light, though long-lived, wine in Tokáj and EGER. A little goes into the TOKAJ blend (cf Muscadelle in Sauternes). V occasionally makes a wonderful ASZU wine solo.

Nagyburgundi Literally "great burgundy": indigenous grape often mistaken for KÉFRANKOS. Sound, solid wine, esp around VILLANY and SZEKSZARD.

Olaszrizling Hungarian name for the Italian Riesling or Welschriesling. Better examples can have a burnt-almond aroma.

Oremus Ancient TOKAJ vineyard of founding Rakóczi family, reconstituted by owners of Spain's Vega Sicilia with HQ now at Tolczva. First-rate ASZU.

Pajzos, Château Tokaj estate and part of TOKAJ TRADING HOUSE/Sárospatak joint venture. See also Ch Megyer. Excellent ASZU.

Pécs Mecsek w (r) ★→★★★ Major S wine city. Esp sp, OLASZRIZLING, Pinot Bl, etc.

Pinot Noir Normally means KÉKBURGUNDI.

Puttonyos Measure of sweetness in TOKAJI ASZU. A "puttony" is a 25-kilo measure, traditionally a hod of Aszù grapes. The number of "putts" per barrel (136 litres) of dry base wine determines the final richness of the wine, from 3 putts to 7.3 is equal to 60 g of sugar per litre, 4:90, 5:120, 6:150. ASZU ESZENCIA must have at least 180. See Eszencia for the *really* sticky stuff.

Royal Tokáji Wine Co Pioneer Anglo-Danish-Hung venture at MAD. 200 acres, mainly 1st or 2nd growth. 1st wine (90) a revelation: 91 & (esp) 93 led renaissance of TOKAJI. 95, 99, 00 to follow. I have to declare an interest as a founder.

Siklós City in S Hungary; part of VILLANY-SIKLOS. Mainly sm producers, known for whites: esp HARSLEVELU. Ripe, fruity Chard: promising; also TRAMINI, OLASZRIZLING.

Somló N Hungary w ★★ Isolated small district N of BALATON: whites (formerly of high repute) from FURMINT & Juhfark (sheep's tail) varieties in both traditional barrel-fermented and fresh, fruity styles. Top prods incl Fekete, Inhauser.

Sopron W Hungary r ★★→★★★ Historic enclave S of Neusiedlersee (see Austria). Traditionally known for lighter reds like KEKFRANKOS and Austrian-style sweet wines but showing promise for whites such as Sauv Bl.

Szamorodni Word meaning "as it was born"; describes TOKAJ not sorted in the v'yd. Dry or (fairly) sweet, depending upon proportion of ASZU grapes naturally present. Sold as an aperitif. In vintage TOKAJ Aszu yrs, the sw style can offer some Aszú character at much less cost. Dry Szamorodni is Hungary's sherry.

Száraz Dry, esp of TOKAJ SZAMARODNI.

Szarvas Royal TOKAJ v'yd, still state-owned, at Tarcal; one of the top classic sites.

Szekszárd r ★★→★★★ District in south-central Hungary; some of country's top reds from Cab and Merlot. Also KADARKA which needs age (say 3–4 yrs); can also be botrytized ("Nemes Kadar"). Good organic BIKAVER and good Chard and OLASZRIZLING, too. Quality wines are lighter, more delicate than those from VILLANY. Producers incl Vesztergombi, Peter Vida, Heimann.

St Ozbán See Szeremley.

Szepsy, István Legendary family name in MAD and an impeccable small production of long-ageing TOKAJI ASZU. Szepsy family "invented" Tokaj in 1630.

Szeremley, Huba The leader in BADACSONY. His Rieslings, SZURKEBARAT, KEKNYELU, and ZEUSZ are the modern models. Also fine KEKFRANKOS from the Tihány Peninsula. SZENT OZBÁNis another label.

Szürkebarát Literally means "grey friar": Pinot Gr. Too many are sw tourist wines from BALATON. But this is one of Hungary's best: wait for great dry wines.

Tarcal TOKAJ commune with the 2 great first-growths and several gd prods.

Tiffán, Ede VILLANY grower producing full-bodied, oaked red wines.

Tokajbor New TOKAJ Cellar at Bodrogkeresztúr. To watch.

Tokaj (Tokáji) Tokáj w dr sw ★★ →★★★★ The ASZU is Hungary's famous liquorous sweet wine (since dirca 1600), comparable to a highly aromatic, dramatically vital Sauternes with a searing finish, from hills in NE nr Ukraine border. Appellation covers 13,500 acres of the Tokajhegyalja. See Aszú, Eszencia, Furmint, Puttonyos, Szamorodni. Also dry table wine of character.

Tokaj Trading House The state-owned TOKAJ co, with 180 acres of the magnificent Szarvas v'yd and many others. Sales 60% in Hungary.

Tramini Gewürztraminer, esp in SIKLOS.

Villány r p (w) ★★ Major region for full-bodied reds, based in this town. Villányi Burgundi: largely KÉKFRANKOS can be gd. Cabs S & F: v promising. Dependable wines. See also Nagyburgundi. A region on the move.

Villány-Siklós Southern wine region named after two towns. High-quality producers incl BOCK, ATTILA GERE, Günzer, Malatinsky, Molnár, Polgar, TIFFAN, Villány Borászat, and Vylyan.

Zéta A cross of Bouvier and FURMINT used by some in ASZU production, also as varietal with a pear/green-apple flavour, but production waning.

Zeusz Recent variety for aromatic sweet whites.

Bulgaria

2001 was the first vintage under the new "French style" Wine Law, which introduced detailed regulations in the 5 wine regions. The drive for higher standards has been reflected by the increased demand for quality wines.

The Danube Plain regions specialize in fruity whites and reds at Svishtov and Rousse, while further south, Lyaskovets, Pavlikeni, and Suhindol produce some well-balanced reds. The Black Sea region is particularly suitable for the production of fresh, dry, and fruity whites at Targovishte, Shumen, and Pomorie. The largest and most productive region is the Thracian Valley with constant high temperatures producing rich reds, especially at Haskovo, Iambol, Sliven, and Assenovgrad. Struma Valley in the southwest is the hottest region, producing substantial reds of great longevity at Damianitsa and Harsovo.

Foreign investment in the modernization of established wineries continues, while newcomers are bringing a welcome diversity to the wine scene.

Assenovgrad r ★★ Main MAVRUD-producing cellar near PLOVDIV. Mavrud (oo) and CAB can last well.

Blueridge, Sliven r (w) ★★★ Bulgaria's newest and largest winery. Australian-designed. Well-received CAB & MERLOT, also CHARD (01).

Boyar Estates Domaine Boyar merged with Vinprom Rousse to form one of largest companies in East and Central Europe, marketing worldwide under Domine Boyar, Blueridge, and Vinprom Rousse labels.

Burgas w p (r) ★→★★Black Sea resort and source of rosé (the speciality), easy whites and some good young reds.

Cabernet Sauvignon V successful (4x Calif's acreage). Dark vigorous fruity, v drinkable young; best quality age well. Good examples: IAMBOL, SLIVEN, SUHINDOL, ROUSSE.

Chardonnay Previously less successful than CABERNET. Better results now from N and E. V dry, full-flavoured wine. Recent examples are promising, esp from TARGOVISHTE, SHUMEN, and SLAVIANTSI.

Controliran Like DOCG and AOC. New wine law published in 2000.

Country Wines Regional wines (cf French Vins de Pays), often 2-variety blends.

Damianitza r ★★ MELNIK winery specializing in native Melnik grape. Also MERLOT and new Redark (oo).

Danube River dividing Bulgaria and Romania. ROUSSE and SVISHTOV vineyards benefit from its proximity, esp for reds.

Dimiat The common native white grape, grown in the E towards the coast. Good examples from Blueridge (**01**) and Black Sea Gold.

Gamza Red grape (Kadarka of Hungary) with potential esp from N region DANUBE plain. PAVLIKENI, NOVO SELO, SUHINDOL, and PLEVEN are specialists.

Harsovo Southwest region, esp for MELNIK.

Haskovo r (w) ★★→★★★★ Recently privatized winery (with v'yds) in S region specializing in MERLOT; STAMBOLOVO, and SAKAR are satellite wineries.

Iambol r w ★★→★★★★ Winery owned by BOYAR ESTATES specializing in CAB S & MERLOT.

Karlovo Town famous for its Valley of the Roses. Whites, especially MISKET.

Khan Krum Satellite cellar of PRESLAV, whites esp Reserve CHARD.

Korten r ★★→★★★ Subregion of SLIVEN. Korten's CAB is more tannic than most.

Lovico Suhindol r w ★★→★★★★ Site of Bulgaria's 1st co-op (1909). GAMZA, CAB, MERLOT blends.

Mavrud Grape variety and darkly plummy red from S Bulgaria, esp ASSENOVGRAD. Can mature 20 yrs+. Considered the country's best indigenous red variety.

Melnik Village in SW and highly prized grape. Dense red; locals say it can be carried in a handkerchief. Needs 5 yrs+; lasts 15. Also ripe age-worthy CAB.

Merlot Soft r variety mainly in HASKOVO in the S. Excellent examples: STAMBOLOVO, IAMBOL, Lyubimets, and Elhovo in the S; SHUMEN & LOVICO SUHINDOL (N).

Misket Mildly aromatic indigenous grape; the basis for most country whites.

Muscat Ottonel Normal Muscat grape, grown in E for mid-sweet, fruity white.

Novo Selo Good red GAMZA from the north.

Oriachovitza r ★★ Satellite cellar of STARA ZAGORA. Major S area for CONTROLIRAN CAB and MERLOT. Rich, savoury red best at 4–5 yrs. Recently gd RESERVE Cab.

Pamid The light, soft, everyday red of the southeast and northwest.

Pavlikeni r ★→★★ Specializes in MERLOT and CAB.

Peruschtitza r ★→★★★ Winery nr PLOVDIV. Reds only, esp MAVRUD, CAB, & RUBIN grapes.

Pleven N cellar for PAMID, GAMZA, CAB. Also Bulgaria's wine-research station.

Plovdiv City in S region source of gd CAB & MAVRUD. Most w'making at ASSENOVGRAD & PERUSCHTITZA. University's Food Technology Dept where most Bulg oenologists study.

Pomorie w (r) ★★ Black Sea Gold Winery in E, whites & reds, esp CHARD & MUSKAT.

Preslav w ★★ Well-known white-wine cellar, in E region. Also good brandy.

Reserve Used on labels of selected and oak-aged wines. Whites for a minimum of two years and reds for at least three years in oak vats.

Riesling Rhine Ries is grown, but most is Italian (Welschries) used for med & dr ws.

Rkatziteli One of the most widely grown grapes in the world, known as Rikat in Bulgaria. Widely used in dry and medium white-wine blends in NE.

Rousse r w r Lge winery in N on the DANUBE. Merged with BOYAR ESTATES. Fresh, high-tech whites esp CHARD, SAUV BL. Gd reds, incl Yantra Valley CAB.

Rubin Bulgarian cross (Nebbiolo x Syrah); often blended with CAB or MERLOT.

Sakar SE wine area for MERLOT, some of Bulgaria's best.

Sauvignon Blanc Grown in E and N Bulgaria esp at SHUMEN, and TARGOVISHTE.

Shumen w r ★★→★★★ E region and winery (owned by BOYAR ESTATES), esp whites and New World-style reds. "Premium Oak" CHARD (**01**) and MERLOT (**00**).

Simeon, Csar Good branded red authorized by the ex-king.

Slaviantsi w (r) ★★→★★★★. Mainly whites, especially MUSCAT, CHARD, MISKET, and Ugni Blanc. Increasingly also reds, especially CABERNET.

Sliven r (w) ★★ Big producing S region, esp for CAB, MERLOT & Pinot N (blended COUNTRY WINE), MISKET, & CHARD. Vini Sliven produces r & w. Promising barrique-aged Cab.

Stambolovo Satellite cell of HASKOVO. Azbuka Merlot 96 recommended.

Stara Zagora S region winery: reds, esp CAB and MERLOT to RESERVE quality.

Sunguarlare Satellite of SLAVIANTSI. MISKET noted for delicate fragrance. Also CHARD.

Svishtov r ★★→★★★★ N region winery on DANUBE. Reds only, especially finely balanced CABERNET. Also good rosé Cabernet (**01**).

Targovishte w ★★→★★★ Winery in E region, quality whites, esp CHARD (incl barrel-fermented) and SAUV BL. Promising new Tuk Tam range.

Varna w ★ Black Sea coast region for whites, esp CHARD (buttery or unoaked), SAUV, DIMIAT, ALIGOTE, and UGNI BL (sometimes blended).

A Bulgarian choice for 2003

Red: Blueridge Cabernet Sauvignon Bin 316 01; Blueridge Merlot Bin 617 '01; Iambol Domaine Boyar Cabernet Sauvignon 01.

White: Slaviantsi Muscat & Ugni Blanc Country Wine; Shumen Chard 01.

Indigenous blends: Blueridge Dimiat 01; Assenovograd Mavrud 00

Reserve wines: Stambolovo Merlot Reserve 94; Iambol Oravnifera Cabernet Sauvignon Reserve 99; Oriachovitsa Merlot/Cab S Res 94; Domaine Boyar Royal Reserve Cabernet Sauvignon 96.

The former Yugoslav states

Before its disintegration in 1991, Yugoslavia was well-established as a supplier of wines of international calibre, if not generally of exciting quality. Now the newly formed states are again working on export, while developing their own distinct winemaking traditions. Current political disarray and competition from other East European countries make commercial contacts difficult (except in Slovenia, whose "Riesling" was the pioneer export, since followed by Cab, Pinot Bl, Traminer, and others). All regions, except the central Bosnian highlands, make wine, traditionally in giant co-ops, but newer small, private producers have emerged. The Dalmatian (Croatian) coast and Macedonia have good indigenous wines. In Dalmatia, for example, new investment and Western technology promise interesting results with some of these. Best results come directly from the producer's cellar.

Slovenia

Barbera Vg sparkling from Janez Istenic and family in BIZELJSKO.

Bela Krajina SAVA, esp "Ledeno LASKI RIZLING" (late-harvest frozen grapes).

Beli Pinot Pinot Bl, a popular grape variety. Belo is white.

Bizeljsko-Sremic In SAVA district. Full-flavoured local-variety reds and LASKI R.

Brda Slovene upper part of Collio DOC (Italy). Many estates on both sides.

Crno vino Red (literally "black") wine.

Curin-Prapotnik Pioneer Slovenian white-wine trader.

Cvicek Traditional rosé or pale red esp from DOLENJSKA. ("Schilcher" in Austria.)

Dolenjska SAVA region: CVICEK, LASKI RIZLING, and Modra Frankinja (dry red).

Drava Valley (Podravski) Slovene wine region. Mainly whites from aromatic (Welschries, Muscat Ottonel) to flamboyant (RIES and SAUV); also Eisweins and Beerenauslesen as in neighbouring Austria.

Drustvo Vinogradnikov BRDA assoc of 45 growers/winemakers (with SAVA, DRAVA, and Moravia equivalents).

Gorna Radgona Winery for sp, late-harvest sweet and Eiswein (Ledeno vino).

Grasevina Slovenian for Italian RIES. The normal "Riesling" of the region.

Hlupic Producer of fine whites from around Haloze.

Jeruzalem Slovenia's most famous v'yd, at LJUTOMER. Its best wines are late-picked RENSKI RIZLING and LASKI RIZLING. Also makes tank-fermented sparklers.

Kakovostno Vino Quality wine (one step down from VRHUNSKO).

Kontrolirano poreklo Appellation. Wine must be 80% from that region.

Koper Hottest area of LITTORAL, between Trieste and Piran. Full, rich MERLOTS and B'x-like Rdeci Capris blend.

Kmetijska Zadruga Wine farmers' cooperative.

Kraski Means grown on the coastal limestone or Karst. A region famous for REFOSK wines, eg Kraski Teran and oak-aged Teranton.

Laski Rizling Yet another name for Italian RIES. Best-known Slovene wine, not best quality. Top export brand: "Cloburg" from Podravski (DRAVA) region.

Littoral (Primorje) Coastal region bordering Italy (Collio) and the Med. Esp good reds: Cab, MERLOT (aged in Slovene oak), Barbera, and REFOSK.

Ljutomer (or Lutomer)-Ormoz Slovenia's best-known, probably best white-wine district, in NE (DRAVA); esp LASKI RIZLING, at its best rich and satisfying. Ormoz winery also has sparkling and late-harvest wines.

Malvazija Ancient Greek white grape for luscious (now also lively, fresh) wine.

Maribor Important centre in NE (DRAVA). White wines, mainly from VINAG, including LASKI RIZLING, RIESLING, SAUVIGNON BLANC, Pinot Blanc, and Traminer; also the blend Mariborcan.

Merlot Reasonable in Slovenia. Comparable with neighbouring NE Italian.

Metlika BELA KRAJINA wine centre with warm Kolpa River v'yds.

Namizno Vino Table wine.

Podravje Region with many small v'yds, producing some good Chardonnays.

Pozna Trgatev Late harvest.

Ptuj Historic wine town with trad-based co-op: wines clean, mostly white.

Radgona-Kapela DRAVA district next to Austrian border, esp late-harvest wines, eg RADGONSKA RANINA, also classic-method sparkling.

Radgonska Ranina Ranina is Austria's Bouvier grape. Radgonska is nr MARIBOR. The wine is sweet. Trade name is Tigrovo Mljeko (Tiger's Milk).

Refosk Vg Italian red ("Refosco") grape in E and in ISTRIA (Croatia) as TERAN.

Renski Rizling Rhine RIES: rare here, but a little in LJUTOMER-ORMOZ. Ages well.

Riesling Formerly meant Italian Ries. Now legally limited to real Rhine Riesling.

Sauvignon Blanc Vg with the resources to make it well; otherwise horrid.

Sava Valley Central Slovenia: light, dry reds, eg CVICEK. Northern bank is for whites, eg LASKI RIZLING, Silvaner, and recent Chard and SAUV BL.

Sipon Hungary's Furmint – locally prized, p'haps has a future. Ages well.

Slamnak A late-harvest LJUTOMER estate RIES.

Slovenijavino Slovenia's largest exporter. Wines (esp Welschries) bought in and blended with care for Slovin, Ashewood, and Avia brands.

Teranton Red made from outstanding grapes; aged 6 yrs[+] before release.

Tigrovo Mljeko See Radgonska Ranina.

Tokaj The Pinot Gr, making rather heavy white wine.

Vinag Huge production cellars at MARIBOR. Top wine: Cloburg LASKI RIZLING.

Vinakras Sezana v'yds for deep-purple, fresh-tasting TERANTON.

Vipava Forward-looking LITTORAL region with a tradition of export to Austria and Germany: good Cab, MERLOT, Barbera, Chard, and Vrtovcan blend.

Vrhunsko Vino Top-quality wine.

Croatia (includes Dalmatia)

Babic Standard red of DALMATIA, ages better than ordinary PLAVAC.

Badel Top négociant of Croatian wines.

Banat Region partly in Romania: up-to-date wineries making adequate Ries.

Baranjske Planote SLAVONIA area for Ries and Bijeli Burgundac.

Benkovac Town and wine cellar: looking gd (esp rosé) as it emerges from war.

Bogdanusa Local white grape of DALMATIAN islands, especially Hvar and Brac. Round, like Chard, refreshing, faintly fragrant wine.

Bolski Plavac Top-quality vigorous red from Bol on the island of Brac.

Burgundac Bijeli Chard, grown in SLAVONIA.

Dalmacijavino Co-op at Split: full range of DALMATIAN coastal/island wines.

Dalmatia The coast of Croatia, from Rijeka to Dubrovnik. Variety of characterful wines. High-alcohol wines are traditional, but fruitier styles are emerging.

Dingac Vineyard designation on Peljesac's steep western slopes (mid-DALMATIAN coast). It traditionally produces heavy, sweetish wine from PLAVAC MALI grape, but it is emerging as a robust, dry red that supports oak and bottle-ageing.

Faros Substantial, age-worthy PLAVAC red from the island of Hvar.

Grasevina Local name for ubiquitous Laski Rizling. Best from Kutjevo.

Grk White grape, speciality of the island of Korcula, giving strong, even sherry-like wine, and also a lighter, pale one.

Grgich, Miljenko California winemaker (cf Grgich Hills) returns to Croatian roots. Western-style cellar on PELJESAC PENINSULA. Makes r PLAVAC and w POSIP.

Istravino Rijeka Oldest wine négociant of Croatia.

Istria Peninsula in the North Adriatic, Porec its centre: a variety of pleasant wines, Merlot as good as any. Very dry TERAN is perfect with local truffles. Good-quality Pinot Gris and Blanc with high alcohol. Locally popular is historic "Malmsey".

Ivan Dolac A good-quality dry, fruity, aromatic red.

Kontinentalna Hrvatska Inland Croatia. Mostly for whites (GRASEVINA).

Krk Island Historic home to Illyric people; source of sp wines & delicate w Zlahtina.

Marastina Strong, herbal, dry DALMATIAN white, best from Lastovo.

Opol Pleasant, pale PLAVAC red from Split, Sibenik, & Hvar and Brac islands.

Peljesac Peninsula Beautifully terraced, quality wine region in DALMATIA. See Grgich.

Plavac Mali DALMATIA red grape; wine of body, strength, age-ability. See Dingac, Opol, Postup; also Tomic. Also white, Plavac Beli.

Plenkovic Zlatan-Hvar-based winemaker producing quality red and white wines. Bogdanusa shows promise as varietal, but is generally blended.

Polu Semi... Polu-slatko is semi-sweet, polu-suho is semi-dry.

Portugizac Austria's Blauer Portugieser: plain red wine.

Posip Pleasant DALMATIAN white. Reputedly the same grape as Furmint.

Postup Soft, heavy DALMATIAN red of Peljesac Peninsula. Highly esteemed.

Prosek Dessert wine from ISTRIA and DALMATIA: 15% (can be almost port-like).

Slavonija N Croatia, on Hungarian border between Slovenia and Serbia.

Stolno vino Table wine.

Teran Stout, dark red of ISTRIA. See Refosk (Slovenia).

Tomic, Andro Producer of renowned PLAVAC on island of Hvar.

Vrhunsko Vino New origin-based designation for quality wines.

Vugava Viska Rare w grape of Vis (DALMATIA). Linked (allegedly) with Viognier.

Bosnia and Herzegovina

Blatina Ancient MOSTAR red grape and wine from pebbled W bank of Neretva.

Kameno Vino White wine of unique irrigated desert v'yd in Neretva Valley.

Mostar Means "old bridge". Was Herzegovina's Islamic-looking wine centre, but cellars destroyed during the civil war. Ljubuski and Citluk are rebuilding. Potentially admirable ZILAVKA white and BLATINA red.

Samotok Light, red (rosé/"ruzica") wine from run-off juice (and no pressing).

Zilavka The white grape of MOSTAR, making wines rather neutral when exported, but can be dry and pungent and memorably fruity with a faint flavour of apricots.

Serbia

Serbia has its own Prokupac grape; used alone it makes a light, fruity red, often blended with Pinot Noir or Gamay. In SE towards Bulgarian border, vineyards of Cab Sauv and Merlot planted in 80s now mature and promising.

Montenegro

13 July State-run co-op; high-tech Italian kit, nr PODGORICA. VRANAC: high quality.
Cemovsko Polje Vast pebbled semi-desert plain; esp VRANAC. Awaits discovery.
Crmnica Lakeside/coastal v'yds esp for Kadarka grape (see Macedonia).
Duklja Late-picked, semi-sweet version of VRANAC.
Krstac Montenegro's top white grape and wine; esp from CRMNICA.
Merlot Since 80: good, wood-aged results.
Podgorica Ancient name reintroduced for capital Titograd.
Vranac Local vigorous and abundant red grape and wine. Value.

Macedonia

Recommended wineries: Povardarie-Negotine, Bovin-Negotino for Cab Sauv, Merlot, Pinot N, and VRANEC. Lozar-Veles for Sauv Bl, Chard, and Zilavka.

Belan White Grenache. Makes neutral blended wine.
Crna Reka River with many artificial lakes for irrigation.
Kadarka Major red grape of Hungary; here closer to its origins around L Ohrid.
Kratosija Locally favoured red grape; sound wines with good potential.
Plovdina Native (S) grape for mild red, white; esp blended with tastier PROKUPAC.
Prokupac Serbian and Macedonian top red grape. Makes dark rosé (Ruzica) and full red of character, esp at Zupa. PLOVDINA often added for smoothness.
Rkatsiteli Russian (white) grape often used in blends.
Temjanika Grape for spicy, semi-sweet whites.
Teran Transferred from Istria, but Macedonia's version is less stylish.
Tikves Much-favoured hilly v'yd region (20,000 acres). Esp for pleasant, dark-red Kratosija; fresh, dry Smederevka – locally mixed with soda.
Traminac The Traminer. Also grown in Vojvodina and Slovenia.
Vardar Valley Brings the benefits of the Aegean Sea to inland v'yds.
Vranec Local name for Vranac of Montenegro (qv); indifferent quality.
Vrvno Vino Controlled origin designation for quality wines.

Former Czechoslovakia

Re-established in January 1993 as Czech (Moravia and Bohemia) and Slovak republics. There was barely any tradition of exporting from this mainly white-wine region, but good wines have emerged since 1989. 1997, 1999, & 2000 are outstanding vintages. Labels will say whether they are blended or single grapes. Privatization and foreign investment and advice bode well for the future.

Moravia Favourite wines in Prague: variety and value. Vineyards situated along Danube tributaries. Many wines from Austrian border: similar grapes, Grüner V, Müller-T, Sauv, Traminer, St-Laurent, Pinot Noir, Pinot Blanc, Blauer Portugieser, Frankovka, Rhine Riesling, Vlassky Riesling; eg from **Mikros Mikulov** (fresh, fruity wines), **Znovin Satov** (modern, mostly white – grapes from local farms and co-ops), **Jaroslavice** (oak-aged reds), **Vinium** (since 1936, now privately-owned & advised by Australian winemakers: mostly white, also light, fruity reds, incl Moravia Hills Dry Red), **Vinne Sklepy Valtice** (Historic South Moravian Château now a privately owned co-op: clean, savoury white and aromatic red), & **Znojmo** (long-est'd, ideal limestone soil; local white grapes, sweetish prize-winning Pinot Gris 93 from Sobes). **Other regions:** Prímetice (full, aromatic whites), Blatnice, Hustopece, sunny Pálava, Saldorf (esp Sauvignon bl, "Rynsky" Riesling), and Velké Pavlovice (good Ruländer, Traminer, St-Laurent, and award-winning Cab 92, still expanding). Moravia also has sparkling.

Bohemia Winemaking since 9th C. Same latitude and similar wines to eastern Germany. Best: N of Prague, in Elbe Valley, and (best-known) nr Melník (King Karel IV bought in Burgundian vines in 15th C; today Ries, Ruländer, and Traminer predominate). Bohemia Sekt from Stary Plzenec is popular: tank-fermented (mostly) with grapes from SLOVAKIA and MORAVIA. Soare sparkling also growing. Also interesting Pinot N. Top wineries: **Lobkowitz** (at Melnik), **Roudnice**, **Litomerice**, **Karlstein**.

Slovakia Most of former Czechoslovakia's wine but number of vy'ds now declining. Best in eastern v'yds neighbouring Hungary's Tokaj region. Slovakia uses Hungarian varieties, international varieties (Ries, Gewürz, Pinot Bl, Sauv Bl, and Cab S) and makes a little Tokaj, too. Key districts: Malo-Karpatská Oblast (largest region, in foothills of the Little Carpathians, incl Ruländer, Ries, Traminer, Limberger, etc), Malá Trna, Nové Mesto, Skalice (small area, mainly reds), and (in Tatra foothills) Bratislava, Pezinok, Modra.

Romania

Romania has a long winemaking tradition, but potential for quality was wasted during decades of supplying the USSR with cheap sweet wine. The political situation has allowed little progress. Quantity is still the goal but modern equipment, foreign expertise, and a growing focus on vineyard management are seeing a fraction of Romania's vast potential realized. The full, soft reds from Dealul Mare (esp Pinot Noir) are gaining an excellent international reputation. Further capital investment, as well as consistency, is now what is needed

Alba Iulia Area in cool TIRNAVE region of TRANSYLVANIA, known for aromatic and off-dry white (Italian RIES, FETEASCA, MUSKAT-OTTONEL), bottle-fermented sparkling.

Aligoté Pleasantly fresh white from 11,000 acres (2nd only to France).

Băbească Neagra Traditional red grape of the FOCSANI area, light body and colour. (Means "(black) grandmother grape".)

Banat Plain on border with Serbia. Workaday Italian RIES, SAUV BL, MUSKAT-OTTONEL, and local Ries de Banat; light red Cadarca, CABERNET, and Merlot.

Burgund Mare Name linked to Burgenland (Austria) where grape is called Blaufränkisch (Kékfrankos in Hungary).

Buzau Hills Gd reds (CAB, Merlot, BURGUND M) from continuation of DEALUL MARE.

Cabernet Sauvignon Increasingly grown, esp at DEALUL MARE; dark, intense wines.

Carl Reh New German-owned 2.5m litre winery in Oprisor.

Carpathian Winery Dealul Mare. Excellent Pinot N. Try Telegraph Hill 2000.

Chardonnay Some sweet styles but modern dry and oak-aged styles, esp from MURFATLAR and TRANSYLVANIA increasingly available.

Cotesti Warmer part of FOCSANI; deep-coloured PINOT N, Merlot, etc, and dry whites. Look for Marom late-harvest Merlot 1995.

Cotnari Region at Moldavia's N vineyard limit; warm microclimate and good botrytis. Famous (rarely seen) historical wine: light dessert white from local GRASA, FETEASCA ALBA, TAMAIIOASA, and Francusa. Like v delicate Tokaj.

Crisana W region including historical MiniS area (since 15th C: reds, esp Cadarca, and crisp, white Mustoasa), Silvania (esp FETEASCA), Diosig, Valea lui Mihai.

Dealul Mare "The big hill". Important, up-to-date, well-sited area in SE Carpathian foothills. R's from FETEASCA NEAGRA, CAB, Merlot, PINOT N, etc. W's from TAMIIOASA. French investment. Look for Dionis label (fine reds).

Dobrogea Sunny, dry, Black Sea region. Incl MURFATLAR. Quality is good.

DOC New classification for higher-quality wines replacing VS, VSO.

DOCG (Was VSOC) Top-range wines. CMD: late-harvest, CMI: late-harvest with noble rot, CIB is from selected nobly rotten grapes (like Beerenauslese).

ROMANIA

Drăgășani Region on River Olt S of Carpathian Mountains, since Roman times. Traditional and "modern" grapes (esp Sauvignon Bl). Good MUSKAT-OTTONEL, reds (CABERNET).

Fetească Romanian white grape with spicy, faintly Muscat aroma. Two types: F Alba (same as Hungary's Leányka, age-worthy and with better potential esp when carefully handled; base for sparkling and sweet COTNARI) and F Regala (good for sparkling).

Fetească Neagră Red Fetească. Difficult to handle, but can give deep, full-bodied reds with gd character and ageing potential. "Black maiden grape".

Focsani Important MOLDAVIA region, incl COTESTI, Nicoresti, and ODOBESTI.

Grasă A form of the Hungarian Furmint grape grown in Romania and used in, among other wines, COTNARI. Prone to botrytis. Grasa means "fat".

Iași Region for fresh, acidic whites (F ALBA, also Welschries, ALIGOTE, spumante-style MUSKAT O): Bucium, Copu, Tomesti. Reds: Merlot, CAB; top BABEASCA.

Jidvei Winery in the cool Carpathians (TIRNAVE) among Romania's N-most v'yds. Good whites: FETEASCA, Furmint, RIES, SAUV BL.

Lechinta Transylvanian wine area. Wines noted for bouquet (local grapes).

Merlot Romania's workhorse grape. Most widely planted red grape.

Murfatlar V'yds nr Black Sea, 2nd-best botrytis conditions (see Cotnari): esp sweet CHARD, late-harvest CAB. Now also full, dry wines and sparkling.

Muscat Ottonel The E European Muscat, a speciality of Romania, esp in cool-climate TRANSYLVANIA and dry wines in MOLDAVIA.

Odobesti The central part of FOCSANI; white wines of FETEASCA, RIES, etc.

Panciu Cool MOLDAVIA region N of ODOBESTI. Good still and sparkling white.

Paulis Small estate cellar in town of same name. Oak-aged Merlot a treasure.

Perla Semi-sw speciality of TIRNAVE: Italian RIES, FETEASCA, and MUSKAT-OTTONEL.

Pinot Gris Widely grown in TRANSYLVANIA and MURFATLAR. Full, slightly aromatic wines, closer to Alsace than Italian Pinot Grigio in style.

Pinot Noir Grown in the south: can surprise with taste and character.

Prahova Winecellars Promising British venture (7 wineries in DEALUL MARE) using native and international grapes, incl Sangiovese. Try Pinot N 99.

Premiat Reliable range of higher-quality wines for export.

Riesling (Italian Riesling) Widely planted. Most poorly made, but has potential.

Sauvignon Blanc Often Romania's tastiest white, esp blended with FETEASCA.

Tămîioasă Românească Traditional white grape known as "frankincense" for its exotic scent and flavour. Pungent sw wines often affected by botrytis.

Tîrnave Transylvanian wine region (Romania's coolest), known for its PERLA and much FETEASCA REGALA. Dry and aromatic wines (especially Pinot Gris, Gewürztraminer) and sparkling.

Transylvania High central region. See Alba Iulia, Lechinta, Tîrnave.

Valea Călugărească "Valley of the Monks", part of DEALUL MARE with go-ahead research station. CABERNET, Merlot, & PINOT NOIR are admirable, as are Italian RIESLING & PINOT GRIS.

Vin de Masa Most basic wine classification – for local drinking only.

Vinexport Est 90, fast developing (80% of Romania's wine exports).

Vinterra Dutch/Romanian venture. Best wine is Merlot 99.

Greece

Since Greece's entry into the EC in 81 its antique wine industry has moved into higher gear. Some is still fairly primitive, but a new system of appellations is in place, and recent years have seen an explosion of good wines onto the world market. Modern, well-made but still authentically Greek wines are well worth drinking.

Agiorghitiko Widely planted NEMEA red-wine grape. Very high potential.

Agioritikos Medium whites and rosés from Agios Oros (Mt Athos), Halkidiki's monastic peninsula. Brand name for TSANTALIS.

Antonopoulos ★★→★★★ Highly reputed producer: w MANTINIA, Adoli Ghis, unoaked, nutty Chard, vg Cab S, Cabernet-Nea Dris (**96 97 98 00**). To follow.

Argyros ★★→★★★ Top SANTORINI producer with delicious (and expensive) Vinsanto aged 20 yrs in cask. Current vintages: 83.

Attica Diminishing vineyards around Athens, the chief source of RETSINA.

Boutari, J and Son ★→★★ Merchants in NAOUSSA. Also wineries GOUMENISSA on SANTORINI and CRETE. Broad range from all over Greece. New varietals, w Assyrtiko, MOSCOFILERO, r AGIORGHITIKO, XINOMAVRO.

Calliga ★ Brand name now KOURTAKIS-owned. Good AGIORGHITIKO sourced for Montenero and Rubis.

Cambas, Andrew ★→★★ Brand owned by BOUTARI. Vg value Chard & Cab S.

Carras, Domaine ★★ Estate at Sithonia, Halkidiki with its own AC (Côtes de Meliton). Old Vine Syrah 98. Under new management 2000.

Cava Legal term for cask-aged still w & r wine. Eg Cava BOUTARI (NAOUSSA-NEMEA).

Cephalonia (Kephalonia) Ionian island: good white ROBOLA and Muscat.

Crete Improving quality. Led by Alexakis, Creta-Olympias, Lyrarakis.

Emery ★★ An historic RHODES producer, specializing in local varieties: brand names Villare and GrandRose. Also gd-quality, trad-method sp wine.

Gaia ★★★ Top-quality NEMEA-based producer. Fruity Notios label. New Aghiorghitiko 01. Top wine Gaia Estate (**97 98 99 00**). Also unoaked and oaked Thalassitis from SANTORINI. Astonishing RETSINA Ritinitis Nobilis.

Gentilini ★★→★★★ Upmarket white ROBOLA from CEPHALONIA. "Fumé": oak-aged.

Gerovassiliou ★★★ Perfectionist miniature estate nr Salonika. Rhône-influenced reds, Krima 99, Syrah 00, and whites of unique style, especially fine Viognier.

Goumenissa (AC) ★→★★ Oaked red from W MACEDONIA. Esp BOUTARI, Aïdarini.

Hatzimichalis, Domaine ★ Small estate and merchant in Atalanti. Huge range. Greek and French varieties. Top wine: CAVA; better red than white.

Katogi-Strofilia ★→★★. The result of a merger between Katogi and Strofilia in March '01. Predominantly Greek varieties but Chard and Cab also produced.

Katsaros ★★→★★★ Sml winery of v high standards on Mt Olympus. Organic. Ktima Katsaros cask-aged Cab S, Merlot (97 98 99 00). New Chard.

Kir-Yanni ★★→★★★ V'yards in Naoussa and at Amindeo – high quality. Vibrant w Samaropetra and Chard (01). Gd Syrah (00). Top Naoussa Ramnista (00).

Kouros ★★ Reliable, well-marketed white PATRAS and red NEMEA from KOURTAKIS.

Kourtakis, D ★★ Athenian merchant with mild RETSINA and good, dark NEMEA.

Ktima Estate, farm. Term not exclusive to wine.

Nico Lazaridis ★★ Family estate in Drama, NE of Salonika. Spectacular post-modernist winery. Rich Merlot 00. Top wine: Magico Vouno 98.

Lazaridis, Domaine Kostas ★★→★★★ Not to be confused with NICO LAZARIDIS. High-quality white, rosé, red Amethystos label. Top wine: red CAVA 99.

Lemnos (AC) Aegean island: co-op dessert wines, deliciously fortified Muscat of Alexandria. New, dry Muscats by Kyathos-Honas winery.

Macedonia Quality wine region in the north, for XINOMAVRO.

Malagousia Rediscovered perfumed white grape. Major producers CARRAS, GEROVASSILIOU (new single varietal in 2001 or blended with Assyrtiko), MATSA.

Mantinia (AC) PELOPONNESE region. Fresh, grapey MOSCOFILERO.

Matsa, Château ★★→★★★ Sml ATTICA prod exploiting native Greek varieties. Top wine: SAVATIANO Vieilles Vignes. Also stylish Laoutari & excellent MALAGOUSIA.

Mavrodaphne (AC) "Black laurel", and red grape. Cask-aged port/reciotto-like, concentrated red; fortified to 15–22%. Speciality of PATRAS, N PELOPONNESE.

Mercouri ★★→★★★ PELOPONNESE family estate. V fine Refosco, delicious RODITIS. New CAVA (oo) Classy Refosco dal Penducolo rosso and MAVRODAPHNE blend.

Moscofilero Rose-scented high-quality, high-acid grape.

Naoussa (AC) r High-quality region for XYNOMAVRO. One of the two Greek regions where "cru" notion may soon develop. Excellent vintages include the following: 94, 97, oo.

Nemea (AC) r Region in E PELOPONNESE producing dark, spicy AGIORGHITIKO wines. Often also the backbone of many (not always Greek) blends. High Nemea merits its own appellation. Koutsi front-runner for cru status.

Oenoforos ★★ Good PELOPONNESE producer. Class leading RODITIS Asprolithi white. Elegant Lagorthi. Fresh Chard, subtle Cab.

Oktana ★ Joint venture of ANTONOPOULOS, KATOGI, MERCOURI, and Strofilia. New winery at Asprokambos, high NEMEA. Many styles and cask-aged.

Papaïoannou ★★→★★★ Top NEMEA grower. V classy red, incl Pinot N; flavourful, oaky w. Top wine: Ktima Papaioannou Palea Klimata (old vines) 97 98.

Patras (AC) White wine (based on RODITIS) and wine town facing the Ionian Sea. Home of MAVRODAPHNE.

Pegasus, Château ★→★★ NAOUSSA estate for gd red to age 10 yrs. Organic.

Peloponnese Mountainous southern land mass of mainland Greece, with half of the country's v'yds, incl NEMEA, MANTINIA, and PATRAS.

Rapsani Interesting oaked red from Mt Ossa. Rasping until rescued by TSANTALI.

Retsina ATTICA speciality white: with Aleppo pine resin added; oddly appropriate with certain Greek food. Domestic consumption now waning.

Rhodes Easternmost Greek island. Home to the creamy (dry) ATHIRI white grape. Top wines include Caïr (cooperative) Rodos 2400 and Emery's Villare. Also some sparkling.

Robola Good-quality, lemony white grape, originating from speciality of CEPHALONIA and other Ionian isles.

Roditis White grape grown all over Greece. Good when yields are low.

Samos (AC) Island near Turkey famed for sweet, pale, golden Muscat. Especially (fortified) Anthemis, (sun-dried) Nectar. Rare old bottlings can be outstanding.

Santorini Volcanic island N of CRETE: luscious, sweet Vinsanto (sun-dried grapes), mineral-laden, bone-dry white from fine Assyrtico grape. Oaked examples: gd. Top producers incl: ARGYROS, GAIA ,Sigalas. Hadjidakis new winery.

Savatiano White grape of RETSINA. Often considered dull, but see Ch Matsa.

Semeli, Château ★★ Estate near Athens. Good white and red, incl Cab S.

Skouras ★★ Innovative PELOPONNESE wines. Viognier (Cuvée Eclectic). Best wine: Megas Oenos red (99). New high Nemea, Grande Cuvée 98.

Spiropoulos, Domaine ★★ Organic quality producer in MANTINIA. Improving oaky, red Porfyros (AGIORGHITIKO, Cabernet, Merlot). Sparkling Odi Panos shows potential.

Tsantalis ★→★★ Merchant/producer at Agios Pavlos. Vineyards in NAOUSSA, Maronia, and RAPSANI. Wide range of country and AC wines. New varietal range w Assyrtiko/Sauv Bl, Athiri, r AGIORGHITIKO, Merlot, and Syrah.

Tselepos ★★→★★★ Top-quality MANTINIA producer and Greece's best Gewürz (o1). Fresh, oaky Chard. Solid Nemea (oo). Very good Cab/Merlot (99). Stylish Merlot (oo). Villa Amalia improving Methode Classique sparkling.

Voyatzi Ktima ★★ Small estate nr Kozani. Fat w Malvasia Aromatica and RODITIS. Top red: Ktima Voyatzi (oo) Xynomavro and Cab S blend.

Xynomavro The tastiest of many indigenous Greek red grapes – though name means "acidic-black". Grown in the cooler north, it is the basis for NAOUSSA, GOUMENISSA, and Amindeo. High potential.

Zitsa Mountainous N Epirius AC. Delicate Debina white, still or fizzy.

Cyprus

Cyprus's finest product is the historic sweet Commanderia – a watery version of which is often used as Communion wine. For years "sherry" paid the bills and reds and whites were basic. Now upgrading has started. Soils are predominantly limestone and the vineyards are located in the foothills of the Troodos Mountains at altitudes of between 250 and 1,600 metres. The majority of the island's wine is produced by 4 organizations, all of which have wineries near the coastal ports for convenience in shipping. Until recently, only 2 local grapes were grown; now another 12 have emerged, including the inevitable international favourites. A recent development is the construction of small regional wineries in vineyard areas. Some of these have been built by the 4 main companies, others by new producers. Significantly, Cyprus has never had phylloxera.

Afames Area on the south slopes of Troodos and a dry tangy r (MAVRO) from SODAP (major wine co-op at LIMASSOL).

Arsinoë Dry, delicate, fruity, dry white XYNISTERI from SODAP, named after an unfortunate female turned to stone by Aphrodite.

Commandaria Good-quality, brown, sweet wine since ancient times in hills N of LIMASSOL. Region limited to 14 villages; named after crusading order of knights. Made by solera maturation of sun-dried XYNISTERI and MAVRO grapes. Best (as old as 100 yrs) is superb: incredible sweetness, fragrance, concentration – a jewel to seek out. But most is just good Communion wine.

Emva Brand name of well-made dry, medium, and cream Sherry-style wines.

ETKO One of 4 lgst prods, based in LIMASSOL. 16 diff wines. Best is Ino red, others incl w: Nefel, r: Olympus, Cornaro Carignan, Cornaro Grenache, and Semeli.

Kalo Khorio Principal COMMANDARIA village, growing only XYNISTERI.

KEO Lgst, most go-ahead firm at LIMASSOL, also operates 3 wineries. Range incl Alkion, Aphrodite (dry XYNISTERI w), Bellapais (fizzy, med-dr w & p), Thisbe (med-dr w), Rosella (dr fragrant p), Heritage (rich, oaked dr r from MARATHEFTICO), Othello (solid, dr r, best drunk at 3-4 yrs), Domaine d'Ahera (velvety, dr r). COMMANDARIA St John (sw fortified). Standard KEO Dry White & Dry Red: vg value.

Kokkineli Deep-coloured, semi-sw rosé: the name is related to cochineal.

Laona The largest of the small regional wineries at Arsos, now owned by KEO. Good range, incl an oak-aged red and a fruity dry white.

Limassol Southern wine port. Home to all the large wineries.

Loel One of major prods. Reds incl Orpho Negro, Hermes, whites incl varietal PALOMINO and Ries, also COMMANDARIA Alasia (sweet fortified), and brandies.

Marathasa Region in the Troodos foothills.

Maratheftico Vines of superior quality make concentrated red wine of tannin, colour, close to Cab S; the future grape of Cyprus.

Mavro The black grape of Cyprus. Can produce quality if planted at high altitude; otherwise gives sound, acceptable wines.

Monte Roya Modern regional winery at Chryssoroyiatissa Monastery.

Muscat All major firms produce pleasant, low-price Muscats.

Opthalmo Black grape (red/rosé): lighter, sharper than MAVRO.

Othello A good standard, dry red (MAVRO and OPTHALMO grapes from the PITSILIA region). Solid and satisfying version from KEO. Best drunk at 3–4 yrs.

Palomino Soft dry w (LOEL, SODAP). V drinkable ice-cold. Imported for Sherry-style.

Pitsilia Region S of Mt Olympus. Some of best wines.

Semeli Good traditional red from ETKO. Best at 3–4 years old.

SODAP A co-op winery and one of the four largest producers. Wines incl: w: Arsino, Artemis, Danae; r: Afames, and varietal Carignan and Grenache. Also new range called Island Vines r & w – modern, fresh, inexpensive.

Xynisteri Native aromatic white grape of Cyprus, making delicate & fruity wines.

Asia, North Africa, & the Levant

Algeria As a combined result of Islam and the EC, once-massive vineyards continue to dwindle. Red, white, and esp rosé of some quality and power come from coastal hills of Tlemcen, Mascara (good red and white), Haut-Dahra (strong red, rosé), Zaccar, Tessala, Médéa, and Aïn-Bessem (Bouira esp good). Sidi Brahim: drinkable red brand. These had VDQS status in French-colonial days. Cork also produced.

China In light of the recent WTO agreement, the Chinese wine industry is being inundated with international investment and technology. Not only are new v'yards springing up in the N Central Heartland areas and in the maritime areas of Shandong, but this investment is leading to further improvements in the lesser-known regions. Even the arid areas of the Turpan Depression are being exploited, accounting for almost 20% of all wine produced in China. Cab S and Merlot have recently been introduced in the Shacheng District, north of the Great Wall. There has been a resurgence of winemaking on the banks of the Yellow River in Anhui and Henan Province. Even in Yunan, above Vietnam, and the northeastern areas next to Korea, there are new wine ventures being established. Huadong Premium Chardonnay 1999 (Shandong) won Bronze at the OIV Chardonnay du Monde in Bordeaux, July 2001. Recommended producers incl Huadong (Shandong), Dragon Seal, and Great Wall Torres (Hebei). The Langfang Castel-Changyu Wine Co Ltd (Shandong) is the new joint venture to watch.

India Tiny industry dominated by Ch Indage (70% of national total), SE of Bombay, with international recognition for Chard- & Pinot N-based sparklers: Omar Khayyám, Marquise de Pompadour (sweeter), and Celèbre (vintage). Still wines incl European varietals as well as blends incorporating local varieties. Labels are Chantilli, Soma, Riviera, & Vin Ballet. Grover is the other significant producer, S of Bangalore. Sula, NE of Bombay, is a new entrant.

Japan Japan's wine industry is based in the central Honshu prefecture of Yamanashi (west of Tokyo). Nagano & Yamagata prefectures (north of Tokyo) and the northern island of Hokkaido are the other significant regions. The sentimental favourite of the Japanese is the Koshu grape, upon which the industry was founded. But 80% of the 55,000 acres under vine in Japan is planted with the *V. labrusca* varieties or *V. labrusca*-based hybrids (eg Delaware, Kyoho, Campbell's Early Muscat, & Muscat Bailey A). The grapes are mainly for the table but are used by winemakers. Plantings of Chard, Cab S, Cab F, & Merlot have created a new de luxe market for Japanese wines; quality can be v high, but quantities are tiny (2,500 acres). To compensate for inappropriate varieties, tricky conditions and high costs, concentrates, must (even grapes), & bulk wine are imported and used for fermenting or blending locally. Labelling laws have permitted a small amount of genuine domestic wine to go a long way. Low-priced "domestic" wine has predominantly imported content; even premium wines receive a boost. Five drinks giants account for two-thirds total production: Mercian, Suntory, Sapporo (Polaire), Manns, and Kyowa Hakko Kogyo (Ste-Neige). The most interesting (and expensive) of their wines are Mercian's Kikyogahara Merlot and Jyonohira Cab of real density and quality. Smaller operations making leading examples of Koshu and/or classic European varieties include Ch Lumière, Marufuji, Grace, Kizan, Katsunuma Jozo, Alps, Takeda, Okuizumo, and Kobe Wines. Tokachi Winery does interesting things with wild vines native to Hokkaido.

Malta Look out for genuine Maltese wines produced under the Meridiana & Marnisi labels. The pioneer, Meridiana has Antinori support in making gd Isis Chard, Melqart Cab-Merlot, Nexus Merlot, a dense, oaky "Bel" Syrah, & premium Celsius Cab Res. Other wines may be made from imported grapes.

Morocco North Africa's best wine is produced from vineyards along the Atlantic coast (Rabat to Casablanca, light, fruity with a white – "Gris" – made from red grapes) and around Meknes and Fez (best-known). Vineyards have declined from 190,000 to 35,000 acres but big investment from French companies such as W'm Pitters & Castel is transforming the industry. Celliers de Meknes is the local leader but has now been joined by Cépages de Meknes, Cépages de Boulaouane, and SADAY in producing quality wines. Look for L'Excellence de Bonassia (aged Cabernet-Merlot blend), Domaine de Sahari, or good-value Atlas Vineyards, and El Baraka.

Tunisia Now has 37,000 vineyard acres (there were 120,000 15 yrs ago). The speciality was sweet Muscats and light rosés. Some drinkable reds are now being produced. Coolest v'yds are on the coast. Selian is one to watch and Accademia del Sole, with investment from Sicily and an Aussie winemaker, is making the best wine.

Turkey Most of Turkey's 1.5 million acres of v'yds produce table grapes; only 3% are for wine. Wines from Thrace, Anatolia, and the Aegean can be v drinkable. Many indigenous varieties: 60 are commercial – eg Emir, Narince (w) and Bogazkere, Oküzgözü (r), and used with Riesling, Sém, Pinot N, Grenache, Carignan, and Gamay. Trakya (Thrace) white (light Sém) and Buzbag (E Anatolian) red are well-known standards of state producer Tekel (21 state wineries). Diren, Doluca, Karmen, Kavaklidere, Taskobirlik are private firms; fair quality. Doluca's Villa Nevar from Thrace is well-made, as is Villa Doluca. Kavaklidere makes gd Primeurs (white Cankaya, red Yakut) from local grapes. Buzbag is Turkey's most original and striking wine.

The Old Russian Empire

The 12 CIS (Commonwealth of Independent States) countries of the former USSR now produce a total of only 3% of the world's wine. Improvements since the 1991 revolution are slow but some producers are producing interesting wines.

Ukraine (incl Crimea) 2nd-lgst wine-producing country in the CIS. Crimea's first-class dessert & fortified wines were revealed in 90 by the auction of old wines from the last Tsar's Massandra Collection, nr Yalta, where production continues today. Alupka fortified classic sp from Novy Svet & Grand Duchess (from Odessa Winery, founded 1896 by H Roederer). Reds: potential (eg Alushta). Whites: Aligoté & Artmovskoe sp (Romanian grapes). To watch.

Georgia Possibly the oldest wine region of all. Antique methods such as fermentation in clay vats (kveris) still exist. Newer techniques used for exports (Mukuzani, Tsinandali); Reluctant to modernize. Kakheti (E): produces two-thirds of Georgia's wine, famed for big red (Saperavi), acceptable white (Tibaani, Rkatsiteli, Telavi). Kartli: central area. Cheap, drinkable sp attracts investment from foreign companies. As equipment, technique, and attitudes evolve, Georgia could be an export hit.

Moldova The most important in size and potential. Wine generates a 3rd of Moldova's income. Wine regions are: Bugeac (most important, S), Nistrean, Codrean, Northern. Grapes incl Cab, Pinot Noir, Merlot, Saperavi (fruity), Ries, Chard, Pinot Gr, Aligoté, Rkatsiteli. A full range of wine styles is made. A startling glimpse of potential was seen in 92 with the release of 63 Negru de Purkar. Top wineries: Purkar, Cahul, Kazayak, Hincesti; also good: Cricova. Western and Antipodean (Penfolds since 1993) investment at Hincesti, and more recently by local company Vininvest, has brought modern, hygienic winemaking practices. Moldova's most modern-tasting wine: Ryman's Hincesti Chard is very good. Most wineries (127) are now privatised; progress has not been smooth, but worth following. Appellations are now in force. Cricova's cellars are an impressive tourist attraction with some 120 km of tunnels).

Russia Wine culture: never strong. Main region: Northern Black Sea coastal region of Krasnodar, produces 80% of Russia's wine. Sw wines prevail, dry growing fast. Fair Cab, Merlot, Ries, & Rkatsiteli (Anapa, & Temruk) & sw sparkling Tsimlanskoye Shampanskoe (Rostov). Abrau Durso brut (speciality): since 1870 classic sp (Aligoté, Chard, Cab F); Champagne-like climate; Muscats. Top prod: Fanagoria (North Black Sea): Merlot, Cab, Ries, Chard.

The Levant

Israel Edmond de Rothschild re-established the modern wine industry in the 1880s but for many years, Israeli wineries produced unsophisticated wines. Recently, with plantings of classic varieties in cool, high-altitude regions such as Upper Galilee and Golan Heights (1,200m) a wine revolution took root. Continued investment in modern technology and internationally trained winemakers have had dramatic effects.

Amphorae r w New but exciting boutique winery. V promising Chard & Cab S.

Barkan r w Israel's 2nd-lgst winery, with new v'yds in Negev Desert. Gd Cab S.

Binyamina r w Reasonable reds aged in American oak, aromatic Muscat.

Carmel r w sp Lgst producer, wineries in Zichron Yaacov, Rishon LeZion, & Ramat Arad. Top wines: Private Collection Cab S "V'yds Selected" wines gd value.

Castel Judean Hills r (w) ★★ Small family estate producing elegant, subtle Cab-Merlot (**96** 97 98). 2nd label Petit Castel; classic, well-made Chard.

Dalton Upper Galilee r w Grassy Sauv Bl & increasingly gd Merlot and Cab S.

Flam r Young boutique winery. Promising Cabernet S and Merlot.

Galil Mountain Upper Galilee r w Joint venture between Kibbutz Yiron and Golan Heights Winery. V'yds on Lebanon border.

Margalit r ★ Boutique w'ry. Full-b'd Cab (**93** 95 99); intense Mer & rare Carignan.

Recanati r w New winery producing Cabernet S, Merlot, and Chard.

Soreq Tal Shahar Vineyard r Small estate. Recent Cabernets showing quality.

Tishbi Estate r w sp Family grower. Oaky Chard and improving Merlot.

Tzora r w Kibbutz winery. Distinctive Mediterranean wines. Cab S & Sauv Bl best.

Yarden Golan Heights r w sp ★★ Leader in Israel's "wine awakening". Multi-layered, oaky Cab S (**85 90** 93 97); complex Merlot (**93** 97); quality Pinot Noir (99), barrel-ferm Chard. Better special res Katzrin Cab S-Merlot-Cab F (**90** 93 96). 2nd label Gamla – gd value.

Lebanon The small wine industry (7,500 acres) is based in Beka'a Valley, E of Beirut. The older wineries are heroic survivors of the civil war. There are some quality reds – made with French influence.

Ch Musar r (w) ★★★ Splendid and unique Cab S with Cinsault, has recently tasted stretched, even volatile: (**86 88** 91 93 94 95). Should Improve with age. Lighter r Hochar Père et Fils (Cinsault and Cab). Also full-bodied, oaky white from indigenous grape, Obaideh.

Clos St Thomas r (w) Small winery. Ch St Thomas is soft, fruity, rounded red.

Kefraya r w ★★ Fragrant Ch Kefraya Comte de M, (**96** 97) – blend of Cab S, Mourvèdre, & Syrah. Also fresh rosé and luscious dessert, Lacrima d'Oro.

Ksara r w Est 1857 by Jesuits. Now modernizing. Château Ksara (**97** 98) – spicy, aromatic Cab S, Reserve du Couvent – fruity red, gd value. Clean Chard.

Massaya r w French-Lebanese collaboration. As yet, promise unfulfilled.

Wardy r w Promising winery. Gd Chard & Sauv Bl. Red label Ch les Cedres.

England & Wales

Over two million bottles a year are now being made here from over 300 vineyards (2,000 acres). Although most are white and made from fruity German crosses, a number of interesting reds come from Pinot Noir and Dornfelder, as well as from a new variety, Rondo. Bottle-fermented sparkling wines are also proving to be one of England's great successes, made of Chardonnay and Pinot Noir and closely modelled on Champagne. Since 1994, an EU-approved "Quality Wine Scheme" has been run by the UK Vineyards Association. Unfortunately, it is only open to vinifera varieties so growers of the (v worthy) Seyval Blanc (and other hybrids) may not apply. NB: Beware "British Wine" – neither British, nor indeed wine, and has nothing to do with the following.

Recent Vintages

2001 Warmest year on record with quality wines made in many wineries. Bacchus wines are very spicy. Reds are good and will keep.

2000 Cool year with a wet harvest. Whites better than reds. Sp wines should be good. The best will keep, but many should be drunk within 2 yrs.

1999 Average yields and a warm summer helped most winemakers produce interesting wines, esp with varieties such as Bacchus and Seyval Bl.

1998 Overall, a warm year with a fine autumn. The west fared better than the east, where early frosts did some damage. Sp wines should be good.

1997 A very hard frost in early May reduced yields in almost all vineyards and the national crop was small. Fruity varieties such as Bacchus did well.

Adgestone nr Sandown (Isle of Wight) 8-acre v'yd on chalky hill site. Est'd 68. New owners; new winemaker.

Astley Stourport-on-Severn (Worcestershire) 99 00 ★★ 5 acres; some fair wines. Madeleine Angevine, Kerner, and Huxelvaner are prizewinning.

Barnsole (Kent) 98 ★★ 3.4 acres planted 1993 and now producing good range of wines. Consistently awarded Quality and Regional Wine status.

Battle Wine Estate Battle (East Sussex) ★★ 33-acres; New Zealand-trained winemaker. Wines of consistent quality.

Bearsted Maidstone (Kent) 98 ★★ 4-acres est'd 86. Gd Bacchus and gd sp.

Beaulieu Abbey Brockenhurst (Hampshire) 00 ★ 1.5-acre v'yd, established 58 by Gore-Browne family on old monastic site. Gd rosé and sp.

Beenleigh Manor Totnes (Devon) 00 ★★★ ⅓ acre of vines grown under polythene tunnels. Award-winning oak-aged Cab/Merlot in tiny quantities.

Biddenden nr Tenterden (Kent) ★★ 20-acre v'yd planted 72: Ortega and Dornfelder worth trying. Sparkling also very good.

Bookers Bolney (W Sussex) 6-acres of Müller-T and others. Wines improving.

Bothy Abingdon (Oxfordshire) 2.6-acres. Good range of well-made wines, esp Ortega-Optima. Sparkling well-thought-of and sweet wines winning awards.

Boze Down Whitchurch-on-Thames (Oxfordshire) ★★ 5.4-acres. Wide range of high-quality wines. Reds worth trying. Good website.

Breaky Bottom Lewes (E Sussex) 96 ★★ 5.5-acre v'yd with cult following. Good, dry wines, esp Seyval Bl and 96 sparkling: gd and getting better.

Bruisyard Saxmundham (Suffolk) 10 acres Müller-Thurgau. Est'd 74: oaked and sparkling worth trying. Winery and herb garden for visitors.

Camel Valley Bodmin (Cornwall) 99 00 ★★ 4.4-acre v'yd; gd quality, esp. Cornwall Brut 99 and Rosé sparkling 99.

Carr Taylor Hastings (E Sussex) 21 acres, est'd 73. Sparkling wines good. Now part of English Wines plc, which incl CHAPEL DOWN & LAMBERHURST.

Carters Colchester (Essex) ★★ 4.2-acres. Dornfelder red won East Anglian trophy in 98. Also gd sp and vg Bacchus. 1998 won East Anglia "Wine of the Year".

Chapel Down Tenterden (Kent) 99 00 ★★★★ Largest UK producer. Epoch Brut sp, Epoch red, Bacchus, Downland Oak best wines. British Airways, House of Commons, & major multiples supplied. Home to English Wines plc which incl LAMBERHURST & CARR TAYLOR.

Chiddingstone Edenbridge (Kent) ★ 36-acre v'yd; stress on dry wines, esp barrel-aged. Good Pinot Blanc de Noir. Chasselas worth trying.

Chilford Hall (Cambs) 98 99 ★ 18 acres est in 72. Wide range of dry wines .

Chiltern Valley Henley (Oxfordshire) 1 acre of vineyards high up on chalk plus grapes from local v'yds. Wines incl Old Luxters Dry Reserve. Good sp.

Danebury Stockbridge (Hants) 5.3 acres: Auxerrois, Bacchus, etc. Improving. Gd sp.

Davenport Rotherfield (E Sussex) 98 99 ★★ Young winery: serious wines. Aus-trained winemaker. Started to win awards. Going organic. Sp coming on.

Denbies Dorking (Surrey) 99 00 ★★★ 261-acre v'yd (England's lgst). Impressive winery: worth a visit. Vg Riesling. Reds and sw improving.

Eglantine Loughboro' (Leics) 3.3 acres, many varieties. Mad Sylv sw wins medals.

English Wine Centre, Alfriston, (East Sussex). No v'yd, but stocks wide range.

Frithsden Hemel Hempstead (Herts) 2-acre v'yd: Ortega & Kerner worth trying.

Frome Valley Vineyard Bishops Frome (Herefordshire) ★ 2.5 acres. Award-winning, well-presented wines made at THREE CHOIRS. Good visitor facilities.

Gifford's Hall Bury St-Edmunds (Suffolk) 9-acre-vineyard for interesting wines (incl oak-aged) and visitor facilities.

Glyndwr Vineyard Llanblethain (Wales) 3.4 acres with v mild conditions nr to sea. Made at THREE CHOIRS. Notable sp & reds. Oldest commercial Welsh v'yd.

Great Stocks Billericay (Essex) ★ 6.5-acre v'yd with interesting wines, esp 95 Symphony blend and oak-aged Orion. Wines made at DAVENPORT.

Hale Valley Wendover (Bucks) 1.5 acre v'yd: wines of interest. One to watch.

Halfpenny Green (Staffordshire) 15-acres; esp gd Madeleine Angevine and sp.

Harden Farm (Kent) 12 acres. Bacchus & Schönburger gd; supplier to CHAPEL DOWN.

Harling Norwich (Norfolk) 6.5-acres Müller-T and Bacchus. Under new ownership. Wines made at SHAWSGATE.

Hendred (Berkshire) 6-acres planted in 71. Interesting Seyval and Mad. Angevine.

Hidden Spring Horsham (E Sussex) ★★ 7.5-acres. Wines consistently gd, esp Sunset Rosé. Wines made at VALLEY.

Horton Estate (Dorset) 9 acres. Bacchus, Reichensteiner, & reds. Shows promise.

Ickworth (Suffolk) 99 00 2 acres. Starting to win awards and be noticed.

La Mare Jersey (Channel Isl) Wines fair but improving; continued investment.

Lamberhurst (Kent) ★ 26-acres. Changed hands in 2000 and now part of English Wines plc. All wines made at CHAPEL DOWN.

Leeds Castle Maidstone (Kent) ★ Long-est'd 3.25 acres of vines. Müller-T and Seyval Blanc. Wines sold only at Castle outlets. Made at TENTERDEN. Winner of Laughton Trophy with 1998 Seyval.

Leventhorpe (Yorkshire) Most northerly commercial v'yd. 5.5-acres, planted 86 and doing well with Mad Angevine, Mad Sylvaner, and Seyval Bl.

Llanerch S Glamorgan (Wales) ★ 5.5-acres, est'd '86. Wines sold under "Cariad label". Individual style developing, worth its awards. Good p and sp.

Meopham Valley (Kent) 99 4.75 acres, established 1991. Starting to make interesting wines, especially Pinot Gris.

Mersea Vineyard East Mersea (Essex) ★★ 6.6 acres. Est'd 85, south-facing v'yd on scenic island. Consistently gd wines. Made at CHAPEL DOWN & VALLEY.

Moorlynch Bridgewater (Somerset) 3.7-acres. Gd wines, Res 97 & pink sp.

New Hall nr Maldon (Essex) 90⁺ acres on mixed farm. Vg Bacchus 00. Grape supplier to other wineries, incl CHAPEL DOWN, THREE CHOIRS, & VALLEY

Northbrook Springs Bishops Waltham (Hampshire) ★★ 13 acres. Improving wines winning medals. Sp showing well. Supports Quality Wine scheme.

Nutbourne Pulborough (W Sussex) ★★ 00 15-acres. Medal-winning Sussex Reserve in 2000.

Nyetimber W Chiltington (W Sussex) ★★★★ 39-acres, planted 88: Chard, Pinots N, & Meunier for classic sp. 94 Cuvée Aurora won Gore-Browne Trophy '01. Excellent quality with gd bottle-age. The way forward for English sparklers.

Penshurst Tunbridge Wells (Kent) 12 acres, since 72, incl good Seyval Bl and Müller-T. Fine, modern winery.

Plumpton College Lewes (E Sussex) Experimental vineyard attached to college running courses on viticulture and winemaking. Sm winery; wines improving.

Priors Dean Alton (Hampshire) 0.9 acre. Made at VALLEY.

Ridge View Ditchling Common (E Sussex) ★★★ 16-acre v'yd planted 95: Chard, Pinots N & Meunier for quality sp. Cuvée Merret Bloomsbury 97 and NV Fitzrovia Rosé are very good. Setting standards in UK sp-wine production.

Rosemary (Isle of Wight) 28 acres, IOW's lgst v'yd. Variable quality, slow to improve.

St Augustine's Aust (Gloucs) ★ Gd Mad Angevine. Wine made at THREE CHOIRS.

Sandhurst Cranbrook (Kent) ★★ 13.6 acres. High-quality Bacchus, red and sw wines. Wines made at TENTERDEN. Major grape supplier to CHAPEL DOWN.

Seddlescombe Organic Robertsbridge (East Sussex) 8 acres; UK's main organic v'yd. Range of wines with quite a following. Some of interest.

Sharpham Totnes (Devon) 99 00 ★★★ 9.8 acres. Award-winning v'yd produces consistently gd wines. 99 Barrel-fermented & 2000 Estate Selection winners.

Shawsgate Framlingham (Suffolk) ★★★ 12.5 acres: under new ownership (2000). Bacchus 2000 won Jack Ward Trophy.

Standen E Grinstead (W Sussex) 2.5 acres. Shows promise. Will specialize in sp.

Sugar Loaf (Wales) ★ 4 acres. Wines made at THREE CHOIRS. Award-winner.

Tenterden (Kent) ★★★ 18.5 acres, est'd 77. Consistently good including Estate Dry & Cinque Ports Classic. Part of English Wines plc & home to CHAPEL DOWN.

Three Choirs (Glos) 99 00 ★★★ 74 acres, est'd 74. Estate Reserve Bacchus, Phoenix, and Siegerrebe are vg. English Nouveau is v popular and sparkling is vg. UK's 2ⁿᵈ-lgst producer.

Tiltridge Upton-upon-Severn (Worcestershire) 99 Small, 1-acre v'yd with good local following. Wines of interest. Elgar Dry sparkling very good.

Titchfield Titchfield (Hampshire) 1.25-acre v'yd planted 88. Good-quality wines made at THREE CHOIRS.

Valley Twyford (Berks) 98 99 00 ★★★★ 20-acre v'yard: UK's most successful producer with serious range of quality wines. Oak-aged Fumé, Clocktower Pinot N, Ascot sp worth trying. Makes for a large number of other v'y'ds.

Warden Abbey (Bedfordshire) 99 ★★ 5.6 acres planted in 86. Wines well made and regularly win prizes. Warden V'yd and sp wines recommended.

Wickham Shedfield (Hampshire) 99 00 ★★ 18-acre v'yd since 84. Wines consistent, esp Vintage Selection 99 and Fumé 00. New owners in 00.

Wooldings Whitchurch (Hampshire) 00 ★ 12-acre vineyard. Wide range of wines available. Quality fair to good.

Worthenbury Wrexham (Wales) 00 0.6 acres of Pinot Noir, Chardonnay, and Sauvignon Blanc produced under polythene.

Wroxeter Roman Shrewsbury (Shropshire) 6-acre vineyard planned on site of Roman town. Wines improving in quality.

Wylye Valley Warminster (Wilts) ★ 8.8 acres planted 89. Wines winning awards.

Wyken Bury-St-Edmunds (Suffolk) 99 5-acre v'yd planted 88. 92 Auxerrois, Bacchus, and Kernling are good. Award-winning restaurant.

North America

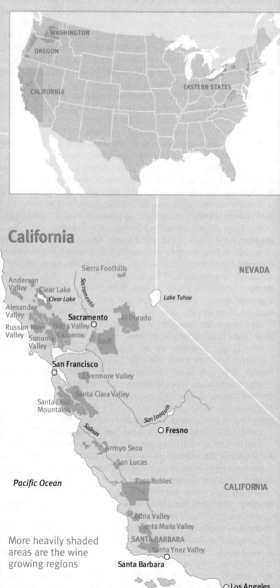

California

More heavily shaded areas are the wine growing regions

Although whipped to and fro by fashion and neo-prohibitionism, the North American wine market has recently enjoyed an unprecedented ten years of steady expansion. Gains in per capita consumption have been modest, but the increase in per capita spending has been significant. New plantings have made the US into the world's fourth largest wine producer; while population growth has made it the world's fourth largest wine consumer. Whether or not these trends can continue is a subject for debate. The effect of the World Trade Center terrorist attack in September 2001 was not a disruption in wine sales, but rather a noticeable shift from restaurant sales to retail stores.

Internet wine marketing has been an equally vexing question in America. From 2000 to 2001 the financial wind went out of the sails of many dot.com ventures. Prior to that they had been mounting a serious political challenge to the anachronistic laws in many American states concerning the sale of wine across state lines. Direct shipment from producer to consumer across state lines is illegal in two-thirds of the states and all the provinces of Canada. Entrenched distributors have always lobbied to keep things that way, while small wineries and hobbyist connoisseurs have always agitated for change. E-commerce may yet carry the day, but the downturn in the fortunes of the technology market has diverted attention away from this issue.

California remains a bastion of strong, fruit-driven, intensely ripe wines destined to carry large amounts of hearty new oak. More attention is paid today to subtle nuances than would have been the case 20 years ago, but the New World style is well represented throughout California. Advances have been very rapid for Syrah and Cabernet Franc. Sangiovese, Pinot Gris, Viognier, Marsanne, and Rousanne are also seeing interest. A veritable boom currently exists for red Zinfandel, with bottle prices routinely in the £$20–40 range.

Appellations (AVAs) are now a fact of life, with more than 120 registered and more on the way. The first stirrings of serious meaning are with us (eg Russian River Valley & Santa Maria Valley Pinot Noirs), but it is still much too soon to use AVAs as a general guide to style. Below are the most commonly mentioned regions. Grapes & makers' names, though, remain key.

The principal California vineyard areas

Central Coast

San Francisco Bay S to Santa Barbara, scattered with increasing wine activity.

Arroyo Grande & Edna Valley The largely maritime districts west of coastal mountains in San Luis Obispo County. Best known for lemony Chardonnay that matures elegantly. Also hosts CA's best Viognier and Pinot Bl.

Carmel Valley Coastal AVA Monterey County. Small production, better known for golf courses than wine. Some wonderful red MERITAGE.

Paso Robles Large, productive district East of coastal range in San Luis Obispo County. Long known for Zinfandel. Inexpensive land converted from alfalfa farms, attracting many major players. Soft Cab S, Syrah: mainstays.

Salinas Valley 100-mile-long flat farming district, too cold for grapes at N on Monterey Bay, but hosts world's largest contiguous v'yd (San Bernabe) at S end. Fine, pineapple-scented CHARD; good nectarine-scented Riesling.

San Benito County Hot, rural county E of Monterey, inland of Gabilan Mountains.

Santa Barbara County Lgst, prestigious district 3 hrs drive from Los Angeles. Many celebrity owners. Lush, layered Pinot N and Chard; superb SYRAH in warmer E canyons; distinctive Sauv Bl, Ries in foggy west. Incl Sta Maria & Sta Ynez AVAs.

South Coast

Los Angeles Megalopolis has a few hobbyist v'yds incl Malibu Canyon AVA, as well as 800 historic acres in Cucamonga AVA, with fine Grenache.

Temecula (Rancho California) In S California, 25 miles inland, halfway between San Diego and Riverside. Mainly whites. 2,000 acres of vines.

Ventura River watershed; productive agricultural district, with a few v'yds.

North Coast

Encompasses Lake, Mendocino, Napa, & Sonoma counties, all N of San Francisco.

Anderson Valley Cool coastal valley in Mendocino County makes America's best sparklers, excellent Gewürz, and rapidly improving PINOT N.

Lake County & Inland Mendocino County Warm to hot districts around Ukiah and SW shore of Clear Lake do very well with Zinfandel, Rhône varietals, Sauv Bl. Italian varieties advancing fast. Full-bodied Cab.

Napa Valley Best-known wine district just N of San Francisco Bay. With its relatively small size and large number of wineries (about 30% of those in CA), Napa's v'yd land has become more expensive than any outside Europe. Great diversity of soil, climate and topography in such a small area can produce a wide range of wines (esp Cab, Merlot, Sauv Bl) very well. A dozen AVAs incl, for example Oakville, Rutherford, Stags Leap, Mt Vedeer, and Carneros at the south end on the Bay (for Chard and Pinot N). Total nearly 40,000 acres. Rapidly developing into international gourmet destination with prices to match.

Northern Sonoma Warm districts (Alexander Valley, Dry Creek, Knights Valley) and cool ones such as Russian River. Healdsburg is the nexus for wine culture. Great Pinot N, Chard all along River Road & Westside Road from Healdsburg almost to Pacific Ocean. Superb Zin in Dry Creek. Lush, accessible Cab S from Alex. Valley.

Sonoma Valley & Carneros Separated from Napa Valley by 2,400 ft Mayacamus mountains. Carneros AVA at S end, bordering San Francisco Bay, is shared by both valleys, and coolest part of either, specialising in sp, Pinot N, Chard. Sonoma town square still feels rural. Sonoma has more v'yd acres than Napa.

Bay Area

Contra Costa County Historic growing district on N slope of Mt Diablo now succumbing to homes. Remaining old vines make fine Zins, red Rhônes.

Livermore Gravel soil on E of mountains defining San Francisco Bay. Urban pressure being relieved by creative planning. CA's best Semillon.

Santa Clara Valley Broad valley south of the Bay, once major wine district, now called Silicon Valley. Remnant areas like Hecker Pass can surprise today.

Santa Cruz Mountains Steep slopes separating S Bay from Pacific Ocean. Room for few v'yds but several top-class wineries (eg Ridge). Cold on the ocean side.

Central Valley

Lodi & The Delta Hydrological centre, from Sacramento to Stockton, is cooler than either the Northern or Southern halves of Central Valley. Clarkesburg in W does Ca's best Chenin; Lodi (E) backs on to Sierras with dense ZIN.

Sacramento Valley N half of Ca's agricultural centrepiece makes affordable Rhône varietals from the Dunnigan Hills AVA.

San Joaquin Valley Fertile and hot, the source of most of the jug, bag-in-a-box, and fortified dessert wines from the state. 200,000+ acresz.

Sierra Foothills

Amador County Warm region famous for old ZIN vineyards producing jammy, intense wines with a signature metallic backnote. Top Rhône reds and Italian varietals are beginning to see good experimental results.

Calaveras County Southernmost of the premium Sierra Foothills districts and gateway to spectacular Yosemite National Park. Good CAB FR.

El Dorado County Cutting edge of high elevation viticulture in Ca with several vineyards at 3,000 ft. Two districts: one around Placerville has four of Ca's best wineries; second called Fairplay is charmingly eccentric.

Recent vintages

California's climate is not as consistent as its "land of sunshine" reputation suggests. Although grapes ripen regularly, they are often subject to spring frosts, sometimes a wet harvest-time and (too often) drought.

Wines from the San Joaquin Valley tend to be most consistent year by year. The vintage date on these, where there is one, is more important for telling the age of the wine than its character.

Vineyards in the Central Coast region have a different pattern of vintage quality from those in the North Coast or Sierra Foothills. Rain arrives later, rarely before mid December, and is much less of a factor. The Central Coast vineyards, also have much cooler maritime mesoclimates. Grapes ripen more slowly and are harvested 3-6 weeks later than inland North Coast regions such as Napa. That said, the following vintage assessment relies most heavily on evaluation of Cabernets and Zinfandels from North Coast regions:

2001 Little winter rain, sporadic heat in March, severe April frost, hottest May on record, and no rain until October. Early signs imply excellent quality, although could be inconsistent because everything ripened at once.

2000 Scares included an earthquake in Napa and a threatened storm from the south in early September, but neither caused any damage. Biggest harvest on record primarily due to new acreage. Good quality.

1999 Very cold spring and summer created v late harvest, but absense of fall rain left crop unscathed. High natural acids and a hot Oct made for intensely flavoured and coloured wines. Crop size off by 10-40%. Outstanding quality.

1998 Erratic harvest stumbled into November. Wines are adequate to dismal.

1997 Huge crop, strongly flavoured reds with lots of extract. Esp enjoyable for youthful exuberance. Significantly better than preceding or succeeding yrs.

1996 Tiny crop, with lots of structure, but lacks aromatic charm. Needs age.

1995 Tiny crop, great vitality but slow to unfold. Good Zins, great Cabs. Best vintage for cellaring since 90.

1994 Mild growing season and dry, late harvest. Superb Zins; Cabs are supple, wonderful for drinking right now.

1993 Modest, plain-faced, serviceable year in the North Coast, but spectacular in the Sierra Foothills with conc'd Zins and refreshing acidity. Drink up.

1992 Oddly inconsistent. Some empty. Some flavourful and vital.

1991 Very late harvest; v large crop: 30-50% bigger than normal and twice the size of tiny '90. Wines are lean, racy, most European styled in years. Took a long time to develop in bottle.

1990 Picture-perfect California vintage and a small crop: wonderful development and strong collectors' value. Cabs magnificent at present.

1989 Rainy harvest gave North Coast winemakers fits. Much derided in the press, which in turn created many bargains because the Cab.s were not really so bad in many instances. Nevertheless, now fading.

1988 Bland, lacking focus and structure.

1987 First year of a long drought. Cabernets and Zins very dark and extracted. Hard and uncompromising for a decade, they have now emerged to show some grace alongside the power. Best will last another five years.

1986 Standard, average wines without great risk or reward.

1985 V cool vintage created a steel rod in the backbone. Bouquet development and balance make them very reliable today.

1984 Warm year. Showy early. In dotage now.

1983 Warm year with El Niño rains at harvest. Never was much good.

1982 Cool year with El Niño rain at harvest. Risky today

1981 Even the best from a hot harvest are well on the down-slope.

1980 V cool growing season with a severe heat wave at harvest. Big wineries had trouble. Little wineries can often surprise today.

California wineries

Acacia Napa ★★★ (Chard) 96 97 98 99 (Pinot N) **91 92 93** 94 95 **96** 97 98 99 Long-time specialist in durable, deep CARNEROS Chard & Pinot returning to single v'yd wines after a phylloxera-induced interlude of extra-oaky Reserves.

Ahlgren Santa Cruz Mtns ★★★ Excellent Chard from VENTANA v'yd in Monterey Cty and noteworthy Cabs from Besson v'yd in Gilroy and Bates Ranch in SANTA CRUZ MTNS.

Alban Edna Valley ★★★ Pioneer planter of Rhône varieties, and benchmark for Viognier, in California. Estate model crisper than Central Coast version. Small quantities of excellent Grenache. Reva Syrah one of CA's best over last 4 yrs.

Alderbrook Sonoma ★★ Winemakers have been playing musical chairs at this winery but new-in-'94 owner resolutely pursuing accessible styles in esp Chard, Syrah, Zin.

Alexander Valley Vineyards Sonoma ★★ Cabernet S most likely of 6 wines to live up to promise of fine vineyard. Whites quirky at best.

Anapamu and Rancho Zabaco ★★ Parts of the large Gallo operation made in Dry Creek. Anapamu is good Chardonnay sourced near Monterey; Rancho Zabaco is good. Zinfandel sourced in Mendocino.

Andrew Murray Sta Barbara ★★ 95 97 98 Sml winery. Vineyards planted on slopes thus reducing yields. Good Syrah, great Roussanne.

Araujo Napa ★★★★ Eisele v'yd, now an estate, its Cabernet as dark and tannic as when JOE PHELPS made it famous.

Arrowood Sonoma ★★→★★★★ (Chard) 97 98 99 (Cab) 85 87 90 91 **92** 94 95 96 97 98 Long-time CHATEAU ST JEAN winemaker Dick A on peak form with supple, age-worthy Cab S. Chard (esp Res) for oak-lovers. Sold to Mondavi '00.

Artesa Napa ★ Still wines made at the fabulously beautiful facility owned by, and formerly called, Cordorniu.

Artisans and Estates Collection of wineries & vineyards owned by Jess Jackson, of KENDALL-JACKSON fame. Each has its own winemaker, and expansion through acquisition since 1988 has been meteoric. Highest end of the stable incl: HARTFORD COURT, Alexander Mtn Estates, MATANZAS CREEK, and Stonestreet (SON), Kristone and CAMBRIA (ST BARB), CARDINALE and Lokoya (NAPA). Mid-range includes La Crema, Edmeades, Robt Pepi, Bailey & Brock. Also has properties in Italy and Chile as well as its own cooperage in France. No end appears to be in sight.

Atlas Peak Napa ★★ Allied-Domecq owned winery to seek for Sangiovese and Sangio-Cab Consenso from Antinori-owned v'yds in east hills.

Au Bon Climat Sta Barbara ★★★ (Chard) **93 94 95** **96** 97 98 99 (Pinot N) **90 93** 94 **95** 96 97 Jim Clendenen listens to his private drummer: ultra-toasty Chard, flavourful Pinot N, light-hearted Pinot Bl. Vita Nova label for Bordeaux varieties, Podere dellos Olivos for Italianates. Sold also on Qupé.

Babcock Vineyards Santa Barbara ★★★ Very cool location in western SANTA YNEZ VALLEY. Strong reputation for Pinot N and Chard; "Eleven Oaks" Sauv Bl is one of CA's better examples. New entry into Syrah is impressive.

Barnett Napa ★★ Intriguing Cabs from tiny estate high on Spring Mtn.

Barnwood Sta Barbara ★★ 98 Located in the remote NW corner of the county, but has purchased LAETITIA for presence on the coast. Good value Cab.

Beaucanon Napa ★★ B'dx owner Lebègue turning out consistently supple stylish Cab S, Merlot, & improving Chard from own 250 acres. La Crosse is 2nd label.

Beaulieu Vineyard Napa ★★→★★★★ (Cab) **58 65 73 78 85 90 91** 95 96 UDV's crown jewel is, rightly, best known for ageable, American-oaked Georges de Latour Private Reserve Cabernet Sauvignon. CARNEROS Chardonnay worth a look. Commodity line is Beautour, experimental one Signet.

Belvedere Sonoma ★★ William Hambrecht uses mostly his own grapes for Alexander Valley Cab S, Dry Creek Valley Zin, Russian River Chard.

Benessere Napa ★★ One of top five Sangiovese from CA.

Benziger Family Winery Sonoma ★★ Called Benziger of Glen Ellen until Proprietors Reserve sold to UDV (then Heublein). Now all SONOMA grapes and dotty for oak across whole range.

Beringer-Blass Napa ★★→★★★ (Chard) **97 98 99** (Cab S) **80 87 90 91** 92 94 95 96 97 98 99 Acquired in 2000 by Australia's Mildara-Blass (Fosters), this century-old winery pursues larger-than-life style from top of line (Reserve, single v'yd Cabs) to recently introduced commodity range called Beringer Founder's Estate (originally named Hudson Estate). Also owns CHATEAU ST-JEAN, CHATEAU SOUVERAIN, MERIDIAN, NAPA RIDGE, and STAG'S LEAP WINERY.

> **Pierce's Disease**
> This bacterial vine infection became a high profile issue in 'oo when an energetic flying insect called the Glassy-winged Sharpshooter arrived borne on ornamental plants. Some districts were particularly hard hit, but despite hysterical press announcements even small growers in those areas soldiered on, fighting back with insect sprays and careful v'yard management. Spread of the problem has since proven to be slow. New research at UC Davis shows strong promise for techniques to ameliorate the problem over the next 5 yrs.

Bernardus Carmel Valley ★★★ Strong MERITAGE wines from densely planted hillside. In town high-end auberge includes top sommelier south of S Fran.

Biale Napa ★★ Small, ZIN specialist using mostly Napa fruit.

Boeger El Dorado ★★ Mostly estate wines. Attractive Merlot, Barbera, Zin; all less bold than many neighbours.

Bonny Doon Sta Cruz Mtns ★★★ Mad punster Randall Grahm still resolutely Rhôneist with pink Vin Gris de Cigare, red Cigare Volant, and Grenache Village. Meditations now extend to Italianates, too. Also bargain Pacific Rim Riesling (incl real Mosel!). Follow the future with Grahm.

Bouchaine Carneros ★★★ (Chard) 94 95 **96** 97 99 (Pinot) **92 93 94** 95 96 97 98 99 Had a renaissance in late 90s which greatly improved PINOT N and CHARD.

Black Sheep Calaveras County ★★ Zins from AMADOR & CALAVERAS get better yearly.

Brander Vineyard, The Sta Barbara ★★ Estate producer in STA YNEZ VALLEY recently prefers power to finesse in Sauv Bl, Cab blend.

Bruce, David Sta Cruz Mts ★★★ (Pinot) **95 96** 97 98 99 Long-time source of eccentric bruiser (now moderated) Chardonnay. Pinot Noir (from own and SONOMA vines) is forte.

Buehler Napa ★★ (Chard) **95 96** 97 98 99 (Cab S) **90 91 92 93 94** 95 96 97 98 In E hills recently "repositioned" with upscale prices on unchanged estate Cab S, Zin and Russian River Chard.

Buena Vista Carneros ★★ (Chard) **96 97** 98 99 (Cab S) **91 92 93 94** 95 96 97 98 Has swapped an earlier taste-the-grapes style for one more heavily marked by winemaking: especially Chardonnay.

CALIFORNIA

Burgess Cellars Napa ★★ Emphasis on dark weighty well-oaked reds; Cab rather plain-faced, Zin begins to be more out-sized.

Bynum, Davis Sonoma ★★ (Chard) **96 97 98** 99 (Pinot N) **91 92 93 94 95** 96 97 98 99 Long-underrated but beginning to draw attention for characterful single vineyard wines, especially Pinot Ns from RRV.

Byron Vineyards Sta Barbara ★★ (Chard) **96 97** 98 99 (Pinot) **93 94 95** 96 97 98 99 Prospering under MONDAVI; estate PINOT N leads with CHARD not far behind.

Cain Cellars Napa ★★★ (Cain Five) 85 86 87 90 91 92 **94** 95 96 97 98 Stylish, supple Cain Five anchored in estate plantings of Cabernet S and four cousins on Spring Mtn; Cain Cuvée (declassified Cain Five) can rival the big brother. Monterey Sauvignon Musqué also fine.

Cafaro Napa ★★★ Winemaker label for sturdy-to-solid Cab and Merlot.

Cakebread Napa ★★ (Chard) **96 97** 98 99 (Cab S) 85 87 90 **91 92** 94 95 97 98 Now up to three bottlings of Cab: all hearty and heartily-oaked.

Calera San Benito ★★★ (Chard) **97** 98 99 (Pinot) **91 92** 93 **94 95** 96 98 97 98 Dry sunny chalky hills near Chalone lead to booming Rhône-weight estate Pinot Ns named after individual vineyard blocks (Reed, Selleck, Jensen). Also for perfumiest Viognier.

Callaway Temecula ★ (Chard) **94 95 96** 97 98 99 Sourcing grapes outside home region for new fighting varietal priced "coastal" line.

Cambria Sta Barbara ★★ Part of KENDALL-JACKSON'S ARTISANS AND ESTATES group. Chard routinely toasty, Pinot N more enticing.

Canandaigua Huge NY firm now No 2 to GALLO in California and long a power in bottom tier of market (Richard's Wild Irish Rose, Taylor California Cellars, etc). Lately reaching up, first tentatively with DUNNEWOOD, more aggressively with SIMI, now acquiring FRANCISCAN Estates along with ESTANCIA and MT VEEDER including '01 acquisition of RAVENSWOOD.

Carmenet Sonoma ★★→★★★ (Cab S blend) 87 **90 91 92** 94 95 96 97 98 Fancifully named variations on ripe Cab (eg Moon Mountain, Dynamite, Vin de Garde) all from mountaintop vineyard. CHALONE-owned.

Carneros Creek Carneros ★★→★★★ (Pinot N) **92 93 94** 95 96 97 98 99 Resolute explorer of climates and clones in CARNEROS offers 5 Pinots each yr: lightsome Fleur de Carneros; Côte de Carneros; darker, richer Estate; Reserve Francis Mahoney Estate. Single v'yd Las Brisas coming.

Castoro San Luis Obispo ★★ Paso Robles estate, as substantial as its wines (Cab S, Zin). Savvy winemaker Nils Udsen has a way with fresh fruit aromas. Nb nouveau wines. Zins: vg & value. Remainder of the line, reliable.

Caymus Napa ★★★→★★★★ (Cab S) 87 90 **91 92** 94 95 96 97 98 Dark quick-to-mature American-oaked Cab Special Selection: celebrated core. Lighter, basic bottling not far behind. Developing v'yds: MONTEREY, SONOMA for other varieties.

Chalk Hill Sonoma ★★ Large estate near Windsor, forever changing styles for Chardonnay, Sauvignon Blanc, Cabernet.

Chalone Monterey ★★★ (Chard) **94 95** 96 97 98 99 Unique estate high in Gavilan Mts; source of flinty Chard and dark tannic Pinot N, both slow-to-open burgundy imitations (Pinot N can go 15 yrs). Pinot Bl and Chenin styled after Chard. Also owns ACACIA, CARMENET, EDNA VALLEY VINEYARD, Echelon Gavilan and Canoe Ridge (Washington). (Lafite) Rothschilds own major share.

Chappellet Napa ★★★ (Cab S) 75 76 78 84 86 87 90 91 92 94 95 **95** 96 97 98 99 Beautiful amphitheatrical hill vineyard. Always age-worthy Cab S has new grace-notes, esp Signature label. Chenin: a NAPA classic now touched with oak. Chardonnay gentle; easy Sangiovese too. Also very good Cabernet Franc, Merlot, Tocai Fruilano, sweet Moelleux.

Charles Mitchell Fairplay, El Dorado County ★★ Entertaining visit, eccentric owner. Gd MERITAGE reds and fine Barbera sourced from LA Cetto (Baja), Mexico.

Château Montelena Napa ★★★ (Chard) **96 97** 98 (Cab) **90 91** 92 94 95 96 97 98 99 Understated age-worthy Chard and recently modified (91 92) but still tannic potent Calistoga-estate Cab to age for ever.

Château Potelle Napa ★★ Expat French couple produce quietly impressive Chard (Reserve edition toastier) and vigorous Cabernet from MT VEEDER estate, outright aggressive VGS Zin from AMADOR.

Château St Jean Sonoma ★★→★★★ (Chard) **96 97** 98 99 Style always bold, heady; more so since bought from Suntory in '96 by BERINGER owners. Known for single-v'yd Chards (Robert Young, Belle Terre); now reds are creating a stir.

Château Souverain Sonoma ★★→★★★ (Cab S) **87 90 91 94** 95 96 97 Top-of-the-line CARNEROS Chard, Alexander Valley Cab, and Dry Creek Valley Zin, all with lots of oak. So too basic SONOMA bottlings. Same owner as BERINGER.

Château Woltner Napa ★★→★★★ Excellent Howell Mt estate Chards (incl expensive Frederique) joined in 1995 by Cab-based red. From ex-owners of Ch La Mission Haut-Brion.

Chimney Rock Napa ★★→★★★ (Cab S) **87 90 91 92 94** 95 **96** 97 98 99 Once racy Stags Leap District Cabernet now fleshier and driven more by cassis aroma due to sophisticated trellising.

Christopher Creek Sonoma ★★★ Ownership by Fred Wasserman has seriously improved already admirable Syrah and Petite Sirah.

Cline Cellars Carneros ★★ Originally Contra Costa (important vineyards still there), now in SONOMA/CARNEROS and still dedicated mostly to husky Rhône Rangers (blends and varietals), eg Côtes d'Oakley, Mourvèdre.

Clos du Bois Sonoma ★★→★★★ (Chard) **96** 97 98 (Cab) **87 90 91 92 94** 95 **96** 97 98 99 Sizeable (400,000 case) Allied-Domecq firm at Healdsburg. Winemaker Margaret Davenport hitting impressive stride with Cab S, Pinot N, Chard. Top are single-v'yd incl Cab Briarcrest, Chard Calcaire.

Clos Pegase Napa ★★ (Chard) **95 96** 97 98 99 (Cab S) **90 91 94** 95 96 97 98 99 Post-modernist winery-cum-museum (or vice versa) intelligently grows Chard in CARNEROS and Cab in Calistoga.

Clos du Val Napa ★★★ (Chard) **94 95 96** 97 98 99 (Cab) **85 87 90 91** 92 94 95 96 97 98 99 French-run. Elegant, reliable, aging candidates. Nice selection of older vintages available in Cabs and Sem/SB blend too.

Cohn, B R Sonoma ★★→★★★ One-time SONOMA estate Cab S specialist now buying grapes as far afield as Paso Robles, thus far to uncertain effect.

Collier Falls Dry Creek ★★ **97** 98 99 Grower at northern tip of valley having exceptional Zin made for him.

Corison Napa ★★→★★★ (Cab) **87 90 91 94** 95 **96** 97 98 99 Long-time winemaker at CHAPPELLET on her own making supple flavoursome Cabernet promising to age well.

Cosentino Napa ★★ (Pinot N) **94 95 96** 97 98 99 Irrepressible winemaker-owner always full-tilt. Results s'times odd, sometimes brilliant, never dull. Crystal Valley is widely distributed down-market brand.

Crocker-Starr St Helena ★★★ **97** 98 Former winemaker from SPOTTSWOODE teamed up with the great-grandson of the Crocker who built the western part of the trans-continental railroad. A range of three Cabernet Franc based offerings. All are exceptional.

Cuvaison Napa ★★★ (Chard) **96** 97 98 99 (Merlot) **87 90 91 94** 95 96 97 98 99 Estate CARNEROS Chard steadily fine though fleshier, oakier than formerly. Recent estate Cab begins to outshine Merlot.

Dalla Valle Napa ★★★★ Hilly estate has become a cult classic with newly supple reds (Cab-based Maya, Sangio-based Pietre Rosso).

Dehlinger Sonoma ★★★ (Pinot) **94 95** 96 97 98 99 Tom D focuses on ever-plummier estate Russian River Valley Pinot N, and rightly. Also Chard, Syrah.

DeLoach Vineyards Sonoma ★★★ (Chard) **94 95 96 97** 98 99 Fruit-rich Chardonnay ever the mainstay of reliable Russian River Valley winery. Gargantuan single-vineyard Zins (Papera, Pelletti) finding an audience.

Diamond Creek Napa ★★★★ (Cab S) 84 **85 87 90** 91 92 93 **94 95** 96 97 98 99 Austere, stunningly high-priced cult Cabs from hilly v'yd nr Calistoga go by names of vineyard blocks, eg Gravelly Meadow, Volcanic Hill. 3,000 cases.

Domaine Carneros Carneros ★★★ Showy US outpost of Taittinger in CARNEROS echoes austere style of its parent in Champagne. Vintage Blanc de Blancs the luxury cuvée. Still Pinot Noir also impressive.

Domaine Chandon Napa ★★ Maturing v'yds, maturing style, broadening range taking Moët & Chandon's California arm to new heights. Look esp for NV Reserve, Etoile Rosé. Still wines a recent addition.

Domaine Saint-Gregory Mendocino ★★ Companion label to Monte Volpe for wines from French grape varieties.

California wines to try in 2003

August Briggs One of the top three PN out of Carneros, and a fine Napa Zin as well

Craig High-end Napa Cab producer with reliable track record

Echelon Very good value wines, particularly PN, from Chalone group

Gott Amador Zin with all the berries and iron you can handle

Kirkland Ranch Big cattle spread SE of Napa making strong Merlot

Plumpjack Damn good Cab, owned by young politico who could be next San Francisco mayor

Rubissow-Sargent Good quality, modestly-priced Cab from Mt Veeder

Spencer Roloson Concentrated Zins from Chiles Valley in Napa

Domaine de la Terre Rouge Amador County ★★★ Former retailer is a Rhone specialist with a strong stable of growers. Syrah and Grenache are both tops. Zins under Eastin label from old Fiddletown v'yds also noteworthy.

Dominus Napa ★★★★ 84 85 87 **90 91 95 96** 97 98 99 Christian Moueix of Pomerol is now sole owner of the fine Napanook vineyard and elegantly austere winery (98). Style, tannic at first, variable with vintages through mid-90s, now much more fruit driven since move into own facility.

Dry Creek Vineyard Sonoma ★★ Unimpeachable source of dr tasty w, esp Chard & Fumé Blanc, but also Chenin Bl. Cab S & Zin rather underrated. 110,000 cases.

Duckhorn Vineyards Napa ★★★ (Merlot) **90 91** 94 **95 96** 97 98 99 Known for dark, tannic, almost plummy-ripe single-v'yd Merlots (esp Three Palms, and Cab-based blend Howell Mountain. Goldeneye PN made in Anderson Valley startled the marketplace with its atypical weight and intensity.

Dunn Vineyards Napa ★★★★ (Cab) **87 89 90 91 92 94 95** 96 97 98 99 Owner-winemaker Randall Dunn makes dark tannic austere Cab from Howell Mt, slightly milder from valley floor. 4,000 cases.

Eberle Winery San Luis Obispo ★★ Burly ex-footballer makes Cab and Zin in his own image. Also look for their polar opposite: Muscat Canelli.

Edna Valley Vineyard San Luis Obispo ★★ (Chard) 96 **97** 98 99 Decidedly toasty Chard from a joint venture of local grower and CHALONE. Pinot N best drunk soon after vintage. 48,000 cases.

Edizione Pennino Napa ★★ Expensive, ZIN is the best item.

Estancia Label for gd variety MONTEREY Chard, Sauv, Pinot N, Alexander Cab S.

Etude Napa ★★★★ (Pinot N) **94 95 96** 97 98 99 Winemaker-owned cellar of highly respected consultant Tony Soter. V gd NAPA Cab overshadowed by burnished CARNEROS Pinot Noir. Engaging experiments in Pinots Blanc, Gris, and Meunier. Soter has moved to, and is opening a winery in, Oregon.

Far Niente Napa ★★★ (Chard) **96 97** 98 99 (Cab S) **91 94 95 96** 97 98 99 Opulence is the goal in both Cab S and Chard from luxury mid-NAPA estate.

Farrell, Gary Sonoma ★★★★ After yrs of sharing, maker of brilliant, age-worthy RRV Pinot N is building own cellar. Also excellent Merlot, Zin, ultra-toasty Chardonnay.

Ferrari-Carano Sonoma ★★ Ostentatious winery draws on far-flung estate vineyards to make range of broad wines well suited to property. New mountain v'yds for Italianate and Bd'x varieties producing leaner models.

Fess Parker Santa Barbara County ★★ Owned by actor who played Dan'l Boone on TV; son Eli is winemaker. Serviceable Chardonnay and Pinot N. Impressive Riesling. Very good Syrahs every vintage back to 1992.

Fetzer Mendocino ★★ 3M case, Brown-Forman owned. Consistently good value from least expensive range (Sundial, Valley Oaks) to most (Reserve). Vineyards increasingly organic. Bonterra is completely organically grown.

Ficklin San Joaquin ★★ First in California to use Douro grape varieties. Since 1948, Tinta California's best "port". Sometimes vintages.

Fiddlehead ★★★ Winemaker Kathy Joseph commutes between home/office nr Sacramento and 2 wineries where she contracts space: one in ARROYO GRANDE AVA, San Luis Obispo; the other in Oregon. Fine Sauv Bl & top-end Pinot N.

Field Stone Sonoma ★★ Flavourful estate-grown Alexander Valley Cab S too often overlooked. Old-vine Petite Sirah can be impressive.

Firestone Sta Barbara ★★ (Chard) **96** 97 98 (Merlot) **94 95 96** 97 98 99 Fine Chardonnay overshadows but does not outshine delicious Riesling.

Fisher Sonoma ★★ Hill-top SONOMA grapes for often-fine Chard; NAPA grapes dominate steady Cab. 10,000 cases.

Flora Springs Wine Co Napa ★★ (Chard) **96** 97 98 99 (Trilogy) **87 90 91 94** 95 **96** 97 98 99 Old stone cellar full of oak. So are wines, esp proprietory Sauvignon called Soliloquy, Cab blend called Trilogy, and varietal Sangiovese.

Fogarty, Thomas Sta Cruz Mts ★★ Fine Gewürz from VENTANA sets the pace; whole line is well made.

Folie à Deux Napa ★★ Winemaking doyen, owner Richard Peterson has hired Scott Harvey, giving this small winery extraordinary Amador Zins to go with their very fine Napa Cabs.

Foppiano Sonoma ★★ Long-est'd wine family turns out fine reds (esp Petite Sirah, Zin) under family name. Whites labelled Fox Mountain.

Forman Napa ★★★ The winemaker who brought STERLING its first fame in the '70s now makes excellent Cab and Chard on his own. 15,000 cases.

Foxen Sta Barbara ★★★ (Pinot) **92 93 94 95** 96 97 98 Tiny winery nestled between Santa Ynez & Santa Maria valleys. Always bold, frequently brilliant Pinot N.

Franciscan Vineyard Napa ★★★ (Cab) **85 87 89** 90 **91 94** 95 **96** 97 98 99 Big v'yd at Oakville for stylish Cabernet, Zin, ultra-oaky Chard takes extra step with wild yeast fermentation. Sale to CONSTELLATION left Agustín Huneuus with QUINTESSA label, and Veramonte in his homeland Chile.

Franzia San Joaquin ★ Penny-saver wines under Franzia Corbett Canyon and other labels. "Bottled in Ripon" is the tip off. Lgst bag-in-box producer.

Freemark Abbey Napa ★★★ (Chard) **96** 97 98 99 (Cab S) **80 85 87 91 92 94** 95 96 97 98 99 Underrated today, but consistent for inexhaustible stylish Cabernet Sauvignons (esp single-vineyard Sycamore and Bosché) of great depth. Vg deliciously true-to-variety Chardonnay.

Frog's Leap Napa ★★→★★★ (Cab S) **87 90 91 94** 95 96 97 Small winery, charming as its name (and T-shirts) and organic to boot. Lean racy Sauv, toasty Chard quite the reverse. Zin. Cabernet, Merlot all take to age.

Gabrielli Mendocino ★★ Essentially a winemaker label for gd value varietals from Ukiah region.

Gainey Vineyard, The Sta Barbara ★★ Pinot N leads the list but Chard, Sauv, Cab worth a look. 12,000 cases.

Gallo, E & J San Joaquin ★→★★ Having mastered the world of commodity wines (with eponymously labelled "Hearty Burgundy", "Pink Chablis", etc) this 40M-case family firm (the world's biggest) is now unleashing a blizzard of regional varietals under such names as Anapauma, Marcellina, Turning Leaf, Zabaco and more, some from Modesto, some via GALLO SONOMA.

Gallo Sonoma Sonoma ★★→★★★ (Chard) 96 **97 98** 99 (Cab S) **91 92 94 95 96** 97 98 99 3 million cases facility run by third generation doing small single v'yd bottlings from Sonoma. Has potential to be impressive.

Gan Eden Sonoma ★★ Kosher producer of traditional single-grape wines has won substantial praise for Chards.

Geyser Peak Sonoma ★★→★★★ Bought from Henry Trione in 1999 by distiller Jim Beam. Aussie winemaker Daryl Groom (who came when Penfolds was a partner) stays aboard, making good Chard, crackerjack Sauv and Syrah outright superior Reserve Alexandre.

Gloria Ferrer Carneros ★★ Original goal of Spain's Freixenet was nothing but classic sp. Now smoky CARNEROS Chardonnay and silky Pinot Noir from diverse clonal selection on equal footing, maybe in forefront.

Grace St Helena ★★★ 90 91 92 **94** 97 One of the original cult Cabs from 2-acre v'yd. Owner is a teetotal, former stockbroker.

Greenwood Ridge Mendocino ★★ (Pinot) **96** 97 **98** Est'd specialist in racy ANDERSON VALLEY Riesling more recently appreciable for melony Sauv, herby Merlot. Pinot N begins to convince, too. 4,000 cases.

Grgich Hills Cellars Napa ★★★ (Chard) **95** 96 97 98 99 (Cab S) **80 85 87 90 91 94** 95 96 97 98 99 Winemaker Grgich and grower Hills join forces on pure Sauv, deftly oaked Chard long-ageing Cab, and – too little noticed – Spätlese-sweet Ries. Also plummy SONOMA Zin. 60,000 cases.

Groth Vineyards Napa ★★→★★★ (Cab S) **85 86 87 90** 91 **94** 95 96 97 98 99 Oakville estate challenges leaders among NAPA Cab & Sauv Bl. Also vg Chard.

Guenoc Vineyards Lake County ★★ Ambitious winery/v'yd in its own AVA just North of NAPA county line. Property once Lillie Langtry's challenge to B'dx. Wines less over-oaked recently.

Gundlach-Bundschu Sonoma ★★ (Chard) 96 **97** 98 99 (Cab) **90 91 94** 95 **96 97** 98 99 Pioneer name solidly revived by fifth generation. Versatile Rhinefarm v'yd signals memorably individual Gewürz, Merlot, Zin, Pinot N. 50,000 cases.

Hagafen Napa ★★ First and perhaps still the finest of the serious kosher producers. Especially Chard and Johannisberg Ries. 6,000 cases.

Handley Cellars Mendocino ★★ (Chard) **95** 96 97 98 99 (Pinot N) **96 97 98** 99 Winemaker-owned. Excellent ANDERSON VALLEY Chard, Gewürz, Pinot N, and (tiny lots) classic sp. Also vg Dry Creek Valley Sauv, Chard from her family's vines.

Hanna Winery Sonoma ★★ 600 acres of Russian River and Alexander valleys v'yds producing sound middle-of-the-road Chard, Cab, Sauv.

Hanzell Sonoma ★★★ (Chard) 96 **97** 98 99 (Pinot N) 94 **95 96** 97 98 99 The late founder revolutionized Calif Chards, Pinot Ns with French oak in late '50s. Three owners later, Hanzell produces powerhouses from same two varieties.

Harlan Estate Napa ★★★★ Cab **91 92 93 94** 95 **96** 97 98 99 Racy Cabs from small estate in hills W of Oakville earning their right to luxury prices.

Hartford Court Sonoma ★★★ Specialist in KENDALL JACKSON'S ARTISANS & ESTATES group shows promise with single v'yd Pinot Ns, tight coastal grown Chard and wonderful old vine Zins.

Hartwell Napa ★★ High-end image, small producer with good Cab potential.

Heitz Napa ★★★→★★★★ (Cab) **74 78 80 87** 91 92 94 95 96 97 98 99 On dark, deep-flavoured Cab S, esp Martha's Vineyard, rests the fame of the place. So it has since the 1960s, when the individualist winemaker-owner (†2000) set new standards for his peers. The newer Trailside Vineyard even rivals Martha.

Heller Estate Monterey ★★→★★★★ (Cab) **83** 95 96 97 New owners reviving estate. Esp look for med-bodied earthy CARMEL VALLEY Cab, rich Chard and seeing Chenin Blanc. Cachagua line is ★★.

Hendry Napa ★★ Long known as a grower on other labels; now making nice Cab and ZIN for self.

Hess Collection, The Napa ★★★ (Chard) **95 96** 97 98 (Cab S) **87 91 94 95** 96 97 A Swiss art collector's winery-cum-museum in former Mont La Salle winery of CHRISTIAN BROTHERS. Ever more impressive Mt Veeder Cabernet S. Chardonnay newly from American Canyon, 60,000 cases. More broadly sourced 300,000 case Hess Selection label gives very good value.

Hill Winery, William Napa ★★ Allied-Domecq property on the rise with subtle (for California) Chard; even more with flavourful, silky Cab.

Hop Kiln Sonoma ★★ Source of sometimes startlingly fine "Valdiguie" (aka NAPA Gamay). Russian River Gewürz is full-flavoured and large-scale.

Husch Vineyards Mendocino ★★ Has ANDERSON VALLEY v'yd for often fine Pinot N, Ukiah one for s'times good Sauv, Cab S.

Indian Springs Nevada County, Sierra Foothills ★★ Large 450 acre v'yd, wines made by consultant Jed Steele. Showing promise with Sangiovese.

Iron Horse Vineyards Sonoma ★★(★)Chard) 95 **96 97** 98 99 Substantial Russian River estate at its best with classic-method fizz that hovers between fine and bold. Chard can excel. Cab-Sangio from affiliated Alexander Valley property.

J Sonoma ★★★ Born part of JORDAN, now on its own in former PIPER-SONOMA cellars. Creamy classic-method Brut (**90 91 92 93**) the foundation. Also still Pinot N.

Jade Mountain Napa ★★→★★★ After sale to Chalone, pursuing lofty goals using Rhône varieties, esp Syrah.

Jarvis Napa ★ Spectacular underground construction easily disguises modest quality of an expensive range, primarily Bordeaux reds and Chardonnay.

Jekel Vineyards Monterey ★★ (Chard) **97** 98 99 Ripe juicy Riesling used to be most noteworthy item. It remains reliable, but red B'dx blends from Sanctuary section of own v'yds have improved dramatically. Owned by Brown Forman.

Jessie's Grove Lodi ★★ Old Zin vines work well for farming family's new venture.

Jordan Sonoma ★★★ (Cab S) 85 **87** 90 91 **94** 95 **96** 97 98 99 Extravagant Alexander Valley estate models its Cabernet on supplest Bordeaux. And it lasts. Chard typical California-toasty.

Kautz-Ironstone Lodi and Calaveras County ★★ Showplace destination in SIERRA FOOTHILLS grew to 300,000 cases in five years. Renovated bulk facility in Lodi to aid growth. Honestly priced broad range led by fine Cab Franc.

Karly Amador ★★ Among more ambitious sources of SIERRA FOOTHILLS Zin.

Keenan Winery, Robert Napa ★★ Winery on Spring Mountain: supple, restrained Cabernet, Merlot; also Chardonnay.

Kendall-Jackson Lake County ★★→★★★★ Staggeringly successful style aimed at widest market: esp broadly sourced off-dry toasty Chardonnay. Even more noteworthy for the development of a diversity of wineries under the umbrella of ARTISANS & ESTATES.

Kenwood Vineyards Sonoma ★★ (Cab S) **87 90 91 95** 96 97 98 99 Single-v'yd Cab (Jack London), Zin (several) the high points. Sauv Bl is reliable value. Recently the same owner as KORBEL.

Kistler Vineyards Sonoma ★★★★ (Chard) **95 96** 97 98 99 Ever more chasing the Burgundian model of single vineyard Pinot Noir, most from Russian River (greatest successes), Chardonnays very toasty, buttery but with taut, sinewy structure which demands several years of bottle age.

Korbel Sonoma ★★ Long-est'd classic-method sp specialist emphazises bold fruit flavours, intense fizz; Natural tops the line. Purchased by Anhauser-Busch.

Krug, Charles Napa ★→★★ (Cab S) **91 92 94** 95 96 97 98 99 Historically important winery with generally sound wines. Cabs at head of list, CARNEROS Pinot N not far behind. CK-Mondavi is relentlessly sweet commodity brand.

Kunde Estate Sonoma ★★ (Chard) **96 97** 98 99 Long-time large grower has emerged as winemaking force with buttery Chard, flavourful Sauv (lightly touched with Viognier). Reds still finding a footing.

La Jota Napa ★★ Tannic Cab S from small estate on Howell Mountain.

Laetitia San Luis Obispo ★★ Now owned by BARNWOOD, concentrating on estate still wines. Pinot N scintillating, Pinot B maybe. Also Chardonnay.

Laird Napa ★★(★) Quickly getting recognized for full-bodied Chard.

Lambert Bridge Sonoma ★★ Revival of briefly defunct Dry Creek Valley winery so far more sound than exciting.

Lamborn Howell Mountain ★★ Excellent site. Wine produced at new facility gives concentrated, peppery Zins. Solid track record.

Landmark Sonoma ★★ (Chard) **96 97** 98 99 Long-time Chard specialist now in the me-too toasty-buttery school.

Lang & Reed Napa ★★ New. Specialist with Loire-style Cab Francs.

Latcham Fairplay, El Dorado County ★★ Making standard range with a standout Petite Sirah under Granite Springs label. Cab F is worth seeking.

Laurel Glen Sonoma ★★★ (Cab S) **85 86 90 91 94 95** 96 97 98 99 Big, austere distinctly regional Cab from steep vineyard in SONOMA Mtn sub-AVA. 5,000 cases. Counterpart good-value, higher-volume second label.

Lava Cap El Dorado ★★(★) Where bold styles rule, a source of singularly understated, intriguing Zinfandels and Cabernets. Buys in grapes for very concentrated Petite Sirah which blossoms around its 5th birthday.

Leeward Winery Ventura ★ (Chard) **97** 98 99 Ultra-toasty CENTRAL COAST Chards are the mainstay. 18,000 cases.

Lewis Napa ★★★ Purchased grapes & custom crush with consultant Paul Hobbes have done wonders with Merlot & Chard. Owned by Indy race car driver.

Lockwood Monterey ★★ Lge v'yd (1,650 acres) in S SALINAS VALLEY. Lockwood, Shale Creek labels virtually indistinguishable by style, but Lockwood ranges wider.

Lohr, J Central Coast ★→★★ Lge, wide-reaching firm at peak with PASO ROBLES Cab S Seven Oaks. Commodity line sub-titled Cypress.

Lolonis Mendocino ★★ Substantial grower at Ukiah with range of consistently attractive varietals from own vines.

Long Meadow W. Mtns Napa ★★ 98 Beautiful new rammed earth winery and olive pressing facility with great potential. Cathy CORISON is winemaker.

Long Vineyards Napa ★★★ (Chard) 96 **97** 98 99 (Cab) **80 85 86 87 90 91 94 95** 96 97 98 99 Tiny n'bour of CHAPPELLET: lush Chard, flavourful Cab, luxury prices.

Longoria Winery Santa Barbara (★★→★★★) Long-time GAINEY winemaker now on own, and brilliant with Pinot Noir.

Luna Napa ★★ Italianate theme executed by former NEWTON winemaker John Konigsgaard is erratic on Pinot Gr but has interesting Sangiovese in barrel.

Lynmar Russian River ★★★ Three vintages in a row of top flight Pinot Noir have launched this new venture. Quail Hill designation is almost a bargain at $30.

MacRostie Carneros ★★ Buttery Chard is flagship. Also well-oaked Merl, Pinot N.

Madroña El Dorado ★★ Loftiest v'yds in SIERRA FOOTHILLS, and pioneer in high elevation styles. Reds always a wrestling match between tannin and acid, but Ries benefits from that same interaction. Standard Ries best after six years, Late Harvest super all the time.

Markham Napa ★★ (Cab S) **87 90 91 94 95** 96 97 98 99 Recently good to excellent, esp Merlot and Cab S grown in own v'yds. Sauv also to note.

Martin Bros San Luis Obispo ★★ Entirely dedicated to Italian varieties (Nebbiolo, Sangiovese), or styles ("Vin Santo", chestnut-aged Chard).

Martini, Louis M Napa ★★ Resolute insistence on making truly age-worthy Reserve Cab S, Merlot, Zin and Barbera from fine v'yds (Monte Rosso, Los Vinedos, Glen Oaks, etc) finally begins to recapture public attention.

Masson Vineyards Monterey ★ CANANDAIGUA'S supermarket label.

Matanzas Creek Sonoma ★★★(★) (Chard) 96 97 98 99 (Merlot) 94 95 96 97 98 99 Merlot and Chard seek to be CA's most expensive with controversial results. Winery sold in 2000 to ARTISANS & ESTATES.

Mayacamas Napa ★★ (Chard) 96 97 98 99 (Cab S) 85 87 90 91 92 94 95 96 97 98 V gd small v'yd with rich Chard and firm (but no longer steel-hard) Cabernet. Some Sauvignon, Pinot. 5,000 cases.

Mazzocco Sonoma ★★ Good and improving Chard, Cab from Alexander and Dry Creek Valley estate vineyards.

McDowell Valley Vineyards Mendocino ★★ Grower-label for family with hearts set on Rhône varieties, esp ancient-vine Syrah and Grenache.

Meridian San Luis Obispo ★★ Fast-growing sibling to BERINGER making mark with single-vineyard EDNA VALLEY Chard, Paso Robles Syrah. Also STA BARBARA Chard, Pinot N, PASO ROBLES Cab S. 300,000 cases.

Meritage Name coined in Calif in the early 80's (rhymes with heritage), and then trademarked, to describe r or w made from blends of B'dx varieties. Whites have been slow to catch on, but reds have transformed Calif thinking on Cabs.

Merry Edwards Russian River ★★(★) Superstar consultant has planted her own Pinot N v'yd in Russian River district. Top quality results in '97 & '98.

Merryvale Napa ★★ Oak aplenty in red, white MERITAGES, Chardonnay. Cab S more middle of the road.

Michael, Peter Sonoma ★★★(★) Partly Knights Valley estate-v'yd and partly bought-in Howell Mountain: larger-than-life, Frenchified Chard, Merlot, Cab.

Michel-Schlumberger Sonoma ★★ Reinvigorated Dry Creek Valley winery at its best with Cabernet Sauvignon.

Miner Napa ★★ Nicely balanced wines with a reputation for Merlot.

Mirassou Central Coast ★★ Fifth-generation grower and pioneer in MONTEREY (SALINAS) gets highest marks for Pinot Bl classic sp. Chard, Pinot worth a look.

Mondavi, Robert Napa ★★→★★★★ Brilliant innovator now applying lessons to varietals for every purse. From top: NAPA Valley Reserves (bold, prices to match), Napa Valley appellation series (eg CARNEROS Chard, Oakville Cabernet, etc), Napa Valley (basic production), Coastal Series (eg CENTRAL COAST Chard, NORTH COAST Zin etc), RM-Woodbridge (California appellation for basic production, also pricier "Twin Oaks" line). Also Famiglia di Robert Mondavi, OPUS ONE, BYRON, Caliterra (Chile), Luce and Ornelia (Italy), Vichon (France). Living memorial, institute devoted to wine, food and art called Copia opened in downtown Napa 01.

Mont St John Carneros ★★ Old NAPA wine family makes good value Pinot N, Chard from own v'yd; buys in for solid Cabernet.

Monteviña Amador ★★ Owned by SUTTER HOME. Now turning more to Italian varieties (30 trial plantings) but hearty SIERRA Zin still the foundation stone.

Monticello Cellars Napa ★★ (Cab S) 87 90 91 94 95 96 97 98 99 Basic line under Monticello label, reserves under Corley. Both include Chard, Cab S. Reserve Pinot is the most intriguing.

Moraga Bel Air ★★★ 95 96 97 Cult Cabs from most expensive 7-acre v'yd in US. Owned by former Northrup CEO, Tom Jones. Tony Soter is consultant.

Morgan Monterey ★★(★) (Pinot) 94 95 96 97 98 Winemaker-owner. Basic Pinot Noir blends MONTEREY, CARNEROS but deep earthy possibly age-worthy Reserve is all Monterey now. Also toasty Chard.

Mount Eden Vineyards Sta Cruz Mts ★★→★★★ (Chard) **96 97** 98 99 Big expensive Chard from old Martin Ray v'yds; gentler MONTEREY version. Also Pinot N, Cab.

Mount Veeder Napa ★★ Once steel-hard Mt Veeder Cab now merely austere, as is more recent red MERITAGE. FRANCISCAN-owned.

Mumm Napa Valley Napa ★★ G H Mumm-Seagram joint venture range incl cheery Blanc de Noirs, distinctive single-v'yd Winery Lake & opulent luxury DVX.

Murphy-Goode Sonoma ★★ Large Alexander V estate. Sauv, Merlot, Cab S to explore. Reserves lavishly oaked.

Nalle Sonoma ★★★ (Zin) **90 94 95** 96 **97** 98 99 Winemaker-owned Dry Creek cellar getting to the very heart of Zin: wonderfully berryish young; that and more with age. 2,500 cases. Master of the claret style.

Navarro Vineyards Mendocino ★★→★★★ (Chard) 95 **96** 97 98 99 From ANDERSON VALLEY, splendidly age-worthy Chard, perhaps the grandest Gewürz in state. Even more special: late-harvest Ries, Gewürz. Pinot Noir not to be ignored. Only self-deprecating prices keep this from being cult favourite of big-shot collectors.

Nevada City Sierra Foothills ★★ Wide range of tourism-designed offerings distract from extraordinary Cab F. Winery is in the cultural capital of the mountains.

Newton Vineyards Napa ★★→★★★ (Chard) **97** 98 99 (Cab S) **87 94 95** 96 97 98 99 Luxurious estate growing more so; formerly ponderous style now reined back to the merely opulent for Chardonnay, Cabernet, Merlot.

Neyers Napa ★★★ Marketing man's label but super winemaking consultant Ehren Jordan, fine quality overall; great on Syrah.

Niebaum-Coppola Estate Napa ★★→★★★ (Rubicon) **91** 92 **94 95** 96 **97** 98 99 Movie-man Coppola's luxuriously wayward hobby much invigorated since acquisition of Inglenook winery and 220-acre vineyard (but not name). Flagship Rubicon is wonderful but lower end blends are uneven.

Oakville Ranch Napa ★★ Stunning property atop ridge east of Yountville. Deep concentrated Cabs are best; buttery, dense Chard has adherents.

Olivet Lane Sonoma ★ Brand made by Merry Edwards. Nice low oak Chard.

Opus One Napa ★★★★ (Cab S) **85 87 90** 91 92 93 **94 95** 96 **97** 98 99 Joint venture of R MONDAVI and Baronne Philippine de Rothschild. Spectacular winery; wines becoming brilliant. Mouton, watch out!

Pacific Echo Anderson Valley ★★ Formerly Scharffenberger, now Pommery-owned, sparkling wine. No longer sourced exclusively in Anderson Valley.

Pahlmeyer Napa ★★★ Cultish MERITAGE producer has 200 acres newly planted south of ATLAS PEAK. Merlot dominated blend is reliable.

Paradigm Napa ★★★ Westside OAKVILLE vineyard has unlimited potential. First three releases have competed with the valley's best.

Paraiso Springs Monterey ★ Up-an-comer owned by v lge grower in Salinas.

Patz & Hall Napa ★★★★ Reputation for CARNEROS Chard from individual v'yds firmly established around crisp structure and opulent winemaking.

Pecota, Robert Napa ★★ Drink-young Cab, Sauv, Chard, Gamay.

Pedroncelli Sonoma ★★ Old-hand in Dry Creek. Reds incl single vineyard, too austere for easy enjoyment. Whites more agreeable.

Perry Creek Fairplay, El Dorado Co ★★ Wide range of tourist wines and cigar sales in tasting room. Obscure extraordinary accomplishments with Zin.

Phelps, Joseph Napa ★★★ (Chard) **96** 97 98 99 (Cab S) **85 87** 90 **91 94 95** 96 97 98 99 Deluxe winery, beautiful v'yd: impeccable standards. Vg Chard, Cab S (esp Backus) and Cabernet-based Insignia. Also look for promising Rhône series under Vin du Mistral label.

Philips, R H Yolo, Sacramento Valley ★→★★ Pioneer in Dunnigan Hills NW of SACRAMENTO trying everything on huge property, succeeding best with Syrah,

Viognier, and great value Chardonnay under TOASTED HEAD brand. Sold in 00 to Canada's VINCOR.

Pine Ridge Napa ★★→★★★ Gentlemanly commune-labelled Cabs are best (Rutherford, Stags Leap, etc), Merlot not bad either. Dry oak-aged Chenin Petite Vigne is intriguing and there is Chard too, of course.

Preston Sonoma ★★ One of Calif's pioneer "terroiristes" concentrating on wines best suited to his Dry Creek v'yds: esp Zin, Barbera, and Rhône varieties.

Pride Mountain Spring Mountain, Napa ★★★ Top hillside location contributes bright fruit characters to fine Bordeaux variety offerings.

Quady Winery San Joaquin ★★ Imaginative Madera Muscat dessert wines, including celebrated orangey Essencia, dark Elysium, and Moscato d'Asti-like Electra. Starboard is a play on port; a better name than wine.

Quintessa Napa ★★★(★) Splendid new estate of Huneeus family, on Silverado Trail, linked to FRANCISCAN. Predictably very high standards.

Quivira Sonoma ★★ Sauvignon, Zinfandel, others, from Dry Creek Valley estate. More enamoured of oak than vineyard in recent vintages.

Qupé Sta Barbara ★★→★★★ Never-a-dull-moment cellar-mate of AU BON CLIMAT. Marsanne, Pinot Bl, Syrah are all well worth trying.

Rafanelli, A Sonoma ★★ (Cab) **90** 91 **94** 95 **95** 96 97 98 99 (Zin) **94 95** 96 **97** 98 99 Hearty, fetchingly rustic Dry Creek Zin; Cab of striking intensity.

Ravenswood Sonoma ★★ Originally major critical success for (or despite) single-v'yd Zins of skull-rattling power.Purchased in 01 by CONSTELLATION.

Raymond Vineyards and Cellar Napa ★★ (Chard) **97** 98 99 (Cab S) 87 **90** 91 **92 94** 95 96 97 98 99 Old NAPA wine family now with Japanese partners. Generations signifies well-oaked top-of-the-line Chard, Cab. Amberhill is consistent good value commodity second label.

Renaissance North Yuba, Sierra Foothills ★★ Spotty track record and quasi-religious fervor of artistic community backing this ambitious wine venture. Question marks remain, but French-Israeli winemaker for last 6 yrs has made remarkable strides. 20 cases of '99 Roussanne was best ever seen in CA.

Renwood Amador ★★ An ultra-ambitious venture capitalist expanding rapidly, but maintains rock hard style of yesteryear. Several single vi'yard bottlings of Zinfandel, Syrah, and Barbera as ripe and monumental as red wine can be. They KO all comers for a few years, but then begin to reveal raisin smells.

Ridge Sta Cruz Mts ★★★★ (Cab S) 85 87 **90** 91 **94 95** 96 **97** 98 Winery of highest repute among connoisseurs. Drawing from NAPA (York Creek) and its own mountain v'yd (Monte Bello) for conc'd Cabs, worthy of long maturing in bottle but needing less than formerly (NB 90 91 more approachable than 80). But power remains in SONOMA (Lytton Springs) and SAN LUIS OBISPO (Dusi) Zins and other red wines. Also outstanding gentle Chardonnays from SANTA CRUZ.

Rochioli, J Sonoma ★★★(★) (Pinot N) **94** 95 96 **97** 98 99 Long-time Russian River grower making four distinct Pinot Noirs from sizeable v'yd long-celebrated under own, other labels. Also very good Sauvignon Blanc.

Roederer Estate Mendocino ★★★ ANDERSON VALLEY branch of Champagne house (est '88). Resonant house style apparent esp in luxury cuvée l'Ermitage. Still stuns the Champenois. 25,000 cases, poised to triple. Sold as Quartet in Europe.

Rombauer Vineyards Napa ★★ Well-oaked Chardonnay, dark Cabernet S (especially reserve-style Meilleur du Chai). Now also owner of the revived Hanns Kornell sparkling wine cellars and NAPA cellars.

Ross, Stephen SLO ★★ Pretty gd Pinot N mostly sourced from Santa Barb Co.

St Amant Lodi ★★ Easternmost section of large LODI AVA, closest to AMADOR County: one of the most adroit at winemaking. Rhônes okay; Zins pretty gd.

CALIFORNIA

St Clement Napa ★★→★★★ (Chard) **96 97** 98 99 (Cab) **85 87 90 91** 94 **95** 96 **97** 98 99 Japanese-owned; turning towards burlier, oakier style in recent vintages of NAPA Sauv Bl, Cab, Merlot, and CARNEROS Chard.

St Francis Sonoma ★★ (Chard) 96 **97** 98 99 (Cab S) **87 90 91 92 94 95** 96 97 98 99 Tasty Chard (Reserve far oakier). Merlot & Cab subtly aged in American oak.

St-Supéry Napa ★★ French-owned (Skalli qv) and much activity since arrival of consulting winemaker Michel Rolland. Most grapes come from Dollarhide Ranch (Pope Valley) E of NAPA. Sauv Bl v crisp and flavourful given hot climate. Red Meritage doing quite well in tastings recently.

Saintsbury Carneros ★★★ (Chard) **95 96** 97 98 99 (Pinot N) **94** 95 96 97 98 99 Contends as AVA's finest and longest-lived Pinot Noir. Lighter Pinot Garnet and oaky Chard also vg. 60,000 cases.

Sanford Sta Barbara ★★★ (Pinot) **92 94** 95 96 97 98 99 Bold to over-the-top, esp Barrel Select but never dull Chard, Pinot N. Intensely regional Sauv worth a look.

Santa Barbara Winery Sta Barbara ★★ (Chard) **96 97** 98 99 (Pinot N) **94** 95 96 97 98 99 Former jug-wine producer, now among regional leaders, esp for Reserve Chard, Pinot Noir. Also Sauvignon Bl, Riesling.

Sarah's Vineyard Hecker's Pass, Santa Clara Valley ★★★ Sold (01) by one of the most charmingly eccentric personalities in the industry. Marilyn Taylor made great wines. One of the best Merlots in CA from Radike Vyd near PASO ROBLES.

Sattui, V Napa ★★ King of direct-only sales (ie winery door or mail order). Lusty Cab, more refined Ries are the wines to seek.

Sausal Sonoma ★★ Lge-scale Alexander V estate noted for its Zin and Cabs.

Schramsberg Napa ★★★ One of CA's top sparkling producers for decades. Historic caves. Res: splendid; Bl de Noir outstanding (2–10 yrs). Luxury cuvée J Schram is America's Krug. Founder Jack Davies died '98: his family presses on.

Schug Cellars Carneros ★★ German-born & trained owner-winemaker dabbles in other types, but CARNEROS Chard, Pinot N are his main interests and wines.

Screaming Eagle Napa ★★★★ The new NAPA paradigm: Cabernet S grower + consulting oenologist = small lots of (delicious) cult wine at luxury prices.

Seavey Napa ★★(★) Tucked in the eastern hills. Makes big, ripe Cab. Mulberry scented Merlot on the way. Chard okay, but not the main attraction.

Sebastiani Sonoma ★→★★ Substantial old family firm working low end of market (August Sebastiani Country, Vendange, Talus) but able to compete above this price level, esp with Sonoma Cask. 4 million cases.

Seghesio Sonoma ★★ Concentrating now on superb, age-worthy Zins from own old v'yds in Alexander, Dry Creek valleys, but don't overlook smaller lots of Sangiovese Vitigno Toscano, Pinot N.

Sequoia Grove Napa ★★ NAPA Cabs (Napa, Estate): dark and firm. Chards recently firmer, fresher, longer-lasting.

Seven Hills San Luis Obispo ★★ V lge new Australian investment E of PASO ROBLES making generous Shiraz. Also co-operating with Paragon V'yds in Edna Valley for Chard and Pinot N. Aussie w'making tricks worth watching on Paso fruit.

Shafer Vineyards Napa ★★★ (Cab S) **90 91 94 95 96** 97 98 99 With '95, oak overshadows grape in single-v'yd Red Shoulder Ranch Chard (CARNEROS), & begins to in Hillside Select Cab S (Stags Leap District), Sangio-based Firebreak.

Sierra Vista El Dorado ★★(★) Dedicated Rhôneist in SIERRA FOOTHILLS. Dedicated "Rhônigade" at high elevation. Style elegant, mid weight and fruit driven. Five Star Reserve Syrah won a panel tasting in London over many top French and Australian examples. Zinfandels very good. Bargain: Châteauneuf-type blend "Fleur de Montagne".

Silver Oak Napa/Sonoma ★★★ Separate wineries in NAPA and Alexander Valleys make Cabernet Sauv only. Owners have ridden extreme American-oaked style to pinnacle of critical acclaim.

Silverado Vineyards Napa ★★→★★★ (Chard) **95 96** 97 98 99 (Cab S) **85 87 90 91 94 95 96** 97 98 99 Showy hilltop Stags Leap District winery (Disney-owned); vineyards also elsewhere in NAPA. Consistently refined Cab, Chard, Sauvignon, Sangiovese.

Simi Sonoma ★★ After trimming line to a select few historic winery (under new owners) is back to making a wide range of varietals. Long-lived Cab S, vg Chard still the heart of the matter. Reserves (like so many) try too hard.

Sinskey Vineyards, Robert Napa ★★ Winery in Stags Leap, v'yds in CARNEROS for boldly oaked, firm Chard, Merlot, Pinot N.

Smith-Madrone Napa ★★ 95 **96 97** 98 99 Chard from Spring Mtn estate has had ups and downs; now up. Ries supports an nr-lost NAPA tradition. Don't miss it.

Names to Look for in 2003

Dutton-Goldfield Impressive stable of Sonoma Pinot Noirs

Paul Hobbs Fine winemaker buying top grapes in Carneros

Kuleto Estate Try Sangiovese from famous reataurant designer

Mueller Extraordinary Pinot Noir from Russian River

Scherrer Dense mouthful of old-vine Zin from Alexander Valley

---

Sonoma-Cutrer Vineyards Sonoma ★★→★★★ (Chard) **95 96** 97 98 99 Ultimate Chard specialist at somewhat diminished best with single-v'yd Les Pierres, Cutrer. FETZER owner Brown-Forman acquired 80% interest in 99.

Spottswoode Napa ★★★(★) (Cab S) **87 89 91 94 95 96** 97 98 99 Firm resonant luxury Cab from sm St Helena v'yd. Supple polished Sauv. 3,500 cases.

Stag's Leap Wine Cellars Napa ★★→★★★★ (Cab S) 78 84 **86 87 90 91 93 94 95** 96 97 98 99 Celebrated v'yd for silky, seductive Cabs (SLV, Fay, top-of-line Cask 23), Merlots; non-estate vg; also Chard, Sauv, Ries. 50,000 cases.

Stags' Leap Winery Napa ★★ Since 1997 purchase by owners of BERINGER, abandoned old reliance on Chenin B, Petit Sirah in favour of Cab S & Chard.

Staglin Napa ★★★ (Cab S) **90 91 94 95 96** 97 98 99 From sm Rutherford v'yd designed by late André Tchelistcheff, consistently fine v silky Cab S & Sangio.

Steele Wines Lake ★★→★★★ Long-time K-J winemaker patrols whole coast for esp single v'yd Chards. Boldly oaked, pricey. 2nd label called Shooting Star.

Sterling Napa ★★→★★★ Scenic Seagram-owned winery; extensive v'yds and inexplicable ups & downs. Look for tart Sauv & firm basic bottling of Cab S.

Stony Hill Napa ★★★ (Chard) **93 94 95** 96 97 98 99 Hilly v'yd and winery for many of California's v best whites over past 30 yrs. Founder Fred McCrea died in 77, widow Eleanor in 91; son Peter carries on powerful tradition. Chard (both estate and non-estate SHV) is less steely, more fleshy than before. Oak-tinged Riesling and Gewürz are understated but age-worthy.

Storybook Mountain Napa ★★★ NAPA's only dedicated Zin specialist makes taut Estate and Reserve wines from Calistoga vineyard.

Strong Vineyard, Rodney Sonoma ★★ (Chard) 96 **97** 98 99 (Cab) **90** 91 **94 95** 96 97 98 99 Formerly Sonoma V'yds; produces gd basic bottlings, better single-v'yd ones (Alexander's Crown Cab, Chalk Hill Chard, Charlotte's Home Sauv, River East Pinot N). Windsor name and facilities purchased in 2000 by Mildara-Blass from Aus for access to direct shipment program.

Summit Lake Howell Mt ★★ Old vine Zins from historic district. Med body, spicy.

Sutter Home Napa ★ Famous for sw white Zin, heady AMADOR Zin. Branching out and reaching up with Signature Series and M Trinchero: mid-priced varietals.

Swan, Joseph Sonoma ★★ (Zin) **90** 91 **94 95** 96 **97** 98 99 The son-in-law of late Joe Swan makes equally ultra-bold Zin, Pinot Noir.

Swanson Napa ★★→★★★ (Cab S) 91 92 **94 95** 96 97 98 99 Reds are the measure of the house, esp heartily oaked Cab, Sangio, Syrah.

Tablas Creek Paso Robles ★★★ Beaucastel owners challenge themselves with cuttings from their Châteauneuf vyds. All are happy with results.

Taft Street Sonoma ★★ After muddling along, has hit an impressive stride with esp good-value Russian River Chards, Merlots. 18,000 cases.

Talbott, R Monterey ★★ Wealthy owner doing well with big toasty Chards from Santa Lucia, Highlands, and CARMEL VALLEY AVAs.

Talley Vineyards San Luis Obispo ★★ Estate in Arroyo Grande (near SANTA BARBARA boundary) growing exceptional Pinot Noir. Chard too.

Tanner, Lane Santa Barbara ★★ (Pinot N) 93 94 **95 96 97** 98 99 Owner-winemaker with often superb single-v'yd Pinot Noirs (Bien Nacido, Sierra Madre Plateau). Drink immediately or keep. Now Syrah too.

Thoma – Sketchbook ★★ Mendocino Located in old Parducci property, new investment from Chicago, now home for Dennis Patton (formerly Hidden Cellars). Great potential, esp old growth Italianate v'yds in the Ukiah area.

Toasted Head Central Valley ★★ New brand from RH Philips. Really great buttered toast '00 Chard.

Torres Estate, Marimar Sonoma ★★★ (Pinot N) 93 94 **95 96 97** 98 99 Sister of Catalan hero makes buttery Chard, lovely Pinot N from RR Valley.

Trefethen Napa ★★★ (Chard) **90** 91 **93** 94 **95** 96 97 98 99 (Cab) **80 85 87** 90 **91 94 95** 96 97 Respected family winery. Very good dry Ries, tense Chard for ageing (late-released Library wines show how well). Cabernet shows increasing depths. Lower priced wines labelled Eshcol.

Truchard Carneros ★★→★★★ From the warmer, inner-end of CARNEROS comes one of the flavoury, firmly built Merlots that give the AVA identity. Cabernet S even better.

Tudal Napa ★★ (Cab S) **90** 91 **94 95** 96 97 98 99 Tiny estate winery N of St Helena; steady source of dark firm ageable Cabs.

Tulocay Napa ★★ (Pinot N) **90 92 94 95** 96 97 98 99 Tiny winery at Napa City. Pinot esp can be v accomplished. Cab is also worth attention.

Turley Napa ★★★ Former partner in FROG'S LEAP, now specializing in hefty, heady single vineyard Zin and Petite Sirah from old vines. Ehren Jordan is consultant. Purchased Pesenti in Paso Robles in 2001.

Turnbull Wine Cellars Napa ★★ Once extra-minty Cab now (95 96) more classical, restrained. New Sangio looks bright too. Estate faces MONDAVI winery.

Ventana Monterey ★★ '78 winery, showcase for owner's v'yds: watch for Chard and esp Sauv from Musqué clone.

Viader Napa ★★ (Cab blend) **94 95** 96 97 98 Argentine Delia Viader fled to Calif to do her own thing: dark Cab blend from estate in hills above St Helena.

Viansa Sonoma ★★ After obligatory Chard, Merlot, roster pays homage to Sam SEBASTIANI'S ancestors with blended, varietal Italianates including such rarities (for California) as Arneis, Dolcetto, Freisa.

Vino Noceto Amador ★★ Estate with California's truest-to-type.

Vyd 29 St Helena ★★★ 96 97 98 Located at 2929, Hwy 29. Tiny vineyard has fine Cabernets made at GRACE.

Wente Vineyards Livermore and Monterey ★★ Historic specialist in whites, esp LIVERMORE Sauv and Sém. MONTEREY sweet Riesling can be exceptional. A little classic sparkling. Also owns Concannon. 300,000 cases.

Whitehall Lane Napa ★★ Boldly oaked Chard and heady Cab head short list. San Francisco family the third owner in 25 years.

Wild Horse Winery San Luis Obispo ★★→★★★ (Pinot) 92 93 **94 95** 96 97 98 99 Owner-winemaker has a particular gift for Pinot Noir (mostly San Luis Obispo and STA BARBARA GRAPES). Also worthy Chard, Merlot.

Williams Selyem Sonoma ★★★ (Pinot) **90 91 92 93 94 96** 96 97 98 99 Intense smoky Russian River Pinot esp Rochioli and Allen vineyards. Now reaching to SONOMA coast, MENDOCINO, too. New majority owner ('98) from NY having a little trouble holding the reins.

Young's Amador County ★★★ Small production of very fine Barbera and Zin.

Zaca Mesa Sta Barbara ★★ Turning away from Chardonnay and Pinot to concentrate on Rhône grapes (especially Marsanne and Syrah) and blends (Cuvée Z) grown on estate.

ZD Napa ★★ (Pinot) 93 **95** 96 **97** 98 99 Lusty Chardonnay tattooed by American oak is ZD signature wine. Pinot N is often finer. 18,000 cases.

The Pacific Northwest

The wine country of the Pacific Northwest spans three adjoining states, Oregon has more than 15,000 acres of vines. concentrates in the Willamette Valley, south of Portland. Washington's 35,000 acres of vineyard are concentrated in the warmer, drier half of the state, east of the Cascade mountain range. Idaho's wine country lies just east of Washington's, along the Snake River.

The grapes of Burgundy and Alsace do well in Oregon; Dijon clones of Chardonnay and Pinot Noir promise earlier ripening, potentially more complex wines. Across the Columbia River in eastern Washington, the warmer, drier climate of the Columbia Valley allows thicker-skinned varieties (Merlot, Cab S, Cab F, and the hot new favourite, Syrah) to ripen well. These same varieties also grow well in the warmer southern appellations of Oregon, and in Idaho.

The largest wineries of the Pacific Northwest seem small in comparison to those in California. Most of the more than 380 wineries – a number that increases every year – produce fewer than 30,000 cases of wine annually, and many wineries make only 2,000 to 5,000 cases. Washington's Walla Walla Valley has recently been the most glamorous and rapidly-expanding appellation, growing from ten to thirty producers within a year and doubling vineyard plantings within the same period.

Recent Vintages

2001 Very promising. Lower acidity and less concentration than previous three years. Softer, earlier-drinking wines.

2000 A solid vintage throughout. High yields, concentrated, structured wines.

1999 Superb. Perfect growing season produced balanced wines. Now – 2008.

1998 Excellent throughout. Reduced yields and concentration in Oregon; quantity and quality in Washington. Now or soon.

1997 Rain in Oregon meant hard, lean wines – drink now. High yields and balanced wines in Washington. Drink now – 2006.

Oregon

Abacela Vineyards Umpqua Valley ★★★ 97 98 99' New producer; full of interest: Tempranillo, Dolcetto, Cab Fr, and Syrah stand out.

Adelsheim Vineyard Yamhill County ★★★ 91 92 93 **94** 95 96 97 **98** 99' Smoothly balanced Pinot N. New Dijon clone Chard, Ries, and Pinots Gris, and Blanc: clean, bracing. Also fruity Merlot.

Amity Willamette ★★ 97 98 **99** 00 Top Gewürz, Ries, Pinot Bl. Patchy Pinot N.

Andrew Rich (Tabula Rasa) Willamette ★★ Small producer; wide range: Pinot N, Washington Cab S, Chenin-Sauv Bl, rosé and Gewürz ice wine.

Archery Summit Yamhill Co ★★★ 93 94 95' 96 97 98' 99' 00' Flashy sibling of NAPA winery Pine Ridge. V impressive oaky Pinot N; Vireton (Pinot Gr blend).

Argyle Yamhill County ★★★ (sp) 89 91 **93 94** 96 98 99' 00 NW's best classic sp (incl NV), consistently well made. Also fine Ries, Chard, and high quality Pinot N.

Beaux Frères Yamhill County ★★★ 91 **92 93 94** 95 96 97 98 99' 00 Excellent, structured Pinot N; more finesse in recent yrs. Part-owned by Robert Parker Jr.

Bethel Heights Willamette ★★★ 91 92 93 **94 95** 96 **97 98** 99' Deftly made Pinot N from estate nr Salem. Also notable Chard, Pinot Bl, Pinot Gr.

Brick House Yamhill County ★★★ 93 94 95 96 97 98 99' 00 Dynamic, organic property operated by former CBS news correspondent. V Burgundian style. Sml quantities of v gd Pinot N, Gamay, & barrel-ferm Chard.

Cameron Yamhill County ★★★ 93 94 95 96 97 98' Eclectic producer of Pinot N, Chard: some great, others conversation pieces. Vg Pinot Bl.

Chehalem Yamhill County ★★★ 91 92 93 94 95 96 97 98 99' (w 00') Top quality Pinot N, Chard, Pinot Gr, Ries. Reserve Pinot N: collaborations with Burgundian winemaker Patrice Rion.

Cooper Mountain Willamette ★★ Steadily increasing quality. Pinot N, Chard, Pinot Gr, Pinot bl. Organic v'yds working towards biodynamic certification.

Cristom N Willamette ★★★ 92' 93 94 95 96 97 98' 99' 00' Delicious Pinot N and buttery smooth Chard. Try the barrel-fermented Viognier.

Domaine Drouhin Willamette ★★★★ 91 92 93' 94 95 96 97 98' 99' 00' Superb estate-grown Pinot N from one of the first families of Burgundy. Laurène Reserve silky and elegant equally fine Chard 96 97 98 99'.

Domaine Serene Willamette ★★ 98' 99' 00 Big, jammy wines. Small production; look for Evenstead Reserve Pinot N; new Rockblock Syrah worth finding.

Elk Cove Vineyards Willamette ★★★ 98 99' Quality range of wines featuring Pinot N, Pinot Gr, Chard, Ries. Excellent dessert wines: Ultima.

Erath Vineyards Yamhill County ★★★ 93' 94 95 96 97 98 99 00 V gd Chard, Pinot Gr, Gewürz, Pinot Bl. Esp lovely old Pinots 76 & Ries 76. New winemaker 2002.

Evesham Wood Nr Salem Willamette ★★★ Sm family winery; fine Pinot N (91 92 93 94 95 96 97 98 99), Pinot Gris and dry Gewürz. Ltd production of Cuvée J in high demand. Newly organic vineyards.

Eyrie Vineyards, The Willamette ★★★ Pioneer ('65) winery with Burgundian convictions. Older vintages of Pinot Noir are treasures (**75' 76'** 80 83 86 89 90); Chards and Pinot Gr: rich yet crisp. All wines age beautifully.

Firesteed ★ Large-volume producer of value-priced Pinot N and a fine DOC Barbera d'Asti (made in Italy).

Ken Wright Cellars Yamhill County ★★★ 93 94 95 **96** 97 **98'** 99 01 Floral Pinot N that has a cult following. Also very gd Chard and Melon de Bourgogne.

King Estate S Willamette ★★→★★★ 94 95 96 97 98 99' Huge beautiful NAPA-like estate. Very good Pinot Gris; Chard and Pinot N improving; fruit sourced from all over, including Cab S, Merlot, and Zinfandel. New estate wines top.

Lange Winery Yamhill County ★★ 98 99' Small family winery; look for excellent reserve Pinot N; Pinot Gr is solid but Res reveals a heavy hand with oak.

Lemelson Yamhill County ★★★ 99' new, well-financed operation producing well-structured fine wines.

Panther Creek Willamette ★★★ 91 92 93 94' **95** 96 97 98' 99' Concentrated, meaty single v'yd Pinot N and pleasant Melon de Bourgogne. Purchased grapes from top v'yds, including Shea.

Ponzi Vineyards Willamette Valley ★★★ 89 90 91 92 93 94 **95** 96 **96** 97 98' 99' Small winery almost in Portland, well-known for Pinot Gr, Chard, Pinot N. Well-made Arneisand Dolcetto.

Rex Hill Willamette ★★→★★★ 91 92 93 94 **95** 96 97 98' 99' Excellent Pinot N, Pinot Gr and Chard from several N Willamette vineyards. Reserves are among Oregon's best; King's Ridge label is great value. New winemaker 2002.

St-Innocent Willamette ★★ 98 99 Gaining reputation for big, delicious, forward Pinot N; pleasant but slightly bitter whites.

Sokol Blosser Willamette ★★ 93 **94** 95 **96** 97 98' 99 Much improved. Pinot N. NV Evolution notable.

Torii Mor Yamhill County ★★★ 93 94 95 **96** 97 98' 99 Established Pinot N v'yd (planted 1977) in Dundee Hills; good Pinot Gr. Several gd single v'yd Pinot N bottlings. New winemaker in '00. First $100 bottle in Oregon.

Tyee S Willamette ★★ Small, family-owned and -run winery is especially good with dry Gewürz, Riesling and Pinot Bl. Pinot N improving.

Willakenzie Estate Yamhill County ★★★ 98' 99' 00 First wines released 1996; delicious Pinots Gris, Blanc, Chardonnay, Pinot Noir. Well-financed, state-of-the-art facility; French owner and winemaker.

Willamette Valley Vineyards Willamette ★★→★★★ 94 95 96 97' 98' 99' Huge winery near Salem. Moderate- to very high-quality Chard, Ries, Pinot Noir. Amazing range from commercial to top flight. Also owns and produces v.g Griffin Creek and Tualatin brands.

Witness Tree Willamette ★★ S'times lovely but inconsistent Pinot N; vg rich Chard.

Yamhill Valley Vineyards ★★★ Increasingly good Pinot Gr, Chard, Pinot N, Pinot Blanc.

Tracking down Northwest wines

Portland Wildwood (1221 NW 21st Avenue, tel 503-248-9663) The quintessential Northwest restaurant, with a dynamite Northwest wine list. Oregon Wines on Broadway (515 SW Broadway, tel 503-288-4655) Wine bar/shop with focus on Pinot Noir. Daily selections for tasting.

Dundee Ponzi Wine Bar (100 7th Street, tel 503-554-1500) A very attractive stop in the epicentre of wine country (45 mins from Portland). While the focus of wines to taste and buy is Ponzi's, you'll also find a broad selection of hard-to-find current releases from other top producers.

Seattle McCarthy & Schiering WIne Merchants (2401-B Queen Anne Ave.N. tel 206-282-8500; 6500 Ravenna Ave. NE, tel 206-524-9500) Seattle's best wine shop, with a stellar line-up of top Northwest names. Owner Dan McCarthy is also co-author of "A Pocket Guide to the WInes if Washington, Oregon & Idaho".

Washington & Idaho

Andrew Will Puget Sound (Washington) ★★★ 89 90 91 92 **93 94 95** 96 97 98' 99' 00 Exceptional Cabernet S, Merlot and barrel-fermented Chard from best E Washington grapes. Fine Pinot Gris.

Arbor Crest Spokane ★★★ New life from 99 when enologist daughter returned; tremendous talent just now showing inn the wines.

Barnard Griffin Pasco, Columbia Valley (Washington) ★★→★★★ Sml producer: well-made Merlot, Chard (esp barrel-fermented), Sem, Sauv Bl. Top Syrah.

Bookwalter Columbia Valley ★★★ 00' Older estate with new life thanks to consultant Zelma Long. Rich, balanced wines, well-priced.

Canoe Ridge ★★★ Walla Walla (Columbia Valley) ★★★ Owned by CHALONE (California). Impressive 93 94 95 96 **97 98** 99 Chard and Merlot. Fine Gewürzt

Cayuse Walla Walla 98' 99' Striking Rhône-styles showing a real taste of place.

Château Ste-Michelle Woodinville (Washington) ★★→★★★ Ubiquitous regional giant is Washington's largest winery; also owns COLUMBIA CREST, Northstar, Domaine Ste-Michelle and Snoqualmie. Major east Washington vineyard holdings, first-rate equipment and skilled wine-makers keep wide range of varieties in front ranks. Vineyard-designated Cabernet, Merlot, and Chard. Successful ventures with Antinori (Colsolare) & Ernst Loosen (Eroica).

Chinook Wines Yakima Valley (Washington) ★★ Owner-winemakers purchase local grapes for sturdy Chard, Sauv, Merlot, and Syrah. Look for Cab Franc.

Columbia Crest Columbia Valley ★★ Separately run CH STE-MICHELLE label for delicious well-made top value wines. Cab, Merlot, Syrah & Sauv Bl best. V gd res wines.

Columbia Winery Woodinville ★★→★★★ (Cab) 79 83 85 87 88 **89 90 91 92 93** 94 95 **96** 97 **98** 99 Pioneer (1962, as Associated Vintners) and still a leader. Balanced stylish understated single-v'yd wines, esp Syrah and Viognier.

DeLille Cellars Woodinville ★★★ **92** 93 94 95 96' 97 98' 99 Exciting winery for vg red B'dx blends: age-worthy Chaleur Estate, D2 (more forward, affordable). Excellent barrel fermented white (Sauv-Sém). Look out for new Syrah, Doyenne.

Dunham Cellars Walla Walla ★★★ **95 96 97** 98' 99 Young exciting wines from former L'ECOLE NO 41 (see below) assistant winemaker. Cabernets and Sém-Chardonnays all well extracted and elegant; lovely Syrah.

Glen Fiona Walla Walla ★★★ Rusty Figgins, brother of Leonetti's Gary Figgins, making only Syrah (oaked and unoaked) since 1995.

Gordon Brothers Columbia Valley ★★→★★★ Tiny cellar; consistent, balanced Chard (Res 91), Merlot, Cab. Recently improving: new w'maker.

Hedges Cellars Yakima Valley ★★★ Made its name exporting its wines to Europe and Scandinavia. Now boasts fine vineyard (Red Mountain), château-style wines, delicious Cab, Merlot, Sauv Bl.

Hogue Cellars, The Yakima Valley ★★→★★★ Large well-established producer known for excellent, good value wines, especially Ries, Chard, Merlot, Cab. Produces quintessential Washington Sauv Bl.

Kiona Vineyards Yakima Valley ★★ Solid Red Mountain producer since 1980. Very good quality/value Lemberger, Syrah, Cabernet Sauvignon.

Leonetti Walla Walla ★★★★ 91 92 **93** 94 95 **96'** 97 98' 99' 00' The Washington estate in highest demand – a major collectable wine. Harmonious individual Cabernet: fine and big-boned. Merlot: bold, ageworthy.

L'Ecole No 41 Walla Walla ★★★ 91 **92** 93 94 95 96' 97 98' 99' 00'

A choice of Pacific Northwest wines for 2003

Ch Ste Michelle Eroica Riesling, Columbia Valley, Washington
Chinook Cabernet Franc, Washington
Bookwalter Merlot, Washington
Chehalem Pinot Gris, Oregon
Cameron Abbey Ridge Pinot Noir, Oregon
Rockblock Syrah (made by **Domaine Serene**), Oregon

Blockbuster reds (Merlot, Cabernet, and MERITAGE blend) with jammy, age-worthy fruit. Good barrel-fermented Sémillon.

Matthews Cellars Woodinville ★★★ 96' **97** 98' 99 Smaller producer of mouth-filling Bordeaux blends since 1993. New Sém worth hunting down.

McCrea Puget Sound ★★★ Small winery for gd Viognier, Syrah, and Grenache. Experiments with Rhône blends continue.

Quilceda Creek Vintners Puget Sound ★★★★ 87 88 89 90 91 **92 93** 94 95 96' 97 98' 99 Expertly crafted ripe well-oaked Cab S from Columbia Valley grapes is the speciality. Exceptional finesse and ageability. Winemaker is the nephew of the legendary André Tchelistcheff.

Reininger Walla Walla ★★★ 99' Small, focused producer of top wines.

Rose Creek Vineyards S Idaho ★★ Small family winery; good esp for Chard.

Ste Chapelle Caldwell (Idaho) ★★ Pleasant, forward Chard, Ries, Cab, Merlot,

Syrah from local and E Washington v'yds. Attractive sparkling wine: good value and improving quality.

Washington Hills Cellars/Apex Yakima ★★ Solid line incl Sém, Fumé, Cab, Chard, Merlot, and late-harvest Ries, Gewürz. Apex label: higher quality.

Waterbrook Walla Walla ★★★ 89 90 91 92 93 94 95 96 97 98 99 Stylish, distinctive Chard, Sauv, Cab, Merlot from a winery that has hit its stride.

Woodward Canyon Walla Walla ★★★ 90 91 92 93 94 95 96 97 98 99' 00'. Quality-driven and loyally followed. Ripe, intense, but elegant Cab, Chard, and blends.

British Columbia

This expanding and significant part of the Canadian wine industry has grown up since the 70s. The biggest concentration of wineries is in the splendid Okanagan Valley, 150 miles east of Vancouver, in climatic conditions not very different from eastern Washington. There are 63 wineries and 4 appellations (Okanagan Valley, Frasier Valley, Similkameen Valley, and Vancouver Island).

Burrowing Owl 98' 99 00 01 Excellent Chard and Pinot Gr; promising reds.

Calona Vineyards ★★ 98' 99 00 01 Large winery. Gd Pinot Bl, Sém and Merlot.

Gray Monk ★★ 98' 99 00 01 Gd Okanagan Auxerrois, Gewürz and Pinot Blanc.

Mission Hill ★→★★★ 98' 99 00 01 Acclaimed Reserve Chard, Pinot Blanc.

Paradise Ranch ★★★ Impressive Icewines.

Quails' Gate ★★ 98' 99 00 01 Chardonnay, Chenin Blanc, Pinot Noir, Riesling Ice Wine.

Sumac Ridge ★★ 98' 99 00 01 Gewürz, Sauv Bl, sp among region's best. Notable MERITAGE and Merlot. (Owned by VINCOR.)

East of the Rockies & Ontario

Producers in New York (there are now 160 in 7 AVAs) and other eastern states, as well as Ohio (66 in 4 AVAs) and Ontario (67) traditionally made wine from hardy native grapes and French-American hybrids. Today, consumer taste plus cellar and vineyard technology largely bypass these, although Seyval Blanc, Chambourcin, and Vidal keep their fans. Chardonnay, Riesling, and Cabernet Sauvignon are now firmly established. Pinot Noir is emerging with some notable results, and Cabernet Franc and Merlot appear overall to be the East's most promising red. Progress, from Virginia to Ontario, is accelerating as the wines gain recognition outside their own immediate region.

Wineries and vineyards

Allegro ★★ 00 01 Pennsylvania. Worthy Chard, Cab.

Andres 2nd-lgst Canadian winery. Owns HILLEBRAND and new Peller Estates.

Antony Road Has risen to the top in Finger Lakes. Fine Riesling and superb late-harvest VIGNOLES.

Bedell ★★★ 98 00 01 LONG ISLAND winery; excellent Merlot and Cab S.

Biltmore Estate ★★ 00 01 Largest of North Carolina's 22 wineries with Vanderbilt mansion, America's largest. Chard and sparkling.

Canandaigua Wine Co NY based. World's 2nd largest wine co. Owns and operates 12 different wineries in California, Idaho, New York, and Washington State. 2002 sales hit 45 million 9-litre cases. Full range of sherry-style wines, table and sparkling (250,000 cases).

Cave Spring Cellars ★★★ 00 01 ONTARIO boutique: sophisticated Chard, Ries, and Gamay. Big restaurant, popular tourist stop, 28-room inn.

Chaddsford ★★★ 99 00 01 Solid Pennsylvania producer since '82: especially for good Pinot Gris and B'dx-style red blend.

Chamard ★★ 99 00 01 Connecticut's best winery, owned by Tiffany chairman. Top Chard. AVA is Southeastern New England.

Château des Charmes ★★★ 99 00 01 Show-place château-style ONTARIO winery. Fine Chard, Viognier, Cab, sparkling.

Clinton Vineyards ★★ 00 01 HUDSON R winery; clean dr SEYVAL & spirited sp Seyval.

Chalet Debonné Vineyards ★★ 00 01 Popular OHIO estate (in Lake Erie AVA): hybrids, eg CHAMBOURCIN and VIDAL; and *vinifera*, eg Chard, Ries, Pinot Gr.

Finger Lakes Beautiful historic upstate NY cool-climate region, source of most of state's wines. Seat of NY State's "*vinifera* revolution". Top wineries: ANTONY ROAD, Château La Fayette Reneau, DR FRANK, FOX RUN, GLENORA, STANDING STONE, Swedish Hill, H WEIMER, Kings Ferry, Red Newt & Shalestone.

Firelands ★★ 00 01 Ohio estate in LAKE ERIE AVA, growing Chardonnay, Cab, Gewürz, Pinot Gris, Riesling sp and Pinot Noir.

Fox Run ★★★ 98 99 00 01 Gd example of new generation FINGER LAKES winemaking; some of the region's best Chard, Gewürz, Ries, Pinot Noir, & B'x style red.

Frank, Dr Konstantin (Vinifera Wine Cellars) ★★★ 98 99 00 01 Sm, influential winery. The late Dr F was a pioneer in growing European vines in the FINGER LAKES. Good Ries, Gewürz, Chard, Cab S, and Pinot N. Vg Chateau Frank sp.

Glenora Wine Cellars ★★ 00 01 FINGER LAKES producer of good sparkling wine, Chard and Ries Restaurant and inn with scenic lake views. Expanding empire includes two new wineries.

Hamptons, The (Aka South Fork) LONG ISLAND AVA. The top winery is moneyed WOLLFER ESTATE. Duck Walk up-and-coming.

Henry of Pelham ★★★ 98 99 00 01 Elegant ONTARIO Chardonnay & Riesling; Cabernet/ Merlot, distinctive Baco Noir.

Hillebrand Estates ★→★★★ 98' 99 00 01 ONTARIO producer attracting attention with Ries, sp, and B'dx-style red blend. Handsome restaurant.

Hudson River Region America's oldest winegrowing district (28 producers) and NY's first AVA. Straddles the river, two hours' drive N of Manhattan.

Inniskillin ★★★★ 98' 99 00 01 Outstanding (VINCOR-owned) prod that spearheaded birth of modern ONTARIO wine industry. Skilful burgundy-style Chard & Pinot N & B'dx-style red. Vg Ries, ice wine (incl sp), Pinot Gr.

Lake Erie Lgst grape-growing district in the eastern US; 25,000 acres along shore of Lake Erie, incl portions of New York, Pennsylvania & OHIO. 90% is CONCORD (mostly used for commercial juice & jelly), generally from New York's Chautauqua County. Also name of a tri-state AVA: NY's sector has 8 wineries, Pennsylvania's 5 and Ohio's 26. Ohio's Harpersfield sets standards for quality.

Lamoreaux Landing ★★★ 97 98 99 00 01 Stylish FINGER LAKES house: promising Chard, Ries, and Cab Franc from striking Greek-revival winery.

Lenz ★★★ 99 00 01 Classy winery of NORTH FORK AVA. Fine austere Chard in the Chablis mode, also Gewürz, Merlot and sparkling wine.

Long Island Exciting wine region East of the Rockies and a hothouse of experimentation. Currently 2,700+ acres, all *vinifera* (47% Chard) and 3 AVAs (NORTH FORK and THE HAMPTONS). Most of its 29 wineries are on the North Fork. Best varieties: Chard, Cab, F Merlot. A long growing season; almost frost-free. Promising new wineries incl: Leib, Galluccio (formerly Gristina), Schneider, Raphael.

Michigan In addition to fine cool climate Ries, impressive Gewürz, Pinot N, and Cabernet F, are emerging; 32 commercial wineries and four AVAs. Best include St-Julien Wine Co, Ch Grand Traverse, Peninsula Cellars (Bulls Eye Pinot bl), and Tabor Hill. Mawby Vyds and Ch Chantal known for sparkling wine from Chard, Pinot Noir, and Pinot Meunier. Fenn Valley and Good

Harbour have lge local following. Black Star Farms, a showplace with inn, creamery and distillery.

Millbrook ★★★ 00 01 Top HUDSON RIVER REGION winery. Dedicated viticulture and savvy marketing has lifted spiffy whitewashed Millbrook in big old barn into NY's firmament. Burgundian Chards: splendid; Cab F can be delicious.

North Fork LONG ISLAND AVA (of 3). Top wineries: Bedell, Macari, LENZ, PALMER, PAUMANOK, PELLEGRINI, PINDAR. 2½ hrs' drive from Manhattan.

Ohio 66 wineries, 4 AVAs, notably LAKE ERIE and Ohio Valley.

Ontario Main eastern Canada wine region, on Niagara Peninsula, Pelee Island and LAKE ERIE north shore: 71 wineries. three small young wineries (Thirty Bench, Malivoire, Thirteenth Street) now raising the quality bar here. Riesling, Chardonnay, Cab F, even Pinot Noir show potential for longevity. Ice wine is international flagship of region. Gewürz and Pinot Gr showing promise.

Palmer ★★★ 00 01 Superior LONG ISLAND (N FORK) producer and byword in Darwinian metropolitan market. High profile due to perpetual-motion marketing. Tasty Chard, Sauv Bl and Chinon-like Cab F.

The Big Apple has local wines – where to find them:

No longer the rarity they once were, NY wines have finally gained a foothold in Manhattan restaurants. Among the top players offering local wines:

Le Bernardin 1er seafood restaurant offering fish-friendly East Coast wines.

Home Cosy Greenwich Village spot where New York wines complement "American Neighbourhood" cuisine.

Gramercy Tavern A cosy mix of urban chic and low-key charm.

Gustavino's New and trendy sunlit space under the 59th Street Bridge.

Jean Georges Sophisticated favourite of NY gourmands – local wine offerings.

Judson Grill Contemporary market-based seasonal fare – serious wine list.

Savoy SoHo hotspot with New York wines.

Zoe Eclectic contemporary American cuisine –strong wine list

Paumanok ★★★ 99 00 Rising fine LONG ISLAND (N FORK) winery; impressive Cab, Merlot, Ries, Chard, outstanding Chenin, savoury late-harvest Sauv.

Pellegrini ★★★ 98 99 00 01 LONG ISLAND's most enchantingly designed winery (on N FORK), opened 1993. Opulent Merlot, stylish Chard, B'x-like Cab. Inspired winemaking. Exceptionally flavourful wines.

Pindar Vineyards ★★★ 99 00 01 Lge 287-acre operation at N FORK, LONG ISLAND (Island's lgst). Wide range of blends & popular varietals, incl Chard, Merlot, sp & esp gd B'dx-type r blend, Mythology. Popular tourist destination.

Red Newt ★★★ Est. 99 in Finger Lakes. Already turning out top Chard, Ries, Cab F, Merlot, and B'x-inspired red blend. Popular bistro.

Sakonnet ★★ 00 01 Largest New England winery, based in Little Compton, Rhode Island (SE New Eng AVA). V drinkable wines incl Chard, VIDAL, dry Gewürz, Cab Fr and Pinot N. Delicious sp Brut cuvée.

Standing Stone ★★★ 98 99 00 01 One of FINGER LAKES' finest wineries with very good Ries, Gewürz and Bordeaux-type blend.

Tomasello ★★ 99 00 01 Est'd New Jersey winery. Gd CHAMBOURCIN. Cab S and Merlot.

Unionville Vineyards ★★ 99 00 01 One of New Jersey's best wineries, est '93. Lovely Ries and good Cab/Merlot blend.

Vincor International ★→★★ 4th lgst co in N America. Recently acquired Calif's RH Phillips and Washington State's Hogue Cellars. Premium wines; varietals, blends. Owns Jackson-Triggs, INNISKILLIN (Chard, Cab), and Sumac Ridge (BC).

Vineland Estates ★★★ 98 00 Gd ONTARIO producer; dry and semi-dry Ries, Gewürz much admired. VIDAL ice wine: good, Chard, Cab, Sauv bl, and B'dx-style red. Excellent restaurant & tasting room.

Vintners Quality Alliance Canada's appellation body, started in ONTARIO but now incl BRITISH COLUMBIA. Its rigid standards have rapidly raised respect and awareness of Canadian wines to high levels. VQA enacted into Ontario law in 2000.

Wagner Vineyards ★★ 00 01 Famous FINGER LAKES winery. Barrel-fermented Chard, dry and sw Riesling and ice wine. Attracts many visitors.

Westport Rivers ★★ 00 01 Massachusetts house est'd '89. Good Chard and elegant sparkling. (Southeastern New England AVA.)

Wiemer, Hermann J ★★→★★★ 97' **98'** 99 00 01 Creative German-born FINGER LAKES winemaker. Outstanding Ries incl vg sp and "late harvest". Vg Chard.

Wolffer Estate ★★★ 99 **00** 01 In operation since '87, has come of age with modish Chard, Merlot and sparkling from German-born winemaker. Proof that gd wine can be made on LONG ISLAND's South Fork.

Wollersheim ★★ Wisconsin winery specializing in variations of Maréchal Foch. Prairie Fumé (Seyval Bl) is a commercial success.

Southern and central states

Virginia Emerging as important wine state since 72. 71 wineries (in 6 AVAs), 2146 (51% increase from 1995) acres of vineyards. Top whites include Chard, Pinot Gr, & Viognier. Best reds are Cab F, Merlot, & Cab S. Top producers include Barboursville, Breaux, Horton (Viognier, other Rhône-style wines), Ingleside Plantation, Jefferson (near Monticello), Linden, Piedmont, Prince Michael, Oakencroft, Rockbridge, Tarara, Whitehall, Williamsburg, and Villa Appalaccia. Exciting newcomers: Chrysalis, impressive Viognier & Valhalla.

Missouri A blossoming industry with 41 producers in 3 AVAs: Augusta (first in the US), Hermann, Ozark Highlands. In-state sales catching fire. Best wines are SEYVAL BLANC, VIDAL, Vignoles (sweet and dry versions). Top estate is Stone Hill, in Hermann (since 1847): rich red from NORTON grape variety; Hermannhof (1852) is drawing notice for the same. St James for both Vignoles and Norton; Mount Pleasant, in Augusta: rich "port" and nice sparkling wine. To watch are Adam Puchta, Augusta Winery, Blumenhof, Les Bourgeois, Montelle, Röbler.

Maryland 11 wineries, 2 AVAs. Basignani makes good Cabernet S, Chardonnay, SEYVAL. Best-known Boordy Vineyards: good Seyval Chard, Cab and sparkling. Fiore's CHAMBOURCIN is interesting. Catoctin AVA: main Cabernet and Chardonnay area. Linganore is second AVA.

The Southwest and the Rockies

Texas

The fifth-largest wine producing state in the US has 37 bonded wineries, with 6 more projected; 7 AVAs. Although Pierce's Disease is a concern, the state has over 3300 acres under vine, primarily *vinifera*. The best wines compare well with California.

Becker Vineyards ★★★ Stonewall. Very gd Merlot, Claret (esp 99). Award winning Cab S and Chard. Good port-style wine.

La Buena Vida Vineyards ★ Tasting room in Grapevine (nr Dallas). Produces tables wines under brands of Springtown, Walnut Creek Cellars and LaBuena Vida. Very good Walnut Creek Ports, esp 96.

Cap Rock ★★★ Nr Lubbock. Reliably good varietals: Cab S, Chard, Merlot. Well-crafted blends, especially Cabernet Royale.

Fall Creek Vineyards Texas Hill Country. Good Chard and Ries.

Hidden Springs Winery Pilot Point. Good merlot and Chard.

Konzelmann ★★★ Top Ries, Chard and Icewine.

Llano Estacado ★★★ nr Lubbock. The pioneer (since 76) continues on award-winning track with Chard, Chenin blanc and Zin. Very good blends, esp Signature series and Viviano.

Messina Hof Wine Cellars ★★★ nr Bryan. Very good boutique wines. Excellent late-harvest Riesling and Cabernet Sauvignon (especially 99 Barrel Res). Now has restaurant and deluxe B&B.

Peninsular Ridge ★★★ Est. Ontario 2000, already showing good Chard, Merlot, icewine. Restaurant with panoramic view of Lake Ontario.

Ste-Genevieve ★ Fort Stockton. Largest Texas winery, linked with Domaines Cordier (France). Well-made NV wines but now has premium label Escondido Valley wines, esp Chard and Syrah.

Spicewood Good Sauvignon Blanc and Chard.

New Mexico etc

New Mexico continues to show promise with more emphasis on *vinifera* grapes, though some French hybrids are still used (historic Mission grape is produced at Tularosa Winery). Three AVAs and over 20 wineries. Casa Rondeña: ★★ good Cab F (esp **99**). Gruet Winery: ★★★ excellent sparkling wines and good Chard & Pinot N. Jory: good Sauv Bl and Zin. La Chiripada: ★★ good blends, some with hybrids and good Riesling and port-style wine. Milagro Vineyards: small, but good chard. Ponderosa Valley: ★★ very good Riesling and blends especially Summer Sage. Santa Fe Vineyards: ★★ very good Chard and Zin, good blends. La Viña: ★★ good Chard and Zin; good blends, esp Rojo Loco.

Colorado continues to focus on *vinifera* grapes, with about 400 acres planted, mostly on the Western Slope. Thirty-six wineries and two AVAs. Carlson Cellars: ★ good blends and good Riesling, Chardonnay, and fruit wines. Canyon Wind Cellars: good Chardonnay and Merlot. Cottonwood Cellars: Rich Cab S and good merlot and Chard. Grande River: good Chard. Plum Creek: good Chardonnay and Merlot. Terror Creek: ★★ very good Pinot Noir, Ries, Gewürz. Trail Ridge: new, shows promise with blends.

Oklahoma – a state to watch in 2003

Oklahoma has made huge strides establishing its niche in the Southwest. A new law allowing wineries to sell directly to liquor stores and restaurants has inspired interest in wine. Some labels call up a "fun" image with wine names such as "Oklahoma Gold" and "Dust Bowl Red"; but winemakers and grapegrowers are serious, and proud, of the dozen or so wineries. Growers are experimenting with Native American and French American Hybrids as well as *vinifera*. **Sparks Vineyards and Winery** shows promise with Merlot, Chard, Zin, Vidal Blanc. Family-owned **Stone Bluff Cellars**, near Tulsa, features hybrids; award-winning Cynthiana and Vignoles.

Arizona progresses in overall quality and the number of wineries (now 10). Success with Rhone and Mediterranean grape varieties: Sangiovese, Syrah, Petit Sirah show promise. Callaghan Vineyards: ★★ Excellent Meritage blend: Buena Suerte Cuvée, gd Syrah. Dos Cabezas: ★ Petit Sirah, Chard, Sangiovese. Kokopelli, Arizona's largest winery, makes sound, reasonably-priced wines. Echo Canyon, new, emphasizes Rhone varietals.

Oklahoma has expanded to 11 wineries. **Utah** continues to show promise but also has limited wineries. **Nevada**'s Pahrump Valley V'yd near Las Vegas has very good Chard, Cab S and Symphony.

EAST OF THE ROCKIES & ONTARIO

Central & South America

More heavily shaded areas
are the wine growing regions

Chile

Sustaining the surge in quality that took place in the 1990s was
always going to be difficult for Chile. Many observers feel that the
country risks being overtaken by neighbouring Argentina in the wine
race. But the Chileans are still on the move. Where once simple varietal
wines dominated production, we're now seeing more interesting
blended wines. Carmenère, for many years mistakenly labelled Merlot,
has emerged as a serious grape variety, although there is an increased
realization that its best role is in blends.

Chile's vineyards (all irrigated) can be found throughout the 300
miles of the Central Valley to the south of Santiago. Most lie on flat
plains, but hillside sites are beginning to be exploited. Casablanca
(between Santiago and Valparaiso) offers excellent *terroir* for
Chardonnay, Sauvignon Blanc, and Pinot Noir, although red-wine
fever means that more Carmenère and even Cabernet Sauvignon
are now being planted.

Recent vintages

As a general rule, whites and cheaper reds should be drunk as young as
possible.

2001 Near-perfect conditions, generally lower yields, very high quality.

2000 Lge, cool vintage. Gd v'yard managers made excellent, aromatic wines.

1999 Low yields and drought produced conc'd but some slightly baked reds.

1998 Cool, El Niño-affected season; erratic ripening and high yields.
1997 Excellent warm vintage, produced small crop of aromatic, conc'd wines.
1996 Summer rains and a cool harvest made for uneven ripening and quality.

Aconcagua Northernmost quality wine region. Incl CASABLANCA, Panquehue.

Almaviva See Baron Philippe de Rothschild.

Antiyal ★★→★★★ New MAIPO venture from Alvaro Espinoza, winemaker at VIÑA CARMEN making fine and complex red from organically grown fruit.

Baron Philippe de Rothschild ★★★→★★★★ Famous B'dx company making good Mapa varietal range, better Escudo Rojo red blend, and expensive but classy, claret-style Almaviva, the latter a MAIPO joint venture with CONCHA Y TORO.

Bío-Bío Sthnmost quality wine region. Wet. Potential for gd whites and Pinot N.

Calina, Viña ★★ Kendall-Jackson (see California) venture. Better reds (esp Selección de Las Lomas Cab S) than whites, with silky Elite Cab S the pick. El Caliz is good, intro-level range.

Caliterra ★★→★★★ Sister winery of ERRAZURIZ, now half-owned by Mondavi (California). Chardonnay and Sauv Bl improving (higher proportions of CASABLANCA grapes), reds becoming less one-dimensional. Reserva range, very good, new Arboleda wines (Cabernet S, Syrah, Carmenère, Merlot, Chardonnay) even better. Seña (★★★★) is high-class Mondavi-inspired Cab S/Merlot/ Carmenère blend launched '97.

Cánepa, José ★★ Still finding feet after company upheaval in mid-1990s; historically good reds, also decent Semillon.

Carmen, Viña ★★★ MAIPO winery under same ownership as SANTA RITA. Ripe, fresh Special Res (CASABLANCA) Chardonnay and deliciously light Late-harvest MAIPO Sem top whites. Reds even better; esp RAPEL Merlots, Maipo Petite Sirah, and Cabs, esp Gold Reserve. Now does vg Maipo Syrah and has new organic range called Nativa.

Carta Vieja ★★ MAULE winery owned by one family for six generations. Reds, esp Cab and Merlot, better than whites, though Antigua Selección Chard is good.

Casa Lapostolle ★★★ Money from the family of Grand Marnier and winemaking expertise from Bordeaux's Michel Rolland result in fine range across the board. Bordeaux-style Sauvignon is good, but the reds, led by stunning (but pricey) Merlot-based Clos Apalta, are even better.

Casablanca Cool-climate region between Santiago and coast. V little water: drip irrigation essential. Top-class Chard and Sauv; promising Merlot and Pinot N.

Casablanca, Viña ★★★ Sister winery to SANTA CAROLINA. Wines now made by Joseba Altuna of Guelbenzu (Spain). RAPEL and MAIPO fruit used for some reds but better wines, notably Merlot, Sauv, Chard, and Gewürz, come from Santa Isabel Estate in CASABLANCA. Look for new super-*cuvée* Fundo.

Casa Silva ★★ Colchagua estate offering pithy Classic Sémillon, spicy, chunky Reserva Merlot, and top-of-the-range Quinta Generación Red and White; the white is a wonderful blend of Chardonnay, Sauvignon Gris, and Viognier.

Concha y Toro ★★→★★★★ Mammoth operation; *bodegas* and v'yds all over Chile. Top wines: meaty Amelia CASABLANCA Chard; rich, chocolatey Marqués de Casa Concha Merlot (RAPEL); and Don Melchor Cab (Rapel); also "Trio" Range (now with 6 wines!); good-value Explorer wines, incl Alicante Bouschet, Pinot Noir, Cab/Syrah; and new Terrunyo range, focusing on specific *terroirs*. See also Baron Philippe de Rothschild.

Cono Sur ★★→★★★★ Chimbarongo winery owned by CONCHA Y TORO for very good Pinots (local and CASABLANCA fruit). Also dense, fruity Cabs, delicious Viognier, and spicy Zinfandel. Top releases appear as "20 Barrels" selection. Also second label Isla Negra.

Cousiño Macul ★★→★★★ Distinguished, beautiful old MAIPO estate. Long-lived Antiguas Res Cab; top wine Finis Terrae (B'dx blend). Also supple Merlot and old-fashioned, very dry Sem, Chardonnay.

Dallas Conté ★★→★★★ Fresh, nutty Casablanca Chard & ripe, fleshy Cab are the stars from collaboration between Australia's Mildara Blass & VIÑA S CAROLINA.

Domus ★★★ MAIPO single, v'yd venture from Ignacio Recabarren (see Viña Casablanca) and Ricardo Peña, making good Chard and vg Cab.

Echeverría ★★ Boutique Curicó (MAULE) winery producing intense, complex Reserve Cabs, v gd oaked and unoaked Chard and rapidly improving Sauv Bl.

Edwards, Luís Felipé ★★ Colchagua (RAPEL) winery; citrussy Chard, silky Res Cab. Wines now made by an ex-Penfolds winemaker.

Errázuriz ★★★ Sole winery in Panquehue district of ACONCAGUA. First-class range, including complex, mealy Wild Ferment Chard (now partnered by a Pinot N); brooding Syrah; Chile's best Sangiovese; earthy, plummy Merlot; fine Cabs topped by Don Maximiano Reserve. Also fine newcomer Viñedo Chadwick (Cab S/Carmenère), 1st vintage 99.

Fortuna, Viña La ★★ Old-est'd winery in Lontué Valley. Range of attractive varietal wines, esp chunky Malbec.

Francisco de Aguirre, Viña ★★ Promising Cabs S and F and Chard under the Palo Alto label from the northerly region of Valle de Limari.

Gracia, Viña ★★ Newcomer with v'yds from ACONCAGUA down to BIO-BIO. Cab S Reserva R is best; gd Pinot N and Chard. Plans for Mourvèdre and Syrah.

Haras de Pirque ★★ New estate in Pirque (MAIPO). Smoky, Graves-like Sauv Bl, stylish Chard, dense, fruity Cab S/Merlot made by A. Espinoza (see Antiyal).

Larose, Viña de ★ RAPEL venture by Médoc Ch Larose-Trintaudon under the Las Casas del Toqui and Viña Alamosa labels. Promising, top-end Leyenda Chard and red blend.

Maipo Oldest wine region, nr Santiago. Quite warm. Source of Chile's top Cabs.

Maule S'most region in Central Valley. Incl Claro, Loncomilla, Tutuven Valleys.

Montes ★★→★★★ Alpha Cab can be brilliant; Merlot, Syrah and Malbec also fine; whites steady. B'x blend Montes Alpha M is improving with each vintage, while new Folly Syrah outstanding; the best in Chile.

Mont Gras ★★→★★★ State-of-the-art winery in Colchagua Valley capable of top-class Merlot and Cabernet. Best wines under Ninquen label. American Paul Hobbs is consultant.

Morande ★★ Vast range including César, Cinsault, Bouschet, and Carignan. "Limited Edition" used for top wines, including a spicy Syrah/Cabernet Sauvignon and inky Malbec.

Paul Bruno ★★ MAIPO joint venture of Paul Pontallier and Bruno Prats from B'dx with Chilean Felipé de Solminihac. Flagship wine slowly improving as vines age. Also good value Uno Fuera Cab S.

Porta, Viña ★★ MAIPO winery under same ownership as Viña Gracia offering reliable range including supple, spicy Cab.

Rapel Central quality region divided into Colchagua and Cachapoal valleys. Source of great Merlot.

La Rosa, Viña ★★ Impressive RAPEL Chards, Merlots, Cabs under La Palmeria and Cornellana labels.

San Pedro ★★→★★★ Massive Curicó-based producer. Gato reds and whites are top-sellers. Best wines: Castillo de Molina and 1865 reds, and Cabo de Hornas Cabernet S.

Santa Carolina, Viña ★★→★★★ Historic *bodega*; increasingly impressive and complex wines. All MAIPO Reserve wines are good, including a rich, limey Sauv Bl. Barrica Selection range, incl earthy Carmenère and supple Syrah, is better still. New Cab S/Merlot/Syrah Trébol is complex and excellent value.

Santa Inés ★★ Successful small family winery in Isla de MAIPO making ripe, blackcurranty Legado de Armida Cab Sauv. Also labelled as De Martino.

Santa Mónica ★★★ Rancagua (RAPEL) winery; the best label is Tierra del Sol. Riesling, Semillon, and Merlot under Santa Mónica label also gd.

Santa Rita, Viña ★★→★★★★ Long-est'd MAIPO *bodega* improving steadily. Range in ascending quality: 120, Reserva, Medalla Real, new Florester (inc. fine red blends), Casa Real. Best: Casa Real Maipo Cab S, but Triple C (Cab S/Cab F/Carmenère) nearly as gd.

Selentia ★★ New Chilean/Spanish venture making Char and Cab S. Reserve special Cab S is fine, B'dx-like red.

Seña See Caliterra.

Tarapacá, Viña ★★ MAIPO winery much improved after recent investment but still inconsistent.

Terramater ★★ Wines made from sources throughout the Central Valley incl v gd Altum range.

Terranoble ★ Talca winery specializing in grassy Sauv and light, peppery Merlot, range now expanded and incl v gd spicy Carmenère Gran Reserva.

Torreón de Paredes ★ Attractive, crisp Chard, age-worthy Res Cab from this RAPEL *bodega*. Flagship Don Amedo Cab S could be better.

Torres, Miguel ★★ Pioneering Curicó winery now back on form with fresh whites and gd reds, esp sturdy Manso del Velasco single-v'yd Cab and Cariñena-based Cordillera. See also Spain.

Undurraga ★★ Traditional MAIPO estate known for its Pinot. Top wines: Reserva Chard, refreshing, limey Gewürz; peachy Late Harvest Sém.

Valdivieso ★★ Major producer with new Lontué winery. Single-vineyard Cab F, Merlot, Malbec and NV blend Caballo Loco are pick of the range. Reserve bottlings also gd, but quality more erratic among the cheaper wines.

Vascos, Los ★★ Lafite-Rothschild-SANTA RITA operation, but no Chilean first growth. Wines: fair but neglect fruit flavours in favour of firm structures. New top blend Le Dix has still to convince.

Veramonte ★★ CASABLANCA-based operation of Agustín Huneeus (formerly of California winery Franciscan); whites from Casablanca fruit, red from Central Valley grapes – all good. Top wine: Primus red blend.

Villard ★★ Sophisticated wines made by French-born Thierry Villard. Gd MAIPO reds, especially heady Merlot, Equis Cab S and CASABLANCA whites. Also v alluring Casablanca Pinot Noir.

Viu Manent ★ Emerging Colchagua winery; best of fine range are plummy Cab S, exotic Merlot, & dense, chewy Malbec. Watch out for Syrah in the future.

Argentina

Despite the recent financial crisis, it is not all doom and gloom in Argentina. Improvements in viticulture and winemaking continue, often aided by investment from overseas. However foreign influence is not entirely positive. "International" rather than Argentinean flavours can dominate. More welcome is the emergence of small labels run by home-grown talent – Benmarco, Susana Balbo, Tikal, and Luca are four to look out for.

Malbec remains the most successful grape variety. Decent Cabernet also exists, although many of the unblended versions can seem hollow. Syrah is beginning to show promise, as are Bonarda, Tempranillo, and Sangiovese. For whites, reasonable Chardonnay and Sauvignon Blanc exist, but the spicy Torrontés makes the most distinctive wines; not to everyone's taste.

The warm dry climate, watered by snow-melt from the Andes, makes grape-growing relatively easy. Vineyard conditions are determined more by altitude than latitude. Mendoza is the most important province, but conditions are far from uniform.

Recent vintages

As a general rule, whites and cheaper reds should be drunk as young as possible.

2001 Quality is variable, but some very good reds.

2000 Rain at harvest and hail caused problems but some excellent reds from those who picked after the rain.

1999 A drought year. Some rich, full-bodied red wines.

1998 The El Niño vintage. Dilute and occasionally unripe reds but some are gd.

1997 Lge harvest affected by storms. Erratic quality – top reds show good fruit

1996 Without the depth and class of 95 but the best reds have good fruit.

Archaval Ferrer ★★★ MENDOZA. Super-conc'd reds, esp Gran Malbec.

La Agrícola ★ Dynamic MENDOZA estate producing gd-value Santa Julia range, led by new blend "Magma" and higher-quality "Q" label (impressive Malb, Merl, Tempranillo). Recently introduced Terra Organica organic wines: good but not great.

Alta Vista ★★★ French-owned MENDOZA venture specializing in Malbec. Dense, spicy Alto among best wines in the country.

Altos las Hormigas ★★★ Italian-owned Malbec specialist, wines made by consultant Alberto Antonini (ex-technical director of Italy's Antinori). Top wine: Viña las Hormigas.

Anubis ★★ New joint venture between Alberto Antonini and Susana Balbo making exciting, juicy reds, esp Malbec.

Arizù, Leoncio ★★ Small MENDOZA (Maipù) bodega with three tiers of quality – Viña Paraiso, Luigi Bosca and Finca Los Nobles. high standards esp gd Los Nobles Malbec/Verdot and Cabernet Bouchet. Alberto Arizù Snr makes fine Petit Verdot, Malbec, and Nebbiolo under Viña Alicia label.

Balbi, Bodegas ★★ Allied-Domecq-owned San Raphael producer. Juicy Malbec, Chard, & delicious Syrah (red & rosé). Red blend Barbaro also v gd.

Bianchi, Valentin ★ San Rafael red specialist Familia Bianchi (Cab S) is excellent flagship, while good-value Elsa's Vineyard label includes meaty Barbera. Also pithy Sauv Bl.

Canale, Bodegas Humberto ★★ Premier Río Negro winery known for its Sauvignon Blanc & Pinot Noir, but Merlot & Malbec (esp those under the Black River label) are the stars.

Catena ★★★ Dynamic Dr Nicolas Catena oversees production of Argento, Alamos Ridge (both for gd-value Cab, Chard, Malbec), Catena (v good Cab, Chard, Malbec), Catena Alta (top Cab, Malbec, stunning Chard) and new flagship Nicolas Catena Zapata. Also new Cabernet/Malbec blend "CaRo" made with the Rothschilds of Lafite, 1st vintage 2000.

Chandon, Bodegas ★→★★ Makers of Baron B and M Chandon sparklers under Moët & Chandon supervision; new promising Pinot N-Chard blend. Mostly sold on home market. Also see Terrazas.

Doña Paula ★ Luján de Cuyo estate owned by Santa Rita (see Chile) making dense, structured Malbec.

Esmerelda, Bodegas See CATENA.

Etchart ★★→★★★ Pernod-Ricard owned, two wineries in SALTA and MENDOZA. Fresh, spicy Torrontés from Cafayate in SALTA, reds from both regions gd, topped by plummy Cafayate Cab S.

Fabre Montmayou ★★ French-owned Luján de Cuyo (MENDOZA) bodega; fine reds and advice from Michel Rolland of B'dx. Also decent Chard.

Finca La Anita ★★ Syrah, Malbec, and Cuarto de Milla (Syrah-Malbec blend) are best wines from this MENDOZA boutique winery.

Finca Colomé ★★★ SALTA *bodega* now owned by California's Hess Collection turning out very Rhône-like Cab-Merlot blend.

Finca Flichman ★★ Old co: two wineries in MENDOZA now owned by Portugal's Sogrape. Varietal range topped by Private Res Cab S. Good-value Syrah. Top wine: Dedicato blend.

Finca El Retiro ★★ MENDOZA bodega making good reds under guidance of Alberto Antonini. See Altos las Hormigas.

Lurton, Bodegas J & F ★★→★★★ MENDOZA venture of Jacques and François Lurton. Juicy, conc Piedra Negra Malbec heads range which also includes decent Pinot G, Malbec and Cab S.

Mendoza Most important province for wine (over 70% of plantings). Best sub-regions: Agrelo, Tupungato, Luján de Cuyo, and Maipú.

Navarro Correas ★★ Good if sometimes over-oaked reds, esp Col Privada Cab S. Also reasonable whites, inc v oaky Chard and Deutz-inspired fizz.

Nieto Senetiner, Bodegas ★★ Luján de Cuyo-based *bodega*. Good-value wines produced under the Valle de Vistalba label, plus recently introduced top-of-the-range Cadus reds. Alberto Antonini (see Altos las Hormigas) is a consultant.

Norton, Bodegas ★★★ Old *bodega*, now Austrian-owned. Gd whites & v gd reds, esp chunky, fruity Malbec and Privada blend (Mer-Cab S-Malbec).

Patagonia, Viña ★→★★ Owned by Concha y Toro of Chile, making gd-value if rather "'international" Malbec, Syrah, Cab S, Mer, Chard under Trivento label.

Peñaflor ★→★★★ Argentina's biggest wine co, reputedly the world's third lgst. Bulk wines for domestic market incl Andean Vineyards, Fond de Cave (Chard, Cab) labels and for finer wines, TRAPICHE.

Río Negro Promising new area in Patagonia.

Salentein, Bodegas ★★ Ambitious new Valle de Uco (MENDOZA) *bodega*, already succeeding with Cab S, Malb, Merl and (under the Primus label) Pinot Noir. Entry-level wins appear as Finca El Portillo or La Pampa.

Salta Northerly province with the world's highest v'yds. Sub-region Cafayate renowned for Torrontés.

San Telmo ★★ Modern Seagram-owned winery making fresh, full-flavoured Chardonnay, Chenin Bl, Merlot, & esp Malbec, & Cab Cruz de Piedra-Maipú.

Santa Ana, Bodegas ★ Old-est'd family firm at Guaymallen, MENDOZA. Malbec Reserva is pick of a wide but rather uninspiring range.

Terrazas ★★→★★★ CHANDON enterprise for still table wines made from Malbec, Cabernet S, Chardonnay, and (soon) Syrah. The three ranges are entry-level Alto (juicy Cabernet is the star), mid-price Reserva, and top-of-the-tree Gran Terrazas.

Torino, Michel ★★ A rapidly improving (and organic) Cafayate enterprise with particularly good Cabernet.

Torontes Aromatic, often fiery whites. An acquired taste.

Trapiche ★★→★★★ Premium label of PEÑAFLOR. Labels in ascending quality order are Astica, Trapiche (pick is Oak Cask Syrah), Fond de Cave (good Malb Reserva), Medalla (decent plummy Cab S), and fine if pricey red blend Iscay.

Viniterra ★→★★ Clean, modern wines under the Omnium, Bykos, and Vinteraa labels. Watch out in future for Pinot G.

Vistalba, Viña y Cava ★★ See Nieto Senetiner.

Weinert, Bodegas ★★★ The Malbec, Cabernet, and Cavas de Weinert blend (Cab-Merlot-Malbec) are among the best reds from Argentina.

Yacochuya ★★★ SALTA. Stunning Malbec from old vines.

Other Central & South American wines

Bolivia With a generally hot, humid climate, annual domestic consumption of just one bottle per capita, only 2,000 ha of grapes (most destined for fiery *aguardiente*), and only ten wineries, this is not a major producing country. Even so, wines from Vinos y Viñedos La Concepción, especially the Cabernets, are good and show what is possible. The vineyards, 1000 km south of La Paz, lie at altitudes of up to 2,800 m, making them the highest in the world.

Brazil New plantings of better grapes are transforming a big and booming industry with an increasing home market. International investments, esp in Rio Grande do Sul and Santana do Liuramento, especially from France (eg Moët & Chandon) and Italy (Martini & Rossi), are significant, and point to possible exports. The new sandy Frontera region (bordering Argentina and Uruguay) and Sierra Gaucha hills (Italian-style sparkling) are to watch. Exports are beginning. Equatorial vineyards (eg near Recife) can have two crops a year – or even five in two years. Not a recommendation. Of the wines that do leave Brazil, 95% are made by the massive Vinicola Aurora (Bento Gonçalves). Look out for Amazon label.

Mexico Oldest Latin American wine industry is reviving, with investment from abroad (eg Freixenet, Martell, Domecq) and California influence via UC-Davis. Best in Baja California (85% of total), Querétaro, and on the Aguascalientes and Zacatecas plateaux. Top Baja C producers are Casa de Piedra (very impressive Tempranillo/Cabernet Sauv), L A Cetto (Valle de Guadaloupe, the largest, especially for Cabernet, Nebbiolo, Petite Sirah), Bodegas Santo Tomás (now working with California's Wente Brothers to make Duetto, using grapes from both sides of the border), Monte Xanic (with Napa-award winning Cabernet), Bodegas San Antonio, and Cavas de Valmar. The premium Chardonnay and Cabernet S from Monterrey-based Casa Madero are also good. Marqués de Aguayo is the oldest (1593), now only for brandy.

Peru Viña Tacama near Ica (top wine region) exports some pleasant wines, esp the Gran Vino Blanco white; also Cab S and classic-method sparkling. Chincha, Moquegua, and Tacha regions are slowly making progress. But phylloxera is a serious problem.

Uruguay Uruguay's point of difference is Tannat, the rugged and tannic grape which, in Southwest France, is responsible for Madiran. Tannat by itself, produces a sturdy plummy red, better blended with more supple Merlot and Cabernet Franc. Beyond Tannat a few producers offer decent Gewürz and Chardonnay, while the promising De Lucca has some Roussanne and Syrah. Five different viticultural zones were established in 1992, but the name of the producer is the most important element. Carrau/Castel Pujol enjoys input from Spain's Freixenet and France's Jacques Lurton, who makes the supple Casa Luntro Tannat at Cerro Chapeu in the north. Amat Gran Tradición 1752, and Las Violetas Reserva *cuvées* show Tannat at its most fragrant. Other wineries include Bruzzone & Sciutto, Castillo Viejo (gd value Catamayor range), Los Cerros de San Juan (working with LVMH), Dante Irurtia, Juanicó (in joint venture with Pape-Clément), Pisano, Carlos Pizzorno, and Stagnari. Flying winemaker wines under the Bright Brothers label are also worth trying.

Australia

Heavier shaded areas are the wine growing regions

The influence of Australia in the modern wine world is out of all proportion to the size of its vineyards. They represent less than 4% of global production, yet Australian wines, ideas and names are on all wine-lovers' lips. In 16 years, her exports have grown from 8 to over 350 million litres and the number of wineries has climbed to over 1,350. Even growers in the south of France listen to Australian winemakers. Australia has mastered easy-drinking wine and is making some of the world's very best.

Her long-term classics are Shiraz, Semillon, and Riesling. In the 70s they were joined by Cabernet and Merlot, Chardonnay, Pinot Noir, and other varieties. In the 90s, Grenache and Mourvèdre were rediscovered. At the same time, cool fermentation and the use of new barrels accompanied a general move to cooler areas. For a while, excessive oak flavour was a common problem. Moderation is now the fashion – and sparkling wine of highly satisfactory quality is a new achievement.

Australia faces a major challenge in managing its own helter-skelter growth. It has to find ways to more than double its exports over the next ten years without damaging its reputation. Chardonnay was its flag-bearer in the 80s and 90s; it is now betting on Shiraz doing the trick in the coming decade. Old World and New World alike will not make things easy in a global market which is still contracting, but Australia has the human and natural resources it needs to succeed.

Recent vintages

New South Wales

2001 Extreme summer heat and ill-timed rain set the tone; remarkably, Hunter Valley Semillon shone.

2000 A perfect growing season for the Hunter Valley, but dire for the rest of the state; extreme heat followed by vintage rain.

1999 Another Hunter success; rain when needed. Other regions variable.

1998 Good to excellent everywhere; good winter rain, warm, dry summer.

1997 Heavy rain bedeviled the Hunter; Mudgee, Orange, and Canberra all starred.

1996 Yields varied (frost, hail), but a perfect close to the season produced very good wine in most regions.

1995 Severe drought slashed yields and stressed fruit; good at best.

1994 Hunter heatwaves and fires followed by torrential rain didn't help; good red wines elsewhere, particularly Mudgee.

1993 Unusually cool, wet spring & summer diminished quality; excellent autumn saved Canberra and Hilltops.

1992 Continuation of the 1991 drought followed by brief vintage flooding soured Hunter, Mudgee, and Cowra; others fared rather better.

1991 A classic drought year produced low yields of very rich wines, esp reds.

Victoria

2001 Did not escape the heat; a fair-to-good red vintage, whites more variable.

2000 Southern and central regions flourished in warm and dry conditions; terrific reds. Northeast poor; vintage rain.

1999 Utterly schizophrenic; Yarra disastrous (vtge rain); some other southern and central regions superb; northeast up and down.

1998 Drought and October frost did not spoil an outstanding year in all regions, particularly for Shiraz, Cabernet, Merlot.

1997 A cool, wet spring gave way to drought; low yields of very high-quality grapes, especially Pinot in the south.

1996 Extremely variable. Far southwest, Grampians, and Bendigo did well.

1995 Mostly disappointing; the summer too hot, the autumn too cool and wet. Grampians (magnificent) and Geelong were the principal exceptions.

1994 Unusually cool and largely dry growing season depressed yields, quality saved by a glorious Indian summer; good to excellent throughout.

1993 A wet winter, spring, and summer partially retrieved by an Indian summer and autumn, most notably in the cooler red-wine regions.

1992 Magnificent for Yarra; gd elsewhere, equable growing conditions.

1991 A v warm, dry summer and autumn produced low yields of outstanding red wines right across the state. Whites good but short-lived.

South Australia

2001 Far better than 2000; winter rain helped combat the searing summer heat; Clare Valley Riesling an improbable success.

2000 The culmination of a four-year drought impacted on both yield and quality, the Limestone Coast zone faring the best.

1999 Continuing drought was perversely spoiled by ill-timed March rainfall; Limestone Coast and Clare reds the few bright spots.

1998 V dry year; low yields, overall quality of reds superb, esp S of Adelaide.

1997 On-again, off-again weather upset vines and vignerons alike, with the exception of Eden and Clare Valley Riesling. Yields down overall.

1996 Good winter/spring rain followed by a warm, dry summer; classic vintage, classic wines, succulent, and long-lived.

1995 Dry winter, frosty spring, and rainy summer reduced yields and quality, the low yields averting disaster.

1994 A long, cool, and dry growing season produced excellent white wines across the state, and elegant reds with above-average yields.

1993 The 2nd-wettest growing season on record promised disaster until a warm and dry March and below-average yields saved the day.

1992 A cool, dry year until vintage rain in all regions except McLaren Vale and Langhorne Creek spoiled what might have been a good vintage.

1991 A warm and dry year, the red wines initially appearing to lack the vinosity of the great 1990 vintage, but which flowered in bottle.

Western Australia

2001 Great Southern, the best vintage since 95; good elsewhere.

2000 Margaret River excellent; variation elsewhere, the Swan Valley ordinary.

1999 An outstanding vintage for Margaret River and Swan reds (best in over a decade) and pretty handy elsewhere, other than the Great Southern.

1998 The Swan Valley shone again, but the sun didn't elsewhere in the state in a rainy March and April.

1997 Wet winter and spring, perfect summer. Gd reds from Margaret River, gd Riesling from Great Southern. North was fried in Jan/Feb heatwave.

1996 The Swan Valley was cooked but the warm year was a blessing for Margaret River and Great Southern, with lovely Cabernet the pick.

1995 Very low yields were (partially) compensated for by wonderful quality in the south and Margaret River; the Swan average.

1994 A textbook vintage – perfect conditions for Great Southern (superb) and Margaret River. Swan Valley as per usual.

1993 A cool and wet spring and summer produced best white wines in the Swan Valley for decades, excellent whites elsewhere, and useful reds.

1992 A mild growing season, marred only by rain in the Swan Valley, produced good white and red wines in the south.

1991 Despite bird damage, a great red year for Margaret River, outstanding whites from Swan, and v good reds (sml quantities) from Great Southern.

Adelaide Hills (SA) Spearheaded by PETALUMA: cool, 450-m sites in Mt Lofty ranges.

Alkoomi Mt Barker r w ★★★ (Ries) 94' 96' 99 01' (Cab S) 93' 94' 97 99 25-year veteran producing fine, steely RIES and potent, long-lived reds.

Allandale Hunter Valley r w ★★ Small winery without v'yds, buying selected local and Hilltops grapes. Quality can be good, esp CHARD.

Amberley Estate Margaret River r w ★★→★★★ Highly successful and rapidly expanding maker of a full range of regional styles with Chenin Blanc the commercial engine, driving sales to 90,000 cases.

Angove's Riverland (SA) r w (br) ★→★★ Large, long-established MURRAY VALLEY family business. Good-value whites, especially CHARDONNAY.

Ashbrook Estate Margaret River r w ★★★ Minimum of fuss; consistently makes 8,000 cases of exemplary SEM, CHARD, SAUV, VERDELHO, and CAB S.

Ashton Hills Adelaide Hills r w (sp) ★★★ Fine, racy, long-lived RIES and compelling PINOT N crafted by Stephen George from 20 yr-old v'yds.

Bailey's NE Vic r w br ★★→★★★★ Rich, old-fashioned reds of great character, especially SHIRAZ (formerly Hermitage), and magnificent dessert Muscat (★★★★) and "TOKAY". Part of BERINGER BLASS.

Balnaves of Coonawarra r w ★★→★★★★ Grape-grower since 75; winery since 96 going from strength to strength, esp SHIRAZ and CAB.

Bannockburn Geelong r w ★★★ (Chard) 96' 97' 98' 00 (Pinot N) 92' 94' 96 97' 00 Intense, complex CHARD & PINOT N made using Burgundian techniques. 7,000 c/s.

Banrock Station Riverland SA r w ★→★★ 1,600 ha property on Murray River, 243 ha v'yd, owned by BRL HARDY producing impressive budget wines.

Barossa (SA) Aus's most important winery (but not v'yd) area; grapes from diverse sources make diverse wines. Local specialities: SHIRAZ, SEMILLON, GRENACHE, etc.

Barwang Hilltops r w ★★ Owned by MCWILLIAMS; Stylish estate wines for Aus market, mass-market brand for joint venture with Brown-Foreman in US.

Bass Phillip Gippsland (Vic) r ★★★→★★★★ (Pinot N) 91' 92' **94' 95** 96' 97' 98' 00' Tiny amounts of stylish, eagerly sought PINOT NOIR in three quality grades; very Burgundian in style.

Beggar's Belief Chardonnay S Aus w Oak and sugar mixture responsible for the majority of recruits to the ABC club.

Bendigo/Ballarat (Vic) W'spread sm v'yds, some vg quality. Balgownie, JASPER HILL.

Beringer Blass See BLASS

Best's Grampians r w ★★→★★★ (Shiraz) **88 91** 92' **93** 94' 96 97' 98' Conservative old family winery; very good, mid-weight reds, CHARD not half bad. Thomson Family SHIRAZ from 120-yr-old vines superb.

Big Rivers Zone (NSW & Vic) The continuation of South Australia's RIVERLAND including the Murray Darling Perricoola and Susan Hill Regions.

Blass, Wolf (Bilyara) Barossa r w (sp, sw, br) ★★★ (Cab blend) **90' 91' 93 94** 96' 97 98' Founded by BAROSSA's ebullient German winemaker, Wolf Blass, now BERINGER BLASS. Brilliant young winemakers Wendy Stuckey (Ries) and Caroline Dunn (reds) are reinventing Blass.

Blue Pyrenees Estate Grampians/Avoca r w sp ★★ Owned by Rémy Martin. Steadily moving from sparkling to table wine.

Botobolar Mudgee r w ★★ Marvellously eccentric little organic winery.

Bowen Estate Coonawarra r w ★★★ (Shiraz) **90' 91'** 94' 95 96' 97 98' (Cab) **90' 91'** 96 98' 99 Sm winery; intense CAB, spicy SHIRAZ, both ripe and alcoholic.

Brand's of Coonawarra Coonawarra r w ★★★ (Shiraz) **90 91' 93** 96' 97 98' 99 (Cab S) **90' 91 93'** 94' 95' 98' 99 Owned by MCWILLIAMS. Going from strength to strength esp with super-premium Reserve SHIRAZ and CAB.

Brangayne of Orange Orange r w ★★→★★★ Reflects potential of relatively new region. Wines of great finesse incl CHARD, SAUV, SHIRAZ, CAB-Merlot. Instant success.

Bridgewater Mill Adelaide Hills r w ★★→★★★ Second label of PETALUMA; suave wines, SAUV BL, and SHIRAZ best. A good restaurant, too.

BRL Hardy See Hardy's.

Brokenwood Hunter Valley r w ★★★ (Shiraz) 87' 91' **93'** 94' 95' 98' 99 Exciting CAB, SHIRAZ since 73 – Graveyard SHIRAZ outstanding. Cricket Pitch SEM-SAUV fuels growth; zooming to 70,000 cases. See also SEVILLE.

Brookland Valley Margaret River r w ★★→★★★ Superbly sited winery and restaurant doing great things, esp with SAUV. Half-share owned by BRL HARDY.

Brown Brothers King Valley r w dr br sp sw ★→★★★ (Noble Ries) **92'** 94' 96' 97 98 Old family firm, new ideas: wide range of delicate, single-grape wines, many from cool mountain districts. CHARD, RIES. Dry white Muscat outstanding. CAB blend is best red.

Buring, Leo Barossa r w ★★→★★★ (Ries) 73' 75' 79' **84' 91' 92 95'** 97 98 99' Old RIESLING specialist, now owned by SOUTHCORP. Great with age (even great age), esp reserve releases under Leonay label.

Cabernet Sauvignon 28,609 ha, 249,288 tonnes Grown in all wine regions, best in COONAWARRA. From herbaceous green pepper in coolest regions through blackcurrant and mulberry, to dark chocolate and redcurrant in warmer areas.

Campbells of Rutherglen NE Vic r br (w) ★★ Smooth, ripe reds and gd dessert wines, the latter in youthful, fruity style other than Merchant Prince Muscat.

Canberra District (ACT) Both quality and quantity on the increase; altitude-dependent, site selection important.

Cape Mentelle Margaret River r w ★★★→★★★★ (Cab) **82' 83' 90' 91'** 93' 94' 95' 96 99' Idiosyncratic, robust CAB can be magnificent, CHARD even better; also Zin and very popular SAUV-SEM. David Hohnen also founded Cloudy Bay, NZ. Veuve Clicquot principal shareholder of both since 90.

Capel Vale Geographe (WA) r w ★★★ Steadily growing and v successful with good whites, incl RIES. Also top-end SHIRAZ and CABERNET.

Central Ranges Zone (NSW) Encompasses MUDGEE, Orange, and Cowra regions, expanding in high altitude, moderately cool to warm climates.

Chain of Ponds Adelaide Hills r w Impeccably made, full, flavoursome wines vinified by PENFOLDS. SEM, SAUV, CHARD to the fore. Elegant Amadeus CAB also gd.

Wineries to watch in early 2000s

Cheviot Bridge Vic Mountain	Newcomer; streetwise owners
Cullen Margaret River	Chardonnay and Merlot
Greenock Creek Barossa	High-scoring wines
Margan Family Hunter	Ultra-clever business family
Palandri Margaret River	Aiming too high? Time will tell
Pinot Noir Generally	2000 vintage superb all over
Shadowfax Geelong	The place to go
Taylors Clare Valley	Spectacular improvement
Tower Estate Hunter Valley	Len Evans's pride and joy

Chambers' Rosewood NE Vic br (r w) ★★→★★★ Good, cheap table and great dessert wines, esp traditional "TOKAY" and Muscat.

Chapel Hill McL Vale r w ★★★ (r) **90' 91' 92' 93** 95' 98' 99 Once tiny, now booming: prizewinning CHARD, SHIRAZ, and CAB from Pam Dunsford.

Chardonnay 18,434 ha, 245,199 tonnes Best-known for fast-developing buttery, peachy, sometimes syrupy wines, but cooler regions produce more elegant, tightly structured, age-worthy examples. Oak, too, is now less heavy-handed.

Charles Melton Barossa r w (sp) ★★★ Tiny winery with bold, luscious reds, esp Nine Popes, an old-vine GRENACHE and SHIRAZ blend.

Cheviot Bridge (Central Vic High Country) r w ★★ →★★★★ 50,000 cases. Export-orientated business, set up in 98 by industry veterans.

Clare Valley (SA) Small, high-quality area 90 miles north of Adelaide, best for Riesling; also SHIRAZ and CABERNET.

Clarendon Hills Mclaren . r (w) ★★★ Monumental (and expensive) reds from small parcels of contract grapes around Adelaide.

Coldstream Hills Yarra Valley r w (sp) ★★★ (Chard) **88' 92' 94 96' 97** 98' 00 (Pinot N) **91' 92' 96' 97'** 98 00' (Cab S) **91' 92'** 93 94 97' 98' 00' Estate winery est'd 85 by wine critic James Halliday. Delicious PINOT N to drink young and Reserve to age, lead Australia. Vg CHARD (esp Res wines), fruity CAB, and Cab-Merlot, and (from 97) Merlot. Acquired by SOUTHCORP in 96.

Coonawarra (SA) Southernmost and finest v'yds of state: most of Australia's best CAB, successful CHARDONNAY, RIESLING, and SHIRAZ. Newer arrivals include Gartner, Murdock, and Reschke.

Coriole McLaren Vale r w ★★→★★★ (Shiraz) **90' 91'** 92 94' 95 96' 98' 99' To watch, especially for old-vine SHIRAZ Lloyd Reserve; best when nicely balanced by oak. Other wines are worthy.

Craiglee Macedon (Vic) r w ★★★ (Shiraz) **86' 88' 90'** 91' **92 93** 94' 97' 98' (00') Re-creation of famous 19th-C estate: fragrant, peppery SHIRAZ, CHARD.

Cranswick Estates Riverina r w ★→★★ Million-case, public-listed winery firmly aimed at export market with accent on value.

Cullen Wines Margaret River r w ★★★ (Chard) **94' 95'** 96' 97 98 99) (Cab S-Merlot) **90' 91'** 92' 93' 94 95' 96 97 98' 99' Mother-daughter team

AUSTRALIA

pioneered the region with strongly structured CAB-Merlot (Australia's best), substantial but subtle SAUV, and bold CHARD: all real characters.

Dalwhinnie Pyrenees r w ★★→★★★ (Chard) **93 94 96** 98' 99' (Cab S) **92'** 93 94' 95' 96 98 99 5,500-case producer of concentrated, rich CHARD, SHIRAZ, and CAB S, arguably the best in PYRENEES.

d'Arenberg McLaren Vale r w (rsw br sp) ★★→★★★ Old firm with new lease of life; sumptuous SHIRAZ and GRENACHE, fine CHARD with lots of new labels.

Deakin Estate Murray Darling r w ★→★★ Part of Katnook group producing over 500,000 cases of very decent varietal table wines.

De Bortoli Griffith (NSW) r w dr sw (br) ★→★★★ (Noble Sem) **87' 91'** 92 93' 94' 96 98 99' Irrigation-area winery. Standard reds and whites but splendid, sweet, botrytized Sauternes-style Noble SEM. See also next entry.

De Bortoli Yarra Valley r w ★★→★★★ (Chard) **93' 94'** 96' 97 98 99' 00'(Cab S) **92'** 94' 97 98 99 00' Formerly Chateau Yarrinya: bought by DE BORTOLI and now YARRA VALLEY's largest producer. Main label is more than adequate; second label Gulf Station and third label Windy Peak vg value.

Delatite Central Vic r w (sp) ★★★ (Ries) **92 93 96 97'** 99 00 Winemaker Rosalind Ritchie makes appropriately willowy and feminine RIES, Gewürz, PINOT N, and CAB from this v cool mountainside v'yd.

Devil's Lair Margaret River r w ★★→★★★ 40.5 ha of estate vineyards for opulently concentrated CHARD, PINOT N, and CAB-Merlot. Fifth Leg is trendy second label. Acquired by SOUTHCORP early 97.

Diamond Valley Yarra Valley r w ★★→★★★ (Pinot) **94'** 96' **97** 98' 99' 00' Outstanding PINOT N in significant quantities; other wines good, esp CHARD.

Domaine Chandon Yarra Valley sp (r w) ★★★ Classic sparkling wine from grapes grown in all the cooler wine regions of Australia, with strong support from French owner Moët & Chandon. Successful in UK under GREEN POINT label.

Dominique Portet Yarra Valley r w ★★ After a 25-year career at Taltarni, now in his own winery for the first time. Much expected.

Dromana Estate Mornington Peninsula r w ★★→★★★ (Chard) **97** 98' 99' 00' (01) Led energetically by Gary Crittenden: light, fragrant CAB, PINOT, CHARD; sudden interest in Italian varieties (grown elsewhere).

Eden Valley (SA) Independent from both the ADELAIDE HILLS and BAROSSA VALLEY; HENSCHKE and MOUNTADAM.

Evans Family Hunter Valley r w ★★★ (Chard) **95 96** 98' 99 00' 01 Excellent CHARD from small vineyard owned by family of Len Evans. Fermented in new oak. Repays cellaring. See also TOWER ESTATE.

Elderton Barossa r w (sp br) ★★ Old v'yds; flashy, rich, oaked CAB and SHIRAZ.

Evans and Tate Margaret River r w ★★★ (Cab) **88 91'** 92' 94' 95' 96' 99' Fine, elegant SEM, CHARD, CAB, Merlot from MARGARET RIVER, Redbrook. Recent stock-exchange listing underpins continued growth.

Ferngrove Vineyards Great Southern r w ★★ Cattle farmer Murray Burton has established over 400 ha of vines since 97; 50,000 cases on the way up.

Fox Creek Mclaren V r (w) ★★→★★★ Produces 20,000 cases of flashy, full-flavoured wines which enjoy much success in Aus wine shows.

Freycinet Tasmania r w (sp) ★★→★★★ (Pinot N) **88' 90 91'** 94' 95 96 97 98' 99' 00' 01' East-coast winery producing voluptuous, rich PINOT N, gd CHARDONNAY.

Gapsfed Wines King Valley (Vic) r w ★★ Brand of large winery which crushes grapes for 50 growers.

Gartner Family Vineyards Coonawarra r w ★★→★★★ Over 400 ha of vines, mainly COONAWARRA and PADTHAWAY; new semi-underground winery.

Geelong (Vic) Once-famous area destroyed by phylloxera, re-established mid-1960s. Very cool, dry climate: firm table wines from good-quality grapes. Names incl BANNOCKBURN, Idyll, SCOTCHMAN'S HILL.

Geoff Merrill McLaren Vale r w ★→★★★ (Cab) **90' 93** 96' **97** 98' 99 Ebullient maker of Geoff Merrill, Mt Hurtle, Cockatoo Ridge. A questing enthusiast; his best are excellent, others unashamedly mass-market oriented. TAHBILK own 50%.

Geoff Weaver Adelaide Hills r w ★★→★★★ 8 ha estate of former HARDY'S winemaker Geoff Weaver, at Lenswood. Very fine SAUV, CHARD, RIES, and CAB-Merlot blend. Marvellous new label design.

Giaconda Central Vic r w ★★★ (Chard) **91 92' 93** 94' 96' **97'** 98 99' oo' (Pinot N) **92' 93 94** 96' **97'** 98 99 (oo') V sml fashionable winery near Beechworth.

Goulburn Valley (Vic) Very old (TAHBILK) and relatively new (MITCHELTON) wineries in temperate mid-Victoria region; full-bodied table wines. Goulburn Valley Vineyard Co is a promising new budget producer. NB: their VERDELHO.

Goundrey Wines Great Southern (WA) r w ★★ Recent expansion seems to have caused quality to become variable.

Grampians (Vic) Region previously known as Great Western. Temperate region in central W of state. High quality (esp sparkling).

Granite Belt (Qld) High-altitude, (relatively) cool region just N of NSW border Esp spicy SHIRAZ and rich SEM-SHARD.

Grant Burge Barossa r w (sp sw br) ★★→★★★ 110,000 cases of silky-smooth reds and whites from the best grapes of Burge's large v'yd holdings.

Greenock Creek Barossa r ★★★ Soaring prices and iconic status for SHIRAZ thanks to Mr Parker and US buyers.

Great Southern (WA) Remote, cool area; GOUNDREY & PLANTAGENET are lgst wineries.

Green Point r w See Domaine Chandon.

Grenache 2,427 ha, 22,563 tonnes. Produces thin wine if over-cropped but can do much better. Growing interest in old BAROSSA & MCLAREN VALE plantings.

Grosset Clare r w ★★★→★★★★ (Ries) 90' **92 93' 94** 95' **97'** 98' 99 00' 01 (Gaia) 86 **90** 91 **92 93** 94' 95 96' 98' 99 Fastidious winemaker. Foremost Aus RIES, lovely CHARD, PINOT N, and Gaia CAB-Merlot.

Hanging Rock Macedon (Vic) r w sp ★→★★★ (Shiraz) **90' 91'** 92 93 **94'** 97' 98 99' Eclectic range: budget Picnic wines; huge Heathcote SHIRAZ; complex sparkling.

Hardy's McLaren Vale, Barossa, Keppoch, etc r w sp (rsw) ★★→★★★★ (Eileen Chard) **93 94** 96' 97 98 99' oo("Vintage Port") 46' 51' 54' 56' **58' 75 77** 82 84' 96' Historic company blending wines from several areas. Best are Eileen Hardy and Thomas Hardy series and (Australia's best) "Vintage Ports". REYNELLA's beautifully restored buildings are now group HQ. 1992 merger with Berry-Renmano and public ownership (BRL HARDY) makes this Australia's 2nd-lgst wine co.

Heggies Adelaide Hills r w dr (sw w) ★★ (Ries) **92** 95 **98** 99 00 01' Vineyard at 500 metres in eastern BAROSSA Ranges owned by S SMITH & SONS. The wines are separately marketed.

Henschke Barossa r w ★★★★ (Shiraz) 58' **60 61' 62 66 67' 68' 72 73 75 76 79 80'** 81' 83 84' 86' 88' 90' **90' 91'** 92' 93' 96' 98' 99 (Cab S) **78 80 81 84 85** 86 **88** 90' **91'** 92 93 94' 95 96' 98' 125-yr-old family business, perhaps Australia's best, known for delectable SHIRAZ (especially Hill of Grace 59), vg CAB and red blends. Lenswood v'yds on ADELAIDE HILLS add excitement.

Hollick Coonawarra r w (sp) ★★ (Cab-Merlot) **90** 91' **92 93** 96' 98' Gd CHARDONNAY, RIESLING; much-followed reds, especially Ravenswood.

Houghton Swan Valley r w ★→★★★ The most famous old winery of WA. Soft, ripe Supreme is top-selling, age-worthy wine; a national classic. Also excellent CAB, Verdelho. SHIRAZ, etc. sourced from MARGARET RIVER and GREAT SOUTHERN. See HARDY'S.

Howard Park Mount Barker r w ★★★ (Ries) 88' **90' 91 93 94' 95'** 96' 97' 98' 99' (Note: the oo and the 01 are not good, over-acidified.) (Cab S) **86 88 90'** 91 **92 93** 94' 96' 98' 99' Scented RIES, CHARD; spicy CAB S. Major winery expansion underway in both MARGARET RIVER and GREAT SOUTHERN with flourishing contract-winemaking business for others. 2nd label: Madfish Bay.

Hunter Valley (NSW) Great name in NSW. Broad, soft, earthy SHIRAZ and SEM that live for 30 years. CABERNET not important; CHARD increasingly so.

Huntington Estate Mudgee r w ★★★ (Cab S) **89** 91' **93' 94'** 95' 97 99' 00' Small winery; the best in MUDGEE. Fine CAB, vg SHIRAZ. Invariably underpriced.

Jasper Hill Bendigo r w ★★★→★★★★ (Shiraz) **83' 85' 86'** 90' **91' 92'** 94 96' 97' 98' 99' Emily's Paddock SHIRAZ-Cab F blend and George's Paddock Shiraz from dry-land estate are intense, long-lived, and much admired. BENDIGO's best.

Regions: Geographical Indications

The process of formally defining the boundaries of the Zones, Regions, and Sub-regions, known compendiously as Geographic Indications (GIs), continues. These correspond to the French ACs and United States AVAs. It means every aspect of the labelling of Australian wines has a legal framework which, in all respects, complies with EC laws and requirements. The guarantee of quality comes through the mandatory analysis certificate for, and the tasting (by expert panels) of, each and every wine exported from Australia.

Jim Barry Clare r w ★→★★★★ Some great vineyards provide good RIES, McCrae Wood SHIRAZ, and convincing Grange challenger The Armagh.

Katnook Estate Coonawarra r w (sp sw w) ★★★ (Cab S) **86** 90' **91'** 92 93 97' 98' 99 Excellent and pricey CABERNET and CHARDONNAY; also RIESLING and SAUVIGNON.

Keith Tulloch Hunter r w ★★★ Ex-Rothbury winemaker fastidiously crafting elegant yet complex SEMILLION, SHIRAZ, etc.

King Valley (Vic) Increasingly important alpine region. 10,000 tonnes chiefly for purchasers outside the region, some wineries of its own.

Knappstein Wines Clare r w ★★★ Reliable RIESLING, Fumé Blanc, CAB-Merlot, and Cab Franc wines. Owned by PETALUMA.

Knappstein Lenswood Vineyards r w ★★★ Estate now sole occupation of Tim KNAPPSTEIN making subtle SAUV BL and powerful CHARD, PINOT N.

Knight Granite Hills Macedon r w ★★→★★★ 30-yr-old family vineyard and winery has regained original class with fine, elegant RIES and spicy SHIRAZ.

Lake Breeze Langhorne Ck r (w) ★★ Long-term grape-growers turned winemakers producing succulently smooth SHIRAZ & CAB.

Lake's Folly Hunter Valley r w ★★★★ (Chard) **92' 93' 94** 95 96' 97' 98 99' 00' (Cab S) **69 75 81 85 88** 91' **93' 94** 97' 98' 99 Small family winery founded by Max Lake, the pioneer of HUNTER CAB. New owners since 2000. CAB is v fine, complex. CHARD exciting and age-worthy.

Lamont Swan V r w ★★ Winery and superb restaurant owned by Corin Lamont (daughter of legendary Jack Mann) and husband. Delicious wines.

Lark Hill Canberra District r w ★★ Most consistent CANBERRA producer, making esp attractive RIES, pleasant CHARD, and surprising PINOT.

Leasingham Clare r w ★★→★★★ Important med-sized quality winery bought by HARDY'S in 87. Gd RIES, SEM, CHARD, and CAB-Malbec. Various labels.

Leeuwin Estate Margaret River r w ★★★★ (Chard) **82' 83' 85' 86** 87' **89 90 91 92' 94** 95' 96 97' 98 99 Leading W Australia estate, lavishly equipped. Superb (and very expensive) CHARDONNAY; vg RIESLING, SAUVIGNON, and CAB.

Limestone Coast Zone (SA) Important zone including COONAWARRA, PADTHAWAY Wratton Bully, Mount Benson, and Bordertown. Rapidly expanding in southeast South Australia.

Lindemans Originally Hunter Valley, now everywhere r w ★→★★★ (COONAWARRA Red) **86'** 90' **91' 92** 96' 97' 98' 99 One of the oldest firms, now a giant owned by SOUTHCORP. Vg CHARD and C'warra reds (eg Limestone Ridge, Pyrus).

Macedon and Sunbury (Vic) Two adjacent regions, Macedon at much higher elevation, Sunbury nr Melbourne airport. CRAIGLEE, HANGING ROCK, VIRGIN HILLS.

Margan Family Winemakers Hunter r w ★★→★★★ Highly successful winemaker incl fascinating House of Certain Views brand.

Margaret River (WA) Temperate coastal area with superbly elegant wines 174 miles S of Perth. Australia's most vibrant tourist wine region.

M. Chapoutier Mount Benson (sa) r ★★ 40 ha biodynamic v'yd, planted to Rhône varieties plus CAB SAUV. Elegant reds from young vines.

McLaren Vale (SA) Historic region on the southern outskirts of Adelaide. Big reds now rapidly improving; also vg CHARD.

McWilliam's Hunter Valley and Riverina r w (sw br) ★→★★★ (Elizabeth Sem) **79' 82** 84' 86' 87' 89' 91' 92 93 **94' 95** 96 98 99' (00') Famous family of HUNTER VALLEY winemakers at Mount Pleasant: SHIRAZ & SEMILLON. Also pioneer in RIVERINA: CABERNET S & RIESLING. Recent show results demonstrate high standards. "Elizabeth" (sold at 5 years) and "Lovedale" (10 years) SEMILLONS: now Australia's best. Honest RIVERINA wines at low prices.

Miramar Mudgee r w ★★ Some of MUDGEE's best white wines, especially CHARDONNAY; long-lived CABERNET and SHIRAZ.

Miranda Riverina r w (sww) ★→★★ Vineyards & wineries in RIVERINA, KING VALLEY and BAROSSA underpin continuing growth of this major producer.

Mitchell Clare r w ★★★ (Ries) **90' 92** 94' 95 **97** 00' 01' Small family winery for excellent CAB and v stylish, dry Ries.

Mitchelton Goulburn Valley r w (sw w) ★★→★★★ Substantial winery, acquired by PETALUMA in 92. A wide range incl a vg wood-matured Marsanne, SHIRAZ; classic Blackwood Park RIES from GOULBURN VALLEY is one of Australia's v best-value wines. Many enterprising blends and labels.

Montrose Mudgee r w ★★ Reliable underrated producer of CHARDONNAY and CABERNET blends. Now part of the ORLANDO group.

Moorilla Estate Tasmania r w (sp) ★★★ (RIES) **91' 93** 94' 95' **97'** 98' 99 00 Senior winery on outskirts of Hobart on Derwent River: vg RIESLING, Traminer, and CHARD; PINOT N now in the ascendant.

Mornington Peninsula (Vic) Exciting wines in new cool, coastal area 25 miles S of Melbourne. 1,000 ha. Wineries incl DROMANA, STONIERS.

Morris NE Vic (br) r w ★★→★★★★ Old winery at Rutherglen for Australia's greatest dessert Muscats and "TOKAYS"; also recently vg low-price table wine.

Moss Wood Margaret River r w ★★★★ (Sem) **86' 87' 92'** 94' 95' 96 97 98' 99 **01'** (Cab S) **80' 86 87 90** 91 92 93' 94' 95' 96 98' 99' To many, the best MARGARET RIVER winery (only 11.7 ha). SEM, CAB, PINOT N, and CHARD, all with rich fruit flavours, not unlike some of the top California wines.

Mount Cotton Estate Queensland Coast r w ★★ 100 ha, striking 75,000-case winery, 200-seat restaurant. Biggest of many such new ventures.

Mount Langi Ghiran Grampians r w ★★★ (Shiraz) **86' 88 90' 91** 92 93' **94** 95 96' 98' 99' Especially for superb, rich, peppery, Rhône-like SHIRAZ, one of Australia's best cool-climate versions.

Mount Mary Yarra Valley r w ★★★★ (Pinot N) **89' 92' 94 95** 96' 97' 98 99' **(00')** (Cab S-Cab F-Merlot) **82** 84' 85' 86' 88' 90' **92' 93'** 95' 96' 97' 98' 99 Dr John Middleton is a perfectionist making tiny amounts of suave CHARD, vivid PINOT N, and (best of all) CAB S-Cab F-Merlot: Australia's most B'x-like "claret". All will age impeccably.

Mountadam Barossa r w (sp) ★★★ (Chard) **90' 92' 93 94' 96** 97' 98' High EDEN VALLEY winery of Adam Wynn. CHARD is rich, voluptuous, and long. Other labels include David Wynn, Eden Ridge. Acquired by Cape Mentelle 2000.

Mudgee (NSW) Small, isolated area 168 miles northwest of Sydney. Big reds and full CHARDONNAYS.

Murray Valley (SA, Vic & NSW) Vast irrigated v'yds. Principally making "cask" table wines. 40 per cent of total Australian wine production.

Nepenthe Adelaide Hills r w First winery to be built here for 10 years (since PETALUMA); severe restrictions apply in water-catchment zone. State-of-the-art kit, excellent v'yds, skilled winemaking: sophisticated wines especially SAUVIGNON, CHARDONNAY, SEMILLON.

Ninth Island See Piper's Brook

Oakridge Estate Yarra Valley r w ★★ New winery, and expanded vineyards; Merlot is a specialty.

O'Leary Walker Wines Clare r w ★★★ Two whizz-kids have mid-life crisis, leave BERINGER BLASS to do their own thing – very well.

Orlando (Gramp's) Barossa r w sp (br sw w) ★★→★★★ (St Hugo Cab) **86' 88 90' 96** 98' 99' Great pioneering co, bought by management in 88 but now owned by Pernod-Ricard. Full range from huge-selling Jacob's Creek "Claret" to excellent Jacaranda Ridge CAB S from COONAWARRA. See also Wyndham Estate.

Alpine Valleys (Vic) Geographically similar to KING VALLEY and similar use of grapes.

Padthaway (SA) Large vineyard area developed as overspill of COONAWARRA. Cool climate; good PINOT N is produced and excellent CHARD (esp LINDEMANS and HARDY'S), also Chard-Pinot N sparkling.

Palandri Wines Margaret River r w ★★ Massive public investment in 210 ha v'yds in Great Southern, 2,500-tonne winery, and relentless advertising campaign.

Paringa Estate Mornington Peninsula r w ★★★ Maker of quite spectacular CHARD, PINOT N, and (late-picked) SHIRAZ winning innumerable trophies with tiny output of 2,000 cases.

Parker Estate Coonawarra r ★★★ Small estate making v good CAB, esp Terra Rossa First Growth.

Pemberton (WA) Rapidly growing region between MARGARET RIVER and GREAT SOUTHERN; initial enthusiasm for PINOT NOIR and CHARDONNAY replaced by Merlot and SHIRAZ.

Penfolds Orig Adelaide, now everywhere r w (sp br) ★★→★★★★ (Grange) 52' 53' 55' **62' 63' 66' 67** 71' **75 76 80 83 85 86'** 88 90' 91' 92 94' 95 96'(Bin 707) **64 65** 66' 76' **78 80 83' 84 86' 88** 90' **91** 92 94' 96' 98' (Bin 389) 66' 70' 71' **76' 83' 86' 88'** 90' **91 92 93** 94' 96' 98' Ubiquitous and excellent: in BAROSSA VALLEY, CLARE, COONAWARRA, RIVERINA, etc. Consistently Australia's best red-wine company. Its Grange (was called "Hermitage") is deservedly ★★★★. P's Yattarna CHARD, the long-awaited "White Grange", released 98. Bin 707 CABERNET not far behind. Other bin-numbered wines (eg Cab-SHIRAZ 389, Kalimna Bin 28 Shiraz) can be outstanding, though prices are rising. Grandfather "Port" is often excellent.

Penley Estate Coonawarra r w ★★★ High-profile, no-expense-spared, newcomer winery: rich, textured, fruit-and-oak CAB; also SHIRAZ-Cab blend and CHARD.

Perth Hills (WA) Fledgling area 19 miles E of Perth with a larger number of growers on mild hillside sites.

Petaluma Adelaide Hills r w sp ★★★★ (Ries) 80' **82 86' 94' 96'** 98 99 00' (Chard) **90' 91 92' 93** 94' **95' 96'** 98 99 00' (Cab S) 79' **86' 88' 90' 91'** 92' **93 94'** 95' 97' 98' A rocket-like '80s success with COONAWARRA CAB, ADELAIDE HILLS CHARD, CLARE VALLEY RIES, all processed at winery in Adelaide Hills. Red wines have become richer from 88 on. New Tiers Chard challenges PENFOLDS' Yattarna and LEEUWIN ESTATE. Also: BRIDGEWATER MILL. Now owns KNAPPSTEIN, MITCHELTON, Smithbrook, and STONIERS. See also Croser.

Peter Lehmann Wines Barossa r w (sp br sw w) ★★→★★★ Defender of BAROSSA faith, Peter Lehmann makes consistently well-priced wines in substantial quantities; now publicly listed and flourishing. NB Stonewell SHIRAZ (tastes of blackberries and rum) and dry RIES.

Pierro Margaret River r w ★★★ (Chard) **90 91' 93' 94** 95' 96' 99 00' Highly rated producer of expensive, tangy SEM, SAUV BL, and v good barrel-fermented CHARD.

Pikes Clare Valley r w ★★ 30,000 case winery (and estate vineyards) run by accomplished viticulturist Andrew and winemaker brother Neil Pike; honest, powerful wines.

Piper's Brook Tasmania r w sp ★★★ (Ries) 81' 82' 84' 89 91 92' 93' 94' 95' 96' 98' 99' 00' 01' (Chard) 92' 93' 94' 95' 97 99' 00' Cool-area pioneer; vg RIES, PINOT N, restrained CHARD from Tamar Vly. Lovely labels. 2nd label: Ninth Island. Acquired HEEMSKERK, Rochecombe in 98; now controls 35% of Tasmanian wine industry.

Pinot Noir 3,756 4,142 ha, 29,514 tonnes Mostly used in sparkling. Exciting wines from S Victoria, TASMANIA, and ADELAIDE HILLS; plantings are increasing.

Pirramimma McLaren V r w ★★ Low-profile, century-old family business with first-class v'yds making underpriced wines incl excellent Petit Verdot.

Plantagenet Mount Barker r w (sp) ★★★ (Cab S) 92' 93' 94' 95 98' (99') The region's elder statesman: wide range of varieties, especially rich CHARD, SHIRAZ, and vibrant, potent CAB S.

Primo Estate Adelaide Plains r w dr (w sw) ★★★ Joe Grilli is a miracle-worker given the climate; successes incl very gd botrytized RIES, tangy Colombard, potent Joseph CAB-Merlot (aka Moda Amarone).

Pyrenees (Vic) Central Vic region producing rich, minty reds and some interesting whites, esp Fumé Bl.

Red Hill Estate Mornington Peninsula r w sp ★★→★★★ One of the larger and more important wineries; notably elegant wines.

Redman Coonawarra r ★→★★ The most famous old name in C'WARRA; red-wine specialist: SHIRAZ, CAB S, Cab-Merlot. Wine fails to do justice to quality of v'yds.

Reynell McL Vale r rsw w ★★→★★★★ ("Vintage Port") 75' 77' 82 87 88 90 Historic winery serving as HQ for BRL HARDY group. Vg "Basket-pressed" red table wines, superb vintage "Port", now under Reynell label.

Reynold's Orange NSW r w ★★ Brand name for 900-ha/20,000-tonne Cabonne Winery, exporting 175,000 cases to US via JV with Sutter Home.

Richmond Grove Barossa r w ★→★★★ Master winemaker John Vickery produces great RIESLING at bargain prices; other wines are OK. Owned by Orlando Wyndham.

Riesling 3,558 ha, 26,980 tonnes Has a special place in the BAROSSA, EDEN and CLARE valleys. Usually made bone-dry; can be glorious with up to 20 years bottle-age. Newer botrytis Rieslings made sparingly but can be superb.

Riverina (NSW) Large-volume irrigated zone centred around Griffith; good-quality "cask" wines (especially white), great sweet, botrytized SEM. Watch for reduced yields and better quality.

Rockford Barossa r w sp ★★→★★★★ Small producer, wide range of thoroughly individual wines, often made from very old, low-yielding v'yds; reds best. Sparkling Black SHIRAZ has super-cult status.

Rosemount Estate U Hunter, McLaren V, C'warra r w (sp) ★★ ★★★★ Rich, unctuous HUNTER "Show" CHARD is international smash. This, MCLAREN VALE Balmoral Syrah, MUDGEE Mountain Blue CABERNET-SHIRAZ, & COONAWARRA Cabernet lead the wide range, which gets better every year. Merged with SOUTHCORP March 01. Links with Mondavi, too.

Rosevears Estate N Tasmania r w Recently opened, spectacularly sited winery/restaurant complex by Tamar River. Wines incl CHARD, PINOT N, and CAB-Merlot under Rosevears and Notley Gorge labels.

Rothbury Estate Hunter Valley r w ★★ Fell prey to Fosters/MILDARA in 96 after long bitter fight by original founder Len EVANS (since departed). Has made long-lived SEM and SHIRAZ and rich, buttery, early-drinking COWRA CHARD to good effect. Old Evans fans should see Evans Family.

Rutherglen and Glenrowan (Vic) Two of five regions in the Northeast Victorian Zone justly famous for weighty reds and magnificent, fortified dessert wines.

Rymill Coonawarra ★★ Descendants of John Riddoch carrying on the good work of the founder of COONAWARRA. Strong, dense SHIRAZ and CABERNET especially noteworthy.

St Hallett Barossa r w ★★★ (Old Block) **84 86 88** 90' **91' 92'** 93' 94' 95 96 97 98 Rejuvenated winery. 60+-yr-old vines give splendid Old Block SHIRAZ. Rest of range (eg CHARD, SAUV-SEM) is smooth and stylish.

St Hubert's Yarra Valley r w ★★→★★★ Successive ownership changes have somewhat dimmed the lustre; now a tiny fragment of BERINGER BLASS.

St Sheila's SA p sw sp **36 22 38** Full-bodied fizzer. Ripper grog, too.

Saltram Barossa (Merged with ROTHBURY in 94.) r w Mamre Brook (SHIRAZ, CAB, CHARD) and No 1 Shiraz are leaders. Metala is assoc Stonyfell label for Langhorne Creek Cab-Shiraz.

Sandalford Swan Valley r w (br) ★→★★★ Fine old winery with contrasting styles of r and w single-grape wines from SWAN and MARGARET RIVER areas.

Sauvignon Blanc Usually not as distinctive as in New Zealand, and made in many different styles, from bland to pungent. Sandalera is amazing long-aged sweet white.

Scotchman's Hill Geelong r w ★★ Newcomer making significant quantities of stylish PINOT N and good CHARD at modest prices.

Semillon 6803 ha, 88,427 tonnes Before the arrival of CHARDONNAY, Semillon was the HUNTER VALLEY'S answer to South Australia's RIESLING. Traditionally made without oak and extremely long-lived, now too often made with too much oak.

Seppelt Barossa, Grampians, Padthaway, etc r w sp br (sw w) ★★★ (Shiraz) 71' **85' 86' 90** 91' **92** 93' 96' 97' 98' Far-flung producers of Australia's most popular sparkling (Great Western Brut); also new range of Victoria-sourced table wines. Top sparkling is highly regarded "Salinger". Another part of SOUTHCORP, Australia's largest wine company.

Sevenhill Clare r w (br) ★★ Owned by the Jesuitical Manresa Society since 1851; consistently good wine; reds (esp SHIRAZ) can be outstanding.

Seville Estate Yarra Valley r w ★★★ (Chard) **92 94'** 97 98 oo' (Shiraz) 85 **86 88 90** 91 **92 94** 97' 98' Tiny winery acq by BROKENWOOD 97; CHARD, SHIRAZ, PINOT N, CAB.

Shadowfax Vineyard Geelong Vic r w ★★→★★★ Stylish new winery, part of historic Werribee Park, also hotel based on 1880s Mansion. NB P Noir

Shaw & Smith McLaren Vale w (r) ★★★ Trendy young venture of flying winemaker Martin Shaw and Australia's first MW, Michael Hill-Smith. Crisp SAUV, vg unoaked CHARD, complex, barrel-ferm Reserve CHARD, new Mer.

Shiraz 33 676 ha, 311, 045 tonnes. Hugely flexible, with styles ranging from velvety/earthy in the HUNTER; spicy, peppery, and Rhône-like in central and southern Victoria; and brambly, rummy-sweet, and luscious in BAROSSA and environs (eg PENFOLDS' Grange).

Simon Gilbert Wines Mudgee r w ★★ AUS$10 million winery as major contract maker plus own wines in major focus for Central Ranges Zone.

Southcorp The giant of the industry, despite its naff name: owns PENFOLDS, LINDEMANS, SEPPELT, Seaview, WYNNS, etc, and, from 2001, ROSEMOUNT.

Southern NSW Zone (NSW) incl CANBERRA, Gundagai, Hilltops, and Tumbarumba districts, Stonehaven, and PADTHAWAY r w ★★→★★★ First large (AUS$20m) winery in PADTHAWAY region built by BRL HARDY servicing whole LIMESTONE COAST ZONE production.

S Smith & Sons (alias Yalumba) Barossa r w sp br (sw w) ★★→★★★ Big, old family firm with considerable verve. Full spectrum of high-quality wines, including HILL-SMITH ESTATE. HEGGIES and YALUMBA Signature Reserve are best. Angas Brut, a good-value sparkling wine, and Oxford Landing CHARDONNAY are now world brands.

Stonier Wines Mornington Peninsula r w ★★★ (Chard) **93' 94' 95 97** 98 oo'o1' (Pinot) **93' 94' 95' 97'** 99 oo' Has overtaken DROMANA ESTATE for pride of place on the Peninsula. CHARDONNAY, PINOT NOIR are consistently vg; Reserves outstanding. 70% owned by PETALUMA since 88.

Swan Valley (WA) Birthplace of wine in the west, N of Perth. Hot climate makes strong, low-acid table wines but gd dessert wines. Declining in importance.

Tahbilk Goulburn Valley r w ★★→★★★ (Marsanne) **92 95 96 97** 98' 99 oo (Shiraz) **8o 84'** 86 **88** 91' **92** 98 99' (Cab) **86** 88 90 92 94 97 98 Beautiful historic family estate: reds for long ageing, also RIESLING and Marsanne. Reserve CAB outstanding; value for money ditto. Rare 186o vines SHIRAZ, too.

Taltarni Grampians/Avoca r w (sp) ★★ Huge but balanced reds for very long ageing; good SAUV and Clover Hill (Tasmania) sparkling.

Tarrawarra Yarra Valley r w ★★★ (Chard) **92' 94' 95** 97 98' oo' (Pinot N) **92' 94' 95 96** 97' 98 oo' Multimillion-dollar investment with limited quantities of idiosyncratic, expensive CHARD and robust, long-lived PINOT N. Tunnel Hill is the second label.

Tasmania Over 700,000 litres produced. Great potential for CHARD, PINOT N, and RIES in cool climate.

Tatachilla McLaren V r w ★★→★★★ Late 2000 merged with St Hallett to form public-listed Banksia Wines; significant (250,000 case) production of nice white and vg reds to increase rapidly.

Taylors Wines Clare r w ★★→★★★ 200,000 case production of much-improved RIES, SHIRAZ, CAB esp under St Andrew's label.

T'Gallant Mornington Peninsula w (r) ★★ Improbable name, avant garde labels for Aus's top Pinot Gris/Grigio producer; also fragrant, unwooded CHARD.

Tower Estate r w ★★★→★★★★ Newest venture of Len EVANS (and financial partners) offering luxury convention facilities and portfolio of seven wines made from grapes grown in various parts of Australia. Initial tastings impress.

Trentham Estate Murray Darling (r) w ★→★★ 50,000 c/s of family-grown & made sensibly priced wines from "boutique" winery on R Murray; gd restaurant, too.

Turkey Flat Barossa Valley r p ★★★ Icon producer of rosé, GRENACHE, SHIRAZ from core of 150-yr-old v'yd's. Top Stuff.

Tyrrell Hunter Valley r w ★★★ (Sem Vat 1) **87'** 89' **90 91 92 94'** 95' 96 98' 99' oo' (Chard Vat 47) **96** 97' 98' 99' oo (Shiraz Vats) **73' 75 79'** 81' 83 87' 91' 92' 94' 96' 97 98' 99' oo' Some of the best traditional HUNTER VALLEY wines, SHIRAZ and SEM. Pioneered CHARD with big, rich Vat 47 – still a classic. Also PINOT N.

Upper Hunter (NSW) Est'd in early 6os; irrigated vines (mainly whites), lighter and quicker developing than Lower Hunter's.

Vasse Felix Margaret River r w ★★★ (Cab S) **85 88 89 91 92 94 95 96** 97 99 With CULLEN, pioneer of the MARGARET RIVER. Elegant CAB, notable for mid-weight balance. Major expansion underway. Second label: Forest Hills (esp RIES, CHARD).

Verdelho Old white grape re-emerging in some light, aromatic wines and CHARD blends. Worth trying.

Virgin Hills Bendigo/Ballarat r ★★★ **73' 74' 76' 81' 82 84 88** 91' 92' 95 97 98' (oo') Tiny supplies of one red (a CABERNET-SHIRAZ-Malbec blend) of legendary style and balance. Rapid ownership changes unsettling.

Voyager Estate Margaret River r w ★★★ 30,000 cases of estate-grown, rich, and powerful SEM, SAUV BL, CHARD, AND Cab-Merlot.

Wendouree Clare r ★★★★ 78 79 **83 86 89'** 90' 91' 92 93 94 96' 98' 99 Treasured maker (tiny quantities) of some of Australia's most powerful and concentrated reds based on SHIRAZ, CABERNET S, MOURVEDRE, & Malbec; immensely long-lived.

Westfield Swan Valley w r ★→★★ John Kosovich's CAB, CHARD, and VERDELHO show particular finesse for a hot climate, but he is now developing a new v'yd in the much cooler PEMBERTON region.

Wignall's Great Southern (WA) r w ★★ In the far SW corner of Australia (near Albany), Bill Wignall makes sometimes ethereal, always stylish PINOT NOIR.

Wirra Wirra McLaren Vale r w (sp sw w) ★★★ (Cab S) 86 90' 91' 92 95 96' 97 98' High-quality wines making a big impact. Angelus is superb, top-of-the-range CABERNET, ditto RSW SHIRAZ.

Woodstock McLaren Vale ★★ Ever-reliable maker of chunky, highly flavoured reds in regional style and luscious botrytis wines from esoteric varieties. 20,000 cases.

Wyndham Estate Mudgee (NSW) r w (sp) ★→★★ Aggressive, large HUNTER and MUDGEE group with brands: Craigmoor, Hunter Estate, MONTROSE, Richmond Grove, and Saxonvale. Acquired by ORLANDO in 90.

Wynns Coonawarra r w ★★★ (Shiraz) 55' 63 65 85 86' 88' 90' 91' 93 94' 96' 98' 99 (Cab S) 57' 60' 62' 82' 85' 86' 90' 91' 94' 96' 97 98' 99' SOUTHCORP-owned COONAWARRA classic. RIES, CHARD, SHIRAZ, and CAB are all very good, especially John Riddoch Cab, and Michael "Hermitage".

Yalumba See S Smith & Sons.

Yarra Burn Yarra Valley r w sp ★★→★★★ Estate making SEM, SAUV, CHARD, sparkling PINOT, Pinot N, CAB; acquired by BRL HARDY in 95, with changes now underway. Bastard Hill CHARD and PINOT N legitimate flag-bearers.

Yarra Ridge Yarra Valley r w ★★→★★★ Very successful CHARDONNAY, CABERNET, SAUVIGNON BLANC, PINOT NOIR, all with flavour and finesse at relatively modest prices. Owned by BERINGER BLASS.

Yarra Valley Superb historic area nr Melbourne. Growing emphasis on very successful PINOT NOIR and sparkling.

Yarra Yering Yarra Valley r w ★★★→★★★★ (Dry Reds)81' 82' 83 84 85 90 91' 92 93' 94' 95 96 97' 98' 99 Best-known Lilydale boutique winery. Esp racy, powerful PINOT N, deep, herby CAB (Dry Red No 1), and SHIRAZ (Dry Red No 2). Luscious, daring flavours in red and white. Also fortified "Port-Sorts" from the correct grapes.

Yellowglen Bendigo/Ballarat sp ★★→★★★ High-flying sparkling winemaker owned by BERINGER-BLASS. Recent improvement in quality, with top-end brands like Vintage Brut, Cuvée Victoria, and "Y".

Yeringberg Yarra Valley r w ★★★ (Marsanne) 91' 92 94' 95 97 98 00' (Cab) 74' 75 76 79 80' 81 82 84 86 88 90 91 92 94' 97' 98' 00' Dreamlike, historic estate still in the hands of the founding family, now again producing v high-quality Marsanne, Roussanne, CHARD, CAB, and PINOT N in minute quantities.

Yering Station/Yarrabank r w sp ★★★ Yarra Valley On site of Victoria's first v'yd; replanted after 80-yr gap. Extraordinary joint venture: Yering Station table wines (Reserve CHARDONNAY, PINOT NOIR, SHIRAZ); Yarrabank (especially fine sparkling wines for Champagne Devaux).

Zema Estate Coonawarra r ★★→★★★ One of last bastions of hand pruning in COONAWARRA; silkily powerful, disarmingly straightforward reds.

Terroir in Australia

Terroir – the conjunction of soil, subsoil, slope, aspect, altitude, and all the elements of site climate – is as alive and well in Australia as it is anywhere else in the world. This vast continent offers a range of *terroir* greater than any other country other than the US, sustaining the creation of styles ranging from the finest bottle-fermented sparkling wines to the richest fortified wines. But over the past five years, and into the future, there has been a move from the warmer to cooler climates, and a progressive matching of *terroir* and variety. Thus Hunter Valley Semillon; Yarra Valley Pinot Noir; Coonawarra Cabernet Sauvignon; Barossa/McLaren Vale Grenache; Clare Valley, Riesling.

New Zealand

More heavily shaded areas
are the wine growing regions

Northland
Auckland
Auckland ○ Waiheke Island
Waikato
Gisborne
Hawke's
Bay
Wairarapa
(incl Martinborough)
Nelson
Nelson ○ ○ **Wellington**
Marlborough ○ **Blenheim**
Waipara
Canterbury ○ **Christchurch**
Central Otago
○ **Dunedin**

Tasman Sea   *Pacific Ocean*

Since the mid-1980s, New Zealand has made its name for wines (mainly white) of quality no one had anticipated, well able to compete with those of Australia or California, or indeed, France. In 1982, NZ exported 12,000 cases; in 2001, over 2.1 million. There are now over 39,000 vineyard acres.

White grapes still prevail though reds are catching up. The most extensively planted are Sauvignon Blanc and Chardonnay (covering over half of the national vineyard). Pinot Noir, Merlot, Cabernet Sauvignon are now well-established, with sizeable pockets of Riesling, Muller-Thurgau (fast-declining), Semillon, and Pinot Gris (newly fashionable). Intense fruit and crisp acidity are the hallmarks of New Zealand. Nowhere matches Marlborough Sauvignon for pungency. Chardonnay has shone throughout the country, Riesling's stronghold is the South Island. Marlborough has also proved itself with fine fizz. Recent reds (esp Cabernet and Merlot) from the warmer Hawke's Bay and Auckland have at least equalled the best NZ whites in quality. Pinot Noir has now proved capable of wonderful wines in cooler Martinborough and the South Island.

Recent Vintages

2001 V dry season in the South, wet in the North. Tiny crop in H Bay and Gisb. Marlb Sauv Bl of variable, often v gd quality. Pinot N should be excellent.

2000 Cool, wet spring and summer, saved by an Indian summer. Low yields. Aromatic whites – gd intensity and vigour. Pinot N better than Cab S.

1999 Promisingly dry and sunny summer, followed in the North by warm, wet autumn. Avge in Gisb and H Bay, but drier and better in Marlb.

1998 Widespread drought. Richly alcoholic wines with low acidity. Tropical fruit-flavoured Marlb Sauv Bl and powerful, conc'd H Bay reds.

1997 Low-yielding. Dry weather at the end of the season, but earlier high rainfall and humidity gave variable quality. Punchy Marlb Sauv Bl.

1996 Bumper harvest of mixed quality. Excellent Chardonnays; ripe and zingy Marlborough Sauvignon Blancs; green-edged Hawke's Bay reds.

Allan Scott Marlborough ★★ Attract Ries, Chard, and Sauv Bl; top label Prestige.

Ata Rangi Martinborough ★★★ Small but highly respected winery. Outstanding Pinot N (96' **97** 99 '00). Rich, conc'd Craighall Chardonnay.

Auckland (r) 93' **94' 96** 99 00' (w) **99** 00' Largest city in NZ. Location of head offices of major wineries. Some of NZ's top Cab-based reds. Incl Henderson, Huapai, Kumeu, Matakana, Clevedon, and Waiheke Island districts.

Babich Henderson (Auckland) ★★→★★★ Med-sized family firm, established 1916; quality, value. AUCK, H BAY, and MARLB v'yds. Rare premium wines: The Patriarch. Fine Irongate Chard (95' **96 98'** 99 00'), Cab-Merlot (single v'yd).

Black Ridge Central Otago ★→★★ World's southernmost winery. Noted for rich soft Pinot N, also gd Chard, Ries, and Gewürz.

Brancott Vineyards ★★→★★★ Brand used by MONTANA in US market.

Brookfield Hawke's Bay ★★→★★★ One of region's top v'yds: outstanding "gold label" Cab-Merlot; rich Chard, Pinot Noir, and Gewürz.

Cairnbrae Marlborough ★★ Small winery; quality Sauv Bl, Chard, and Ries.

Canterbury (r) 98' **99'** 00 01' (w) 00 01' NZ's 5th-largest wine region; v'yds at Waipara in N and nr Christchurch. Long, dry summers favour Pinot N, Chard, Ries.

Canterbury House Waipara ★→★★ Sizeable North Canterbury winery, American-owned, with firm spicy Pinot N and flavoursome flinty Sauv, Ries, and Chard.

Cellier Le Brun Marlborough ★★ Small winery: very gd, bottle-fermented sp, esp vintage (96) and Bl de Blancs (96). Terrace Road table wines are solid.

Central Otago (r) 99' 00 01' (w) **99'** 01 Small, cool, mountainous region in S of South Island. Ries and Pinot Gr promising, Pinot N rivals MARTINB's best.

Chard Farm Central Otago ★★ Good Chard, Ries, and perfumed silky Pinot N.

Church Road Hawke's Bay ★★→★★★ MONTANA winery. Wines include rich ripe Chard and elegant B'dx-like Cab S/Merlot. Top wines labelled Reserve.

Clearview Hawke's Bay ★★→★★★ V small producer. Burly flavour-packed Res Chard; dark, rich Res Cab Franc, Res Merlot, and Old Olive Block (Cab blend).

Cloudy Bay Marlb ★★★ Founded by WA's Cape Mentelle; now owned by the vast LVMH group. Intense Sauv Bl (**01**) & bold Chard were initially thrilling now just gd. Pelorus sp also impressive. Pinot N (**99'**) one of NZ's best.

Collard Brothers Auckland ★★→★★★ Long-est'd small family winery. Whites esp Rothesay V'yd Chard and Sauv Bl, MARLB Ries, and Sauv Bl.

Cooper's Creek Auckland ★★→★★★ Mid-sized producer. Excellent Swamp Res Chard, H BAY Ries, MARLB Sauv Bl.

Corbans Auckland ★→★★★ Est'd 1902, NZ's 2nd-largest wine company until purchased by Montana in 2000. Key brands: Corbans (top wines: Cottage Block; Private Bin), Huntaway Res, STONELEIGH (MARLB), LONGRIDGE (H BAY), Robard & Butler. Top GISBORNE Chards, S Isl Ries, & sp wines can be superb.

Craggy Range Hawke's Bay ★★ New winery established large v'yds in HAWKE'S BAY and MARTINBOROUGH. Immaculate Sauv Blanc, and Chard since 99.

Cross Roads Hawke's Bay ★→★★ Sm winery. Satisfying Chard, Ries, Cab S, Pin N.

De Redcliffe Waikato ★→★★ Med-sized Japanese-owned winery; "Hotel du Vin" attached. Gd Chard, Ries, & Sauv Bl, plain reds. Firstland range is excellent.

Delegat's Auckland ★★→★★★ Mid-sized family winery. V'yds at H BAY and MARLB. Proprietor's Res label dropped; replaced by Res label less oaky Chard, Merlot, and Cab S. OYSTER BAY brand: deep-flavoured MARLB Chard and Sauv Bl.

Deutz Auckland ★★★ Champagne co gives name and technical aid to fine sp from MARLB by MONTANA. NV: lively, yeasty, flinty; vintage bl de blancs: rich and creamy.

Domaine Georges Michel Marlborough ★→★★ French-owned, based at former Merlen winery. Stylish, full rounded Sauv Bl & crisp appley Chablis-like Chard.

Dry River Martinborough ★★★ Tiny winery. Penetrating, long-lived Chardonnay, Riesling, Pinot Gris (NZ's finest), Gewürztraminer (ditto), and notably powerful Pinot Noir (94' **96' 97'** 99' 00')

Esk Valley Hawke's Bay ★★→★★★ Now owned by VILLA MARIA. Some of NZ's most voluptuous, Merlot-based reds (esp Res label 95' 96' **98' 99** 00'), v gd dry Merlot rosé, oak-aged Chenin Bl, satisfying Chards, and Sauv Bl.

Fairhall Downs Marlborough ★★ Rich vibrantly fruity whites, notably weighty, peachy, spicy Pinot Gr and scented, pure, deep-flavoured Sauv Bl.

Felton Road Central Otago ★★★ New star winery in warm Bannockburn area. Pinot N Block 3 and Ries outstanding; excellent Chard and regular Pinot N.

Forrest Marlborough ★★ Small winery; fragrant, ripe Chard, Sauv Bl, and Ries; stylish H BAY Cornerstone Vineyard Cab-Merlot.

Framingham Marlborough ★★ Specializes in aromatic white wines, notably Ries (Classic Ries is slightly sw, intensely flavoured and zesty; Dry Ries even finer).

Fromm Marlborough ★★ Small winery, Swiss-founded, focusing on red wines. Fine Pinot N, esp under Fromm Vineyard label.

Gibbston Valley Central Otago ★★ Pioneer winery with popular restaurant. Greatest strength Pinot N, esp fleshy firm Res (99' 00). Racy local whites (Chard, Ries, Pinot Gr, Sauv Bl).

Giesen Estate Canterbury ★→★★ German family winery, now region's largest. Known for Ries, incl honey-sweet Late Harvest. Grapes now from CANTERBURY except Chard, Sauv Bl (MARLB). Chard and Pinot N good especially Reserve.

Gillan Marlborough ★→★★ Small winery producing fresh, vibrant Sauv Bl and Chard, promising sparkling wine and leafy Merlot.

Gisborne (r) 98' 00 (w) 00' NZ's third-largest region. Strengths in Chard (typically fragrant, ripe and appealing in its youth), and Gewürz (highly-perfumed and peppery). Abundant rain and fertile soils ideal for heavy croppers, esp Müller-T. Reds typically light, but Merlot shows promise.

Goldwater Waiheke Island ★★★ Region's pioneer Cab S-Merlot (**96** 97 99') still one of NZ's finest: Médoc-like concentration and structure. Also crisp, citrussy Chard and pungent Sauv Bl, both grown in MARLB.

Greenhough Nelson ★★ One of region's top producers, with immaculate and deep-flavoured Ries, Sauv, Chard, and Pinot N. Top label: Hope Vineyard.

Grove Mill Marlborough ★★→★★★ Attractive whites, incl vibrant MARLB Chard; excellent Ries, Sauv, slightly sweet Pinot Gr.

Hawke's Bay (r) 95' 98' 99 00 (w) 98' 00' NZ's 2nd-largest region. Long history of table-winemaking in sunny climate, shingly and heavier soils. Full, rich Cab S and Merlot-based reds in gd vintages; powerful Chard; rounded Sauv.

Highfield Marlborough ★★ After hesitant start, now Jap-owned with quality Ries, Chard, Sauv Bl, and Pinot N, and piercing, flinty, yeasty Elstree sp.

A choice from New Zealand for 2003

Merlot Esk Valley Res (99), Villa Maria Res (99), Unison Selection (99)
Pinot Noir Martinborough V'yard (99), Gibbston Valley Res (99), Isabel (00)
Chardonnay Clearview Res (00), Kumeu River Mate's Vineyard (00), Ata Rangi Craighall (00)
Sauvignon Blanc Palliser (01), Babich Winemaker's Res (01), Seresin (01)
Bottle-fermented fizz Nautilus Cuvée Marlborough NV, Elstree Cuvée Brut (97), Lindauer Grandeur
Sweet wines Dry River Chardonnay Botrytis Berry Selection (00), Cloudy Bay Late Harvest Riesling (99), Virtu Noble Semillon (98)

Huia Marlborough ★★ Mouth-filling, subtle wines that age well, incl savoury rounded Chard and perfumed well-spiced Gewürz.

Hunter's Marlborough ★★★ Top name in intense immaculate Sauv (oaked and not). Fine, delicate Chard. Excellent sp, Ries, Gewürz; light, elegant Pinot N.

Huthlee Hawke's Bay ★★ Small, low-profile winery with crisp zingy Sauv Bl and Pinot Gr and concentrated, claret-style reds (esp Merlot and Cab S-Merlot).

Isabel Estate Marlborough ★★→★★★ Family estate with limey clay soil. Outstanding Pinot N, Sauv Bl, & Chard, all with impressive depth & finesse.

Jackson Estate Marlborough ★★→★★★ Large vineyard, no winery. Rich Sauv Bl, good Chard (esp weighty Res). Rich complex sp, gorgeous sw whites.

Kemblefield Hawke's Bay ★→★★ American-owned winery. Light reds, buttery, ripely herbal, oak-aged Sauv Bl, soft, peppery Gewürz, and fleshy, lush Chard.

Kim Crawford Hawke's Bay ★★ Personal label of former COOPER'S CREEK winemaker, launched 96. Rich oaked GISBORNE Chard, robust, unwooded MARLB Chard, high-flavoured MARLB Sauv Bl, and vibrant supple HAWKE'S BAY Cab Fr.

Kumeu River Auckland ★★★ AUCKLAND grapes, v rich, mealy Kumeu Chard (00'); single-v'yd Mate's Vineyard Chard even more opulent. Rest of range solid, including fresh, pure Pinot Gris and oaky savoury Pinot Noir. Brajkovich is second label.

Lake Chalice Marlborough ★→★★ Small producer with bold creamy-rich, softly-textured Chard and powerful Cab S and Merlot. Ries and Sauv Bl of good quality. Platinum is premium label.

Lawson's Dry Hills Marlborough ★★→★★★ Weighty wines with rich, intense flavours. Distinguished Sauv Bl (esp), Gewürz, and Ries.

> **The best Pinot Noirs from New Zealand**
> Pinot Noir is the hot new Kiwi red, yielding perfumed, supple, richly varietal wines in Martinborough and several South Island regions, notably Central Otago but also (recently) Marlborough. Quantities are small but rising swiftly, and the best are of exciting quality. Top labels include Ata Rangi, Martinborough Vineyard, Dry River, Palliser, Walnut Ridge (all from Martinborough), Cloudy Bay, Fromm La Strada, Fromm Vineyard, Neudorf, Pegasus Bay, Gibbston Valley Reserve, and Felton Road Block 3.

Lincoln Auckland ★ Long-est'd, medium-sized family winery. Good value sound varietals: buttery GISBORNE Chard (President Selection).

Lindauer See MONTANA.

Linden Hawke's Bay ★→★★ Smallish producer with soft, buttery Chard, solid but not exciting Sauv, and smooth berryish Merlot, and Cab S.

Longridge See CORBANS

Margrain Martinborough ★★ Small winery with firm, concentrated Chard, Ries, Pinot Gr, Merlot, and Pinot N, all of which reward bottle-age.

Marlborough (r) 98' 99 00 01' (w) 01 NZ's largest region. Sunny, warm days and cool nights give intensely flavoured, crisp whites. Extraordinarily intense Sauv, from sharp, green capsicum to riper, tropical-fruit character. Fresh, limey Ries. High-quality sparkling. Too cool for Cab S, but Pinot N is highly promising.

Martinborough (r) 98 99' 00 01 (w) 00 01 Small, high-quality area in S WAIRARAPA (foot of North Island). Warm summers, dry autumns, gravelly soils. Success with white grapes (Chardonnay, Sauvignon Blanc, Riesling, Gewürztraminer, Pinot Gris) but most renowned for Pinot Noir.

Martinborough Vineyard Martinborough ★★★ Distinguished small winery; one of NZ's top Pinot Noir (98' 99' 00'). Rich, biscuity Chardonnay. Also intense Riesling, Sauvignon Blanc.

Matakana Estate Auckland ★★ Lgst producer in Matakana district. Since 1998, classy Chard, Pinot Gr, Sem, and Merlot/Cab blend. Volume label: Goldridge.

Matariki Hawke's Bay ★★ Stylish, conc'd w and r, extensive v'yds in stony Gimblett Road. Rich, ripe, oak-aged Sauv; robust, spicy Quintology red blend.

Matawhero Gisborne ★→★★ Formerly NZ's top Gewürz specialist. Now has wide range (also Chard, Sauv Bl, Cab-Merlot) of varying but often gd quality.

Matua Valley Auckland ★★→★★★ Highly rated, mid-size winery with large estate v'yd, now owned by Beringer Blass. Excellent oaked Matheson Sauv Bl. Top wines labelled Ararimu incl fat, savoury Chard, dark, rich Merlot-Cab S. Numerous attractive GISBORNE (esp Judd Chard), H BAY, and MARLB wines (latter branded Shingle Peak).

Mills Reef Bay of Plenty ★★→★★★ The Preston family produces impressive wines from H BAY grapes. Top Elspeth range incl lush, barrel-ferm'd Chard and dense, rich Bx-style reds. Middle-tier Reserve range also impressive. Two quality sparkling wines: Mills Reef and Charisma.

Millton Gisborne ★★→★★★ Region's top sm winery: mostly organic. Top med-sw Opou V'yd Ries. Soft, savoury Chard Opou V'yd. Robust complex dr Chenin Bl.

Mission Hawke's Bay ★→★★ NZ's oldest wine producer, est'd 1851, still run by Catholic Society of Mary. Solid varietals: sweetish, intensely perfumed Ries esp gd value. New Reserve range incl excellent Bordeaux-style reds, Semillon, Riesling, and Chardonnay.

Montana Auckland ★→★★★★ NZ wine giant, 60%+ market share after buying Corbans in 2000. Wineries in AUCKLAND, GISBORNE, H BAY (see CHURCH ROAD), and MARLB. Extensive co-owned v'yds. Famous for Marlb whites, incl top-value Sauv Bl, Ries, and Chard (new Reserve range esp good). Strength in sp, incl DEUTZ, and stylish, fine-value Lindauer. Elegant H BAY Church Road reds and quality Chard. Bought by UK-based Allied-Domecq in August 2001.

Morton Estate Bay of Plenty ★★→★★★ Respected mid-size producer with v'yds in H BAY and MARLB. Refined, rich Black Label Chard one of NZ's best (**98'**), but mid-tier White Label Chard also good. Brilliant Coniglio Chard is NZ's most expensive.

Mount Riley Marlborough ★→★★ Fast-growing company with extensive v'yds but no winery. Beautifully balanced easy-drinking Chard; piercing Ries; punchy Sauv Bl and dark flavoursome Cab/Merlot. All good value.

Mt Difficulty Central Otago ★★★ New producer in relatively hot Bannockburn area. Powerful, firm, toasty Chard and v refined, intense Pinot N.

Muddy Water Waipara ★★ Sm, high-quality producer since 96 with beautifully intense and poised Ries, lush powerful Chard, & very bold, conc'd Pinot N.

Nautilus Marlborough ★★ Small range of distributors Négociants (NZ), owned by S Smith & Son of Australia (cf Yalumba). Top wines incl Sauv Bl and fragrant, yeasty, smooth sp. Lower tier wines: Twin Islands.

Nelson (r) 99 00 01' (w) 00 01' Small region west of MARLBOROUGH; similar climate but little wetter. Clay soils of Upper Moutere hills and silty Waimea Plains. Strengths in whites, esp Ries, Sauv Bl, Chard. Pinot N is best red.

Neudorf Nelson ★★★ One of NZ's top boutique wineries. Strapping, creamy-rich Chard, one of NZ's best (**99'** 00). Fine Pinot N, Sauv Bl, and Ries.

Nga Waka Martinborough ★★→★★★ Dry, steely whites of v high quality. Outstanding Sauv Bl; piercingly flavoured Ries; robust, savoury Chard.

Ngatarawa Hawke's Bay ★★→★★★ Med-sized. Top Alwyn Reserve range incl powerful Chard and strapping Cab S and Merlot. Mid-range Glazebrook.

Nobilo Auckland ★→★★ NZ's 3rd-lgst wine company. Acquired SELAKS 98; now owned by BRL Hardy. Early reputation for reds faded. Marlb Sauv: gd, sharply priced. Superior varietals labelled Icon. V gd Drylands Sauv Bl. Cheaper wines labelled Fernleaf and Fall Harvest.

Okahu Estate Northland ★→★★ NZ's northernmost winery, at Kaitaia. Hot, humid climate. Reds: stuffing and warm, ripe flavours. Kaz Shiraz 94 NZ's first gold-medal Shiraz. Savoury, complex Reserve Clifton Chard.

Omaka Springs Marlborough ★ Small producer with solid Sauv Bl, Ries, Chard and Merlot. New Reserve: Chard and Pinot N more impressive.

Oyster Bay See DELEGAT'S.

Palliser Estate Martinborough ★★→★★★ One of the area's largest and best wineries. Superb tropical-fruit-flavoured Sauv Bl, excellent Chard, Ries, and Pinot N. Top wines: Palliser Estate; lower tier: Pencarrow.

Pask, C J Hawke's Bay★★ Med-sized winery, extensive v'yds. Gd to excellent Chard (esp Res). Cabernet S and Merlot-based reds fast improving, with rich, complex Res releases.

Pegasus Bay Waipara ★★→★★★ Small but distinguished range, notably taut cool-climate Chardonnay, lush complex oaked Sauv/Sém; and zingy, high-flavoured Ries. Cab S-based reds: region's finest. Pinot N lush and silky.

Peregrine Central Otago ★★ Emerging star with strikingly good debut Sauv Bl (98); steely, incisive Ries; fleshy, rich Pinot Gr and Gewürz.

Quartz Reef Central Otago ★★ Quality producer with weighty, flinty Pinot Gr; substantial rich Pinot N; yeasty, lingering,Champagne-like sp, Chauvet.

Rippon Vineyard Central Otago ★→★★ Stunning v'yd. Fine-scented, v fruity Pinot N and slowly evolving whites, incl steely, appley Chard.

Robard & Butler See CORBANS.

Rongopai Waikato ★→★★★ Small winery using local, AUCKLAND, and GISBORNE fruit. Softly mouth-filling ripe Sauv Blanc, and Chardonnay. Renowned for botrytized sw whites, esp Reserve Riesling.

Sacred Hill Hawke's Bay ★★ Sound "Whitecliff" varietals; good, oaked Res Sauv Bl (Barrel Fermented and Sauvage). Gd Basket Press Cab S and Merlot-Cab. Powerful, creamy Rifleman's Reserve Chard v distinguished.

Saint Clair Marlborough ★★ Fast-growing export-led producer. Substantial vineyards. Fragrant, full Riesling, Sauvignon Blanc, easy Chardonnay. Plummy, early-drinking Merlot. Rich, concentrated Reserve Sauvignon Blanc, Chardonnay, and Merlot.

St Helena Canterbury ★→★★ The region's oldest winery, founded near Christchurch in 78. Light, supple Pinot N (Res is bolder). Chard variable but gd in better vintages. Cheap, earthy, savoury Pinot Bl is fine value.

Seifried Estate Nelson ★→★★ Region's only medium-sized winery, founded by Austrian. Known initially for well-priced Riesling and Gewürztraminer, but now also producing good-value, often excellent Sauvignon Blanc and Chardonnay. Light reds. Best wines labelled Winemaker's Collection.

Selaks ★★→★★★ Mid-size family firm bought by NOBILO 98. Sauvignon Bl is their strength but the reds are plain.

Seresin Marlborough ★★→★★★ Est'd by expat NZ film producer Michael S. First vtge 96. Stylish, immaculate Sauv, Chard (esp Res), Pinot N and Gr, Ries, Noble Ries.

Sherwood Canterbury ★→★★ Tart austere Ries and Chard and two Pinot Ns, notably fresh, plummy, berryish Res model. Bold, peachy, nutty Res Chard.

Shingle Peak See MATUA VALLEY.

Sileni Hawke's Bay ★★ Major new winery (from 98) with extensive v'yds and v classy Merlot/Cab, Chard, and Sém.

Soljans Auckland ★ Long-est'd sm family winery. Good, supple Pinotage.

Spencer Hill Nelson ★★ Known for Chard (rich, creamy, smooth): 1st vintage 94. "Tasman Bay": larger volumes. "Spencer Hill": v'yd-designated and oaky.

Stonecroft Hawke's Bay ★★→★★★ Small winery. Dark, concentrated Syrah, more Rhône than Australian. Also very good Cab/Syrah/Merlot blend ("Ruhanui"), Chardonnay, Gewürztraminer, Sauvignon Blanc.

Stoneleigh See CORBANS.

Stonyridge Waiheke Island ★★★★ Boutique winery. Two Bordeaux-style reds: Larose exceptional (93 **94'** 96 97 99 00'); Airfield: second label.

Te Awa Farm Hawke's Bay ★★ Newish winery; lge estate v'yd. Classy Chard, Cab-Merlot, and Merlot under Boundary, Frontier, and larger vol Longlands labels.

Te Kairanga Martinborough ★★ One of district's larger wineries. Big, flinty Chard (Res: richer), perfumed, supple Pinot N (Res: complex, powerful).

Te Mata Hawke's Bay ★★★→★★★★ The Bay's most prestigious winery. Fine, powerful Elston Chardonnay; v good, oaked Cape Crest Sauvignon Blanc; stylish Coleraine Cabernet-Merlot (91' **95** 98'). Awatea Cabernet-Merlot (v gd): 2nd label, less new oak.

Te Motu Waiheke Island ★★ Top wine of Waiheke V'yds, owned by the Dunleavy and Buffalora families. Dark, concentrated, brambly red of very good quality, first vintage 93. Dunleavy Cab-Merlot is second label.

Torlesse Waipara ★→★★ Small, gd-value Canterbury producer of weighty conc'd Sauv Bl, fresh, flinty Ries and firm, toasty, citrussy Chard.

Trinity Hill Hawke's Bay ★★→★★★ Part-owned by John Hancock (ex-MORTON ESTATE). Impressively dark, firm, conc'd reds since 96, and elegant Chard.

Unison Hawke's Bay ★★ Red-wine specialist with dark, spicy, flavour-crammed blends of Merlot, Cab S, and Syrah. Selection label is oak-aged longest.

Vavasour Marlborough ★★→★★★ Based in Awatere Valley. Immaculate, intense Chard and Sauv Bl; promising Pinot N. Dashwood: second label.

Vidal Hawke's Bay ★★→★★★ Established 1905 by Spaniard, now part of VILLA MARIA. Reserve range (Chardonnay, Cabernet-Merlot) uniformly high standard. Other varietals good.

Villa Maria Auckland ★★→★★★ NZ's 2nd-largest wine company, incl VIDAL and ESK VALLEY. Owner: George Fistonich. Top range: Reserve (Noble Riesling NZ's most awarded sweet white); Cellar Selection: middle-tier (less oak); third-tier Private Bin wines can be excellent and top-value (esp Riesling, Sauvignon Blanc, Gewürztraminer).

Waipara Springs Canterbury ★★ Small producer with lively, cool, climate Ries, Sauv Bl, and Chard; reds promising.

Waipara West Canterbury ★★ Co-owned by London-based Kiwi wine distributor Paul Tutton. Finely scented lively Ries; freshly acidic, herbaceous Sauv; firm citrussy Chard, and increasingly ripe and substantial Pinot Noir.

Wairarapa NZ's 6th-largest wine region. See MARTINBOROUGH.

Wairau River Marlborough ★★ Intense Sauv Bl; succulent, toasty Chard.

Wellington Capital city and name of region; incl WAIRARAPA, Te Horo and MARTINB.

West Brook Auckland ★★ Long-est'd underrated, full Chard, Sauv Bl and Ries. Top wines labelled Blue Ridge.

Whitehaven Marlborough ★★ Emerging firm (first vintage 94); excellent wines: racy Ries, scented, delicate lively Sauv Bl, flavourful, easy Chard.

Wither Hills Marlborough ★★★ Vineyard owned by former DELEGAT's winemaker Brent Marris. Exceptional Chardonnay and Sauvignon Blanc. Serious, concentrated, spicy Pinot Noir.

The best Sauvignon Blancs from New Zealand

Marlborough produces inimitably zesty and explosively flavoured Sauvignon Blancs, best drunk young (at six to 18 months). Hawke's Bay's more robust, ripely herbaceous and rounded Sauvignon Blancs are less punchy, but better suited to barrel maturation. Classic labels include Cloudy Bay, Hunter's, Grove Mill, Palliser, Vavasour, Villa Maria Reserve, Montana Reserve, Wither Hills, Lawson's Dry Hills, Isabel, and Seresin.

South Africa

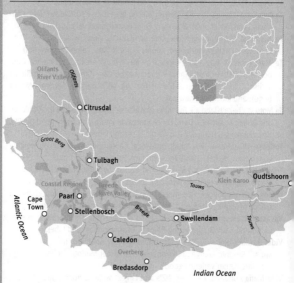

A younger, well-travelled, wine-savvy generation is taking charge in the Cape winelands. It has been little more than a decade since the country emerged from its enforced isolation and apartheid sanctions to encounter much-changed markets and fashions. Initially, the Cape's strong and long 350-year-old wine tradition slowed the transformation. The wine establishment had taken years to abandon its price-fixing powers and monopolistic production quotas. And, except for a small, independent minority, they were in denial about their rampant viruses and sloppy vineyard management. But all that is changing.

Pinotage is no longer regarded with such reverence. Today's movers take much more care over their vineyards – of all varieties. And the effort to grow first-rate fruit has the inevitable knock-on effect in the winery.

South Africa's rich wine diversity remains one of its great attractions. Its vineyards, clustered spectacularly around the mountains and coastlines of the southern tip of Africa, amid wild flora and fauna found nowhere else, are another. For a time, these will remain a plentiful source of sound, cheap (mainly white) supermarket wines. But the new-wave Cape winemakers are not aiming to hang about on the lower levels. Their sights are set much higher.

Recent Vintages

2001 Lower-than-avge yields, conc'd fruit: dry summer and winter. Should be among the best red vintages. Big wines, deep colours, should keep well.

2000 Difficult, 3rd successive year of high temps – many v'yd fires – then isolated hailstorms. General improvement in v'yd management yielded promising reds. Heat not ideal for crisp, fruity whites.

1999 Stop-start beginning played havoc with flowering, harming yields in early varieties. Prolonged heatwave prior to harvest pushed up alcohol; some massive – unbalanced – wines, for long ageing.

1998 Searingly hot, dry vintage from outset – curtailing season. Low yields helped quality. Big, high-alcohol reds, for keeping.

1997 Longest, coolest season in decades, allowing for gradual ripening; finest red year of decade for growers not panicked by a few showers.

1996 Generally cooler with some showers, but record yields. Overall, a patchy vintage, esp for growers unable to intervene early to limit crop.

African Terroir Wines ★→★★ Revamped, big, Swiss-owned ST'BOSCH- and PAARL-BASED winery (formerly Sonop Wines). Grapes sourced from around the Cape feature in several gd-value ranges. "Azania Range" SHIRAZ (01) and "Big Five Collection" – gd Cab S, PINOTAGE, Merlot (all 01). "Diemersdal" range Cab S and Pinotage, and excellent Shiraz (01) in "Out of Africa" range.

Allesverloren r ★★ Old family estate in Swartland W of Cape Town, best known for port-style (**89 90 93 96** 97). Also hefty Cab (**95 96 98**) and Shiraz (**94 96 99**)

Amani r w ★★ ST'BOSCH. Smart, deteremined newcomer with strong, bold CHARDONNAY (00 01) and gutsy MERLOT (99 00).

Avontuur r w sw ★★ ST'BOSCH. Winning many awards. Full, lemony Chard (00), solid, fruity res PINOTAGE (**99 00**). Gd sparkling Brut NV, from Pinot N/Chard. Barrel-aged, botrytis Riesling label, "Above Royalty" (99).

Axe Hill r sw ★★★ Outstanding tiny specialist producer of vintage style "port" at Calitzdorp. Touriga National, Tinta B (**97 98** 99).

Backsberg r w sw ★→★★ 395-acre PAARL estate undergoing extensive (incl organic) v'yd & winery renewal. Competitive pricing with loyal following. Leads with B'x blend "Klein Babylonstoren" (**97** 98). Also Shiraz (99), barrel-ferm Chard, Sauvignon, rosé, sparkling brut, and outstanding cask-aged "Sydney Back" brandy, from CHENIN.

Beaumont r w ★★ Walker Bay. Family-run, rustic winery: v gd PINOTAGE Res (97 99), Chard, and CHENIN (**99** 00). Promising dense, dark Mourvèdre.

Bellingham r w ★→★★ Gd specialist reds in "Spitz" premium range. Cab F (**98** 99), PINOTAGE (**97** 99), Shiraz (**98 99 00**). Popular whites (all DYA), esp Chard, Sauv bl, and Chard-Sauv blend "Sauvenay". Sweet, soft Cape Ries-based Johannisberger wines (exported as Cape Gold).

Bergkelder ST'BOSCH co, owning and/or marketing several estates (Le Bonheur, Uiktyk, Alto). Brands incl JC Le Roux (sp) & Fleur de Cap (r w sw). See Distel.

Beyerskloof r ★★→★★★ STELLENBOSCH. Popular small specialist. Deep-flavoured Cab S-Merlot blend (**95 97** 98 99) and PINOTAGE (**98 99 00**). Same team produces Bouwland label. Good PINOTAGE Res (98) and Cab Merlot (99 00).

Boekenhoutskloof r w ★★ Franschhoek winery. Leading prod of spicy, assertive Shiraz (97 98 99); Cab S (**97 98** 99), and Sémillon (99 00). Gd-value 2nd label Porcupine Ridge.

Boland Kelder r w sw ★★ PAARL. Winemaker of the Year 01. Gd Cab S (99 00), PINOTAGE (**97** 99 00), full-bodied Shiraz (98 00). Gd, fortified white Muscadels.

Boplaas r w sw ★→★★ Estate in dry, hot Karoo. Earthy, deep Cape Vintage Reserve port-style (**91 94 96** 97 99), fortified Muscadels & "Cape Tawny Port" NV.

Boschendal r w sp ★★ 617-acre estate near Franschhoek. Known for good whites, sparkling Chardonnay Reserve (**99** 00). Very good Shiraz (97 98 99). Also Bordeaux blend "Grand Reserve" (**97** 98 99), Merlot (**95 97 98** 99).

Bouchard-Finlayson r w ★★→★★★ Walker Bay. Leading Pinot Noir producer: "Galpin Peak" (**96 97** 99 00) & "Tête de Cuvée" (99). Excellent Chard sp "Missionvale" label, also "Kaaimansgat" (both **99** 00 01). Vg Sauv Bl (DYA).

Breede River Valley Fortified and white wine region E of Drakenstein Mts.

Buitenverwachting r w sp ★★→★★★ German-owned estate in Constantia suburbs of Cape Town. Outstanding Sauv (**99** 00), Chard (**99** 00), B'x blend "Christine" (**95** 96), Cab S (**91** **92** 95), Merlot (**95** 99).

Cabrière Estate ★★ Franschhoek. Gd NV CAP CLASSIQUE under Pierre Jordan label (Brut Sauvage, Chard-Pinot N, and Belle Rosé Pinot N).

Cap Classique, Méthode South African term for classic-method sp wine.

Cape Point Vineyards r w ★★ Cape Point. Atlantic on both sides of these v'yds on the Cape Peninsula. Outstanding Sauv Bl and Sauv/Sém (00). Gd Chard (00).

Cederberg Wines r w ★★→★★★ Cederberg. High Cape v'yds. Scintillating, fruity, crisp whites: Sauv Bl & Chenin Bl (00 01). Superb Cab-based blend.

Château Libertas Big-selling blend of mainly Cab S made by SFW.

Chenin Blanc Most widely planted grape; v adaptable. Sometimes very good; much upgrading by leading growers, incl barrel-fermented examples. Generally, short-lived as dry, fruity; often lasts better when sweet. Also called Steen.

Clos Malverne ★★ Small ST'BOSCH estate, with established reputation for PINOTAGE Res (**96** **97** 98), Cab/Merlot/PINOTAGE blend "Auret" (**95** **97** 98).

Constantia Once the world's most famous sweet Muscat-based wine (both red and white), from the Cape. See KLEIN CONSTANTIA.

Constantia Uitsig r w ★★ Chard Res. (01) Sémillon Res. (**99** 00 01) (plus Cab. S) from Constantia v'yds. Wines made at neighbour Steenberg.

Cordoba r w ★★→★★★ Highly regarded winery/v'yds on Helderberg mountains, ST'BOSCH. Stylish Cab F-based claret blend – labelled "Crescendo" (**95** **97** 98 99); plus ripe, rich Merlot (**95** **96** **97** 98).

Darling Cellars r w sw ★→★★★ Atlantic Coast w of Cape Town, "Onyx" label tops large range, PINOTAGE-Shiraz blend (99), PINOTAGE (98 99); good "Groenekloof" Shiraz (98 99). Good-value "DC" range.

De Toren r ★★★ ST'BOSCH. First release of "Fusion V" (Cabs S and F, Merlot, Petit Verdot, Malbec). Obssesive berry selection makes for elegant, complex wine.

De Trafford Wines r w ★★★ ST'BOSCH. Small-scale *artisanal* – unfiltered, natural yeast fermentation B'x blend Res (98 99); Cab S (**97** 98 99 00); Shiraz (98 00), Merlot (**97** **98** 99 00). Also CHENIN BL – dry – in oak (00), dessert CHENIN "Vin de Paille" (**97** **98** 99).

De Wetshof w sw ★★ Robertson. Chardonnays of varying style – top are flagship barrel-selected "Bataleur" (**98** **99** 00) and "D'Honneur" (00). Also Sauv Bl, Gewürz, "Danie de Wet" Rhine Ries, "Edoloes" (99 00). Bottles own-brand Chards for British supermarkets.

Delaire Winery r w ★★→★★★ High mountain v'yds at Helshoogte Pass above ST'BOSCH. Rich Chard (**97** **98** **99** 00), massive Cab "Botmaskop" (98), emphatic Merlot (98 00), Cab-Merlot (00).

Delheim r w dr sw ★→★★★ Big winery; mountain v'yds nr ST'BOSCH. Much-acclaimed Vera Cruz Shiraz (98 00); plummy "Grand Res" B'x blend, Merlot, Cab S, and Cab F (**95** **96** 97 98 99). Gd Cab S (**95** **97** 98 99); consistent PINOTAGE (**98** 99); also Chard, Sauv, and sweet wines, sparkling Gewürz, outstanding botrytis Steen, "Edelspatz" (00).

Devon Hill r w ★★ ST'BOSCH. New Swiss-owned winery in Devon Valley. Rich, award-winning Cab S (00), Merlot (00), PINOTAGE "Bluebird" (00).

Die Krans Estate ★→★★★ Karoo semi-desert v'yds making rich, full Vintage Res port-style. Best **91** **94** 95 97. Also traditional fortified sw r & w Muscadels.

Distel Newly formed conglomerate, merging several of SA's biggest wine operations, BERGKELDER, Distillers, ST'BOSCH FARMERS' WINERY (SFW); marketing big, steady – no recent fireworks– FLEUR DE CAP, ZONNEBLOEM, Grundberger, NEDERBURG, etc.

Durbanville Hills r w ★★ Grapes from maritime cooled vineyards in Durbanville. Fine, elegant reds: Cabernet, Merlot, PINOTAGE (all 99 00), Chardonnay. (00 01) intriguing Sauvignon Blanc. (00).

Edelkeur ★★★ Excellent, intensely sw, noble rot white from CHENIN BL by NEDERBURG – like all full-blown botrytis desserts, officially designated Noble Late Harvest.

Eikendal Vineyards r w sw ★→★★ Swiss-owned 100-acre vineyards, winery at STELLENBOSCH. Merlot (**96 97** 98 99). Very good Chardonnay (98 99 00 01); Cab S Res (**94 96** 99).

Estate Wine Official term for wines grown and made (not necessarily bottled) exclusively on registered estates. Not a quality designation.

Fairview r w dr sw ★★→★★★ Enterprising PAARL property in vanguard of Cape's push to modern fruity styles. Wide range of labels. Tasty Viognier (**98 99** 00). Best regulars: Shiraz Res (**97** 98 00); "Cyril Back" Shiraz (**98** 99); Amos Pinotage (**98** 99); Primo Pinotage (00); Rhône-style blend cheekily named "Goats do Roam"; substantial Oom Pagal Sém (00); Akkerbos Chard (00); barrel-ferm CHENIN. Also Malbec, Gamay, Carignan, Mourvèdre.

A choice from South Africa for 2003

Cabernet Sauvignon Kanu, Rustenberg Peter Barlow, Thelema, Neil Ellis V'yard Selection, Boekenhoutskloof

Merlot Thelema Res, Delaire, Veenwouden, Spice Route Flagship, Steenberg

Shiraz Graham Beck The Ridge, Neil Ellis V'yard Selection, Waterford Kevin Arnold, Delheim Vera Cruz, De Trafford, Havana Hills, Fairview Cyril Back

Pinotage Fairview Primo, Uiterwyk Top of the Hill, Simonsig Red Hill, L'Avenir

Pinot Noir Newton-Johnson, Bouchard-Finlayson "Tête de Cuvée", Glen Carlou, Hamilton Russell, Meerlust

Chardonnay Seidelberg, Eikendal, Kanu, Fairview Akkerbos, De Wetshof D'Honneur. Always outstanding: Thelema, Vergelegen Res, Glen Carlou Res, L'Avenir

Sauvignon Blanc (DYA) Mulderbosch, Steenberg Res, Vergelegen Res, Neil Ellis "Groenekloof"

Chenin Blanc Kanu, Cederberg, Villiera, Mulderbosch "Steen op Hout", L'Avenir, Seidelberg, Ken Forrester

Dessert Constantia "Vin de Constance", Avontuur Above Royalty, Vergelegen Sémillon Noble Late Harvest

Sparkling Villiera Brut Natural Chardonnay, J C Le Roux Pinot Noir, Graham Beck Brut

---

Flagstone r w ★★ Cape Town. Enterprising Aussie winemaker trucks in grapes from 39 vineyards. Best label so far is "Music Room" Cabernet S (00).

Fleur du Cap r w sw ★→★★ Value range from Bergkelder at ST'BOSCH, incl. "Unfiltered Collection". Good Cab S. (**96** 98), Merlot (**96** 98), fine Gewürz, botrytis CHENIN, Chard (00). Gd Sauv Bl (DYA).

Glen Carlou r w ★★→★★★ Top Cape winery, v'yds at PAARL, tie-up with Donald Hess of Napa, California (qv). Outstanding Chardonnay Reserve (**98 99** 00); B'x blend "Grand Classique" (**95 97** 98); full Pinot N (96 98 00); Spicy, new Shiraz (00). Among the best Cape CHENINS – off-dry – labelled "Devereux" (**99** 00); Cape Vintage "port" style (**96 97** 98).

Graham Beck Winery r w sp ★★→★★★ Two avant-garde ROBERTSON properties producing three classy METHODE CAP CLASSIQUE bubblies: Brut RD NV, Blanc de Blancs – all Chardonnay (**93** 96); Cuvée 2000 NV, mainly Pinot Noir, light blush launched oo; well-regarded Chardonnay (99 oo). Cult-status Shiraz "The Ridge" (**97 98** 99). New "Coastal" operation producing Cornerstone Cab (99) and Old Road Pinotage (98 99). Also claret-style Estate Blend (99).

Grangehurst r ★★→★★★ Small, top STELLENBOSCH winery, buying in grapes, specializing in reds. Outstanding "Cape blend" Nikela (**97 98**) – Cabernet, PINOTAGE, Merlot. Good PINOTAGE (**95 97** 98) and concentrated Reserve Cabernet-Merlot (**95 96 97** 98).

Groot Constantia r w ★→★★★ Historic gov't-owned estate near Cape Town. Superlative red & white Muscat desserts in early 19th century. Good Cab-Merlot "Gouverneur's Reserve" (**92 94 95 97** 99), PINOTAGE (**97 99** oo), Chard Res (**oo o1**), Shiraz (99), Weisser (Rhine) Ries-Gewürz botrytis sp (**98 99**), also gd Sauv Bl (DYA).

Hamilton Russell Vineyards r w ★★→★★★ Walker Bay. Cape's "burgundy" specialist estate at Hermanus. Fine Pinot N (**96 97** 98 99 oo) and classy, fine-edged Chard (**97 98** 99). Small yields, French-inspired vinification, careful barrelling. "Ashbourne" label now discontinued.

Hartenberg r w ★★→★★★ STELLENBOSCH Respected producer usually releasing reds only after long maturation. Shiraz (**93 95 96** 97); Merlot (**95 96** 97); Cab. S (94 96 97). V individual Pontac (**93** 98); Zinfandel (**95** 97); Chard Res (**oo o1**); sweet Weisser (Rhine) Ries.

Havana Hills r w ★★ Durbanville. Splendid debut for new winery behind Cape Town. Reserve Du Plessis range tops bill: deep, brooding Cab S-Merlot (oo), Merlot (oo), and Shiraz (oo).

Hazendal r w ★→★★ Old STELLENBOSCH estate. Russian-owned. Gd Chard (**oo o1**) and flagship Cab-Shiraz (**97 98** 99 oo). Also sparklers, PINOTAGE, CHENIN.

Hidden Valley r ★★★ Small Devon Valley, ST'BOSCH v'yd. Outstanding Cape (a standard-bearer) PINOTAGE (**96 97** 99 oo). New classic Cab S (99 oo).

J C le Roux ★→★★ Gd, large (620,000 cases p.a.) ST'BOSCH-based sparkling-wine house. Best is Pinot Noir (98). Also *blanc de blancs* Chard, long – 5-9 yrs – maturation in bottle. Well-priced Pinot-Chard NV blend "Pongràcz". By MÉTHODE CAP CLASSIQUE.

Jordan V'yds r w ★★ ST'BOSCH. Cab S-Merlot Res named "Cobbler's Hill" (**97 98** 99), Cab S (**95 96** 97 98); very good Sauv Bl (DYA), Chard (**99 oo o1**). California-trained husband-and-wife team, Gary & Cathy Jordan.

J P Bredell ★★→★★★ STELLENBOSCH v'yds. Rich, dark, deep Vintage Res port-style (Tinta Barocca and Souzão grapes) (**91 95** 97 98). Also rich PINOTAGE (**96** 98), recently Merlot (98) and Shiraz (**97** 98).

Kaapzicht Estate r w ★★→★★★ ST'BOSCH Recently topping local listings with "Steytler" PINOTAGE (**98** 99) and "Vision" blend – Pinotage, Cab S, Merlot (oo); also well-crafted Cab S (**96 97** 98 99).

Kanonkop r ★★→★★★ ST'BOSCH. Grand local status. Sets the pace for friendlier, oak-finished PINOTAGE (**89 91 94 97** 98 99). Equally distinctive, emphatic B'x-style blend Paul Sauer (**89 91 94 95 97** 98 99). Individual, powerful Cab (**89 91 94 95 97 98** 99).

Kanu Wines r w sw ★→★★ ST'BOSCH. Prominent newcomer. Cab S "Limited Release" (98 99); Merlot (**98** 99); barrel-aged, new-style CHENIN BL; Chard (**99 oo**); outstanding Sauv Bl (DYA); botrytis Harslevelü.

Ken Forrester Vineyards ★★ Imaginative STELLENBOSCH Helderberg producer (and restaurateur at "96 Winery Rd" – a winemakers' hangout). Full "Grande Chenin" from 25-plus-year-old bush vines (**97 98 oo**); Unusual light-textured savoury blend, Grenache-Syrah.(99 oo) 35 year-old plus v'yd.

Klein Constantia Estate r w sw ★★ →★★★ Immediate neighbour of historic Groot Constantia Estate. Always standout, bold, crisp Sauvignon Blanc,

DYA, which can hang on for years. Solid Chardonnay (**97 98** 99); taut Cabernet, Bordeaux-style blend Marlbrook (**94 95 96** 97); generous Shiraz (**94 95** 97 99). From 1986, Vin de Constance revived the 18th-century Constantia legend – mint-lime-coffee aromas – dessert from Muscat de Frontignan (**93 94 95 96** 97 98).

Kleine Zalze r w ★→★★ STELLENBOSCH. Making comeback. Cabernet S (98 99) and ripe-tasting Shiraz (00). Barrel-fermented CHENIN BL (**99** 00).

Kumala r w sp ★→★★Gd-value range by British-based Western Wines; biggest-selling Cape brand in UK (1.2 million cases p.a.). Sound Cab S Reserve, Merlot Reserve (99 00), Chard Brut, MÉTHODE CAP CLASSIQUE.

KWV International r w sw ★→★★★ PAARL. The Kooperatieve Wijnbouwers Vereniging, formerly S Africa's national wine co-op. Controlled Cape wine for most of the 20th century until controversial privatization 1997. Vast premises in PAARL, a range of gd-to-excellent wines, esp Cathedral Cellar reds, Cab S (**94 95 96** 97), Merlot (**94 95** 96 97 98), PINOTAGE (**94 95 96** 97), B'x blend "Triptych" (**94** 95 96 97 98), Shiraz (**96** 97 98), Chard (00). Also 'Regular' KWV labels incl traditional blend of Shiraz, Merlot, Cab S called Roodeburg, legendary name in Cape wine (**96 97** 98)**;** vast range of dry whites and others, incl "port" styles, "Vintage Port" (97); Millenium Vintage "Port" (99), and "Full Ruby" NV. KWV-run La Borie Estate Cab. S (**96 97** 98), luxurious, rich, fortified dessert from PINOTAGE, "Pineau de Laborie".

La Motte r w ★★ Lavish Rupert family estate near Franschhoek. Lean, stylish reds: Bordeaux-style blend Millennium (**95** 97 98), good Shiraz (**95 96 97** 98).

L'Avenir ★★→★★★ Outstanding ST'BOSCH estate. Leading producers of PINOTAGE (**97 98** 99) and top, rich, sturdy Cape CHENIN BL (98 99 00 01); also impressive Cab S (**95** 97 99), Chard (00 01), flavour-filled, weighty Sauv Bl. (**00** 01). Also Botrytis dessert Vin de Meuveur (97 00).

Landskroon Estate r w ★→★★ Solid, old (uninterrupted eight generations) family property in PAARL. Recently upgraded reds with "Paul de Villiers" Cab S (99) and Shiraz (00); good range of other Cab S and Merlot. Outstanding "port" (96 97 99).

Le Bonheur Estate r w ★★ STELLENBOSCH estate, fine, minerally B'x blend, "Prima" (**95** 96 97 98 99). Cab S (**95** 97 98); big-bodied Sauv Bl (**99 00** 01).

Le Riche Wines r ★★→★★★ ST'BOSCH. Outstanding boutique wines, hand-crafted by respected Etienne Le Riche: Cab S Res (**97** 98 99 00), Cab S (**97** 99), Merlot-Cab (99 00).

Linton Park r w ★★ Large British-owned winery at Wellington. Gd "Summer Hill" Shiraz first release (99 00), Cappell's Court is 2nd tier.

Long Mountain Wine ★→★★ Pernod-Ricard label, buying grapes from co-ops under peripatetic Aussie Robin Day and local Jacques Kruger. Good, well-priced Cab S, Ruby Cab, Cab S-Merlot Res, Chard, CHENIN BL. Big presence in UK supermarkets.

L'Ormarins Estate r w sw ★★ One of two beautiful Rupert family estates nr Franschhoek. Best red is B'x blend "Optima" (94 95 96 97), Cab S (**91 94** 95), forward oak-aged Sauv Bl (01).

Meerendal Estate r ★★ Excellently sited Durbanville property, emerging from long trough. Cab S, PINOTAGE, Shiraz, Bordeaux blend "Cabochon" all 98s, deep-flavoured, strong.

Meerlust Estate r w ★★→★★★ Prestigious old family estate nr ST'BOSCH; present incumbent, Hannes Myburgh, is 8th generation to own Meerlust. With Cape's only – and longtime – Italian winemaker, Friulian Giorgio dalla Cia. Fine – stressing elegance over impact – "Rubicon" B'x blend (**91 92 95** 97); Merlot (**91 95** 96 97); Pinot N Res. (**96 97** 98 99). Ripe, heavy Chard (**97 98** 99). Also lusty SA estate "grappa", from Cab S.

Middelvlei Estate r ★★ STELLENBOSCH Well-run family estate: very good reds, sparkling Shiraz (**95 96 97** 98 99); PINOTAGE (**94 95 96** 97 98); Cab S (**91 94** 95 96); Chardonnay (00).

Morgenhof Estate r w sw ★★→★★★ French-owned ST'BOSCH estate on a roll. Outstanding Merlot Res (98), Merlot regular (**96** 97 98), Bordeaux blend "Premiere Sélection" (**95** 96 97), Cabernet S Res (98), excellent Sauv Bl (**00** 01), Chard (**99** 01), "port" style LBV (**95**), and Vintage (98), black and rich. Gd, dry CHENIN BL (**96** 99 00).

Mulderbosch Vineyards r w ★★★ ST'BOSCH. Among Cape's best; penetrating Sauv Bl from mountain v'yds (**97 99 00** 01); Chard, one oak-ferm'td (**98** 99 00 01), other fresh, bold, unoaked (**98** 00). Vg barrel-ferm CHENIN "Steen op Hout" (**97 98** 99 00). Easy, B'x-style blend, "Faithful Hound" (**94 95** 97 98).

Muratie Estate r ★★ Old STELLENBOSCH estate, revival began with Bordeaux blend "Ansela" (**94 95** 96 97), now with very promising Cabernet Sauvignon (00). Pinot Noir (97) 98). Sumptuous, opaque "Vintage Port" (**98**), smoky, ruby-style NV "port" – all Portuguese varieties. Fortified Muscat "Amber", with loyal following since 1925. Gd Chardonnay "Isabella" (00).

Nederburg r w p dr sw s/sw sp ★→★★★ Large, modern PAARL winery (6–700,000 cases pa; 50 different wines). Est. 1937. Own grapes and suppliers. Gd Reserve Cab S (**97** 98 99), Cab-Merlot blend "Edelrood" (**97** 98); plus Chard, Sauv Bl, Ries, and sparklers. Small quantities Limited Vintage, Private Bins for auction, some outstanding – recently Private Bin PINOTAGE (**97** 99, plus botrytis desserts). Was 70s pioneer of botrytis sw wines. Stages Cape's biggest annual wine event, the Nederburg Auction. See also EDELKEUR.

Neethlingshof r w sw ★★ Large ST'BOSCH estate, many labels. Lord Neethling Cab S (**97** 98); Cab S (**94** 96 97 98); PINOTAGE (97) 98); Shiraz (**95 96** 97 98); Chard (00 01); Sémillon Res (98 99); excellent Gewürz and blush Blanc de Noirs. Since 1990s consistently judged among national champion botrytis wines from Ries (Weisser Riesling) NLH (all very good, sparkling 98).

Neil Ellis Wines r w ★★→★★★ Among most-respected Cape wine names. Full, forthright wines from widely sourced grapes, vinified at Jonkershoek Valley, STELLENBOSCH. Quality-price tiering begins with top-flight Reserve Vineyard Selection (**97 98 99**), Shiraz (**97** 98 99). STELLENBOSCH range: Cab S (**94 96** 97 99), PINOTAGE (98 99 00) Shiraz (**97** 98 99), Cab-Merlot (97) 98 99). Always excellent Sauvignon Blanc from various sites, sparkling Groenkloof (**99 00** 01), full, bold Chardonnay from STELLENBOSCH (**99** 00 01). Inglewood is value range.

Nelson Wine Estate r w ★→★★ PAARL winery, v'yds: gd Cab S (**95** 98 99), PINOTAGE (98 99), Chard (99). Among first Cape grower-worker partnerships, under Klein Begin (Small Beginnings) label, incl PINOTAGE, Cabernet.

Newton-Johnson Wines r w ★★→★★★ Sourcing grapes widely, supplemented by own harvests/labels: family-run winery at Walker Bay. Now joins small list of vg Cape Pinot Noirs with (00), Cab S (98 99), PINOTAGE (98 00), lemony Chard (**99** 00), Sauv Bl (**00** 01). Gd value under "Cape Bay" labels.

Overgaauw Estate r w ★★ Old (since 1783) family estate nr STELLENBOSCH; excellent Merlot (**95 97** 98 99) and Bordeaux-style blend "Tria Corda" (**95** 97 98 99), v gd Cabernet Sauvignon (**95** 97 98). Also Cape Vintage (port-style) (**88 89 90** 98), includes Touriga Nacional from 94 – S Africa's first.

Paarl Town Thirty miles northeast of Cape Town and the demarcated wine district around it.

Paul Cluver Estate r w ★★ Elgin coastal region, east of Cape Town with reputation for dessert and off-dry Rhine Weisser Riesling (**97 98** 00 01), good notices for recent Pinot Noir (98), also improving Cabernet Sauvignon (**97** 98).

Pinotage S African red grape cross of Pinot N and Cinsault – "born" in 1926. Can be delicious – intriguing boiled-sweets, banana flavours, and has shown potential if carefully matured in oak. But coarse, estery flamboyance can dominate.

Plaisir de Merle r w ★★ Grand, SFW-owned cellar, vineyards near PAARL. Good, modern, approachable-style Cabernet (**95 98** 99), Merlot (**95 98** 99), also Chardonnay (**99** 00), Sauvignon Blanc DYA.

Rickety Bridge r w ★★ Franschhoek. Very good Shiraz (**96** 97 98), Merlot (**97 98** 99), Cab S-Merlot flagship Paulinas Reserve (96). Also good Chardonnay, Sémillon, Sauvignon Blanc (99).

Robertson District Inland from Cape. Mainly dessert (notably Muscat) and white wines, determined effort to increase red v'yds recently.

R&R at Fredericksburg Winery r w ★★→★★★ Top v'yds, cellar at Simondium, PAARL. Initials stand for joint venture, Rothschild and Rupert, two old French and S African wine families. So-so start, (97 Cab-Merlot), followed by much better oak-matured B'x blend "Baron Edmond" (**98** 99); Chard "Baroness Nadine" (98 99), deep-flavoured classic.

Rustenberg Wines r w ★★★→★★★★ Prestigious old STELLENBOSCH estate, founded 300 yrs ago, making wine continuously for more than 100. Major cellar, v'yd revamp since mid-90s. Terrific latest release of flagship, single-v'yd "Peter Barlow" Cab S (**96 97 98** 99) latter among finest Cape Cab S ever; "Rustenberg" B'x blend "John X Merriman" (**96** 97 98 99). Outstanding Chard "Five Soldiers" (**98 99** 00). Also top class 2nd label "Brampton", Cab S-Merlot (**97 98** 99'), plus Chard, Sauv Bl.

Rust en Vrede Estate r ★★★ Estate just E of STELLENBOSCH: best-known for strong, individual, mainly Cab S blend "Rust en Vrede Estate Wine", superb in latest releases (**91 94 96** 97 98). Solid Cab S (**91 94 96** 98), Shiraz (**94 96** 97' 98), also Merlot, Tinta Barroca.

Savanha r w ★★ Label for newly est, ST'BOSCH-based Wine Corp. Attractive, medium-weight "Sejana Merlot" (99) and "Naledi" Cab S (99). Range incl Shiraz, Chardonnay, Sémillon, Sauvignon Blanc.

Saxenburg Wines r w dr sw sp ★★→★★★★ Swiss-owned STELLENBOSCH vineyards and winery, owned and jointly run with the French Château Capion nr Montpellier, specializing in Syrah/Shiraz. Distinctive, powerful Cape reds: (Private Collection – PC labels), Shiraz "PC" (**91 94 95 96 97 98**) & Shiraz "Saxonburg Select" (**97** 98). Robust, deep-flavoured "PC" PINOTAGE (96 98 99), "PC" Cab S (**91 92 94 95 97** 99). Also Merlot (**94 95 97** 98), plus Chardonnay, Sauvignon Blanc, and sweet Gewürztraminer.

Seidelberg Estate r w ★★ PAARL. Very promising start from major re-vamp of beautifully situated v'yds, (formerly De Leuwen Jagt) with Chardonnay (99), CHENIN BLANC (01), and Merlot (99).

Simonsig Estate r w sp sw ★★ Malan family winery at STELLENBOSCH; extensive range: Cabernet-Merlot "Tiara" (**91 94 95 97 98** 99). Much behind new Cape blend – Frans Malan Reserve, mainly PINOTAGE with Merlot, Cabernet Sauvignon (98 99), rich, "Red Hill" PINOTAGE (**97 98** 99), Syrah Reserve "Merindol" (**97** 98 99), very good Chardonnay (**98 99** 00), dessert-style Gewürztraminer. First – 30 years ago – Cape Méthode CAP CLASSIQUE, Kaapse Vonkel brut (96) Pinot Noir, Chardonnay.

Simonsvlei International r w p sw sp ★ One of South Africa's best-known co-op cellars, just outside PAARL. Many tiers of quality, from "Hercules Paragon" (Merlot) to "Mount Marble".

Spice Route Wine Company r w ★★→★★★ Malmesbury, now fashionable West Coast region. V intense, dark, rich, gripping flagship Syrah (98 99), Merlot (98 99), PINOTAGE (98 99); full, barrel-ferm CHENIN BL (**98 99** 00).

Spier Cellars r w ★★ ST'BOSCH winery. A Wine Corp label. New releases: "Private Collection" Cab S (98), Merlot (98 99). Also in "regular" range: PINOTAGE (99), CHENIN BL (00), botrytis dessert (98), Fresh Sauv Bl (01).

Springfield Estate Robertson ★★ ROBERTSON growers known for original approach: "whole-berry fermentation" reds, for juicy Cab S (98 99), crisp Sauv Bl (DYA), and rich, wild, yeast Chard named "Méthode Ancienne" (97 98 99 00).

Steenberg Vineyards r w ★★→★★★ CONSTANTIA. Serious recent entrant, winery v'yds in Cape Town golf course. So far, outstanding Merlot (97 98 99 00); equally distinguished, lasting Sauv Bl (99 00 01); Sémillon (00 01). Also good, leaner Cab S, Chard, sp brut "1682" NV Chard/Pinot N.

Stellenbosch Town and demarcated district 30 miles E of Cape Town (2nd-oldest town in S Africa). Oak-lined university town and heart of the wine industry. Many top estates, especially for reds, are in mountain foothills; extensive wine routes, many restaurants.

Stellenbosch Farmers' Winery (SFW) world's fifth-largest winery, now part of South Africa's biggest wine conglomerate DISTEL, biggest after KWV: equivalent of 14M cases pa. Range incl NEDERBURG; top is ZONNEBLOEM. Wide selection of mid/low-price wines.

Stellenbosch Vineyards ★→★★ Dynamic regional venture by some 150 ST'BOSCH growers merging forces (from former ST'BOSCH co-ops Welmoed, Eersterivier, Helderberg, Bottelary). Top range is "Genesis". Big, juicy Merlot (99), vg Shiraz (97 98 99), Chard (99 00); "Kumkani" label features excellent – tropical fruity – Sauv Bl. (99); Gd-value wines, incl CHENIN-based dry white "Versus".

Stellenryck Collection r w ★★ Gd BERGKELDER range. Cab S (94 98), Chard (98 99 00), Rhine Ries, Fumé Blanc.

Stellenzicht ★★→★★★ STELLENBOSCH. Modern winery, neat mountainside v'yds. Outstanding Syrah (94 95 97 98 99), plus attractive B'x blend "Stellenzicht" (94 95 97 98), PINOTAGE (98 99), Sauv Bl DYA, Sémillon Res (98 99 00), Chard (98 99 00). Remarkable noble late-harvest botrytis dessert wines from Rhine Riesling (96 98).

Swartland Wine Cellar r w dr s/sw sw sp ★→★★ Vast range from hot, dry wheatland: big-selling, low-price; esp CHENIN and dry, off-dry, or sw, but (recently) penetrating Sauv Bl; big, ripe Cab-Merlot Res. (97 99 00), Shiraz (99 00) Chard (01), soft PINOTAGE. (99 00) Vg "Vintage Port" (97), and other fortified desserts from Muscat varieties.

Thelema Mountain Vineyards r w ★★★→★★★★ ST'BOSCH mountainside winery v'yd (first release '87) Winemaker Gyles Webb and Thelema, top international names for nearly a decade. Outstanding, individual (ripe berry/mint) reds; fresh, fruity, focused whites. Cab S (91 92 93 94 95 97 98 99), Merlot (94 95 97 98 99) – incl ultra-rich Merlot Res (99). Chard (93 97 98 99 00), Sauv Bl (01). Individual, spicy, rich Chard named "Ed's Reserve" (98 99 00). Immaculate v'yds.

Twee Jonge Gezellen Estate w sw sp ★→★★ Old Tulbagh. In Krone family (18th-C founder). Best is Méthode CAP CLASSIQUE "Cuvée Krone Borealis Brut" from Chard/Pinot. Gd blended whites, many Muscat-based, dry to sweet; most popular: TJ39, dry, blend of a dozen varieties.

Uiterwyk Estate r w ★★ Old estate SW of STELLENBOSCH. Striking single-vineyard PINOTAGE "Top of the Hill" (96 97 98). Very good Cabernet Sauvignon based blend, incl Pinotage (94 96 97 98), Shiraz (99). Also sweet whites, incl Viognier, Chardonnay, Sauv Bl.

Veenwouden r ★★★ Immaculate family-run PAARL property owned by Geneva-based opera singer, Deon Van der Walt. Outstanding Merlot (95 96 97 98 99 00), and B'x blend "Veenwouden Classic" (95 96 97 98).

Vergelegen r w ★★★→★★★★ ST'BOSCH – Helderberg. One of Cape's oldest wine farms, founded 1700 and currently hottest names, lifted by talented, outspoken winemaker André van Rensberg, brilliant, complex, like his reds: Cab S (**97** 98), Bordeaux blend flagship "Vergelegen" (98 99), Merlot (**95** 98). Superb Chardonnay Reserve (**97** 98 99 00) and racy, exciting Sauvignon Blanc Reserve. "Schaapenberg" (**98** 99 00). Cracker dessert: Noble Late Harvest Sémillon (98 99).

Vergenoegd r w sw ★★ Old STELLENBOSCH family estate. B'x blend reserve (94 95 97 98 99), Cabernet Sauvignon (**94** 95 98), Shiraz (**96** 97 98). Cape Vintage "Port" (**93 94** 95 96 97).

Villiera Wines r w sp ★★→★★★ Big PAARL winery with extensive, good-quality range, including 4 MÉTHODE CAP CLASSIQUE bubblies: new Brut National Chardonnay – virtually organic, "Tradition Brut" and "Tradition Brut Rosé" (both NV), "Monro Brut Première Cuvée" (**95** 96) from Pinot Noir/Chardonnay. Sound reds: Bordeaux blend "Cru Monro" (**95 96** 97 98 99), Merlot (**98** 99), Merlot Reserve (98), single-vineyard, spicy-mushroomy Shiraz since (99 00). Top "Bush Vine" Sauvignon Blanc (99 00), consistently good – plus good value – dry CHENIN BLANC (**98 99 00** 01), dessert botrytis Chenin Blanc (00), "Port" (95 97).

Vredendal Cooperative r w dr sw ★ S Africa's largest co-op winery in warm Olifants River region. Improving reds, sp Shiraz Mt Maskam (98 99). Huge range, mostly white. Big exporter of various supermarket labels.

Vriesenhof-Talana Hill r w ★★ Highly rated ST'BOSCH property, run by one of Cape's favourite wine (and rugby) characters, Jan Boland Coetzee. Winning approving notices with new Pinot N (00). Firmly structured B'x blend flagship "Kallista" **93 94** 95 97 98), Cab (**94** 95 97 98), penetrating PINOTAGE (**97** 98 99). Good Chard (**98 99** 00). Good-value Paradyskloof label.

Warwick Estate r w ★★ STELLENBOSCH estate. Consistently gd B'x blend "Trilogy" (**92 94** 95 97 98), individual Cab F (**94 95** 97 98). Top "Old Bush Vine" PINOTAGE (**95 96** 97 98 99) from 25-yr-old vines; red blend "Three Cape Ladies" – Cab S, Cab F, Pinotage (**98 99** 00 01). Vg Chard (**98 99** 00 01).

Waterford r w ★★ STELLENBOSCH. Show-piece new winery, plantings; acclaimed debut with bought-in grapes: Kevin Arnold Shiraz (98 99), Cabernet S (98 99). Very good Sauvignon Blanc (00 **01**), Chardonnay (00 01).

Welgemeend Estate r ★★ Boutique PAARL estate: Médoc-style blend (**94 95 96** 97 98). Malbec based blend "Duelle" (**96 97** 98).

WhaleHaven Wines r w ★★ Walker Bay. Local reputation for Pinot Noir "Oak Valley" (**95 96** 97 98 99), cool-climate, limey crispness in Chardonnay (**99** 00). Also good line-up of Cabernet Franc, Merlot, Sauvignon Blanc, plus slightly fizzy pink, "Baleine Noir".

Wine Corp Newly established (2000) umbrella group at ST'BOSCH, controlling SPIER CELLARS, Longridge, SAVANHA, Capelands. Already under new management by 2001 – currently being overhauled, some labels on hold, or being "retired".

Wine of Origin The Cape's appellation contrôlée, but without French crop-yield restrictions. Certifying the following: vintage, variety, region of origin.

Worcester Demarcated wine district round BREEDE and Hex river valleys, E of PAARL. Many co-op cellars. Mainly dessert wines, brandy, dry whites.

Zonnebloem r w sw ★★ (Cab S) SFW's top wines, with new "fine art" labels for Cabernet S, Merlot (99 00), Shiraz (99), Sauv Bl (00). Good regular range, including Cabernet S (**94 95** 98), Merlot (95 97 98), Bordeaux blend Laureat (**91 93 94** 96 97 98), Shiraz (**96 97** 98 99), PINOTAGE (**95** 98 99), Sauvignon Blanc DYA, Chard (00 01). Blanc de Blancs one of the Cape's best available dry CHENINS (with touch of Sauvignon Blanc).

A little learning...

A few technical words

The jargon of laboratory analysis is often seen on back-labels, especially of New World wines. It creeps menacingly into newspapers and magazines. What does it mean? This hard-edged wine-talk, unsympathetic as it is to most lovers of wine, is very briefly explained below.

The most frequent technical references are to the ripeness of grapes at picking; the resultant alcohol and sugar content of the wine; various measures of its acidity; the sulphur dioxide used as a preservative; and occasionally the amount of "dry extract"– the sum of all the things that give wine its character. And about the barrels.

The **sugar** in wine is mainly glucose and fructose, with traces of arabinose, xylose and other sugars that are not fermentable by yeast, but can be attacked by bacteria. Each country has its own system for measuring the sugar content or ripeness of grapes, known in English as the **"must weight"**. The chart below relates the three principal ones (German, French, American) to each other, to specific gravity, and to the potential alcohol of the wine if all the sugar is fermented.

Sugar to alcohol: potential strength

Specific Gravity	°Oechsle	Baumé	Brix	% Potential Alcohol v/v
1.065	65	8.8	15.8	8.1
1.070	70	9.4	17.0	8.8
1.075	75	10.1	18.1	9.4
1.080	80	10.7	19.3	10.0
1.085	85	11.3	20.4	10.6
1.090	90	11.9	21.5	12.1
1.095	95	12.5	22.5	13.0
1.100	100	13.1	23.7	13.6
1.105	105	13.7	24.8	14.3
1.110	110	14.3	25.8	15.1
1.115	115	14.9	26.9	15.7
1.120	120	15.5	28.0	16.4

Residual sugar is the sugar left after fermentation has finished or been stopped, measured in grams per litre. A dry wine has virtually none.

Alcohol content (mainly ethyl alcohol) is expressed in percent by volume of the total liquid. (Also known as "degrees".) Table wines are usually between 11.5° and 13.5°.

Acidity is both fixed and volatile. **Fixed acidity** consists principally of tartaric, malic and citric acids, all found in the grape, and lactic and succinic acids, produced during fermentation. **Volatile acidity** consists mainly of acetic acid, which is rapidly formed by bacteria in the presence of oxygen. A small amount of volatile acidity is inevitable and even attractive. With a larger amount the wine becomes "pricked"–to use the Shakespearian term. It turns to vinegar. Acidity may be natural, in warm regions it may also be added.

Total acidity is fixed and volatile acidity combined. As a rule of thumb for a well-balanced wine it should be in the region of one gram per thousand for each 10° Oechsle (see above).

Barriques Too much of the flavour of many modern wines is added in the form of oak; either from ageing and/or fermenting in barrels (the newer the barrel the stronger the influence) or from the addition of oak chips or – at worst – oak essence. Newcomers to wine can easily be beguiled by the vanilla-like scent and flavour into thinking they have bought something luxurious rather than something cosmetically flavoured. But barrels are expensive; real ones are only used for wines with the inherent quality to benefit long-term. French oak is classic and most expensive; especially that from the Allier, the famous Tronçais forest, in Burgundy, the Vosges, Nevers, and Limoges. Each supposedly has a different flavour and influence – which can be altered by "toasting" the inside to different degrees when the barrel is constructed. American oak has a strong Bourbon flavour. Baltic oak is more neutral.

Malolactic fermentation is often referred to as a secondary fermentation, and can occur naturally or be induced by the winemaker. The process involves converting tart malic acid into softer lactic acid. Unrelated to alcoholic fermentation, "*la malo*" can add complexity and flavour to both red and white wines. In hotter climates where natural acidity may be low canny operators avoid it.

Micro-oxygenation is a technique developed in MADIRAN, to allow the wine controlled contact with oxygen during maturation. This mimics the effect of barrel-ageing, reduces the need for racking, and helps to stabilize the wine.

pH is a measure of the strength of the acidity, rather than its volume. The lower the figure the more acid. Wine usually ranges from pH 2.8 to 3.8. Winemakers in hot climates can have problems getting the pH low enough. Lower pH gives better colour, helps stop bacterial spoilage and allows more of the SO_2 to be free and active as a preservative.

Sulphur dioxide (SO_2) is added to prevent oxidation and other accidents in winemaking. Some of it combines with sugars etc and is known as "**bound**". Only the "**free**" SO_2 that remains in the wine is effective as a preservative. **Total SO_2** is controlled by law according to the level of residual sugar: the more sugar, the more SO_2 needed.

Wines to drink now in an ideal world
The successful wines (see text) of:

Red Bordeaux
Top growths of 90, 89, 88, 86, 85, 83, 82, then 78, 70, 66, 61, 59, 49, 47, 45
Other crus classés of 95, 90, 89, 86, 85, then 88, 82, 70, 61
Petits châteaux of 99, 98, 96, 95, then 90, 89

Red Burgundy
Grands crus of 95, 93, 90, 89, 88, 85, then 78, 69, 64, 59

Premiers crus of 98, 97, 96, 95, 93, 90, 89, 85
Village wines of 99, 98, 97, 96, 95

White Burgundy
Grands crus of 97, 96, 95, 92, 90, 89, then 86, 85
Premiers crus of 98, 97, 96, 95, then 93, 90, 89
Village wines of 00, 99, 98, 97, 96, 95

Rhône reds
Hermitage/top northern Rhône reds of 98, 96, 95, 91, 90, 89, 88, 85, 83, 78, 61
Châteauneuf-du-Pape/Gigondas of 98, 95, 94, 90, 89, then 88, 85, 83

Sauternes
Top growths of 95, 90, 89, 88, 86, 85, 83, then 81, 79, 76, 75, 71, 70, 67, 59, 55
Other wines of 97, 96, 95, 90, 89, 88, 86, 85, 83

Alsace
Grands crus 98, 96, 95, 94, 93, 90, 89, 88, 85, 83, then 76, 67
Standard wines of 00, 99, 98, 97, 96, 95, 94, then 90, 89, 88

Sweet Loire wines
Top growths of 97, 96, 95, 90, 89, 88, 86, 85, 78, 76, 75, then 71, 64, 59, 47

Champagne
Top wines of 96, 95, 93, 90, 89, 88, 86, 85, then 83, 82, 79, 75

German wines
Great sweet wines of 97, 96, 95, 94, 93, 90, 89, 88, 86, 85, 83, 76, 71, then 59, 53
Auslesen of 98, 97, 95, 94, 93, 90, 89, 88, 86, then 85, 83, 76, 71
Spätlesen of 00, 99, 98, 97, 96, 95, 94, 93, 92, 91, 90, 89, 88, then 86, 85, 83, 76
Kabinett and QbA wines of 00, 99, 98, 97, 96, 95, 94, 93, 90

Italian wines
Top Tuscan reds of 97, 95, 93, 90, 88, then 86, 85, 82
Top Piedmont reds of 96, 95, 93, 90, 89, 88, 85, 82

Spanish wines
Top Rioja 96, 95, 94, 91, 90, then 82, 70, 84
Top Ribera del Duero 96, 95, 94, 91, 90, 89   Priorato 98, 96, 94

California wines
Top Cabs, Zins, Pinot N of 99, 98, 97, 96, 95, 94, 91, 90, then (but not Pinot N) 87, 86, 85, 84
Top Chardonnays of 00, 99, 98, 97, 96, 95, 94

Australian wines
Top Cabs, Shiraz, Pinot Noir of 98, 96, 94, 91, 90, then (but not Pinot Noir) 88, 86, 85, 84, 82, 80
Top Chardonnays of 00, 99, 98, 97, 96, 95, 94, 92
Top Semillons & Rieslings of 00, 99, 97, 95, 94, 93, 92, 90, 89, 88, then 86, 84, 83

New Zealand wines
Marlborough Sauvignon Blanc 01, 00
Pinot Noir (Martinborough or South Island) 00, 99, 97, 96
Hawkes Bay Cabernets 98, 95

Vintage Port 91, 85, 83, 82, 80, 77, 70, 66, 63, 55, 48, 45...

And the score is...

It seems that America and the rest of the world will never agree about the idea of scoring wines. America is seemingly besotted with the 100-point scale devised by Robert Parker, based on the strange US school system in which 50 = 0. Arguments that taste is too various, too subtle, too evanescent, too wonderful to be reduced to a pseudo-scientific set of numbers fall on deaf ears. Arguments that the accuracy implied by giving one wine a score of 87 and another 88 is a chimera don't get much further.

America likes numbers (and so do salesmen) because they are simpler than words. When it comes to words America likes superlatives. The best joke about it – at least I hope it was a joke – was the critic who came up with a 150-point scoring system. He argued that if 50 was no score at all you needed 150 to reach 100. Logical, but if it catches on there will be chaos. It might just ridicule the whole unreal business to death.

The Johnson System

I offer a tried and tested alternative way of registering how much *you* like a wine. The Johnson System reflects the enjoyment (or lack of it) that each wine offered at the time it was drunk with inescapable honesty. Here it is:

The minimum score is 1 sniff

One step up is 1 sip

2 sips = faint interest

A half glass = slight hesitation

1 glass = tolerance, even general approval

Individuals will vary in their scoring after this (they do with points systems, too). You should assume that you are drinking without compunction – without your host pressing you or the winemaker glowering at you. But you have time and you are thirsty.

Two glasses means you quite like it (or there

is nothing else to drink);

Three glasses – you find it more than acceptable;

Four – it tickles your fancy;

One bottle means satisfaction;

A second bottle is real thumbs up. The steps grow higher now:

A full case means you are not going to miss out on

this one...and so on.

The logical top score in the Johnson System is,

of course, the whole vineyard.

Quick reference vintage charts

These charts give a picture of the range of qualities made in the principal "classic" areas (every year has its relative successes and failures) and a guide to whether the wine is ready to drink or should be kept. Generalizations are unavoidable.

✓	drink up	ⴓ	needs keeping
ⴓ	can be drunk with pleasure now, but the better wines will continue to improve	ⵝ	avoid
		o	no good
		10	best

(Symbol key: ⴓ = glass symbol; ✓ = drink up; ⵝ = avoid)

Vintage	Germany Rhine		Mosel		Italy Piedmont reds		Tuscan reds		Spain Rioja	
2001	7–9	ⴓ	8–10	ⴓ	6–8	ⴓ	6–7	ⴓ	7–9	ⴓ
2000	5–8	ⴓ	5–8	ⴓ	7–9	ⴓ	7–9	ⴓ	7–8	ⴓ
99	7–10	ⴓ	7–10	ⴓ	8–10	ⴓ	8–10	ⴓ	7–9	ⴓ
98	6–9	ⴓ	6–9	ⴓ	8–10	ⴓ	6–8	ⴓ	7–8	ⴓ
97	7–9	ⴓ	7–10	ⴓ	8–10	ⴓ	8–10	ⴓ	5–7	ⴓ
96	7–9	ⴓ	6–8	ⴓ	7–9	ⴓ	5–7	ⴓ	8–10	ⴓ
95	7–10	✓	8–10	✓	6–8	ⴓ	5–8	ⴓ	7–9	ⴓ
94	5–7	ⴓ	6–10	ⴓ	4–6	✓	5–8	ⴓ	8–10	ⴓ
93	5–8	ⴓ	6–9	ⴓ	6–8	ⴓ	5–7	ⴓ	5–7	✓
92	5–9	ⴓ	5–9	ⴓ	2–5	ⵝ	2–5	ⵝ	6–8	✓
91	5–7	ⴓ	5–7	ⴓ	3–5	ⵝ	4–7	✓	7–9	✓
90	8–10	ⴓ	8–10	ⴓ	8–10	ⴓ	8–10	ⴓ	7–9	ⴓ
89	7–10	ⴓ	8–10	ⴓ	8–10	ⴓ	2–5	ⵝ	6–8	✓

Vintage	Australia Shiraz		Chardonnay		Champagne Vintage (97 = NV)			Port Vintage (97 = declared)	
2001	6–8	ⴓ	5–7	ⴓ	2001	1–3	ⴓ	2001	N/A	ⴓ
2000	6–8	ⴓ	7–9	ⴓ	2000	7–9	ⴓ	2000	8–10	ⴓ
99	7–9	✓	5–7	✓	99	6–8	ⴓ	99	4–6	ⴓ
98	7–9	ⴓ	7–9	ⴓ	98	5–7	ⴓ	98	4–6	ⴓ
97	6–8	ⴓ	8–10	ⴓ	97	5–7	ⵝ	97	8–10	ⴓ
96	8–10	ⴓ	4–7	✓	96	8–10	ⴓ	96	4–6	ⴓ
95	8–10	✓	3–5	ⵝ	95	7–9	ⴓ	95	4–6	ⴓ
94	6–8	✓	7–9	ⴓ	94	2–4	ⵝ	94	7–9	ⴓ
93	5–7	✓	5–7	ⴓ	93	5–6	ⴓ	93	2–5	ⴓ
92	6–8	✓	6–8	ⴓ	92	5–7	ⴓ	92	6–8	ⴓ
91	7–9	ⴓ	7–9	✓	91	4–6	ⴓ	91	2–5	ⴓ
90	7–9	ⴓ	8–10	✓	90	8–10	ⴓ	90	3–6	ⴓ

Vintage	California Cabernet		Chardonnay		New Zealand Red		White		S.Africa Red	
2001	6–8	ⴓ	5–7	ⴓ	5–7	ⴓ	6–8	ⴓ	6–8	ⴓ
2000	6–7	ⴓ	5–8	ⴓ	6–8	ⴓ	7–9	ⴓ	4–6	✓
99	7–8	ⴓ	5–8	ⴓ	6–8	ⴓ	7–9	✓	6–8	ⴓ
98	5–7	ⴓ	5–7	ⴓ	7–9	ⴓ	7–8	✓	7–9	ⴓ
97	8–10	ⴓ	8–10	ⴓ	5–8	✓	6–9	✓	8–10	ⴓ

France

| Vintage | Red Bordeaux | | White Bordeaux | | Alsace |
	Médoc/Graves	Pom/St-Em	Sauternes & SW	Graves & dry	
2001	6–8	7–8	8–10	7–9	6–8
2000	8–10	7–9	6–8	6–8	8–10
99	5–7	5–8	6–9	7–10	6–8
98	5–8	6–9	5–8	5–9	7–9
97	5–7	4–7	7–9	4–7	7–9
96	6–8	5–7	7–9	7–10	8–10
95	7–9	6–9	6–8	5–9	6–9
94	5–8	5–8	4–6	5–8	6–9
93	4–6	5–7	2–5	5–7	6–8
92	3–5	3–5	3–5	4–8	5–7
91	3–6	2–4	2–5	6–8	3–5
90	8–10	8–10	8–10	7–8	7–9
89	6–9	7–9	8–10	6–8	7–10
88	6–8	7–9	7–10	7–9	8–10
87	3–6	3–6	2–5	7–10	7–8
86	6–9	5–8	7–10	7–9	7–8
85	7–9	7–9	6–8	5–8	7–10
83	6–10	6–9	6–10	7–9	8–10

France continued

| Vintage | Burgundy | | | Rhône | |
	Côte d'Or red	Côte d'Or white	Chablis	Rhône (N)	Rhône (S)
2001	6–8	7–9	6–8	7–8	7–9
2000	7–8	6–9	7–9	6–8	7–9
99	7–10	5–7	5–8	7–9	6–9
98	5–8	5–7	7–8	6–8	7–9
97	5–8	5–8	7–9	7–9	5–8
96	6–8	7–9	5–10	5–7	4–6
95	7–9	7–9	6–9	6–8	6–8
94	5–8	5–7	4–7	6–7	7–9
93	6–8	5–6	5–8	3–6	4–9
92	3–6	5–8	4–6	4–6	3–6
91	3–6	4–6	6–9	6–9	4–5
90	7–10	8–10	6–9	6–9	7–9
89	6–9	8–10	6–8	6–8	6–8

Beaujolais 01, 00, 99 Crus will keep. **Mâcon-Villages** (white) Drink 01, 00, now or can wait. **Loire** (Sweet Anjou and Touraine) best recent vintages: 97, 96, 95, 93, 90, 89, 88, 85; Bourgueil, Chinon, Saumur-Champigny: 00, 99, 98, 97, 96, 95, 93, 90. **Upper Loire** (Sancerre, Pouilly-Fumé): 00, 99, 98, 97 **Muscadet** 01, 00, 99: DYA.

The right temperature

No single aspect of serving wine makes or mars it so easily as
getting the temperature right. White wines almost invariably taste
dull and insipid served warm and red wines have disappointingly
little scent or flavour served cold. The chart below gives an
indication of what is generally found to be the most satisfactory
temperature for serving each class of wine.

	°F	°C	
	68	20	
	66	19	
Room temperature	64	18	Best red wines especially Bordeaux
	63	17	
Red burgundy	61	16	
	59	15	Chianti, Zinfandel Côtes du Rhône
Best white burgundy Port, Madeira	57	14	
	55	13	*Ordinaires*
	54	12	Lighter red wines eg Beaujolais
Ideal cellar Sherry	52	11	
	50	10	
Fino sherry, Tokaji Aszú Most dry white wines Champagne	48	9	Rosés Lambrusco
	46	8	
Domestic fridge	45	7	
	43	6	Most sweet white wines Sparkling wines
	41	5	
	39	4	
	37	3	
	35	2	
	33	1	
	32	0	

wine
catalogue

The following titles are just a
selection from the Mitchell Beazley Wine
List and are available
from all good bookstores.

To order direct from the publisher
in the UK call our Credit Card Hotline
number: **01903 828800**

In the USA call Phaidon Press Inc
on 1877 Phaidon (toll-free)

In Canada call McArthur & Co
Publishing Ltd on 416 408 4007

Alternatively visit our website on
www.mitchell-beazley.com

MITCHELL BEAZLEY

The Hugh Johnson List

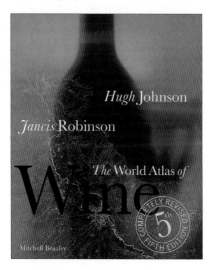

THE WORLD ATLAS OF WINE *5th Edition*
HUGH JOHNSON AND JANCIS ROBINSON

For this brand new extended edition of the best-selling *World Atlas of Wine*, Hugh Johnson has teamed up with Jancis Robinson to create the most comprehensive revision of the book so far. The maps, text, photographs, and illustrations have all been extensively updated, with additional pages dedicated to the fastest developing wine regions of the 1990s. In keeping with the *Atlas's* reputation for cartographic excellence, all the maps have been digitally updated and in some cases extended, and thirty new maps detail the vineyards in the wine world's emerging regions.

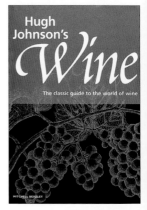

HUGH JOHNSON'S WINE
The classic guide to the world of wine
HUGH JOHNSON

For an accessible, all-round guide to the complex world of wine, *Hugh Johnson's Wine* covers everything from how wine is made to detailed tours of the wine regions, explaining what makes a "great" wine and how to select the right wine when dining out or entertaining at home.

THE WORLD ATLAS OF WINE
ISBN: 1 84000 332 4
£35 / US $50 / CN $70 Hardback 352 pages

HUGH JOHNSON'S WINE
ISBN: 0 85533 039 2
£14.99 / US $24.95 / CN $34.95
Hardback 272 pages

To order: **UK 01903 828800 / USA 1877 Phaidon (toll-free)/Canada 416 408 4007 McArthur**

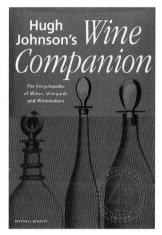

HUGH JOHNSON'S WINE COMPANION
The Encyclopedia of Wines, Vineyards and Winemakers
4th Edition
HUGH JOHNSON

In its fourth edition, this classic wine encyclopedia explores each of the world's wine countries in fascinating depth, detailing the styles, traditions, growers, and winemakers. Also profiled are the classic grapes, revealing where they grow best. This book explains how wine is made, from the vineyard to the bottle.

HUGH JOHNSON'S HOW TO ENJOY YOUR WINE
everything you need to know to get the most from wine
HUGH JOHNSON

Aimed at those who already enjoy a glass of wine, but who want to deepen their understanding of it. Hugh Johnson explains everything you need to know about handling wine in all social situations. With tips and guidance on all aspects of storing, serving, and tasting wine.

HUGH JOHNSON'S
HOW TO ENJOY YOUR WINE
ISBN: 1 84000 074 0
£9.99 Hardback 120 pages
*This edition not available from Phaidon / McArthur

HUGH JOHNSON'S WINE COMPANION
ISBN: 1 85732 274 6
£30/ US $40/ CN $50 Hardback 592 pages

To order: UK 01903 828800 / USA 1877 Phaidon (toll-free)/Canada 416 408 4007 McArthur

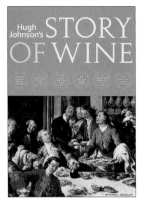

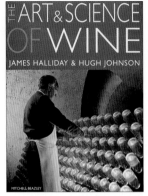

HUGH JOHNSON'S STORY OF WINE
HUGH JOHNSON

A fascinating examination of the history of wine written with all the characteristic wit and enthusiasm of Hugh Johnson, unveiling the cultural perspective of wine in enthralling episodes. Illustrated with 220 full-colour photographs, maps, and diagrams.

THE ART AND SCIENCE OF WINE
HUGH JOHNSON & JAMES HALLIDAY

An approachable guide to the process behind winemaking. Hugh Johnson and James Halliday examine how nature, art, and science combine to provide the infinite variety of the world's wines; from the vineyard, vatroom, and cellar to the bottle.

HUGH JOHNSON'S CELLAR BOOK
HUGH JOHNSON

Keep cellar records in order with this indispensable book. Useful tips on storing, opening, enjoying and recording wine. Followed by how to plan a cellar. The *Cellar Book* also includes space for personal notes.

HUGH JOHNSON'S STORY OF WINE
ISBN: 1 84000 120
£22.50/US$40/CN$60
Hardback 480 pages

THE ART AND SCIENCE OF WINE
ISBN: 1 85732 422 6
£15.99 Paperback
232 pages
*This edition not available from Phaidon/McArthur

HUGH JOHNSON'S CELLAR BOOK
ISBN: 1 84000 093 7
£18.99/US$29.95/CN$39.95
Hardback 224 pages

HUGH JOHNSON'S CELLAR BOOK
ISBN: 1 84000 094
£80/$120/CN$100 Special hardback, leather bound edition, 224 pages

To order: UK 01903 828800 / USA 1877 Phaidon (toll-free)/Canada 416 408 4007 McArthur

THE WINE ATLAS OF FRANCE
and Traveller's Guide to the vineyards
HUBRECHT DUIJKER, HUGH JOHNSON

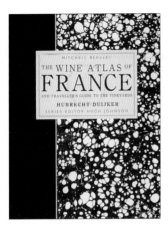

The Wine Atlas of France offers unique cartographic coverage of the wine regions and absorbing insights into the producers and their wines. This is complemented by useful touring information and places of interest to visit. Hotels and restaurants are also recommended.

TUSCANY AND ITS WINES
HUGH JOHNSON
PHOTOGRAPHY BY ANDY KATZ

Tuscany and its Wines combines the inspirational writing of Hugh Johnson with the sparkling photography of Andy Katz. This is an irresistible portrait of Tuscany's culture, history, landscapes, people, foods and, above all, wines.

THE WINE ATLAS OF FRANCE
ISBN: 1 85732 336 X
£27.50/US$45/CN$50 Hardback 264 pages

TUSCANY AND ITS WINES
ISBN: 1 84000 274 3
£16.99 Hardback 144 pages
*This edition not available from Phaidon/McArthur

To order: **UK 01903 828800 / USA 1877 Phaidon (toll-free)/Canada 416 408 4007 McArthur**

THE NEW FRANCE
ANDREW JEFFORD

This groundbreaking and authoritative book on French wine draws on painstaking research by leading wine writer Andrew Jefford, who has travelled extensively in each of France's fourteen wine regions to investigate the personalities and producers who have masterminded the resurgence of the French wine industry. Includes vintage charts and fifteen full-colour maps.

New

TOURING IN WINE COUNTRY
SERIES EDITOR HUGH JOHNSON

Each book in this best-selling series offers a comprehensive and inspirational guide to travelling in one of the world's top wine regions. Evocative descriptions of wine routes are accompanied by detailed maps showing the route and surrounding vineyards. Each title also includes the author's recommendations for hotels, restaurants, and producers.

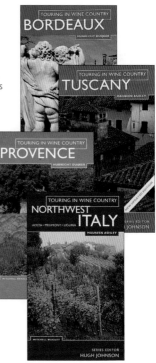

BORDEAUX
ISBN: 1 84000 246 8

BURGUNDY
ISBN: 1 84000 245 X

NORTHWEST ITALY
ISBN: 1 85732 864 7

PROVENCE
ISBN: 1 84000 046 5

TUSCANY
ISBN: 1 84000 247 6

£12.99/US$19.95/CN$21.95
Paperback

THE NEW FRANCE
ISBN: 1 84000 410 X
£30/US$45/CN$70 Hardback 256 pages

To order: UK 01903 828800 / USA 1877 Phaidon (toll-free)/Canada 416 408 4007 McArthur

Mitchell Beazley Wine Guides

Mitchell Beazley relaunches its bestselling Wine Guides series, presenting each title with a new, clearer layout and boasting a more thorough update than ever before. The larger format has also been given a stylish new cover treatment.

New

WINE GUIDES
£9.99/us $14.95/cn $21.95 Hardback

WINES OF ITALY
BURTON ANDERSON
ISBN: 1 84000 553 X

WINES OF BORDEAUX
DAVID PEPPERCORN
ISBN: 1 84000 550 5

WINES OF CALIFORNIA
STEPHEN BROOK
ISBN: 1 84000 393 6

POCKET GUIDES
£8.99/us $14.95/cn $21.95 Hardback

WINES OF AUSTRALIA
JAMES HALLIDAY
ISBN: 1 84000 249 2

WINES OF BURGUNDY
SERENA SUTCLIFFE
ISBN: 1 84000 015 5

WINES OF SPAIN
JAN READ
ISBN: 1 84000 389 8

FORTIFIED & SWEET WINES
JOHN RADFORD & STEPHEN BROOK
ISBN: 1 84000 248 4

WINES OF THE LOIRE, ALSACE AND THE RHÔNE & OTHER FRENCH REGIONAL WINES
ROGER VOSS
ISBN: 1 84000 016 3

WINES OF NEW ZEALAND
MICHAEL COOPER
ISBN: 1 84000 020 1

CHAMPAGNE & SPARKLING WINE
MICHAEL EDWARDS
ISBN: 1 84000 077 5

SCOTCH WHISKY
CHARLES MACLEAN
ISBN: 1 84000 327 8

MICHAEL BROADBENT'S WINETASTING
MICHAEL BROADBENT
ISBN: 1 84000 325 1

MICHAEL BROADBENT'S WINE VINTAGES
MICHAEL BROADBENT
ISBN: 1 84000 326 X

New

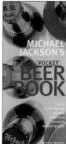

MICHAEL JACKSON'S POCKET BEER BOOK
MICHAEL JACKSON

This handy guide will keep beer lovers abreast of the world's best breweries and their beers.

MICHAEL JACKSON
ISBN: 1 84000 252 2
£8.99 Hardback 208 pages
*This edition not available from Phaidon/McArthur

To order: UK 01903 828800 / USA 1877 Phaidon (toll-free)/Canada 416 408 4007 McArthur

LANGUEDOC-ROUSSILLON
THE WINES AND WINEMAKERS
PAUL STRANG

The sudden renaissance of the Languedoc-Roussillon, one of France's oldest wine regions, is the most exciting development in the wine world in the last twenty years. This is the first illustrated book to explore the terroir, traditions, winemaking practices, laws, personalities, and, most importantly, the wines of the region.

New

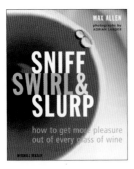

SNIFF SWIRL & SLURP
MAX ALLEN

For no-nonsense advice on how to get maximum enjoyment from drinking wine, you will find everything you need in Sniff Swirl & Slurp. Straight-talking wine writer Max Allen explores how countries, regions, grapes, and winemaking affect the taste of wine. This equips you to understand why wines taste the way they do.

New

GIRLS' GUIDE TO WINE
SUSY ATKINS

Bewildered and befuddled by wine? So many styles, labels, and grapes, so little time – what's a girl to do? No problem – this portable, lively guide demystifies the tricky process of picking the perfect wine every time. Packed with savvy tips on how to buy it, try it, serve it, and even identify the perfect man with it, NO girl's handbag should be without this sassy, no-nonsense guide to wine.

New

LANGUEDOC-ROUSSILLON	SNIFF SWIRL & SLURP	GIRLS' GUIDE TO WINE
ISBN: 1 84000 500 9	ISBN: 1 84000 513 0	ISBN: 1 84000 682X
£25/US$40/CN$60	£12.99/US$19.95/CN$29.95	£4.99/US$7.95/CN$12.95
Hardback 192 pages	Hardback 192 pages	Paperback 144 pages

To order: UK 01903 828800 / USA 1877 Phaidon (toll-free)/Canada 416 408 4007 McArthur